International Federation of Library Associations and Institutions
Fédération Internationale des Associations de Bibliothécaires et des Bibliothèques
Internationaler Verband der bibliothekarischen Vereine und Institutionen
Международная Федерация Библиотечных Ассоциаций и Учреждений
Federación Internacional de Asociaciones de Bibliotecarios y Bibliotecas

IFLA Publications 80/81

Human Development: Competencies for the Twenty-First Century

Papers from the
IFLA CPERT Third International Conference on
Continuing Professional Education
for the Library and Information Professions

A Publication of the Continuing Professional
Education Round Table (CPERT)
of the International Federation of
Library Associations and Institutions

Edited by
Patricia Layzell Ward and Darlene E. Weingand

K · G · Saur   München 1997

IFLA Publications
edited by Carol Henry

Recommended catalogue entry:

Human development: competencies for the twenty-first century :
papers from the IFLA CPERT Third International Conference on
Continuing Professional Education for the Library and Information
Professions ; a publication of the Continuing Professional Education
Round Table (CPERT) of the International Federation of Library
Associations and Institutions / ed. by Patricia Layzell Ward and
Darlene E. Weingand. – München : Saur, 1997, p. XII, 1–400, 21 cm
  (IFLA publications ; 80/81)
  ISBN 3-598-21806-0

Die Deutsche Bibliothek – CIP-Einheitsaufnahme

Human development: competencies for the twenty-first century :
papers from the IFLA CPERT Third International Conference on
Continuing Professional Education for the Library and Information
Professions ; a publication of the Continuing Professional Education
Round Table (CPERT) of the International Federation of Library
Associations and Institutions / ed. by Patricia Layzell Ward and
Darlene E. Weingand. – München : Saur, 1997
  (IFLA publications ; 80/81)
  ISBN 3-598-21806-0

Printed on acid-free paper
The paper used in this publication meets the minimum requirements of American National
Standard for Information Sciences – Permanence of Paper for Printed Library Materials,
ANSI Z39.48.1984.

Printed/Bound by Strauss Offsetdruck GmbH, Mörlenbach

ISBN 3-598-21806-0
ISSN 0344-6891 (IFLA Publications)

TABLE OF CONTENTS

Acknowledgements...IX

Foreword

    Patricia Layzell Ward & Darlene E. Weingand...................................... X

WEDNESDAY August 27, 1997

INAUGURATION OF THE CONFERENCE

Welcome: Ole Harbo

KEYNOTE ADDRESS: Minister of Research Jytte Hilden

SESSION 1. Continuing Education Planning: Individual and Institutional

A Distance Independent/Open Learning Education Model For The Continuing Professional Education Of Librarians
    Maxine K. Rochester & Ken Eustace 1

Continuing Professional Development And Flexible Information Workers: Problems And Opportunities
    Anne Goulding and Evelyn Kerslake 10

Future Academic Library Skills: What Will They Be?
    Steve Morgan 19

SESSION 2a. Models to Cope with Growing Continuing Education Needs

Hungarian CPE Efforts Intensified Through International Co-operation
    Mihaly Palvokyi, Agnes Teglasi and Niels Ole Pors... 30

Users Training Programs Developed By The Brazilian University Libraries
    Maria N. 0. Silva 40

Constructs For Investigating Lack of Persistence In Experimental Distance Education: A Study Of Health Science Librarians
    Diane Tobin Johnson, MaryEllen C. Sievert, Teresa Hartman and Timothy Patrick.......... 49

SESSION 2b. Continuing Education Planning: Individual and Institutional

The Changing Nature Of Continuing Education For The Individual: Will Libraries And Librarians Continue To Play A Role In Supporting Learners?
    Clive Cochrane 60

On The Education Of Information Resources Management Professionals At High Level In China
    Peng Feizhang and Zhang Jin.. 67

*Closing The Information Technology Gap: Typical Training Concerns In A South African University
   Library In The 1990's*
      Clare M. Walker 72

SESSION 3. Models to Cope With Growing Continuing Education Needs

LIS Educational Systems Within CMC (Computer Mediated Communication)
      Augusta Maria Paci 81

Group Mentoring. : A First Experience In Continuing Education
      Ann Ritchie and Paul Genoni 88

Facilitating Workplace Learning
      Jana Varlejs.. 98

THURSDAY August 28, 1997

SESSION 4a. Training the Trainer

Training Of Trainers And Professional Development: Estonian Prospective
      Aira Lepik 105

New Times - New Possibilities
      Euginia M Rossinskaya.. 114

Librarians As Change Agents In The HE Community
      Kay Flatten 118

SESSION 4b. Measuring Continuing Education Needs

*Theory And Practice Of Law Librarianship Through Continuing Professional Education:
   The Nigerian Experience*
      Oluremi Jegede.. 122

Continuing Education And Information Technology: A Study Of Content And Deliverables
      Niels Ole Pors and Trine Schreiber 133

*Differences Between Librarians And Library Directors In Their Perception Of Continuing
   Professional Education*
      Gabriella Dotan and Irith Getz.. 140

*Information Technology Developments As A Factor In Determination Of Continuing
   Education Needs In Some Southern African Academic Libraries*
      Lesley M Moyo 151

SESSION 5. Workshops

*Measuring Continuing Education Needs And Results Competency For The Twenty-First
   Century*
      Blanche Woolls.. 161

SESSION 6a. Continuing Education Planning: Individual and Institutional

Personal Professional Development: Competencies For The Solo Librarian
Sue Lacey Bryant 179

Growing With The Customer: Challenges To The Estonian Librarian In The 21st Century
Aili Norberg 189

Planning Professional Excellence In Library And Information Organisations - A South African Perspective
Fransie Terblanche 193

SESSION 6b. Models to Cope with Growing Continuing Education Needs

LIS Professionals In The Networked Learning Environment
Irene Wormell 201

Russian System Of Continuing Education In Transition
Irina L. Klim 211

Continuing LIS Professional Education Through Distance Mode: Prospects For India
Uma Kanjilal 219

SESSION 7a. Models to Cope with Growing Continuing Education Needs

The Internet And Continuing Professional Education
Laurel A. Clyde 225

The Impact Of National Training Reform And The Restructuring Of Industrial Awards On Staff Development In Australian Academic And State Libraries
Angela Bridgland 235

Distance Education As A New Possibility For Library And Information Science Education In Estonia
Sirje Virkus 249

SESSION 7b. Continuing Education Planning: Individual and Institutional

Evaluation As A Human Development For Professionals In The Twenty-First Century; A Brazilian Experience
Sueli Angelica Do Amaral 255

An Approach To Identifying Skills Within An Information Culture: The Application Of Information Policy To Information Cultures
Michael Kristiansson and Leif Kajberg 264

Continuing Education For Croatian Librarians: Needs And Opportunities
Tatjana Aparac 271

FRIDAY August 29, 1997

SESSION 8a. Training the Trainer

The Academic Librarian And Scholarship: A Vision For The Twenty-First Century
Araxie Paula Churukian 278

Measuring Continuing Education Needs: Identifying Transferable Skills Through Mentoring
Jane Farmer and Fiona Campbell 284

Training The Trainer: A Perspective From The ALA / CLENE-RT'
Darlene E. Weingand 290

SESSION 8b. User Education: The Librarian as Educator

Effectiveness Of An Academic Library As A Continuing Education Provider
Abdus Sattar Chaudhry 306

*Applying Principles For Effective Staff Development To Large Urban Public Library
Systems In Canada*
Ken Haycock 316

The New Role Of Librarians As Internet Trainers
Diann Rusch-Feja 324

SESSION 9. User Education: The Librarian as Educator

*Information Exchange And Communication Between Researchers: The Specialised
Librarian's Part In Scientific Research*
Viviane Couzinet and Arlette Bouzon 334

Information Skills Teaching In The Age Of The Electronic Library In The United Kingdom
Graham Walton, Joan Day and Catherine Edwards 342

Libraries As Learning Organisations
Ganga B. Dakshinamurti 350

SESSION 10a. Continuing Education Planning: Individual and Institutional

The Higher School Of Information Service In Prague
Marcela Burilová 358

*Continuing Education Of Information Professionals In A Changing Environment: With
Special Reference To Brazil*
Tania Mara Botelho 366

The Library And Bibliometrics
Ona Voverienë 370

SESSION 10b. Continuing Education Planning: Individual and Institutional

Polish Experiences In Continuing Education For Librarians
Maria Kocojowa and Wanda Pindlowa.. 374

Asian Institute For Education In Librarianship And Information Science: A Continuing Professional Development Proposal
Russell Bowden 378

Librarians Continuing Education in the Libraries of Estonia
Krista Talvi 385

Appendix A
Organising Committee.. 392

Appendix B
Authors of the Papers... 393

ACKNOWLEDGEMENTS

The Organising Committee wishes to acknowledge the support of:

Emeritus Professor Elizabeth Stone for her continuing inspiration;
K.G. Saur for the publication of the proceedings which disseminate the ideas of CPD;
IFLA Headquarters staff for their friendly advice;
Danida for the support for some overseas delegates;
the membership of CPERT for their enthusiasm;
the authors of papers and presenters of workshops and poster sessions who provided the intellectual content of the conference;
and finally, but not least to the Royal School of Librarianship for providing the Secretariat and hosting the conference. Particular thanks are due to Ole Harbo, Director of the School, Niels Ole Pors, and to Lone Laurberg who handled the planning and administration effectively with a good sense of humour.

FOREWORD

The First World Conference on Continuing Education for the Library and Information Science Professions took place in Palos Hills, Illinois, USA, in August 1985. The dream of the conference planners was to create "a worldwide network for library leaders in continuing education, to explore mutual concerns, share research, and demonstrate the state of the art in practice."

This dream was carried forward through the establishment of the Continuing Professional Education Round Table as part of the Division of Education and Research within IFLA. A Second World Conference was held in Barcelona, Spain, in August 1993, and the Third International Conference in Copenhagen, Denmark, in 1997. The Third Conference is co-sponsored by CPERT and the Royal School of Librarianship in Copenhagen.

The main theme of the Conference is "Human Development: Competencies for the Twenty-First Century. Six sub-themes were identified:

- Continuing Education Planning: Individual And Institutional
- Models To Cope With Growing Continuing Education Needs
- Measuring Continuing Education Needs
- User Education: The Librarian As Educator
- Training The Trainer

The call for papers produced many more papers than had been expected, all of a high quality, and from around the globe. The members of the Organizing Committee deputed to make the selection had a difficult task, and regret that all papers submitted could not be found a place in the programme.

Two workshops - presented by Margaret Redfern on appraisal and staff development, and Neil Greeve on the delivery of CPD via the Internet - involved practical work and have not been included in the proceedings. A number of poster sessions were presented and they too could not be included.

The papers in this volume reflect the substantial changes in the information professions that are sweeping us forward toward a new century. There is a focus on the future in these papers, and an emphasis on the ways in which distance education will assist the upgrading of the professional skills and knowledge of the professional librarian. The impact of information technology bringing an emphasis on access rather than holdings, coupled with political and economic change, underlines the need for continual professional development that is accessible and effective. There is concern about an information technology gap and the requirement that centres of learning be appropriately equipped for training. Emerging from the process of change is a recognition of the ever increasing importance of learning and training in the workplace, and the need for there to be a partnership between management and staff.

In addition, participants are also being asked to consider future directions for CPERT, and the theme for the next international continuing education conference. It is anticipated that such an international gathering of library leaders interested in continuing professional education will take place approximately every 3-5 years.

Patricia Layzell Ward   Darlene E. Weingand
University of Wales Aberystwyth   University of Wisconsin, Madison

Acknowledgements IX
Foreword

    Patricia Layzell ward & Darlene E. Weingand X
    Maxine K. Rochester & Ken Eustace 1
    Anne Goulding and Evelyn Kerslake 10
    Steve Morgan 19
    Niels Pors and Mihaly Palvokyi and Agnes Teglasi 30
    Maria N. O. Silva 40
    Diane Tobin Johnson, MaryEllen C. Sievert, Teresa Hartman, and Timothy Patrick 49
    Clive Cochrane 60
    Peng Feizhang and Zhang Jin 67
    Clare M. Walker 72
    Augusta Maria Paci 81
    Ann Ritchie and Paul Genoni 88
    Jana Varlejs 98
    Aira Lepik 105
    Eugenia M. Rossinskaya 114
    Kay Flatten 118
    Oluremi Jegede 122
    Niels Pors and Trine Schreiber 133
    Gabriella Dotan and Irith Getz 140
    Lesley M. Moyo 151
    Blanche Woolls 161
    Sue Lacy Bryant 179
    Aili Norberg 189
    Fransie Terblanche 193
    Irene Wormell 201
    Irina L. Klim 211
    Uma Kanjilal 219
    Laurel A. Clyde 225
    Angela Bridgland 235
    Sirje Virkus 249
    Sueli Angelica do Amara 255
    Michael Kristiansson and Leif Kajberg 264
    Tatjana Aparac and Dubravka Stancin Rosic 271
    Araxie Paula Churukian 278
    Jane Farmer and Fiona Campbell 284
    Darlene E. Weingand 290
    Abdus Sattar Chaudry 306
    Ken Haycock 316
    Diann Rusch-Feja 324
    Viviane Couzinet and Arlette Bouzon 334
    Graham Walton, Joan Day, and Catherine Edwards 342
    Ganga B. Dakshinamurti 350
    Marcela Burilova 358
    Tania Mara Botelho 366
    Ona Voverienë 370
    Maria Kocojowa and Wanda Pindlowa 374
    Russell Bowden 378
    Krista Talvi 385

Appendic A
    Organising Committee 392
Appendix B
    Authors of the Papers 393

A DISTANCE INDEPENDENT/OPEN LEARNING EDUCATION MODEL FOR CONTINUING PROFESSIONAL EDUCATION OF LIBRARIANS

Maxine K. Rochester and Ken Eustace
School of Information Studies
Charles Sturt University
Australia

Abstract: This paper considers harnessing new technology to enhance CPE for librarians, proposing a learner centred model. Used as a case study is the experience of one of the authors, Ken Eustace, in undertaking a course with Paideia University, a virtual university on the Internet.

INTRODUCTION

Harnessing new technology to enhance Continuing Professional Education (CPE) for librarians is considered here and builds upon a paper given at the IFLA CPERT Second World Conference on Continuing Professional Education for the Library and Information Science Professions held in Barcelona in 1993 (Rochester and Pearce 1993). That Conference identified five trends in CPE; one of these trends was increasing use of technology to provide continuing education at remote sites. Findings from the Lyceum Project (Eustace 1995), which considers the learner or end-user position, across a range of factors including the user interface, computer literacy and access to the suitable technology level, will be used. The challenge for online educators and librarians is one of computer literacy, where the teacher/participant is overtly and covertly developing skills with object-oriented technology, data communications, data modelling, multimedia and object-oriented programming.

The role of educators and librarians has been challenged by the use of World-Wide Web (WWW or WEB) and MOO services for borrowers. The MOO (multi-user domain or MUD, object-oriented) is a text-based virtual reality existing in a real-time on an Internet server. New technology is an essential component in the weaving of the online educator's tapestry, whether it be electronic publishing or the use of text-based virtual reality. Higher bandwidth options on the Internet such as the desktop video environment of CU-CeeMe or the M-Bone provide a superior form of communication, but are not truly global at the moment to the same extent as the use WEB and the MOO. Even in third world countries where only e-mail and telnet services exist, users can still access WWW and MOO sites with a simple command-line interface.

Internet access gives each librarian a platform for individual expression, opening up new opportunities for professional development and collaboration, notwithstanding the personal development benefits gained by experiencing other perspectives. A good example of this was the use of listservers and WWW sites in running the first virtual conference for teacher librarians (Henri and Hay 1996), in June 1996. Henri and Hay of the School of Information Studies at Charles Sturt University organised the conference through a WWW site at http://www.itec.com.au/ where fifty-five papers were offered by an international cast of educators and practitioners.

The authors propose a learner centred model using:

- IFLA official languages on the Internet;
- interactive dialogue;
- increased involvement of the teacher/supervisor in the learning process;
- a higher staff/student ratio;
- modern communications technology;
- a wide range of teaching and learning strategies.

Program development is model-driven, employing new technology as it becomes available, to achieve its aims.

CASE STUDY: PAIDEIA AND THE LYCEUM PROJECT

The use of interactive online services in the development of distance independent education appears to be growing at a rate which will see major changes in the twenty-first century. The experiences gained by Ken Eustace at Paideia, a university on the Internet will be used as a case study. Since May 1994, Ken Eustace has been involved in study for the Master of Arts (Liberal and Policy Studies) as part of an ethnographic study in the Lyceum Project. The structure at Paideia is an exciting and challenging alternative global open learning model that has also been used with the supervision of higher degree students at Charles Sturt University. The model can be applied to a wide range of continuing professional education, including for librarians (Eustace, 1997). For information on Paideia, uses the WWW links available at http://silo.riv.csu.edu.au/paideia/ or go directly to the http://www.best.com/~attictwo/ site for course participation and advice.

The development of Paideia as a "Virtual University" has been a rewarding challenge, not without ist problems. Paideia sits at the virtual end of the traditional-virtual spectrum of niches for a modern university.

```
                    <-----[Paradigm Shift]>B>
          Virtual<_________________________>Traditional
          ^
          Paideia
```

GLOBAL ISSUES: EQUITY AND ACCESS TO THE 'HIGH ROAD'

In the developed world there has been concern about the use of new technology leading to inequalities of access to education; this concern is magnified for the developing world. We have been reminded that equity of access must be built in as a goal in the development of programs (Hall 1996, p. 86).

Desktop Videoconferencing as the High Road

According to Brownlee and Ingham (1996), desktop videoconferencing systems such as Cu-SeeMe, still have a long way to go before they can be used for a wider section of the learning community. The technology level required raises equity issues, as many users and indeed some countries do not have the audio-visual equipment (monitor, camera, microphone, and speaker) to participate at this time.

Videoconferencing supports two-way video and audio communication so that two or more people at different locations can see and hear each other at the same time. The basic system must have as well a means of transmitting information between sites. As the broadband satellite connection is expensive, recent advances in communications technologies have created an interest in compressed video systems, which transmit information via today's Internet or telephone network, greatly reducing the cost of videoconferencing.

Some common reasons exist for using videoconferencing or WWW/MOO technology:

- To provide equitable access to resources;
- To share resources, especially for scattered or rural populations;
- To provide a virtual experience when the real experience is not feasible;
- To facilitate collaboration, information searching, problem solving, and decision making within a learning environment based on dialogue, distributed expertise, and problem solving;
- Visual connection can help to foster active participation;
- Remote experts can help validate understanding, provide feedback, and introduce practical examples and improve motivation;
- Supports use of diverse media;

- User can share applications and documents with real-time feedback.

WWW and MOO as the Low Road.

The WWW and MOO software tools are available now on the desktop and can use common telecommunications infrastructure such as modems and the local telephone exchange. The client/server relationship and the protocols used make less demand upon bandwidth than videoconferencing. The bottom line is that for most of us, we get our information and communication as text - a format that exists for WWW as well as for MOO.

Language as the Vehicle of Knowledge and Understanding.

Offering a global course for three years in English was seen as the normal mode as English was determined as the standard language of the Internet, although some observers have commented that such action is creating a virtual monoculture as a new kind of imperialism. We should consider offering international CPE courses in the five IFLA official languages. Even to adopt French and Spanish as well as English on the Internet, would go a long way to opening up participation by African and Latin American countries with colonial roots. Unfortunately there are some developing countries lacking ready access as they do not have the legacy of a colonial language.

Equity and access issues in Australia has led the Australian Library and Information Association (ALIA) to form a strategic partnership with Edith Cowan University in Perth WA. This partnership will make available, online courses for continued professional development. ALIAs reasons for this were to provide a flexible delivery mode and access for as many ALIA members as possible, because of their geographic isolation in a sparsely populated continent.

ECONOMIC FACTORS

The development of electronic teaching is expensive, but this may be offset by delivery to a larger number of students. Because of the expense and time involved in developing courses, there have been agreements between institutions nationally and internationally to share courses or subjects, and for cross accreditation. Also the use of such technology may lead to higher staff/student ratios than in traditional teaching methods, again increasing costs.

ACCREDITATION

It is desirable for CPE courses whether long or short to receive some kind of formal accreditation or recognition process. Participants need this for personal reassurances of quality, for use in the flexible academic environments where credit may be given for prior learning, and also for purposes of staff evaluation and use as a performance indicator. This is even more important in the global education environment opened up by new technology, and when professionals are so mobile.

Procedures to maintain the technical and academic quality of electronic teaching programs in an Australian university show the additional demands electronic delivery add to existing course evaluation requirements (Audley 1996). A technical evaluation of the course is added to the traditional academic merit evaluation. There is also a financial evaluation of the course, with a cost/benefit analysis carried out. The accreditation or recognition process for CPE courses may be carried out by the national professional association, e.g., the Australian Library and Information Association, or by national accrediting bodies and then recognised internationally, or by international consortia. The experience of Paideia University in seeking accreditation for a virtual MA degree is instructive. As a consequence of the Paideia experience, Ken Eustace is employing online course evaluation in postgraduate subjects offered by the School of Information Studies at Charles Sturt University. Online evaluation allows for just-in-time changes to be made as teaching proceeds rather than at the end of the subject.

Paideia originally sought accreditation in the Netherlands but the Dutch authorities required that any such MA course should be offered in Dutch as well as English (so that all Dutch citizens had an equal opportunity to participate). While it would have been possible for GlobalNet Associates to translate the course outline and curriculum materials, such as the 132-page self-study guide, into

Dutch, none of the team was fluent in the Dutch language. Since conference dialogue (both asynchronous via e- mail and WWW and synchronous or real-time via MOO) is an integral part of learning transactions, Paideia sought accreditation elsewhere without the bilingual restriction encountered in the Netherlands.

At this time some slight disparities in the approaches by various Open Learning Agency (OLA) members towards the accreditation process for a "virtual degree" were discovered. Australia in 1995 was not prepared at all for such an accreditation process to happen. During 1996, the Paideia team has been active in seeking accreditation of its global Master's degree program through the Open Learning Agency, the Private Post-Secondary Education Commission (PPSEC) of British Columbia, Canada. The Open University of British Columbia was also keen to help out with the "traditional needs" of a virtual degree. A lot of debate over the qualification of a global Master's has concerned the assessment procedure governing participants and their supervisors, even though almost all evidence of participant interaction is available online via the Internet. Constructivism, scaffold learning, portfolio reporting of learning transactions (e.g., weekly assignments/exercises, electronic publishing of journal and/or conference papers, participation in the regular conference agenda (dialogue) with peers and mentors) are all part of the Paideia pedagogy. The final accreditation process in Canada was progressing towards completion until the Minister for Education in BC suspended all out-of province accreditation pending a review of the process.

Handling academic perspectives has been difficult at times where some disdain has been expressed at what is happening, partly as a concern for defending the "status quo" in earning a higher degree than for any sound pedagogical basis. The current paradigms for earning a Masters degree (e.g., coursework, coursework/dissertation or thesis) are being protected under the "real vs. virtual" scenario.

PEDAGOGIC PARADIGMS

A wide range of teaching and learning strategies are necessary to cater for individual needs and differences, over many parts of the world. The book metaphor remains the most popular form of learning, along with competition among student as part the learning process. Flexible learning paths is now a major paradigm in professional education as a result. The World -Wide Web is now a major part of resources-based learning. At the first International WWW conference held at CERN in Geneva during May 1994, 380 delegates attended. The Third International Conference in Washington, in December 1994 had 11,000 participants (Ragget, Lam and Alexander 1996, p. 27).

THE LEARNER CENTRIC MODEL

Individual Needs of the Professional Librarian.

Not all librarians will embrace the same level of technology in their learning style. A global online course structure will develop a learning environment where several interdependent factors are meshed. Here the technical, social, political, cultural and conceptual factors of the online course are woven into a single learning fabric where each factor is a fibre. Pull out one of the fibres and the fabric is weakened.

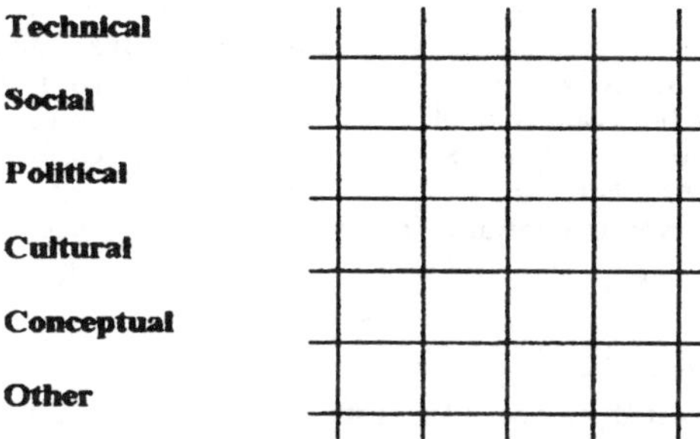

Figure 1. The Online Educators Tapestry

If this is the case then how much of each fibre will the individual professional librarian tolerate?

This is an issue for all educational institutions now facing distance education methods across a broad spectrum of traditional to virtual courses due the impact of multimedia and communications technology on learning in the last four years.

ASYNCHRONOUS AND SYNCHRONOUS LEARNING

The use of electronic mail and the World-Wide Web/CD-ROM based multimedia has seen a growing trend towards resource-based learning where all the teaching resources are available online. Indeed this trend has seen communications technology terms such as synchronous and asynchronous, being applied to pedagogy. Here we find the debate over synchronous and asynchronous learning methods illustrated using two students:

Student A " I have to work hard to get my assignments in on time as I have a full-time job. I would like to be able to hand the work in when it is ready.....

Lecturer A " Hand it in at the end of the course. I would hate to see the quality of the project ruined by a hasty submission caused by a due date..."

Student B " I am a highly organised person and I hate asynchronous learning. I have to know all the due dates for my assignments and like working to schedule. You can expect me to hand in my work ahead of schedule..."

Lecturer B " I expect all the assignments to be in on time and I will be holding three online conferences via MOO so that the dialogue can be easily recorded and used as a learning resource off-line..."

At Paideia (Eustace, 1996) we found that a mix of both in combination with a flexible participation strategy by treating each student as a *tourist* on a journey making forward progress all the time but opting for a personal combination of tours (synchronised) and free days (asynchronous).

COMPUTER LITERACY STANDARDS FOR PARTICIPATION

WWW is described as having a static client, since connection to the WEB server is broken after each request. It gives access to information as hypertext or hypermedia, has some useful search tools and can empower users to publish their own information. It can be made more interactive with the use of programming scripts on the server side, but how real is the interaction without communication with other users? The MOO, although a text-based system has the real-time interaction with other users but lacks the visual and audio environment of the WEB. By linking the WEB to the MOO, the interface captures the best and worst of both systems, where WWW inherits the real-time communication and the MOO inherits the lag of the WEB, as one example. It is this sort of result that may lead to a new client/server architecture for true interaction - a precursor to interactive TV!

COLLABORATIVE WORKSPACE

The role of computer-supported co-operative work (CSCW) is growing as a tool in documenting research. Some of the common MOO developments for teaching and research are listed below, from the TecfaMOO site (Schneider, 1995) in figure 5:

<table>
<tr><td>
Virtual Meeting spaces for researchers (desktop conferencing)
Tutorial support for classroom teaching
Tutorial support for distance teaching
Environments for 'Just-in-time' Open Learning
Learning by doing educational environments
Spacial organisation of information retrieval;
Dynamics of interactions in a virtual space;
Social and Political issues in virtual worlds.
</td></tr>
</table>

Figure 5. The use of MOO technology in teaching and research

CASE STUDY: THE INTERNET PUBLIC LIBRARY

As part of his five new laws of librarianship, Gorman (1995) states that *each new type of communication not only enhances, but can also extend the strengths of the previous methods.* Respect of all forms by which knowledge is communicated, is now a tenet that the librarian should uphold. Putting such ideas to the test by first-hand experience seems appropriate at this stage. The Internet Public Library (IPL) has been set up at the University of Michigan by staff and students at the School of Information and Library Studies (http://ipl.sils.umich.edu/) as an experimental Internet project combining traditional library culture with the dynamic software services on the Internet, such as WWW and MOO. This virtual library environment contains eight essential services at this point of time. These include:

- **Reference center** with ready reference collection and a MOO service which provide the mechanism for handling online reference questions;

- **Youth Division** which include a listserv for discussions of childrens books;

- **Services to Librarians Division;**

- Exhibit Hall;

- Classroom for time and distance independent teaching;

- Reading Room which has pointers to other full text resources on the Internet;

- Building Directory, an essential service in an expanding IPL structure which lists all   the resources within the IPL;

- WEB searching tools.

IPL MOO: THE INTERNET PUBLIC LIBRARY INTERACTIVE VIRTUAL ENVIRONMENT

Part of the growing WWW/MOO environment at the IPL is the Reference Center. The following text extract is taken from the IPLMOO WWW page which is located at http://ipl.sils.umich.edu/moo/

IPLMOO will be an important part of the reference center. It will provide real-time many-to-many communication with others around the world, including our crack IPL Reference Center staff. Areas within IPLive will include the Real-Time Reference Desk and the Chat Room.

The IPL Reference Center is part of the new wave in networked librarianship in cultivating collections, collaboration, co-operation and on-line services. It is here that the virtual student and the virtual librarian can a common locus. Any interactive environment has to be allocated staff to maintain its quality of service. This is already apparent with the WWW-manager links on numerous Home pages and now the IPLMOO also plans to provide a live, on-line reference service. Dorman (1995) illustrates the importance of allocating staff responsibilities to libraries on the WEB. The New York Public Library (http://www.nypl.org) has used a 15-person task force to structure the WWW design by allocating staff who would be responsible for EACH of the home pages to be developed. The aim is to assign the creation of online resources to the appropriate subject specialists within the library. This approach must be taken with any Internet services including MOO, chat and desktop video.

By linking the MOO to the WEB and adding a virtual librarian presence at AussieMOO, we can provide an enhanced quality of interaction for online education. McAfee and Eustace (1995) described how interaction on a MOO using a style called the *written conversation*, invokes the thought process in the user.

COMPETING TECHNOLOGIES

Competing technologies such as video conferencing generally require high bandwidth connections and a high performance machine. The MOO is a low bandwidth service and WWW is also available at low bandwidth, using hypertext clients such as lynx. Lynx is an efficient text client for the WWW, especially when most information accessed exists as text.

Equal opportunities for access are then provided to users with limited technology levels, as you don't need the latest technology to participate. Many countries only have e-mail and telnet services, but that would still provide access to text-based WWW and MOO resources.

Emerging Pedagogy. Educators are embracing new teaching pedagogy related to:

- Interactive processes,
- Flexible participation,
- Student student control of learning,
- Communication communication in real time,
- Criterion-referenced learning,
- Electronic publishing;
- Fascination by users with text-based systems;
- Building and maintaining knowledge for the organisation.

Electronic Publishing. WEB and MOO server management will become popular as users want greater control over the media using new object-oriented scripting languages such as Python or Java can open scripting to more users.

WWW/MOO interface and the Popularity of Text-based Virtual Reality. The developers of lambdaMOO did not conceive the popularity of their MOO with over 5000 users, but the text-based interaction of the MOO and Internet Relay Chat (IRC) are still gaining in popularity.

A MOO is a type of multi-user virtual environment that allows interaction between players and objects in a form that is similar to adventure games. It is a rich environment, but is limited to a text-based or keyboard interface. The MOO is the dynamic or synchronous partner of the WWW/MOO interface. WWW is the static or asynchronous partner and most attempts have identified that there are four ways to go beyond the WEB and the MOO:

- multiple windows on the local screen;

- a new WWW client;

- a large set of server-side perl or python scripts for dynamic documents (forms, maps)

- Java programming language and the promise of dynamic clients

A new client or a set of CGI (Common Gateway Interface) scripts may have to be developed to cope with a MOO server. Certainly Java is going to make the client software more responsive to the incoming data, but it is a proprietary product, it has been slow to migrate down to the MS Windows and Macintosh platforms and will require a high performance machine like video conferencing, in some cases. Fellows and Eustace (in preparation) have determined that a new WWW/MOO like protocol, server and client may be the answer to building the interface required for distance education needs. Such an architecture may be built using the object-oriented language called python and will be the subject of a forthcoming paper on the *ROO Project*.

CONCLUSIONS

Harnessing new technology to enhance CPE for librarians offers new opportunities, and if offered via the Internet need not restrict access nor teaching methods. The learner centered model using

- IFLA official languages on the Internet;

- interactive dialogue;

- increased involvement of the teacher/supervisor in the learning process;

- a higher staff/student ratio;

- modern communications technology;

- a wide range of teaching and learning strategies

offers ways of pooling our resources globally to provide the quality CPE needed in the time of change occasioned partly by the new communications technology itself.

REFERENCES

Audley, D. (1996), "Development of a policy for the accreditation of electronic flexible delivery programs," *The Virtual University? Symposium*, 21-22 November 1996. Parkville, University of Melbourne, pp. 85-90.

Anderson, T. (1994), "Using the Internet for distance education delivery and professional development," *Open Praxis*, Vol. 2, pp. 8-11.

Bates, A. W. (1994), "Educational multi-media in a networked society." *Open Praxis*, Vol. 2, pp 22-26.

Brownlee, R. and Ingham, J. (1996), Cu-SeeMe Report Discussion. [Online]. Available as e-mail from VIDEOCON@ASUVM.INRE.ASU.EDU, VIDEOCON: Video Conferencing list.

Curtis, P. and Nichols, D.A. (1993), MUDs Grow Up: Social Virtual Reality in the Real World Xerox PARC, Palo Alto, USA: [Online]. Available FTP: file://parcftp.xerox.com/pub/MOO/papers/MUDsGrowUp.txt

Dimitroyannis, D. (1994), Virtual Classroom: A Case Study. 1st International World-Wide-Web Conference - WWW '94, Geneva, Switzerland, (May 25-27). [Online]. Available at http://www.elsevier.nl/WWW94preview.html

Dorman, D. (1995), "Untangling the Web at the Exhibits," *American Libraries,* Vol. 26, 8 (September), pp. 806-808.

Duffy, T.M. et al eds. (1993), *Designing Environments for Constructive Learning,* Berlin, Springer-Verlag.

Eustace, K. (1995), "The Lyceum Project: Some aspects of networked interactive technologies in university teaching," Research in progress, Available as e-mail: keustace@csu.edu.au

Eustace, Ken (1996), "The Lyceum Project ," Masters thesis: Available online at http://www.csu.edu.au/research/sda/Reports/paideiat.html

Eustace, Ken (1997), "The Paideia Experience : A Challenging Global Open Learning Initiative" in preparation.

Eustace, K and McAfee, M. (1995), "Beyond the WEB and the MOO in Education. " *Proceedings of the Australian Computers in Education Conference, ACEC'95,* July 9-13, Perth, Australia. [Online]. Available WWW: http://www.csu.edu.au/research/sda/Papers/webmoo2.html/

Gorman, M. (1995), "Five New Laws of Librarianship." *American Libraries,* Vol. 26, 8, (September), pp. 784-785.

Habermas, J. (1987), *The Theory of Communicative Action. Vol. 1, Reason and the Rationalisation of Society.* (translated by Thomas McCarthy). London, Heinemann.

Hall, P. (1996), "Distance education and electronic networking, " *Information Technology for Development* Vol. 7, pp. 75-89.

Henri, J. and Hay, L. (1996), "Commentary - TLS and the Internet: Opportunities for Professional Development." *Access* , Vol. 10, 3, pp 10-12.

Lipman, M. (1991), *Thinking in Education.*, Cambridge, Cambridge University Press.

McAfee, M. (1994), "Teaching and Learning on the Web: Paideia. 1st International World-Wide-Web Conference - WWW '94, Geneva, Switzerland, (May 25-27).

Raggett, D., Lam, J. and Alexander, I. (1996), *HTML3: Electronic Publishing on the Web.* Harlow, England, Addison-Wesley.

Rheingold, H. (1988), "Virtual Communities," *Whole Earth Review,* (Winter).

Rochester, M. K. and Pearce, Wendy (1993), "Use of distance education strategies for continuing education: progress, issues and challenges" in *Continuing Professional Education and IFLA,* Munchen, Saur, pp. 63-84.

Schneider, D. (1995), The TECFAMOO Home Page. [Online]. Available at http://tecfa.unige.ch/tecfamoo.html

Sparkes, J. (1984), "Pedagogic differences between media," In Bates, A.W. (ed.) *The Role of Technology in Distance Education.* London, Croom Helm.

CONTINUING PROFESSIONAL DEVELOPMENT AND FLEXIBLE INFORMATION WORKERS: PROBLEMS AND OPPORTUNITIES

Anne Goulding
Evelyn Kerslake
Department of Information and Library Studies
Loughborough University, UK.

Abstract:	Today's fast-changing information environment means that initial professional library and information qualifications have a limited shelf-life. This paper explores flexible workers' CPD needs and opportunities, drawing on the findings of a British Library-funded study involving 575 libraries from the public, commercial, academic and health sectors (Goulding and Kerslake, 1996a).

INTRODUCTION

Today's fast-changing information environment means that initial professional library and information qualifications have a limited shelf-life. In response, systematic, career-long, continuing professional development (CPD) has been advocated as the way to maintain the longevity and effectiveness of those qualifications. This seems a reasonable solution, unless, that is, you are one of the growing numbers of professional library workers who are part of the flexible labour market and do not work on permanent and full-time employment contracts. For these professionals who make up an increasing proportion of today's information labour market, the need for CPD has never been greater, while the chances of receiving high quality CPD appear slim.

This paper explores flexible workers' CPD needs and opportunities, drawing on the findings of a British Library-funded study involving 575 libraries from the public, commercial, academic and health sectors (Goulding and Kerslake, 1996a). A general lack of CPD opportunities for flexible workers is identified which could result in the down-skilling of these workers in direct contradiction to the numerous calls from the European Union, the UK government and professional bodies to maintain and, if at all possible, increase skill levels in the labour market. Failure to develop flexible workers could have serious implications for the skills profile of the information workforce and, thus, for the quality of services. The paper also explores the possibility that in failing to offer CPD to these workers, who are predominantly women, library and information services may also be contravening sex discrimination legislation.

BACKGROUND

Continuing Professional Development.

The benefits of CPD for information and library workers have been well rehearsed in the pages of the professional and academic press (see e.g. Hendry, 1996; Kinnell Evans, 1995; Freeman, 1993). According to Webb, (1991) CPD plays a dual role:

> CPD is seen not only as a means of offering job enrichment to the individual, but also as the key to developing a top quality workforce, capable of taking initiatives and making a maximum contribution to each organisation's changing needs. (p. iv)

In the United Kingdom the Library Association's Framework for CPD has been the main force highlighting the need for continuing education, post-initial qualifications. It aims to encourage library and information workers to monitor and chart their own development, and then to assume responsibility for learning.

Employees are thus facing pressure from their own organisations, professional associations and even national and European governments to keep pace with change by maintaining and extending their skills and knowledge through participation in CPD activities. While this pressure applies to all employees, certain types of workers may find it more difficult to meet these expectations and, as a consequence, fall by the wayside in terms of knowledge and expertise. This is certainly a danger as regards the growing numbers of flexible library and information service (LIS) workers.

Flexible Workers.

The human resource management issues surrounding numerical and temporal flexibility are of growing concern in all sectors, particularly in services like LIS where use of part-time and temporary workers is high (Goulding and Kerslake, 1996b).   There are many types of flexible workers employed in the LIS sector including those who:

* work part-time on a permanent basis: although, as the Equal Opportunities Commission (1995, p. 4) notes, part-time working "means different things to different people";

* job-share: where "two or more people voluntarily share the responsibilities of what is normally a full-time job" (New Ways to Work, 1993, p. 14);

* are on full or part-time temporary or casual contracts: those who are employed on daily, weekly, monthly or other short-term contracts which end at the employer's discretion; and,

* work term-time: those who work only when the academic institution is teaching, and not during vacations or holidays;

* have annualised hours contracts: defined by New Ways to Work as "a system whereby the period of time within which employees must work is defined over a whole year" (1993, p. 27). Thus the average 37.5 hour working week becomes 1,702.5 hours (after holiday and bank holiday entitlements) which are worked in the course of the year.

The British Library-funded research mentioned above covered all but the last of these different types of flexible workers.

The Research.

Although flexible workers have long been part of the information workforce (see e.g. Weibel and Heim, 1979; Severns, 1953; Layzell Ward, 1966) there is little information available to managers on their characteristics and management; a worrying situation at a time when their numbers are increasing. The British Library study aimed to redress this dearth of information focusing specifically on flexible workers' training and development needs and opportunities. The research consisted of a questionnaire survey and case study interviews with a variety of types of flexible workers and their managers. This paper will concentrate on the interviews conducted with flexible workers and their managers, specifically their perception of flexible workers' CPD needs and opportunities and the barriers they consider prevent their full participation in CPD activities.

FLEXIBLE WORKERS' CPD NEEDS AND OPPORTUNITIES

The Managers' Position.

According to the CBI (1994), employers may question the extent to which part-time and temporary workers can and should benefit from long-term career development on the same basis as permanent full-time staff. When flexible workers are measured against these 'real' workers (Coote and Campbell quoted in Purdy, 1988, p. 157) they are found lacking by employers who assume that 'real' work means long hours. This leads to a perception of flexible workers as less committed, less ambitious, as generally lesser workers than their full-time colleagues. Consequently, this is used to justify the lack of training and development offered to flexible workers and the differentiation between the types of training offered to flexible workers on the one hand, and permanent full-time workers on the other (Beechy and Perkins, 1987). This position was clearly expressed by one case study manager:

> ...there's even more of a distinction in our minds between the casual staff who are here for a very short period, compared to all out permanent staff who tend to be here for thirty years and we accept the responsibility in developing them as people. (Special library manager)

This manager later stated quite categorically that there was no policy of developing these workers for the future although they were equipped with the necessary skills for their current jobs.

Not all managers took this blinkered view, however, and others did accept responsibility for the future employability of their services' flexible workers. One manager said of temporary workers:

> I think we try and give them the opportunity to do as much long-term development as possible because we know that the situation is temporary ... so rather that say you can only do things that are related to the work we do here ..., where things have arisen that people have wanted to go on, we have said 'just go', because it's important. (Academic library manager)

Similarly, a manager of job-sharers said:

> ...basically we try to make sure that we can provide encouragement and development that will enable them to go on and be broader and better all-rounders and broaden their horizons. It won't just be relevant to the job and we don't say, 'Well you're an indexer so you can only have training on indexing'. (Special library manager)

Both these managers recognised the importance of the maintenance and development of skills in an era of rapid change and also stressed the organisation's responsibility to facilitate access to development opportunities, and to encourage all workers to participate regardless of their employment status. This attitude, however, was the exception rather than the rule as development training was not offered as a matter of course to the flexible workers who participated in the group discussions.

The Flexible Workers' Position.

Opportunities for flexible workers to participate in development training were rare. Flexible working patterns can mean that workers miss out on CPD activities, as illustrated by this comment from a job-sharer:

> ...that was specifically one area which I'd lost out on through being part-time because I wanted to do French refresher basically and it was organised ... for days when I could attend and then it was changed and I sort of said, 'Hey, you've got me down for this course and I won't be able to attend if you change it', but it didn't make any difference. It was still changed to a day when I couldn't come ... So I just had to drop that. (Special library)

This group of job-sharers also gave examples of workers who had taken part in these types of development activities when they were permanent full-time workers but had stopped doing so when they changed to flexible working patterns. The flexible workers in the discussion groups often noted that some workers in their library/information service were more likely to have access to development opportunities than others, but even where flexible workers did have access to development opportunities this was usually restricted in some way. A job-sharer said:

> ...you're actively encouraged if it is job specific, but you're not encouraged or you're actually refused if it's not job-specific. (Special library)

Despite difficulties flexible workers faced in accessing development opportunities, they were aware of the benefit of this type of activity. Although certain individuals within the discussion groups expressed a lack of interest in training and development, they were a small minority. Generally workers realised that their organisations were undergoing change and that new skills were needed. The personal benefits of CPD were also recognised:

> C   I think it has a concrete effect in affecting your daily work and also you can show to management that you're interested and active in developing the job, so I think it does help. It's just like a signal, 'I am here' sort of thing.

A   And it's something to add to your c.v. (Job-sharers, Special library)

The chance to meet other LIS workers was also frequently mentioned as a valuable element of CPD activities.   A group of temporary part-time workers felt that this kind of informal communication between workers was vital:

C   The internet course that I went on ... there were other librarians
           from other colleges in the area, and I liked that aspect of it. It was
           quite interesting to meet other librarians from different types of
           libraries.

A   Actually, that's the best bit, meeting the people from the other colleges.

D   ... a lot of what you gain in going to another place is the interaction with
           other people, and a lot more can be gained from lunchtime and coffee-time
           than -

B   Than listening to the lectures, yeah.

Although this is true for permanent full-time workers and flexible workers equally, due to marginalisation within their own organisations, opportunities for flexible workers to meet other similarly situated workers and generally to network are extremely important. The results of a lack of development training was illustrated by the comments of a job-sharer who was becoming de-skilled because of her non-participation in CPD activities:

           I was quite familiar with computers when I came to work here because I'd
           had training where I'd worked before, but it's all changed since then and I haven't
           had any training since I came here. (Public library)

The extracts from interviews with both managers and workers above suggest that although they are often aware of the need for CPD, there are certain barriers preventing flexible workers participating fully in CPD activities. These can broadly be divided into physical and attitudinal barriers.

BARRIERS TO FLEXIBLE WORKER PARTICIPATION IN CPD

The ideology of flexible work encourages the assumption that flexible workers are not interested in development opportunities. This can then be used by managers to justify their reluctance to offer CPD activities to flexible workers. During the focus group discussions a minority of workers did indeed express diffidence. These reservations on the part of both managers and workers will hereafter be referred to as *attitudinal* barriers. Overwhelmingly, however, flexible workers in the group stated that they were unable (rather than unwilling) to attend development opportunities, i.e. there were certain *physical* barriers preventing their full participation in CPD.

Physical Barriers.

The physical barriers which prevent flexible workers taking advantage of development opportunities can be summarised as financial, logistical, and organisational.

i)   <u>Financial</u>: financial barriers operated to inhibit flexible workers' participation in
           CPD in two main way. Firstly, flexible workers, especially those working fewer
           than full-time hours, may earn low wages and this has a direct impact on their
           ability to participate in training opportunities. Secondly, flexible workers in some
           groups were in no doubt that their library/information service did not want to invest
           in their training.
The first of these obstacles is felt especially acutely by those with caring responsibilities. A job-sharer, for example, had to spend extra on child-care because her employer would not allow her to swap her working days for time spent training outside her normal working hours. This worker was

thus, unwillingly, picking up a substantial part of the cost of training which appears to be provided by her employer. While this worker may have had as equal access to development opportunities as full-time workers, this equality came at a cost which her full-time colleagues did not have to bear. This raises the very important issues of who pays for workers' development. Recent government policy in the UK has shifted responsibility for training away from itself and towards the immediate beneficiary. Similarly, the British Library Association's Framework for Continuous Professional Development aims to encourage individuals to take responsibility for the education and training required to maintain their employability. This does not mean, however, that employers can abrogate all their responsibility in the CPD process. Organisations still need to ensure that they, at the very least, cultivate a climate in which CPD can take place, if they do not actively support it.

Flexible workers in the focus groups often criticised this shift of responsibility for funding CPD from organisations onto workers, especially if they felt that the organisation was going to benefit, as this extract from a focus group discussion with job-sharers illustrates:

B	...we both asked to go (on the course) and it was £10 and we were refused so (worker A) paid for herself and I said 'forget it'!
AG	So neither of you were going to be paid for?
B	Our line manager wouldn't pay £10.
A	That's right. I actually managed to get the time back but he was reluctant to do that, but in fact the library displays have benefited a lot from just that short course and it's a shame because we both would have benefited enormously from it, and the service would have done.

The criticism here stems from the small cost involved and the 'enormous' benefit gained. While this situation is not perhaps unique to flexible workers, because they generally earn less that permanent full-time workers the cost of subsidising their own training is comparatively greater.

The second of the financial barriers - the cost of training flexible workers - can be a major obstacle for those organisations with large numbers of part-time or job-share staff. A manager of a public library service which employed a lot of job-sharers said:

> ...you have to train two people to get a whole in a sense. So there are issues where perhaps both of them need health and safety training ... and you've got to train both halves, and if you're paying for that it pushes up all the training costs.

These financial implications can lead managers to formulate training and development policies which penalise job-sharers and deliberately exclude them from receiving the same amount of development as other workers, including other flexible workers:

> ...one of the things that we've come up against is that we've been told that job-sharers can't do the same course because we're one post. Unless you can convince them, they will only pay for one of us to go, and then the idea is that you come back and tell you partner.

Job-sharers are therefore treated differently because of their working pattern and, as will be discussed below, organisations pursuing this policy may be in danger of contravening sex discrimination legislation.

ii)   <u>Logistical barriers</u>: Flexible workers in the focus group discussions described a whole host of logistical barriers that prevented them participating in developmental opportunities. The flexible workers often worked a 'double-shift', combining paid employment with domestic/caring responsibilities, studying, other part-time jobs or self-employment. Ensuring that all commitments are met means that a delicate balance has to maintained. Development activities organised outside regular working hours disturbs this balance and for focus group participants this was a significant barrier preventing their participation. Difficulties in rearranging child-care for day-long training courses, for example, were often mentioned as a major obstacle.

Lack of knowledge of CPD activities was also commented upon. This particularly affects those flexible workers who do not work full-time hours as there may be significant periods of time when they are not in the workplace and by the time they hear of the activity it may be too late to apply. Minimal staffing levels in LIS services can also make it difficult for flexible workers to attend, especially as they are often deployed to cover periods of peak service demand. A job-sharer in a public library said that participation was "always governed by the ability to release you". Flexible workers were also aware that if they were absent on courses, very often somebody else had to do their duties:

> You were made very aware that if you're not there staff are going to be left
> short, and they resent you for it. There's no two ways about it; they resent you if you
> go off on a course. (Job-sharer, public library)

Again, although this could apply equally to permanent full-time workers, flexible workers working fewer that full-time hours possibly felt more pressure to be at their work station for all of their contracted hours. This issue is discussed in more detail below in the section headed 'attitudinal barriers'.

iii) <u>Organisational barriers</u>: There were some examples given in the discussion groups of barriers created by organisational policies which prevented flexible workers from participating in development activities. As has been discussed above, organisational policies about training for job sharers in some services restrict development opportunities to the post rather than the number of workers in that post. To compound problems, cascading training between job-share partners can be made more difficult if there is little, or no, overlap time in the job-share.

A potential impediment to CPD facing part-time term-time workers in an academic library was that there was no way of recompensing them for any training taken outside their working hours. Time-off-in-lieu was not available, nor was it the policy of the service to pay for hours spent training, so any training would have to be within their regular hours of work. As these workers were employed part-time and only in term-time to cover the service's peak demand period, this was difficult.

Refusal to back an application for training can itself form a barrier to training as it may deter others from making requests. Job-sharers in a special library, for example, had made a mental note that a colleague had been refused development training which was not directly job related, and they gave this as the reason that they had not asked their manager about similar development opportunities. This emphasises the need for managers to explain fully when refusing training requests as rumours can snowball leading to resentment and feeling of being a second class worker.

The financial, logistical and organisational barriers outlined above demonstrate the variety of physical hurdles which may come between flexible workers and development opportunities. There are, however, other less obvious psychological barriers that prevent flexible workers' full participation in CPD.

Attitudinal Barriers.

The attitudes of managers towards developing their flexible workforce and the attitudes of flexible workers themselves towards their work raise two more subtle obstacles to flexible workers' participation in development activities.

i) <u>Managers' attitudes</u>: As already discussed above, managers may feel that training and development for flexible workers represents a waste of organisational resources and, generally, the managers of flexible workers interviewed for this study were not keen to support education and training which was not related to their flexible workers' jobs. Despite the widespread use of, for example, part-time staff, there is still a common view among managers that any employee working less than permanent full-time hours lacks the necessary commitment to their work and the organisation:

> ...psychologically work is almost more of a sideline for a lot of the female part-timers that we have, and that's not to say that they're not committed and they're not competent and they're not able, but they just have a lot of other things going on. (Academic library manager)

In one sentence this manager stereotypes both women and part-timers as workers whose main concern in life is not in the workplace. Although the manager qualifies this generalisation by stressing the capabilities of part-time workers, attitudes like these can lead to discrimination in the workplace. In a similar vein a manager of term-time workers said:

> They are not initially as interested as perhaps a full-time worker might be. I'm not saying they are not interested at all, but perhaps their reasons for having the job are slightly different. (School library manager)

Managers often believed, therefore, that flexible workers have different motivations for working and want different things from work compared with permanent full-time staff, and that this reflects in their attitudes to work. There are, perhaps, elements of truth in all these assertions but their differences should not be used by managers as an excuse to treat flexible workers in an adverse manner and, in particular, they should not be used to deny them development opportunities. It was not only managers who constructed psychological barriers to flexible workers' participation in CPD, however, the workers themselves also expounded individual, internally motivated reasons which prevented their own participation.

ii)   <u>Workers' attitudes</u>: As well as the physical and logistical barriers to their participation in CPD discussed above, flexible workers also experienced psychological pressures which prevented them taking these opportunities. These were generally time pressure associated with the nature and organisation of their flexible working positions into which CPD activities were difficult to fit:

> If you are part-time every minute counts. I don't think you have quite the same flexibility with your time that you do if you are full-time ..., perhaps I felt that because I was a newer member of staff that something more general like equal opps training or assertiveness training, I felt would be more difficult to justify - especially if it was a whole day course - more difficult for me to justify for me to attend, especially if it was on a day when I wasn't normally in, than if I were full time. That's partly the workload and ... feeling kind of you're letting that down if you went on something, if it was kind of perhaps more for you than specifically of direct benefit or immediate benefit to the job. (Job-sharer, special library)

The time-pressured nature of flexible work meant that the flexible workers in the discussion groups often viewed CPD activity as a distraction from the main purpose of their job:

> ...when you work two and a half days a week your workload is such that I think you have to be much better about managing your time, so that if you do decide to do something like spend a day out, I was going to say waste a

> day going out, if you spend a day going on a course it means that you have a lot more work to do when you come back... (Job-sharer, special library)

Although permanent full-time workers may feel a similar pressure, flexible workers feel that, as one job-sharer said, "every minutes counts" and that their tight working schedule made devoting working time to general development activities more difficult to justify. The worker's choice of words in the last quote, i.e. "waste a day going out" are particularly revealing suggesting that development training is considered a somewhat indulgent activity, peripheral to the main purpose of the job. Even more significant, perhaps, the worker acknowledged her inappropriate turn of phrase.

CONCLUSIONS

The attitudes toward CPD displayed by the flexible workers participating in this study were mixed. It should be remembered, however, that any negative attitudes could be as much the result of a lack of a training culture within their organisation as their own lack of enthusiasm. Furthermore, those with positive attitudes towards developing themselves were not always participating in this kind of activity which suggests that good intentions on the part of workers is not sufficient to motivate them to participate; there also needs to be commitment and encouragement from the organisation. Managers' readiness to encourage their flexible workers to participate in CPD activities was conditioned by their general attitudes towards flexible workers. On the one hand, those who believed that flexible workers are not as committed or ambitious as their permanent full-time colleagues saw little need for development training and assumed a lack of interest on the part of the flexible workers in their services. On the other hand, managers with more enlightened views of the capabilities of flexible workers encouraged their workers to participate in development opportunities and, recognising the uncertain nature of the labour market, felt obliged to facilitate training and development activities.

Organisations neglecting to offer development and training to their flexible workers need to be aware that they may be contravening sex discrimination legislation. Although flexible information workers are not all women, they are overwhelmingly women (Goulding and Kerslake, 1996b) and this may be enough to bring training for flexible workers under the jurisdiction of a 1994 House of Lords ruling, which stated:

> ... the application of different qualifying conditions for part-timers in employment legislation discriminated against women contrary to European equal pay and equal treatment laws ... (Employment Gazette, 1995, p. 43)

Employment law experts Leighton and O'Donnell observe that this could be extended to cover training opportunities:

> If, for example, part-timers and temporary staff who are predominantly female ... are denied access to ... training, this will probably be seen as discriminatory and unlawful. (Leighton and O'Donnell, 1995)

Another imperative which should compel library and information service to act on the findings reported here is the need to pursue quality initiatives which demand new skills of staff and should encourage managers to evaluate their current training provision and recruitment criteria. By excluding from training a large section of workers on which the library service is heavily reliant, library and information services are in danger of compromising the quality of their provision.

The evidence suggests that flexible workers do not have equal access to CPD activities for a variety of reasons. To encourage flexible workers to participate, library and information services need to develop a training culture, and establish and encourage the use of facilitation systems such as time-off-in-lieu and financial assistance with additional care provision. Managers should also make the effort to stress to all flexible workers that development training is not a perk but is their right and responsibility to keep up with developments and maintain their skills for the service and their own career development.

REFERENCES

Beechey, V. and T. Perkins, T. (1987), *A matter of hours.* Cambridge: Polity.

CBI (1994). *Flexible training markets. Who pays for training?* London: CBI.

Employment Gazette (1995), "Statutory rights for part-time workers," *Employment Gazette,* February, p. 43.

Equal Opportunities Commission (1995), *Part-time workers, not second class citizens.* Manchester: Equal Opportunities Commission.

Freeman, M. (1993), "Education and training for librarianship and information services in the UK," *New Library World*, 94 (1108), pp. 12-14.

Goulding, A. and Kerslake, E. (1996a), *Developing the flexible library and information workforce: a quality and equal opportunities perspective*, Boston Spa: British Library Research and Innovation Centre, BLR&I Report No. 25.

Goulding, A. and Kerslake, E. (1996b), "Flexible working in libraries: profit and potential pitfalls," *Library Management*, 17 (2), pp. 8-16

Hendry, J. (1996), "On the fast track or the road to nowhere," *Library Association Record*, 98 (7), pp. 356-357.

Kinnell Evans, M. (1995), "Adding value: Management education and continuing professional development in the library and information sector," *In:* M Haycock-Beaulieu and N. Ole Pors eds. *Proceeding of the 1st British-Nordic Conference on Library and Information Studies, 22-24 May 1995, Copenhagen.* Copenhagen: Royal School of Librarianship, pp. 147-156.

Layzell Ward, P. (1966), *Women and librarianship.* London: Library Association.

Leighton, P. and O'Donnell, A. (1995), *The new employment contract: using employment contracts effectively.* London: Nicholas Brearly.

New Ways to Work (1993), *Change at the top. Working flexibly at senior and managerial levels in organisations.* London: New Ways to Work.

Purdy, D. (1988), *Social power and the labour market.* Basingstoke: Macmillan.

Severns, H. and Sarah B. Askew (1953), *In:* E. M. Danton, ed. *Pioneering leaders in librarianship.* ALA: Chicago, pp. 13-21.

Webb, S. P. (1991), *Best practice? Continuing professional development for library/information staff in UK professional firms.* Berkhamsted: British Library Research and Development Department, BLRD&D Report No. 6039.

Weibel, K. and K. Heim, K (1979), *The role of women in librarianship 1876-1976: the entry, advancement, struggle for equalization in one profession.* Phoenix: Oryx.

FUTURE ACADEMIC LIBRARY SKILLS:
WHAT WILL THEY BE?

Steve Morgan
University of the West of England

Abstract: The academic library of the future will require certain skills and academic credentials. This paper explores those areas, plus the personal qualities needed.

INTRODUCTION

Speculation on what the library of the future will look like has become an increasingly popular pastime. The issue has been explored not only in the professional literature (Joint Funding Councils' Libraries Review Group 1993;Heseltine 1994) but also through electronic discussion lists and bulletin boards. The question also continues to intrigue those conducting job interviews in academic librarianship. Of course, such forecasting is partly dependent on the timescale envisaged but can cover a number of different scenarios. These range from the idea of information technology retaining its role in support of printed texts for many years to come through to the library as a physical entity disappearing completely. In this scenario the library becomes almost independent of time and place. Although similar discussions have taken place in the past in relation to microform formats and the early experiments with automation, recently this issue has acquired a more urgent and focused edge. Rapid technological developments are taking place in a number of areas, in particular, global networking and telecommunications, digitisation and electronic publishing and delivery. These are acting as catalysts in focusing the attention of information professionals, the academic community and, thanks to the interest shown by the mass media, the general public. The virtual library, the library without walls and the electronic campus are just some of the terms regularly used to conceptualise the library of the future. A more cautious note is struck by Stoll (1995, p.214) who warns against the danger of a "library without value" rather than without walls.

Inevitably, the discussion then turns to the future role of the academic librarian - or is it cybrarian? - in this envisaged world of technological and educational sophistication. How will it change? What new skills will be needed? Which of the librarian's traditional skills will be retained? How will the convergence of support services affect staffing structures, responsibilities and working conditions? What effect will unemployment and increased competition for jobs have on the types of skill requirements? Will the librarian as a species disappear alongside the library as a physical entity?

KEY SKILLS

It is safe to assume that the current plurality of information formats - the electronic sitting alongside the printed - will remain with us for some while yet. It is difficult and possibly futile to be more precise about the likely balance between the two. This is the premise on which this paper is based. However, only one set of skills highlighted here is related to information technology. Important though such skills are and will be in the future, there is a danger that people- and service-based skills will become neglected particularly in the professional literature. There is a certain irony here. The more the debate revolves around information technology, the greater the realisation that it is the people - the various constituents within the academic community - who are the significant players. Information technology will continue to be the means rather than the end. Helping to connect people with the required information regardless of format will remain a basic tenet of academic librarianship. Information technology will continue to develop and represent one vehicle among many through which this connectivity will be achieved. The time when students and academic staff interact regularly and effectively with library and information services without the need for guidance and advice is still some way off.

Periodically, there is a debate about the best model to provide library and information services within further and higher education. Unlike Heseltine (1995), I reject the suggested demise of subject librarianship. Currently, it remains the model most suited to the provision of support for teaching, learning and research. It is through this subject-based approach that the various academic library services are delivered most effectively. This view is also supported by Fielden (1993), National Board of Employment, Education and Training (1990) and House and Moon (1994).

Before turning to the particular skills required for the future, it needs to be stressed that there are key areas of traditional information work where proficiency is still required. These will apply to any librarian or information professional regardless of the sector into which (s)he operates. These are some of them:

- Identifying and meeting the information needs of the clientele

- Identifying, accessing, organising, interpreting and evaluating knowledge and information

- Interpersonal and communication skills

- Professional development including updating IT-related skills

- Generic management skills

This paper highlights some of the essential core skills for the academic librarian of today and the foreseeable future. The skills and qualities are grouped under the following headings:

- Educational credibility

- User education

- IT-related skills

- Management skills

The final part of the paper suggests that for these skills to flourish, they have to be managed in such a way that there is co-ordination, consistency and continuity.

EDUCATIONAL CREDIBILITY

In my view it is vital for librarians to gain credibility in an educational role. This represents the key to their effective integration into the academic community. There are few quick and easy ways of developing these skills and attitudes. How to achieve credibility with academic staff is difficult to describe. However, rather like politicians possessing that quality of gravitas, you know it when you see it! Hidden behind the notion of "credibility" are a variety of elements including status, academic qualifications, subject-based knowledge, academic activities, personal qualities and professionalism. These are discussed in turn.

Status.

The status of the librarian within the faculty or department has been a continuing source of debate in the US (Mitchell 1992; Krompart 1992; Major 1993). Resolution appears no nearer as librarians strive to reach a consensus on two issues:

- Are librarians' responsibilities suitably scholarly, academic and professional to qualify as faculty?

- Should librarians have the same conditions of service, performance criteria etc. as academic staff?

In the UK professional literature less prominence is given to the librarian's formal status within institutions. There is, however, a wide variety of different perceptions on their role within the academic community. Are they administrators, educators, some kind of hybrid, providers of support, scholars, professionals or curators who stamp books? The perceptions of academic staff can be reinforced or altered in a number of ways:

- Improving the standing of the library service within the institution generally raises the standing of the librarians as individual professionals.

- The librarian who has confidence in the library's role in relation to academic departments is able to speak convincingly about meeting their information needs.

- Librarian visibility within academic departments is an important source of awareness raising. This may include participating in and presenting papers at influential meetings. It may also take in more subtle activities such as e-mailing staff for their opinions, involvement in social events or organising departmental workshops.

- It is unhelpful for librarians who may be highly paid and whose conditions of service may resemble their academic counterparts to be seen carrying out tasks which are inappropriate for that level of staff. It may also be inadvisable on purely economic grounds.

Basically, the academic librarian is seeking parity of esteem within a community of scholars.

Academic Qualifications and Subject Knowledge

The librarian who has a graduate or postgraduate qualification in a subject relevant to a particular department or faculty will gain credibility by virtue of subject familiarity. Where there are no formal subject qualifications, a broad knowledge of the areas covered by the departments is usually a prerequisite for dealing with ease with the academic staff. A higher degree obtained in library and information studies demonstrates an affinity not only with postgraduate students and their problems of studying at that level but also with the academic staff many of whom will have a similar level of qualification. Increasingly, academic librarians are recognising the importance of their educational role by gaining teaching qualifications.

Academic Activities.

To be able to participate in scholarly activities undoubtedly increases the librarian's credibility. This may take the form of:

- Publishing journal articles, books, chapters, book reviews etc.

- Editorships of journals, newsletters

- Presenting papers at or organising conferences

There are also a variety of institutional activities in which librarians can take part - to the benefit of the institution, the department, the library and the individual. These may include visits from validating bodies, inspections by Government officials, teaching and research assessments, institutional reviews, cross-departmental bodies etc. The effect which the librarian's contribution to such high-profile events has on other academic staff should not be underestimated.

Personal Qualities.

The librarian who is positive, proactive, highly motivated and assertive is likely to foster productive relationships with academic staff and give them confidence in their ability. Effective librarians will not allow themselves to be intimidated. The library profession is obsessed with its own image (Atkinson 1994) which is partly self-generated but continually fuelled by the mass media. Although the problem is less pronounced in academic libraries, there still remains a hard-core of perceptions which include lack of confidence, modesty, resistance to change, inferiority and introversion. Employers and Library Schools have a responsibility to ensure that entrants to the profession possess the appropriate personal qualities. When such qualities are accompanied by effective interpersonal skills - in particular, communication skills - credibility is enhanced.

Professionalism.

Librarians who demonstrate a "professional" approach to their work gain the respect of academic colleagues and users alike. This professional/client relationship may work at an informal level e.g. ensuring that agreed action resulting from a enquiry is actually followed up or at a formal level e.g. an appointments or surgery system. This kind of system demonstrates the value of the librarian's time and has parallels with other professions such as solicitors, doctors, dentists etc.

USER EDUCATION

The librarian's educational role forms the central plank on which his/her other duties and responsibilities are built (Heery and Morgan 1996). This approach is also recognised by Fielden (1993, p.6):

"Subject librarians will have to understand teaching/learning skills if they begin to fulfil para-academic functions".

It is vital that the librarian develops a range of methods to train students in the skills of self-reliance. This is particularly important given the shift from teaching to learning, the higher profile of transferable skills and the increasingly electronic environment. These changes have profound implications for librarians as trainers as well as the student body.

In addition to the core skills required for providing effective user education, it is apparent that the librarian needs to become more adaptable and flexible in the teaching and learning environment. Increasingly there are encouraging examples in which the librarian (in conjunction with academic staff) has the freedom to organise the structure, methods, location and evaluation of programmes. All too often in the past, much of the programme detail has been imposed by others. The ability to take either of these scenarios and turn it into an experience which benefits the student requires flexibility and adaptability.

So what are some of the elements that the librarian has to take into account?

The librarian needs to:

- Be equally comfortable whether user education takes place with one person or over 200

- Be equally comfortable whether the session takes place in an informal but familiar setting (a tutorial in the librarian's office) or in a formal but unfamiliar one (a room within the academic department with minimal equipment)

- Understand how students organise their studies and how they go about learning. In this way library programmes may be tailored to majority needs and styles of learning

- Become familiar with a wide variety of teaching and learning methods including coaching, facilitation, workbooks, joint or group teaching and, increasingly nowadays, the opportunities provided by the electronic classroom

- Be aware of different types of users. These include part-time and distance learning students, overseas and disabled students, those students coming directly from schools, tertiary and further education colleges, higher education colleges, universities, mature students, women returners etc.

- Aim to turn constraints - staffing, time, size of group, facilities - into opportunities where negotiations have proved unsuccessful

- Build into user education programmes appropriate provision for short- and long-term skills acquisition

- Be prepared to innovate and take risks whenever the opportunity presents itself
-
- Be able to apply his/her pedagogical skills and knowledge to each of the components of Fielden's (1993) matrix of learner support

- Become involved, where appropriate, in helping academic staff to design and develop course material. This may be particularly helpful where open and distance learning operate

- Become involved in wider study skills programmes

It goes without saying that IT-related skills will continue to be highly prized assets in the coming years. To transfer some of these skills successfully from librarians to ever increasing numbers of students is a formidable challenge.

IT-RELATED SKILLS

It is information technology which generates the most vigorous debate in relation to the changing role of the librarian. Technological advances continue to ask questions of the support services including the library. Library services - whether converged or not - are examining their policies on the balance between collection development and accessing information electronically. Most academic libraries have some degree of involvement in this latter process whether through more traditional interlibrary loan services or via more sophisticated document delivery.

The importance of information technology to the modern academic library has been recognised in a number of ways including the highly successful UK eLib Programme. This now consists of over 40 projects. How these projects develop - if, indeed, they do - when the funding runs out will be particularly interesting.

These IT-related skills and competencies are discussed under two headings:

- Tailored navigational support

- IT-related infrastructure

Tailored Navigational Support.

This term was coined in the Follett Committee's supplementary report on IT (1993). This continually evolving set of skills - somewhat removed from the custodial role of the past - implies that the librarian

- Keeps up-to-date with subject-based knowledge and accompanying IT developments

- Has an advisory role in guiding users through the maze of electronic sources and formats

- Is fully conversant with sometimes highly sophisticated search methods

- Has the necessary skills to train library staff and users

These navigational support skills work on two levels - the operational and the strategic.

Operational.

At the operational level the librarian requires the skills to gain access to electronic sources of information including knowledge of licenses, protocols, modems, interfaces etc. This role is sometimes termed access engineer. Having gained access to a source, the ability to find one's way to the required information efficiently and effectively is vital. The diversity of software and charging formats makes this particularly difficult. The librarian has to demonstrate a consistent level of competence whether searching a CD-ROM database, accessing an expensive online service or making hypertextual links across cyberspace. Naturally, communication and training skills are essential to transfer the operational competencies to others. A particularly sensitive approach is required when training technophobes. For the librarian who only uses some electronic services irregularly, it is advisable to ensure that a personal or organisation skills updating programme operates. If this is impractical, designating individual librarians as "experts" in particular electronic services is one way forward.

Strategic.

The navigational support provided at the strategic level requires the application of critical, evaluative and interpretative skills. The diverse range of sources available to the librarian or user means that decisions have to be made about which are best suited to meet the information needs. As House and Moon (1994 p.79) rightly point out:

> "The key contribution of the subject librarian may well be not simply the tracking down of a wider and wider range of less and less useful information, but the interpretation of the likely value of that information to potential users".

The librarian's knowledge, experience and skills are all important in offering advice and guidance on the appropriateness of sources. For example, decisions have to be made between printed and electronic, between online and CD-ROM, between CD-ROM and Internet sources, between different sources on the Internet, between indexing, abstracting and full-text services. This resembles more the role of information or knowledge manager part of whose remit is to facilitate the productive use of the virtual library.

The importance of acquiring these navigational skills has been recognised and is reflected not only in the eLib programme but also in the Library Schools. An example of current trends is given by Hodges (1995):

> "Trainee librarians of today have to know how to use the machine, and how to interrogate the system through the machine, but the important thing is which information is useful to the individual being helped".

This brings us back to the key area - the relationship between librarian and user in which interpersonal skills and a service-oriented approach are paramount regardless of the involvement of IT.

The information technology elements of most Library School curricula have expanded enormously. It is important that this trend continues so that the right calibre of librarian possessing skills appropriate to current and future academic libraries feeds the profession.

IT-related Infrastructure.

The technological developments in networking, electronic publishing and digitisation make it understandable that other IT-related skills are sometimes relegated to a less prominent position. The academic librarian of this decade and beyond has to possess a portfolio of other IT-related skills in order to complement and support the navigational skills. Such skills help library staff to manage the information more widely and, in turn, transfer these skills to the users as appropriate. These skills include:

- Word processing
- Desktop publishing
- Use of bibliographic software packages
- Spreadsheets
- Graphics packages
- Bulletin boards
- Dexterity with data and file manipulation
- Developing and maintaining World Wide Web files
- Familiarity with local automated systems
- IT troubleshooting
- Familiarity with different operating systems

In institutions which have converged services or which foster close relations between library and other support staff, these skills can be acquired incrementally through locally organised training programmes.

MANAGEMENT SKILLS

We need to ensure that external developments are turned to the advantage of the library service. The staff who are required to adopt the skills and techniques of sound management practice will depend largely on the ethos, organisation and structure of the service. There are a number of factors suggesting that managerial responsibilities need to be more widely adopted (Morgan et al forthcoming). These include:

- The breakdown of hierarchical staffing structures
- Increasingly participative decision-making
- Greater emphasis on accountability and performance evaluation
- Widespread financial constraints
- Recognition that change has become a way of life
- Greater emphasis on teamwork
- The need for flexibility in working arrangements
- The devolution of responsibilities and budgets
- The importance of individual time management

This view is reinforced in the Fielden report (1993 p.39) which indicates that "basic managerial skills are required for a range of staff" and that these should not be restricted to heads of library services.

I would like to highlight three areas of management which reflect the path along which academic librarians will be increasingly treading. They are:

- Change management

- Financial management

- Strategic awareness

Change Management.

Changes taking place in the academic environment need to be treated positively and optimistically. To the cynical this may seem naive in the extreme. Whenever possible, changes need to be perceived as opportunities. This philosophy, however difficult it may be for some, applies to all strata of the library service. It need not be viewed as blind acceptance of "the way it has to be". For example, it does not preclude the continuous striving for additional resources or the search for innovatory methods of meeting user needs. Change has to be harnessed and turned to the advantage of the service and the users. After all, what is the alternative? The service becomes reactive to events "outside of its control", is driven in a direction decided by other parties who inevitably have their own agendas and moves further and further away from the library's main aims and objectives. It is easy to become part of a downward spiral in which the library receives less and less support - politically and financially - and is viewed as a "whinging" resource-sapping central service.

Within a supportive managerial framework it is possible to reduce the resistance to change by ensuring effective channels of communication and by obtaining the commitment and involvement of the staff.

Communication.

This seemingly simple suggestion is the most frequent cause of failure to adapt to changing circumstances. Two-way communication is required to explain and answer questions about new services and strategies. Successful academic integration cannot be achieved without effective communication between library and academic staff in all its many forms.

Obtaining commitment and involvement.

Participative management lies at the heart of dealing with change whether as manager or participant in the process. Whenever library staff are involved in strategic decision-making - and there are a variety of models to choose from - there is a greater chance of staff ownership and commitment. It comes as no surprise that decisions arrived at in a vacuum by a few people are often resisted by staff affected. Experience suggests that the earlier that individuals or teams are involved in decision-making, the more effective those decisions are. One way of encouraging a participative approach is to offer meetings training.

Although these activities are time consuming, the long term benefits will be significant. Whether our depressing desire for short term solutions can be overcome is, however, debatable.

Financial Management.

Increasingly, academic librarians are having to make decisions which require budgetary skills, accounting skills and techniques of economic analysis. As a result of devolved budgets, the establishment of cost centres and the internal market, many more librarians are responsible for budgets than was previously the case. The budgets may cover books, journals, furniture, IT equipment, binding, staff training, database services, document delivery services etc. Delegation of such responsibilities to subject or functional librarian has become quite common. Whilst in-depth knowledge of accountancy is unnecessary, a familiarity with both resource allocation models and the conducting of financial negotiations would be desirable.

Perhaps even more beneficial in the current climate are the skills of economic analysis. The provision of library services is becoming increasingly complex. Decisions have to be taken about the balance between different service elements e.g. printed v electronic, networked v stand-alone, staffing v material. Indeed, the access and collection debate has a significant financial perspective. Technology has further muddied the economic waters for librarians generally. Careful judgements have to be made on the basis of often scant information. The variety of charging modes - subscriptions, licensing, pay-as-you-use etc. - for electronic services further complicates effective financial decision-making. A rudimentary knowledge of cost-benefit analysis is becoming a necessity rather than a luxury.

Strategic Awareness.

While it may be unnecessary for subject or faculty librarians to have well-developed strategic planning skills, it is vital that they demonstrate an awareness of matters of strategic importance to the library service. In the proactive participative service referred to above, these librarians are likely to be involved in the library's strategic decision-making process. Where this is not the case, the librarians need to show a keen awareness of:

- The institution's mission and strategy
- The library's mission and strategy
- The interrelation between these two strategies
- The external environment and its effects
- The planning and policy cycles of library and institution

This awareness enables the librarian to understand the context in which and the constraints under which the library service continually operates. It is sometimes easy for librarians to concentrate their attention on their own areas of responsibility and become detached from the wider picture. Academic integration, gaining credibility with the academic staff, the educational developments that underpin services to groups and individuals, co-operative ventures would all be enhanced by an awareness of strategic issues.

PROFESSIONAL DEVELOPMENT AND TRAINING

Ultimately, a partnership between the library and the individual librarian is the most effective means of ensuring the development of appropriate skills. Each constituent has a responsibility to the other. Benefits then accrue to the individual, the other library staff, the users and the parent institution. This partnership helps to retain the motivation of the library staff and maintain a positive attitude. For each constituent to gain maximum benefit from staff development and training there needs to be co-ordination and continuity.

Co-ordination.

Staff development and training should be the formal responsibility of a senior member of staff. That person then formulates and co-ordinates policies across the service through consultation and discussion. The priorities for staff development and training need to reflect the strategies of the parent institution and the library. Responsibility for dispensing the Staff Development and Training budget in accordance with equitability and need would also lie with that member of staff. Co-ordination takes place in a number of ways:

- Between and within different levels of staff
- Collating collective SD and T issues following appraisal
- Across campuses, satellite libraries, converged services
- Between in-house and externally provided events
- Between individual and group events
- Between assistance with qualifications and other types of events
- Between institutions e.g. co-operative events
- Between methods of staff development e.g. shadowing, job rotation, courses, individual study, visits, conferences etc.

It is important that the co-ordinator has methods of identifying staff development needs e.g. appraisal, review, delegated representatives, committees etc. This information may then be taken alongside the strategic priorities to inform the decision-making process.

Consistency.

The co-ordinator can also ensure that there is consistency in the level of service provision. From this position it becomes easier to identify areas where the quality of service falls below the recognised standard and requires investigation (and possibly additional training). A good example of this is an enquiry point where the library is expected to provide an efficient and effective service regardless of the nature of the enquiry or the member of library staff who is required to answer it. Co-ordinated refresher and updating training sessions help to equalise competence across the service. My own University library has held regular staff development events - three per year - for the last five years under the co-ordinating eye of a member of the Library Management Team. These events organised for the 16 subject librarians ensure that the senior staff develop skills, attitudes and services that benefit all. Not only is it an opportunity to share good practice but it also provides a check on strategic direction.

Continuity.

Individual librarians are responsible for their own personal professional development. This may be an informal arrangement formulated by the individual and modified as the nature of the job develops and as skills are acquired. Alternatively, the process may be formalised adapting, for example, the UK Library Association's Framework for Continuing Professional Development. This framework is systematic but flexible so that individuals can modify it to suit their needs. The diverse range of skills required by current librarians has only been touched upon in this paper. From the complexity of interpersonal skills training to the dynamic changes within information technology it is increasingly necessary to formalise personal professional development. This view is reinforced by Sylge (1995 p.31):

> "A personal programme of training needs to be built up by an individual as part of their working life - it is not pre-planned by an organisation".

Such programmes need to recognise the importance of updating skills. In order to maximise the benefits of SD and T events, participants need to practice the new skills continually or apply new knowledge as soon as possible.

Increasingly, training and awareness are provided by means other than course attendance. Networking amongst librarians within and between institutions is developing rapidly. The format may be informal, conferencing, single issues, electronic newsletters etc. The Internet continues to be fraught with problems but provides the main vehicle for national and international networking. It can also be an antidote to professional isolation from which some academic librarians suffer. The establishment of a web of contacts has always loomed large in more specialised library services but information technology has made this available to a wider range of constituents.

It is important that the skills highlighted in this paper and those outlined in any staff development and training policies are integrated into the fabric of the service. These skills and competencies should form a consistent thread through recruitment, selection, induction, on the basis of need and through the appraisal/review process.

FINAL THOUGHTS

We in the academic library profession are living in exciting times. It is not just the speed of change which provides the excitement but the recognition that we can make a significant contribution to progress within the academic community. We must continue to develop our interpersonal (in the broadest sense) and IT-based skills and apply them to the people/information interface. We need to ask ourselves continually whether we are providing the quality of service which we - as recipients - would expect. We need to view the service through the eyes of the users - something that is easier said than done. We need to embrace innovation, eschew modesty and display what Bean (1987 p.232) describes as "constructive arrogance". Our approach to meeting the information needs of the early twenty-first century requires us to be positive, proactive, participative and professional. My main purpose in this paper has been to offer some practical suggestions to making it possible.

REFERENCES

Atkinson, J (1994), The image of the academic librarian <u>in</u> Harris, C ed. *The new university library: issues for the 1990s and beyond.* London: Taylor Graham, pp.89-100.

Bean, E (1987), "Polish up your image", *Catholic Library World* 58(5) pp.232-236.

Fielden, J (1993), *Supporting expansion: a report on human resource management in academic libraries for the Joint Funding Council's Libraries Review Group.* Bristol: Higher Education Funding Council for England.

Heery, M and Morgan, S (1996), *Practical strategies for the modern academic library.* London: Aslib.

Heseltine, R (1994), "Vices and virtues in the virtual library". *Times Higher Education Supplement* 14 October (Multimedia Section) pp.IV-V

Heseltine, R (1995), "The challenge of learning in cyberspace". *Library Association Record* 97(8) pp.432-433.

Hodges, L (1995), "Content with a starring role". *Times Higher Education Supplement* 13 October (Multimedia Section) p.IX

House, D and Moon, C (1994), "The new university librarian" <u>in</u> Harris, C ed. *The new university library: issues for the 1990s and beyond.* London: Taylor Graham, pp.73-88.

Joint Funding Councils' Libraries Review Group (1993), *Report.* Bristol: Higher Education Funding Council for England.

Krompart, J (1992), "Research Notes: researching faculty status: a selective annotated bibliography". *College and Research Libraries* 53(5) pp.439-449.

Libraries and IT: working papers of the Information Technology Subcommittee of the Higher Education Funding Councils' Libraries Review. Bath: United Kingdom Online Network.

Major, J (1993), "Mature librarians and the university faculty: factors contributing to librarians' acceptance as colleagues". *College and Research Libraries* 54(6) pp.463-469.

Mitchell, W and Morton, B (1992), "On becoming faculty librarians: acculturation problems and remedies" *College and Research Libraries* 53(5) pp.379-392.

Morgan, S, Heery, M and Gallacher, C (forthcoming), *Managing change in libraries*. London: Aslib.

National Board of Employment, Education and Training (1990), *Library provision in higher education institutions*. Canberra, Australia: NBEET.

Stoll, C (1995), *Silicon snake oil: second thoughts on the information highway*. New York: Doubleday.

Sylge, C (1995), "Your investment is you: personal professional and career development in the 90s". *Managing Information* 2(10) pp.30-32.

HUNGARIAN CPE EFFORTS INTENSIFIED THROUGH INTERNATIONAL CO-OPERATION

Niels Ole Pors
Mihaly Palvolgyi
Agnes Teglasi

Abstract   Brief introduction to CPE efforts in Hungary at various levels (national, regional and local) and offered by various institutes. Needs for co-ordinated CPE efforts are identified: harmonisation in course development, making CPE a coherent part of LS education system, more sensitivity to job market requirements.

A new CPE model for Hungarian LIS Departments was elaborated by LISTEN TEMPUS JEP (1994-97) efforts, with help of EU partners (Royal School of Librarianship, Hochschule für Bibliotheks- und Informationswesen, The Robert Gordon University, De Montfort University) whose experiences were studied. CPE actions should make best use of expertise and infrastructure acquired through a set of short intensive courses.

Two-year postgraduate specialisation courses (preparation of teacher-librarians for the Library and Computer skills module of the new National Curriculum, creating and introducing an Information Management course.)

New CPE course materials and research and development aspects of offering CPE through flexible, open and distance learning schemes have been established within the frame of a PHARE project. Co-operation with other Departments as well as with business and industry are highlighted.

In addition, experiences of joint actions with British Council (Management course) and Open Society Institute (English language and online searching workshop offered jointly with the University of Wales) are also analysed.

Plans for the future include intensifying CPE efforts based on more systematic needs assessment, more harmonised actions. Offering multiregional CPE training events in East-Central Europe is suggested.

1. BRIEF HISTORY OF CPE IN HUNGARY

CPE in a systematic way was initiated in Hungary by the Ministry of Culture in the early 1960s, and carried out centrally, as well as by network centres. From the 1970s the Centre for Library Science and Methodology at the National Library played a leading role in CPE through offering both long (80-240 hours) programmes in a variety of areas (computers, management, music librarians, reader service, indexing and abstracting, etc.) as well as short courses (ranging from the one-day to 30-40 hours, like research methodology, AACR2, etc.)

In the late 70s and early 80s issues of basic and continuing library education were broadly discussed (Tóth, 1981), and the endeavours of the Centre for Library Science and Methodology, the National Technical Development Commission and the National Council on Librarianship focused on development issues. Material was prepared, and concept for the development of the systematic CPE of librarians elaborated (Katsányi, 1984). The following were considered as CPE providers:
- University and college level LIS Departments (to offer second-degree and postgraduate specialisation courses e.g. for school librarians)
- The Centre for Library Science and Methodology (offering both long and short courses mainly to present new products and developments in special areas of the library and information work)
- co-ordination and network centres (e.g. National Technical Information Centre and Library, county libraries etc.) offering updating courses, and CPE of people they have trained
- Association of the Hungarian Librarians (MKE)
- Other institutions not directly related to libraries

CPE included general updating courses, specialised courses leading to a new degree, job-related courses, short target-oriented courses. Acquiring university doctoral and so called 'candidate' degree were also considered as kind of CPE. The latter one could only be offered within the frame of other scientific disciplines.

Unfortunately the well designed concept could not have been realised fully due to insufficient financial support, legal support, as well as disintegration of LIS departments and insufficient harmonisation.

2. NEEDS FOR CPE

In the first half of the 1990s new developments have taken place in Hungarian librarianship due to the social, political and economic reorganisation as well as spreading of new information technology, leading to
- new conceptual understanding of the library system, and libraries' role within society,
- changes in financing the libraries
- new focus on library economy,
- integration into international networks and systems,.
- the appearance of new electronic media.

There has been some major changes along with new demands arising from the external environment
- the introduction of the market economy brought with new management approach and showed very clearly - among others - he gap in the production of sufficient business information sources and the lack of business information services. The training element and the preparation of professionals for these new roles was a challenge for the LIS Departments as well
- access to a wider range of information made many people realise that insufficient information skills and language skills do not allow utilising the information available.
- reorganisation of primary, secondary and higher education, and related legislation lead to new initiatives in specialised CPE programmes
- information society is now more and more getting a reality in Hungary. This calls for need for new information professionals: a new postgraduate programme of information management is being developed at Berzsenyi College with the financial support of PHARE

The needs of the profession is of course important to consider in the context of CPE. There has only been few surveys carried out about the profession's needs. (Vidra Szabó, 1995). It showed a general need for revival in both basic and continuing professional education. The needs of Szentendre county library staff was surveyed in 1996 (while offering a CPE course), and showed that computer skills, management skills, communication skills, English language skills - in this order - are among the most required ones. A regional survey in 1996 confirmed the needs of companies, state and local administration, as well as other organisations (chambers of commerce, business centres) for the career of information professionals or managers.

There are clear distinctions among priorities depending on the type of the library. It is obvious as they are facing different challenges. In public libraries there is a great demand for courses in word processing, in evaluating and selecting integrated library software, and in introducing OPACs. In academic libraries, being the most advanced ones, due to central and international financial support through foundations, homepage building, and network navigation in Internet are strongly demanded.

Reorganisation and restructuring higher education strongly affected the functions and roles of academic libraries. In the early 1990s a proposal for a World Bank support was elaborated, and a plan was worked out, in co-operation with Western consultants. The plan included intensive staff development. 2 LIS Departments (Eötvös University, Berzsenyi College) and some regional training centres were identified to carry out the systematic postgraduate training of library managers, network administrators, and information service providers. (The proposal has not been approved.) (Darányi, 1993)

In 1994 the Library Department Ministry of Culture and Education prepared a medium-range plan for LIS training and continuing education which was discussed broadly through the Association of Hungarian Librarians Presidential Board and Council, and became a central topic of the Debrecen conference held 25-26 October, 1994 about the state of the art and development of LIS education in Hungary. It was elaborated on the following

- training programme should be based on the development plans of the profession, as well as based on real training need analyses,
- initial training and CPE should build a system, initial training having the function for preparing for the profession, and CPE having the function for specialise for jobs, and for types of libraries, these departments should be strengthened,
- thus initial education, postgraduate and second-degree should be based on university and college departments,
- contents and methods of CPE should be systemically updated, to facilitate international contacts, which should be supported by the profession and other forum and authorities
- legal regulation should promote basic and continuing professional training.

Based on and authorised by the Debrecen conference the heads of departments have worked out detailed recommendation for CPE.

3. MAJOR ORGANISATIONAL SET-UP FOR CPE COURSES

Conferences, seminars organised regularly by professional organisations and other training activities cannot substitute CPE, but all formats together can create a good structure of professional development for the benefit of both the individuals and their organisations.

CPE are offered by some *colleges and universities*. The idea of developing the CPE capacity of college departments was approved in the 80s, a concept elaborated by the middle of the 1980s, and again reconsidered in the middle of 1990s, but so far the realisation has been severely hindered by

- the decentralised tertiary education with too many LIS departments with insufficient staffing and infrastructure resources,
- LIS departments have been understaffed and overloaded with general BA/BSc courses,
- lack of integration of initial LIS education and CPE in a harmonised system,
- the lack of legal/financial base, CPE being not acknowledged as work load, consequently no resources provided for it

There are two university LIS Departments (Budapest, Debrecen), and four LIS departments at teacher training colleges (Szombathely, Nyiregyháza, Szeged, Budapest) not to count smaller ones, having only 1 or 2 staff members.

The TEMPUS project of the LIS Department at Eötvös University (with Deventer, and Hanover in 1992-93) and that of Berzsenyi and Bessenyei College (with Copenhagen, Stuttgart, Aberdeen and Leicester in 1994-97) focused - in addition to establishing basic computer infrastructure - on adapting Western experiences in basic and continuing professional education.

Eötvös University introduced from 1990 on a postgraduate specialisation programme in old and rare books. It also participated in the CPE courses organised for school librarians in the late 1980s and early 1990s. The 2-year second-degree CPE programme in information science in 1995 was revised with more focus on the management of information, to incorporate the latest achievements in information technology.

The Librarianship Department in Szombathely has also been involved in providing CPE courses for teachers and school librarians. The 120hour course was organised three times between 1987 and 1990 and involved 37 participants. The experiences were presented to the CPE Round Table in Martin, Slovakia in October 1988. In 1992-93, and 1993-94 the CPE courses for teachers and school librarians continued with 40 participants (70-90 hours course) focusing already on the new National curriculum requirements and related library and information endeavours.

In Autumn 1995 the *University LIS Department in Debrecen* hosted a management course for future librarians. The programme was organised and financed by the British Council in co-operation with the Hungarian Ministry of Culture.

If we look at *the professional bodies*, it seems there has been some kind of specialisation established here. The Chamber of Libraries and Information Centres (KIK) organises programmes supported by the National Cultural Fund (NKA) and occasionally jointly also by the British Council, mainly in the area of management. The Association of Hungarian Librarians (MKE) ,organises one-day intensive courses, such as Internet use, database search, etc. The sections and the county organisations of the Associations are also very much involved to develop their members through various means, seminars, work-shops, study tours, etc.

The *individual libraries* have a very important part to play. Individual libraries offer or „buy" programmes when they feel the immediate need for introducing new services, technologies changing the structure etc. A good example is the Szentendre County Library. As they are involved in a PHARE project to establish new services for the local community, the management recognised the need for providing professional education courses for their staff. The project has been expanded so further three public libraries are in the process to establish health and community information services It was the LIS Department at Berzsenyi College that was asked to provide the education programmes and run the courses in-house.

Some good examples can be drawn form other libraries (Katona József Public Library Kecskemét) where in-house training with outside consultants - from the U.K. - was established and will run as a three year British Council funded project to establish new services and a whole new structure of a service oriented library. It is essential to mention this, because unfortunately the system of in-house training or on the job training is almost non-existent in Hungary.

The Berzsenyi Dániel County Library (Szombathely) can also set a very good example, as it has organised two major types of in-house training courses for its own staff and that of the other town libraries in the county. In 1995-96 they ran information technology related courses (Word processing, networking, e-mail, database management software), and courses focusing on special areas of library work (for reader service staff one coursed about the digital services of major Hungarian scientific libraries, and an other focused on developing self-knowledge, and conflict management skills) while a set of course for children's librarians focused on drama pedagogy for better communication with children.

It is important to emphasise that *academic libraries* at the Budapest University of Economics and Veszprém University are in the process to develop training labs. These are with double purpose as partly they will serve as staff development facilities and also will fulfil information kills development for the users.

The following programmes were *held* in the last two years at LIS Berzsenyi College, Szombathely between 1994-96:

Course name	Time-frame	Number of participants	Funding body
Business information	120 hours course work	14 enrolled 9 completed	Ministry of Culture and Education, Hungary
Library management	28 hour course-work	18 people	British Council + Ministry of Culture and Education, Hu.
Combined training in English	120 hours course work	14 enrolled and completed	Open Society Institute

language and online searching				

Besides these short term courses two major postgraduate programmes were *design and elaborated:*
- Information Literacy TEMPUS specialisation programme, to be started from 1997
- Information Management PHARE programme, to be started from 1997

Programme	Time frame	Level	Funding body	Starting date
Information literacy	4 semester	post-graduate	TEMPUS for design and preparation	September 1997.
Information management	4 semesters	post-graduate	PHARE for design and preparation	September 1997

The Business information course, 1994-95 included 120 hours of course work, and the same amount time for independent study, and additional consultation time for writing a project paper. (Téglási, 1995). The aim of the course was to prepare librarians for offering business information in their libraries and to tailor their services to existing needs, and to increase information awareness of SMEs. The course was provided by LIS staff, and invited speakers from various organisations (Business Chamber, University of Economics, etc.). 14 people were enrolled, and out of them 9 completed the course, most of them from libraries participating in the nation-wide project of VIP (information project for small and medium size businesses), supported and financed by the Ministry of Culture and Education. Professional initiatives were provided by experts from the U.K. with British Council funding.

The course contents included supporting parts, such as communication block to develop oral and written communication (10 hours), English language use (12 hours), introduction to network communication (6 hours), and general information on SME-s (20 hours).The main body of the course focused on SMEs (types, structures, information needs), relevant information services and management issues. The overall feedback was very positive about the content and the methods, though the ratio among the different elements was not satisfactory for everyone. Participants appreciated the opportunity for establishing their contacts with major „players" in business information, and the lively discussions about major issues. They reacted positively to real-life exercises and hands-on experience in online searching of databases.

The Library Management course, Szombathely, 5-8 February 1996 was financed by the British Council in co-operation with the Hungarian Ministry of Culture. The major aim was to prepare trainers to provide management courses. The course was attended by a heterogeneous group of 9 LIS lecturers from various LIS departments (Szombathely, Budapest, Nyiregyháza, Debrecen, Szeged) and professionals (involved in management training and CPE) and 9 students who enjoyed the benefit of having an English language management course with interesting new methods and discussions. The course helped in getting acquainted with the British experience in library management (strategic and project management, collections management) and gave a through insight to the current situation through the practice of a particular library.

The methods of the course involved several small discussions and short exercises that allowed active participation for everyone. The feedback was very positive, especially SWOT analysis, project management steps, the collection development issues with a tight budget. Costing and charging proved to be also very interesting issue for Hungarian professionals, an area we have to learn more. It was suggested that in the future courses should be organised for more homogenous groups. It was also raised to have courses run by both a practitioner and a lecturer based on team teaching.

An intensive course in *English language and Online searching* for Hungarian librarians, were held jointly at Szombathely and Aberystwyth, Summer 1996. The course was designed and run by the Department of Information and Library Studies, University of Wales and LIS Berzsenyi College, and supported by the Open Society Institute Regional Library Programme. The major aim of the course was to provide Hungarian library/information professionals with communication skills:

- oral and written forms of general and special English and
- electronic/network communication also developing English language skills by using the Internet, online search, etc.

The target group was practising professionals, who currently have medium level English language and online searching skills, but for whom those skills are or will be a high priority. Participants were selected on the basis of the individual's appropriateness. The selection committee was keen on keeping a balance having participants from different types of institutions and from all around the country. The course started with a one week intensive preparatory special language course in Szombathely, and continued with a two week programme in Aberystwyth to participate in the English language programme at the English Language Unit of the University of Wales as well as undertake a specially designed course on online searching, and Internet use at the Department of Information and Library Studies.

Methods included lectures and demonstrated sessions with related practical exercises. Language assistance was on hand in both the lecture and practical sessions. Participants had a very positive feedback to the special combination of developing both language and online searching skills, they appreciated both the lectures and discussions (e.g. use of Dialog, analysis of databases, search strategies and management issues) as well as hands-on sessions. The course was regarded as a successful pilot by the Open Society Institute, which regards it as a model course that should be offered for librarians and information professionals of other Eastern European countries as well.

TEMPUS has played an important role in this context. The LISTEN TEMPUS co-operation with four Western and four Eastern partners (1994-97) has lead to the renewing of the basic LIS programme, based on a critical analysis of the situation after the first year of TEMPUS (Tóth, 1995), and in addition specialised continuing education programmes have been designed after a set of intensive courses focusing on training of CPE trainers (from the second year).

In the second year of the project a number of intensive courses have been held in Hungary (Szombathely and Nyíregyháza) by Western colleagues in the areas of business information and information user education. The Central library of the University of Economics (Budapest), and that of Veszprém University, as well as College of Finance and Accountancy (Zalaegerszeg) were also involved. The CPE intensive courses were of introductory nature, involved lectures, demonstrations, hands-on sessions in online and CD-ROM searching, database management and discussions. Both contents, and methods used were appreciated. It was also valuable that it brought together LIS staff, librarians and network management staff, as well students in getting acquainted with latest developments in business information and user education.

The one week-intensive course in November 1995 in Copenhagen at the Royal School of Librarianship for 12 Hungarian colleagues was especially useful as it provided models of how to carry out basic and continuing education in a systematic way (frames, contents, structures, interrelationships, methods). (Kajberg, Pors, 1995) (Pors, 1995) A number of examples of different types of CPE courses were analysed and discussed.

In the final phase of the second year (Spring 1996) selected Hungarian staff (10 people altogether from the 5 Hungarian partner institutes) could receive intensive „Train the trainer" courses in Aberdeen and Leicester. Getting acquainted with issues of business information course design, implementation and evaluation in a systematic way, and the related discussions and project work represented a kind of model, Hungarian LIS staff and librarians have to follow. Database marketing, use of databases and Internet in business information have offered new knowledge for Hungarian staff. Hands-on experience in using business databases has developed related practical skills. It was also adequately presented how information use in general and in business information especially can be facilitated through the intensified education role of librarians. These intensive „Train the trainer" courses can be considered as models for Hungarian LIS staff while planning their own courses, with a view on the special Hungarian environment.

Two types of CPE courses have been considered in future course design and implementation by LIS staff:
- short intensive courses, focusing on new areas (Internet, homepage building), and synthesising knowledge in growing areas (business information), developing foreign language skills of librarians.
- 2-year postgraduate programmes to follow basic LIS education: the curricula of the Business information/information management, and Information literacy programmes have been elaborated. Both courses represented a mixed mode of CPE, both involving open distance features (independent study based on packages, and assigned reading) as well as face-to-face sessions (in a time duration of 500 contact hours) in each programme.

The new experience gained at the Western partners has motivated Hungarian LIS Departments to find strategic alliances in Hungary with business and management schools and departments to be able to carry out the new tasks   effectively. (Budapest University of Economics Central Library Janus Pannonius University, Faculty of Economics). This especially relates to the Information Management programme, which involves management, marketing, finance, and system analysis modules as well.

A *new National Curriculum* (NAT) for primary and secondary schools has been elaborated and will be implemented in 1997. One of the major modules of NAT to be taught is *Information literacy*. As new information technology has been introduced broadly in Hungarian schools as well, effective use of computers and networks has become very important, as well as the emphasis on individual study. There is little staff expertise to teach the modern information literacy skills. Thus there is a strong need to undergo professional CPE in this area. So a 2-year postgraduate programme developed by LIS Department, Berzsenyi College has to focus on preparing staff able to guide learners to access and use information resources effectively, help them learn independent study skills, thus respond to the challenges of life-long learning in information society. It is obvious that school librarians will play a major part and act as educators and facilitators of learning, supporting both staff and students in resource based learning, computer and „traditional" library skills.

The curriculum for the 2-year Information literacy module has been worked out for teacher-librarians to teach Information literacy, with emphasis on adequate management, technical and communication skills as well as transferable skills problem solving, presentation, keyboard skills, word processing, searching in networks). There is a separate programme for teachers of different subjects (Biology, etc.) to incorporate information skills development in their related courses. The curricula were submitted for accreditation, and it is planned that the programme begins in September 1997. The training efforts go parallel with a nation-wide development to update computer infrastructure in primary and secondary schools.

The PHARE - programme looks very promising in relation to Information Management development. The fundamentals of this programme were created by the LISTEN TEMPUS JEP and can be regarded as a follow up of that. The demand for information managers has grown considerably in Hungary due to influx of capital into the country, and development of medium and large often joint enterprises. *The PHARE project (1995-97)* focuses on the design and implementation of a two-year postgraduate programme according to Hungarian requirements to promote development of Hungarian economy. The information managers will acquire the necessary communication, information, technical and foreign language skills according to European standards.

In addition to LIS staff of Berzsenyi College and Eötvös University the regional business link, business chamber, and the local government, as well as the regional labour development centre are also members of the consortium. The major Western partner is the Royal School of Librarianship, while ASLIB and FID also offer consultation and contributes to CPE staff training. The IM programme will be a mixed mode course mainly based on individual study, including open distance learning, as well as group and individual consultations for learner support.

The project includes 5 work packages: (1) assessment of training needs for the carrier of information managers (2) survey and adaptation of international expertise in IM training and distance education, related staff training. (3) Design and development of curriculum and open learning materials. (4) Infrastructure development to offer alternative, electronic ways for open learning via open forum, open classroom. (5) programme implementation , evaluated, and further development. (Pálvölgyi, Bobok, 1996).

To sum up the experiences of the above course examples, it is a special advantage for LIS Departments that through these initiatives they can keep close touch with the library and information reality, and keep the Departments in contact with the profession which helps to be much more sensitive to CPE needs.

4. PROBLEMATIC AREAS

As it was discussed above, even though there is a growing consensus as regards a national CPE strategy and concept, there are a couple of issues that hinder the efforts:

Unfortunately we cannot talk about a systematic, well-established CPE structure. Though the Higher Education Act (1993 and modifications 1996) states that postgraduate programmes are within the authority of Higher education institutions in Hungary, no resources are assigned to this task. Neither the libraries nor the individual professionals are in the position to pay for tuition and additional expenses to participate in CPE courses. The only possible way is to seek grants.

As it was described and analysed above, about 30 Hungarian LIS staff and librarians, network specialists are prepared for training in CPE. This has a multiplicative effect, as knowledge acquired is being disseminated in broader circles through both short and long courses. It is now to find the opportunities to provide this facet also in the future through close co-operation with Western partners, through short intensive courses as well as through consultation tours, and joint research and development.

The infrastructure for CPE has developed considerably recently. At national level we can say that the National Infrastructure Development Project (NIIF) provides local and wide area network connection for more and more institutions within the country and the LIS Departments are reasonably well equipped for holding classes, laboratory sessions, and they also have some facilities for open learning. On the other hand the situation is very fragile, as infrastructure development needs constant efforts of updating, maintenance, and it is difficult to follow the fast changes in IT considering the miserable financial situation of Hungarian higher education, having even difficulties in paper and overhead supply...

CPE programmes based at LIS departments have the benefit to join Dialog (Knight Ridder Information) CIP project, free - of charge. New opportunities for CPE are provided by Internet, for continuous updating of staff skills through WWW, mailing lists, news communities, full-text electronic materials in library and information science (Hungarian Electronic Library, URL http://mek.hu) that can be considered as assigned reading in any updating or refreshing CPE course.

It is also positive that supported by TEMPUS and PHARE new distance education materials have been prepared to assist individual learning, as well as guided hands-on experience, in on-line and CD-ROM searching events. The translation and adaptation of some English language materials and development of other teaching aids are also vital means for successful CPE. Despite all efforts there is still a lack of professional literature and CPE materials.

The efforts to develop mixed mode universities (involving both traditional, distance, open and flexible schemes) focus on the following:
- to create optimum conditions for accessing local, national and international DOFL resources and services, implementing efficient means of learner support
- to develop innovative and user friendly DOFL products and services
- to explore the flexible interaction and optimum co-ordination of new and traditional methods

- survey and adapt quality standards and know how used at EC partners and promote international co-operation (Pálvölgyi, 1995).

Unfortunately job training and CPE requirements have not been clarified, until know, and legal regulation of library jobs is controversial. The legal regulation has been changed several times during the past couple of decades that resulted a chaotic situation in various levels of diplomas, degrees and certificates in librarians training and education. Parallel with this the salary scheme and the acknowledgement of different educational formats have been changing very rapidly. There is no systematic and compulsory scheme for providing updating, retraining or specialising courses though the new library law (having passed several approval but not accepted by the Parliament yet) deals with the necessity of CPE as a professional job requirement.

In a society with several unsettled issues it is up to the individual institutions and their leadership how they support or reward employers with their CPE efforts. Experience shows that at present CPE provides benefit rather to the individuals than to their institution. The libraries don't utilise their employers' newly acquired knowledge or/and skills partly because they cannot donate it properly and partly because staff development is almost non-existent in Hungary. To support our statement we would like to refer to a survey carried out at the end of the business information course (VIP) in 1994-95. The question, whether the newly acquired knowledge and skills can be utilised and in what way at the current work-place there was only one positive response out of nine. Most of the participants found the course very useful and good for self-development and expressed their hope that some day they would utilise it but not at their current work-place and not in their current position.

5. FUTURE POSSIBILITIES

CPE should be an organic, necessary and integral factor of LIS education, and not seen just an optional supplement to initial training. As we have our organisational, technical, financial and personnel limitations, it is especially important to intensively concentrate our resources to offer quality CPE. The following should be considered as priorities for CPE development in Hungary:

Society being in transition hinders our efforts, so we can only be hopeful that in many areas of our external environment better leadership and organisation will bring fruitful results. The much needed and waited acts and regulations, especially the ones directly effecting our profession - Library Act, the Act of Non-profit institutions - are in preparatory phase and both of them can cause major breakthrough in the CPE field as well.

Surveying and monitoring the market is not in our culture yet, but it has to be a very vital part of assessing the needs. It is important to focus at both the traditional library sector (public, school, academic) as well as the non-traditional (profit and non-profit organisations) market as well. There should be a thorough assessment of the offer side of CPE as well.

There should be a more strategic approach to planning and harmonisation of CPE in Hungary with a better co-operation of CPE providers, as regards institutions and types of courses,

Better harmonisation and integration of basic professional education and CPE as regards contents, structures and methodologies, introduction of specialising minor programmes (e.g. Information services management) in LIS Departments concentrating on the growing side of the market, and offering better chances to be employed.

International CPE experiences should be studied and adapted to the Hungarian needs and environments, joint CPE course development with international partners, e.g. multi - regional offers in East-Central European countries

It could be useful to a greater extent to introduce library and information management consultation, and research and development services by associates off LIS departments and libraries

REFERENCES

(Darányi, 1993) Darányi Sándor: A felsőoktatásban dolgozó könyvtárosok át- és továbbképzése. Tervezet. In: Könyv, könyvtár, könyvtáros, 1993. July 8-19. pp. August, 19-25. pp. (Retraining and extension training of academic librarians. A proposal. - English language abstract in Hungarian Library and Information Science Abstracts, Vol.23. No. 1. 1994. 9. p.)

(International, 1995) International Conference "For the Development of Academic Libraries". System plan demonstration, know-how transfer, case studies. A Felsőoktatási Könyvtárak Fejlesztéséért. Budapest, May 15-16 1995.

(Kajberg, Pors, 1995) Kajberg, Leif - Pors, Niels Ole: The Royal School of Librarianship, Denmark: presents educational programmes and envisaged curricula. *Librarian Career Development*, Vol. 3. No. 4. pp. 19- 25.

(Katsányi, 1984) Katsányi, Sándor: A továbbképzés rendszerének fejlesztése, *Könyvtáros*, 1984.7. 380-385. (Developing a system for CPE)

(Murányi, Pálvölgyi, Téglási, 1996.) Murányi Péter - Pálvölgyi Mihály - Téglási Ágnes:Információs menedzserképzés a szombathelyi BDTF Könyvtár-Informatika Tanszékén (KIT) Elôadás. Debrecen, Networkshop, Informatika a felsôoktatásban konferencia, 1996. augusztus 27-29. 7,7 p. (Information management programme development at LIS Department Berzsenyi College, Szombathely)

(Pálvölgyi, 1988.) Pálvölgyi, Mihály: Methodological and technological foundation of the continuing education by the primary professional education. Presentation at the IFLA Round Table on Continuing Professional Education seminar, Martin, 1988. October.

(Pálvölgyi - Bobok, 1996) Pálvölgyi Mihály - Bobok Beáta: elaboration and implementation of an Information management postgraduate programme via distance learning scheme (IM DLS) Paper presented to the FID Pre-Congress Symposium in Graz, October 21 1996. 12 p.

(Pors, 1995) Pors, Niels Ole: Curriculum development and students perceptions. In *Proceedings of the 1st British-Nordic conference on library and information studies*, 22-24 May 1995, Copenhagen. Ed. by Micheline Haycock-Beaulieu, Niels Ole Pors. Copenhagen, The Royal School of Librarianship, 1995. Copenhagen, 1995. 7-15. p.

(Téglási, 1995) Téglási, Ágnes: Teaching management and management related courses at KIT, Library and Information Science Department of Berzsenyi College. In *Marketing and development of new information products and services in Europe. Proceedings of the 3rd International BOBCATSSS Symposium, Budapest, January 1995.* Ed. By Jan P. Brouwer, and Martijn Vermeulen, pp. 183-190.

(Tóth, 1995) Tóth, Gyula: *Objectives of general curriculum development at the Department of Librarianship and Information Studies at Berzsenyi College in view of experiences of LISTEN TEMPUS JEP - Points for the TEMPUS seminar.* Szombathely, 1995. 9 p.

(Tóth, 1981) Tóth Gyula: A könyvtárak káderhelyzete, könyvtárosképzés - és továbbképzés, Kt. 1981.2. 85-93.) (the staffing situation in libraries, the basic and continuing professional education of librarians).

(Vidra Szabó, 1995) Vidra Szabó Ferenc: A könyvtárosok képzettsége, In *Könyvtári figyelő*, 1995. No.2. 236-250. p. (The qualifications of librarians)

USERS TRAINING PROGRAMS DEVELOPED BY
THE BRAZILIAN UNIVERSITY LIBRARIES

Maria N. O. Silva
Federal Senate Library
Brasilia, DF, Brazil

Abstract: This paper covers descriptive research surveying the theory and practice of users education programs developed by the Brazilian University Libraries. The data were collected by means of a Brazilian and international literature review and by questionnaire application to all 102 higher education institutions considered as universities by the Brazilian Education Ministry. The final results of this study indicate the necessity of changes in the training programs structure, so that the users' actual needs can be met.

INTRODUCTION

The users training in Brazilian and foreign countries university libraries is an activity which has been developed over several years. Despite the fact that it is more recent in Brazil, where the first programs were presented in the literature in the sixties, it is an activity which has already completed 30 years of existence in our libraries.

Since the first work was registered in the "Universidade de Sao Paulo," other similar training courses were developed in different areas and institutions, initiating many didactic texts, bibliography research manuals, etc. (Belluzzo, 1989). Regardless of the multiplication effect along the years, the users training programs in Brazilian university libraries have not received much attention by the national authors, resulting in low Brazilian production in this area. The few texts found in the literature are basically practical experiences. In fact, the national production, in theoretical and practical terms, is not significant if compared with the users education works presented in the international literature.

The experience as a librarian in the Reference Section of the Biblioteca Central of the Universidade de Brasilia (UnB), dealing directly with development of users education programs, showed that there is a lack of theoretical and practical substantiation in the planning out and development of users training in that university, as well as in other universities. In most cases, the users training became isolated initiatives which are not continued. Each new initiative seems not to take advantage of the past experiences.

Looking to reduce this lack of substantiation, a study was made about the users training practices adopted by the Brazilian libraries by means of a documentary analysis. Since the national literature doesn't present enough updated data about the subject, a survey was conducted involving the Brazilian university libraries by means of a questionnaire application.

USERS TRAINING - DEFINITION

Users training is an activity of the Reference Service of a library which has as an objective to "give knowledge to the users and not users about the services and products offered by the library to the community, by means of different instruction methods." (Medeiros, 1984) Users education programs comprise orientation visits around the library, illustrative speeches and also folders, guidelines and audio-visual media with information about the services and products of the library, lectures about the rules to elaborate scientific works, orientation about on-line and CD-ROM data base utilization, lectures with bibliographical instruction of specific subjects and computer aided orientation. In most cases, users training is offered by librarians and university professors and, due to the characteristics of the clientele and its needs, it is normally related to university libraries.

In specialized libraries, the users would hardly agree to do their own bibliographical research. However, more and more voices are being heard insisting on the need that users education be included in the services offered by public libraries. The American Library Association recommends that "all libraries (must) include an instruction about the use of the libraries as one of the priorities of the service (Grogan, 1995) and Macedo (1990) includes users education as one of the five fields of reference work services offered by every library.

In spite of the fact that authors and institutions dictate rules about how, when and why the libraries must include users education programs in their activities, Harris (1992) states that "academic libraries, public or specialized, with similar levels of education and experience, have different points of view about bibliographic instructions."

Kemp, Nofsinger and Spitzer (1986) go further, defending the idea of the "construction of a bridge between the secondary school and the university." They attribute to the librarians of the universities the "responsibility to work with secondary schools, to guarantee the adequate preparation of the students to their transition from the secondary level to the university level," and affirm that several American university libraries have already developed this type of activity successfully.

RESEARCH

The study was developed using a descriptive method of research where, according to the literature, the reality is known and interpreted without interference or modifications. The users training programs developed by the Brazilian university libraries were studied in terms of description, classification and interpretation;, having as an objective to know their nature, composition and the processes involved.

The universe of the research comprises the 102 higher education institutions considered as universities by the Brazilian Education Ministry. The study involved the federal higher education institutions and the state, municipal and private ones as well.

Table 1 shows the representation of the institutions by region of the country.

Table 1
Institutions of Higher Education by Region of Brazil

Region	No. Of States	No. Of Higher Education Institutions (SEI)	Percentage of SEI in Relation to the Country's Total
North	7	7	6.86%
Northeast	8	22	21.57%
Southeast	4	44	43.14%
South	3	24	23.53%
West-Center	4	5	4.90%
TOTAL	26	102	100%

The percentage of answers received was satisfactory (81.37%) regarding the number of institutions involved, mainly if it is considered that: only two States, Amapá and Rio Grande do Norte, each one represented by only one university, had zero percentage of response; in the West-Center Region, the percentage of response was 100% and in the most representative regions of the country (South and Southeast Regions) the rate of response was greater than 80%.

To evaluate the size of the libraries, the size of their collections (number of cataloged volumes and the number of subscribed periodicals) was considered as a parameter. The libraries were so classified as "small," "medium," or "big," according to the following criteria:

small = less than 31.999 volumes;
medium = 32,000 to 109,999 volumes;
big = more than 100,000 volumes

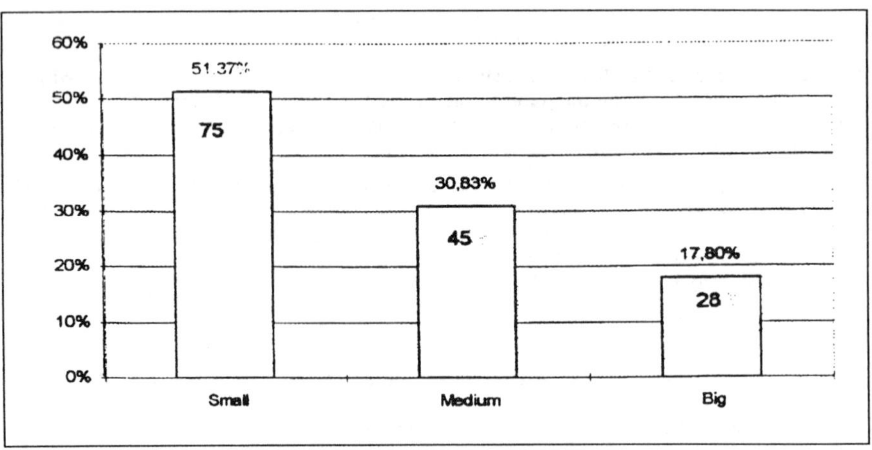

Number of Libraries by the Size of the Collection
Figure 1

USER TRAINING

Most of the 146 respondent libraries (75) indicate that the users education programs are important to give to the users the knowledge about the library, its services and products, so that he becomes able to use the sources of information and to optimize its use.

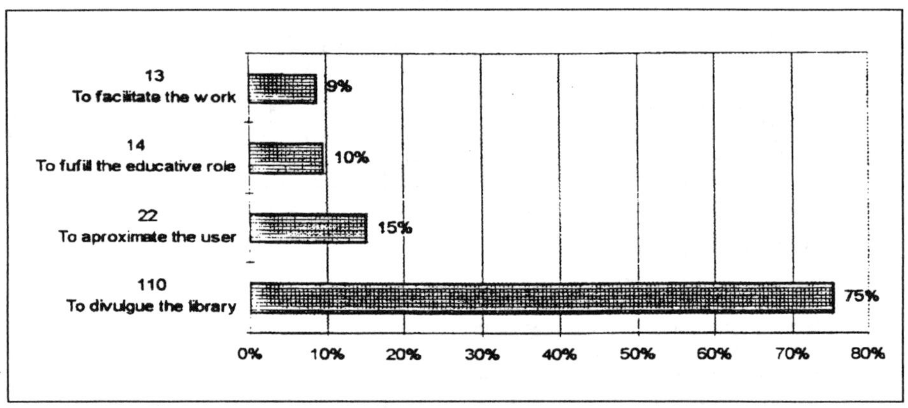

Importance of the Users Education
Figure 2

These results confirm the objectives of the users training programs presented in the literature: teach the users about how to use a library (Ah-Ton & Valéio, 19797; Ufrs, 1982; Cunha, 1986) and facilitate the integration of the library into the university's teaching/learning process (Brunetti, 1983; Oliveira, 1986; Silva, Amaral, Dias, 1986).

Among 146 respondent libraries, 74% do some kind of users training, 23% said that they don't do users training, and 3% didn't answer this question. Among 34 libraries (23% that did not develop any training, 22 (15%)don't do it because they don't have adequate personnel and organizational structure and 12 (8%) affirm that they don't see any necessity to develop this type of activity.

TARGET

The 108 university libraries developing users education programs have programs which are, in most cases, mainly directed to graduation students (95%) and, in second place, also with a high percentage (76%) to post-graduation students.

The training programs also concern the professors (54%) and employees of the universities (47%); 50% of the respondents still do some kind of training directed to other segments of the community, such as high school students, research students of other higher education institutions, and also to the community as a whole.

The data found in the literature confirm these results. In general, the clientele of the training is composed first of new students and graduation students, followed by the post-graduation students, professors and employees (Moreira, 1979; Ufrs, 1982; Brunetti, 1983; UnB, 1986; Costa, 1987; Nicz & Marchiori, 1991; Esteves, 1992; Ínsfran, 1992; Glogoff, 1995).

TRAINING METHODS AND TECHNIQUES

Among the university libraries developing users education programs, 69.18% use at least one of the methods listed in the questionnaire with high frequency; 5.48% make a little use of the methods presented and 25.34% don't use any method in their training.

Figure 3 shows that the oriented tours are the main form of training, since 103 (95%) from the total of 108 libraries developing users training use this method; only 2 (2%) don't use it, and 3 (3%) didn't answer this question.

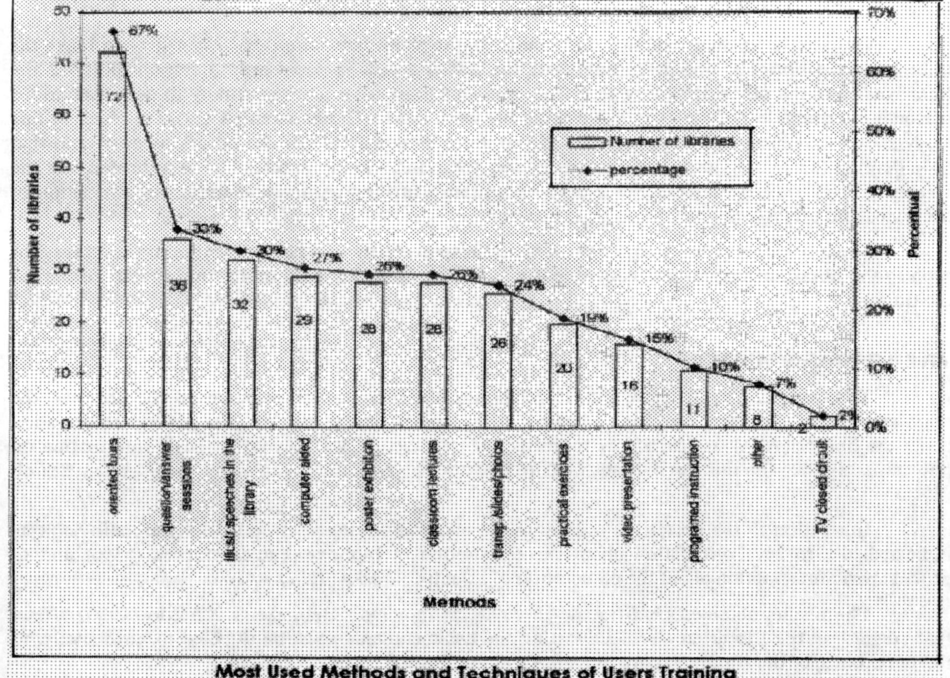

Most Used Methods and Techniques of Users Training
Figure 3

The classroom lectures, done by 74 libraries (69%) are extensively used. Following this method appear the speeches in the library, utilized by 66 libraries (61%); the question-answer sessions, by 57 (53%); the posters exhibition, by 53 (49%); the transparencies, slides and/or photographs presentation, by 47 (44%); the computer-aided instruction, by 43 (40%) and practical exercises, by 43 (40%).

Only 10 libraries (9%) reported that they use methods not presented above. The most relevant are: guidelines, folders about the library, pamphlets containing instructions about research and training on the data base of the university. The other 98 libraries (91%) didn't inform if they use other methods not listed in the questionnaire.

Although the oriented visit is fully utilized, some authors disagree about its utility to the users. Eadie (1990) believes that, "a good sign system is better than hundreds of oriented tours" and Radford (1980) affirms that "almost every study that has been done on the guided tour and lectures to new students are largely in vain; and two, despite this, almost every library provides orientation tours and lectures."

REALIZATION PERIODS

The period of realization of the users training was researched taking into account each segment of the users community of the university libraries: graduation students, post-graduation students, professors, university employees and also external public. The results show that the libraries develop most of their training programs in the beginning of the school year (30%), the highest percentage (61%) is related to the realization of the training when requested by the users, independent of the school year. This result meets the Ah-Ton & Valério (1979) recommendation that "the right moment to training will vary according to the clientele [and that], any way, a training like this will be offered only if it is found useful and necessary."

THE RESPONSIBILITY ATTRIBUTION

Despite the existence of two different thoughts about who would be responsible to make the training in the libraries, one defending that "the training task is necessarily a responsibility of the librarians" and the other defending that "the professor must have the opportunity to demonstrate his personal interpretation of the knowledge about his work field" (Cunha et alii, 1979), the result of this study shows that most training programs (56%) are a responsibility of the librarians only, and that 24% develop this activity together, professors and librarians. Some libraries (10%) indicated that the responsibility varies, being sometimes only a librarian's attribution and sometimes an attribution of librarians and professors.

Some libraries (2%) delegate the training responsibility to other employees of the library, or even to the librarianship trainees course, but any library indicated only professors as responsible for the training.

THE TRAINING SUBJECTS

The research results show that, in relation to the services and resources of the libraries, the main subjects of the users training indicated in the questionnaire are: to give general information about the library (98%); to teach how to utilize the catalogs (92%); to provide basic information on how to manipulate the indexes and abstracts (69%) and to give orientation about the on-line research (55%).

In relation to the objectives regarding the elaboration of scientific works, the main subjects indicated are: to give orientation about the elaboration of bibliographic references (81%) and to provide basic information about the elaboration of scientific works (72%).

The results obtained confirm the literature statements. Belluzzo & Macedo (1990) affirm that "regarding the Librarian Users Education the basic contents must be directed to, principally, to the importance of the library, its organization and use."

EVALUATION

Since the validation and evaluation of the results are one of the four steps which necessarily comprise the training process (Chiavenato, 1985), it was identified which libraries, among those that develop users training, do any kind of evaluation of the results obtained and what are the methods used to make this evaluation.

Among 108 libraries that develop users training, most of them (54%) don't make any kind of evaluation of their training process and 46% do evaluate. Among those libraries that don't evaluate, 15 declared that they don't have plans to do so, 9 pointed out the lack of personnel as the cause for not evaluating, and 7 don't evaluate because "the results of the training are very evident."

Kokkonen (1992), reporting a research done by UNESCO about the state of the libraries and the users education in underdeveloped countries, shows that "very few institutions of the countries involved in the study have experience with some type of evaluation of the courses they offer" and Robertson (1992), in a study about the Scottish higher education institutions, observed that only 20% of the institutions involved evaluate their users training programs.

Despite being considered of great importance by the literature, the evaluation of the users training programs done by the libraries is very little developed. The literature shows results that confirm this fact.

CONCLUSIONS

The results of this research indicate that the general view of the users training programs undertaken in the Brazilian university libraries differs very little from those reported in the national and international literature, and that the nowadays great polemic about the validity of the conventional training is being a concern to some libraries. The breaking of the barriers and the approximation of the library users begin to become the main objective of some training, in substitution of the old ideal of turning the user self-sufficient and independent. The users needs start, gradually, to be faced as the starting point for a plan of users education programs, in opposition to the belief that the librarians are the ones who know what is better for their users.

If, as affirmed by Eadie (1990), "the sixties and seventies were the periods of expansion and experimentation [when] libraries and librarians searched new rules [and when] were created new and specials services [and if] the eighties and nineties are the periods to the reexamination, reduction, elimination of superfluous [...]," it is expected that the results of this study can contribute, in any sense, as a theoretical base to those who look forward to evaluating their users training programs. Considering that the aim of the training is the user, he can only take a great advantage of education programs if they are directed to the satisfaction of his real needs.

> To say that the user:
> "[...] don't have any interest to learn
> how to efficiently utilize the library" (Radford, 1980)
> or that
> "[...] what users want is to find the information they need
> to make a concrete work, like write a paper or
> solve a problem" (Pinzelik, s.n.t.)
> or even that
> "[...] the users education may be really prejudicial,
> leaving the users with the mistaken idea that
> to find information is a simple task and
> sowing the seeds of frustration, blame and irritation
> that attack them when they discover that this is not true" (Grogan, 1995)
> is to commit the same mistake very criticized by these same authors;
> we are always working over conjectures.

The defenders of the users education affirm that the user needs to be trained to supply his needing of information and become a self-sufficient person in the search and retrieval of information. The critics of this activity affirm that the user doesn't want to participate in the users training programs and that he doesn't have interest in learning anything about the library, what he wants is only the information important in that specific moment.

Once more, the user is not being considered and his opinion is not being taken into account.

The user must have the option to: "1) learn to use the library and its resources or 2) not learning and even though be able to have integral, complete and total attention to his needs by the reference librarians" (Katz, 1982). Different users with the same request may demand different answers or, yet, the same user with different requests may demand different types of attending. Ranganathan used to say: "to each reader his liberty."

If the user is the main reason of the libraries, before planning activities which probably interest them or before eliminating activities which may not interest them, one must remember that: 2) the user can only wish to obtain something of the library if he knows that it exists and that, 2) any activity undertaken to attend the user must be based on his real needs and not on conjectures.

Today, not only the users education is being discussed. The survival of the traditional library itself and the information professional is being extensively debated, too.

In the same way, the discussions about the continuity or not of the profession are made by those who foresee the death of librarianship, libraries and librarians and those who defend the idea that there will be a great change, that the profession will be reborn, "but, with new components of new education programs in which communication, computation, education and other elements of arts and liberal and natural sciences will be together in a holistic curriculum" (Billings, 1995).

The truth is that, since the beginning, when the support of the information was a tablet made of clay and the writing was cuneiform inscriptions (Milanesi, 1983), until today, when the information is stored in microchips, the libraries have already undergone thousands of transformations and always followed the world evolution. If new technologies are now established, if virtual libraries are already reality, probably the library and its professionals will also follow these evolutions, adapting themselves once more to the new reality. David Hoekema (1994), philosophy professor of the Calvin College, United States, affirms that "we always need interpreters, appraisers and guides [...] and even when all cultural patrimony of the east and west is in a chip...the need of explanation, interpretation and dialog will persist and will not be found in the machine."

Dunn (1988) makes an addition saying that "the sources of reference are so many, in press and electronic formats, that it would be unfair and unreal to expect that any user could keep himself informed about at least the minimum. This is a librarian job."

A survey made by Ching-Chih Chen and Raitt (1990) proved these statements. The results demonstrate that "the CD-ROMs are being most used by libraries personnel, in the United States and also in the Occidental Europe, [...] [and that] albeit the fact that the number of searches done in the CD-ROMs by the users is high if compared to the on-line searches, the reference librarians are being forced to dedicate a great part of their time in helping these users, analyzing their search strategies, assisting them on choosing the most adequate data-base for a specific subject, explaining them the structure of the data-bases and supervising the search itself.

As libraries have their objectives based on the objectives of the institutions they belong to, the users education, in the same way, is also based on the library goals. If the future of the libraries is being discussed, obviously, the education programs are being debated as well. It is a time of adaptations and changes, and so the users education must be restructured to follow the crisis of modern technologies, always looking forward to the satisfaction of the interests and needs of the final user.

It is important to remember what Tom Eadie (1990) said: "Anything that fits everyone fits no one well."

REFERENCES

Ah-Ton, Ah-Tin and C. H. Valério (1979), "A formaçao dos usuários no meio universitário: uma revisao bibliográfica (1974-1978)," In *Congresso Brasileiro de Biblioteconomia e Documentaçao*, 10, *Anais*...Curitiba: ABPr, v. 1, pp. 177-200.

Belluzzo, R. C. B. (1989), *Educaçao de usuários de bibliotecas universitárias; da conceituaçao e sistematizaçao ao estabelecimento de diretrizes*, Sao Paulo: Universidade de Sao Paulo (Dissertaçao de Mestrado).

Belluzzo, R. C. B. And N. D. de Macedo (1990), "Da educaçao de usuários ae treinamento do bibliotecário," *Revista Brasileira de Biblioteconomia e Documentaçao*, Sao Paulo, n. 23, v. 1-4 (jan./dez), pp. 78-111.

Billings, H. (1995), "The Tomorrow Librarian," *Wilson Library Bulletin* (January), pp. 34-37.

Brasil, Ministério da Educaçao Secretaria de Educaçao Superior (1993), *Catálogo geral de instituiçoes de ensino superior: graduaçao de pós-graduaçao*, Brasilia: SESU.

Brunetti, M. I. S. (1983) *Proposta de uma metodologia para integrar os programas de educaçao de usuários aos objetivos educacionais da universidade*, Campinas: PUCC (Dissertaçao de Mestrado).

Chiavenato, I (1985), *Recursos Humanos*, Sao Paulo: Atlas.

Ching-Chih Chen, D. I. Raitt (1995), 1990 apud Grogan, D. *A prática do serviço de referencia*, Trad. De Antonio A. Briquet de Lemos, Brasilia: Briquet de Lamos/Livros.

Costa, M. C. M. (1987), "Consideraçoes sobre a necessidade de implantaçao de treinamento de discentes na Universidade Federal de Pernambuco," *R. Esc. Bibliotecon. UFMG*, B. Horizonte, v. 16, n. 1 (mar.), pp. 97-113.

Cunha, L. G. C. Et alii (1978), "Metodologica da pesquisa documentária," In Seminário Nacional de Bibliotecas Universitárias, 1, Niterói, *Anais*...Niterói: UFF-NDC, 1979, pp. 373-391.

Cunha, M. (1986), B da, Biblioteca universitária e educaçao de usuários, *Revista de Biblioteconomia de Brasília*, Brasilia, v. 14, no. 2 (jul./dez), pp. 175-188.

Dunn, E. B. (1995), 1988 apud Grogan, D. *A prática do serviço de referencia*. Trad. De Antonio Agenor Briquet de Lemos, Brasilia: Briquet de Lemos/Livros.

Eadie, T. (1990), "User Instruction for Students Does Not Work," *Library Journal*, v. 115, n. 17 (oct.), pp. 42-45.

Esteves, C. D. L. (1992), "Treinamento de usuários na BC/UFRRJ: uma experiencia em andamento," In Seminário Nacional de Bibliotecas Universitárias, 7, 1991, Rio de Janeiro, *Anais*....Rio de Janeiro: SIBI/UFRJ, pp. 526-541.

Glogoff, S. (1995), "Library Instruction in the Electronic Library: The University of Arizona's Electronic Library Education Centers," *Reference Services Review*, v. 23, n. 2 (summer), pp. 7-12.

Harris, R. M. (1992), "Bibliographic Instruction: the Views of Academic, Special, and Public Librarians," *College & Research Libraries*, v. 53, n. 3 (may), pp. 249-256.

Hoekema, D. (1994), "Quotable: In the Electronic Age, the University Library Can Be 10 Times Larger on the Inside Than It Is on the Outside," *Chronicle of Higher Education,* (jan.), p. B5 apud Billings, H., "The Romorrow Librarian," *Wilson Library Bulletin* (jan. 1995), pp. 34-37.

Insfrán, A. A. De et alii. (1992), "Interaçao bibliotecários/corpo docente/corpo discente: relato de uma experiencia," In *Seminário Nacional de Bibliotecas Universitárias*, 7, Rio de Janeiro, Anais....Rio de Janeiro:SIBI/UFRJ, pp. 317-324.

Katz, W. A.(1982), *Introduction to Reference Work*, 4. Ed., New York: McGraw-Hill Book Company, 2 v.

Kemp, B. E., M. M. Nofsinger and A. M. Spitzer (1986), "Building a Bridge Articulations Programs for Bibliographic Instruction," *College & Research Libraries*, (Sept.), pp. 470-474.

Kokkonen, O. (1992), "User Education Around the World: the UNESCO Survey of Library and Information User Education Programmes in Some Developing Countries," In IFLA General Conference, 58 (153-USER-2-E).

Macedo, N.D. De (1990), Principios e reflexoes sabre o serviço de referencia einformaçao (continua), *R. Bras.Bibliotecon.e Doc.*, Sao Paulo, v. 23, n. 1/4 (jan.dez), pp. 9-37.

Medeiros, M. B. B. (1984), *Levantamento e análise da terminologia brasileira em ciencia da informaçao*, Brasilia: Universidade de Brasilia (Dissertaçao de Mestrado).

Milanese, L. (1983), *O que é biblioteca?* Sao Paulo: Brasiliense (Coleçao Primeiros Passos, 94)

Moreira, A. C. P. Et alii (1978), Treinamento de usuários da informaçao para alunos de graduaçao da área biomédica da UFF, In *Seminário Nacional de Bibliotecas Universitárias*, 1, Niterói, *Anais...*Niterói: UFF- NDC.

Nicz, S. N. S., and P. Z. Marchiori (1991), Reformulaçao didática da disciplina orientaçao bibliogrzefica do Departamento de Biblioteconomia da Universidade Federal do Paraná, In *Congresso Brasileiro de Biblioteconomia*, 16, Salvador, *Anais...*Salvador: Assoc. Profissional dos Bibliotecários da Estado da Bahia, v. 2, pp. 1191-1201.

Oliveira, Z. C. P. Et alii (1986), O treinamento de usuários universitários com base na relaçao biblioteca/corpo docente, *Revista de Biblioteconomia de Brasilia*, Brasilia, v. 14, n. 1 (jan./jun), pp. 139-146.

Pinzelik, s.n.t.

Radford, N. A. (1980), "Why Bother With User Education?" *New Zealand Libraries,* v. 43 (dec.), pp. 53-58, apud Grogan, D. *A prática do serviço de referencia,* Trad. De Antonio A. Briquet de Lemos, Brasilia: Briquet de Lemos/Livros, 1995, p. 17.

Robertson, J. E. (1992), "User Education for Overseas Students in Higher Education in Scotland," *Journal of Librarianship and Information Science,* v. 24, n. 1 (mar.), pp. 33-51.

Silva, M. N. O. E Amaral, S. A. Do, Dias, W. M. D. (1986), *Projeto de treinamento de usuários da Biblioteca Central da Universidade de Brasília,* Brasilia: Universidade de Brasilia.

Universidade de Brasília (1986), Biblioteca Central, Seçao de Refencia, *Projeto de treinamento de usuários da Biblioteca Central da Universidade de Brasilia,* Brasilia: UnB.

Universidade Federal do Rio Grande do Sul (1982), *Programma de treinamento de usuários,* Porto Alegre: UFRGS (Padroes para os serviços bibliotecários na UFRGS, 5)

CONSTRUCTS FOR INVESTIGATING LACK OF PERSISTENCE IN EXPERIMENTAL DISTANCE EDUCATION: A STUDY OF HEALTH SCIENCES LIBRARIANS

Diane Tobin Johnson
MaryEllen C. Sievert
Teresa Hartman
Timothy Patrick
University of Missouri
USA

Abstract: This study examines distance education as a continuing education delivery system, with special application to health sciences librarians.

In many professions, including the profession of librarianship, distance education has been heralded as a solution to the problem of bringing new knowledge to the practising professional, chiefly because the "cost" to the professional is seen as less. Some forms of distance education offer the ability to access new knowledge at one's own pace, at one's convenience in terms of time, and certainly at one's own location. Reducing the demands of pace, timing, and location for the professional is presumed to mean that more professionals will participate in continuing education, an argument that stems from basic marketing practice—if price is reduced or benefit is enhanced, increased volume should result.

In many fields, the development of distance education programs has been neither rapid nor widespread. In library and information science, for example, correspondence courses (one of the first forms of distance education) have existed since the late 1800's. The majority of the institutions accredited by the American Library Association have offered courses conducted off-campus using a variety of methods during the past ten years, a practice that began in 1947 (Barron, 1996). The use of audioconferencing, videoconferencing, and videotaped courses began more than ten years ago, but is not widespread (Barron, 1996). Entry into distance education delivery by the professional programs and associations serving librarians has been characterized by an anxiety about the market (Hannigan, 1993). That anxiety seems to be somewhat justified by provider experience. For example, only 12% of the membership of the Medical Library Association (MLA) participate in MLA's Journal Club or other self-study programs, while 60% report attending continuing education courses sponsored by organizations other than MLA. Broad concepts about reducing perceived costs and enhancing perceived benefits seem to have limitations in terms of predicting the responses of professionals.

Nevertheless, reaching practising professionals with new knowledge is important in all areas of librarianship, and it is particularly important in the area of health sciences librarianship. Access to timely, appropriately-evaluated resources can literally be a matter of life or death, a matter of health or wellness. The U.S. National Library of Medicine (NLM) and the Medical Library Association (MLA) have been extremely interested in the investigation of distance learning technologies as a way of diffusing new knowledge and reaching larger numbers of practising professionals.

Health sciences librarians, like other professionals (Cervero, 1988), function under an implicit public assumption that their education will be continuous so long as they are employed in information service. There are, however, no requirements for continuing practice in the field. Even if such requirements did exist, delivering instruction and assessing continued competency would still be widely acknowledged as problematic. The profile of health sciences librarians prepared by the NLM suggests why (U.S. National Library of Medicine, 1995). First of all, the group is small; no more than 10,000 professionals work in more than 3,600 medical libraries and other health-related agencies in the U.S. and Canada. Secondly, health sciences librarians are scattered. About 37% work in large cities; less than 5% work in rural communities. About half work in hospital libraries; another quarter work in academic health sciences centers, usually affiliated with schools of medicine and nursing.

The majority of health sciences librarians are members of their professional group, the Medical Library Association. The association offers an annual conference, a quarterly publication, and several certified continuing opportunities each year at locations other than the conference. MLA chapters hold their own conferences and events. Events offered outside the association may qualify for continuing education units through a certification process offered by the association. Members also have access to some self-study programs, such as those mentioned above.

The roles and functions of health sciences librarians are changing as the health care delivery system is affected by several trends in the larger environment (Detre, 1994). The first is the trend toward regional health networks, accompanied by the merging of outpatient, inpatient, rehabilitation, patient education and home care functions. The increased emphasis on managed care will likely change the roles of primary care providers and specialists as a way of coping with both an exploding knowledge base and an increased number of patients. The increased number of patients will come not from an increase in catastrophic illnesses, but from the technological ability to identify, early in life, those people at risk for developing specific disorders. Particularly in the managed care scenario, it makes economic sense to intervene with patient education to prevent illness or to cope with it effectively. Librarians who have typically served in stand-alone facilities with responsibilities only to specialists and primary care physicians face much broader responsibilities as they become part of the patient education team. Applying emerging information technology to quickly retrieve and evaluate relevant knowledge for a variety of health care professionals, patients, and families will become an ever more important function. The response to programs anticipating these trends offered by and through the Medical Library Association has been good. However, the need for continuing education in this profession continues to grow.

Recent efforts have been made to address this need. In 1987, the U.S. National Library of Medicine published a Long Range Plan, forecasting the use of new technologies in delivering information to an increasingly diverse biomedical community. Continuing education was seen as integral to this process, both in terms of retraining highly skilled librarians and in terms of "training the trainer" so that librarians could effectively train end-users. Meanwhile, the Medical Library Association created the educational policy statement *Platform for Change*, published in 1991, which echoed NLM's theme and called on the NLM to specifically define support available to assist with training and retraining health sciences librarians. This request resulted in the formation of a steering committee and finally the Planning Panel on the Education and Training of Health Sciences Librarians. The four national goals cited in their report (1995) focused on the areas of recruitment, professional education, lifelong learning programs, and evolving roles for health sciences librarians. While emphasizing that professionals should take responsibility for their own development, the panel urged professional schools to become more involved in continuing education, and specifically to explore the possibilities of alternative methods and courses of study.

The U.S. National Library of Medicine issued a Request for Applications in February 1995; seven planning grants addressing various aspects of the Planning Panel's report were funded in October 1995. The School of Library and Informational Science at the University of Missouri-Columbia planning grant had two aims (Sievert, Johnson, Schmidt, Reid, and Mitchell, 1996). The first was to develop a model curriculum for health sciences librarianship at the master's level, including field rotations with problem-based-learning medical students; the second was to develop materials that could be delivered via alternative instructional methods. In order to test materials and alternative methods of delivery, the School decided to offer an international satellite broadcast, a series of instructional modules via the World Wide Web, a listserv discussion group, and a traditional face-to-face intensive four-day seminar under the title *Libraries, Medical Informatics and Health Care*. Over 400 librarians throughout the United States and in four other countries participated in these various events. Over 200 made inquiries or signed up for various aspects of this training but did not complete the actual work. Portions of that experience form the basis for this research.

Distance education has been justified primarily by appeals to reduction in cost (broadly conceived). Professional association involvement, chiefly through reviewing proposed content and certifying providers to offer continuing education units, has been justified primarily by appeals to enhancement of benefits. If perceived costs can make continuing education offerings attractive to professionals and if professional associations can appropriately promote enhanced benefits, it would seem to follow that great numbers of professionals would be apt to take advantage of continuing education offerings and that professional associations and providers would team up rapidly to produce appropriate learning experiences. However, experience seems to suggest that many professionals decide not to take advantage of learning opportunities or not to completely follow through with initial commitments. It is important for providers to learn what factors play an important role in those decisions, particularly as providers stand at the brink of investing their resources in new modes of delivery.

There is some existing evidence concerning deterrents to participation in continuing education which may prove useful in the distance education context. A review of adult learning theories, particularly motivational models, and distance learning concepts will assist in framing the concept of deterrents within a larger motivational picture. Then data provided by a portion of the population of non-persisters from the project *Libraries, Medical Informatics and Health Care* are examined in order to propose some potential additional deterrent factors to consider in distance contexts.

LITERATURE REVIEW

According to Merriam (1993), much of the developmental research on adult learning has been drawn from the field of psychology. As adult educators have attempted to differentiate adult education from the field of education in general, a number of models have been proposed. Some of these models have been widely accepted as informal "theories," that is, they form the basis for research investigations. No empirical theory of adult education yet exists. Models are adopted based on their intuitive explanatory power.

One of the most popular models is Cross's (1981) Chain of Response (COR) Model, an interactive, non-linear model to explain adult participation in educational endeavors. Cross proposes seven interacting elements:

(1)   evaluation of self;
(2)   attitudes toward education in general;
         attitudes towards making and meeting goals;
         impact of life transitions;
         assessment of opportunities and barriers;
         access to and use of information; and
         previous experiences of participation.

The strength of the Cross model is that any element may interact with any other element. Hence, the professional who is experiencing divorce (life transition) may experience a re-evaluation of the self which may in turn interact with her assessment of opportunities and barriers associated with a particular continuing education offering. The model thus provides a rich contextual approach to explaining behavior, including personal characteristics, situational constraints, and institutional factors, as well as information availability and assessment.

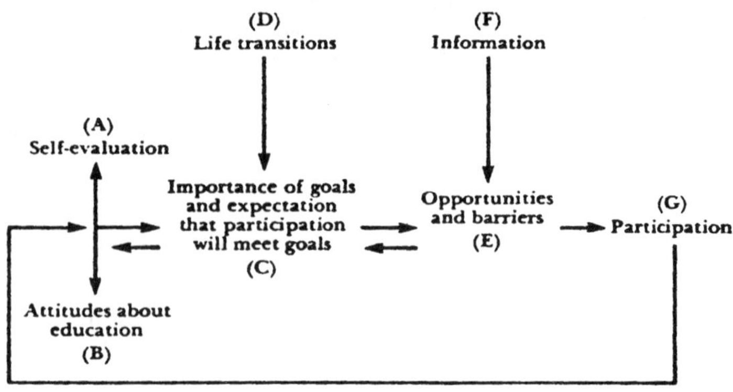

From *Adults as Learners* by K. Patricia Cross, Jossey-Bass Publishers, 1981.

Cost Construct, Correlation Matrix

Item	Q24	Q32	Q46
Q24	1.000		
Q32	.3554	1.000	
Q46	.6952	.3808	1.000

Alpha= .7396

Q24 Cost of travel, lodging, books, tuition, and food for the face-to-face seminar was too much for me.

Q32 My employer does not assist with cost.

Q46 The location of the face-to-face seminar was inconvenient for me.

More recently, MacKinnon-Slaney (1994) created a slightly different model for counselling adult students, the Adult Persistence in Learning (APIL) Model, focusing on three interacting components: personal issues, learning issues, and environmental issues. The personal issues component includes the following factors: self-awareness, willingness to delay gratification, clarification of career and life goals, mastery of life transitions, and a sense of interpersonal competence. The learning issues component includes educational competence, and intellectual and political competence.   The environmental issues component includes the following factors: information retrieval, awareness of opportunities and impediments, and environmental compatibility.

Figure 2. The Adult Persistence in Learning (APIL) Model

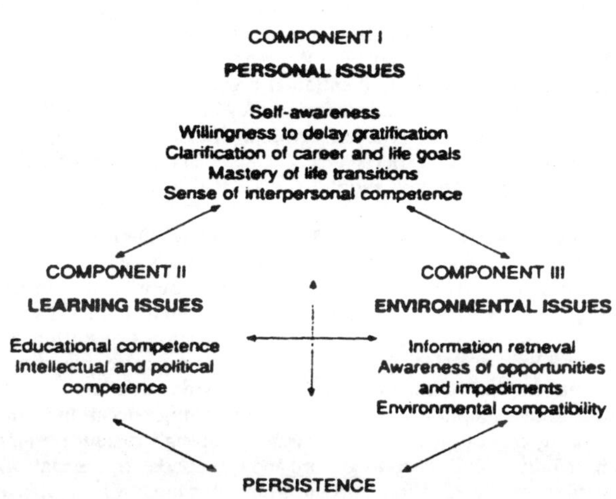

From "The Adult Persistence in Learning Model: A Road Map to Counseling Services for Adult Learners" by Fiona MacKinnon-Slaney, <u>Journal of Counseling and Development</u>, volume 72, January/February 1994, p. 269.

Although the APIL Model contains some of the elements in the COR Model, its strength is that it has a more contemporary thrust.   Including elements such as interpersonal competence, political competence, and environmental compatibility might seem to have predictive power with regard to the participation behaviors of today's professionals.

Both of these are complex models; their interactive dimensions make them difficult to test as a whole. However, both models use the concept of barriers/impediments as a variable in predicting participation.   The COR model includes these as the fifth element.   The APIL model includes awareness of impediments under the third component, environmental issues.   Further, some research exists which suggests specific deterrent factors.

Scanlan and Darkenwald (1984) and Darkenwald and Valentine (1985) posit that participation behaviors are directly influenced by specific sets of deterrents (barriers/impediments in the Cross/MacKinnon-Slaney models). Using factor analysis, Scanlan and Darkenwald (1984) isolated six factors (disengagement, lack of quality, family constraints, cost, lack of benefit, and work constraints) which in combination accounted for 41% of the variance in a study of allied health professionals. A larger study of an adult population in a New Jersey county yielded some parallel results (Darkenwald & Valentine, 1985) with such factors emerging as lack of confidence, lack of course relevance, time constraints, low personal priority, cost, and personal problems. In each study, participants were queried about reasons why they might have rejected one or more continuing education opportunities. Some motivational process, such as those described in the COR and APIL models was assumed to be operating. It is important to note that a specific decision not to participate had not been observed.

Is it possible to extend the concept of deterrent factors to participation in continuing education through distance education opportunities? Moore (1993) suggests that problems typically experienced in education may be exacerbated by distance. By logical extension, deterrents could play a stronger role in distance education offerings. On the other hand, the perceived cost to the potential participant may be substantially reduced, as mentioned previously, thereby modifying the effects of deterrents. Moore's assessment of distance education in the U.S. (1993) notes that the development of a strong student support element lags behind the development of course design and communication delivery systems. A study of deterrents experienced by distance education participants could assist in determining whether perceived poor student support is experienced as a deterrent.

What import might such a study have for the field of library and information science? Barron (1996) traces the development of distance education in MLS degree programs, noting that 17 colleges and universities are currently using some form of telecommunicated instruction within their degree programs, although only one program offers the degree primarily in a distance format. Barron notes that the Library and Information Science Distance Education Consortium (LISDEC) changed focus in 1994 from providing distance education modules for degree programs to assisting with provision of continuing education. The American Library Association has recently formed a multi-unit task force to address access to and requirements for continuing education in the field. A national level network of continuing education resources provided through distance education technologies seems to be at least a possibility. Understanding more about what deterrents may operate for potential distance education participants in continuing education offerings would appear to be a useful endeavor. According to the National Center for Educational Statistics, approximately 146,000 professionals are engaged in employment in the nation's academic, public, and school libraries. The world of health sciences librarianship is much smaller, encompassing approximately 10,000 professionals . Because of the rate and volume of change in the medical field, participation in continuing education is particularly critical in this area of librarianship. Therefore, the study of deterrents to participation in continuing education in a distance format within this group seems especially useful.

PROBLEM STATEMENT

The research reported here focuses on the deterrents experienced by potential participants in each distance education format. What deterrents did they experience? Did their experience of deterrents suggest an approximation of the factors discovered by Scanlan and Darkenwald (1984) or were different factors operating? Did the use of technology in itself generate additional deterrent factors not identified in the Scanlan and Darkenwald study but consistent with the models proposed by Cross (1981) and MacKinnon-Slaney (1994)?

METHODS AND PROCEDURES

An attempt was made to capture all inquiries about any aspect of *Libraries, Medical Informatics, and Health Care* including inquiries made by mail, e-mail, telephone, and fax. These inquiries were generated by project publicity through traditional press releases to library publications, distribution electronically to several library listservs (including MEDLIB-L), and through direct mail to over 200 health sciences consortia and libraries.

Some inquirers changed options during the course of the project. A decision was made to classify the inquiry based on the final disposition of the inquirer's effort. As a result, an inquirer who had first asked about the telecast (Option 1) would have been counted under inquiries about the combined telecast/Internet option (Option 3) if he or she had eventually chosen that option. There was no direct charge to any participants except those who chose the face-to-face four-day seminar; in that case, tuition was incurred. As each registration was received, a notation was made about whether continuing education units (CEUs) from the Medical Library Association were desired by the registrant. A record was kept of those completing the requirements for CEUs. Follow-up telephone calls were made to registrants who had indicated a desire for CEUs but for whom there was no record of requirements met.

Accordingly, a database of persisting students (those who had completed the requirements for an option) could be constructed, as well as a database of "non-persisters" (those who had indicated initial interest, or who had signed up for an option, and for whom no record of completion existed). This database of 238 non-persisters was contacted an average of three times and asked to complete a 48-item survey concerning the deterrents to participating that they might have experienced. Only 16% were contacted by traditional mail; the rest were contacted through e-mail.

In order to identify elements that could potentially explain non-persistence, all e-mail and verbal messages (taken from phone messages and conversational notes) from inquirers and participants were content analyzed. Using this process, an additional 41 elements were added to elements from the Deterrents to Participation Scale previously identified (Scanlan & Darkenwald, 1984; Darkenwald and Valentine, 1985). Although Darkenwald and Valentine (1985) sought to identify deterrents for a much more diverse adult population, elements unique to that study also seemed to fit with the MacKinnon-Slaney model and the content of the messages from the non-persisters in this group. Accordingly, elements from both studies were modified to better fit this particular audience. These processes resulted in a pool of 94 items which was then reviewed by a small group of health sciences librarians. Items perceived as duplicates, unclear items, and irrelevant items were identified and eliminated. The resulting 77-item instrument was then tested with a group of online health sciences librarians for item reliability, noting amount of time taken to complete the instrument. Respondent comments and item statistics implied that the instrument could be shortened without significantly affecting reliability. The revised 48-item instrument was formulated around nine hypothesized constructs, seven adapted from the earlier studies and two originating from the research team's ideas about the impact of technology. The adapted constructs included: Confidence, Perceived Benefit, Cost, Disengagement, Personal Problems, Work Constraints, and Perceived Quality. The two hypothesized technology factors included Distance Education Concerns and Technology Frustration. The 48 items included 18 items from earlier research and 30 items derived from the content analysis described above.

The instrument was then distributed via e-mail and regular postal mail (including a self-addressed, stamped return envelope) to all inquirers and enrolees who had not persisted with any intended aspect of *Libraries, Medical Informatics, and Health Care*. Respondents were instructed to indicate the importance of each reason in their decision not to participate or continue participating. The scale used was a Likert-type scale, with values of "not important", "slightly important", "somewhat important," "important" and "very important." They were also invited to respond to an open-ended question regarding their reason(s) for not participating. A brief demographic section was appended, including information about the age, gender, education, and employment status of the respondent.

It seemed reasonable to expect that it might be difficult to retrieve completed surveys from people who had already made at least one decision not to participate in the offering. That expectation proved to be correct. A series of follow-up attempts was made (averaging three contacts per respondent), including additional e-mail contacts, postal contacts, and telephone calls. A monetary incentive was used during the final round of follow-up correspondence.   Despite these efforts, less than 25% of the non-persisters responded to the survey. Because the response level was low, factor analysis was not attempted. Coefficient alpha was used to determine the reliability of the new deterrents suggested and to confirm the reliability of the deterrents suggested by previous research.

DATA ANALYSIS

Establishing reliability with coefficient alpha simply indicates how well the items used in a scale reflect an underlying construct. Each of the factors identified in the previous research cited, as well as those factors posited as an effect of distance and technology, would be considered an underlying construct. Because items from previous research were mixed with items from the content analysis, the supported constructs tended to vary slightly from those earlier identified. Straightforward support was found for the *Cost* construct identified by Scanlan and Darkenwald (1984), shown in Table 1.

Table 1

Cost Construct, Correlation Matrix

Item	*Q24*	*Q32*	*Q46*
Q24	1.000		
Q32	.3554	1.000	
Q46	.6952	.3808	1.000

Alpha= .7396

Q24 Cost of travel, lodging, books, tuition, and food for the face-to-face seminar was too much for me.

Q32 My employer does not assist with cost.

Q46 The location of the face-to-face seminar was inconvenient for me.

Some items identified in previous research in separate lack of quality and lack of course relevance constructs show reliability here in an augmented construct termed *Content Deemed Unsuitable* construct.   This construct included items concerning interest in the content, content perceived to be at the wrong level, content perceived as impractical, or content that was perceived as too general for the respondent's more specific purpose. Coefficient alpha for the reliability of these items was fairly high, at 0.89, as shown in Table 2.

Table 2

Content Deemed Unsuitable Construct, Correlation Matrix

Item	*Q5*	*Q30*	*Q35*	*Q16*
Q5	1.000			
Q30	.6245	1.000		
Q35	.5631	.7156	1.000	
Q16	.5773	.7623	.7826	1.000

Alpha= .8898

Q5 The content didn't seem interesting.

Q30 These kinds of programs tend to be geared toward the wrong level for my needs.

Q35 The content didn't seem useful or practical.

Q16 I wanted to learn something specific; this was too general.

MacKinnon-Slaney's work (1994) offered some insight into how personal issues might become barriers for continuing education participants in a distance education environment. General concerns shown in previous research (competing with younger students, lack of self-discipline) were combined with concerns evidenced in content analysis (lack of background in this field, competing with experienced librarians, and appearing a fool in online discussions).

Table 3
Confidence Construct, Correlation Matrix

Item	Q1	Q12	Q14	Q28	Q29
Q1	1.000				
Q12	.4913	1.000			
Q14	.4792	.5631	1.000		
Q28	.7384	.3859	.3859	1.000	
Q29	.5799	.5804	.7724	.4074	1.000

Alpha= .8277

Q1	I didn't feel I had the right background to undertake this work.
Q12	I didn't want to make a fool of myself in online discussions.
Q14	I felt I couldn't compete with younger students.
Q28	I felt I couldn't compete with more experienced librarians.
Q29	I don't always have the discipline to set learning priorities for myself.

More specific concerns about the experience of distance education itself merged to form a *Distance Education Concerns* construct with a reliability coefficient of 0.88. These concerns included having enough variety in the types of material used, being able to do learning activities that did not feel like tedious "busy work." A general feeling about poor quality in previously-experienced distance education and previous poor experiences with teleconferences also figured into this construct. It is important to note that this construct is separate from *Content Deemed Unsuitable*, in that the prior construct speaks to specific content and this construct speaks to the expected or actual quality of the learning experience. The correlation matrix for this construct, associated coefficient alpha, and specific questions are shown in Table 4.

Table 4
Distance Education Concerns Construct, Correlation Matrix

Item	Q2	Q37	Q48	Q40
Q2	1.000			
Q37	.5251	1.000		
Q48	.7211	.5481	1.000	
Q40	.6924	.7663	.7662	1.000

Alpha= .8822

Q2	There wasn't enough variety in the material.
Q37	The learning activities were too tedious, it felt like "busy work."
Q48	Distance education programs in general tend to be of poor quality.
Q40	I have had poor experiences with teleconferences.

Lastly, frustration with specific aspects of the technology used in distance education produces a *Technology Concerns* construct. Specific aspects of not being able to control the changes associated with the technology (finding co-ordinates, making a lesson on the Internet work, adjusting to accommodate availability of modules on the Internet) come together with a general feeling that participants do not get the attention they need in distance education programs. This correlation matrix, associated alpha of 0.77, and questions are shown in Table 5.

Table 5
Technology Concerns Construct, Correlation Matrix

Item	Q18	Q45	Q9	Q13
Q18	1.000			
Q45	.3387	1.000		
Q9	.5213	.3222	1.000	
Q13	.6850	.5008	.4686	1.000

Alpha= .7701

Q18	The Web modules didn't come up on time; it was too confusing.
Q45	I couldn't find the appropriate teleconference co-ordinates.
Q9	I couldn't get a specific module or lesson to work.
Q13	I don't think participants get the attention they need in distance education programs.

DISCUSSION

The major limitation of this report is that, at the time this volume goes to press, less than 25% of the non-persister target population have responded to the survey. The strength of this report is that it was done with a target population who had not persisted with a specific continuing education opportunity. The recency and specificity of the non-persisting behavior helps ground the responses assessed here differently than the responses assessed in previous research.

The coefficients reported here range from 0.74 to 0.89. Previous research has already established the viability of cost, content, and confidence constructs. The intercorrelations reported here are, for the most part, strong enough to suggest that future studies on deterrents to participation in distance education contexts could include elements which address those contexts. They suggest that a distance education confidence construct might include items addressing a fear that one's background is not adequate in the subject matter or in the technical competence needed, fear of losing face in online environments and fear of competing with knowledgeable others. In addition, it may be expected that poor experiences with distance education technologies and/or poor estimation of the capability of distance education could serve as deterrents to participation and that non-persisters might be sensitive to the variety of learning materials available as well as whether the learning activities are perceived as "busy work." Even as technologies and learner's experiences change, the existence of a distance concerns construct in deterrent research seems supportable. This suggests that the market for distance education for continuing education professionals is, or is becoming, a sophisticated market with expectations of offerings that will meet their personal standards for quality.

Frustration with operating the technology which makes distance education possible also seems to be a strong candidate for inclusion in deterrent research. The coupling of that frustration with a perceived lack of attention seems to indicate that participants feel that technical difficulties, wherever they originate, should be attended to by the continuing education provider. If that is the case, then distance education providers must include a substantial component of student support in the technology area in order to attract and retain professionals who are potential continuing education participants.

One additional note seems in order. It seems unlikely that specific items in deterrent research will always configure themselves in constructs revealed in previous research. Items or elements may produce different factors given different populations and different contexts, simply because the learning environment continues to change. This dynamic interplay, while not particularly comforting, does follow from the fluid structure of the models introduced here. Future research might fruitfully use the models to identify elements which then can be expected to configure themselves differently from context to context. The stability may be in the models and the elements, rather than in the factors.

REFERENCES

Anderson, R. E. and Darkenwald, G. G. (1979), *Participation and Persistence in American Adult Education,* New York: College Board.

Barron, D. D. (1996), "Distance education in North American library and information science education: applications of technology and commitment", *Journal of the American Society for Information Science*, 47, pp. 805-850.

Cervero, R. M. (1988), *Effective Continuing Education for Professionals,* San Francisco: Jossey-Bass Publishers.

Cookson, P. S. (ed.) (1989), "Recruiting and retaining adult students", *New Directions for Continuing Education*, 41, San Francisco: Jossey-Bass Publishers.

Cross, K. P. (1981), *Adults as Learners: Increasing Participation and Facilitating Learning,* San Francisco: Jossey-Bass Publishers.

Darkenwald, G. G. & Valentine, T. (1985), "Factor structure of deterrents to public participation in adult education", *Adult Education Quarterly*, 35 , pp. 177-193.

Detre, T. (1994), Statement by the panel chair. NLM Planning Panel on the Education and Training of Health Sciences Librarians, Sept. 15, 1994.

Hannigan, J. A. (1993), "Distance learning and interactivity", in: *Project Century 21: A Research and Action Program for Meeting the Information Needs of Society—Background Papers,* pp.19-40, Chicago: American Library Association.

MacKinnon-Slaney, F. (1994), "The adult persistence in learning model: a road map to counseling services for adult learners", *Journal of Counseling and Development*, 72, pp.268-275.

Medical Library Association (1991), *Platform for Change: the Educational Policy Statement of the Medical Library Association,* Chicago: Medical Library Association.

Merriam, S.B. (ed.) (1993), "An update on adult learning theory", *New Directions for Adult and Continuing Education*, 57, San Francisco: Jossey-Bass Publishers.

Moore, M. (1989), "Recruiting and retaining adult students in distance education", in P. S. Cookson, (ed.), *Recruiting and Retaining Adult Students,* San Francisco: Jossey-Bass Publishers. pp. 89-98.

National Library of Medicine. (1995), "The education and training of health sciences librarians", in *National Library of Medicine Long Range Plan, Report of Planning Panel on the Education and Training of Health Sciences Librarians.* Bethesda, MD: National Institutes of Health.

National University Continuing Education Association. (1994),: *Lifelong Learning Trends A Profile of Continuing Higher Education* (3rd ed.), Washington, D.C.: National University Continuing Education Association.

Scanlan, C. S. & Darkenwald, G. G. (1984), "Identifying deterrents to participation in continuing education", *Adult Education Quarterly*, 34, pp. 155-166.

Sievert, M.C., Johnson, D.T., Schmidt, D., Reid, J.C., and Mitchell, J.A. (1996), "The Missouri planning grant for the education and training of health sciences librarians", *Bulletin of the Medical Library Association*, 84, pp. 553-559.

THE CHANGING NATURE OF CONTINUING EDUCATION FOR THE INDIVIDUAL: WILL LIBRARIES AND LIBRARIANS CONTINUE TO PLAY A ROLE IN SUPPORTING LEARNERS?

Clive Cochrane
Head, Management & Information Systems Division
Queen's School of Management
The Queen's University of Belfast
Northern Ireland, UK

ABSTRACT: In a period of rapid change continuing education for the individual is vital. More open approaches to learning are developing with the greater use of information technology. It is suggested that because the nature of continuing education is changing, library and information professionals must not only alter their professional practice when supporting the continuing education of others, but they must embrace these new approaches in their own continuing education.

INTRODUCTION

The recent White Paper "Towards the learning society" (Commission of the European Communities, 1995) acknowledges the importance of education and training in Europe in a period of rapid change. Within this broad context the aim of this paper is to stress the significance of continuing education for the individual and suggest that developments in information technology are encouraging more open approaches to learning. Library and information science (LIS) professionals have always supported the continuing education of individuals. In view of the dramatic changes taking place in the delivery of continuing education and the importance now attached to the acquisition of new skills it is proposed that LIS professionals consider new rather than traditional approaches to provision. In doing so they need to have a fundamental appraisal of their own continuing education. Before examining these issues personal reflection highlights the need for each individual to take greater responsibility for his or her own continuing education at a time of economic, social and technological change.

Personal Reflection 1977-1997

With the new millennium approaching personal reflection enables me to identify three major trends in my own continuing education over a twenty year period from 1977-1997. Firstly, there was the necessity to update my knowledge and skills as the nature of my work changed. Secondly, I relied on the flexibility offered by distance learning for the majority of my continuing education. Thirdly, with the passage of time new technology played increasing importance in the delivery of learning material. By examining each area in turn the nature of my own continuing education will serve as a case-study epitomising the experiences of many others.

When I was initially appointed a lecturer in Library and Information Studies at the Queen's University of Belfast (QUB) in 1977 my qualifications comprised a BA degree and a post-graduate Diploma in Librarianship. I was appointed to develop courses in the emerging field of audio-visual librarianship. In 1979 I enrolled for a Diploma in Educational Technology, an appropriate cognate field of study enabling me to develop my teaching and research interests. By the mid-eighties I embarked on a research degree in the field of moving image archives to deepen my knowledge of one particular area of interest. In 1988 I enrolled for a Diploma in Post-Compulsory Education with the aim of enhancing my theoretical and practical understanding of adult education. This was followed by a Certificate in On-Line Education & Training which provided me with an introduction to a new area, namely computer conferencing. Finally, in the early nineties, after taking a free-standing module about multi-media developments I subsequently enrolled for an M Sc in Information Technology & Learning to equip myself for developments which would influence both my research and teaching.

These courses were undertaken against a background of constant change emanating from a variety of sources. The name of my department changed four times - Library & Information Studies, Information Studies, Information Management, Management & Information Systems - reflecting changes within the LIS profession in general and within the University in particular. With each name change the mission of the department altered, moving further and further away from its traditional roots in librarianship. As the aims of the department changed so did the nature of the programmes delivered to students. The disappearance of the word "library" from the department's name and its substitution by the word "information" was accompanied by a substantial increase in student numbers. As our programmes placed emphasis on management and information technology they were viewed in a positive light by students who perceived them to be relevant to a broad rather than a narrow range of jobs.

Changes in Government policies towards higher education manifest themselves in various ways. During the nineties there was a rapid expansion of student numbers. Greater emphasis was placed by Government on ensuring that universities improved the quality of the learning experienced by students. Many subject areas, including LIS, were encouraged to pay more attention to the use of information technology in teaching and learning. The quality of research in every subject area was subject to periodic peer review.

In summary during twenty years there have been substantial changes regarding what I teach, whom I teach, how I teach, the research I undertake and the ways in which my teaching and research are evaluated. Continuing my education enabled me to develop as the nature of my work changed.

Although I lived and worked in Belfast I was able to take the following programmes, geared to my own learning needs, offered in distance learning mode by institutions throughout the United Kingdom:

- Diploma in Educational Technology - Dundee College of Education (Scotland)
- M Phil (research) - University College, Aberystwyth (Wales)
- Diploma in Post-Compulsory Education - Open University (Milton Keynes, England)
- Certificate in On-line Education & Training - Institute of Education, London University (England)
- M Sc in Information Technology & Learning - Lancaster University (England)

Through distance learning I was not tied to what was available in my immediate locality. A variety of educational opportunities were available, yet there was minimum disruption to my professional life.

Personal reflection on the learning I acquired during two decades inevitably leads to some consideration of methods of delivery. These formal courses were characterised by a mixed media approach to learning. Packages of printed material of varying quality were delivered to my home. Over time other methods of delivery increased in sophistication. A variety of audio-visual materials was used to support my learning. Slides, filmstrips and audiocassettes were sent by Dundee College of Education. The Open University transmitted radio and/or television programmes and/or distributed audio and video cassettes. Face-to-face meetings ranging from one-day workshops to residentials lasting a week enabled students and tutors to meet. At London University a one-day training workshop about the CoSy computer conferencing system opened what turned out to be one of my most interesting learning experiences - a course about computer conferencing taught via computer conferencing. The students came from various parts of the British Isles, several European countries, USA and Israel. As the students were communicating with each other via computer conferencing it was an excellent example of the "virtual classroom" in action. Although asynchronous communication was the focus of the course it ended with the experimental use of synchronous communication. Students in Belfast, Aberdeen and London were able to communicate with each other via audio- and videoconferencing. At Lancaster University students were encouraged to communicate with each other and their tutors via e-mail and computer conferencing using the Caucus system.

An important general conclusion to emerge from this personal reflection is the fact that developments in information technology have enabled students and tutors to overcome the physical barriers of distance. Technologies such as computer and videoconferencing permit new forms of communication to take place and encourage participation in learning events irrespective of where a student lives or works.

Like many other professionals I have faced great changes at work in recent years. Accountants, engineers, lawyers, managers, medics and teachers have been forced to recognise that lifelong learning is now an integral part of work and career development. LIS professionals in the United Kingdom, for example, are no exception and are now encouraged to take greater responsibility for their own continuing professional development, although there is no legal obligation on employers to implement such schemes. In view of the changing nature of jobs undertaken by LIS professionals (Cronin, 1993), the growing use of information technology and new organisational structures in the organisations in which they work, it is vital that LIS professionals develop a proactive rather than a reactive stance and acquire new skills, attitudes and knowledge. Rather than look at this in isolation it is vital to consider some of the changes taking place elsewhere. For too long the response of LIS professionals to the continuing education of members of their user communities has lacked vision. A traditional approach to service has been the norm. While there is room for traditional lending and reference services it is time to reflect on some of the changes taking place beyond library walls and consider how they might influence the continuing education of LIS professionals.

INFORMATION TECHNOLOGY AND ITS IMPACT ON LIFELONG LEARNING

Many individuals now have access to computer terminals at work and at home. In a relatively short period they have become fully integrated into our daily existence. The functions of the stand-alone PC have been transformed in recent years. Rather than being used just for running applications software, facilities are now available to exploit an increasing range of multi-media material on formats such as CD-ROM. With developments in networking and telecommunications the individual has the ability to access on-line databases, communicate with others using asynchronous communications media such as e-mail and discussion lists and access resources via the Internet. In effect the individual's multi-media workstation is becoming his personal access point to friends, colleagues, fellow students and resources of all kinds nationally and internationally. In the last few years there has been much interest in the educational world in the development of desktop videoconferencing systems (DTVC) which permit one-to-one communication and various forms of collaborative learning to take place. Unlike other more expensive forms of videoconferencing aimed primarily at inter-group communication, DTVC products are relatively low-cost hardware/software packages. This fact, plus the increasing availability of P Cs to individuals means that DTVC could spread rapidly as costs decrease. Referring to higher education Morgan and Thorp (1995) predict not only growth in the use of DTVC, but also changes for users:

"Within five years it is quite likely that most members of staff in HE and large numbers of students will have access to a multimedia PC with many other components of a videoconferencing system built-in...If the desktop videoconferencing technology delivers on its promise and the products do indeed enhance people's working lives and increase the level of "communication at a distance" then we could see dramatic developments in working practices in the next few years."

Mason (1994) notes that "desktop systems will support online help facilities, tutorials, browsing tools and search and reference facilities. These will put the user centre-stage as manager of the learning process. Teachers have just as important a role in this new future, but it is as a preparer of material, facilitator of interaction, expert on how to find, access and use information."

If the scenarios envisaged above materialise individual learners in future, irrespective of location, will be able to communicate by sound and vision in real-time with colleagues and other professionals. LIS professionals should have the appropriate facilities to enable them to play the role Mason envisages for teachers. If potential users of library and information services are able to express their needs and communicate with professionals from a distance rather than visiting a library this will alter the relationship between client and service provider. Already experiments in telemedicine show that healthcare professionals can communicate with patients at distant locations. Bank personnel will be able to communicate with their customers via strategically placed video-booths. Although these ideas may now appear to be futuristic, it is clear that in other professions new technology is influencing the nature of the relationship between the service provider and the client. There is no reason to suppose that the traditional concept of a user visiting a library to receive service is likely to remain permanent. Perhaps the time has come to envisage a new kind of service for some, if not necessarily all users.

VIDEOCONFERENCING AND THE LIBRARY AND INFORMATION PROFESSION

The potential of DTVC for the profession has been indicated above. Although this tends to support one-to-one communication, many institutions, particularly in the educational sector, use videoconferencing systems to support learning between individuals and groups in different locations. There are signs that the LIS profession is beginning to recognise the value of these technologies. There is evidence from North America (Littman, 1995) and (Pagell, 1966) that group videoconferencing and DTVC systems are being used by libraries for a variety of reasons and some new academic libraries in the United Kingdom (Brockhurst, 1966) are equipped with videoconferencing facilities. A small-scale survey of UK library schools conducted by Cochrane (1966) indicates that LIS lecturers envisage many interesting uses of videoconferencing technology by the schools in particular and the profession in general. Suggested uses for library schools included support for distance learning students, inter-unit teaching, joint seminars with a guest "expert" in one location, demonstrations and presentations. Suggested uses of videoconferencing in academic libraries included user education, advisory or reference work and contact with students, academic or other staff at various locations/ campuses. Uses suggested for public libraries included new patterns of communication between the central library and its branches and potential links with schools, further education colleges, businesses and other institutions in their areas.

Actual practice and potential uses indicate that the competent use of videoconferencing technology will enable LIS professionals to support the continuing education of others and indeed themselves in innovate ways. For the continuing education of LIS professionals videoconferencing will enable courses, workshops, seminars and demonstrations to be more accessible to practitioners, especially those in more remote locations.

FROM DISTANCE TO OPEN LEARNING

Returning to my own personal reflection it is clear that although distance learning was of great benefit it had certain disadvantages. These included the fact that I had to submit assignments on particular dates, follow a set curriculum, attend scheduled residential sessions. In other words although distance learning can overcome the barriers of physical distance it is not necessarily open in its approach. There are signs, however that new technology is helping to achieve a more open approach to learning.

Currently I am eagerly following a discussion list which was established by Sheffield University following a successful conference on networked learner support in 1996. Professionals in different locations are able to discuss ideas in an asynchronous manner. At the same time I am able to participate in a similar system established for former postgraduate Lancaster University students. The significance of these developments is that the use of information technology by two separate educational institutions enables me to learn, develop and communicate with professional colleagues about different issues irrespective of location.

The idea of receiving one's continuing education from a particular institution at any one time is no longer valid. Looking at this on a wider perspective it is conceivable that a librarian using his workstation would be able to offer reference advice to a post-graduate student at home via DTVC, participate in a discussion list developed by a specialist group of the Library Association and work for a further qualification offered by another institution by using DTVC and asynchronous media to communicate with fellow students and tutors and access course resources on the Internet. This scenario indicates that work and continuing education (and training) can become ongoing activities rather than separate events as is the case at present. Maybe we should also think less about the acquisition of formal qualifications by the individual and focus on the acquisition of new skills,

attitudes and knowledge in a more informal manner in view of the fact that people are now required
to adjust more quickly to change than in the past.

IMPLICATIONS FOR THE CONTINUING EDUCATION OF LIBRARY AND INFORMATION PROFESSIONALS

Looking beyond the LIS profession it is inevitable that more open approaches to learning
embracing the greater use of information technology will play a key role in the delivery of continuing
education to other professional groups.   More and more conventional educational institutions are now
offering open learning opportunities. Some even state that they provide all the learning materials a
student requires.   Rather than assume that other professionals will inevitably visit libraries in
connection with their continuing education perhaps the time has come to suggest that librarians
consider using new technology to support learners in innovative ways. These might include guiding
users through the growing range of electronic and on-line resources available, preparing materials
that are accessible via the Internet and communicating directly with users at home or in their
workplace using a range of synchronous and asynchronous media, rather than face-to-face in the
library.

To assist in the continuing education of other professionals, the continuing education of LIS
professionals requires a fundamental re-think. Topics to be covered might include the following:

- Continuing education - to address issues such as lifelong learning, workplace learning and
  professional development.
- Theories of adult learning - to cover aspects of cognitive psychology, experiential learning,
  andragogy and networked learner support.
- Learning needs analysis - to cover the techniques used to establish what the learning needs of
  particular groups may be.
- Instructional design - to provide guidelines regarding the structuring of content and suitable
  methods of delivery.
- Information technology for learning - to provide an understanding of the Internet, groupware,
  computer and videoconferencing, electronic journals, multimedia and other relevant
  developments.
- Moderating and netiquette - to provide guidelines regarding the moderation of learning events
  using computer or videoconferencing, including an understanding of social presence and the most
  appropriate approaches to stimulate participation and learning in these.
- The creation of learning resources - to include the design of Internet resources, the use of "html"
  and an introduction to authoring systems.

Not only do LIS professionals need to learn about these areas, but they need to experience
them so that they can empathise with their clients. The "library schools", libraries and professional
bodies such as the Library Association must, for example, experiment themselves with new
technology to deliver continuing education for LIS professionals. Rather than rely entirely on a diet
of one-day workshops, seminars and annual conferences new approaches need to be considered. If a
group of six medical schools can collaborate to teach surgery to students via videoconferencing
(Jameson et al, 1995) then it is possible for a group of "library schools" to collaborate and offer
continuing education opportunities for LIS professionals. Rather than hold a conference at one
location the Library Association could experiment and relay lectures by videoconferencing to
delegates at a number of locations throughout the United Kingdom. The fact that a training package
about the Internet called TONIC is available on the Internet means that more resources could be
created for the continuing education of the profession by the profession.   By exposing LIS
professionals to these methods of delivery not only can they become aware of the practical issues
involved in networked learner support, but they can experience more open approaches to learning.

The LIS professional equipped with the appropriate mix of knowledge, skills and attitudes
would be able to support the lifelong learning of other individuals. With advances in technology, the
need to develop new skills and have a flexible approach to work in particular, a new type of adult
learner is beginning to emerge. LIS professionals should take a proactive stance to prevent other
groups moving into areas which they should be competent to tackle.

In a period of rapid change the need for continuing education in our profession is as important as it is in others. There is however a gap between rhetoric and reality. Many philosophical and practical issues need to be addressed. Observations by Biggs (1995), Webb (1995) and Weingand (1995) highlight important issues such as whether or not continuing education should be voluntary or compulsory and how managers should cope with practical issues such as limited funds, problems of staff coverage and memories of bad courses. If the more informal, open and workplace based approach to the continuing education of LIS professionals emerges then there would be a greater variety in methods of delivery, less need to rely entirely on traditional seminars, workshops and conferences, and consequently fewer practical difficulties in ensuring that professionals gain continuing education. If more barriers to the acquisition of continuing education by LIS professionals could be removed then attitudes to implementation would be more positive.

LIBRARY AND INFORMATION PROFESSIONALS AND THE LEARNING WORKFORCE

The need for all workers, not just professionals, to develop their skills in an age of rapid change is now recognised. Research by Forrester et al (1995) shows that the recurrent education and training of all employees is vital for the individual, the enterprise and the economy. They argue that in the United Kingdom a learning workforce is required in which people not only increase their capacity to learn, but do so more quickly to keep up with the pace of change. Many individuals are only too aware that the shelf-life of their own skills is becoming increasingly short and employers are beginning to consider the full implications of concepts such as the learning enterprise. As a consequence of technological and management developments the nature of organisations is changing. Organisational hierarchies are flatter, greater emphasis is being placed on teamwork and collaborative learning, employees are expected to be multi-skilled and flexible in their approach to work. It is in this environment that staff are developing their learning. Forrester et al (1995) consider that workplace learning is vital for employee development. As shown already new technologies enable employees to learn flexibly at work and/or at home. If LIS professionals think about their own and the continuing education of others in a new light then it possible that they will play a key role in continuing education along with other professionals such as lecturers, trainers, courseware developers and educational technologists. Clearly change will be gradual and will influence some professional groups more quickly and significantly than others.

CONCLUSION

Libraries and librarians will continue to play a role in supporting learners. Many learners still rely on public and academic libraries for borrowing materials, using reference services and accessing data-bases. Nevertheless the way in which continuing education is delivered to individuals at home and at work is changing. It is up to LIS professionals to determine whether or not they will participate in the tele-learning scenario envisaged by Collis (1996). If they are to do so their own continuing education must change and embrace new technologies and open approaches to learning. Personal reflection has shown that in a relatively short time major changes in the delivery of continuing education have taken place. It is likely that the pace of change during the next twenty years will be even more profound.

REFERENCES

Biggs, Mary (1995) Reflections on continuing education...near a window. *Journal of Education for Library and Information Science* Vol 36 (2). p.174-179.

Brockhurst, Chris (1996) Building for the future. *Library Association Record_* Vol.98 (11). p.584-585.

Cochrane, Clive (1996) The use of videoconferencing to support student learning and its implications for the library and information profession. *1st International Symposium on Networked Leaner Support.* 17-18 June. Sheffield: Department of Information Studies, Sheffield University. http://panizzi.shef.ac.uk/nls_symp/

Collis, Betty (1996) Tele-learning in a digital world: the future of distance learning. London: International Thomson Computer Press.

Commission of the European Communities (1995) Towards the learning society. Brussels: Commission of the European Communities.

Cronin, Blaise et al (1993) The emergent market for information professionals: educational opportunities and implications. *Library Trends* Vol.42 (2). p.257-276.

Forrester, Keith et al (1995) Workplace learning: perspectives on education and training at work. Aldershot: Avebury.

Jameson, D G et al (1995) Teaching on the Information Superhighway. <u>in</u> Held, Paul and Kugemann, Walter F (eds.) Telematics for education and training. *Proceedings of the Telematics for Education and Training Conference,* Dusseldorf / Neuss, 24-26 November, 1994. Amsterdam: IOS Press, p.81-84.

Littman, Marlyn Kemper (1995) Videoconferencing as a communications enhancement. *Journal of Academic Librarianship* September. p.359-364.

Mason, Robin (1994) Using communications media in open and flexible learning. London: Kogan Page.

Morgan, Steve and Thorp, Mary (1995) Videoconferencing on Unix workstations to support helpdesk/advisory activities. Liverpool: University Computer Services Department. (SIMA Report 13)

Pagell, Ruth A (1996) The virtual reference librarian: using desktop videoconferencing for distance reference. *The Electronic Library* Vol. 14 (1).p.21-26.

Webb, Reneta (1995) Continuing education: mandate or option? *Journal of Education for Library and Information Science* Vol.36 (3), p.261-264.

Weingand, Darlene (1995) Continuing education and competencies: whose responsibility? *Journal of Education for Library and Information Science* Vol.36 (1). p.63-65.

ON THE EDUCATION OF INFORMATION RESOURCES MANAGEMENT PROFESSIONALS AT HIGH LEVEL IN CHINA

Peng Feizhang, Zhang Jin
School of Library and Information Science,
Wuhan University, Wuhan, Hubei, 430072
P. R. of China

Abstract   This paper reviews the history of information resources management education in China, analyses its development, current problems from the evaluation system, the impacts of new technologies on the education, the construction of faculty and reform of the education system etc.

1. INTRODUCTION.

With the rapid development of the culture and information industry in China, the information resources management is becoming a hot issue in the library and information science and other related sciences. Either scholars and experts in academic institutes or government officials at different levels recognize the significance of training information resources management professionals at high level in the future social, economic, cultural and technical developments.

Information resources management is a broader concept that should include traditional library science, information science, archival science etc. The education of the professionals at high level refers to the master and doctoral education in this field. The objectives of the education in this field should be to develop an understanding of the concept, content, methods, theories of librarianship, management and information science; to prepare students for higher levels of library management, research, teaching, consulting in library, enterprise, archival department, and information agency. Schools (departments) of library and information science are mainly responsible for training the professionals.

Traditional library education in China has a long history. In 1920, Ms. M. E. Wood established the Boone library school at Wuchang [3], the predecessor of the school of library and information science at Wuhan University. It was the first institute of library science education in China. In 1978 the master program of library and information science restarted in China. In 1990, the doctoral program of library and information science was initiated. Now it has formed a scale, see Table 1.

Table 1

academic institutes	master degree		doctoral degree	
	Library Science	Infor. Science	Library Science	Infor. Science
Wuhan University	q	q	q	q
Nanjing University	q	q		q
Beijing University	q	q	q	
China People University	q		q	
Northeast Normal University	q			
Nankai University	q			
Zhongshan University	q			
Beijing Normal University		q		
Jiling Industry University		q		
China Academy of Sci.	q	q	q	
China Sci. & Tech. Infor. Research Institute		q		
China East Normal University	q			
Shanghai Force Political College	q			
Hunan Medical College		q		
China Defense Sci. & Tech. Information Center		q		
Beijing Xiehe Medical University		q		
Nanjing Polytechnic University		q		
China Academy of Agriculture		q		
China Space Research Institute		q		
Chinese Medicine Research Institute		q		
Shanghai Jiaotong University Library		q		
Total	10	15	4	2

The number of the graduated doctoral students in the field is presented in Table 2.

Table 2.

academic institute	1994	1995	1996
Wuhan University	5	4	7
Beijing University	1	2	2
Total	6	6	9

2. CURRENT STATE AND ANALYSIS

2.1 the evaluation system

In order to fulfil the education objectives, to provide qualified information resources management professionals at high level, and to make the education system to catch up with the dramatic change in the world, an effective evaluation system must be set up to monitor the whole education system, including a current curriculum, adaptability of the graduated students to the society, content of each course offered to students, and teaching methods of the faculty etc. Without such a system it is impossible to train competitive and qualified professionals.

Rapid society development, especially in the science and technology fields, requires that these changes in the society be quickly reflected in the education system. It is the evaluation system that guarantees the channel we could get feedback information from the society, dynamically adjust the education objectives and curriculum etc.

We have to admit that it is a tough task. A powerful evaluation system has not been set up so far. The changes of the education objectives, modification of each course content and adjustments of the curriculum in a school (department) of library and information science, in most cases, depend only on opinion of leaders, professors and experts at that school (department), curriculum construction mainly bases on faculty knowledge structure and background rather than it should be. It is a common model. The weaknesses of this model are: the student perspective is ignored, outside factors are not fully considered.

A good evaluation system should receive advice from (1). experts, professors, the faculty within school (department); (2). experts, professors, faculty outside the school (department); (3). current students at the school (department); (4). students who graduated from the education system; (5). society needs. Here the society needs mean the agencies, institutes where students work and will work.

Advice from student perspective is indispensable. Advice from graduated students even more important because they not only experienced the complete course system, but also work in practical agencies like libraries and information centers. They really understand which parts they learnt at the school (department) are useful, which parts are not. The society need information is necessary, it directly influences education objectives and curriculum. The ways getting the advice are various: questionnaire, seminar, consulting, survey etc.

2.2 The Impacts of New Technology on the Education

The new technology development in recent decades was impressive, particularly in information processing field like the telecommunication, CD-ROM, multimedia, INTERNET etc. However, the impacts on the education of information resources management professionals have both the positive and negative sides. New technology development does enrich the contents of information resources management, facilitate information storage, process and retrieval, make nation-wide long distance information resources management education possible.

The negative side reflects in follows:

The new technology develops so fast that the schools (departments) could not afford to buy new facilities, today's advanced equipment may be out of date tomorrow. For instance, 486 type microcomputers which were very powerful and popular in the last year have been replaced by more powerful Pentium computers. Accesses to the Internet are not available in most universities and colleges in China.

Some faculty who do not have a scientific and technical background, or are not active to learn and to use new technologies, do not feel comfortable with the current and emerging technologies. Sometimes they refuse to integrate the new technologies into their textbooks. The technophobia prevails in the faculty. It impedes the education program.

The reasons that result in the technophobia are that some of the faculty are too conservative to adapt to the rapid changing technical environment; many faculty are already overworked in their routing teaching and research works; lack of facilities in schools (departments) prevents them from accessing to new technologies; not strong background in science and technologies is another key obstacle.

Without doubt, information resources management is closely related to technologies. It seems that the requirements for jobs in library, information center, archival agency demand more and more technology competence, the information resources management professionals must face the challenge from new technologies.

One of the controversial issues about the new technologies is what role an information resources management professional will play: an operator of an information system or designer of an information system. The result will directly influence the objectives and the curriculum, determine to what extent we integrate the new technologies into our classes.

Apparently the society needs the two types of the professionals. We could not focus on one and ignore another.

2.3 The Construction of the Faculty

In the United States and other western countries, if the academic institutes are accredited by a national professional library and information science society, not only full professors in these institutes but also associate professors can be doctoral advisors. In China the system is quite different from those in the United States and western countries. The doctoral advisor is a professional title higher than a full professor like full professor, associate professor, or lecturer. They are elites in the field. The faculty who do not have such a professional title are not qualified for training doctoral students. Of course, the academic institutes where doctoral advisors work are accredited by the State Education Commission. Frankly speaking, this system did promote the development of education at high level in China when China restored its high education in the late of 1970'. But now it no longer meets the needs of the society. First the number of doctoral advisors is limited. Second the system prevents other faculty, especially the young faculty, from involving in training doctoral students. Both factors impede the development of information resources management education on a large scale. Now the officials of the State Education Commission and experts have recognized the weaknesses of this system, they try to take concrete steps to overcome them.

Visiting professors (or part time instructors)at a school (department) of library and information science as a supplement to the instructors are very useful if they really give lectures at the school (department) on a regular basis. Employing visiting professors can reduce budget of the school(department). In addition, they can promote academic exchange, introduce new teaching methods, and add what the faculty lack to students. However, in most cases a visiting professor at academic institutes in China is a kind of social honor. They do not function as they should do. They rarely give lectures or are responsible for an independent course at a school (department) of library and information science, let alone on a regular basis. On the other hand, the school (department) could not afford to pay for hiring visiting professors, the visiting professors who usually are officials, headers or famous experts in government agencies, academic institutes are too busy to leave their jobs for long time.

Another problem about the construction of the faculty is the optimization of knowledge structure of the faculty. The school (department) should recruit some instructors with backgrounds of computer science, telecommunication, linguistics, psychology and management. The traditional, single discipline structure will be not competitive for future development. Multidiscipline structure of the faculty will be necessary.

2.4 The Reform of the Management System of Library and Information   Science

In China master degree requires about eight required courses and a thesis. It takes three years for a student to complete it. In fact two years is enough. The education aims at this level should be to master the basic skills and fundamental theory about information resources management. The more specific research fields should be left to doctoral students. A specific research field for a master student will limit his future development after his graduation and narrow his career choice range.

A strict and scientific education system is one of the important factors that guarantees qualified doctoral students. A preliminary examination should be required to assess the breadth of the student's discipline knowledge, academic achievements and potential research abilities. A comprehensive examination should be designed to evaluate mastery of the general field of information resources management, acquisition of both depth and breadth in the specialization within the field. In addition, English or other foreign languages, as a dispensable tool, must be emphasized. Students should have a good command of spoken English and writing English. A computer language should be specified for a doctoral student based on his research topic. Students should use skilfully a computer to do his research. They should apply scientific research methods like survey, experiment, history etc. to his research.

3.CONCLUSION

Rapid economic development, booming of information industry and revolution of the new technologies, on the one hand, provide development opportunity for education of information resources management at high level in China; on the other hand, they also challenge the old education system and produce some new problems.

Modern information resources management education in China stays in the developing phase, funding scarcity and obsolete facilities still restricts its development. Reconstruction of the curriculum is an impeding problem. New curriculum not only keeps the traditional and useful parts, but also absorbs new ideas and new technologies like expert system, artificial intelligence, modern linguistics, psychology, telecommunication, modern management etc. In addition, they should be scientifically integrated into current curriculum.

In order to promote the development of information resources management education at high level in China, we should work out a rational evaluation system, dynamically adjust the curriculum, carefully analyze the impacts of the new technologies, actively face the challenge of the new technologies, optimize the knowledge structure of the faculty, establish the effective evaluation system, learn foreign successful experiences in the field. Only in this manner, the information resources management in China would make great progress in future development.

REFERENCE

Peng Feizhang (1996), Library Science Graduate Student Education Be New Century-Oriented, *Knowledge of Library and Information Science*, No. 2, pp.2-4.

Dong Xiaoyin (1996), The Pattern Change and Problems of the Chinese Library and Information Education, *The Journal of the Library Science in China*, No.1, pp.28-36.

Ma Feicheng (1996), The Current State and Development of Library and Information Science Education in China, *The Library and Information Service*, No.1, pp.12-15.

Liao Pan (1992), The Reform Trend of Library and Information Science Education, *Library Works and Research*, No.2, pp.2-4.

Zhang Jin (1994), The Analysis on American and Canadian Library and Information Science Education, *The Journal of China Scientific and Technical Information Society*, No.6.

CLOSING THE INFORMATION TECHNOLOGY GAP: TYPICAL TRAINING CONCERNS IN A SOUTH AFRICAN UNIVERSITY LIBRARY IN THE 1990s

Clare M Walker
Librarian: Education and Training
University of the Witwatersrand Library, Johannesburg
South Africa

Abstract: This paper describes approaches to developing and maintaining a staff training and CPE programme in the Library of the University of the Witwatersrand, Johannesburg (Wits Library).

INTRODUCTION: TRAINING IN THE SOUTH AFRICAN CONTEXT

Challenges facing librarians in South Africa are not only caused by the technological developments but also by the major political change from an oligarchic Apartheid society to that of a democratic one... The transformation process now under way calls for the library and information service to also undergo transformation and address the social responsibility of libraries... (Paris, 1996:6-7)

In these words, Julie Paris, a subject librarian at the University of the Western Cape, highlights the South African context within which all training and development, whether it is focused on technological, academic or managerial issues, must take place.

The present paper describes approaches to developing and maintaining a staff training and CPE programme in the Library of the University of the Witwatersrand, Johannesburg (Wits Library). Current implementation and planned extensions and upgrading of the Library's electronic information systems and networks requires intensive in-service training (INSET) and continuing education (CPE), as it does in other libraries in South Africa and elsewhere. South African library staff have qualifications that may range from educationally impoverished basic school-leaving certificates, with English as a second or third language, to graduate professional qualifications which not only vary in information technology content, but often reflect educational positions that were current in the `old' South Africa. Consequently, the skills, knowledge and understanding that library staff should develop and maintain range from basic keyboard, mouse and screen skills to sophisticated electronic database and Internet information retrieval, the broader understanding of academic subject fields and the increasing `para-academic' role particularly needed in the development and support of information literacy, and greater awareness of management and leadership skills.

A study of some recent international and local professional and report literature (as reflected in the list of references) confirms that Wits Library finds itself in a position very similar to that of many other university libraries. The additional historical and contemporary South African socio-political dimension, however, highlights problems (and challenges) that are unique and must be taken into account in any proposed actual or potential development of new training and development initiatives. An overview of current discussion documents and reports in the field of higher education gives an indication of some of the national problems facing LIS in this sector and directions that further development of INSET and CPE might take, particularly within the proposed National Qualifications Framework (NQF).

TRAINING AND DEVELOPMENT AT WITS UNIVERSITY LIBRARY

In January 1996, Wits Library installed a 10-workstation electronic classroom linked to the Library's LAN, with an instructor's workstation controlled by a TECH Commander console and equipped for large screen output through a ceiling-mounted LCD projector for demonstrations to larger groups. This was the first such installation in a university library in South Africa and it was a direct outcome of training priorities identified in the Library's `vision' for its future (University of the Witwatersrand... The Library, 1994).

The development of this 'vision', based on the input of several Library task groups, was a response to the University's 'mission project', a redefining in the early 1990s of how the University saw itself and its responsibilities, and an acknowledgement of areas which required redress of past (apartheid-era) inequalities:

> " ...members of under-represented groups should be given the opportunity to advance their skills so that they can compete effectively and on equal footing... [there is] an urgent need for a well-planned, comprehensive and integrated programme of staff development" (University of the Witwatersrand..., 1994:26)

The Library's own vision, however, was particularly concerned with the implications of the computer revolution:

> "Library staff... are eager to move forward and take advantage of the opportunities created by technology... Vision and adaptability are required of all members of our academic community if the Wits Library is to play its vital role successfully in the future of the University " (University of the Witwatersrand... The Library, 1994:1)

and the importance of staff development and training to fulfil this role was acknowledged: "The importance of hi-tech continuing education for existing library staff cannot be sufficiently emphasised" (University of the Witwatersrand...The Library, 1994:21), although a cautionary note emerged from discussions on staffing: "individual abilities of staff need to be recognised. Those at the lower levels feel they are given no credit for doing what they believe is a lot more than the requirements of the job..." (University of the Witwatersrand... The Library, 1994:40). The issue of appropriate recognition of skills in the workplace, in libraries as in industry, has been one of the forces behind the development of a South African National Qualifications Framework, which will be discussed in greater detail below (Human Sciences Research Council 1995; South Africa. Department of Education, 1996a).

Following the University's 'mission' and the Library's own 'vision', a Library Systems Needs Analysis Task Group was established in September 1995 and specialised working groups, including one on training, were again convened among the Library staff. The reports of these working groups and the main Needs Analysis Task Group were incorporated into a Review Committee Report. The task of the Review Committee was to make recommendations with respect to information technology and technological structures in the Library and the University, including a new fully integrated library software system and the possibility of a regional libraries consortium.

The opinion of the working group on training was that:

> "Library staff training is a never-ending, self-reinforcing process in which the input of the specialist trainer, the support and creation of opportunity by supervisors and managers, and the positive attitude of individual members of staff are all mutually supportive and interactive" (University of the Witwatersrand... The Library... 1996a)

and the Review Committee recommended that "provision be made for training as an integral feature of the implementation of all new software" (University of the Witwatersrand... Review Committee... 1996:21).

The work of the Needs Analysis Task Group has become an integral element in the establishing of a regional consortium of libraries in the higher education sector, the Gauteng and Environs Library Consortium (GAELIC), which is seen as becoming "an exciting new entity -- a Gauteng Virtual Library". The envisaged co-operation between participants will cover a variety of areas, including software and networking, sharing of material resources, and co-operation in human resources and the empowerment of information users (Multi-million volume library... 1996:5). Human resource development to support this venture will necessarily incorporate intensive staff training programmes at the preparatory, implementation and ongoing stages in all involved libraries.

Systematic in-service training of Wits Library staff, however, has taken place for many years, on an informal and individual basis until very recently, as the applications of electronic information technology expanded from online searching in the 1970s to a fully networked system in the 1990s. A recent paper given at IATUL 96 by a colleague (Wilcocks 1996) documents this expansion of the campus network to more than 60 departments and research units now linked to the Library's LAN. The need for Library staff skills in information retrieval has grown as information access has decentralised and more users need assistance. Not only basic staff training but practice and confidence are essential for the provision of this service, and the appointment in 1993 of a full time librarian for education and training (the present writer) and the installation of the electronic classroom (ECR) in 1996 have greatly enhanced the quality and volume of staff training and development in this and other areas.

TRAINING IN THE ELECTRONIC CLASSROOM (ECR)

The central purpose of this paper was to give a practical account of the staff training conducted during 1996 in the Wits Library ECR. The installation of the ECR has transformed the training of library staff (and of academic library users) from an ad hoc, improvised and to a certain extent peripheral activity to a formally structured and much more central and productive function within the Library.

The ECR provides a physically comfortable teaching and learning environment and is equipped as an ordinary classroom as well as a practical computer laboratory. For security reasons it is not an open walk-in computer facility. In addition to the purpose-built workstation desks and the instructor's workstation and console, the ECR is equipped with a projection screen, ordinary overhead projector, white board and flip chart. It is cabled on the same principles as a language laboratory (as well as being linked to the Library LAN). The instructor's console allows several screen and instructor/student workstation permutations: student keyboards can be locked; the instructor's screen can be shown at each workstation and, simultaneously if required, through the LCD projector on to the large screen. Student screens and keyboards can be released for independent work. The console can be set to scan each screen in rotation, or show any particular student screen, on the instructor's monitor or, if required, on the large screen. Student screens can be blanked out if the instructor only wishes to demonstrate on the large screen (if for example, a larger class than can be accommodated at the workstations, is present). While headphone links would enhance the ECR, it is still possible for the instructor to monitor and intervene very effectively with individual users on the basis of the scanning process. All console settings can be changed with a keystroke at any stage in a training session.

The increasingly networked access to electronic information resources in the decentralised Wits Library system has created an urgent need for more staff training at every level. There are two large "main" libraries on campus, two off-campus professional libraries (medical and business) and several smaller divisional ones physically linked to different teaching faculties. The staff in these libraries are not always trained subject librarians but must act as such; most library assistants are required, through chronic staff cutbacks, to carry out a range of "professional" information functions which may include considerable guidance to academic staff and student users in information work. The ECR has helped enhance and extend this support through greater numbers of more regular and interconnected training sessions and demonstrations, with hands-on opportunities for each person to practice with assistance during training sessions.

The training covers all of the Library's networked and stand-alone electronic systems and resources and the Internet, as well as the more basic office skills such as WordPerfect and Windows. The contents of training programmes is updated continually by library staff whose field of subject expertise this is. In addition, software vendors and outside organizations arrange to use the ECR to demonstrate new features or versions of their products or to offer training courses for the Library. The ECR has thus become a powerful means for "re-tooling" Library staff to meet the challenges of new information technology. The overarching aim of this training is the development and empowerment of university information users at all levels, to develop information handling skills not only in technical fields but in the broader arena of information literacy, and for Library staff as much as for academic staff and student users. (Walker, Laburn and Ward, 1996:317-318).

Between May and November 1996, 29 internal 90-minute staff training sessions were given in the ECR and 208 attendances were registered. Five external demonstrations and training sessions were also held. The training included general introductory talks and demonstrations on electronic resources, citation indexes and a comparison between WordPerfect 6.1 for Windows and MS Word;

hands-on training sessions were given on ISI and NISC CDROM databases (5); Pegasus Mail (5); Netscape (2); Windows 3.1 (8) and WordPerfect 5.1 (7). Although the informal current measure of computer literacy on the University campus is knowledge of Windows 3.1, not all staff yet have access to a Windows environment.

The structured contents of training programmes is deliberately very flexible, to accommodate a variety of levels of ability and needs expressed during any training session. Initially, in 1994 and 1995, training sessions were held in response to demand and waiting lists were kept. This became increasingly cumbersome to administer as the demand for training grew. When the ECR became available, more people (up to 20) per hands-on session could be accommodated and longer, more frequent sessions could be held. The standard training session now is 90 minutes long and two sessions a week are arranged in all but the busiest weeks of the year, or when other training and development workshops are being held. The Library staff responsible for training plan sessions only two weeks ahead and Library staff are invited by email to attend. Email notification is in itself a training opportunity: not all staff log on to their email each day and training information is used as an incentive for them to do so.

A standardised structure for training sessions, and a two or three part modular progression from one session to the next, have been developed over the year. Each session begins with a short introduction describing in basic language why the session is being offered, an elementary explanation of unfamiliar concepts that the session will cover, and ways in which the contents of the session may be relevant to Library services and practices. Internally developed guides and instruction sheets, with practical exercises and examples, are distributed and where online tutorials are available (as in Windows and WordPerfect), these are also incorporated into training sessions. The trainer usually switches between three different approaches: description and demonstration, try-outs on instruction, and supervised practice sessions. The ECR instructor's monitor and console allow close tracking of individual progress and a change of training pace or direction if this seems appropriate at any particular time. Each group of staff has a very distinctive character and it is the responsibility of the trainer to be sensitive to this.

EVALUATION OF TRAINING

All staff are required to give advance notice of attendance and to sign an attendance list, for analysis and records of training rather than mere monitoring. At the end of each session all staff are asked to complete a 5-question anonymous evaluation sheet before leaving. Comments, though very brief, are indicative of whether the training sessions are fulfilling their purpose. A bulk retrospective review of these evaluations reveals difficulties and anxieties common to the training situation as a whole rather than any single session.

The evaluation sheet asks staff 1) to rate the training session on a scale from excellent to poor and 2) to say why; 3) to state whether or not the session seemed relevant to their work in the Library and, if so, 4) in what way. The fifth question asks for suggestions for further training.

Although this evaluation sheet was designed to be as simple as possible, many staff spend a surprisingly long time completing it. Comments are often pedestrian and what one might expect; yet occasionally a training session seems to have been an inspiration; while sometimes one has clearly not been effective. The naivete of the small selection of unedited comments quoted below reflects a deeply felt need for training, and a typically optimistic and positive attitude towards personal training opportunities.

"I improved a lot compared to my previous experience and believe that in the next course I will be excellent."

"I learnt making of notices, not just notices but bold and beautiful."

"From knowing nothing about citation searches I now have a good idea. I probably need more practice before doing it for real."

"I learnt what I did not know, quite interesting to play around with words."

"Not really pertaining to what I do but there's a computer monitor in a library and people ask how it works and I don't know."

"I love learning something new and interesting, especially using of the mouse."

"Because I know little about CD-ROM and it gave me interest in knowing more."

Such comments bear out perceptions recorded in the Library's earlier `vision' document: "Staff feel they need opportunities to further themselves through acquiring new skills... More training would enable them to keep up with new developments; a wider range of training than that needed for the immediate job would motivate them" (University of the Witwatersrand... the Library 1994:41).

Nevertheless, despite such motivated attitudes, training sessions can seem very labour-intensive work, on occasion "wading through mud", as one trainer put it. One of the problems of this kind of training in the South African context is trainees' significant lack of basic technological or computer background knowledge. Much of the training still takes place in a vacuum, unconnected to personal or even other work experience. The broadening of horizons and the creation of a more general information and knowledge platform on which to train remains one of the major challenges of staff training and development in the Library.

TRAINING IN OTHER UNIVERSITY LIBRARIES

So that the Wits Library training should not be seen in isolation, an informal "quick and dirty" email survey of training practices and policies in other South African university libraries was carried out, together with a search for recent local literature on staff training in academic libraries. Recent articles on the impact of new areas of information technology in libraries in the United States, and the importance of staff training and development for this (Hastings and Tennant 1996; Liebscher and McCaffrey 1995; St Lifer 1996; Tennant 1995; Tenopir 1995) reflect an intensive atmosphere of change that is not yet present in most South African institutions, as Paris comments (Paris 1996).

The informal email survey incorporated three questions in requests for information about training: whether the library offered formal (class or group) training in information technology; whether the library offered formal training to build up specific subject knowledge for academic information retrieval; and whether the library had a formal staff training and development policy or policy document. Colleagues at seven other university libraries responded.

The response to the first question was mostly positive; the structure of the training varied from refresher workshops to regular monthly sessions to formal registration at distance education college.

Responses to the second question indicated that this was considered overall to be the responsibility of the individual member of staff, who was put in a subject area and had to "sink or swim" and acquire the necessary subject knowledge by whatever means seemed available. The comment that "general knowledge, gut feeling and common-sense take a long time to develop" is unconsciously indicative of a lack of appreciation of the need to redress in some more directed way the poor general knowledge background that hinders the advancement of many South African library staff, particularly those from "disadvantaged" educational backgrounds. Comments from all respondents showed that this was an area of concern, but no formal solutions were suggested.

In response to the third question, about a formal training and development policy, only two indicated that a policy had been drawn up and was in the process of either of approval or on trial. General input suggests that training is not mandatory and that there is a minimum degree of formality or structure at most university libraries. Training certainly takes place, and is considered important, but is not yet central to library planning and management.

In addition to this email survey, two recent sources describe in detail library staff training programmes at the University of Botswana (Chiware and MacLeod, 1993) and at Vista University (Lessing 1994). In each case structured formal training programmes of different kinds have been developed. When designing these programmes, trainers at both institutions had to take into consideration the lack of familiarity with automated systems in libraries, and few computer or even keyboard skills, particularly among more junior staff. The programmes accommodated the need for structured and to some extent personalised training, opportunities for repetition and practice, and work-related, task-oriented training that allowed trainees to experience as far as possible a "real" work situation.

Chiware and MacLeod highlight many of the special socio-economic circumstances that affect library automation, and staff training, in African countries. They describe the University of Botswana Library programmes designed to overcome these problems, particularly among the high proportion of staff without prior knowledge or experience of computers. Lessing, working in the geographically decentralised Vista University system spread over a number of campuses, with limited availability of high level trainer time, encountered similar problems. She has focused on the design and development of computer-assisted, task-oriented training programmes as an alternative to the labour-intensive personalised training that 94% of staff considered desirable, and found it a more satisfactory approach than leaving staff to train themselves without the necessary motivation, skills or background knowledge to do so (Lessing 1994:149-150). Training in the Wits Library ECR seems to address some of the problems addressed by each of these other institutions.

RECOGNITION OF HUMAN RESOURCE DEVELOPMENT

In a more general paper on continuing library education (CLE) in South Africa, Kuhn writes that "CLE can be described as 'all learning activities and efforts, formal and informal, by which individuals seek to upgrade their knowledge, attitudes, competencies, and understanding in their special field of work...'" and believes that it should build on previously acquired knowledge (Kuhn 1994:48). CLE should not be self-centred: its purpose is to deliver quality performance in the work setting. She points out, however, that "little CLE for paraprofessionals heightens awareness of the overall nature of, or developments in, the field of librarianship ... and is not necessarily broadbased" (Kuhn 1994:50). Paris is emphatic that "any training or retraining... should be done in line with the needs of those wanting and needing the services", specifically in helping users by sifting and analysing information to help them manage their information overload and assist them in making "wise decisions in what they need (Paris 1996:9-15).

The view that the training and development of library and information workers should result in improving the quality of information service to users, particularly in the South African context addressed by both Kuhn and Paris as cited above, is an important perspective. This is reflected in the Appendix on libraries and information technology in the recent report of the National Commission on Higher Education, the NCHE (South Africa. National Commission on Higher Education 1996:361-363). For those participating in training programmes, however, recognition and reward is of paramount importance, and Kuhn acknowledges that any system of certification is not likely to be successful without "a linked system of rewards and promotion prospects, which in turn has implications for the financial resources of an institution as well as organizational structure" (Kuhn 1994:51). These resources and structures do not as a rule significantly accommodate in-service training programmes.

Both the report of the NCHE and the subsequent Green Paper (South Africa. Department of Education 1996b) acknowledge the importance of "human resource development" in libraries and information technology. The NCHE report here follows closely the British "Follett Report" (Joint Funding Councils' Libraries Review Group 1993:68) in stating that "If the full potential of the investment proposed by the library and information technology sectors is to be realised, there needs to be a concomitant investment in human resources development". The NCHE recommends that library budgets should include an allocation which will enable staff members to participate in training and development programmes, and so acquire the skills necessary "to develop their role... in the new networked environment" (South Africa. National Commission... 1996:372-373). The Green Paper adds merely that the Ministry of Education endorses the key conditions proposed by the NCHE, including "provision of appropriate human resources development..." (South Africa. Department of

Education 1996b:38). The contrast, however, between the brief comments in the South African report and the extensive separate report on human resource management in higher education libraries in the United Kingdom (Supporting expansion 1993), is disappointing.

THE NATIONAL QUALIFICATIONS STRUCTURE (NQF)

As Kuhn points out (Kuhn 1994:51), and Wits Library staff discussions reflect, a certification mechanism to reflect skills and competence acquired on the job, as much as through formal learning processes, is needed for the paraprofessional sector particularly. The British system of National Vocational Qualifications (NVQs) was piloted in a very small number of libraries in South Africa in 1994-95 by Dakers (Dakers 1995), and the potential advantages of a system that might "provide a flexible and supportive framework for ordered and visible equipping of the workforce with much needed skills and competencies" and might lead to "self-confidence, employment, reward and progression" were described in a paper given in Cape Town in July 1996 (Oldroyd 1996).

South Africa established the South African Qualifications Authority, SAQA, and the outline of a South African National Qualifications Framework, NQF, in 1995 (Human Sciences Research Council 1995; South Africa. Department of Education 1996a). The NQF is still under considerable discussion regarding structure and development at all the levels beyond Adult Basic Education and Training (ABET). Its objectives are in general "to create an integrated national framework for learning achievements", expressed specifically as "outcomes-based" education and training (Human Sciences Research Council 1996). The Department of Education discussion document suggests that the establishment of the NQF

> "will enable all existing public and private sector education and training providers to assist in formulating and registering appropriate national standards in their specialist fields through their respective Standards Bodies and to seek recognition for their programmes in terms of such defined standards" (South Africa. Department of Education 1996a)

CONCLUSION

In developing programmes for staff training in the Wits University Library, several features have contributed to bringing training into a more central position in the Library. Since 1993, the Library has had a full time senior member of staff, the Librarian (Education and Training), with responsibility for developing and co-ordinating all staff and academic user training and education. As a result the Library now also has a formal and detailed *Training and development policy* document included in the Library's policy manual (University of the Witwatersrand... The Library 1996b), which was widely discussed and supported at all staff levels during its formulation. The installation of an electronic classroom in 1996 has led to more structured, more frequent and, according to the evaluations, more motivated training for staff at all levels and in all sections of the Library. This in turn should lead to greater confidence in assisting academic users throughout the University to raise their own levels of information literacy, particularly with regard to electronic and networked resources.

As this paper makes clear, training has been identified and supported as an integral and essential element in the planned expansion of electronic information resources and networks, both for the Wits Library and for the new consortium of higher education libraries in the region, GAELIC. The University, in its submission to the NCHE, emphasises the critical role of libraries in higher education (University of the Witwatersrand... 1995:5-6,5-7.5-15), but the problems and challenges of fulfilling this role remain: beyond daily routine tasks, staff lack opportunities, background experience and confidence in exploring new directions in information resources and technology. The legacy of decades of apartheid education systems, in a society that discouraged questioning and inquiring minds, is for many a passive learning and information seeking habit. "It is our responsibility as well as that of employers to ensure that the knowledge base and expertise of information workers is kept up to date" (Paris 1996:15). These are socio-political issues which will no doubt change as South Africa changes.

Above all, the problem of formal recognition of skills acquired through training, of certification and reward, remains to be addressed, not only within the University but at the national level. Accredited competence-based programmes within a National Qualifications Framework, that might be developed from in-service training sessions such as those currently offered in the Wits Library and other institutions, might give library and information workers the opportunity to progress through a more immediately motivating career path in the library than is currently possible. At present, however, this Library and others in South Africa like it, are faced with the dual challenge of expanding and enhancing electronic access to information resources, and encouraging and empowering staff, through training programmes of various kinds, to develop their own information skills and abilities within the Library, while offering only minimal incentives or rewards for this. It will take a considerable input still of material and human resources before the information technology gap in South African libraries is truly closed.

REFERENCES

Chiware, Elisha R T and Roderick A. MacLeod (1993), "Training for automation in an academic library," in *Info Africa Nova conference, Pretoria, 1993: proceedings,* edited by A G Coetzer. Pretoria, South Africa, Info Africa Nova, v.2, pp. 347-367.

Dakers, Hazel (1995), *Global transferability of NVQs.* Unpublished MSc dissertation, University of Leicester, England.

Hastings, Kirk and Roy Tennant (1996), "How to build a digital library," *D-Lib magazine,* (November). (http://www.dlib.org/dlib/november96/ucb/llhastings.html)

Human Sciences Research Council (1995), *Ways of seeing the National Qualifications Framework,* Pretoria, South Africa, the Council.

Joint Funding Councils' Libraries Review Group (1993), *Report.* Chaired by Sir Brian Follett. Bristol, Higher Education Funding Council for England, (December).

Kuhn, Rose (1994), "Some notes on continuing library education (CLE) for library and information workers," *Innovation,* (December), 9: pp. 48-53

Lessing, Anetta J (1994), *Die benutting van rekenaartegnologie vir indiensopleiding van biblioteekpersoneel [The utilization of computer technology for inservice training of library staff].* Unpublished Masters thesis, University of Pretoria, South Africa.

Liebscher, Peter and Nancy McCaffrey (1995), "Continuous education and training of information professionals:the virtual classroom," in *16th National Online Meeting, New York, May 1995: proceedings,* edited by Martha E Williams. Medford, NJ., Learned Information, pp. 263-273.

Multi-million volume library to be established: GAELIC (Gauteng and Environs Library Consortium) (1996). *SAILIS Newsletter*, (December), 16(11), pp.1,5.

Oldroyd, Robert E (1996), "Vocational qualifications as an aid to development," Paper given at *ICEL96,* Cape Town, South Africa, (July).

Paris, Julia D (1996), "The need to train librarians in data-related issues," Paper given at *JASSIST'96 conference*, University of Minnesota.

South Africa. Department of Education (1996a), *Lifelong learning through a National Qualifications Framework: report of the Ministerial Committee for Development Work on the NQF: discussion document.* Pretoria, the Department, (February).

South Africa. Department of Education (1996b). *Green paper on higher education transformation.* Pretoria, the Department, (November). (http://www.polity.org.za/govdocs/green_papers/hegreenp.html)

South Africa. National Commission on Higher Education (1996), *A framework for research.* Pretoria, The Commission.

St. Lifer, Evan (1996), "Network: new roles, same mission," *Library Journal*, 15 November 121(19), pp. 26-30.

Supporting expansion (1993): a report on human resource management in academic libraries for the Joint Funding Councils' Library Review Group, (1993), Bristol, Higher Education Funding Council for England, (July), revised September 1993.

Tennant, Roy (1995). "The virtual library foundation: staff training and support" (http://www.lib.berkeley.edu/ISIS/ITAL.html)

Tenopir, Carol and Ralf Neufang (1995), "Internet use and training in university libraries," in *16th National Online Meeting, New York, May 1995: proceedings*, edited by Martha E Williams. Medford, NJ., Learned Information, pp. 387-293.

University of the Witwatersrand, Johannesburg (1994), Mission statement project: final report to the Senate Planning Committee, Senate and Council, (May). Unpublished report.

University of the Witwatersrand, Johannesburg (1996), Review committee on library systems: report. Unpublished report.

University of the Witwatersrand, Johannesburg (1995), Submission to the National Commission on Higher Education. Unpublished report.

University of the Witwatersrand, Johannesburg. The Library (1996a), "Library systems needs analysis: Training needs working group," Preliminary report. (February). Unpublished report.

University of the Witwatersrand, Johannesburg. The Library (1996b), *Manual of library policies.* 2nd edition. September 1996. Unpublished.

University of the Witwatersrand, Johannesburg. The Library (1994). "The Wits Library of the future," Unpublished report.

Walker, Clare M, Norma Laburn and L Ruth Ward (1996), "Raising information consciousness through IT: the Wits Library electronic classroom," in *NIT'96: 9th international conference: New information technology for library and information professionals...*, *Pretoria, South Africa*, edited by C-C Chen. West Newton, Mass., MicroUse Information, pp. 315-322.

Wilcocks, J (1996), "Bringing staff (faculty) up to speed: CDROM access via a WAN at the University of the Witwatersrand, South Africa," Paper given at *IATUL 1996, "Networks, networking and implications for digital libraries", University of Irvine, California.* (http://educate.lib.chalmers.se)

LIS EDUCATIONAL SYSTEMS WITHIN CMC (COMPUTER MEDITATED COMMUNICATION)

Augusta Maria Paci,
Researcher
Institute For Studies On Research And Scientific Documentation Of The CNR
(The Italian National Research Council)
Roma, Italy

Abstract   The paper assumes the condition of the information professional as a life long learner in relation with the innovative education systems based on information and communication technologies. The distance education systems have already shown their limitation: the new phase is led by the so-called computer mediated communication in education (CMC) which is a wide scenario of applications, networked distribution and access to electronic resources. The other feature of the CMC is its role of fully integration of formal (person to person) teaching activities. In order to develop innovative model for LIS students and professionals a new model of educational system is needed based on libraries of LIS courseware. Early initiatives which originated learning packages are now superseded by more recent ones based on sophisticated authorware and networked resources. A new LIS educational system could attack this obstacle in order to improve their usage in formal education and offer wider, easy and qualitative access to a dynamic collection of packages and teaching aids and materials which may be retrieved, selected and delivered at the user site.

1. THE INFORMATION PROFESSIONAL AS A LIFELONG LEARNER

A characteristic feature of information professionals today is their heterogeneous educational needs.

The evident expansion of areas of learning as a result of the pervasive use of information and communication technologies directly affects traditional LIS content (typical examples being the parallel and mix modes of publishing, collection development criteria, statistical indicators, the quality approach in information and services, the preservation and consumption of traditional and new recording materials, user education and new services and evolving knowledge models for libraries in the net age).

Further evidence is provided by emerging new issues fuelled by external phenomena, such as the ethical approach to information access, the implications of knowledge societies and multicultural communities, the unstable nature of documents, the structural modification of commercial publishers, the copyright scenario and so on.

The community of librarians and information professionals has to assimilate new modes of behaviour and hence to undertake a new mission.

To meet this need, the horizon of education systems has to expand. The first step is to open up traditional country-based LIS education to a global approach, embracing different cultures, styles of working and document typologies.

Initiatives to create new courses within academic contexts generally encounter considerable obstacles in the form of reorganisation, financial restrictions and market finalisation.

New models of education and training have to be developed to test the new potent of information and communication technologies.

In the eighties, many LIS departments offered their students computer facilities. On-line information services, classroom training programmes, on-line connection to automated catalogues and software to develop applications were the basic teaching tools used by the LIS departments in some North American and northern European universities.

In the early nineties, lecturers and librarians started to develop stand-alone education packages to achieve aims, which ranged from the acquisition of computer skills to system training and the explanation of specific library services.

Although the experience had a generally positive outcome, the packages in question failed to prompt the start-up of a more intensive production of courseware applications. Nor did distance learning university programmes really catch on in the library sector.

At present, the technological and communications situation ensures easy connection over geographical networks. Against this scenario, on-line education has the capacity to develop new models of production, distribution and usage, as well as related service-like tutoring of multimedia educational. The growth in the population of users of networked publications is a trend which will not be limited only to professionals attending courses at their workplace, but will also extend to citizens who are prepared to assimilate professional contents.

The experience of computer-based educational packages will benefit from new networking solutions, conceived as Internet usage with broadband transmission technology based on B-ISDN and ATM technologies, and open to support multiservice and multimedia applications.

In the networking conception, the multimedia educational content can be transmitted to remote sites for use on local networks or stand-alone work stations and used by individual operators, users or classes of students tutored in library and information studies. Educational applications are thus not handled on the various work stations, but information is centralised and transmitted through high-speed networks either from a single computer or from groups of computers.

Educational materials production, maintenance and delivery to interested bodies (universities, schools, libraries, state institutions) thus become a cost-effective service. New or expanding themes, comments, teaching aids, videoconferences and lectures and electronic messaging can be managed interactively. The value of applications and related information increase since the service is accurate and handled dynamically, efficiently taking care of aspects as vital as content quality, obsolescence detection, client request monitoring and communication.

The prospects are highly promising, and respond to a broadly emerging need to develop networking services capable of improving conditions for accessing systems of applications to obtain value-added data and information. Thanks to the network, it is possible to exploit data -like money in the banking system - by virtue of its circulation.

2 WHAT IS COMPUTER MEDIATED COMMUNICATION?

The concept of computer mediated communication is a very broad one, the result of major experiences in distance education. It relies on intensive bibliographies.

Computer mediated communication is defined as the transmission and reception of messages using computers as input, storage, output and routing devices. CMC includes information retrieval, electronic mail, bulletin boards and computer conferencing.

Recently, an interesting debate arose among specialists in this domain to outline the need, role and content of educational techniques. The question is a critical one, since CMC designers are not always familiar with educational aspects and learning implications, yet the convergence of these two components is regarded as crucial for the system's success.

CMC is based on four paradigms:

- the on-line resource paradigm, which includes on-line information retrieval in data bases, journals, applications, software libraries and interest groups;
- the E-mail paradigm (individualised teaching and learning);
- the bulletin board paradigm (a conference or bulletin board system guided by an expert or experts);
- the conferencing paradigm (all the participants take part in the interaction).

All four paradigms are of relevance to an LIS system: on-line data bases and journals are classic component of LIS education, while on-line information systems, bibliographical and full texts have always been core themes in the LIS curricula, such systems being widely used to train information specialists to become skilled in information retrieval techniques.

Through the Internet, on-line resources have expanded dramatically: they now encompass software applications, electronic messaging and people themselves (i.e., discussion lists and interest groups). These resources for group learning activities and self-directed student learning are, as Paulsen has pointed out, playing a vitally important role in education.

A great many information specialists are already connected to information highways and will be increasingly so in the near future. Although the primary form of net usage for library and information professionals will, as in other sectors, be access to external resources[1], the network will soon be regarded by increasingly large groups of information specialists as the general medium for communicating, sharing opinions, collecting data for investigations, applying for vacancies, subscribing to events and publications and, last but not least, for attending courses, delivering educational materials, verifying exercises with teachers and experts around the globe within the LIS knowledge domain.

The expanding scenario of CMC stresses the importance of educational and software programs that can be accessed on a remote computer via a computer network, extending access to collections of courseware that can be downloaded and studied off-line by educators and classroom or independent learners. A stack of options of heterogeneous educational software applications and other facilities will be made available to support teaching/learning activities and to educate, train and retrain professionals. Value-added services for on-line education - tutor/student remote interaction via direct E-mail systems or educational mail boxes, interactive remote exercise monitoring and assessment, remote access to courses, aid material and exercises, co-operative production of teaching handouts or documentation for wide-scale distribution - will also be integrated into teaching activities.

There are great expectations for these educational applications at European level: the White Paper on education and training stressed the importance of actions and interventions in this sector as a means of solving the employment problems of youngsters and adults alike. In general, as the European Commission White Paper on education and training pointed out, the educational quality of the products available is not as yet so satisfactory as to persuade educators to use multimedia. There are also many other aspects - such as the computer/student ratio and the ability of teachers and their familiarity with the use of technologies - which do not stimulate the use of educational.

2.1 The development of courseware

The development of educational packages is generally hampered by excessive cost factors, limited internal human resources and lack of market exploitation strategies. Recognised weaknesses are content-related; among the most generally mentioned are the rapid obsolescence of technical data, the lack of consistency and reliability of revised editions, textual errors, poor content coverage and weak structure, the need for better integrated competencies among experts in design, graphics, image and text organisation, the relative inconsistency of hypertextual links and dubious iconographic or colour choices.

Other issues regard industrial authoring software, whose cost is very high, sometimes varying according to the number of licences and run time, and which generally requires external third-party programming specialists. In addition, the application allows for only limited interventions of revision and no for no updating at all. As far as delivery is concerned, the most commonly used media are floppy disks and CD-ROM.

The methodology for the design, development and production of multimedia educational is now passing through a transition phase. Although there are signs of scepticism among educators, prospects of great potential are emerging in society at large. In fact, multimedia attracts vast communities of users, can help to train and retrain for new jobs, can provide individualised and flexible learning tools, can be used in various locations at home, in libraries and in educational institutions: in short, they can innovate the traditional and formal structure of education.

However, since the multimedia age is only just beginning, more experience will of course be necessary. LIS educators should actively participate in these pilot experiences and see the advantages and disadvantages of multimedia educational for themselves, within their own subject field.

The library and information community should also be informed about the potential, social relevance and, last but not least, should be made aware that the library sector can play an important role in facilitating and sharing educational resources.

3. EDUCATIONALS IN LIS SYSTEMS

Expanding educational needs cannot be met by developing new courses or new computer-based courseware.

Only a new model of educational system can provide the solution. For example, European mobility programmes, such as Erasmus and Socrates, have been developed in the nineties to create a framework of actions to offer greater flexibility and an exchange of initiatives and opportunities among European universities.

Communication technologies can provide the infrastructure which will add a new dimension to a phenomenon which is still in a transition phase.

In library and information studies, the educationals available - comprising printed documents, a-v materials, computers and software and real database remote connections - may be considered as valid complementary aid to a wholes set of teaching materials.

They serve to present topic overviews, summaries of technical knowledge and situation simulation to facilitate the tasks of educators.

They can also be extremely effective for repetitive training on specific systems or techniques, ensuring students enjoyable experiences and improved knowledge retention, for the simulation effect and direct interaction are sure to characterise a lifelong exercise in the information universe. In the last five to ten years, a large number of courseware applications have been generated in North American and European universities for a variety of topics and subjects. Some experiences have been also been carried forward in LIS departments and libraries. Many more initiatives are to expected over the forthcoming years as part of the stream of research fundings for educational multimedia developments for higher education.

Based on local expertise, LIS courseware has been implemented and sometimes referenced in the literature to facilitate identification, usability, aims and objectives[2].

Early initiatives originated computer packages designed to allow librarians or students to be trained in specific systems and to acquire basic skills. They were developed to support self-learning experience. Later it became clear that the courseware had to be evaluated and the following mixed criteria were singled out to evaluate product use:

- functionality: i.e., assistance to help teach or learn better;
- capacity to characterise particular subjects;
- ease of use and impact to attract attention;
- ease of installation and user guidance;
- courseware educational and product design;
- stand-alone or networkable application;
- use and duration;
- standard design criteria in terms of screen layout, use of colour, icons and error handling[3].

4. STRATEGIC CONVERGENCE: STAND-ALONE AND DISTRIBUTED EDUCATIONAL SYSTEMS

Multimedia educationals will be the applications of the next decade.

Stand-alone courseware applications have proved to be best suited for personal use. Difficulties of identification and rigid market distribution make it very hard to know exactly how to locate and purchase these educationals. Internet homepages now make it possible to detect and view the list of educationals produced at a specific university or institution[4].

Recent commercial authoring systems are network-oriented; that is, they allow the product to be made viable and interactive via the network, thus facilitating access and downloading onto local workstations.

A networkable multimedia will permit the distribution of educationals through local and geographical networks, thus enlarging potential recipient communities.

However, the real innovation will be the possibility of interactive and real time management of network applications: teachers, educators, tutors, but also students and experts will be able to write, modify and integrate comments, make exercises and tests on-line on a remote system, handling the whole application and downloading sets of information to the connected client station.

The educationals will be centralised and downloaded according to user requests.

5. ONGOING EXPERIENCES

Our experience began as a specific educational application[5] capable of satisfying the needs of teachers and students of information study subjects at the postgraduate library school of the 'La Sapienza' University in Rome. The educational collected into a single, flexible environment a selection of concepts and definitions capable of providing an introductory set of fundamentals currently disseminated in books and professional literature, as well as third party tutorials, glossary and literature catalogues and exercises on information studies. It made use of the available commercial technologies.

The educational has yet to be delivered: The test phase is already under way but, due to the results of the prototype and the interest it has raised, there are now plans to enhance the application by taking into account the network performance of the recent release of authoring software.

This experience has now evolved into another project which considers all the above-mentioned issues in a networked context.

The improvement of networked services and the experience of developing, using and distributing educationals among different centres serves can serve to extend and enrich its significance. Instead of purchasing or transferring single educationals, pinpointed on the network among millions of resources, the European Muriel[6] project seeks to develop a service to build up a client/server educational system capable of sharing interactive comments and videoconferences, writing documents co-operatively and downloading elements of interest for all courseware for local use at library school sites. The project exploits the ISDN high-speed transmission multiservice network for the rapid delivery of electronic documents.

Muriel is intended as an innovative educational system model for library and information studies[i]. The basic concept is to serve and manage the electronic documents produced by the schools involved, integrating this function with service attributes.

The production of educationals is decided by each library school according to their experiences and interests, so the other European schools can benefit from topics already described and approached by another European educational establishment.

The model is able to meet growing educational needs; it can expand the number and typology of documents on various topics, offer a global choice to users in a specific domain and add service value to data and increase their usability.

It also envisages a new approach to the copyright of electronic documents.

The project is in line with the network explosion and with the user needs that are emerging in other sectors. This concept has to some extent anticipated the new approach in network computing, where no applications are resident on the user client and are transferred via the network by specific request. This characteristic well suits the need for the use of applications as opposed to their permanent acquisition and conservation.

6. CONCLUSIONS

The world library community ought to devote attention to educational products and develop criteria for their evaluation. It can also contribute to the definition of a standard.

The CMC offers the possibility of studying the new method of accessing and delivering a great variety of educational contents related to teaching issues.

European countries are characterised by heterogeneous curricula in information studies and library schools can benefit form the exchange of documents and educationals.

The information professional, who is to be considered a lifelong in the new decade, will encounter difficulties in identifying places and documents for his continuing education programme. Various strata of professional knowledge have accumulated in recent decades, ranging from library topics, technical and technological solutions, operational contexts and services, consolidated procedures and practices, through the interaction of the library service with the external world and marketing dependencies right to the conception of the library as a structural part of the knowledge society, with the need to identify responsibilities, ethical issues, economic and social roles and the internationalisation and globalisation of information.

National contexts of the education of information specialists should consider moving from a country-based approach to library and information-based science towards a multilateral, educational one. This is the only way to drive and mobilise nation-wide professional resources to interact with the new dimension of information. The new educational model should refer not only to educators' capacities, but also to the potentialities of a multimedia educational network-based model.

Many libraries and commercial organisations have accumulated significant experiences in courseware design, project definition, authoring platforms, content collection and prototyping. fewer experiences have been recorded vis-à-vis market strategies, targeted communities and financial revenues.

The network service experience can open up new paths for better exploitation of the resources accumulated and the deployment of new, more specialised applications.

FOOTNOTES

1   On these subject it is worth mentioning the work done by the FID Special Interest Groups FID/Modern Information Professionals, and particularly the survey report, 1996, and FID/Education and Training activit for the information professionals.

2   The Resources Centre of the CTI Centre for Library and Information Studies (CTILIS) is situated in the UK Dpt of Library and Information Studies at Loughborough University. CTILIS publishes *Infocus* journal and maintains a WWW server http:/www.lboro.ac.uk/departments/dils/cti/cti.html

3   These criteria have been synthetised by Ann Irving, a member of the evaluation panel of the British CTILIS.

4   Examples are the homepages of Glasgow University and the TILT Project pages.

5   Info-doc ©, ISRDS-Cnr, 1996.

6   Muriel, a two-year project partially funded by the European Union, is co-ordinated by the German Teles Gmbh of Berlin with the participation of the British Library Copyright Office, the Hogeschoole of Maastricht and the University for Library and Information Studies of Shuttgart-ULIS (FHS) CNR-

REFERENCES

Irving, A. (1996), ÒEvaluating Courseware,Ó *Infocus*, v, 1, i, 1, 1996.

Kuehn S. A. (1994). ÒComputer mediated communication in instructional settings: a research agenda.Ó *Communication education*, 43 (2),(April), pp. 171-183.

Overview of TILT Project (1993-95), University of Glasgow. TILT Project was within the UK - wide

Teaching and Learning Technology Programme, 1993-95,http://www.elec.gla.ac.uk/TILT/TILT.html.

Paci, A. M. (1993), ÒThe role of laboratory structures and their integration in Academic courses: considerations and experience in Italy,Ó*Continuing Professional Education and Ifla: Past, Present, and a vision for the Future*, ed. by Blanche Woolls. Proceedings, Munchen, KE Saur, pp. 270-279.

Paci, A.M. (1996), *Valutazione e sperimentazione del sistema Muriel. Muriel Fields trial evaluation*, technical report, 15/96, Isrds-Cnr, 1996.

Paulsen, Morten Flatwe. *The On-line report on pedagogical techniques for computer-mediated communication*, http:/www.nki.no/morten..

Stoppoloni, S. (1996), *Evoluzione e ruolo dei sistemi di formazione a distanza. La Documentazione in Italia. Scritti in occasione del centenario Fid*, Augusta Maria Paci (ed.), Milano, FrancoAngeli.

GROUP MENTORING : A FIRST EXPERIENCE IN CONTINUING EDUCATION

Ann Ritchie
Librarian
Hollywood Private Hospital
Nedlands
Western Australia

Paul Genoni
Lecturer
Department of Information Studies
School of Social Sciences and Asian Languages
Curtin University of Technology
Perth, Western Australia, 6001

Abstract   This paper outlines the role of mentoring as an emerging form of continuing professional development. In particular it describes the development and implementation of a Group Mentoring Programme for graduate librarians. Group mentoring is defined, the current programme is described, the relationship of group mentoring to more traditional forms of one-to-one mentoring is examined, and the ways in which the Programme contributes to the learning process and continuing education are explicated. An impact evaluation of the Group Mentoring Programme was conducted and the short term effects of the programme are discussed. A three stage model designed to outline the ongoing role of various forms of mentoring in the development of the new professional is provided.

INTRODUCTION

For the newly graduated librarian the question will arise as to how they should begin to pursue their continuing professional education and development. At university, their education needs have been identified for them and structured into a coherent curriculum; and the learning outcomes, which are recognised by the relevant accrediting professional bodies, have been tested and graded according to means specified by the course controllers. At the point at which graduates complete a first professional qualification they are transposed from an environment where their education needs have been met by the provision of programmed exposure to suitably qualified and experienced teachers, to an environment in which they are responsible for their own learning, there is no compulsion and few guidelines.

At this crucial point in their professional life graduates are also faced with many other challenges created by the transition from student to professional. Not only are they deprived of the structure provided by their programme of study; they may also be separated from the support of their student peer group; their job prospects may be doubtful; and they are uncertain as to how they should make progress in order to gain acceptance in the wider professional groups. In such circumstances they are almost certainly unsure (or even unaware) of the needs they have for continuing professional education.

It is because of the very particular and personal nature of the stresses faced by newly graduated professionals that mentoring has been seen as a means of providing for their continuing education needs. It is a key feature of mentoring that it provides a means by which young or new members of a professional group can negotiate transitional phases of their careers with the assistance of a senior member of the profession.

In discussing the nature of individual, informal mentoring relationships, Kram and Isabella (1985 : 110-111) describe the functions and roles which characterise mentoring relationships in the following terms:

> Mentors provide...career-enhancing functions, such as sponsorship, coaching, facilitating exposure and visibility and offering challenging work or protection, all of which help the (mentoree) to establish a role in the organization, learn the ropes, and prepare for advancement. In the psychosocial sphere, the mentor offers role modelling, counseling, confirmation, and friendship, which help the (mentoree) to develop a sense of professional identity and competence.

This description of the functions and roles of mentoring incorporates both the career and psychosocial goals that are characteristic of most definitions. Clearly it is aimed, however, at the prospect of providing mentoring to employees in the workplace. Many organisations have introduced mentoring schemes as a mechanism for induction into the organisation or orientation to a new job, as well as a strategy for ongoing training, and management and leadership development.

In the context of organisational culture, mentoring has been used either as a strategy for socialisation (or acculturation), which aims to perpetuate the existing cultural values and norms and maintain the status quo, or for the purpose of cultural change (for example, affirmative action and minority group programmes).

Whatever the organisation's purpose, mentoring is an attempt to draw upon the acquired wisdom and skills of more senior employees, in recognition of the more inexperienced employees' needs for support during transitional stages in their careers.

New graduates of a particular profession, however, are looking for support of a different kind. Their needs relate not to induction into the work practices and philosophy of a particular organisation but to socialisation into the broader responsibilities, roles and networks that are a vital component of professional life. Exposure to professional colleagues and networks will lead to a deeper understanding of the attitudes and ideology of the profession, and this in turn helps the new professional to meet other immediate job and career-related goals. Library schools will provide some exposure to these aspects of the professional socialisation process, in particular through the provision of work-based practicum placements. To overemphasise the professional socialisation process at this stage would, however, be both distracting and premature for the student.

It was in response to the particular needs of new graduates that the authors developed and implemented a group mentoring programme, a concept which is designed to combine the benefits of both one-to-one mentoring and peer support, and to ease the transition of newly graduated librarians into professional life. As such, it also becomes their first experience in continuing professional education, and is therefore crucial to their recognition of the importance of this professional responsibility, as well as in the identification of their particular ongoing educational and developmental needs.

GROUP MENTORING DEFINED

Group mentoring is a relatively new concept, inadequately defined and poorly represented in the literature to date. Although the term 'group mentoring' has been used to express the function of professional associations in influencing the career outcomes of members of that profession (Dansky, 1996) no adequate definition has been created to describe the concept of group mentoring as it has been implemented by the Australian Library and Information Association (ALIA) in Western Australia. It appears that this Group Mentoring Programme is a new and unique means of providing members of a professional association with opportunities for professional socialisation and a first experience of continuing education.

Incorporating and building on Kram and Isabella's definition of conventional mentoring, the following three essential characteristics of mentoring have formed the basis of the Group Mentoring Programme. Mentoring is:

1. a two-way learning relationship which draws upon the knowledge and wisdom of suitably experienced practitioners;

2. designed to fulfil two broad purposes of career development and psychosocial development, with the specific goals of the relationship being determined by the individuals involved; and

3. a relationship which develops over time, i.e. there is more than just a passing interest on the part of the mentor in the mentoree, and the relationship passes through a series of developmental stages. (This is one of the features of mentoring which distinguishes it from other forms of professional development and training, such as coaching.)

Thus, the term group mentoring is used to describe the process in which the functions and roles of mentoring are shared by the group's leaders and participants and carried out in a group environment.

THE ALIA (WA) GROUP MENTORING PROGRAMME

Programme aim and objectives

The central aim of the Group Mentoring Programme is to facilitate the transition of newly graduated librarians into the profession. In their broadest sense, the programme objectives relate to continuing education in librarianship and professional socialisation. Du Toit (1996 : 164-165) defines professional socialisation as:

> a developmental process of adult socialization. Not only does it involve the recognition of an assumed identity by the outside world; it also involves individuals' recognition of the identity within themselves and the non-deliberate projection of themselves in its terms - referred to as *internalization.*

Thus professional socialisation results in the recognition and projection of a professional identity. This concept may be equated to the career and psychosocial functions and outcomes of mentoring as outlined in Kram and Isabella's definition of mentoring i.e. the career outcomes which help the individual to gain recognition and establish a role in the organisation (or, in this case, the professional association); and the development of a professional identity and competence, which are suggested as the main outcomes in the psychosocial sphere.

The stated, formal objectives of the Group Mentoring Programme are:
1. to provide opportunities for continuing professional development in librarianship;
2. to facilitate the sharing of information, ideas and feedback in a supportive environment;
3. to encourage the application of the theory learnt in formal education to practical issues and experiences;
4. to assist participants to develop and achieve their career plans;
5. to provide opportunities for participants to learn and practice mentoring and peer support skills;
6. to encourage the development of leadership roles within the group;
7. to introduce the participants to ALIA committees, groups and networks.

Description of the Programme

Information about the programme was circulated prior to the end of the final semester to graduating students from the two Western Australian universities' library schools. Seventeen new graduates attended the first meeting. Numbers fluctuated slightly and eventually stabilised with eleven completing the year, the other six having dropped out due to relocation or clashing commitments. The programme is now in its second year, and there are approximately thirty participants in 1997. The following discussion will be limited to describing the 1996 programme.

In the original group of seventeen participants there were fourteen females and three males. There were eight graduates of the three year Bachelor degree, and nine who had completed the one year Graduate Diploma. ALIA membership was an eligibility criterion for participation in the programme. Only six were already student members of ALIA and most had not previously attended an ALIA event.

The meetings were held monthly from December 1995 to November 1996. A pre-test was administered at the first meeting to collect baseline data to assist in the final evaluation of the Programme. The needs analysis and formulation of the group's learning objectives was carried out in the first session. The participants discussed their individual objectives for the year and from this, nineteen learning objectives for the group were developed and prioritised. These fell into two main categories corresponding to the mentoring functions of career and psychosocial development.

The objectives were prioritised with the most important and urgent chosen as topics for the first few months' meetings. These related to writing *curriculum vitae*, job applications, addressing selection criteria, and interviewing skills. As the programme progressed participants' interests broadened to consider issues related to establishing professional contacts (an introduction to ALIA and other networks); coping with the demands of a professional role (stress issues, time management and relaxation strategies); and dealing with matters related to the creation and maintenance of a professional profile (personal authority in the workplace and marketing).

Strategic objectives were adopted by the leaders to ensure that some progress was made on the programme's seven formal objectives. These included training in mentoring skills (such as giving and receiving feedback, coaching, self-evaluation and providing supervision); reinforcing leadership roles within the group by encouraging participants to take responsibility for achieving particular learning objectives by organising and facilitating meetings; providing opportunities for more informal discussions and social activities in order to develop a supportive environment.

Other roles of the facilitators have been :

* provision of leadership in the form of initial establishment and ongoing administration of the group;
* ensuring the maintenance of a supportive environment;
* suggestions for learning activities;
* teaching mentoring skills;
* providing introductions to the wider ALIA networks;
* monitoring progress on the achievement of the group's objectives;
* evaluation of the Programme.

During the course of the Programme attempts were made by the facilitators to maintain the personal contact with participants that is the feature of more traditional one-to-one mentoring partnerships. This has included encouraging participants to meet individually with the facilitator of their choice; providing feedback on *curriculum vitae* and written job applications prior to submission; and arranging introductions to selected practitioners or visits to libraries as requested by the participants.

GROUP MENTORING AND CONTINUING EDUCATION

There are a number of ways in which the Group Mentoring environment provides the structural and attitudinal context for continuing education to occur. The qualities of continuing education outlined by Stone, Patrick and Conroy (1974:23) are consistent with the philosophy of the Programme and have been reiterated throughout this discussion. These qualities are:

1. It implies a notion of *lifelong learning* as a means of keeping an individual up-to-date with new knowledge; it prevents obsolescence
2. It includes *updating* a person's education (e.g. makes an individual's education comparable to that of a person receiving a like degree or like certificates at the present time)
3. *It allows for diversification to a new area within a field* (e.g. supervisory and management training)
4. It assumes that the *individual carries the basic responsibility* for his or her own development
5. It involves education activities which are *beyond those considered necessary for entrance into the field*

Mentoring relationships are typically supportive of individuals' learning, and this is translated into the group by creating a 'safe' learning environment. Norms which are supportive of individuals are consciously reinforced (e.g. maintaining confidentiality within the group, encouraging peer coaching and other paired or small group learning activities, and noting individuals' successes and achievements).

The learning objectives

Professional socialisation is a developmental process, beginning in the student's first year of tertiary study, and continuing on through the early years of professional life. It involves learning (or internalising) new knowledge, skills and attitudes which are the distinguishing characteristics of a particular profession. Once internalised, this professional identity is then 'non-deliberately' projected by the individual and is recognisable to the outside world.

Although the ages and life experiences in the group vary from those who have proceeded through university immediately following their secondary schooling, to those who have returned to study at a mature age, in terms of professional experience and knowledge, the group is a fairly homogeneous one. Because participants have just achieved their first qualification in librarianship, a similar baseline level of knowledge and skills can be assumed.

The most obvious and clearest stimulation to learning is apparent in the needs analysis when the gap between the participants' current levels of knowledge, skills and attitudes and those of a professional librarian, is identified. In this initial needs assessment the group's learning objectives are created through a process of brainstorming, and formulating and prioritising the learning objectives; these then form the focus of the monthly meetings. The learning objectives are thus not simply the sum of all the individuals' personal objectives. They are the result of the first piece of work that the group performs as a group. This is the first step towards establishing a cohesive group which is conducive to a self-directed, adult learning style; a group in which the individuals involved take responsibility for their own learning.

Throughout the year the topics which have been selected are subject to a process evaluation and ongoing review. This responsiveness, flexibility and 'point of need' learning is one of the main advantages of the mentoring process. In accordance with the principles of adult learning and in order to maximise the learning for all the group members, the group leaders for the session are encouraged to plan the sessions carefully, ensuring that the methods are congruent with the objectives they are hoping to achieve and utilising a variety of different teaching strategies to accommodate different learning styles. The sessions are highly participative, with didactic methods minimised.

MENTORING ROLES AND SKILLS

The concept of mentoring implies a two-way learning relationship, incorporating the joint functions of career and psychosocial development. In particular, the mentoring roles of role modelling, coaching and counselling highlight the educational aspects of the mentoring process.

Within the group context, the facilitators, as experienced practitioners, are de facto professional role models, and participants are presented with an ongoing opportunity for vicarious or observational learning. Perry, Baranowski and Parcel (1990 : 171-172) draw on Bandura's Social Learning Theory, to describe this concept of observational learning. Regarding the efficiency of using role models for learning complex behaviours, they note:

> A person can learn from other people, not only by receiving reinforcements from them but also through observing them and utilizing his or her symbolic capability... In observational learning... the learner discovers rules that account for the behavior of others by observing the reinforcements they receive for their behavior.

In the more direct teaching roles of mentoring, the facilitators offer individual coaching and counselling. The counselling role is used mainly as a mechanism for clarifying and monitoring individual objectives and providing feedback to help the individual to learn from their own experience.

One of the Programme's objectives is to provide opportunities for participants to learn and practice mentoring and peer support skills. Mentoring skills are modelled by the group facilitators, but deliberate strategies need to be set in place if this is to occur on a peer level. For this reason the session leaders are encouraged to incorporate ongoing coaching, feedback and supervision exercises into their teaching strategies.

Group processes

The group context provides an opportunity for the formal learning to be enhanced by group processes. Not only is there an opportunity for information sharing and discussion; there is also the added dimension of the synergistic effect and creative outcomes of the group work, which will have repercussions beyond the scope of the formal evaluations. In addition, the group process (and the individual's role in the group) may be viewed as paralleling the larger organisational and professional environments, in which committees, teams and project work form a large and growing influence. Thus individuals have an opportunity to learn about themselves, and experiences gained and new skills practised in the safety of the group can often be a stimulus to reflect on and apply the new learning in the larger environment.

PROGRAMME EVALUATION

An impact evaluation of the programme to assess the short-term outcomes was conducted at the end of 1996. A post-test questionnaire was administered to the eleven participants who completed the year's programme, and the results were compared to the pre-test data. This programme has been considered a pilot, and the information gathered will be used to improve subsequent programmes and refine the measuring instruments for future use.

Since the main aim of the programme has been to facilitate the transition into the profession, the main outcome measures relate to the achievement of a professional identity. For the purpose of the programme evaluation, sub-objectives relating to the two dimensions of mentoring i.e. career and psychosocial development, were developed in order to indicate the achievement of a professional identity. Career development was measured quantitatively by recording employment outcomes; psychosocial development (developing a professional identity and competence) was conceptualised as having a positive attitude regarding one's own level of ability as a professional and involvement in professional activities.

CAREER DEVELOPMENT

By the end of 1996, ten of the original group of seventeen had achieved full-time, professional positions. Two participants had to drop-out from the group as they relocated to take up professional positions; others returned to further studies or dropped out for various reasons.

Of the eleven participants who completed the programme, seven have been employed as professional librarians in twelve month contracts or permanent positions; one is participating in a volunteer programme, and one is employed in another area and continues to apply for jobs and pursue professional interests. The two remaining group members are not currently seeking employment.

An unexpected development of the programme was that there were a number of occasions when we were contacted by librarians who were looking for someone to fill a position at short notice. While we acknowledge that using our professional networks is sometimes the way that such appointments are made and we were happy to provide a list of names and contact numbers, it was not our intention to act as an employment agency and it is advisable to be cautious about taking on this role. It should be noted, however, that these informal networks do exist and are at times the mechanism by which employment is found. Three participants were employed in this way as a direct result of their networking in the Programme.

PSYCHOSOCIAL DEVELOPMENT

The development of a professional identity and competence was measured by participants' self-ratings in the areas of professional ability and involvement. A Likert scale was used to measure participants' perceptions of their own levels of activity and involvement in professional and peer networks, their levels of knowledge and skills in librarianship and their ability to apply these in the workplace. Their ability to plan and create twelve month professional objectives, and their levels of self-confidence to achieve these objectives were also used as indicators of psychosocial development.

Individual's pre- and post-test scores were compared, and were found to have increased, suggesting that the Programme had a positive influence on the participants' self-perception of their professional identity and competence. The numbers were too small to test for statistical significance. There was, however, a larger difference in the pre- and post-test scores between those holding a Graduate Diploma (a one year course) and those having a Bachelor (a three year course). Scores for the latter group also measured a rise, although the increase was slightly smaller. This suggests the positive influence of a more gradual transition into the profession. The longer the period involved in study and the more prolonged the contact with educators, peers and practitioners, the greater the likelihood of a higher level of professional identity at the point of graduation.

In addition to the time element, the hypothesis that activities in the informal curriculum are important in the development of a professional identity is supported by the research conducted by Fidler (1995). In Fidler's study of the influence of informal interactions of masters students of librarianship with faculty, peers and practitioners, it was found that peer activity was the only predictor of professional identity. This suggests that the peer support aspect of the Group Mentoring Programme is a crucial ingredient in the professional socialisation process.

PROFESSIONAL OUTCOMES

As previously stated, ALIA membership was a pre-condition for participation in the programme. An immediate outcome of the programme therefore was that ALIA acquired eleven new members. This had return benefits for the new graduates in that they gained access to ALIA publications; became informed of and involved in the activities of the Association's special interest groups, and were eligible for discounted rates for attendance at professional development activities sponsored by the Association.

Participants had reported an average of one attendance for continuing education events and meetings in the year prior to joining the programme (1995). In the post-test the number had risen to an average of 9.1 attendances for 1996. In addition, one of the participants has joined the 1997 Programme to assist in the facilitation of the group. This increased contact is interpreted as a clear indication of the exposure to opportunities that participation in the programme offers, as well as an indication of a desire on the part of the participants to engage with their professional colleagues, to expand their professional networks, and to become involved in continuing professional education activities.

ALIA received immediate benefits from the Group Mentoring Programme through the new memberships which were generated. It is hoped that this can be converted into a longer term benefit for the Association. That is, by introducing new members to the Association by providing them with an immediate benefit; by easing their transition phase from student to practitioner; and by providing a path to other forms of participation such as committee membership, the Group Mentoring Programme will help ensure that participants begin an active and ongoing involvement in the life of their professional association.

It is also hoped that the Programme will provide participants with an early introduction to the concept of mentoring as an important means of continuing professional development, and some of the skills that are required to be effective in a mentoring partnership. By doing so, it will assist the profession to prepare a new generation of practitioners who are willing and able to share with newcomers the benefits of their developing expertise.

COMMENTS FROM THE PARTICIPANTS

A further element of the evaluation of the Group Mentoring Programme was the holding of a focus group meeting for participants in the Programme. This was conducted as a part of the final meeting, and was held with the intention of soliciting more unstructured and qualitative feedback than was possible using the formal measuring instruments. It was hoped that this feedback would help the facilitators to understand the impact of the Programme on the participants, and provide useful information in planning subsequent programmes.

Although some minor problems were raised with the conduct of individual meetings, the feedback was generally very positive, with participants providing further evidence of the benefits that had been provided by the group mentoring experience. Comments made included the following:

- the group offers support for professional development, assistance in applying for and obtaining work and support of peers in a similar position
- we were a group of beginners learning what it is to begin
- it is a 'stepping stone' into the networks - next year I will be able to contribute
- I leant it's not a 'closed shop' out there
- Group mentoring provides a friendly environment where you have no fear of failure
- I learnt about participation - that you get as much out as you put in

- I would have dropped out of the profession if I didn't have the peer support and also being able to refer to the group leaders about my CV and applying for jobs
- the meetings meant that I had someone to talk to in the outside world. For example, I knew people at public library committee meetings
- you hear about jobs and can pass on the information and recommend others because you know them
- I learnt that the profession cares.

A MODEL FOR THE ROLE OF MENTORING IN PROFESSIONAL EDUCATION

A typology for describing mentoring within a profession with the broad general purpose of professional education can be constructed by means of a three-stage model. It has been the intention that the Group Mentoring Programme contributes the second stage in which new graduate makes the transition from student to practitioner.

Stage one : Preservice training with a practicum supervisor in the role of mentor
Stage two : Transition into the profession facilitated by the Group Mentoring Programme
Stage three : Continuing education with the guidance of an individual mentor

Stage one : Preservice training with a practicum supervisor in the role of mentor

All first qualification courses in librarianship offered by universities in Western Australia include at least one, and sometimes two, practicum experiences. Students and practicum supervisors alike are encouraged to look upon this as a 'mentoring' experience. That is, the role of the supervisor has the potential to go beyond introducing the student into the particular work environment and the tasks required of them during the practicum. Ideally, the supervisors see their role as furthering the students' professional education and socialisation by discussing with them and where appropriate, advising them about broader issues related to the development of their professional profiles, skills and networks.

As indicated earlier, one of the characteristics of a true mentoring relationship is that it develops over time. This is not always possible in the practicum context. However, it is often the case that many relationships commenced during a practicum placement are ongoing, with both partners choosing to maintain contact beyond the duration of the practicum. For the student, this partnership is an important part of their 'informal' or 'extracurricular' professional education, and later their continuing education.

Stage two : Transition into the profession facilitated by the Group Mentoring Programme

For the twelve month period immediately following completion of their first qualifying course in librarianship, the new graduate is assisted by participation in the Group Mentoring Programme. For most, this will be their first exposure to continuing professional education.

Stage three : Continuing education with the guidance of an individual mentor

ALIA (WA) also facilitates an individual mentoring programme, whereby members who self nominate are placed in contact with a practitioner with experience relevant to the needs of the prospective mentoree. Those who complete the Group Mentoring Programme are encouraged to continue to benefit from mentoring by joining in the individual mentoring programme. Intending mentorees are asked to nominate an individual who can be approached with a view to becoming their mentor. By having undertaken the Group Mentoring Programme, the new professional is in a far better position to nominate an individual (or at least to describe the characteristics they would like in a mentor) than if they had been required to make such a nomination immediately upon graduation.

The new professional who benefits from these three stages will not only develop more rapidly as an effective practitioner, but will also become far more able to return some of the benefits of mentoring to their profession. That is, they will in turn have made progress towards developing their own skills as a partner in a mentoring relationship. This recognises the two-way aspect of the mentoring relationship and implies that the mentoree has gained some knowledge and skills in how to make a mentoring relationship work well. As a result of the mentoring experience, they will in the future be able to make a significant contribution to the continuing education process, whether called upon to act as a practicum supervisor, an assistant facilitator in the Group Mentoring Programme, or an individual mentor.

CONCLUSION

The continuing professional education needs of library and information professionals can be accommodated in many ways. There are numerous providers of continuing education, both from within and from outside the information professions, who supply education and training courses based on the variety of skills required in order to remain an effective practitioner.

Inevitably, however, such courses are generic. They cannot cater for individual needs or provide 'point of need' learning opportunities; nor can they give the personal support, encouragement and wisdom that are needed as we continue to develop our professional careers. This is a function that can be performed most effectively by some suitably qualified and experienced person (or persons) taking on the role of mentor.

Group mentoring as practiced in Western Australia offers a means by which the concept of mentoring can be implemented in such a way that it:

facilitates the process of professional socialisation;

invites the participation of mentorees at a time when they have particular continuing education needs;

utilises and strengthens their existing network of peer support;

provides access to senior practitioners who are available for personal mentoring;

models and promotes the attitudes and skills needed for effective mentoring.

For participants the Group Mentoring Programme has been a very particular form of continuing professional education, one which has built upon the knowledge and networks that have been gained as part of first degree courses, and has helped them to find their own way and develop their own voice within the profession.

REFERENCES

Dansky, K. H. (1996). The effect of group mentoring on career outcomes. *Group and Organization Management*, 21(1), 5-21.

Du Toit, D. (1996). A sociological analysis of the extent and influence of professional socialization on the development of a nursing identity among nursing students at two universities in Brisbane, Australia. *Journal of Advanced Nursing*, 21, 164-171.

Fidler, L. M. (1995). *Interactions with faculty, peers and practitioners in the informal curriculum as predictors of professional identity*. Unpublished PhD, University of Wisconsin.

Kram, K. E., & Isabella, L. (1985). Mentoring alternatives : the role of peer relationships in career development. *The Academy of Management Journal*, 28, 110-132.

Perry, C. L., Baranowski, T., & Parcel, G. S. (1990). How individuals, environments, and health behavior interact: Social Learning Theory. In K. Glanz, F. M. Lewis, & B. K. Rimer (Eds.), *Health behaviour and health education: Theory, research and practice*. Oxford: Jossey-Bass.

Stone, E., Patrick, R. J., & Conroy, B. (1974). *Continuing library and information science education: final report to the National Commission on Libraries and Information Science.* Washington D.C.: American Society for Information Science.

FACILITATING WORKPLACE LEARNING

Jana Varlejs
Rutgers School of Communication
Information and Library Studies

Abstract:
In-service and formal continuing education receive most of the attention in library/information science literature, but account for the least amount of time invested by library staff. The results of a study documenting participation in self-directed learning versus formal continuing education by members of the American Library Association are reported. Workplace resources and policies for professional development are related to learning measures, and recommendations for practice and further research are made.

INTRODUCTION

The professional literature is rife with admonitions about the need for libraries to become learning organizations, for administrators to invest in staff development, for librarians to maintain old skills while learning new ones (Harris, 1996; Shaughnessy, 1992; Tenopir, 1996). A survey of subscribers to a library personnel listserv found that 90% of the respondents saw a greater need for training, attributing this to changing technology (Shoaf, 1996). Response to the need can be seen in the recent increase in how-to staff development manuals (e.g., Bessler, 1994; Lipow & Carver, 1992; Trotta, 1995; Whetherly, 1994). There is also evidence that new modes of delivering continuing education are on the rise, broadening access. The very technology that has spurred the need for more learning is also generating alternatives to location-bound instruction, giving individuals more choices not only in what to learn, but also in how and when to learn. Distance education using telecommunication has been tracked in the annual statistical reports issued by the Association for Library and Information Science Education since the 1986

volume. While only five schools were using some form of this type of delivery in 1984-85, 17 schools were doing so 10 years later (Sineath, 1996; Walling, 1996). Much of this effort is directed toward students enrolled in master's degree programs, but some of the courses could also serve individuals seeking continuing education. Lately, library staff with access to the Internet have been able to avail themselves of a variety of online courses, some at no charge (Weissinger & Edwards, 1996). Simply subscribing to a number of listservs in one's professional speciality can be a convenient means of maintaining current awareness and participating in discussion with peers.

QUESTIONS OF QUALITY AND QUANTITY

Despite signs of progress, problems remain. There is evidence that the payback on continuing education is not commensurate with the time and money invested (Burgin & Smith, 1993). This concern about the efficacy of training is not unique to librarianship: Studies reported in the management literature suggest that only about 20% of what is taught is actually applied in the workplace (Brinkerhoff & Montesino, 1995). No one is suggesting that traditional continuing education and in-service training be jettisoned. Rather, the thrust is to pay more attention to improving quality and "transfer of training," and to integrating on-the-job learning facilitation with the institution's service objectives (Smith, 1992; Bessler, 1994). Despite the fact that there seem to be more opportunities, there is still a gap between what the library/information field needs and what its continuing education providers can supply (Kevil, 1996). It is not likely that there will ever be a superstore of learning resources, where a librarian can find precisely the right course at the right time at the right price. As a recent survey has shown, over 60% of library staff who responded cited changing job responsibilities within the last year, primarily due to technology (St. Lifer, 1996). While about 79%

reported participation in formal training, it is probably safe to assume that a great deal of the learning demanded by new assignments was of the "do-it-yourself" variety. In business and industry, researchers have found that as much as 90% of workplace learning occurs outside of formal training (Sorohan, 1993). The prevalence of informal learning is supported by a study of health care administrators, which showed that they spent 20 times as many hours on informal than on formal continuing education (Brown & Easton, 1994). Data such as these suggest that the kind of learning that has received the most attention -- in-service training, workshops, courses, etc. -- may not be the most significant, at least in terms of the time invested. A model that presents a more accurate version of the overall continuing education system might include:

In the workplace:

- In-service training, coaching, and mentoring
- Incidental learning
- Self-directed learning projects
- Current awareness

Outside the workplace:

- Professional meetings, conferences
- Workshops, courses, etc.
- Visits, job exchanges

SELF-DIRECTED LEARNING STUDY

In an effort to document the extent of librarians' self-directed workplace learning in comparison to participation in formal continuing education, a study of personal members of the American Library Association (ALA) was conducted (Varlejs, 1996). Questionnaires were sent to a random sample of personal members, resulting in 521 usable responses (67% return rate). Work-related, self-directed learning -- defined as highly intentional learning undertaken on the individual's own initiative and conducted at a pace and with resources of one's own choosing -- was reported by 77%. The number of hours devoted to this kind of learning was three times that spent in formal continuing education.   The questionnaire also sought information about professional development resources and policies, on the assumption that these would have an impact on learning. Within ALA, there is considerable agreement on what should be in place in order to enable staff to pursue professional development. For example, in the ALA's division on Library Administration and Management (LAMA) statement on "The Library as a Humanistic Workplace" (1991, p. 6), the following criteria for professional and personal development are proposed:

Organization:
- Writes and makes available a staff development plan
- Allocates money in the budget for staff development
- Includes development goals and strategies in the performance evaluation process
- Schedules periodic needs assessment
- Provides released time for staff development activities
- Provides training for job related skills and especially for skills needed for new services and procedures
- Promotes from within the organization
- Supports involvement in professional organizations
- Provides opportunities for job enrichment

Manager:
- Provides the information, tools and training for staff to do their jobs
- Communicates performance expectations
- Gives feedback to staff
- Includes staff in appropriate decision making
- Utilizes talents of staff
- Develops areas of potential
- Provides opportunities for job enrichment

Individual:

> - Seeks ways to contribute skills and talents
> - Accepts joint responsibility for developing job-related skills
> - Participates fully in appropriate training activities

As in the inside/outside the workplace learning model presented above, the LAMA list recognizes that professional development takes place both internally and externally, formally and informally. In reviewing this list, it is clear that the library that subscribes to these policies and practices is placing a high priority on staff development and is willing to commit considerable resources to it. This makes sense since 66% of some libraries' budgets may be spent on staff (Wright, 1996) and that investment should be protected. But what is the reality? In the United States, business spends 1.4% of payroll on training, while academic and public libraries spend 1.04% (Library staff development funds, 1995). If they do not spend much, do libraries at least provide the supportive policies and environment prescribed by LAMA?

LIBRARIES' PROVISION OF PROFESSIONAL DEVELOPMENT RESOURCES

In the aforementioned study of ALA members' learning, a number of variables related to the work setting and staff development policies were included. The first set that the respondents were asked to check comprises work setting resources that help staff keep up to date and support professional activities: library literature current awareness system (e.g., routing journals/tables of contents); fax machine; e-mail account; reporting from colleagues on workshops and conferences attended; in-service training; indexes to library literature, either print or online; staff meetings for updating/ information sharing. The findings are summarized in Table 1.

Table 1
Frequency of Workplace Access to Professional Development Resources

	Available	Not Available
Current awareness system	399 (77%)	122 (23%)
Fax machine	450 (86%)	71 (14%)
E-Mail account	355 (68%)	166 (32%)
Reports from colleagues	358 (69%)	162 (31%)
In-service training	366 (70%)	155 (30%)
Indexes to library lit.	344 (66%)	177 (34%)
Staff meetings	416 (80%)	105 (20%)

Another set of questions addressed policies, specifically the provision of release time and financial support for professional development activities. The results are presented in Table 2.

Table 2
Provision of Release Time and Financial Support for Professional Development

Purpose	Release time		Financial support	
	Provided	Not provided	Provided	Not provided
Research	103 (20%)	418 (80%)	54 (10%)	467 (90%)
Professional meetings	480 (92%)	41 (8%)	438 (84%)	83 (16%)
Continuing education	379 (73%)	142 (27%)	350 (67%)	171 (33%)
Academic courses	183 (35%)	338 (65%)	204 (39%)	317 (61%)

In order to gain an idea of how substantial the financial support was for professional development activities such as conference and workshop attendance, respondents were asked what part of their expenses in the preceding year were repaid by the employer. Of the 513 who answered this question, 402 (78%) received some reimbursement, but the median dollar amount was a modest

$267. Nevertheless, the professionals in this study seemed not to be deterred by minimal financial support: 78% attended professional meetings, and 83% participated in formal continuing education. Comparing these findings with the LAMA guidelines, it appears that most libraries employing ALA members do provide money, release time, in-library opportunities and tools for staff development. They also seem to encourage involvement in professional organizations, at least in ALA. The individuals in the sample, as demonstrated by the rate of continuing education attendance, show that they have largely accepted the responsibility for participating in developmental activities.

RELATIONSHIP BETWEEN LEARNING AND RESOURCES

In addition to documenting the extent of self-directed and formal continuing education, the study sought to examine the relationship between library characteristics supportive of professional development and librarians' involvement in learning. When the variables in Table 1 are correlated with the self-directed learning and formal continuing education variables, only two relationships prove to be significant. As shown in Table 3, the number of self-directed projects is significantly correlated with having an e-mail account, and participation in formal continuing education is significantly correlated with working in an institution that provides in-service training. It must be recognized, however, that the coefficients are very small, and at best indicate relative strengths of association.

Table 3

Correlations Between Learning Measures and Workplace Professional
Development Resources

	Current Awareness Meetings	Fax Machine	E-Mail Account	Colleague Reports	In-Service Training	Indexes to Libr. Lit.	Staff
No. of Self-Directed Learning Projects	.0211	.1090	.1888**	.0686	.0994	.1128	.0952
No. of Hours Spent on Self-Directed Learning	.0459	.0135	.1021	.0647	.0693	.0815	.0798
No. of Hours Spent on Formal Continuing Ed.	.0216	.0180	-.0549	.0701	.1278*	.0005	.0373

No. of cases: 506   2-tailed significance: * p<.01 ** p<.001

Table 4 summarizes relationships of release time and financial support policies and actual reimbursement with learning measures. The correlation between reimbursement and meeting attendance was significant, if not very substantial, but the correlation between reimbursement and continuing education participation was almost non-existent. Moreover, self-directed learning (SDL) is negatively related to support for formal continuing education (CE). It seems that either the motivation to learn surmounts inadequate support, or encouragement to participate in formal continuing education decreases the need for self-directed learning.

Table 4
Correlations Between Institutional Support and Learning Measures

Support for Professional Development Activities	Participation in Professional Development Activities			
	No. of Meetings Attended	Formal CE Hours	No. of SDL Projects	No. of Hours Spent on SDL
Time off for meetings	.1135	.0751	.0752	.0568
$ for meeting attendance	.0869	.0456	.1126	.0832
Time off for CE	.0826	.0421	-.0237	-.0340
$ for CE	.1098	.0813	.0433	-.0206
Dollars reimbursed	.2655**	.0197	.0817	.0496

Minimum no. of cases = 500   2-tailed significance: * p<.01 ** p<.001

The 400 respondents who indicated that they had conducted self-directed learning projects were asked to focus on one of the projects and to answer a series of questions about that project, including what types of resources were used. The findings are summarized in Table 5.

Table 5
Resources Used in Learning Projects

Resources Used	Number of Times Checked
Print/online materials	331 (83%)
Communication with colleagues	318 (80%)
Workshops/courses	265 (66%)
Other	68 (17%)

As the number of projects and the hours spent on them increase, so does the use of materials (correlation coefficients of .1830 and .2989, respectively, p<.001). Also, communication with colleagues is significantly correlated with the number of project hours (.2247, p<.001). One would expect that reliance on colleagues for assistance would increase with staff size and with access to e-mail. Similarly, greater use of materials might be expected by those working in libraries that hold more library/information science journals and provide access to the indexes. Table 6 shows the correlations between resources available in the employing institution and the use made of them by those who conducted self-directed learning projects.

Table 6
Correlations Between Resources and Use by Self-Directed Learners

Use of Resources	Current Awareness System	E-Mail Account	Libr/Info Literature Indexes	FTE Staff Size	Libr/Info Literature Journals
Print/Online Materials	.0650	.0858	.0491	.1694*	.1805**
Communication with Colleagues	.0742	.0252	.0360	.0297	.0358

No. of cases: 357   2-tailed significance: * p<.01 ** p<.001

As anticipated, the library literature holdings correlate significantly with the use of materials, but other expected relationships are not evident. Staff size does correlate with material use, but not with communication with colleagues.

DISCUSSION

Since the findings presented above are not strongly supportive of expectations, other explanations of what facilitates workplace learning need to be considered. It may be that the nature of the skill or knowledge sought influences the choice of resources, but many other factors can affect the process of self-directed learning. If learning is conceptualized as a form of information seeking, then professionals' roles, tasks, awareness of sources, career stages, and other variables should be taken into account (Leckie, Pettigrew, & Sylvain, 1996).

It is likely that a different research methodology would elicit better explanations of the influences of workplace environment on learning. For example, open-ended questions about problems encountered would reveal a great deal about what kinds of support would be most useful. One would also want to evaluate the quality of the experience, both in terms of process and product. Workplace learning, just as off-site continuing education, can vary in effectiveness. For example, the available resources may not be appropriate or sufficient for the task at hand, and colleagues may lack expertise or be unwilling to share (Billett, 1995). While many principles of staff development are understood by those responsible for it, there has been a considerable gap between what should be and what actually exists (Weaver-Meyers, 1990).

A number of researchers have found evidence that organizational culture is an important factor in facilitating, or hampering, workplace learning (Billett, 1995; Kops, 1993; Young, 1986). As exemplified by the LAMA guidelines quoted above, the creation of a culture that fosters professional development involves much more than the limited number of variables included in the study of ALA members described in this paper. The provision of resources and policies that allow librarians to learn is a passive -- necessary but not sufficient -- measure. It may be that proactive practices such as maintaining a staff development plan, tying development to performance evaluation, and challenging staff to achieve their potential through job enrichment, etc., go much further toward creating a learning culture. Shared goals and performance expectations, along with a positive attitude toward change, would seem to be basic attributes. On the other hand, it is hard to imagine effective learning without appropriate resources. Facilitating learning in the workplace requires not only a climate and tools for learning, but also an ongoing effort to evaluate both processes and outcomes of learning. Averaged across the entire sample, ALA members spent 79 hours on self-directed learning projects, and 20 hours on formal continuing education. Such an investment of staff time merits evaluation.

REFERENCES

Bessler, J. M. (1994). *Putting "service" into library staff training: A library manager's training guide*. Chicago: American Library Association.

Billett, S. (1995). "Workplace learning: Its potential and limitations," *Education and Training*, 37(5), pp. 20-27.

Brinkerhoff, R. O., & Montesino, M. U. (1995). "Partnerships for training transfer: Lessons from a corporate study," *Human Resources Development Quarterly*, 6(3), pp. 263-274.

Brown, R., & Easton, P. (1994). "The effects of continuing professional education on the upward career mobility of health services administrators," In M. Hyams, J. Armstrong, & E. Anderson (Eds.), 35th Annual Adult Education Research Conference Proceedings, (May 20-22),University of Tennessee, Knoxville, pp. 61-66. (ERIC Document Reproduction Service No. ED 381 616)

Burgin, R., & Smith, D. (1993). "Ensuring that training pays off: Transfer of training in libraries," *The Bottom Line*, 7(1), pp. 22-25.

Harris, H. (1996). "Retraining librarians to meet the needs of the virtual library patron," *Information Technology and Libraries*, 15(1), pp. 48-52.

Kevil, L. H. (1996). "Continuing education and the reinvention of the library school," *Journal of Education for Library and Information Science*, 37(2), 184-190.

Kops, W. J. H. (1994). Self-planned learning efforts of managers in organizational context (Doctoral dissertation, University of Toronto, 1993). Abstract from: *Dissertation Abstracts International,* 54(9), pp. 3294-3295A.

Leckie, G. J., Pettigrew, K. E., & Sylvain, C. (1996). "Modeling the information seeking of professionals: A general model derived from research on engineers, health care professionals, and lawyers," *Library Quarterly,* 66(2),pp. 161-193.

Library Administration and Management Association. (1991) "The library as a humanistic workplace," *A report to the LAMA Board.* (ERIC Document Reproduction Service No. ED 364 253)

"Library staff development funds average less than American businesses" (1995), *Library Personnel News,* 9(6) (November-December), pp. 1-2.

Lipow, A. G., & Carver, D. A. (1992). *Staff development: A practical guide* (2nd ed.). Chicago: American Library Association.

Shaughnessy, T. W. (1992). "Approaches to developing competencies in research libraries," *Library Trends,* 41(2), pp. 282-298.

Shoaf, E. C. (1996).Staff training needs in transition. *Library Personnel News,* 10(4), (July-August), pp. 4-7.

Sineath, T. W. (Ed.). (1996). *Association for Library and Information Science Education statistical report 1996.* Raleigh, NC: Association for Library and Information Science Education.

Smith, D. (1992). "The greening of librarianship: Toward a human resource development ecology," *Journal of Library Administration,* 17(1), pp. 37-53.

Sorohan, E. G. (1993), "We do; therefore we learn," *Training & Development,* 47(10), , (October), pp. 47-48, 50, 52-55.

St. Lifer, E. (1996). "Net work: New roles, same mission," *Library Journal,* 121(19), (November 15), pp. 26-29.

Tenopir, Carol (1996). "Online databases," *Library Journal,* 121(14), (September 1), pp. 129-130.

Trotta, M. (1995). *Successful staff development: A how-to-do-it manual.* New York: Neal-Schuman.

Varlejs, J. (1996). *Librarians' self-directed continuing professional learning.* Doctoral dissertation, University of Wisconsin-Madison.

Walling, L. L. (1996). "Going the distance: Equal education, off campus or on," *Library Journal,* 121(20), (December), pp. 59- 62.

Weaver-Meyers, P. (1990). "ARL libraries and staff development: A suggested model for success," *College & Research Libraries,* 51(3), pp. 251-265.

Weissinger, N. J., & Edwards, J. P. (1995). "Online resources for Internet trainers," *College & Research Libraries News,* 56, (Septembe), pp. 535-539, 572.

Whetherly, J. (1994). *Management of training and staff development.* London: Library Association.

Wright, L. A. (1996), "Public library circulation rises along with spending," *American Libraries,* 27(9), (October), p. 58.

Young, D. J. (1987). An exploratory study of the relationship between organizational climate and self-directed learning among organizational managers (Doctoral dissertation, University of Missouri-Kansas City, 1986). Abstract from: *Dissertation Abstracts International,* 47(10), p. 3638-A.

TRAINING OF TRAINERS AND PROFESSIONAL DEVELOPMENT: ESTONIAN PROSPECTIVE

Aira Lepik
Associate Professor
Department of Information Studies
Tallinn Pedagogical University, Estonia

Abstract: The growth in responsibility of librarians under a country's changed conditions requires high-quality professional education, flexible continuing education and professional development in at all levels. These areas will be discussed, alongside the possibilities and prospects of Estonian librarians for integration into the modern library world. To a large extent it is the responsibility of today's librarian and information specialist competently to lead a demanding information seeker into the expanding information society. The great variety of information and library services and the rapidly increasing amount of information requires competence of librarians and information providers, particularly skills in the use of reference sources and information technology.

INTRODUCTION

Estonian librarianship evolved in the first quarter of the twentieth century, influenced by German and Anglo-American librarianship. After the Second World War it changed to conform with Soviet librarianship of that time. Today we have several reasons to speak of changes in Estonian librarianship and of the need for a librarian to change:

- We have become free of the development models forced on us and Estonian librarianship has to find its own reasonable way of development and integration in the changed context and integration;

- Estonia, independent again for merely five years (since August 1991), needs sufficient, accurate and easily accessible information for the development of its social and political institutions (e.g. parliamentary information services, information provision for management decisions on all levels);

- Changes in the information society demand constant readiness for a additional training or retraining, as information technology influences, either directly or indirectly, all areas of library and information services;

- Some changes in Estonian libraries indicate that continuity of the so-called First Estonian Republic, from 1918 to 1940 (IFLA-membership, activities of a professional association, certification examinations for the staff without LIS degree).

The librarians' increased responsibility demands good professional education, flexible continuing education and professional development at different levels. These areas will be discussed further on, alongside the possibilities and prospects of Estonian librarians for integration into the modern library world.

According to the data of the National Library of Estonia's (NLE) department of library science, the 745 research, special and public libraries of our country had 3,149 staff on 1 January 1996, of whom 2,545 worked as librarians. Consequently, Estonia has about 2,500 professionals responsible for the collections, processing, storage and dissemination of information to the 1,46 million inhabitants of our country.

GROWING CONTINUING EDUCATION NEEDS:

How Are They Expressed And Related To LIS Education?

The history of professional library training in Estonia is 70 years long. Librarians' training became a regular issue for the Estonian Librarians Association in the 1920s; in 1927 librarianship became an optional subject in the curriculum of Tartu University; 1944 saw the opening of the department of bibliography, and 1954 that of the faculty of librarianship. Two-hundred-and-six graduates majored in librarianship or in philology and librarianship from 1945 to 1968 (Noodia, 1969).

Since 1965 it has been possible to get a degree in librarianship at Tallinn Pedagogical University (TPU), witch was until 1992 Tallinn Teacher Training Institute. Unified curricula, compulsory in the whole Soviet Union, did not allow librarians to prepare for the peculiarities of the information environment in witch they had to work later on. The transition to an Estonian curriculum for a five-year undergraduate course took place in 1988. Since 1990 it has united credit courses and the former course system.

Today Tallinn Pedagogical University offers courses in information studies, not in librarianship and bibliography as before, and the graduates get a bachelor's degree. The department of information studies is a part of the TPU faculty of social science, and the faculty is 13 strong. In 1996/97 the department had 102 undergraduates, and next year 20 freshmen will be enrolled. The admission for correspondence courses in information studies ended in 1993. In recent years the number of applicants per student place has ranged between 4,8 and 5,6 on average. The number of TPU graduates in the field of information science and librarianship from 1969 to 1996 is 1,350, of whom 592 were correspondent students. The overall number of Estonian librarians with a university degree in librarianship or information science is 1,556. Of these, 724 studied by correspondence (Lepik, 1996a).

Beginning with the autumn term of 1994, the TPU offers full-time university credit courses. The undergraduates of the department of information science study major, general and additional subjects. The basic degree course provided by the department of information studies is the bachelor's degree (160 credits), with information studies as the major component. The allocation of credits to components is as follows:

> (1) Information studies (105 credits) comprising:
> - *Approbatur*: lower level (15 credits)
> - *Cum laude approbatur*: intermediate level (15+25=40 credits)
> - *Laudatur*: higher level (15+25+55=95 credits)
> - Bachelor thesis on information science (10 credits).
>
> Moving to each following level presumes that the previous level has been achieved.
> (2) Additional subjects (30 credits).
> (3) Optional subjects (5 credits),
> (4) General subjects (20 credits).

This flexible structure of studies allows the students to complete their own curricula according to their interests and goals, and gives them better opportunities to complete in the employment market (Lepik, 1996).

Graduates, with an information degree, are prepared to provide information services and compile databases; they know how to search for information and they have research skills. They are able to process documents and analyse their content; they are acquainted with the traditional and electronic methods of information provision, and they know various reference sources and are able to put them to the use of readers.

Current curricula: What's New?

- In the development of the new curricula in the department of Information Studies, the practice and experience of several European and Scandinavian universities and library schools has been considered. Till 1988, the curricula was centralised and adopted by Soviet authorities in Moscow, changes in curricula on that time were allowed only to 5 % for local needs;

- The system of course studies/training lasted 4 years and only compulsory subjects were taught and have transferred into the system of subject studies. The possibility for Information Studies students to choose additional and optional subjects from the variety of courses taught in other Departments of the University (Public Administration, Computer Studies, Psychology, Languages etc.) gives graduates a better chance to compete at the labour market;

- The education does not any more focus only on different types of libraries. The Department of Information Studies trains professionals for service, administrative planning and research tasks in the whole sector of information management, including library and information service;

- Students are offered greater possibilities for individual specialisation on major studies and they can plan their individual syllabus. The flexible structure of studies allows the students to complete their own curricula according to their interests and goals;

- The principles of modern information handling, information retrieval systems, computer-based library systems and networking are integrated into the curricula (Lepik, 1995a).

Since 1991, it has been possible to take advanced degree courses at TPU's department of information studies and to study for a Master's degree. It is the first time that a degree can be obtained in Estonia, and in the Estonian language. In addition to a 40-credit taught course, the Master's degree requires a written dissertation and its verbal defence. Ten Master's degrees have been awarded from 1993 to 1996 and, at present, 19 researchers are studying for it. It is also possible to do research for a PhD in humanities. This academic year four doctoral students are pursuing that goal. Previously Estonian librarians had to seek advanced degrees outside Estonia and study in the Russian language. Sixteen candidates' dissertations were defended in the Leningrad and Moscow Institutes of Culture and today considered to be the equivalent of a PhD in Estonia (Lepik, 1995b).

The time has come for a thorough analysis of librarians' and information providers' curricula, a matter in which the Estonian Librarians Association and experts of the Librarians Education Board have a lot to say. The certification of Estonian universities in the near future will be a basic for the assessment of LIS education as well.

The analysis of the new LIS curricula is connected to:

- the changes in the society (development in media policy, telematics etc.);
- changes in the information technology used in libraries and other
- informational institutions (integrated library systems, Internet etc.);
- certification of curricula planned to take place in 1997-2000.

During the certification process LIS staff has to inspect the curricula from the following aspects:

- the proportion and character of major and additional subjects;
- the permanent and compulsory parts of the curricula;
- diversity through additional subjects.

CHANGES IN LIS CURRICULA - NEED FOR TRAINING OF TRAINERS

Changes in LIS curricula are not possible without training of trainers. The aim of training of trainers in LIS education is to offer the teachers adequate opportunities to discuss aims, content and teaching methods with colleagues.

On a regional level, since autumn 1993 there has been organised Nordic-Baltic training of trainers seminars for LIS academic staff. This long-term project (October 1993-April 1997) is an effective way to develop curricula and co-operate with Nordic and Baltic LIS educators.

Seminars have been conducted on following subject matter:

- "Nordic library system: development and co-operation"
    October 1993, Vilnius, Lithuania
    The Royal School of Librarianship (Copenhagen, Denmark);

- "Library marketing and public relations"
    April 1994, Tallinn, Estonia
    The Royal School of Librarianship (Copenhagen, Denmark);

- "Information management and business information systems"
    October 1994, Vilnius, Lithuania
    bo Akademi University, Department of Information Studies (bo, Finland);

- "The role of libraries in an changing environment"
    April 1995, Riga, Latvia
    Swedish School of Library & Information Science in Bors (Bors, Sweden);

- "Information technology & information retrieval"
    October 1995, Tallinn, Estonia
    Swedish School of Library & Information Science in Bors (Bors, Sweden);

- "Classification and indexing"
    April 1996, Vilnius, Lithuania
    Oslo College, Faculty of Journalism, Library and Information Science (Oslo, Norway);

- "Information seeking & retrieval"
    October 1996, Tallinn, Estonia
    Tampere University, Department of Information Studies (Tampere, Finland);

- "Library management"
    April 1997, Riga, Latvia
    The Royal School of Librarianship (Copenhagen, Denmark).

Conference between teachers from the Baltic and Nordic institutions will take place in the autumn 1998, where we could evaluate the courses and discuss further co-operation between our institutions.

Extensive changes in the professional field require more continuing education. Librarians do not reckon merely with the development of information technology and the demands of new equipment, but also with changes in political and social spheres. In the 1970s and 1980s the continuing education of librarians was connected with the centralised library system and methodological supervision of libraries. The content of librarians' continuing education started to change according to the inherent library demands only at the beginning of the 1990s (Siitonen, 1993).

Librarians' continuing education may be analysed on different levels:

- *State-wide*: The Centre for Continuing Education of Cultural Workers (established in 1985), the National Library of Estonia and the Training Centre of the Department of Information Steadiest TPU organise a various courses and workshops for the staff of different types of library. The Estonian Children's Library takes care of children's and school librarians' continuing education.

- *Local*: The research and special libraries arrange courses for their own similar library staff (e.g. by Tallinn Technical University Library for the other technical libraries, and by the Estonian Medical Library for hospital libraries, etc.), and the central city and county libraries do the same for other librarians in their region (Lepik, 1996b).

The Department of Information Studies offers continuing education arrangements from evening lectures to seminars of several days' duration, a large range of topics. Training Centre of Department of Information Studies was set up within the Department of Information Studies in June 1995. The Centre has two main aims:

- to provide a consultancy service to meet the needs of individual clients or organisations and embodies the skills, expertise and experience of the Department's academic staff;

- to organise courses and seminars for librarians to help the profession to grow and to meet new challenges.

So far the courses have been conducted on the following topics:

- courses linked with information technology (databases and information retrieval, new information media, information handling etc.);

- courses connected with library management (library marketing and public relations, new library and information services, new rules of bibliographic description etc.);

- courses on different topics (for example, history of books and writing, local bibliography and databases etc.).

From January 1996 to January 1997, 405 librarians have participated in these courses.

The TPU has plans to start a distance continuing education project for the staff of research libraries. Short- and long-term courses should facilitate ongoing continuing education.

During recent years, Estonian Universities and staff of the department of Information Studies have participated in several international projects aimed to facilitate the using of distance education methods:

- FEUCODE - Finnish-Estonian University level Co-operation in Distance Education on methods and forms of distance education (1993-1995);

- FEUCODE II - Finnish-Estonian University level Co-operation on Distance Education, organised by Helsinki, Turu, Jyvskyl and Tartu University, Tallinn Pedagogical University and Tallinn Technical University for continuing professional education of the teachers on methods and forms of distance education (November 1995-June 1996);

- pilot project "Train the Trainer in Distance Education (DE)", arranged in the framework of the PHARE Technical Assistance Programme (TAP) for the Implementation of the Trans-Regional Component of the PHARE Pilot Project for Multi-Country Co-operation in Distance Education (June 1995-February 1996) (Virkus, 1996).

More details and analysis is available on the paper of Sirje Virkus "Distance Education as a New Possibility for LIS Education in Estonia" presented also on this Conference.

The Law on Public Libraries (adopted in 1992, amended in 1993), Regulation of the Ministry of Culture and Education (Nr. 3) of 31 March 1993 - "Educational requirements for public librarians and guidelines for salary differentiation within one level" - requires that public library staff should be trained professional librarians(Valm, 1993). The number of Estonian public librarians on 1 January 1996 was 1,199, of whom 754 had LIS education. Therefore, definite professional requirements and continuing education for those willing to stay on in public libraries after certification are of utmost importance.

In March 1993, the Ministry of Culture and Education set up an advisory body, the Librarians Education Board. Its task is to put forth proposals for different levels of LIS education, develop professional standards and work for the improvement of librarians' education in Estonia. The Board members represent the Estonian Librarians Association (ELA), the National Library of Estonia (NLE), TPU's department of information studies, Viljandi College of Culture, the Estonian Children's Library, Tartu University Library, the Central Library of Harju County and the Ministry of Culture and Education.

One of the main tasks of the board was to set certification standards and to organise the required tests. Examinations are taken in the following fields: librarianship and information science; library management; collection development; cataloguing; library services; bibliography; history of the Estonian books; libraries and bibliography (Aasmets, 1994). So far the examinations have been conducted four times and over 80 librarians certified.

Continuing education is varied and flexible, catering for the needs of those librarians who have an LIS degree and for those without it. The system has been devised so that it embraces qualification improvement, in-house training, continuing education and retraining.

ESTONIAN LIBRARIES IN THE WORLD LIBRARY COMMUNITY

In order to make the international professional community aware of Estonian libraries, our librarians should keep track of the world-wide developments and keep in mind the need to promote Estonian librarianship.

ELA AND IFLA

The highlight of Estonian librarians' professional life in the 1980s was the revival of the Estonian Librarians' Association (ELA) in order to carry on the traditions of the organisation that was active from 1923 to 1940.

This event gave librarians more opportunities for self-realisation and for dealing with professional problems. In its statutes ELA states that it aims to develop librarianship, promote professional education and defend professional interests. Today the organisation has 562 members, about one-fifth of all Estonian librarians. ELA has been active in organising international seminars with the participation of library specialists from Germany, Finland, Great Britain. The relations developed through this organisation are valuable for arranging professional study trips, participation in workshops, courses and other continuing education activities. In recent years study trips to the Finland, Sweden and Denmark have been an important step in the professional development of many Estonian librarians [(Valmas, 1996).

At ELA's instigation, Estonian librarians re-established their relations with IFLA. Since 1989, however, when ELA restored its status in IFLA (ELA was an IFLA member from 1928 to 1940), ELA has started to participate in the activities of various IFLA sections and round tables. Estonian librarians are standing committee members in the following sections:

- parliamentary libraries (Associate Professor Ivi Eenmaa, general director, NLE);
- education and training (Associate Professor Aira Lepik, department of information studies, TPU);

- classification and indexing (Aili Normak, deputy director, Library of the Estonian Academy of Sciences);
- public libraries (Tiiu Valm, library counsellor, Estonian Ministry of Culture and Education) (Lepik, 1996b).

Since 1991 Aira Lepik has been a member of the round table on research in reading (since 1995, the section on reading), the pre-session seminar, "Advanced reading in multicultural countries", took place in Tallinn in 1991 (*Advanced...*1992).

IFLA membership facilitates Estonian librarians' international professional co-operation and participation in joint projects and helps to develop and initiate research projects. The NLE became an IFLA institutional member in 1993 (sections of parliamentary libraries, information technology, interlending and document delivery) and the Library of Academy of sciences joined IFLA in 1994 (sections of science and technology libraries, rare books and manuscripts).

OPPORTUNITIES OF ESTONIAN LIBRARIANS FOR CO-OPERATION AND DEVELOPMENT

International associations of research and special libraries have an essential role in dealing with librarians' professional problems and their development. The NLE and Tartu University Library are Ligue des Bibliotheques Europennes Rechereche (LIBER) members, and Tallinn Technical University Library joined the International Association of Technological University Libraries (IATUL) in 1990. In 1992 Tallinn hosted the IATUL seminar, "Universal availability of scientific and technical literature" ("Universal...", 1993).

Participation in international professional organisations became more active in 1993: the NLE joined the International Association of Music Libraries (IAML); Tallinn Technical University Library Joined the CDS/ISIS User Association and UNESCO's Network of Associated Libraries (UNAL); and the Estonian Children's Library joined the International Association of School Librarianship (IASL). TPU's department of information studies is a founding member of the European Association for Library and Information Education and Research (EUCLID, 1991); students belong to BOBCATSSS (Organisation of European Library and Information Science Education School Students). In 1995 the NLE joined the International Association of Law Libraries (IALL), an associate membership of the European Bureau of Library, Information and Documentation Association (EBLIDA) is being negotiated. In the near future, the Library of Academy of Sciences will become an institutional member of the International Society for Knowledge Organisation (ISKO) (Lepik, 1996b).

Several professional organisations, IFLA, IATUL and ABDOS, have lately arranged their regular meetings in Estonia, thus enabling our librarians to participate in the international library scene without much cost. as our meagre library budgets do not stretch to cover foreign travel, Estonia welcomes international professional activity at home. Estonian librarians participate also in the work of Bibliotheca Baltica, founded in 1994 in Tartu, with the aim of uniting library institutions of the Baltic Sea region countries ("Bibliotheca...", 1996), and of ABDOS (Arbeirgemeinschaft der Bibliotheken und Dokumentationsstellen der Ost-, Ostmittel- und Sdeuropaforschung). The ABDOS'94 conference took place in Tallinn ("ABDOS-...", 1994).

A noticeable international trend in the professional life of librarians, is the spread of regional co-operation. The 1960s and 1980s saw close co-operation between different types of Baltic library (LiLaEst, a joint workshop of Baltic national libraries; Bibliopolis, a summer camp of the academy of sciences libraries; joint faculty meetings of LIS departments in Riga, Vilnius and Tallinn). In the 1990s it is possible to speak also about joint Baltic-Nordic projects (Baltic-Nordic Training of trainers seminars, since October 1993, Nordic-Baltic library meetings, since May 1993, etc.).

At the initiative of Stockholm University, some Baltic University and all national libraries are involved in a library management development project (1992-1995) ("Organization...", 1993; "Library...", 1994). Our integration with Nordic and Scandinavian libraries, experienced in regional co-operation, is utmost importance (Äyräs, 1993). Traditional Baltic co-operation is being revived - the 4th Congress of Baltic Librarians took place in Riga in 1991, some 50 years later than originally planned[18]. The 5th Congress of Baltic Librarians "Independence and Libraries" took place in Tallinn in 1996 ("Independence...", 1996).

Estonian librarians have tried to make as much use as possible of the opportunities offered for professional development by foundations, libraries and training programmes in Europe and America. The Congressional Research Service (CRS) of the Library of Congress has been active in training parliamentary librarians since 1992, including a workshop in Tallinn in 1993. Estonian parliamentary librarians have also been trained in the parliamentary libraries of Finland and Sweden. Good training opportunities have been offered by the Library of Congress - Soros Foundation librarian intern programme for the Washington metropolitan area. So far, four Estonian librarians have qualified. Since 1991, more than ten Estonian librarians have been on study tours or attended training sessions in Germany organised by Deutsches Bibliotheksinstitut, Bibliothekarische Auslandstelle.

CONCLUSIONS

The chances for Estonian librarians' success in the changing professional world increase with their growing skill and readiness to have a say in the analysis and development of library work and information provision. Joint efforts in these areas, moreover, are good indicators of individual proficiency and stimulate self-development. Growing continuing education needs will nowadays be expressed and related to LIS education. Flexibility of the system of continuing education must give an opportunity for permanent training and retraining. Training of trainers is an integrated part of professional education and professional development as well.

REFERENCES

Aasmets, M. (1994), "Raamatukoguhoidjate kutseeksami vajalikkus" ("The necessity for librarians' certification"), *Eesti Raamatukoguhoidajte hingu aastaraamat*, Vol. 5, pp. 26-31.

"ABDOS-Tagung, Tallinn, 9. bis 12. Mai 1994: Referate und Beitrge", Berlin, 1994, XVI, 145 S. (Staatsbibliothek zu Berlin, Preussischen Kulturbesitz: Verfentlichungen der Osteuropa-Abteilung; Bd 18).

Advanced reading in multicultural countries, (1992), IFLA preseminar of Round Table on Research in Reading, 14-16 August 1991, National Library of Estonia, Tallinn, p. 104.

Äyräs, A. (1993), "Nordic and Baltic countries - forward toether", *Scandinavian Public Library Quarterly*, Vol. 26 Nr. 4, pp. 4-5.

"Bibliotheca Baltica. 2. Symposium vom 11. bis 15. Mai 1994 in der Universittsbibliothek Tartu", Hrsg. von Malle Ermel und Robert Schweizer. Tartu, 1996.132 S.

"The IV Baltic Librarians Congress, Riga, Latvia, June 20-21, 1991: a report" (1991), *Baltic Studies Newsletter*, Vol. 15 Nr. 3, pp. 16-20.

"Independence and libraries" (1996), Papers of the 5th Congress of Baltic Librarians, October 21-22, 1996, Tallinn, Estonia. Tallinn, 209 p.

Lepik, A. (1996a), "Infoteaduse eriala Tallinna Pedagoogikalikoolis: traditsioonid ja vimalused" ("The Speciality of Information Science in the Tallinn Pedagogical University: traditions and possibilities"), *Infofoorum*,, Vol. 1, Nr.1, Available http://www.tpu.ee/~i-foorum/air.htm

Lepik, A. (1995a), "Possibilities and needs in the Development of curricula: a look from Estonia", Paper presented at the EUCLID-FID/ET Conference "Improved Practice and Integrated Skills in the LIS Field", 21-22 November, Copenhagen.

Lepik, A. (1995b), "Raamatukogu ja infottajate erialakoolitusest Tallinna Pedagoogikalikoolis: vimalused ja vajadus" ("Library and information science education at Tallinn Pedagogical University: opportunities and needs"), *Eesti Raamatukoguhoidjate hingu aastaraamat*, Vol. 6, pp. 82-104.

Lepik, A. (1996b), "Librarians in changing Estonia: professional education and development", *Library Management*, Vol. 16 Nr. 8, pp. 27-32.

"Library Management Development Project, 2nd report" (1994), Stockholms universitetbibliotek, Rapport 24, Stockholm.

Noodla, K. (1969), "Raamatukogunduse petamisest Tartu likoolis 1927-1967" ("Education in librarianship at Tartu University 1927-1967"), *Teadusliku Raamatukogu tid*, Vol. 2, pp. 3-24.

"Organization and structure of research library systems in Estonia, Latvia, Lithuania, and Sweden" (1993), Stockholms universitetsbibliotek, Rapport 21, Stockholm.

Siitonen, L. (1993), "Continuing education for librarians in post-socialist countries: a case study on Estonia", *Continuing Professional Education and IFLA: Past, Present, and Vision for the Future*, Papers from the IFLA CPERT Second World Conference on Continuing Professional Education for the Library and Information Science Professionals, Munchen: Saur, pp. 225-39.

"Universal availability of publications in science and technology including those on the history and philosophy of science and grey literature" (1993), *Proceedings of the IATUL Seminar*, 8-11 June 1992, at Tallinn, Vol. 2 (New Series), Helsinki Technlogy University, Helsinki, p. 176.

Valm, T. (1993), "Estonian libraries of today", *Scandinavian Public Library Quarterly*, Vol. 26 Nr. 4, pp. 6-10.

Valmas, A. (1996), "Advanced professional training contemporary requirements: librarians expectation and reality", Paper presented at the 3. Symposium of Bibliotheca Baltica, 16-18 May 1996, Riga.

Virkus, S. (1996), "Distance education in LIS education in Estonia", Independence and Libraries. Papers of the 5th Congress of Baltic Librarians, October 21-22, 1996 Tallinn, Estonia, Tallinn, pp. 84-91.

NEW TIMES - NEW POSSIBILITIES

Eugenia M. Rossinskaya
Ministry of Culture of Russia

ABSTRACT: The paper describes a training project in the changing circumstances curently experienced in Russia. The project's purpose was to prepare librarians from the CIS to train other librarians in the tools and technologies of librarianship, in developing senior administrative cadres for the times of change, and in library management.
"If you want to help a hungry man do not do the fishing for him but provide him with a fishing-rod."

Free and effective access to information for students, scholars, businessmen and the general public is a fundamental precondition of a democratic society and is a key building block in the creation of democratic institutions and the promotion of economic development. In the CIS, historical, political, and economic circumstances have hindered the development of information access on a scale appropriate to these countries' needs. With the fall of the Communist system in the region, the time is ripe to begin to address the problems of access to the region's information resources. Normalization and stabilization in the region will progress more surely and more quickly in an atmosphere that supports effective information access. Besides we were forced to start this activity by the fact that the existing system of professional upgrading in the country is a bit far from the needs of practical librarians and library managers. Very often they seem to feel isolated in the new environment where market economy dictates its rules. It is not so easy to live in the period of transition, and for a person who according to his/her position is responsible for his/her staff - i.e. many people - all the problems are doubled.

Our project's purpose was to prepare librarians from the CIS to train other librarians in the tools and technologies of librarianship, in developing senior administrative cadres for the times of change, and in library management. I want to stress that, in this conception, training in library management is a means to attain the desired end of building a democratic society rather than a goal in and of itself. Indeed, we see this as a crucial step; the development of management in libraries and information centers will promote creating an atmosphere characterized by respect for the value of free and open access to information in a democratic society.

The main idea of the project is to help librarians to understand the new situation and to work under new conditions. Library is a forum of information and ideas, an advocate of free and open access to information. Each library must no longer be a lone agent but a part of the whole global community with an access out through networks - such as the Internet - available to every citizen. Traditional funding of libraries (from the state, local bodies, etc.) has been hard hit in these times of economic hardships and the fund-givers are unable to maintain current level of fundings, much less to provide additional support to allow libraries to move forward. It is important to teach librarians to find other sources of funding so that their libraries can provide for free and open access to information, all kind of materials and services. Social, economic and political changes are also affecting the essence - and thereby inducing a revision - of library policies and of librarianship as a profession.

Consequently, there is a perceived need to create new library policies in democratic Russia and Ukraine based on free access to ideas, library materials and services. It is up to librarians to establish, promote, implement and carry out these new policies. This however requires a change in the mentality of librarians since under the administrative command system librarians and bibliographers were viewed as "soldiers of the battle of ideologies".

Electronic communications are a major feature of current library practices world-wide. It is important to provide a comprehensive training of librarians in the tools and technologies of librarianship, with special emphasis on the use of electronic communications, particularly electronic mail and the Internet, in order to provide for appropriate access to information.

This new situation prompted a search of ways of redeveloping and restructuring continuing library education - mostly as a priority for library managers and mid-managerial personnel.

The joint Russian-Ukrainian special library project successfully started in 1995. It began on the Mortenson Center's initiative and with the generous sponsorship of the Eurasia Foundation, the International Research and Exchanges Board (IREX) and the International Renaissance Foundation. The project's purpose is to develop the foundations of an effective training program for librarians in Russia and other CIS countries.

The project (program) entitled "Library Management Training in the CIS" was to include three stages as planned. Firstly, a seminar on contemporary library management and maintenance was to be held for about 50 librarians (mainly directors or deputy directors) from the former Soviet Union. The seminar did take place at VGBIL on February 13-15, 1995. It was conducted by a team of four American consultants with expertise in the areas of personnel management, electronic communication, fund-raising and library promotion, automation and library collections preservation, and intellectual freedom and access to information. In reality the number of participants at the main sessions (on February 13) exceeded a hundred librarians representing different regions of the Russian Federation and some other newly independent states. During the last two days the participants were given an opportunity to discuss (at small group sessions) contemporary library management issues and the concepts of organizing professional workshops for librarians. The seminar held at VGBIL was a great success.

The purpose of the project's second stage was to prepare trainers who can share their knowledge and expertise with other librarians in their home countries. Two Russian librarians were selected on the competitive basis. The co-ordinator of the project in Russia was chosen from the VGBIL staff since the whole project is carried out by the Mortenson Center with active participation of this library.

The Ukrainian librarians joined in the project at its second stage with the support of the International Renaissance Foundation and the Regional Library Program (RLP). Six librarians from Russia and Ukraine (4 trainers - for three months and 2 co-ordinators - for one month) had intense training at the Mortenson Center in September-December of 1995. In the second stage, six individuals were selected from among the seminar participants to go to the United States for further training at the Mortenson Center. During their stay at the Center they were provided comprehensive training in the tools and technologies of librarianship, with special emphasis on problems of management and in the use of computer communications and electronic mail:

1. Fund-Raising and Library Promotion;
2. Using E-mail and the Internet;
3. Intellectual Freedom and Access.

An integral part of this stage of the project was to prepare the participants to share their knowledge and experience with their colleagues in their home countries.

At the beginning of 1996 the third stage of the project began. At this stage the project provided funds for the trainers to go to Russia and Ukraine to conduct workshops for librarians on the topics mentioned above. According to the decision made by the project participants at the working meeting held at VGBIL on January 12, 1996, the joint efforts were aimed at conducting at least three seminars each year (in 1996 and 1997). Two of them were to take three days each. The first one was planned for 24-26 April in Kharkov (Ukraine), the second was to take place in Rostov-on-Don in December (Russia). In June 1996 during the International conference "Crimea-96" in Foros Russian and Ukrainian participants of the project conducted the presentation of the professional development program and orientation sessions. In addition to these joint arrangements there will be several workshops conducted by individual trainers and co-ordinators.

A three-day workshop for Ukrainian librarians (Kharkov, Ukraine - April 24-26, 1996) was conducted by four Ukrainian and Russian librarians trained at the Mortenson Center on the tools and technologies of librarianship with special emphasis on the use of computer communications and electronic mail, the ways of library development and promotion and the issues of free and open access to information in libraries.

The number of participants was more than 50 people including directors and senior specialists of some major Kharkov and other Ukrainian libraries (mostly of the East of Ukraine).

The theme of the "Crimea -96" Conference was "Libraries and Associations in the Transient World: New Technologies and New Forms of Co-operation". Its aim was to extend and strengthen co-operation of Russian, Ukrainian and other CIS countries' libraries with the world library community. The professional program of the conference took place on June 3-7. The project's participants (trainers and co-ordinators) had an opportunity to present the program to librarians from different countries. The purpose of the joint Russian-Ukrainian project and the prospects for its future implementation were stated. This was done in the form of orientation sessions. The participants also evaluated the previous workshops and other events which had taken place since the start of the project.

Among the coming events is a three-day workshop for Russian librarians (Rostov-on-Don, Russia - December, 1996). The workshop will be conducted by the same team of four trainers. The place of the workshop is the Don State Public Library. This workshop is planned as a regional one for librarians from the South of Russia. Among those present there will be representatives of the Culture and Art Department of the Rostov Region, directors and leading specialists of libraries, journalists. The expected number of the participants totals provisionally up to 23 people.

The following workshops are planned for the second year of the Project implementation (1997):

1. Meeting of the project's participants for summing up and evaluation of the workshops and other events held in 1996; planning for the future will also be on the agenda of the meeting (VGBIL, Moscow, Russia - January, 1997). Besides the co-ordinators and trainers taking part in the joint Russian-Ukrainian project some members of the LFL administration, representatives of Russian and Ukrainian Ministries of Culture, library programs co-ordinators of the Open Society Institute and of the International Renaissance Foundation and other persons concerned are going to attend this meeting - all in all about 30 people.

2. A three-day workshop for Russian librarians (Belgorod, Russia - April, 1997). The place of the workshop is the Belgorod Regional Scientific Library. The workshop will be conducted by the same team of trainers and co-ordinators. The estimated number of the workshop's participants will total up to 30 people. Among them there will be representatives of the Belgorod Region Board of Culture, directors and senior librarians from the Belgorod Region libraries and other regions next to Belgorod.

3. Presentation of the program "Professional Development of Russian and Ukrainian Librarians" at the 4th International Conference "Crimea -97" (Foros, Ukraine - June, 1997). The round table is planned to take place in the frame of this conference.

4. A three-day workshop for Ukrainian librarians (Kiev - October, 1997). The Ukrainian Library Association is responsible for the organization of this workshop. The expected audience of the workshop will consist of directors and senior specialists of the major Kiev and other Ukrainian libraries. Representatives of the Ukrainian Ministry of Culture, the main library journals, the Ukrainian State University of Culture will also be invited. The total number of Ukrainian participants will be about 25 people.

A few words about the partners of the joint Russian-Ukrainian Project. The All-Russian State Library for Foreign Literature is the library in the CIS with a rich, acquired in many decades experience of work with foreign materials and co-operation with foreign libraries and information institutions and with cultural agencies in the service of different regions of Russia and the CIS.

For that reason the LFL may well be viewed as a model of open access and modern management practices in libraries for the rest of the country. This can be proved by the professional activities of this institution and the place which the Library occupies among the Russian libraries.

The LFL is a training center for library and information science in Russia and the CIS. In this capacity, the Library organizes no less than 10 seminars each year, inviting foreign experts on various aspects of librarianship and information science and book studies. Each seminar attendance varies from 20 to 80 librarians from around the country and CIS. The LFL is one of the libraries in

Russia to demonstrate new functions of libraries in society, thus providing a new image of libraries and librarians.

In addition, the LFL maintains relations with libraries in Tatarstan, Bashkortostan and other Republics of the Russian Federation, and with many cities within Russia proper, including Ekaterinburg, Yuzhno-Sakhalinsk, Omsk, Tiumen, Voronezh, Saratov, Yaroslavl, Tver, Tula, St.Petersburg, and many others, acting as a resource centre for the professional community in Russia.

Continuing library and information science education is among the priorities of the Ukrainian Library Association which was founded in 1995. The long-term conception of continuing education and training of library and information specialists was elaborated. The first attempts to bring new ideas and forms of continuing library education into life were made at the international conference "Libraries in a Democratic Society" (Kiev, November, 1995). The new trends in library and information science education adopted by the institutions which currently train librarians in Ukraine: 3 higher institutions in Kiev, Kharkov and Rovno and 25 library colleges of culture which train medium = level library personnel. Besides there is the Institute for Continuing Education in Kiev. However, the activities of these training institutions seem to be not enough to provide for functioning of a modern library in the conditions of market economy.

Educational innovations in this are a now in need of more permanent support. The Ukrainian Library Association looks for new continuing education opportunities for Ukrainian libraries.

One significant benefit of the project's focus on management and administration issues is that the skills involved are valuable to both the private and the public sectors. The participants will gain experience of the work of institutions in a democratic society, and this experience will be shared as they participate in the recasting of their society. The economic conditions prevailing in post-Soviet society often result in a wide labor mobility. Whether or not individual participants stay in the library profession, their knowledge gained through the program can be useful to society in other spheres.

Indeed, new times very often bring new possibilities. The only thing is just to take a risk and do something one has never done before. But if you have strong confidence in this challenge, you invite your professional colleagues who hold the same views as you do, and thus you can overcome all the troubles and obstacles which the new times may bring in, and the new possibilities will be discovered and made useful to the benefit both of your profession and the society as a whole.

If you want to help a hungry man do not do the fishing for him but provide him with a fishing-rod.

LIBRARIANS AS CHANGE AGENTS IN THE HE COMMUNITY

Dr Kay Flatten,
TAPin Project Manager,
Faculty of Computing and Information Studies,
University of Central England
Birmingham, UK

ABSTRACT: TAPin is a project funded by the Joint Information Systems Committee (JISC) of the Higher Education Funding Councils, as part of its Electronic Libraries Programme (eLib). One of the project outcomes is the continued professional development of TAPin subject librarians through a planned infusion of the United Kingdom eLib Programme. Two years into this process these librarians are emerging as change agents within their LIS services and the academic departments they support. This paper focuses on the new role of these subject librarians, the barriers they face, and the themes from previous national initiatives designed to integrate technologies into subject departments.

DIFFUSION THEORY AS APPLIED TO LIBRARIANS

The possibility of TAPin subject librarians acting as change agents in the use of networked information by academic staff is consistent with the three phases of Brown's model by which organisations diffuse innovations (Brown, 1981). Firstly, the LIS represents the change organisation through which innovations are to be made available. Secondly, the eLib Programme develops strategies to promote and adopt networked information, and finally, TAPin provides a framework for successful adoption.

Theories on the strength-of-weak ties in organisational change are also applicable to subject librarians. They are the outsiders who channel information between individuals and groups in their subject disciplines. "Weak ties thus provide the basis for both microlevel change (by broadening group horizons) and macrolevel integration (by expanding inter-group connections)." (Schwartz, 1994, p 535) The role of the librarian as change agent was discussed as early as 1991 by Callahan and more recently by Biddiscombe, Reid and Rafferty (Biddiscombe, 1996).

It is by no means certain that subject librarians will play such an important role in the changing communication technologies in HE. Richard Heseltine has spoken of the vanishing need for subject specialists in LIS (Library Resources Exhibitions, 1995). He envisaged the workstation world of academics providing information without the need for such intermediaries. This future role, should it evolve, will not come with ease. The TAPin experience to-date has identified a number of barriers to networked information support for academics.

BARRIERS TO NETWORKED INFORMATION SUPPORT

The barriers likely to hinder the librarians in their own development and the support of the academic staff were more prevalent in the TAPin universities which had been polytechnics until 1992. These new universities stand to gain the most from initiatives like eLib; however, the TAPin IT Infrastructure Audit and Academic Staff Survey pointed to the following serious concerns for their librarians:

* limited access to the Internet
* lack of a mature research culture

The universal pressures of time and money plagued the LIS at all TAPin universities (Flatten and MacKenzie, 1996).

ACCESS TO THE INTERNET

Of the academic staff who had access to a computer in their offices, those from old universities were twice as likely to have their computers connected to Internet/JANET (Chi Square = 30.75; 1df; p<.01). This difference as illustrated in Figure 1 was independent of the age or sex of the staff member.

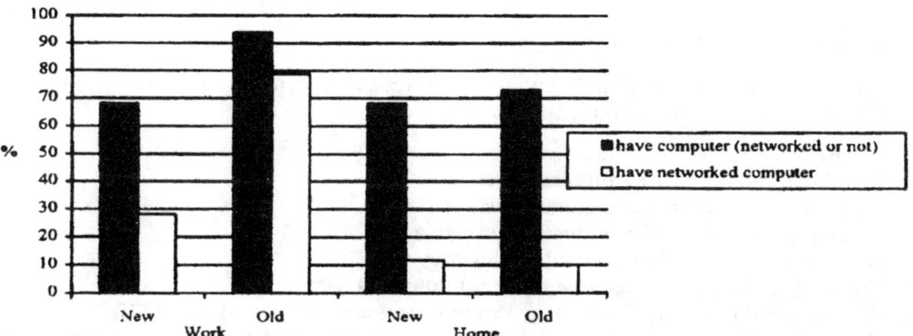

Figure 1: Percentage of staff having a computer and network access at work and/or at home

As with academic staff, the quality of librarian access to networks varied between TAPin universities. One older university had excellent access where the librarians had desktop access to networked information systems and a training room with networked PCs for user education. The university infrastructure was well developed and a good support relationship existed between library staff and computer services staff. Whereas, three newer universities libraries were not directly connected to a campus Internet service. One librarian accessed his email and the WWW by going into a student lab. As the two years have progressed Internet access at the new universities has improved and this barrier has lessened.

RESEARCH CULTURE

Analysis of the Academic Staff Survey data concluded that staff from the old universities devoted significantly more of their time to research (39.5%) while new university staff assigned research 16% of their time (t=7.56; p<.01). Thus academic staff at newer universities were less likely to need information from sources which transfer easily across computer networks. They were inclined to use books and multimedia in their teaching roles.

This research culture was reflected in the agreement staff expressed during interviews with the assumption that global communication is desirable. Academic staff at the old universities agreed with this assumption in 82% of the interviews while new university staff agreed in 66% of the interviews. Those staff agreeing with this assumption referred to contact with colleagues in their research speciality who often delivered information to them before it appeared in print.

TIME AND MONEY PRESSURES

The academic staff in both old and new universities agreed on the time pressure in their jobs. Time pressures affected their attitudes about IT. Those with limited understanding of IT felt they didn't have the time to learn the new technologies. Those with IT experience reported disappointment with past training in IT, many indicating it was a waste of time. They wanted networked information support at the time of need, and only then with information highly relevant to that need. They reported wasting time with earlier experiences at desktop document delivery, and too much information and "junk" on the WWW.

Most of the TAPin librarians worked in a decentralised financial structure where responsibility and finances were allocated directly to each individual faculty. The faculty then allocated moneys to the Library for the purchase of subject related resources. For these librarians to extend the range of electronic services further, more resources are required. This increased access would have to be obtained via negotiation with individual faculties for "contributions" to relevant subscriptions. The demand for electronic information was not yet realised from the faculties; therefore, librarian access was hindered.

ISSUES IN NATIONAL IT INITIATIVES

The following UK national initiatives have all attempted to bring the information technologies into teaching and learning at universities:

> Advisory Group on Computer Graphics (AGOCG)
> The Electronic Libraries Programme (eLib)
> Information Training Technology Initiative (ITTI)
> Learning Technology Dissemination Initiative (LTDI)
> National Council for Educational Technology (NCET)
> Teaching and Learning Technology Programme (TLTP)
> Teaching and Learning Technology Programme Support Network (TLTSN)
> The New Technology Initiative of the JISC Technology Applications Programme (JTAP)

Only the Electronic Libraries Programme has specifically looked at the role of the LIS professional; however, there are issues common throughout all these initiatives which have important implications for network information support by the LIS staff. These are:

*   Institutional strategies which endorse Computer Assisted Learning (CAL) - this will lead to a coherent management structure into which both the technological and pedagogical aspects of librarian support will fit. It also indicates a commitment to CAL leading to internal funding instead of heavy reliance on external funds for IT innovations. In the case of the LIS, central commitment and funding will decrease the reliance upon faculties to provide funds for the LIS products and services.

*   Quality of the information products must be high - this will help librarians with their use of such information and increase their confidence in referring others to the resource. The quality of the networked resource also effects how easy it is to use. Well designed interfaces save time and deliver more relevant information.

*   Standards are important - they make communication across campus networks and between organisations easier. This again saves time for the LIS and academic staff and decreases frustration and pressure.

*   Motivation must be encouraged - If the strategies, quality and standards are in place it is likely that motivation will be high; however, the time pressures of academic staff would suggest that special managerial support techniques are needed. Staff promotion procedures, scheduling CAL development time, supporting training and staff development opportunities are all ways mentioned to encourage changes in behaviours.

The Electronic Libraries Programme, like the initiatives which preceded it, is made up of projects; however, the scope of the eLib programme extends beyond individual projects to include these broader issues. Culture change is a re-occurring theme in eLib activity. The programme aims to address the way in which such issues translate (or resist translation) into an electronic environment (Russel, 1996). The TAPin librarians are the litmus test for many of these changes.

REFERENCES

Biddiscombe, R (ed) (1996). *The End-User Revolution: CD-ROM, Internet and the changing role of the information professional*. London: Library Association. pp. 79-95.

Brown, L A (1981). *Innovation diffusion: a new perspective*. London: Methuen.

Callahan, D R (1991). The librarian as change agent in the diffusion of technological innovation. *Electronic Library*, 9 (1), pp.13-15.

Flatten, K and MacKenzie N (1996). *TAPin Annual Report*. Birmingham: University of Central England. http://www.uce.ac.uk/tapin/reports/annual.htm

Graves, J (1996). *Implementation and Integration of CAL: issues for senior management*. Nottingham: University of Nottingham. http://www.ccc.nottingham.ac.uk/tltsn/calnott.htm

Heseltine, R (1995). *The impact of the SuperHighway on Higher Education*. Lecture at the 6th Library Resources Exhibition 6-8 June NEC Birmingham.

Holland, M (1996). MSc Proposal Draft. Birmingham: University of Central England. P. 6.

Reid, B and Rafferty Brown, P (1996). The changing role of professional education for information professionals (in) Biddiscombe, R (ed). *Ibid.* pp. 173-186.

Russell, K (1996). A snapshot of the Electronic Libraries Programme. *TLTP newsletter* No. 8. Bristol: Northavon House Coldharbour Lane. p 10.

Schwartz, C A (1994). The strength of weak ties in electronic development of the scholarly communication system. *College and Research Libraries*, 55 (6), pp. 529-540.

THEORY AND PRACTICE OF LAW LIBRARIANSHIP THROUGH CONTINUING PROFESSIONAL EDUCATION: THE NIGERIAN EXPERIENCE

Oluremi Jegede
The Institute Librarian
Nigerian Institute of Advanced Legal Studies
University of Lagos Campus
YABA - LAGOS
NIGERIA

ABSTRACT The essay is the three parts. The first part deals with issues/indicators for the need of the continuing professional education (CPE) for librarians working in law libraries. The next segment of the essay discusses the introduction of the CPE programme: objectives, whom is it designed for? etc. Reasons for choosing the faculty members are analysed. The changes in the course-content reflect the changing needs of the librarians. The concluding part advocates that the CPE programmes should commensurate with the general level of the practice of librarianship in the individual countries. What is important however is that each CPE programme should be continuously evaluated to make sure its original objectives are achieved.

The CPE programme by the Nigerian Institute of Advanced Legal Studies, serves not only the librarians from the law libraries and later on the librarians from other special libraries to up date their knowledge and practice of librarianship; but also serves library users, and policy makers to achieve better library and information services for national development.

INTRODUCTION

The running of the continuing professional education (CPE) programmes by the Nigerian Institute of Advanced Legal Studies (hereinafter referred to as the Institute) can be regarded as a direct compliance with the spirit of and to the letters of the law (Decree No. 18 1984 now cap 380 of the Laws of the Federal Republic of Nigeria, 1990 as amended by the Decree No. 6 of 1995) setting up the Institute. The Institute identifies two professional groups which form its own constituency and thereafter set out to fashion CPE programmes for each of them: legal men - (Legal practitioners, company secretaries, members of the magisterial bench, Chief Registrars, Deputy Chief Registrars and the newly appointed judges of the High Courts); and the law librarians. (Librarians working in the courts, ministries of Justice, private law firms and the universities). It may be of interest to state part of the enabling law which enjoins the Institute to develop CPE programmes: Section 4 The functions of the Institute shall be -

(c)   from time to time to organise, host, arrange and conduct national or international seminars, symposia, conferences, workshop, lectures on any branch of the law or related subject;

(d)   to prepare and publish books, records, reports, journals, as may seem desirable for the dissemination of research findings, seminars, symposia, conferences, findings of workshops and the lectures as aforesaid;

The first group i.e. legal men enjoyed the pride of place when the Institute organised the first programme under the title: Advanced Course in Practice and Procedure in 1981. The annual course continues to attract large number of participants. Among its stated objects is the need to expose the participants to the research methods which is hoped will better prepare them for work on the higher bench. The library was asked to plan lectures, seminars and the like to achieve the particular object.

It was not therefore a surprise when the Institute mounted a seminar in 1984 under the title Effective Law Library Services in Nigeria, June 5 - 7 1984. The seminar was a huge success. It brought together seasoned librarians, legal scholars, legal practitioners, judges and even graduates from other disciplines. It was the first of its type in the country.

HISTORICAL BACKGROUND

Thus the foundation for CPE course for librarians working in special libraries especially law libraries was inaugurated. There were however a number of other factors that impelled the inauguration. Earlier on there was a national seminar on law library from February 24 to March 7 1975 which dealt with entire spectrum of the law library services with emphasis on Nigeria's needs. The focus of the seminar was more on the courts and the ministries in that order of precedence. It was clear at that time that the courts were demonstrably deprived of effective law library services. It was assumed that the ministries of justice were well-serviced, and that the academic law libraries give adequate services. Experience has shown that even in 1975 both the Ministries of Justice and Academic law libraries were not in the position to provide good library service due to a large number of factors which are outside our consideration but however, they had been documented elsewhere (Jegede, 1985).

In 1975 Nigeria was made of a Federal Territory and 12 states. The vast majority of the states were few years old and consequently only the ones with their capitals based in the old regions had anything in the shape of a ministry of justice library. The creation of more states in the country has had its toll on law libraries collection especially in the states judiciaries and the ministries of justice. Collections have been depleted. I was told of how two states planned to divide the library collection of a ministry of justice for example a single set of *Encyclopaedia of Forms and Precedents* will be divided into two - you can imagine the effect of such division.

Since 1975 more academic law libraries have been established. In 1987 the Council of Legal Education set up Board of Studies which in turn set up the Accreditations Panel. The Institute Librarian, the present writer, serves on the Accreditation Panel. She is therefore in a position to assess the weaknesses and strengths of each academic law library. It was obvious as it was in 1975 that the legal scholars were demonstrably deprived of effective law library service even in 1987. For example Noter-up Service - amendment of the laws was not done in many of the academic law libraries and where it is done, it is done in a haphazard manner. The visitation of the Accreditation Panel to the Faculties of Law in Nigerian universities brought a new dimension to the administration of law libraries and also gave breath of life to their law library services(Jegede, 1989).

Another factor that should be mentioned came in form of a request for assistance from the Court of Appeal, Lagos, to train its library staff from all the divisions of the Court: Benin, Enugu, Ibadan, Jos and Kaduna. They were about 28 in number. They were divided into 7 groups and each group spending three weeks in the Institute. The training spread over one year - from April 8, 1985 to June 20, 1986. Many problems arose in the course of implementing a friendly agreement in training staff on the job free of charge. At the end of it, the Institute was flooded with request to train staff from ministries of justice, state judiciaries etc., and such training at the time that suited the requesting organisation and on specific area of library work. It was a tedious experience for the Institute Library staff. It should be mentioned that letters of appreciation were written even if such letters contain another request:

> Dear Sir,
> I am directed to register the appreciation of this Court [of Appeal] for assistance extended to us in organising a course for different categories of the Court's Library staff. As a result, the Court has decided to switch over to Moys' classification scheme for law libraries as obtains in your Institute. Kindly allow the following Library staff of our Court, three days refresher course at the Institute Library beginning 1st September, to enable them master the scheme properly.

The last factor that should be discussed is the fact that librarians working in the libraries are of mixed grill having obtained their qualifications from different institutions. It should be mentioned with all emphasis that none of the library schools in Nigeria offer course(s) on any aspect of law librarianship. A teacher from one of the library schools recently commented on the library schools curricula:

> "Over the years there has been little development in the existing curricula of almost all the library schools, with possible exception of ARCIS. Most courses have remained from inception of these schools to date without revision. And where such revision has been

undertaken it is largely cosmetic. New courses are hardly introduced on the basis of actual need or in response to the demand of the changing environment, but mostly for the sake of variety - to break the long monotonous routine" (Diso, 1996).

One then can imagine a graduate from any of the Nigerian library school being appointed as temporary assistant reference librarian in the judiciary, how much helpful he is going to be to a lawyer in a hurry to check on his citations before the judge sits! It is no surprising then taking all the indicators for the need for continuing professional education programme/activities that the Institute instituted the Course in Law Library Services which was first organised in 1988.

THE COURSE OBJECTIVES

At this period of economic recession it is certain that professionals are not able to attend international courses, conferences, etc. in order to update their professional skills. Librarians working in law libraries are no exception. Furthermore the information industry is dynamic and it becomes imperative for librarians and information workers to up date their knowledge. The Institute however views the course as part of its establishment for serving policy makers at all levels. The Institute also sets up the course as part of its Consultancy Services with the aim of generating fund to supplement whatever the government allocates to it.

The main object of the course is to introduce participants from law libraries to research methods in law library services, expose them to current thoughts in librarianship so as to achieve a measure of professional and self development to enhance better performance on their job. A few subsidiary objects are identified as follows:

(i)   Collection Development in a Law Library: the multi-disciplinary approach.

(ii)   Processing legal materials so that the Bench, the Bar, legal practitioners and legal scholars can fully exploit contents of a law library.

(iii)   The different methods of providing effective readers services:
        compilation of bibliographies
        indexing and abstracting of legal materials
        provision of current awareness services, etc.
        techniques of communication in law libraries.

However, it became necessary to expand the objective in 1991 in view of the federal government political transition programme to civil rule so as to include "Library Services to the National/State legislature. At this juncture it should be pointed out as the course is continuously revised, the title changed from Course in Law Library Services to Course in Special Library Services.

COURSE DESIGNED FOR:

The course was originally designed for professionally qualified librarians in charge of law libraries. After four years there was a shift in the category of prospective participants to include group of professionally qualified librarians and graduate staff in charge of special libraries. Some reasons for the shift are:

(a)   More and more special libraries collect law books example Banks and Banking Institutions have appreciable number of law books in their collection.

(b)   The training of legislative librarians is necessary and a vital contribution of the Institute to the government transition political programme to the civil rule.

(c)   It is the only course as of date that serves as continuing education for librarians working in special libraries.

(d)   Limiting the attendance to librarians working in law libraries per se would be a waste of human and material resources.

COURSE CONTENTS

The course contents is revised during the planning of each course and also at the end. A great period is devoted to law library services, so that the participants could have a deeper understanding of the importance of law library services because of the enormous and complexity of legal literature in a country with a federal structure that advocates the rule of law under a military regime. Emphasis is placed on promptness and accuracy of services; and, also the importance of source of information in giving current awareness service is stressed. The course contents include the following:

Introduction to the Nigerian Legal system

Development of law Libraries

Collection Development

- the need to acquire non-legal books to support research in law

- acquisition procedure and records

Cataloguing and Classification

- theory of cataloguing & classification

- major classification, etc.; modifications, etc.

- need for the establishment of divided catalogue in research libraries

- the consistency in the use of subject headings.

Readers Services

- Level of reference services

- Necessity for Noter-up services

- Collation of laws at the end of each calendar year

- Bibliographies, indexes, reading lists, etc. their purpose and need.

- General compilations versus subject compilations

- Indexing of the superior courts judgements

Current Awareness Services

- Library bulletin with or without annotations

- routing of current journals

Selective dissemination of information

Standards in Law Libraries

- Why standards

- Application of standards:
    * to the collection
    * to the services
    * to the personnel

Users expectation of law library services from

- the bench

- the bar

- the rescarcher

- law teachers

- researchers in institutions & Commissions

- the legal secretaries in commercial companies, etc.

- the media people.

In 1989 when the then Federal Military government announced its political transition to civil rule new courses were added to the content to reflect the anticipated change in the government:

- library services to the legislature

- library services to the corporations and commercial institutions

- new dimension in library education

In recent times much attention has been focused on computerisation of library collection. Therefore in tune with practice of revising the course content to reflect current practices the Institute included a tele-conferencing programme (organised in conjunction with the United States Information Service, Lagos) with Professor G.W. Betty Taylor, the Law Librarian and Director of the Legal Information Center, College of Law, University of Florida, Gainesville, Florida, primarily on *"computerisation of a law library."* The programme was excellent and served as the introduction to the two added topics on:

Application of technology to library operations

Effect of technology on library routines:

Acquisitions, etc.

Services/retrieval, etc.

In addition other varied activities are built into the course contents to broaden the outlook of the participants and help in their self-development. Such activities will be further discussed under the sub-title Course Sessions.

THE FACULTY MEMBERS

The faculty members are carefully chosen, and changes are made every three years - new people brought in and some people dropped. The changes are made in accordance with the cumulative evaluation reports on each faculty member by the participants.

The faculty members are drawn from the following groups of professionals:

Librarians

Teachers in the Library Schools

Very Senior and retired Librarians

The Bench

The Bar

Legal Scholars

Teachers of Law

Research Fellows in Law

Media practitioners

The choice of faculty members is premised on the Institute's aim to involve the library policy makers and administrative bosses of the librarians in the course. It is thought that when some of the judges are involved in running the course, they will

(i)   sponsor their library staff,

(ii)   suggest to the Institute which area of librarianship should be emphasised in the interest of better service, and also

(iii)   give the Institute a feed back on the performance of their staff after attending the programme.

The participation of the legal practitioners as faculty members should be seen as a deliberate effort on the part of the Institute authority to break down the wall of unacceptability and apathy between law libraries and law librarians on one hand and the law library users - legal practitioners etc. Furthermore the Institute built in all its continuing professional education programmes for the Bar and the Bench (such as Advanced Course in Practice and Procedure; Course in Legislative Drafting; and Course in Drafting Commercial Agreements and Banking Documentation) the "*Use of Law Library*." This is in order to assist the lawyers to exploit services of law libraries and to appreciate the contribution of effective law library services to the legal practice both at Bar, on the Bench, and in the Commercial and Banking institutions, etc. The Legal Scholars contribute to the programme by teaching the substantive law subjects for example the Nigerian Legal System. It should be borne in mind that none of the library schools in the country offers any aspect of Law Librarianship, as it has been pointed out earlier. One of the participants commented on the inclusion of substantive law subjects as follows:

> "The novelty of an organised course in Law Library Services for those of us who do not have a law background is that you get exposed to the intricacies of legal jargons and legal practice which will never hitherto attract your attention and psyche to legal education."

And so the Institute has succeeded in making use of people from all parts of legal profession: Bar, Bench, and the academics to participate in running the course.

COURSE SESSIONS

Each course is intensive and time consuming and stretches participants in terms of their time and intellectual output. The day starts at 9.00 am and ends at 5.30 p.m. and thereafter participants proceeded to the Institute Library to work on their assignments. Saturdays - 9.00 am to 2.00 p.m. are devoted to practical in cataloguing, classification and reference services. It is not work all the way. As it has been mentioned before other activities to stimulate the participants to realise higher potentials and for self-development are included in the programme. Such activities referred to as co-course activities include visits to selected places of interest, public lectures, and etc., to which other people are invited.

During the 1991 course a tour of the different departments of the Lagos State House of Assembly was organised. During the tour the participants had the opportunity to watch the proceedings of the House of Assembly while in session. It was the first time that many of the librarians working in the law libraries watched a House of Assembly debating a bill. The 1993 participants visited the Concord press, the publishers of *National Concord*, a daily newspaper, and watched the different stages of the production of the daily newspapers, weekly magazines and other publications. The 1988 course participants visited the Supreme Court Library and paid courtesy call on the Chief Justice of Nigeria. The Director of the Nigerian Law School received them at the Nigerian Law School. The 1995 course set went to see the computerised library operations at the Nigerian Institute of International Affairs Library. It was equally educative to the participants as the proceedings of the Lagos State House of Assembly was to the 1991 set.

As it has been mentioned before, seminars, symposia are built into the course contents in order to stimulate the participants on national current issues and also create an informal atmosphere for them to meet people from different walks of life. The 1993 participants enjoyed the lecture by the doyen of the Nigerian press - Ray Ekpu on "Libraries: The Lifeblood of Newspapers." The 1991 set participated in a tele-conferencing programme at the United States Information Service, Lagos which was referred to earlier under the course content. The Institute held one of its seminar series during the 1995 course. The seminar on "Publications Laws of Nigeria: The Need for a Review." brought together lawyers from the Law Reform Commission, the Federal and Lagos State Ministries of Justice, Librarians, Authors, Publishers, Printers, Booksellers, the Officials from the Copy Right Council, and Academia.

The last few days of each course were full of activities. Participants would submit their scripts for grading. The assignment papers are usually distributed during the first week of each course. The pattern during the past years is to set six questions in all. Two questions each on Acquisition, Cataloguing and Classification; and Readers' Services. Participants are encouraged to attempt all. However it is compulsory to answer three questions and one from each section. The nature of the assignment is of such that all participants would use the library collection - indexes, bibliographies, digests, forms and precedents and even the library public catalogues to answer the questions for example (2b) of reference question is as follows:

"Find the following enactments and instruments stating the exact resources and
full details of laws:
(a)   Companies and Allied Matters Decree
(b)   Civil Service (Re-Organisation) Decree
(c)   The Decree lifting the ban on political activities
(d)   Commencement dates of:
    (i)   The Constitution of the Federal Republic of Nigeria
        (Promulgation) Decrees, 1989
    (ii)   Regulated and other profession (Private Practice Prohibition)
        (Exemption) Order, 1987"

In the last week of the course the appraisal forms are distributed to the participants to fill and return at least the day before the formal end of the course.

APPRAISAL OF THE COURSE BY THE PARTICIPANTS

The participants are encouraged to fill/answer all the questions truthfully. They are free to sign or not sign the forms when completed. The questionnaire is reproduced here below:

COURSE ASSESSMENT QUESTIONNAIRE

Please Tick as Appropriate
1.   Length of Course: a. Too Long   b.   Just Right   c.   Too Short
2.   Content of Course:
    a.   Should be expanded to include (Specify Topics) ....
    b.   Just Right
    c.   Should be shortened/deleted(Specify topics)............
    d.   Any Other ....
3.   Daily Programme: a. Too Tedious   b. Good   c. Manageable   d. Too Slack
4.   Services: *Please tick as appropriate*: Excellent   Very Good   Good   Fair   Poor

    A   General Co-ordination
    B   Library
    C   Secretariat
    D   Catering (lunch)
    E   Guest House (if applicable)
5.   (a)   Faculty (Seminar Leaders)
        (Please give us a general assessment of the choice of Faculty)
    (b)   In order to assist in planning future courses, please indicate any of the Course Leaders who you think should not be invited again, should be assigned a different topic or requested to improve on presentation:
6.   Would you rather make your own arrangements for lunch?
7.   **Literature and Course Materials**
    Were these sufficient:
8.   In what ways can the Institute assist you in building the library collection?
9.   General Assessment and Suggestions (indicate possible areas where you think you may require Institute input in your career).

Then the answers are collated and discussed with the participants during the closing session. Over the years, the participants demanded more sessions on substantive law. Another point that should be mentioned here is that the participants would like a course in Library Management. Such request showed that the participants had gained from the course and even suggest to the Institute to organise another programme for them.

CLOSING CEREMONY FOR THE COURSE

The Institute closes each of its courses with a luncheon. Faculty members are invited to join the participants. It is always a congenial and relaxed atmosphere and participants again are encouraged to appraise their course and stay at the Institute. Usually the participants would choose one of their members as a spokesman. On such occasion Mohammed A. Yaro a participant of the 1991 course gave the valedictory speech:

> "At the beginning of the Programme, many people felt lost or at the very best found the environment very strange especially if they were attending this course for the very first time.
>
> After the first week people started interacting with one another and the environment was no longer strange to most of us because we made a lot of friends. Ideas were exchanged on the professional aspects of the course which, to my mind I think should be the benefit of attending the course. A forum where you meet people from all walks of life and representing at least 17 States of the 21 States with a fair distribution between the South and the North is highly commendable. Bringing such people together to interact and exchange ideas on their various backgrounds and professions is by no means a mean feat for the faculty members of the Institute. In fact the course assessment done this afternoon had said it all.
>
> I must confess, I got so inspired and impressed by the great number and quality of the legal literature in the Institute Library. So much so that I fell in love with the law profession as such I promised myself that I must enrol for a part-time degree programme in Law as soon as it is practicable to get the law background for my future endeavours.
>
> This kind of inspiration is one of the objectives of interacting with a large group like the one we have on this course. I am sure I am not alone in this dream as many other participants must have shared this experience with me."

Then the lists of participants with office and home addresses and the Certificates of attendance are distributed to the participants. Prizes are awarded to the best three participants using the marks obtained from their written assignment.

FOLLOW-UP OF THE PARTICIPANTS

It is appropriate to conclude the essay on how the Institute has been able to carry out a follow-up assessment of the course participants in order to evaluate the course as a continuing professional education programme achieving its objectives of updating the knowledge of the professional librarians, developing new skills and thereby promoting individual competence for better library services.

EVALUATION OF THE COURSE BY THE INSTITUTE

It should be mentioned that the Institute evaluates all its courses to make sure;

> that the courses are of standard quality
>
> meet the expectation of the participants
>
> meet the expectation of the sponsors
>
> that they are in tune with current thoughts and practices in the particular subject or discipline.

The course for the librarians is no exception. Each course is evaluated two times by the participants: (i) at the end of the course as has been described above; (ii) after one year of their attendance of the course by sending questionnaires to them. The questionnaire is reproduced below:

Dear Colleague,

Course in Law Library Services: Follow Up

You will remember you participated in the above named course in 19.................... We hope you enjoyed your stay with us and that the course content has been beneficial to you in discharging your duties.

This simple form is for you to fill and return to us in the enclosed stamped envelope. Your answer is invaluable as it will be taken into consideration in reviewing the course content to make the course relevant to the librarians to achieve effective services.

Yours sincerely,

Course Co-ordinator

1. Which aspect of course content have you found useful in:

 (i) serving the library clientele

 (ii) acquiring library materials

 (iii) processing library materials [Please rate them]

  (a) most useful

  (b) more useful

  (c) useful

2. Would you like to attend the course again if you are sponsored? Yes or No.

3. If no. 2 is `Yes' which other areas of library science would you like to be included in the course content?

4. Would you like more time on practicals or the theories?

5. How would you rate visits to places of interests or co-course content activities? Are they contributory to total self-development of participants or they are mere distractions?

6. Would you recommend the continued running of the course?
If yes, annual or biannual basis?

The response from the former participants has been very encouraging. More than 90% of each set of participants returned the forms filled. The analysis of their answers shows that:

1. 85% of the respondents scored No. 1 (i) as the most useful.

2. 75% of the respondents would not mind to attending the course again.

3. 95% of respondents in no, 2 emphasised the need to include topics on computerisation of library routines and operations.

4. 100% - all respondents emphasised the importance of practical - life situation of library operations.

5. 100% - all respondents like the visits etc. to enrich their knowledge and broaden their outlook.

6. 100% - all the respondents want the continuation of the course. 40% want it to be annual and should include more course on computerisation, etc.

[Total number of participants from 1988 - 1995 is 235 from all parts of the country- see graph.]

It can be seen from above that the participants have found the course useful; but the course should be re-designed in the light of application of computer to library operations and services.

Finally the professional activities of the course co-ordinator present excellent opportunities for her to evaluate the former courses' participants at work in each person's base. Although such activities are outside the control of the Institute, the fact that they present opportunities to undertake a continuous assessment of the library course cannot be denied.

In the first place, the visits of the Accreditation Panel, Board of Studies of the Council of Legal Education to the Faculties of Law of the Nigerian universities provides excellent opportunities to the course co-ordinator, the Institute Librarian who is a member of the Accreditation Panel as mentioned earlier to undertake a follow up of the former courses' participants. She is able to observe and discuss with the Faculty of Law Librarian - invariably a former participant of the Institute Course in Law Library Services - on one to one basis. Such discussion brings out how much the course has assisted the librarian in providing library services to the community. Furthermore during interactions and discussion with the faculty members, the course co-ordinator is able to assess how the law librarian is responding to new challenges and the level of reference services the librarian is able to provide.

Secondly there is an opportunity to assess the former participants from the federal and state judiciaries during appointments with and/or visits to the Chief Justice of Nigeria and the Chief Judges of the States by the Course Co-ordinator in her position as the President of the Nigerian Association of Law Libraries. During one of such visits to the Chief Judge of Benue State, the law librarian of the State High Court gave her a copy of his report on the Institute course to the Chief Judge on his return:

"On the whole my Lord, the course is not only interesting but of immense importance as I can now boast of being in a better position to effectively manage our library. My boast notwithstanding, I have to say that without the necessary tools, I would not be able to put into practice what I have learnt. (Signed A.P. Afikwu)."

It can be seen from the above that the Course in Law Library Services organised and run by the Institute is continuously assessed and its participants are monitored. This is possible because the targeted group is small. And moreover the Institute sees it as a duty in providing continuing professional education programmes for the lawyers as well as the law librarians.

Although there are other CPE programmes for librarians, the particular programme being discussed is the only one of its type for librarians working in law and other special libraries. It can be said that the course has achieved a measure of success: it is nationally accepted, and the Nigerian Library Association recognises it as a CPE programme. In 1991 the participants came from 17 states (Nigeria was made up of 21 states as at that date): Bauchi, Bendel, Benue, Cross River, Gongola, Imo, Kaduna, Kano, Kwara, Lagos, Niger, Plateau, Ogun, Ondo, Oyo, Rivers and Sokoto and from the following libraries:

1. Law Libraries:

    (a) Judiciary Law Libraries:

         Supreme Court Library

         Court of Appeal Libraries

         Federal High Court Libraries

         State High Courts Libraries

    (b) Federal/State Ministries of Justice Libraries

    (c) Private Practitioner's Library

    (d) Faculties of Law/Law School Libraries

2. Legislative Libraries

3. Newspapers/Electronic Media Libraries

4. Corporation and Commercial Institutions Libraries

5. National Library of Nigeria

It should be pointed out that many factors have had adverse effect on running the course:

    (i) the political upheaval in the country after the annulment of June 12 1993
         Presidential election nearly ruined the 1993 course because would-be
         participants were afraid of leaving their homes.

<table>
<tr><td>(ii)</td><td>the location of the Institute - situated in the University of Lagos Campus often militates against attendance at its courses because of students demonstrations, crisis, university closures, etc.</td></tr>
<tr><td>(iii)</td><td>The down turn in Nigerian economy has led to cut in fund allocation to the Institutions, and as a result staff training and development is regarded as a semi-necessary luxury that may be overlooked for as long as possible. And what is more attendance at conferences (local and/or in other countries) for professionals is a luxury to be overlooked permanently!!</td></tr>
</table>

The CPE programmes for the librarians working in special libraries in Nigeria are yet to include topics such as using computer networks for creating, sorting, sharing and searching for information resources and etc. This is not due to the lack of knowledge on the part of the providers of CPE programmes. It is the state of underdevelopment of the country which in turn reflects the inadequacy or even total lack of social services. The current state of libraries and library services are part of the underdevelopment which takes time to overcome.

REFERENCES

Diso, Lukman Ibraheem.   (1996),   *Library and Information Science Education in Nigeria for the Challenges during the next millennium.*   Ibadan: - 27p (typescrpt). Paper delivered during the 34th Nigerian Library Association Conference and the Annual General Meeting 8-9 May, 1996. Paper delivered on Tuesday 7th May, 1996.

Jegede, Oluremi.   (1985),   "Development in law libraries and their services." in *The challenge of the Nigerian Nation an examination of its legal development 1960 - 1985.* Lagos. pp229-252.

Jegede, Oluremi.   (1989),   "Policy options in structural organisation and administration of law libraries." in *New dimensions in Nigerian Law.* Lagos. Pp.285-318.

Nigeria. Laws, statutes, etc. (1990),   *The laws of the Federation of Nigeria in force on the 31st day of January 1990.* Revised edition. Lagos: Federal Ministry of Justice. 25v. Chapter 310: Nigerian Institute of Advanced Legal Studies Act. pp. 11,750-11,775. Amended by Decree No. 6 of 1995.

CONTINUING EDUCATION AND INFORMATION TECHNOLOGY
A STUDY OF CONTENT AND DELIVERABLES

Niels Ole Pors

Trine Schreiber

Abstract   The purpose of the paper is to present the study of continuing educational needs of librarians in relation to an increased use of information and communication technology in libraries. The study has been funded by the European Commissions Libraries Programme. The study consists of, firstly, an analysis of the required information technology skills of librarians and information professionals in libraries with regard to the I&CT applications; secondly, a survey of the present supply of continuing education for librarians in the EU member states; and finally, an analysis of the delivery methods appropriate for imparting the required knowledge and skills. In the paper we first discuss how to analyse the required IT skills and in that connection the required content in continuing educational activities. Next, we discuss how to analyse the required delivery methods in continuing education. Below here, a model, which differentiate a selected number of delivery methods in relation to training needs, is made. Finally, a concluding proposal is given concerning a co-ordinated effort in the future analysis of training needs.

INTRODUCTION

Continuing education is a concept, which can be defined in more than one way. Firstly, it can be defined as those educational activities leading to an academic degree. The intention of being engaged in the activities may be the acquirement of a personal professional development. Secondly, it can be defined as educational activities primarily designed to keep practising librarians and information professionals abreast of their particular domain in the library or information centre, and to provide them with training in new fields. In this last case, its ultimate aim is to improve the library and information services. In the following, we are working with the last definition.

The rapid changes in information technologies within the past two or three decades have altered the activities of information professionals and the functions of libraries. Thus, a subject like continuing education has been of importance for information professionals and for libraries trying to cope with the technological development. However, planning of education and training for the increased use of information technology in libraries is not a simple thing.

The planning implies the knowledge of the needs. We can talk about needs in relation to the knowledge and skills required of librarians to run the information and communication technology (I&CT) applications. We can call it the question about the content of continuing education. We have also to observe the needs in relation to the presentation of the knowledge and skills. This is the question about the delivery methods. One of the reasons why planning of continuing education is not a simple thing, is that both kinds of questions have more than one answer. Further, none of the two questions have a fixed scientific basis from which the answers can be developed.

If we take the first question about the content of continuing education, an answer will involve many different elements. Firstly, the content may depend on the demands from the organisations and the labour market. Secondly, it can also depend on the interests of the staff in relation to a personal development. Thirdly, it depends on the qualifications, which the staff already has. Fourthly, the content may be influenced by the present course supply, for instance the content and the delivery methods in course programmes from present providers of continuing education. However, the investigation of each of these elements involves further problems. Concerning the first element, we have to ask: Who can decide which demands we lay on the labour? Concerning the second: In what degree can the interests of the librarians themselves (result from, for instance, an user investigation) determine the content of the educational activities? And the third: Which of the present qualifications of the staff have relevance in relation to continuing education for developing the I&CT skills? Finally: Which kinds of providers influence the content? Is it providers in the private or public sector? Play the providers in the LIS sector any role in determine the content of continuing education?

If we take the second question about those delivery methods, which could be useful in continuing education, we are in the same situation as above. Again, an answer about the existing needs in relation to the delivery methods involves many different elements. Firstly, the choice of methods depends on which definition of continuing education we use in the present situation. Is the aim of the educational activities an acquirement of a academic degree or an improvement of the library and information services? The first one may in greater extent imply training on campus than the second one. Secondly, an element, which also affects the assessment of the needs and further the choice of methods, is the formulations of personal, local, regional or national interests. However, we still have the question in what degree these formulations (which for instance can result of an user investigation) can determine the choice of methods? Thirdly, the choice may be influenced by different theories of pedagogy about delivery and presentation of knowledge and skills in relation to I&CT, and below here, theories developed with specific regard to continuing education. In addition, some of the theories of pedagogy draw attention to models of communication in their proposals. However, the advice of these theories and models can be very different and we have not any absolute measure by which we can find the best one.

The purpose of this paper is to present the study of continuing educational needs of librarians in relation to the I&CT applications in libraries. The aim of the study was to provide information for planning continuing education for an increased use of I&CT in libraries in the EU member states. It was prepared for the European Commissions Libraries Programme, DG-XIII in Luxembourg, named Prolib/Train 10278.

The study contains an analysis of the required information technology skills of librarians and information professionals in libraries with regard to the I&CT applications; secondly it contains a survey of the present supply of continuing education for librarians in the EU member states; and finally, an analysis of the delivery methods appropriate for imparting the required knowledge and skills. Going through these different parts of the study we will discuss the limitations of the kinds of analyses with regard to the identification of the needs concerning the content and the deliverables in continuing educational activities to run the I&CT applications in libraries. The conclusion is, that in the future it is important to co-ordinate the efforts of trying to identify these needs..

The methods in the study consisted of both a desk-research and a survey. The survey was based on a questionnaire. The purpose of the survey was to get information about the present supply of continuing education in the EU member states. The questionnaire was sent to selected providers of continuing education.

THE ANALYSIS OF THE REQUIRED SKILLS

First, we will discuss how to analyse the required information technology skills (IT skills) to run the IT implementations in libraries. In the study, we took the starting point in an abstract model of the IT development in libraries. Together with a literature study about the development of the profession of librarians with regard to the IT applications in libraries, this model became the basis for the construction of a list of required knowledge and skills in the I&CT field.

The information technological development in libraries in Europe can logically be described by a spectrum from the most advanced I&CT libraries to the libraries based on manual or partly manual routines. We can decide, that it contains four levels and each level requires some information technology skills (IT skills) by the staff.

We have chosen to characterise the highest technological level, which we call level 1, by the implementation of workstations in WAN and LAN and of accessibility to different kinds of information media (multimedia objects, CD-ROM, Marc-records, full-text documents, etc.). The consequences are integrated library systems where workstations have both local and remote access to information and integration of library processes like cataloguing, information retrieval, acquisition, circulation and serials control and download options from external databases. In relation to this, the level below, level 2, will be described as libraries that are automated with catalogue data of own holdings accessible in machine-readable form, but yet not fully integrated. Unlike level 1, the libraries at this level deliver services as information retrieval in a wide range of databases, possibly with remote accessibility, but yet not fully integrated with workstation access to local systems. If we continue, we will arrive down at a level 3, and, again in relation to the level above, we can characterise the libraries as having online access to a national bibliography or a union catalogue, but their stock is not filed in online form. They may have some office automation and/or access to a few CD-ROM but it is far from the rule. Finally, when we arrive at the last level, level 4, it has to be contrary to level 1. Thus, we define it as a level, where the libraries are based on traditional, manual routines.

When it concerns public libraries, a great amount of the libraries in Europe are placed at the level 4.[ii] In contrast, regardless of the kind of libraries we talk about, level 1 contains very few libraries. At this level we have the 'pioneers'. Between these levels we have a great amount of libraries which maybe are on their way up to level 1. This is the abstract model of the IT development.

We acknowledge the limitations of the model. It is not based on a empirical study of the demands of the libraries in the next decade, or on a study of how the development really looks like in the library sector as a whole. In spite of this lack the model seems useful. We can use the two levels, level 1 and 4, to conclude that the required IT skills for libraries at the two levels have to be at a basic/ introductory level respectively at a more advanced level.

The basic level of the required IT skills is in our opinion characterised by six topics, namely 'introduction to automated library system, 'online information retrieval', 'CD-ROM information retrieval', 'CD-ROM as a media itself', 'office automation' and 'word processing'. This assessment is based of how we see the IT development just now.

At the more advanced level it can not be viewed only as a support for the day-to-day operations and processes of the library, but IT must be considered as an integral part of the development of new kind of services. Once again, this assessment builds on how we understand the IT development today. In recent years articles and books, produced by people in the LIS sector, are dealing with the kind of services in the libraries which are going to be developed now or in the future.[iii] On the basis of some of these publications, we have defined five service-dimensions, which seem to contain a central part of the many new functions.

The first dimension is *network integration*. The services of this dimension concentrate on the connection between the local library collection and the large quantities of external information accessible in electronic formats. The required IT skills can be described by the following topics: 'network-integration with access to national bibliography', 'network-integration with access to local systems', 'interlibrary networking (i.e. OPAC)', 'electronic document delivery', 'software for handling fulltext documents', 'database design for local documents' and 'multimedia objects'.

The second dimension is *network navigation*. Central functions of the librarian are interpreting information, repacking and synthesising information, and doing content analysis of a wide range of media. Thus, central topics are 'network-navigation (i.e. Internet)', 'electronic document delivery', 'software for fulltext documents', 'homepagebuildings for libraries', 'client/server architecture' and 'document management'.

The third dimension is *user interfaces*. By this we mean the design of IT-based contact between the library collections and the user. Central topics are 'interactive library presentations', 'homepagebuildings for libraries', 'user education in the use of I&CT tools' and 'design of user manuals'.

The fourth dimension is *networked learning*, defined as learning programmes or activities implemented via Internet-based computer-mediated communication, and using networked information resources. The networked learning is becoming an essential part of education, and this will give the librarians a new professional practice termed networked learner support. The required topics are already mentioned under the dimensions network-integration, -navigation and user interfaces.

The fifth dimension is *scientific communication*. The global connection of universities, of departments of research by networks has led to the rise of electronic conferences, bulletin boards and electronic discussion communities. The role of librarian will be to assist participation in net communities and acquire/deliver the electronic documents of research to the scholar. Relevant topics are 'network-navigation (i.e. Internet)', 'electronic document delivery', 'software for fulltext documents', 'client/server architecture' and 'document management'.

For libraries at level 4, in accordance with the model described above, the topics at the basic/introductory level could be of relevance. For libraries at level 1 the topics under the different dimensions could be of interest. However, according to the definition of level 1, the pioneers have maybe already the skills to handle dimensions like the network-integration and -navigation. In other words, the topics under the dimensions user interfaces, networked learning and scientific communication could be of relevance.

Now, what about the libraries at level 2 and 3? Libraries at these levels are at different positions in the change process. Several of these libraries can be characterised as being newly fully or partly automated or as undergoing an automated process. For libraries at these two levels, an educational effort designed to impart both basic and more advanced knowledge of library systems and online retrieval will be necessary.

For libraries at level 2, there exist training needs with regard to all the five service-dimensions. For libraries at level 3, these dimensions seem to be of importance as well, but for these libraries some of the training needs related to the basic/introductory level can very well be essential too.

As shown, the principal limitation of the analysis with regard to the identification of the needs is, that we do not give attention to all the different kinds at elements involved in defining course content. We need more knowledge about the demands, which organisations lay on the labour concerning the IT applications; we have not any knowledge about the interests of the staff itself in relation to personal IT-development; and we do not know anything about the qualifications the staff already has. We took a short cut by help of a model of the IT-development in the libraries, but here again there was a limitation. For the EU member states as a whole, we do not have a empirical based model of the development but only a logical determined one.

THE PRESENT SUPPLY OF CONTINUING EDUCATION IN EU MEMBER STATES

The literature study has involved an investigation of the programmes and activities of the educational institutions in library and information science in the European countries and an investigation about experiences of continuing education for librarians and information professionals with regard to IT-skills [iv].

The survey looked into the course programmes for the years 1995 and 1996 of providers of continuing education from the LIS sector in the EU member countries with special regard to the topics concerning the I&CT field and the delivery methods they were using.

The literature study of the programmes and educational activities showed, that the situation of continuing education throughout Europe is very diversified. The educational activities are organised in very different manners in the different countries. Schools, departments of universities, private and professional associations are active on the continuing educational scene in a very different extent. The frequency of courses, seminars etc. seem in a number of countries very low. The other literature-study, about experiences of continuing educational activities, gave the impression that some educational arrangements have had its starting point in libraries themselves, and more specific in libraries which according to the model above belong to level 1. Thus, we have to add some of this kind of libraries to the list of active institutions in the continuing educational field. At the same time, the literature-study confirmed a picture of continuing education as an uncoordinated field. It indicated a need of gathering the many spread contributions.

Finally, we shall look at the survey. The questionnaire was sent to 131 different institutions, i.e. mainly library schools, departments of universities, professional associations, academic and national libraries. The response rate was 31%. In addition, we got a letter from other 19%. Thus, about 50% answered. Of the 31%, who answered the questionnaire, it was not all, who worked with continuing education as activities primarily designed to improve the library and information services. Of the total 41 providers, who answered the questionnaire, 32 had continuing education which fulfil our definition of the term. These 32 institutions were distributed as follow: 5 library schools, 14 departments at universities, 8 professional associations, 4 national and academic libraries, 1 international organisation. The response rate was rather low. It could be a indication of the situation of continuing education in Europe today, i.e. a situation with very few. On the other hand, the result could also hide a problem concerning the questionnaire itself. It may have had a form which did not "map" well to the activities of the institutions receiving it.

The majority of the 32 providers, responding our questionnaire and fulfilling our definition of continuing education, gave I&CT-courses high priority as part of their course programme. The topics of the activities were very often spread on both basic and more advanced level. 'Network navigation (i.e. Internet)'was the topic that most of the 32 respondents had in their programme for 1995 and intended to have in their programme for 1996. Topics as 'online information retrieval' and 'CD-ROM information retrieval' were next on the list. Many were planning activities about 'homepagebuilding for libraries'. The majority of the respondents were using 'training on campus' as delivery method. In addition, on third of the group used to some degree 'distance learning' and on third 'on-the-job training'. It was not a specific kind of institution among the 32, who used either distance learning or on-the-job training. Fewer of the professional associations were using on-the-job training compared with distance learning. One more of the library schools and one more of the libraries were using on-the-job training compared with distance learning.

As described above there is reservations concerning the findings of this survey. We can not make any generalisations about the providers of continuing education in the EU member states. The study as a whole gave the impression, that the extent of the present supply of continuing education for librarians and information professionals concerning the I&CT field (fulfilling our definition of continuing education) seems low in relation to the needs. Many of the activities are carried out without co-ordination between institutions. Many of the institutions, who are active in the field, have topics like online information retrieval and network navigation in the programmes, but we do not know anything about whether the activities have a basis in an investigation of the training needs in relation to the demanded improvement of library services. Some of the listed service-dimensions, like networked learning and scientific communication, are fields that do not seem to be represented in particularly extent in the programmes.

Now, what information gave this study to the question about the required content of continuing education concerning the I&CT field? First of all, the sporadically efforts, which characterised the situation of continuing education in EU member countries as a whole, will not be able to fulfil the training needs. Unfortunately, it is not a question of giving proposals about supplementary topics to the already existing supply. We are rather in a situation, where the quantity of providers/programmes and the structure of the educational activities are limited in such degree, that it is the building up of continuing education we have to be occupied with.

THE ANALYSIS OF THE REQUIRED DELIVERABLES

Next, we will discuss how to analyse the required deliverables. In the study, this analysis was based first of all on a literature study. In the survey, described above, we asked in the questionnaire the selected providers about the used deliverables. Unfortunately, the findings cannot be generalised to the continuing educational field in general. Anyway, the question is: In what extent can this material form the basis of the construction of a list of needs with regard to the methods delivering the required knowledge and skills?

In the literature the following delivery methods received particular attention: Short courses, diploma courses, seminars, training on campus, on-the-job training, self-directed learning, distance learning and teleconferencing. One of our findings of the literature study was the underlining of specific needs in relation to the delivery of skills. A general opinion was that the educational efforts had to be, on the one hand, local adjusted, i.e. adjusted to the needs of the local library and of the staff. On the other hand, it had to be more planned and co-ordinated than it had been so far. Another general opinion was, that the efforts had to look out for the existence of both a face-to-face communication and a more direct information transmission during a training session.

Each of the delivery methods, which, as mentioned, got special attention throughout the literature, can be described in relation to fulfil these demands. As said, the articles recommended both a level of a co-ordinated continuing education (with national or for instance European settings) and a level of local development of training (with the individual and the employing authority as responsible). For the link between these levels, the role of distance learning as delivery method was underlined. According to the demand about planned educational effort such method as diploma course was pointed out as important. This method contains of standardisation and control. Concerning the other kind of demand, i.e. face-to-face communication, methods like seminars or teleconferencing was proposed as useful possibilities. To fulfil the general demand of information transmission the methods mentioned could be supplemented by for instance training on campus, on-the-job training and self-directed learning. Training on campus has the advantage, that the teacher can keep a check on the learning situation; on-the-job training support the wish to develop educational activities locally adjusted; finally, self-directed learning involves the personal initiative of the participants in the development of the activities.

In the figure below we have summarised our findings concerning the different methods. All the mentioned methods are arranged according to, for the first, the spectrum from face-to-face communication to one-way information transmission, and, for the second, the spectrum from stand-alone activity locally adjusted to the planned, co-ordinated educational effort. In the figure, self-directed learning is placed nearer the site of the stand-alone and local adjusted activity than on-the-job training, because the first one often involves a lesser degree of planned effort than the last one. Diploma courses are placed nearer the site of the planned effort than training on campus, because the first one often have a higher degree of planned and co-ordinated effort than the last one. Seminars have often a high degree of face-to-face communication compared with the other delivery methods. Distance learning and teleconferencing was enhanced in many articles. Teleconferencing is a kind of distance learning. Distance learning can be carried out with a high degree of one-way information transmission, but it can also involve teleconferencing which implies a degree of computer-mediated face-to-face communication. The term 'distance learning' cover more than one method, so in the figure below, we have placed it twice.

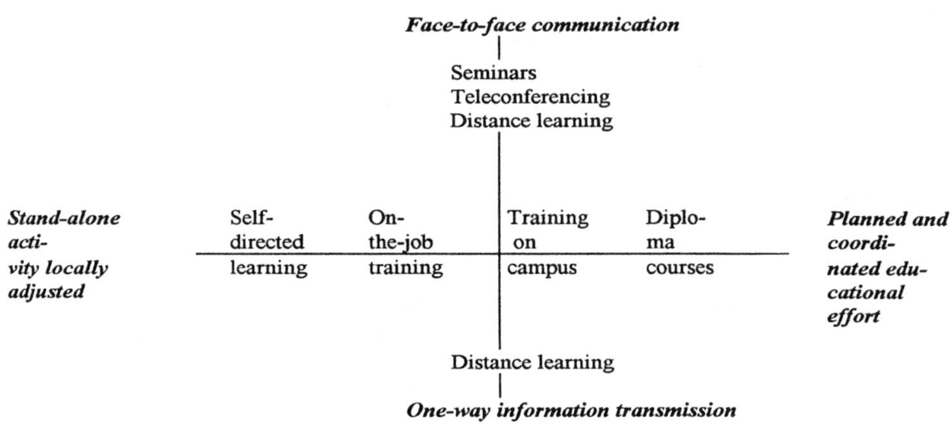

Figure 1. Model for delivery methods meeting needs like stand-alone activity local adjusted, planned and co-ordinated effort, face-to-face communication and one-way information transmission.

What kind of limitations have the analysis? Firstly, such an analysis ought to involve the list of required IT skills. The required knowledge and skills should be included in the decision making of deliverables. However, we actually did that too. Thus, in the study, we took one step more than we have shown above. In the report of the study, we discussed the chosen deliverables on the basis of the chosen content in continuing education and we made conclusions about what deliverables were most appropriate for imparting the listed kind of knowledge and skills. These conclusions are omitted in this paper.[v]

Secondly, it is problem, that it was not a representative selection of interests from the LIS sector, who spoke in the literature. However, the next problem in this connection is, that we have not any criteria for deciding what is a representative selection with regard to continuing education.

Thirdly, the choice of deliverables might have involved theories of pedagogy. There exists a kind of theories, which for the learning situation propose a combination of practical and theoretical experiences. There is the theories of Kolb[vi]; another example is the theory about the Problem-Based Learning[vii]; and also the so called 'active learning' has this element. Surely, we could find more theories which focus at this kind of element, and we could find other theories focusing at other relevant kinds of elements. But, again, we have not any criteria for deciding what is the best one.

CONCLUSION

We have summarised different parts of the study and emphasised limitations of the kind of analyses with regard to the identification of the needs. The investigations, which are necessary for better identification, are extensive. Probably, it is not possible to achieve the necessary knowledge in a single study. Rather, it is important to combine many efforts and to involve many different organisations in the work. In the following we give some proposals, based at the comments above, of what could be central contributions in analysing the needs in the future and who might joint the work.

First of all we need more knowledge about how the IT development actually takes place in libraries, not only at the national level but for instance at the European level. In this connection, it is also important to know more than we do today about both the qualifications, which the librarians at different institutions already have, and the demands, which the environment places at the libraries. On basis of this, further studies of the required knowledge and IT skills to cope with the IT applications in libraries will be possible, and a co-ordinated continuing education for libraries at different IT levels could be planned. Both the professional associations and the educational institutions could contribute to this kind of studies.

For the same purpose, it is necessary to get more information about the providers of LIS continuing education programmes throughout Europe. As shown above, the profile of the group of continuing education providers is still unclear. Therefore, more detailed evidence about the supply is desirable. The future interaction and co-ordination between providers in the area need also further information than we have today. The conducting of such an ongoing study of the profile of the providers could take place at an European level.

Secondly, we need more knowledge about pedagogy theories, which could support for instance a development of distance learning and networked learning with regard to the needs. This could be a task for educational institutions. Networked learning was described as one of the five service-dimensions. In agreement with this, networked learning is and will be an important part of the method 'distance learning' in continuing education. By help of the networked learning, it will be possible to get more institutions or states integrated into continuing education. Still, networked learning needs to be handled, discussed, evaluated and improved. At any time, new courseware arrives at the market and it is necessary to assess the usefulness of these packages in relation to networked learning, and, again, in relation to the needs. It is the interest of both the educational institutions, the professional associations and the providers of continuing education to assess the new courseware in relation to the required skills.

New courseware has also to be discussed and evaluated in relation to the more traditional delivery methods as for instance training on campus or on-the-job training. As shown in the survey, training on campus seemed to dominate among many of the respondents. Studies of the effect of combining training on campus with other delivery methods, for instance distance learning, are of interest both for the providers of continuing education and for the libraries planning their local educational activities. In addition, it could be the task of the providers and the libraries themselves to carry out local studies of the experiences of the activities. And it could be an object of the educational institutions and the professional associations to collect and discuss these experiences.

DIFFERENCES BETWEEN LIBRARIANS AND LIBRARY DIRECTORS IN THEIR PERCEPTION OF CONTINUING PROFESSIONAL EDUCATION

Gabriella Dotan
Beit Berl College
Doar Beit Berl, Israel

Irith Getz
Beit Berl College
Doar Beit Berl, Israel

Abstract: This study compares the preferences of school and public librarians in Israel with the opinions of library directors with regard to topics, modes and incentives conducive to participation in CPE activities.

BACKGROUND – ISRAELI PERSPECTIVES

Public and school libraries

The information revolution, social and economic changes and new theories and practices in public administration have presented new challenges for the library and information world in Israel, as elsewhere. There are 187 public library systems under the auspices of the Ministry of Education, Culture and Sport employing 664 FTE library staff (Ben Naim, 1997). Most of the libraries are small, and many library functions are handled by non-professional or para-professional workers. The majority of librarians are employed part-time (CCIR, 1993).

Public libraries have adopted information technologies since the mid 1980's. Internal library activities (particularly the catalog) were the first to be automated; with the advent of Hebrew language databases, public libraries started to add CD-ROMs to their collections and began to offer information retrieval services to the public. By the end of 1993, 51% of the public library systems had computerized some of their library operations (Ben Naim, 1997). More recently, public libraries have begun to develop media collections, especially videotapes and music CDs.

Elementary school libraries in Israel are usually staffed by teachers with teaching duties, leading to under-use of the library. Professional librarians are generally employed only in the secondary schools, where the libraries are seldom open after school hours (Shoham and Itzhaki, 1989). As a result, many school children use neighborhood libraries to gain access to resources they need for their school assignments, and public librarians are increasingly required to provide school-related reference services and bibliographic instruction. Matters such as co-operation with teachers and school librarians and acquiring an understanding of the new educational methods are of great concern to the public library staff .

The policy of establishing school media centers, which began a decade ago, has engendered closer co-operation between librarians and faculty and has enlarged the collections with non-print resources. The penetration of school management systems, which became widespread in the nineties, facilitated the integration of automated library systems in school libraries as well. By the end of 1994, 31% of the   secondary school libraries had   automated their operations,   and   many   now   offer access to at least the Hebrew databases subsidized by the Ministry of Education for school use (CCIR, 1997).

Basic library education

In Israel there are six library education programs: three academic departments within universities, awarding academic degrees or post-graduate diplomas in information and library studies, and three programs at teachers' colleges, granting professional diplomas ("certified librarian"). Beit Berl College is the largest teachers college in Israel, with a total enrolment of approximately 6000 students. The Department of Library Studies, part of the Division of Special Programs, educates librarians for public and school libraries sector. In addition to library and information studies, the two-year program includes general education courses in various fields of the humanities and social sciences.

As the scope of the library and information work has enlarged, it has become increasingly difficult to accommodate new subjects in the already crowded curriculum, and some topics are now optional. As a result, many novice librarians have only a general awareness and passing knowledge of important professional issues and practices. For example, students in the Department of Library Studies at Beit Berl are required to take four courses in the field of information technologies. Although the department offers several more advanced courses, they are optional. The students have to choose only five courses from a list of 15 electives, including technological topics, library management, children and school librarianship, and various courses in community librarianship.

Although new librarians are generally computer-literate, by the time they assume their first professional post, their expertise in information technologies may already be outdated. And this is a general rule, not only true for computers. Houle's (1981) conclusion, "what a student learns in his first year must be outdated by the time he graduates," now seems more apt than ever.

CONTINUING PROFESSIONAL EDUCATION (CPE) FOR LIBRARIANS

Experienced librarians, as well as novice ones, are required to keep learning in order to fulfil new expectations and work demands. CPE can also provide a sense of personal development, and in many cases, a promise of job promotion (Burgin, 1992; Bryant, 1995).

Employers, too, derive tangible benefits from the CPE of their employees, as it is widely recognized that well-educated staff increase productivity and contribute to the vitality of the organization. To this end, administrators are urged to encourage and support continuing education activities (Heim, 1987; Creth, 1989; Senge, 1991). Nonetheless, library directors do not always agree with their employees with regard to the CPE needs of library staff (White and Paris, 1985; Burgin, 1992).

For the past decade, continuing education for library and information workers has been the subject of a considerable number of surveys and investigations. Several studies dealt with the topics, the types, and the modes of CPE activities, as well as with the incentives (and deterrents) likely to influence participation in CPE. MacDougall et al. (1990) and Lewins et al. (1991) investigated the participation in CPE of professional librarians working in various library sectors throughout the UK, focusing on organizational and managerial perspectives. Their results showed that public librarians preferred short courses organized by their own institutions. Deterrents to attendance highlighted organizational and cost factors. Williams (1992) investigated the educational opportunities made available to rural librarians in the US, and observed that one-day workshops held on-site predominated. Most state agencies specified that lack of replacement staff was the major deterrent to participation in CPE activities.

Burgin (1992) compared the motivations of public librarians to participate in continuing professional workshops with the reasons given by staff from other information sectors. The study affirmed that better service to users is a strong motivator for public librarians, and the author urges library directors to encourage participation in CPE. In another related study, Burgin and Smith (1992) examined the degree to which library directors understood the reasons their subordinates chose to participate in CPE activities, and found significant differences between the directors' perceptions of the motivations and the motivations as reported by librarians.

In the only study of CPE conducted in Israel, Peritz and Shagam (1990) reported the attitudes towards and needs for continuing education among the graduates of the Hebrew University School of Library and Information Science. Since very few graduates (only 13%) were employed in public and school libraries, these findings relate primarily to academic and special librarians.

The present study focuses on CPE activities of public and school librarians in Israel, as expressed by librarians and library directors employed in public and secondary school libraries.

METHODOLOGY

This paper presents data from a study conducted in 1994. The objective of the research was to compare and contrast the opinions of librarians with the opinions of library directors with regard to various CPE components: topics, modes and time of CPE activities, as well as the incentives and benefits for attendance at CPE events. Two questionnaires were designed: one was mailed to the alumni of the first five graduating classes of the Department of Library Studies at Beit Berl College (1989 - 1993); he other was mailed to potential employers of the alumni, namely library directors of public and secondary school libraries in the central region of Israel where Beit Berl College is located.

The questionnaires posed similar though not identical questions regarding CPE. While graduates were asked about their own *preferences*, library directors had to express their opinions regarding the CPE for their employees, thus adding the dimension of *perceived needs*. The respondents indicated their preference for *topics* of CPE and selected the topic which interested them most. Two questions dealt with the preferred types (*modes*) of CPE events, in order to investigate the "how" of continuing education: the first question referred to the format of the event (conference, course, etc.), the second question examined the preferred *structure* (such as field report or in-depth study of one topic). The questionnaires also explored the perceived *motivators* for participation in CPE and elicited factual information from the directors regarding the *support* their organization could actually provide to encourage attendance at CPE activities.

During the first five years, 148 students graduated from the Department of Library Studies, and all were sent questionnaires. One hundred and fifteen (78%) replied. Forty-two percent of the respondents had less than five years of work experience at the time of the survey (thus 58% had some work experience prior to their enrolment in the library studies program at Beit Berl). One hundred and two graduates (89%) indicated that they are employed in a school or public library, and all the ensuing statistics refer to them.

Fifty-six library directors replied to the questionnaire mailed to them (a return rate of 50%): 30 of them administer public libraries, and 26 are in charge of libraries in secondary schools. One third of the public libraries surveyed are small (three to four librarians), and only two libraries employ a large staff (42 and 94 librarians). School libraries employ a very limited staff: only eleven libraries have more than two librarians, and only three school libraries have four positions. Seventy-six percent of the staff employed in school libraries hold librarian diplomas, as opposed to 58% in the public library sector. School libraries are therefore small but highly professional.

Fifty-three percent of the public libraries in the survey employ 46 Beit Berl graduates and six school libraries (23%) employ ten; thus, 56 graduates (55%) are subordinates of the library directors surveyed. Throughout the study, the graduates are occasionally referred to as "librarians" or "employees"; "library directors" are sometimes called "employers."

The contribution of the study will be in gathering basic descriptive information about the CPE *preferences* and *needs* of public and school librarians in Israel, and in using the information in order to develop a program of continuing education at Beit Berl College, designed for public and school library professionals.

ANALYSIS OF PREFERENCES FOR CPE ACTIVITIES

Topics of CPE activities

The questionnaire included a list of thirteen topics of interest, and respondents were asked to indicate their preference by selecting as many as applicable. The results are presented in Table 1.

Table 1 : Distribution of library directors and graduates' preferences for topics for CPE

chi-square	% graduates (N=102)	% library directors (N= 56)	TOPIC OF CPE ACTIVITY
2.18	62.2	74.1	Information retrieval and new library procedures
5.17*	41.8	61.1	New media in libraries (video, cable, courseware)
7.83 **	35.7	59.3	Reading promotion
15.22 ##	25.5	57.4	Curriculum support
3.15	38.8	53.7	Library exhibits
10.64 **	25.5	51.9	Library computer software
1.55	37.8	48.1	Information skills: academic writing

1.27	31.6	40.7	Interpersonal communication
2.59	21.4	33.3	Children's literature
.40	34.7	29.6	Management
.73	30.6	24.1	Bibliotherapy
2.87	13.3	24.1	Storytelling
1.1	12.2	18.5	Special- needs users

* p< . 05;   **p< .005;   ## p< .001

Although both the graduates and the library directors indicated "information retrieval" as their first choice for CPE, followed by "new media," there are several statistically significant differences between the preferences of the groups. The percentage of library directors who indicated these areas as important for CPE was much larger than the percentage of the graduates. Additional significant differences between the groups related to activities in the area of curriculum support (57.4% of the directors vs. 25.5% of the graduates) and library computer software (51.9% vs. 25.5%) -- both new areas of activity in the library, and "reading promotion," deemed important for CPE by 59.3% of the directors, as opposed to 35.7% of the graduates.

It is interesting to note that management appears to be one of the few topics in which there is much more interest among the graduates (first preference of 34.7%) than among library directors (29.6%).

The study also compared the opinions of library directors with those of librarians employed in the same type of library. Table 2 presents the statistically significant differences found in public libraries, and Table 3 introduces the significant differences between the two groups in school libraries.

It appears that directors of public libraries continue to be concerned about the traditional work with children -- reading promotion, children's literature and storytelling -- and would like their staff to be well-versed in these fields; in addition, they indicated the ongoing need for computer abilities.

Table 2 : Comparison of preferences of directors of public libraries and graduates employed in public libraries regarding topics of CPE activities

TOPIC OF CPE ACTIVITY	% directors of public libraries (N= 19)	% graduates employed in public libraries (N= 32)	chi-square	df	p <
Library computer software	53	25	3.99	1	. 05
Reading promotion	79	31.3	10.85	1	. 001
Children's literature	58	12.5	11.83	1	. 001
Storytelling	53	3.1	17.27	1	. 0001

As evident from Table 3, a large percentage of library directors in secondary schools would like their employees to enlarge their knowledge of curriculum-related subjects, as opposed to the relatively few graduates who showed interest in this topic (70.4% vs. 26.8%).

Table 3 : Comparison of preferences of directors of school libraries and graduates employed in school libraries regarding subjects of CPE activities

TOPIC OF CPE ACTIVITY	% directors of school libraries (N=27)	% graduates in school libraries (N=41)	x	f	d p <
Library computer software	56	19.5	9.45		1 005

Curriculum support	70.4	26.8		1	1 .
			2.52		001
New media in libraries	63	37			1 .
			4.55		05

When asked to select <u>one</u> subject of highest preference, the differences between the two groups (all the library directors and all the librarians) became more apparent. Both ranked "information retrieval" first (38% and 35%, respectively); directors ranked "library computer software" second (22%), followed by "reading promotion" (16.4%). Graduates ranked "management" second (11%), and gave third ranking to three topics equally (7.4% each): reading promotion, interpersonal communication, and bibliotherapy. Only 4% of the graduates ranked computer software as their first preference. Not one director ranked management as the first preference. The differences between directors and graduates are statistically significant (p< .01).

Modes of CPE

Previous studies differ greatly in their definition and selection of modes and in their grouping of the modes by various categories (Stone, 1974 ; Ritchie, 1988; Slater, 1991). In the present study, the respondents were asked to indicate their preference for a mode out of four possibilities given, all related to group activities: two educational modes (formal course and one-day seminar) and two interactive modes (conference and short meetings).

Both groups (library directors and graduates) preferred educational modes, as evident from the data in Table 4. This contrasts with the past attendance in CPE activities, as reported by the graduates: 71% participated in one-day seminars, 55% attended conferences, 45.5% took formal courses, and 35% attended short meetings.

Table 4: Distribution of library directors and graduates according to their preference for mode of CPE activity

MODE	Library Directors (N=55)	Graduates (N=94)
Course	40.0	48.9
One-day seminar	32.7	25.5
Conference	18.2	13.8
Short meeting	5.5	10.6
Other modes	3.6	1.1
Total %	100	100

The respondents were also asked to rate their preference for ten different *structures* of formal CPE events, an approach which has not been used in previous studies. The results are presented in table 5.

Table 5: Mean ratings of structures of CPE activities (on a 1-5 scale)

MODES	Library Directors (N=51-54)	Graduates (N=90-95)
Topics related to work requirements	4.60	4.43
Academics as lecturers/instructors	4.37	4.27
In-depth study of one library-related topic	4.25	4.16
Several library-related topics	3.84	3.92
Site-visits to other libraries	3.78	3.83
Workshops	3.71	3.23 **
Informal get-together with peers	3.58	3.33
Field-reports from other libraries	3.36	3.33

| Readings from professional literature | 3.13 | 2.91 |
| General topics | 2.96 | 3.27 |

    * based on t-test   ** p=.034

The results show that the great majority of the graduates gave highest ratings (a mean average of 4.43 on a 5-point scale) to "topics directly related to work requirements." "Lecturers from schools of library and information science" (4.27), and "in-depth study of one subject" (4.16) also received high ratings. Library directors gave highest ratings to the same three options. The only statistically significant difference related to the ratings of workshops.

Additional statistical analyses showed that public library directors rated workshops higher than did the school library directors (4.10 vs. 3.36; t = 5.053; p< .05), and directors as a group rated workshops higher than did the graduates (3.71 as opposed to 3.23; t= -2.14; df=123.88; p< .05). Graduates employed in public libraries rated CPE activities on non-library topics much higher than did the directors of public library (3.62 as opposed to 2.79; t =2.19, df=36.38; p=.037).

Time preference

Both graduates and library directors were asked to rate their preferences for four possible time schedules. Overall, librarians preferred to participate in morning activities (47.9%), but directors indicated their preference for day-long events (46.9%). School librarians were evenly divided (41.5%) between morning and day-long events; the majority of public librarians (62.5%) indicated their preference for morning activities, with one third opting for day-long events.

There are several statistically significant differences between library directors and librarians, when compared by library type: in the public library sector, 14.3% of the directors indicated their preference for evening events, while 100% of the librarians avoided this choice; in the school libraries environment, many directors opted for evening and afternoon activities (27.3% and 31.6% respectively), as opposed to the graduates employed in school libraries (4.9% marked evening activities and 9.8% indicated their preference for afternoon events).

Incentives to participation in CPE activities

The respondents were asked to choose three incentives from a list of ten which, they believe, are most likely to encourage participation in CPE events. The list included six extrinsic factors, which can deter attendance at CPE activities when lacking, and four intrinsic ones, which encourage participation in CPE (based on Herzberg's, 1959 theory). Table 6 presents the findings of the survey.

INCENTIVE	PUBLIC LIBRARIES		SCHOOL LIBRARIES	
	graduates (N=32)	directors (N=19)	graduates (N=41)	directors (N=29)
Intrinsic factors				
Job change/ promotion	53.1	31.6	39.0	31.0
Credit accumulation	43.8	36.8	41.5	3.4 **
Work-related topic	43.8	47.4	61.0	48.3
Reputable organizer	21.9	15.8	26.8	24.1
Extrinsic factors				
Fees paid	40.6	57.9	26.8	48.3 **
Salary increment	40.6	63.2	31.7	44.8
Release from work	28.1	36.8	41.5	31.0
Convenient location	18.8	5.3	17.1	27.6
Convenient time	---	---	---	6.9
Peer influence	---	---	3.4	---

p<.05

While the majority of graduates indicated that factors connected to professional development (intrinsic factors) are most responsible for participation in CPE, library directors were consistent in their perception of the extrinsic factors, specifically those involved with material rewards, as the prime motivators for their staff to attend CPE activities. Directors of school libraries indicated four out of six extrinsic motivators as the prime reasons for their subordinates' participation in continuing education activities (see Table 6): payment of fees by the employer, salary increments as a result of participation in CPE events, convenient location, and convenient time. The difference of opinion between directors and employees regarding the first factor -- payment of fees -- is statistically significant (chi-square 3.42, df=1, p<.05). In general, comparing all the directors of libraries with all the graduates working in both the public and school sectors, 90% of the directors recorded at least one reason from a cluster of three material rewards factors as the chief motivator for CPE attendance, significantly higher than indicated by the employees themselves.

Almost two-thirds of the graduates employed in school libraries said that the topic of the CPE activity, if related to work requirements, serves as a very effective motivator. Credit accumulation towards an academic degree was indicated by 41.5% of the school librarians as significant, but only 3.4% of the school library directors perceived this factor to be of importance to their staff. The difference was found to be statistically significant (chi-square 12.85, df=1, p<.0005).

Overall, 58% of the graduates selected two or three factors relating to professional and personal development as most important motivators, as opposed to only 37% of the directors. In the school library sector the differences are even greater: 95% of the graduates marked at least one of the reasons in this cluster as most important (64.5% indicated two or three factors), as opposed to only 31% of the directors who marked two or three reasons. Both differences are statistically significant (p<.05). The difference between the opinions of public library directors and school library directors regarding the possibility of credit accumulation as a motivator is statistically significant.

Library directors were asked to indicate which benefits their libraries actually grant to librarians participating in CPE events. Three possibilities were given: job promotion/change, payment of registration fees for the CPE activity, and time off from work (see Table 7).

It appears that public libraries offer more benefits than school libraries for participation in continuing education. One third of the public libraries surveyed are in a position to offer job promotions following participation in continuing education activities, four times the rate at the school libraries studied. Although library directors estimated that payment of fees is of major importance in the librarians' decision to attend CPE events, only half of the school libraries offer this benefit to their employees.

Table 7: Benefits given to employees in recognition of participation in CPE activities (%)

BENEFIT	Public libraries (N=30)	School libraries (N=25)	chi-square
Job promotion/change	33.3	7.7	.3054 **
Payment of fees	73.3	53.8	.1815
Time release from work	80.0	80.8	.0516

** $p < .05$

DISCUSSION

This study described the continuing education preferences of Israeli public and school librarians and their CPE needs, as perceived by library directors, and revealed, as well, several differences of opinion between librarians and library directors. The findings can be used to plan and implement CPE programs congruent with the needs of professionals employed in these library environments.

Topics

Both library directors and librarians indicated "information retrieval" and "new media in libraries" as their preferred subjects of interest for CPE. This was not surprising as public and school libraries in Israel are now in the process of expanding their computer and media bases. A large percentage of library directors selected "library software" as an essential subject for CPE, affirming a continuing need in the library, but few of the librarians surveyed opted for this topic. Perhaps, as recent graduates of the library program, the librarians might feel confident in their computer skills. Previous studies show that despite the fact that libraries have been computerized for a long time and various topics in the area of IT have been included in most library and information science courses, this subject has remained popular, perhaps due to the rapid and frequent changes occurring in the field (Stone, 1974; Durrance, 1986; Lewins at al. 1991; Park, 1992). A similar trend occurred in the past, shortly after non-print materials were just introduced in libraries, and librarians expressed a high interest in CPE in the various aspects of the new media (Peritz and Shagam, 1990; Lewins at al. 1991).

Topics connected with library work with children (reading promotion, bibliotherapy, information skills) continue to draw interest, perhaps in reaction to the alternative media offered by the information age, or to better teach users how to cope with the multiplicity of resources. Library directors, particularly in public libraries, expressed a very strong interest in these topics, significantly more than the librarians did. One reason might be that library directors are more aware of the need to maintain and improve the traditional services offered to regular users, whereas new librarians might be predisposed to the new "information" components of library work. School library directors expressed the need for more CPE in areas of contact with the teachers, signalling an awareness of the new trends in school librarianship.

Librarians would like to acquire more management skills through CPE, but library directors do not think their employees need these skills. The same discrepancy between employers and employees was observed also by Slater (1988) and MacDougall et al. (1990). There are very few opportunities for promotion in Israeli libraries, especially school libraries, , which might explain the directors' lack of interest. On the other hand, among the graduates there are "solo librarians" who might feel the need for advanced management skills.

It is noteworthy that library directors expressed a keener interest than did their employees in 11 out of the 13 topics on the list. One can only speculate about the reasons for this. It is possible that library directors want staff with a high level of expertise, who are capable of introducing and implementing changes in the library. In addition, social desirability may have played an important role in the responses of library directors who are anxious to be perceived as innovators and agents of change.

Modes

Although most of the studies, particularly in the UK, have shown that in-service training and internal CPE are most effective, our study has examined only methods of external training, which are more appropriate for Israel's small library systems.

No significant differences were found between the preferences of librarians and the perceived needs as stated by directors. The preferred modes for CPE are formal and highly structured (courses and seminars). Our study did not inquire specifically about short courses, which were found most suitable for CPE activities by Ritchie (1988), Slater (1988, 1991), and Peritz and Shagam (1990), but it is quite possible that some of the respondents who checked "courses" on the questionnaire might have had "short courses" in mind.

The predilection for topics directly related to work requirements confirms previous findings (MacDougall et al. 1990; Williams, 1992). The preference for the in-depth study of one subject, taught by college professors is congruent with the respondents' earlier choice of the course as the preferred method of CPE. The rating of workshops was rather low, in contrast with the results of other previous studies which showed a clear inclination for this format of continuing education (McCrossan, 1988; Williams, 1992). The lack of popularity might be due to the scarcity of workshops being offered in Israel to librarians. General topics and reports from the professional literature were least favored foci of CPE among both librarians and library directors.

Time

Librarians prefer morning CPE events, as opposed to library directors who favor day-long activities. Since librarians are usually released from work for a full day to attend CPE events, it is possible that the directors would like to know that the time off was used to the maximum. School library directors would like their staff to participate in CPE activities in the afternoons or evenings, i.e. after the workday, probably to avoid staff shortages.

Incentives

The results of this study found discrepancies between the motivations of librarians to attend CPE activities and the perceptions of library directors regarding the motivations of their subordinates, confirming the conclusions of Burgin and Smith (1992) and Burgin (1992). The graduates declared that their chief motivators are: (a) topics related to new requirements at work (53%); (b) the prospect of a job change or promotion (44%) and (c) credit accumulation toward an academic degree (41.2%). Conversely, library directors (particularly in school libraries) indicated salary increments and payment of fees as the most important reasons for staff participation in CPE activities. This difference proves that library directors estimate the intrinsic motivation of their employees to be much weaker than the employees themselves indicate. The big difference between directors and librarians in school libraries regarding credit toward an academic degree is noteworthy (3.4% vs. 41.5%), if inexplicable .

Having examined the results of the survey, one is left with a feeling of inconsistency. Library directors in Israel would like their staff to participate in many different CPE programs, but seem to misunderstand the motivations of their employees, attributing them mainly to personal and material considerations. Consequently, the only active support given to CPE attendance is related to material benefits (payment of fees and time off from work). As MacDougall et al. (1990) and Williams (1992) noted, a major problem for most libraries is insufficient staff to cover for those attending CPE events. In this context, time release from work is definitely beneficial to librarians. The majority of library directors in Israel are unable to promote their staff, due to organizational constraints (only one third of the public library directors and less than 10% of the school library directors stated that this is a benefit they can confer). The survey revealed that library directors underestimate the professional interests of the staff as motivators to CPE , and one wonders whether this attitude is not a justification of a situation not under the directors' control.

Summary

The survey revealed agreement between library directors and librarians with regard to the modes of CPE activities. Both groups prefer formal and structured events, particularly the course mode. Concerning the topics of CPE, directors and employees alike are most interested in "information retrieval" and "new media." Several differences of opinion related to the need expressed by directors for more CPE in the areas of "reading promotion," "children's literature" and "library software." School library directors indicated the need for CPE in "curriculum support," as opposed to school librarians who showed little predilection for this subject. Librarians' preferences for incentives conflict with the perceptions of the directors, who significantly underestimate the motivational strength of the professional and job-related interests of their employees.

CONCLUSION

This study was based on the preferences of graduates of the Department of Library Studies at Beit Berl College who are employed in public and school libraries. Additional research is necessary to obtain a more complete picture. Directions for future studies include the CPE preferences and attitudes of all librarians in Israel, the CPE needs of non-professional librarians in Israel (who make up a sizeable proportion of the library staff), and an in-depth exploration of the reasons librarians choose to participate in continuing education activities.

FOOTNOTE

This study was made possible by a grant from the MOFFET Institute. We would like to thank the Research and Evaluation Unit at Beit Berl College, and especially Boaz Shani, for the statistical and methodological assistance.

REFERENCES

Ben Naim, Victor (1997). Interview with G. Dotan, January 5.

Bryant, Sue Lacey (1995). *Personal Professional Development and the Solo Librarian.* London: Library Association.

Burgin, Robert (1992). "Public Librarians and Continuing Education: A Motivational Study." *Public Library Quarterly* 12 (4): 29 - 41.

Burgin, Robert and Duncan Smith (1992). "The Perceptions of Library Directors Regarding Subordinates' Motivations for Participating in Continuing Education Activities." *Journal of Library Administration* 16 (4): 77 - 107.

CCIR [The Center for Cultural Information and Research of the National Council of Arts and Culture] (1993). *Sikum Pe'ilut ha-Sifriyot ha-Tziburiyot be-Israel li-shnat 1991 [Summary of the Activities of Public Libraries in Israel in 1991].* Jerusalem: Ministry of Education and Culture. (in Hebrew).

CCIR [The Center for Cultural Information and Research of the National Council of Arts and Culture] (1997).

Seker Sifriyot Bate Sefer 1993/94 [Survey of School Libraries, 1993/94]. Jerusalem: Ministry of Education and Culture. (in Hebrew) (in publication).

Creth, Sheila (1989). "Staff Development and Continuing Education" in Creth, Sheila and Frederick Duda (eds.), *Personnel Administration in Libraries*, 2nd ed. New York: Neal- Schuman.

Durrance, Joan (1986). "Library Schools and Continuing Professional Education: the De Facto Role and the Factors that Influence It." *Library Trends* 34 (4): 679 - 696.

Heim, Kathleen (1987). "Educating the Future Information Professional." *Library Hi Tech* 5 (2): 33 - 36.

Herzberg, Frederick (1959). *The Motivation to Work.* New York: John Wiley and Sons.

Houle, Cyril (1981) *Continuing Learning in the Professions.* San Francisco, London: Jossey Bass.

Lewins, Helen, Jennifer MacDougall and Gwyneth Tseng (1991). "Public Librarians and Their Continuing Education." *Public Library Journal* 6 (2): 43- 46.

McCrossan, John (1988). "Public Library Administrators' Opinions of Continuing Education Activities." *Public Libraries* 27 (4): 47 - 49.

MacDougall, Jennifer, Helen Lewins and Gwyneth Tseng (1990). *Continuing Education and Training Opportunities in Librarianship.* BL Research Paper 74 (London: BLR&DD).

Park, Betsy and Jane Row (1992). "A Survey of Continuing Education Needs in Tennessee." *Tennessee Librarian* 44 (fall): 39 - 45.

Peritz, Bluma and Tamar Shagam (1990). "Continuing Education in Library and Information Science: a Survey of Needs and Attitudes in Israel." *Education for Information* 8: 23- 31.

Ritchie, S. (1988). *Training and Management Development in Librarianship.* (Library and Information Research Report, 34). London: British Library Research and Development Department.

Senge, Peter (1991). *The Fifth Discipline -- The Art and Practice of the Learning Organization.* New York: Doubleday.

Shoham, Snunit and Moshe Itzhaki (1989). "Sifriyot Bate ha-Sefer ha-Al-Yessodiim bi-Mdinat Israel" [Libraries of Secondary Schools in the State of Israel]. *Yad la-Kore* 24 (1-2): 8-25. (in Hebrew).

Slater, Margaret (1988). *Internal Training and External Short Courses.* (British Library Research Paper, 52). London: British Library Board.

Slater, Margaret (1991). "Training Provision Through Professional Events." *Journal of Information Science* 17: 175 - 184.

Stone, Elizabeth (1974). *Continuing Library Education as Viewed in Relation to Other Continuing Professional Education Movements.* Washington, DC: American Society of Information Scientists.

White , Herbert and Marion Paris (1985). "Employer Preferences and the Library Education Curriculum." *The Library Quarterly* 55 (1): 1-33.

Williams, Mlou (1992). "Survey of Continuing Education Opportunities for Rural Librarians." *Rural Libraries* 12 (1): 19 - 47.

INFORMATION TECHNOLOGY DEVELOPMENTS AS A FACTOR IN DETERMINATION OF CONTINUING EDUCATION NEEDS IN SOME SOUTHERN AFRICAN ACADEMIC LIBRARIES

Lesley M. Moyo
Department of Library and Information Studies
University of Botswana

ABSTRACT This paper is based on a study that was undertaken to survey technological developments and changes in TEN Southern African academic libraries in the following universities: Copperbelt University (Zambia), University of Fort Hare (South Africa), University of Zimbabwe (Zimbabwe), University of Botswana (Botswana), Rhodes University (South Africa), University of Lesotho (Lesotho), University of Port Elizabeth (South Africa), University of Pretoria (South Africa), University of Namibia (Namibia), and North-West University(South Africa).

The study was a survey of the major **IT** (information technology) developments and changes that have occurred in the said academic libraries, over the last decade (1986 - 1996) and the corresponding changes in human resources requirements, and how these are being met. Specific areas surveyed include developments and activities associated with:

- Automation of library main systems (i.e. acquisitions, cataloguing, serials control, circulation, OPAC)

- CD-ROM search stations and networking of CD-ROM

- Access to On-line bibliographic and other networks (e.g. SABINET and UNINET of RSA)

- Access to Internet

As a result of the need for advanced technical skills in "High-tech" libraries, there is now a convergence of the roles of computer professionals and information professionals. The study surveyed how this trend has affected the said libraries: Whether they are now employing computer specialists or re-training existing staff to acquire the needed technical skills.

The study investigated the specific areas that existing library staff have been trained in, and the competencies that have been sought-after when recruiting staff over the last decade, to determine the extent to which **IT** has been an influential factor.

The study further surveyed the common approaches to training that have been adopted by these libraries, and also, the level of integration of continuing education and training in library strategic plans, particularly those concerning automation.

The following are the major findings of the study:

- 70% of the surveyed libraries are fully automated, while 30% are in the process of automating.

- There is an increasing demand for IT competencies resulting from automation of library systems.

- Lack of IT skills is ranked second among the major problems identified as hampering library automation in the said libraries. The first is lack of funding. Others are problems of keeping up with the technology drive, lack of vendor support, inadequacy of IT infrastructures to support required technologies, technical hardware and software problems, and lack of innovation among staff.

- The current demand for IT competencies in not likely to change significantly in the next 5 years because the extent to which the libraries can keep up with the technology drive is very limited.

- Surveyed libraries prefer to train/re-train information professionals to acquire the needed IT skills/competencies, rather than appoint trained computer professionals possessing the required IT skills.

- There is inadequate strategic planning for human resources for IT.

Major recommendations include:

- Need for exploring both continuing education and training programs in meeting human resources requirements for IT development in academic libraries.

- Need for personnel reconfiguration and re-definition of basic professional competencies for the " IT driven world"

- Need for training multi-skilled personnel who can offer a "one-stop-service" to the client

- Need for Library and information science schools, particularly those training within/for Africa to respond by introducing more IT content in curricula, particularly content relevant to the identified areas of need.

- Need for strategic planning with IT focus, and development of IT policies within libraries

- Need to 'cultivate' management skills orientated to IT within the libraries.

1. INTRODUCTION

As we approach the twenty first century, there is a lot of speculation on what lies ahead for the information profession. However, all indicators seem to point to the fact that the next century will see an IT-driven world, with the Internet and related technology becoming universal phenomena. Selim (1993) suggests that as we approach the twenty first century, information will increasingly control our world. This will create a high demand for IT tools and skilled personnel. In this scenario, Information will be a key resource, suggesting that the information profession will very much still be in business in the next century.

However, for the information professionals to continue to meet the demands of an "information controlled world" they will need to have the skills and competencies that will enable them to interact with the technology that facilitates information retrieval, storage, manipulation, and dissemination. Moreover, the number of stakeholders concerned with information acquisition, storage, dissemination and manipulation will increase with development of information technology. Information professionals will no longer have a monopoly over the world of information. How they fare among the various stakeholders, will be largely determined by the significance of the role they play, which in turn will be influenced by the possession of skills and competencies relevant to IT-based information provision. Maliconico (1992) notes that technological developments have increased the visibility of libraries through increased technical capabilities. These enhanced capabilities of automated library systems and increased demand for access to them have resulted in need for technical specialists and operations staff. This, in turn, has led to the rapid convergence of the roles of libraries and computer centres. This can be viewed with alarm if we assume that libraries and computer centres will become competitors, or with optimism if we assume that they will form symbiotic partnerships. According to Kocojowa and Pindlowa (1996) our concern in this situation should not be to try and save "libraries" but rather to concern ourselves with providing a better education for information professionals so that they may competently perform well in the new information environment dominated by use of IT. Even with the Internet, the need for information professionals will NOT end. For example, there is the issue of quality control, and user direction to information sources on the Internet. These are areas where information professionals can take the lead.

IT in Southern Africa

The Southern African region in general, South Africa in particular has a relatively superior IT infrastructure to elsewhere in Africa. This has enabled countries in the region to make some progress in terms of adoption and utilisation of IT for development. One area which has met with some success is the academic arena.

In Southern Africa, IT adoption and utilisation has been spearheaded, to a large extent, by academic institutions particularly universities. For instance in South Africa, networks , such as UNINET exist which link all universities and Technikons. There is also SABINET (South African Bibliographic Information Network) which not only services South Africa but most of the other countries in the region.

This study surveyed some of the university libraries in the region to determine the extent to which IT adoption and utilisation has altered, and is likely to continue altering skills and competencies required for information work over the recent years and into the next century. The study further attempted to determine what implications this has for continuing education for the information profession.

2. OBJECTIVES OF STUDY

The specific objectives of the study were to
- Survey the IT developments in Southern African University libraries over the last decade
- Determine the changes in human resources requirements brought about by adoption and utilisation of IT
- Identify methods used by libraries in meeting the human resources requirements for IT
- Establish the skills and competencies likely to be required for management of information in the next five years in the university libraries of Southern Africa
- Based on the findings of the study, make recommendations with regard to the above areas.

3. METHODOLOGY

The study was conducted using the survey method. A questionnaire was developed incorporating questions on information technology and human resources.

A random sample of 17 university libraries was taken, and questionnaires distributed. 10 questionnaires were received back and analysed. The libraries that responded were:

Copperbelt University Library (Zambia), University of Fort Hare Library (South Africa), University of Zimbabwe Library, University of Botswana Library, Rhodes University Library, Thomas Mofolo Library (University of Lesotho), University of Port Elizabeth Library(South Africa),Academic Information Service (University of Pretoria, South Africa), University of Namibia Library, and North-West University Library (South Africa).

4. MAJOR FINDINGS OF THE STUDY

Overview of technological developments in participating libraries

Out of the ten libraries that responded, one can deduce that most university libraries in Southern Africa are fully or partially automated. 7 out of 10 libraries were fully automated. 3 out of 10 were in the process of automating(see Table 1 for details)

Table 1: Overview of Automation level in Southern African University Libraries

Area of Automation	Number of Libraries	Percentage of Respondents
Full Automation of library		

Main system	7	70
Partial Automation of library main system	3	30
CD-ROM Search Stations	9	90
Networking of CD-ROM	3	30
Online Databases	7	70
Direct Internet Access	6	60
Dial-Up/ Part-time Internet Access	1	10

Automation of main systems

Out of the 7 libraries that were fully automated, 3 used the URICA system, 3 used the ERUDITE system and 1 used the STYLIS system. Of the 3 libraries that were in the process of automating, 1 was using the TINLIB system, one the STYLIS system, the other had not yet selected a suitable system.

The automation in most of the libraries had taken place over the last decade(i.e. between 1986 and the present).Only one library had started automation as early as 1980. In most cases the automation was done "piecemeal", over an average period of 3 years.

CD-ROM search stations

Out of the 10 libraries that responded, 9 have CD-ROM search stations, and out of the 9, 3 have networked their CD-ROMs. The number of search stations ranged from 2 to 250; and the number of databases in use ranged from 7 to 23.

The CD-ROM service constituted the single major information resource for teaching, research and scholarship in 6 of the libraries.

On-line Databases

On-line databases are available in 7 of the 10 libraries as follows: SABINET in 7 libraries, DIALOG in 3, OCLC in 1, FIRST SEARCH in 1, FT profile in 1, and INCH in 1.

Use of these on-line databases was largely restricted to academic staff and graduate students.

Internet access

6 of the 10 libraries had direct access to the Internet. One had dial-up part-time access and 3 had none. So far the Internet facility is not widely used among the libraries having access. In most of the libraries, it was mainly for e-mail queries, and distribution of acquisition lists etc. and interlibrary loan requests. Only 2 libraries were using the Internet substantially as an information retrieval tool, and in those libraries it has been incorporated as part of information literacy skills training. In some libraries, Internet was just used for accessing other databases such as SABINET and NEXUS

Problems of library automation in Southern Africa as articulated by the respondents

- Lack of funds
- Absence of relevant skills(systems people)
- Problems of keeping up with the technology drive
- Lack of innovation among staff
- Technical and hardware/software problems
- Lack of vendor support

- Inadequate staff
- Inadequate IT infrastructure within the institution (to facilitate connectivity)

To determine the major/most common problems, the problems were ranked based on the frequency of occurrence within the entire group of libraries (see table 2). Lack of IT skills is ranked second on the list of problems militating against automation efforts in the libraries. Lack of funding is ranked as first and still remains the main problem, which also underlies the other problems. For instance, absence of funds would also restrict the extent to which libraries are able to secure suitably qualified staff, or implement continuing education programs for their staff.

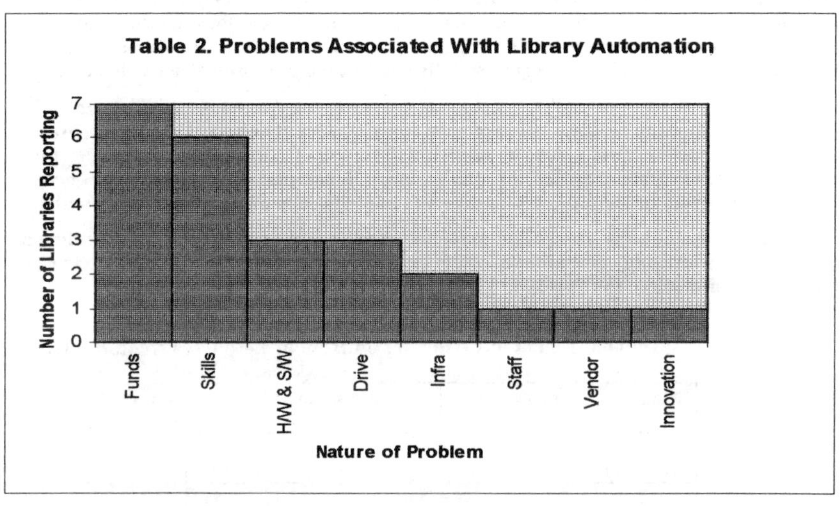

<u>**KEY**</u>

Funds = Lack of funding
Skills = absence of relevant skills
H/W & S/W = Hardware and Software problems
Drive = Problems of keeping up with technology drive
Infra = Lack of IT infrastructure
Vendor = Lack of vendor support
Staff = Inadequate staff
Innovation = Lack of innovation

5. HUMAN RESOURCES FOR *IT* ADOPTION IN SOUTHERN AFRICAN UNIVERSITY LIBRARIES

Changes in human resources brought about by automation

According to Zhou (1996) acquisition of computer-related skills has become one of the most visible concerns of the information profession. The growth in demand for computer-related skills has generated a training need that has to be addressed urgently.

Although the training needs of academic libraries in the US, as revealed by Zhou, may not be the same as those in Southern Africa because of the differences in levels of automation, nevertheless, the need exists on a smaller scale and has to be met if proliferation of IT as an academic resource is to be encouraged. Burrows(1995) states that:

" The proliferation of electronic resources poses a formidable challenge to
academic libraries, by adding a whole new layer of complexity to the

process of teaching, learning, research and scholarship. Libraries must be able to offer effective access to these electronic resources, as well as guidance in the use of them"

One of the critical issues in achieving this is the recognition and fulfilment of human resources needs. This study revealed that management in all the surveyed libraries recognise the need to now have IT literate staff, or at least staff with capacity for IT training as the key to success in automating in the first instance, and offering effective access to electronic resources in the second. Apart from appointment of systems specialists at the high level, Southern Africa academic libraries have also engaged in activities to raise the general IT literacy among all levels of staff, particularly professional grades. 2 libraries have trained ALL their staff, and 3 others are in the process of doing so. Further more 2 of the libraries stated that there is a movement towards the need for multi-skilled staff as far as possible who will be able to provide a "one-stop-service" to the user. In this respect, the libraries are keen to develop a diversity of skills within each professional staff member.

Continuous change and technological advances in the information industry have affected librarians in such a way that not only are new competencies required, but also new ways of thinking and behaving, hence there is a need to re-visit definitions of minimum competencies for information professionals. Apart from the need for staff to have IT competencies, there is also need for them to have a broader vision of the service, and diversity of skills, as well as be innovative and dedicated.

All libraries surveyed reported moderate to very significant impact of IT on human resources requirements, in terms of alteration of skills and competencies required for library service since the beginning of automation in the respective libraries.(see Table 2.)

Table 3. Extent of IT Impact on Human Resources Requirements

Magnitude of impact	Number of Libraries	Percentage
Minimal	1	10
Moderate	3	30
Significant	5	50
Very significant	1	10
TOTAL	**10**	**100**

Specific skills/competencies sought-after by the surveyed libraries with respect to library automation

- Basic IT skills
- High IT aptitude
- Systems knowledge for installation and maintenance/administration of systems(including hardware and software support, general trouble-shooting etc.)
- HTML coding and design
- Networking skills
- Database management
- Internet navigation skills
- Design and maintenance of Internet home pages
- Digitization
- Skills for on-line database searching
- Proficiency in use of a wide range of application software (such as spreadsheets, graphics, word-processing, database management, Desk top publishing etc..)

Other skills/qualities other than IT, but related to automation:

- management skills
- dedication
- innovation
- adaptability

The management skills referred to above are those required for an IT environment because, as Cartee (1990) suggests, technological innovations mean an unstable, unpredictable environment which demands a new kind of manager. This manager should be able to develop and align IT strategies.

Computer professionals or Information professionals?

Although there is now a convergence of the roles of computer professionals and information professionals resulting from a need for advanced IT skills to support automation in libraries, in the surveyed libraries there is still a clear preference to appoint information professionals and if necessary re-train them to acquire IT skills. 8 out of the 10 libraries preferred to train/re-train their information professionals to appointing computer professionals as systems specialists. 2 out of the 10 libraries suggested using both avenues depending on circumstances and cost-effectiveness of approach taken. The Copperbelt University Library argued that IT is only a tool necessary for performance of information service and that staff who are already committed to professional achievement should be trained/re-trained, rather than employing people who have IT skill but devoid of information training. In recognition of the rapidly converging roles of information professionals and computer professionals, the Copperbelt University Library's strategic goals include the merger of the library and computer centre to make one academic information resource centre.

Current staffing for IT

Only one of the libraries has employed 2 systems staff who have no librarianship training (B.Sc. computer science with mathematics). 5 of the libraries have systems people with librarianship training. 3 of the libraries have positions for systems people but they are currently vacant. One of the libraries is depending on the central IT department of the university for its automation, and this has been cited a major drawback (inferior treatment of the library by the IT department)

So far most of the libraries have already been re-training staff to meet IT skills requirements to a great or less extent. As said earlier 2 libraries have re-trained ALL their staff. 3 libraries have each trained one staff as systems librarian, occupying position of systems analyst. One library is in the process of training 2 systems librarians. 3 of the libraries have not had any major training.

Implications for continuing education of information professionals

Fayose (1996) states that:
> "Library and information work is a very dynamic profession. No graduate
> of the profession can hope to achieve utmost competence with only the
> knowledge acquired from the library school. Continuing education should
> be a part of the information profession. It should not only afford the
> professionals the opportunities of advancement or transfer from one level of
> professional competence to another, it should provide opportunities for
> keeping abreast of new technologies, the information explosion and other
> changing aspects of the profession....the whole concept of continuing
> education is to effect change"

Havard-Williams (1993) suggests not only continuing education but also training. He argues that continuing education is only *one* aspect of the concerns which one must have in any discipline these days when ideas, opportunities, threats and challenges are arising so quickly, but there is *also* the concern for the development of the individual, hence the need for "professional development".

For more than 25 years, schools of library and information studies (LIS)have been adapting their curricula and teaching activities to the new information technologies. All of those changes, however, have occurred within the broad umbrella of library and information studies. The new networked electronic environment creates a major shift in the paradigm of the information transfer process. Documents, information and knowledge are being atomised and become ubiquitous on the network. Storing and retrieving networked electronic information, although theoretically a similar process in nature to cataloguing, indexing, and reference, also require additional knowledge, skills and competencies. Technological knowledge and know-how have now become a pre-requisite to networked electronic information related activities (Deschatelets(1996).

Suitable continuing education and training programs should be designed/implemented and staff should be encouraged to attain skills that enable them keep abreast of new technologies as far as possible. The education and training staff undergo should be relevant to the identified areas of need. These education and training needs are identified as the gap between what library and information science schools are currently offering i.e. terms of curricula, and what the market needs are, in terms of skills and competencies. Continuous curricula adaptation is a major issue if the needs have to be continuously met.

The information profession needs to respond to this challenge by re-visiting the curricula of library/information schools to ensure that incorporation of IT skills into the curricula.

Most of the library schools in Africa are still grappling with incorporation of IT into the curricula. The major problem being that there is inadequate IT facilities within most training schools to support permeation of IT into the entire curricula.

For synchronisation of the African market needs for IT skills/competencies and LIS training programs to take place, the matter of curriculum would need to be addressed. Right now it falls out of the scope of this paper.

Meeting continuing education needs in Southern African University Libraries

All libraries surveyed do have education and training programs. However, within those programs, there largely seems to be no specific strategic plans for human resources to meet IT skills requirements in particular. However, 3 libraries decide on areas of training/specialisation that staff members pursue, to ensure that they are in line with library plans. 7 libraries let staff choose their areas of specialisation (but with recommendation and encouragement from library). There is need to align these programs to the library strategic plans.

In the study, most of the questions on projections of human resources needs were not responded to by most libraries. De-Bruin's(1995) comments about the inadequacy of strategic human resources planning in South Africa, seems to be also true for the rest of the surveyed countries. From the responses, it would seem as though there are programs for developing professional staff, but the actual projection of needs for the short term to medium term future is lacking.

Most common approach to continuing professional education among the surveyed libraries is formal continuing education programs with IT content. i.e. staff going for post-graduate diplomas, masters or doctoral studies. Also identified to a lesser extent is employment of short courses zeroing in on specific technologies or products, particularly the trendy technologies.

Because of the rate of development of technology, there is a greater gap between the time of a technological innovation and the time that innovation would be incorporated into the LIS curricula. This factor, compounded with the length of the turn around time of professionals undergoing training makes it impossible for the trendy technologies to be effectively taught through formal continuing education programs. The use of short courses, attachments, commercially run courses would be more effective as they are generally more in touch with the latest innovations.

6. CONCLUSIONS

The following conclusions were drawn:
- There is a high occurrence rate of automation in Southern African university libraries. 70% of the surveyed libraries are fully automated, while 30% are in the process of automating.
- There is an increasing demand for IT competencies resulting from automation of library systems.

- Lack if IT skills is ranked second among the major problems identified as hampering library automation in the said libraries. The first if lack of funds. Others are problems of keeping up with the technology drive, lack of vendor support, inadequacy of IT infrastructures to support required technologies, technological hardware and software problems, and lack of innovation among staff.
- The current demand for IT competencies in not likely to change significantly in the next 5 years because the extent to which the libraries can keep up with the technology drive is very limited.
- Surveyed libraries prefer to train/re-train information professionals to acquire the needed IT skills/competencies, rather than appoint trained computer professionals possessing the required IT skills.
- There is inadequate strategic planning for human resources for IT. Although strategic plans exist in the surveyed libraries, projections for human resources in terms of anticipated IT development don't seem to receive specific attention.
- Libraries endeavour to keep up with the technology drive in as far as IT infrastructures can permit, and finance is available, but in fact the latter is always a limiting factor.

7. RECOMMENDATIONS

- Need for exploring both continuing education and training programs in meeting human resources requirements for IT development in academic libraries.
- Need for personnel reconfiguration and re-definition of basic professional competencies for the " IT driven world".
- Need for training multi-skilled personnel who can offer a "one-stop-service" to the client.
- Need for Library and information science schools, particularly those training within/for Africa to respond by introducing more IT content in curricula, particularly content relevant to the identified areas of need.
- Need for strategic planning with IT focus and development of IT policies within libraries.
- Need to 'cultivate' management skills orientated to IT within the libraries.
- IT skills on their own would not suffice without supplying management skills orientated to IT, dedication, innovation, adaptability, and other information profession ethos. Therefore, need for continued sound training in librarianship and information science principles - will give professionals a superior role in an environment where the number of stakeholders concerned with information acquisition, storage, dissemination, and manipulation will increase with development of IT.
- Need for development of strategic technology policy within overall library policies because IT will require a focused attention as it is going to increasingly play a central role in information work in the 21st century and beyond. Kelley(1992) recommends an approach to technology policy development that includes a review of the technology base, continuing education, improved training practices, and innovative organisational design.
- Need for co-operation among libraries in solving some of the common IT related problems in common areas. e.g. 3 of the surveyed libraries in the same region use the same library systems software. It is possible for one library to source technical assistance from another, or to exchange ideas on IT experiences for mutual benefit. It is also possible to engage in co-operative education and training programs, or to collectively have an input into the design of curricula in library and information science schools.

REFERENCES

Alemna, Anaba A.(1990) "Information technology and information training in West Africa." *Information Development* 6(4) pp 204-208.

Burrows, Toby (1995) "Education for the Internet in an academic library: the Scholars Centre at the University of Western Australia." *Education for Information* 13(1995) pp 229-242.

Cartee, L. D. (1990) "Is Library automation producing a new kind of manager?" *Journal of Library Administration* 13(2) pp 117-138.

Cowan, B. and B. Userwood (1992) "Automation routes past and present: the training implications." *Journal of Librarianship and Information Science* 24(3) pp 139-148.

De-Bruin, H. (1995) "Strategic human resources planning for library and information services in South Africa." *Mousain* 13(1/2) pp 59-80.

Deschatelets, Gilles (1996) "Opening LIS curricula to the new worlds of electronic and strategic information." *Paper presented at the FID/ET Seminar on Working and Learning in a Networked Environment,* Graz, Austria. 21-22 October.

Dyer, H., Fossey, D. and McKee, K.(1993) "The impact of automated library systems on job design and staffing structures." *Program* 27(1) pp. 1-16.

Fayose, P.O. (1996) "Challenges of education for library and information work in Nigeria in the 21st century." *Paper presented at the FID/ET Seminar on Working and Learning in a Networked Environment,* Graz, Austria. 21-22 October.

Havard-Williams, P. (1993) "Professional development from an African point of view." *Librarian Career Development* 1(3) pp. 9-15.

Kelley, Kimberly Banks(1992) "Managing technology in libraries." *Library Administration and Management* 6(3) pp 141-145.

Kocojowa, M. and Pindlowa, W. (1996) "The role of the Internet in the education of librarians and information scientists." *Paper presented at the FID/ET Seminar on Working and Learning in a Networked Environment,* Graz, Austria. 21-22 October.

Maliconico, S. M. (1992) "What librarians need to know to survive in an age of technology." *Journal of Education for Library and Information Science.* 33(3) pp 226-240.

Ochogwu, M. G.(1993) "Producing basic competencies in information science education in Nigeria", *Education for Information* 11(1993) pp 147-154.

Selim, E. O. (1993) "Co-operative training of the African IT workforce for a computer driven world", In: *Information Technology Utilisation in Developing Countries.* S. O. Ojo, D. J. Parsons, J. A. Ige (eds) CISNA, Gaborone, 1993. pp21-31.

Zhou, Y(1996) "Analysis of trends in demand for computer related skills for academic librarians from 1974 to 1994". *College and research Libraries* 57(3(pp 259-272.

MEASURING CONTINUING EDUCATION NEEDS AND RESULTS COMPETENCY FOR THE TWENTY-FIRST CENTURY

Blanche Woolls
University of Pittsburgh
Pittsburgh, Pennsylvania
USA

Abstract: In this workshop, the value of continuing education programs is examined. Topics covered include defining action research, how to collect data, and how to analyze and report findings. Specific examples and forms are given.

Programs may be of great value to participants, but when administrators are unaware of the value, the less obvious programs such as continuing education become vulnerable. To demonstrate the value of a continuing education program means convincing both administrators and participants of the worth so it can be offered and will be attended. If a cost factor emerges to be offset by charging participants, selling the program relies on "evidence" of its worth. Action research provides information about need and value for continuing education programs.

A first step is to understand the meaning of action research, to define the difference between action research and "real research," and to look at the characteristics and methodology of action research. A second step is to choose evaluation for continuing education events and the third is to analyze the results of the evaluation. We will begin with a definition of action research.

DEFINING ACTION RESEARCH

Paraphrasing from Isaac and Michael (1995), one may define action research as developing new skills or approaches and solving problems with direct application to the management of programs. Our definition describes the process as informal, of looking at continuing education programs and what we are doing at the present time, not what we have done in the past. Different from a longer study that would set up an elaborate plan with random assignment to groups, action research does not require the care taken with formal research which is conducted to test and create theories for the profession.

Action research "intends to draw together research and practice" rather than viewing these as separate activities (Carson, 1990), whenever research studies acknowledging action research can be cited here, the methodology or results will be interwoven into the discussion. Academicians conduct real research for a variety of reasons, one of which is to remain in the academic community. Action research is practitioner led and helps librarians become more aware of what is happening in their libraries and beyond. Action research focuses on practice and provides individuals with findings to relate to administrators when change should be implemented.

One researcher divides action research into technical and practical saying that technical action research answers "What can I do and how best can I do it?" while practical action research questions "What should I do and why ought I to do it?" (Tripp, 1990). Whether identified as technical or practical, this research helps us analyze our activities for their worth. McNiff (1988) suggests that an action research study would answer four questions:

- What is your concern?
- Why are you concerned?
- What do you think you could do about it?
- What kind of evidence could you collect to help you make a judgement about what is happening?

The premise of action research, to study the present, results in improvements to be made in the future, a process bringing about a direction for change for practitioners. Action research comes from the social sciences as a test of social phenomena and can be easily related to practice in libraries. This explains the practitioner-as-researcher assumption and why action research is useful. It

- helps solve problems
- encourages effective change
- revitalizes
- empowers decision-makers
- identifies effective methods
- promotes ownership of effective practices
- verifies which methods work
- widens the range of professional skills.
- provides a connection between methods and results
- helps apply research findings to individual situations
- helps individuals becomes change agents (Secondary Perspectives, 1989)

We become better managers by assessing what we see, what we are doing, why, how, and how well we are doing it, and if we need to be doing it. How do we determine if we should offer a program, how do we decide if what we did was successful, and, finally, to whom do we take our findings so we can continue offering our programs.

A review of current action research practice indicates that action research has been adopted by teachers in school classrooms working with university professors so that research results help improve classroom teaching. For this group, action research, "informal" type, is carried on in classrooms as a practical way to identify effective ways to improve teaching and learning (Secondary Perspectives, 1989). Issues of interest are studied to improve practice rather than to publish in research journals.

Educators make some common assumptions concerning action research. These assumptions include democracy, external, change, reflection/action, and the practitioner-as-researcher (van Manen, 1990). The first, democracy assumption, implies a partnership so that real change can occur in situations rather than being dictated in a top-down environment. External knowledge operates when researchers encourage practitioners to conduct research. Because action research encourages reflection and its relation to action, practical concepts are enmeshed in the theoretical. These assumptions fit continuing education for librarians when action originates with those planning rather than administrators insisting on cost accountability. Certainly the author of this paper is a researcher encouraging practitioners and hoping the proposed methods will be undertaken by practitioners.

Frost, in reporting his efforts to have teachers "integrate systematic inquiry into their everyday professional practice" (1995, p. 307), stated "that rigor and validity depend on researchers being prepared to situate themselves in terms of the framework of professional imperatives within which they work and in terms of the values which underpin their professional action" (1995, p. 308). Continuing education providers in libraries believe in their service and work within a framework that anticipates analysis of outcomes. A major problem arises when this program lacks support. After completing his study of teachers and an in-service, curriculum development project, Frost found that success would be more likely when a program:

- provides support and sanction for open-ended enquiry;
- provides a framework of guidance for individuals' professional action planning;
- provides a confidential forum for critical analysis;
- challenges participants' assumptions about issues; and
- facilitates career development through the award of further professional qualifications.

These criteria can be applied as measures to test success of continuing education programs. Which criteria are the most important to any planned event?

In planning action research, two assumptions are made, the first remains an imperative. One should not add appreciably to the burden on participants in the action research process. Lack of time and competing priorities will lessen the desire to conduct action research even when it is a "professional imperative." The second is not to overlook the ability to use your action research evaluation as a public relations opportunity to sell your programs and to let potential participants understand that such programs are being build upon their needs rather than a whim.

With a need for open-ended inquiry, a framework for planning, and critical analysis, data collection devices proposed for continuing education include base line data, journals, peer assessment from the education area as well as generic techniques from the world of research. A second step is apply action research to continuing education events using correct evaluation techniques.

HOW TO COLLECT DATA

The information you are seeking determines the choice of what and how to measure. Suggested measures test both the need for continuing education as well as outcomes of programs. While these focus on continuing education within an institution, the research models apply to programs for agencies and professional associations as well.

No single set of research techniques or procedures can be applied to action research for continuing education. The same procedures measure needs for continuing education as well as the results of any continuing education experience. An array of possibilities will tell you what you need to know. You must determine if, from a practical standpoint, you can afford to collect the information you need. When the amount of time and money required for gathering the information exceed the potential use to be made of it, one should consider an alternative. Do not be deceived by what might appear to be lack of cost to having staff collect data. Staff who are conducting research are not doing their regular task and that has a cost factor.

Baseline data: Evaluating continuing education experiences for librarians begins with an evaluation of needs and an assessment of current level of skills or competencies of the proposed participants. Gathering the baseline data comes from many sources, but one of the most common would be a self-completed questionnaire.

Journals: A study of teachers' experiences in university-based teacher preparation programs as compared to their day-to-day experiences in actual classrooms was based on the premise that "best practice means encouraging reflection about teaching" (Herndon and Fausko, 1994). Teachers collaborated in teams of at least two, and data was collected from both mentors as well as apprentice teachers with journals being maintained by both. One university faculty member was assigned to read the journals and identify themes from them.

While keeping a journal may seem less applicable to information professionals, writing down occurrences in more detail helps retrace steps when analyzing what was done well, what might need improvement, and reflective thinking. Often the exigencies of a situation make refection difficult, and journals bridge this gap between doing and thinking about doing.

Peer Assessment: A two and a half year leadership study was designed as "a conscious effort not only to develop a theory of professional development for school leaders generally but in so doing, to provide professional development which would help these 12 school leaders to understand and then change their situation." A process of "shadowing" meant observing each other's practices and providing both descriptions of observed behaviors and quality evaluative feedback (Robertson, 1995). They also conducted reflective interviews and collaborated in planning and implementing action plans. Modifications were made after they learned from their actions moving them "systematically and collaboratively" towards their desired outcome.

The opportunity to shadow a colleague in the continuing education process promotes direct sharing and learning. Because we often work with colleagues in the provision of staff development, asking for qualitative evaluative feedback builds expertise in both provider and assistant.

Self-assessment: Self-assessment belongs with both participant and provider. Potential participants in continuing education experiences may or may not be good judges of their competencies, but questions may indicate their attitudes toward the proposed program. If no formal self-assessment is provided, their registration for a continuing education program signals a perception of need.

Providers need to recognize their strengths and weaknesses so they include individuals on their team who correct any deficiencies. The strongest program happens when weaknesses are acknowledged and overcome.

Interview: (Isaac and Michael, 1995, pp. 145-148) Some information is more reliably obtained through direct interviews of staff or participants. While this seems a more effective method to collect data than a mailed questionnaire, it is much more expensive. When choosing this method, the information comes more directly and the evaluator sees that the person understands exactly what is needed. However, interviews are more time consuming and may be biased by the interviewer. In addition, data gathered may be more difficult to reduce to quantitative measures.

When developing interview schedules, choose a series of questions to ask. These are asked of everyone who is surveyed, so it is important to make sure you have exactly what you want to know BEFORE you begin. Once the interview is over, it becomes difficult to get additional information from that person.

Interview questions may have evaluation scales (as shown in the questionnaire discussion) or specific answers, or the interviewee asks open ended questions. Structured interviews are easier to code than those which have open ended questions. Those to be interviewed may be all persons in a potential user group or a randomly chosen sample of intended users.

Questions in the interview each lead to the evaluation objective, should be clear, and should not bias the response. Checks for honesty of the interviewee may be appropriate; however, this is very difficult to build into your interview schedule.

The example below determines user satisfaction with a continuing education event. A structured question limits patron response and responses can be tabulated quickly. Open-ended responses allow the patron to specify exactly what they considered the most effective, but it makes counting the replies difficult to place into discrete categories.

Example of an open-ended question

What did you like best about the workshop?

Example of a structured question:

What did you like best about the workshop?
_____ demonstrations
_____ hands on practice
_____ small group discussion
_____ exhibits of equipment

Questionnaire: Questionnaires are often used to determine which prospective continuing education experiences participants wish to attend. You may wish to select your survey respondents at random when the potential group numbers under 50, in which case all users should be queried. For more than 50, a random sample is drawn. Statistics books tell how to draw the sample properly. When properly chosen, a sample group can reliably predict how the total population would have responded.

Questionnaires are a frequently used method to collect data because they **seem** to be easy to prepare, distribute, and tabulate. They appeal to the respondent who will have time to prepare and, if desired, revise answers. Further, they allow you to reach more people, are more economical than interviews, and can be "administered" with little loss of time. One problem occurs when the response rate is low. Another problem occurs when you aren't sure the respondents understood your questions. This would make their answer invalid, but you might not know this.

If it is decided that the needed information can be most efficiently secured though a questionnaire, the following suggestions should help prepare the questions.

- Whenever possible, borrow from an existing questionnaire that seems to be asking what you need to know.

- Create your questions from the perspective of your respondent.

- Make the questions clear and as free from different interpretations as possible. Test your questionnaire by having another person(s) similar to your respondents answer it and then tell you how they interpreted the answers (pilot test) to all questions to determine if they are clear. If not, reword.

- Provide careful directions to the respondent as to how to complete the form and report the answers.

- Define all technical terms.

- Whenever possible, offer a set of suggested answers:

1. My knowledge of the Internet is ___ none at all ___ basic ___ can search easily ___ have used for reference ___ can teach the Internet to staff and patrons.

2. My knowledge of the WWW is ___ none at all ___ basic ___ can search easily ___ have used for reference ___ can teach the WWW to staff and patrons

3. I prefer workshops ___ one hour only, ___ a half-day, ___ a full-day, ___ shorter times over one or more days

- Suggested answers may use rating scales. Examples of rating scales include the following:

Frequency			
Yes	Sometimes yes	Sometimes no	No
Regularly	Occasionally	Rarely	Never
Daily	Weekly	Monthly	Yearly
Always Frequently		Occasionally	Seldom Never
Value or Approval			
Superior	Above average	Average Below Average	Poor/Missing
Very important	Somewhat important	Of little importance	Of no importance
Entirely satisfactory	Usually Satisfactory	Unsatisfactory/ needs improvement	
Much improvement needed		Little improvement needed	
Degree of Acceptance			
Unacceptable	Questionable	Accept with reservations	Accept in general	Endorse
Like_____:_____:_____:_____:_____:Dislike (semantic differential)				
Strongly agree	Agree	No opinion	Disagree	Strongly disagree
Degree of implementation				
Adequate	Inadequate			
Excellent	Good	Average	Fair	Poor
Super cool	Cool	So-So Gross	Super gross	

    Many persons must mail or in another way distribute their questionnaire. If so, a cover letter explaining the purpose of the questionnaire must accompany the actual questionnaire. It should be neat, brief, and should explain the purpose of the study.

Random samples: For researchers who are conducting studies and need responses of a smaller number to generalize to a total population, the choosing of a random sample is done with great care. If you wish to report that your research is as accurate as possible, pick a random sample carefully. As stated earlier, statistics books describe the process in detail. Everyone in your community must have an equal chance of being chosen. Some "purists" would make you use a random number table for selection. Because action research is to help make management decisions and not to find a cure for a fatal disease, samples are less critical, but should be chosen with as much care as possible. If major change is anticipated and a good reading of the community is needed, you may consider a stratified random sample which means you have representation from all strata in the community. It is up to you to define the layers of that strata, e.g., if you consider technology training you would need answers from small, rural libraries, branches in metropolitan cities, local school districts among others.

Counting Items and Tally Sheets: To answer the question, "How many?" counts are made to assess quantity such as timing tasks. Most of us are familiar with counting items. The most often used method of collecting data, careful collection and well planned analysis ensures an understand what the data represents. Most often, results are reported as simple percentages or translated into an average (the mean), sometimes the median (the middle number in a series from the highest number to the lowest), and, at other times, the mode (the number appearing most often in a series of numbers.) To count items, use tally sheets to record observations, success/failure analysis, relevance, before/after studies, and an inflation/deflation index.

A tally sheet is a simple way to collect data. It is developed using the categories you are measuring and the measures should be as concise and clear as possible. This sample tally sheet collects data on the length of time used to answer reference questions. Collecting information concerning the reasons for delays provides the evidence needed to provide a reference workshop for staff.

```
Time Measure
In-House Reference Date:
______ less than 5 minutes    Reasons for delays:
______ 5-15 minutes
______ 15-30 minutes
______ 30-60 minutes
        > 60 minutes
```

Providing continuing education events has a cost attached to planning as well as presenting that is often neglected in assessing expenses. Calculating what staff make per hour and the number of hours spent BEFORE the continuing education event provides a more realistic picture of salary costs than assuming that because staff receive a salary, their time planning costs nothing. However, this is not true because when staff are planning, they are not doing another task that needs to be completed. Planning time and salary can be measured. Use a tally sheet to track the time spent planning.

PLANNING TALLY SHEET
time expended in minutes

Activity:	# staff	# min	Total min.
Planning program	10	30	300
Phoning speakers	1	60	60
Arranging meals	1	15	15

Collecting data over a long period of time may not be possible because of an unacceptable loss of administrative or clerical time. In this case, you may wish to collect your data on randomly selected days. This method requires greater care in the collection process so that the numbers are more exact or can be substantiated estimates. When you have your data collected, you will then tabulate what you have found. These, depending upon the situation will be compiled and reported.

Trained Observation: One form of "trained" observation occurs when an expert is asked to judge staff or activities in order to determine what types of continuing education events are most needed. While this also belongs in the section on qualitative assessment, the process for conducting the test is one of personal observation. If you wish to make personal observations of work habits or work flow to determine the degree of need for continuing education rather than query the potential participants, information may be gathered from tally sheets that would indicate a particular information session was needed by staff. Observations are made by someone who observes an activity or service and places what is observed on a predetermined checklist. The rater should be capable of judging when a criteria has been met or a specific activity has taken place. For the tally sheet below, you would need to describe the difference between "stern" and "distracted." If you wished to analyze the degree of customer service given at the charge-out desk, a tally sheet similar to the one which follows could be adapted to meet your needs.

Customer Service Analysis				
At 10 minute intervals on __________________ (date), the following was observed:				
Task	Warm	Smiling	Distracted	Stern
Ignored				
Greeting patrons	______	______ ______		______
______				
Checking materials	______	______ ______	______	______
Responding to questions				

Observation becomes very expensive in terms of time. In some cases, only a professional can properly observe an activity. In other instances, a volunteer or support person may receive a short orientation and be quite capable of handling an observational checklist.

Best Professional Judgment: This evaluation is conducted by individuals who are using their learning and experience to judge some element of the program. Choose carefully those persons to ask to judge for their level of experience and expertise affects the outcome of the evaluation. The evaluator must step aside from personal experience to view a situation, remaining helpful rather than recommending a replication of another setting because of its familiarity.

Persons who are asked to make their best professional judgment about a situation are usually "trained" in the way the scoring sheet works to ensure that the observers are treating the observation in the same way. Uses of best professional judgment come when you organize a focus group and when you apply consensus/discrepancy measures. Measures of consensus and discrepancy help action researchers understand the degree of differences between perceptions of participants, trainers, and administrators. Before a perception can be changed, we must understand what that perception includes.

Rubrics: Developed to "test," those who create rubrics must determine exactly what they are going to test before beginning to write the rubric. Wording the rubric sets not only data to gather but it establishes levels of acceptance for achievement.

Rubrics transform expectations into degrees of success. This type of measure has been used for some time in those areas where it is very difficult to apply a numerical assessment when no exact right or wrong answer exists.

We can create one of three types of rubrics, either conventional, checklists, or combinations. With the conventional rubric, categories are stated and defined with degrees of acceptance. For each category, both evaluator and one being evaluated know the level of what is unacceptable, what is acceptable, and what shows greater quality. While these measures are clear, concise, and consistent, they may require quite detailed descriptions of performance measures and may be better at defining success than helping point out how to improve flaws. A series of negative responses to questions will indicate training needs.

Degree of competency with the Internet	Yes	No
Knows how to use e-mail		
Knows how to ftp		
Knows how to access a listserv and respond to queries		
Knows how to search on the Internet		
Knows how to locate a Web site		
Knows how to search on the WWW		
Knows how to create a home page		

Checklists are made of what is expected in great detail. The criteria for low to high achievement, the steps to check to see if the appropriate pattern was applied to creating the product, and the "items" needed for a quality performance are determined.

Customer Service
(for reference personnel)
Name

SKILL	always	usually	sometimes	seld
Is polite to library users				
Conducts reference interviews				
Provides prompt help				
Answers information questions accurately				
Provides sufficient information to satisfy most patrons				

Comments:

The last rubric is a combination of the conventional rubric and the checklist. This permits review of progress from many categories such as on both a one-to-five scale and either/or (acceptable/unacceptable) measures. Because it does allow more rating, it is often preferred.

Reference Department
Name   high to low

REFERENCE SERVICES	5	4	3	2	1	0
Conducts reference interview						
Provides prompt answers to questions						
Provides enough information to satisfy patron						
ACQUISITION						
Analyzes and writes critical reviews of potential purchases						

In building a rubric, you need to consider two parts, the categories of evaluation and the levels of quality. Consideration of the categories is the first element of the rubric. These are placed on the side of a grid and may have a wide variety of considerations. The levels of quality show what can be attained for each category with a score of 0 to 5 or not acceptable to highest quality.

<u>**Success/Failure Analysis**</u>: Participants will often become apathetic if they fail to learn or improve, or if the level of instruction which they do receive is below their expectations. A study of

participant achievement might seem difficult but will pay dividends in the end. Attempt to establish an "acceptable" failure rate and analyze when why any program might fall below what should be tolerated. An analysis is then made to determine what can be done to improve the offering. Reasons for failure (or success) should be compiled using **tally sheets** which may be taken by hand (observation, interview, or questionnaire) or the information may be gathered by electronic or other appropriate measure. If failure is due to a need for a longer training session, this signals rethinking a continuing education event.

Failure Chart	Success Chart
E-Mail expertise	Storytelling Programs
Date:	Week of:
____can read	____told stories
____can send message	____read aloud
____can forward, FTP	____showed film
____can create listserv	____puppet show
	____more than one

If the aim of the children's co-ordinator is to have more storytelling sessions with multiple types of sharing of literature and children's librarians are successful at only one or two types of presentation, this "success" measure may signal a need for continuing education.

Relevance: Any continuing education event must be evaluated for its usefulness to the participants. Such a measurement will help plan future events. An interview or questionnaire at the close of the session allows the participant to indicate which items have been useful and which have not. The user, given a list of the "events" of the workshop could rate each item.

<table>
<tr><td colspan="2" align="center">Relevance</td></tr>
<tr><td colspan="2">The following is a list of recent sessions for staff development. Would you please rate your experience on the following scale:

0 - not relevant
1 - of peripheral value
2 - of some value
3 - good
4 - exactly what was needed</td></tr>
<tr><td colspan="2">__________references on the Internet
__________references on the World Wide Web
__________creating a home page
__________etc.</td></tr>
</table>

Before/After Measures: Almost any technique may be used in a measure-treatment-remeasure analysis. Various treatments can be tested in this manner to determine the most effective treatment for the improvement of a specific activity. Care should be taken that the measure selected will really measure the effect of the treatment to see if it does make a difference.

Which treatment produces the greatest increase in attendance at a continuing education event?

Before/After Measures			
Attendance before	Treatment	Attendance after	% increase (+) or % decrease (-)
______	CE credit given	______	______
______	extensive PR	______	______
______	paid registration	______	______
	etc.		

Inflation/Deflation Index: An analysis over time of inflation/deflation rates for budgetary categories such as materials or transportation, cost of paper to duplicate materials or food for continuing education events or even total cost of programs, can be very useful in preparing dollar budgets. In order to calculate the inflation/deflation rates, a constant unit of measure must be selected and measured against the cost of the same unit the previous year or against the base year. For some items, general information may be available. For others, you will need to keep your own records.

Inflation/Deflation Index				

Total Cost of Programs Offered		Years		

	97	98	99	100
A. Total cost of programs				
B. Total dollars expended				
C. average cost for programs*				
Inflation (+)/Deflation(-) percentage over previous year				

*to calculate cost per item, divide B (total dollars) by A (total number of programs offered.)

Focus Groups: A focus group includes individuals who gather or are gathered to react to a situation. This may mean analyzing a problem, developing an evaluation process, or determining the needs before developing a strategic long-range plan for continuing education.

The use of focus groups to problem solve increased steadily in the 1990s. Guided by a facilitator and focused on a pre-determined situation, small numbers of people are asked to express their opinions. While often used as a market research method, it works equally well with continuing education program evaluation. Although focus groups represent a smaller number of staff, they provide more in-depth information than can be collected on a survey form. The personal attention paid during each session elicits better information because it goes beyond pleased staff who respond positively thinking that is what the administrator wishes to hear or staff who believe their last bad experience remains their regular treatment.

Focus groups help establish strategic long range plans and design evaluation. Their opinions concerning training to be offered, the quality of current training, and ideas for improving staff performance are most helpful.

Choosing persons for a focus group means selecting a representative sample. This group may be the leadership as represented by department chairpersons or representatives from the entire staff. When selecting members for the group, pick from any specialized part of the population as well for no group will react as well to being told they need to learn something as they will to having one of their own make that decision.

As with any group process, numbers are limited from seven to twelve. Fewer than seven may not provide sufficient numbers to discuss; more than twelve means it becomes much more difficult to have every member participate. If a larger number of participants is needed, they should be divided into groups of no more than twelve and each group takes responsibility for reporting back to the larger group at the end of the discussion.

Focus groups need to know the purpose of the group before they agree to participate. They should be reminded of their task when you begin the session.

Choose questions you wish to have answered. On survey forms, multiple choice and yes/no answers are appropriate. For a focus group, all questions should be open-ended to encourage in-depth answers and to allow for discussion after each answer has been given.

As with any good survey, pilot test questions to ascertain that they reflect what you wish to know and that they are clear as stated. When you are uncertain about your skills as a focus group facilitator, you will build your confidence if you use the pre-test as a practice focus group session.

Focus groups sit in a circle. Any other room set-up prohibits the give and take exchange essential for the session. Make sure participants are comfortable and relaxed. Encourage each member of the group to speak. It may take some practice to learn how to get those who talk all the time to "wait their turn" and to get those who are reluctant to speak to do so.

Ask someone to volunteer to take notes if you do not have a recorder with you. In some situations, groups will decide their most important points and these are then placed on overhead film or flip charts. Take care not to let the process of "editing" the information on a flip chart become the most important part.

Thank those who participate for their efforts. They will have given their time and consultation to the betterment of the library's services and programs.

Consensus/Discrepancy Analysis: The testing of perceived consensus/discrepancy can be very valuable in evaluating library services. "Perceptions" often count as much as "reality." For example, a staff's perceptions of their need for training and the administration's willingness to support such endeavors may vary.

Multiple perceptions by two or more individuals are recorded on a questionnaire/interview/observation checklist and charted for comparison. The checklist which follows has a scale from -1 to 5.

Circle box	-1	0	1	2	3	4	5
This workshop met needs	not very well	don't know	almost as good as	as good as	better than	much better than	best we've had
Information should be given to	don't know	no staff	clerical only	some professio nals	most professio nals	all professio nals	all staff
In general information was	out of date	periphera l value	some ideas	several ideas	many practical ideas	will impleme nt some ideas	many ideas
This should be repeated	never	don't know	occasiona lly	every six months	once a month	every two weeks	once a week

Recording and comparing from the checklist data shows the following. Choosing which interval measure is considered "agreement" and "disagreement" is your choice. If the interval is too wide, you may be identifying the wrong perception. That is, your group may be disagreeing when you have rated them in agreement. **You need to set your interval _before_ you distribute your checklist.** Otherwise, you might bias the responses by your own interpretation of what you think you have found. Remember that you are trying to get information, even though the results may be painful at first reading. You can make improvements only when you address problems, especially if a discrepancy can be clarified with facts some of which you gather using other action research techniques.

Item #	Staff Rating	Staff Mean	Administrator Mean	Administrator Rating
1	3 5 1	3.0	2.6	5 4 1 1 5 1 1
2	1 1 1	1.0	4.9	5 5 5 4 5 5 5
3	5 5 5	5.0	2.4	1 2 5 1 2 5 1

In this case, on item #1, the three workshop leaders gave ratings of 3, 5, and 1 for an average of 3. The staff gave it ratings of 5, 4, 1, 1, 5, 1, 1, for an average of 2.6. If ratings are less than .5 difference, they indicate agreement, and in this instance, the staff and users agreed on items #1.

The opposite situation prevails on Item #2 where the leaders' mean was at 1.0 and the participants rated it at 4.9. When ratings are more than .5 difference, this would indicate disagreement. The evaluator should try to determine why ratings are so different. It may be the respondent did not understand the question, is a nonuser, or is belligerent.

Once you have collected your data, the choice becomes how to analyze the data and report the results.

HOW TO ANALYZE AND REPORT FINDINGS

The method(s) chosen to analyze the data depend(s) upon the question to be answered. The easiest, most understood method of analyzing data is to use measures of central tendency.

<u>Measures of Central Tendency: Mean, Median, Mode</u>: The mean is perhaps the easiest statistic to calculate and to explain, for we recognize it from elementary school, e.g., the average score on the spelling test. We might add the amounts charged for 25 workshops offered throughout the region, then divide the total by 25 to learn the average fee for workshops.

	Median		**Mode**
30.00	30		30, 30, 30, 30
25.00	30		28
23.00	30		25, 25, 25, 25, 25---most frequent score
22.00	30		24
30.00	28		23
30.00	25		22
30.00	25		20, 20
25.00	25		19, 19
25.00	25		18, 18
25.00	25		15, 15
25.00	24		12
10.00	23		10, 10, 10
10.00	22	mid point	
15.00	20	in ranked	
15.00	20	list	
10.00	19		
12.00	19		
18.00	18		
18.00	18		
19.00	15		
19.00	15		
20.00	12	528 divided by 25 = $21.12	
24.00	10		
28.00	10		
20.00	10		
528.00			

When we report this, we say the average workshop fee was $21.12, the median cost was between $20 and 22 (which means the median and the average are about the same the most often charged fee was $25. This means most workshops cost below $20. Also, $25 as the mode raises your average and your median. We could also say that the range of fees for workshops from $10 to 30 meaning the least expensive workshop was only $10 and the most expensive was $30. The next measure would be the number in attendance and the cost of the workshop. If you have 50 people attending a workshop, the amount charged is the net revenue.

	Fee	**Number attending**	**Net revenue**
	$30.00	30	
$900			
	25.00	30	750

23.00	30	690
10.00	90	900

If a workshop needs $900 to cover costs of speaker, food, handouts, the cost to be assessed would depend upon the number that could be accommodated. While this seems simplistic, having a reminder that costs must be recovered should be helpful.

The first priority of librarians in any type of library is to assist users in their quest for information especially when they cannot locate appropriate materials on their own. On our earlier tally sheet, librarians make note of reasons for user lack of success. This can be used to design staff development programs to improve services.

If you were to interview staff and patrons concerning their success in finding materials you could design an interview schedule and then create a consensus/discrepancy scale to see if staff and patrons agreed upon the success. The scale is from 1=low to 5=high.

TASK	1	2	3	4	5

TASK	1	2	3	4	5
Conducted reference interview					
Provided prompt information					
Was satisfied with information					
Information was accurate					

Your tabulations here would be a simple could of the number who found everything they needed or not or were well satisfied or were not. You would then need to collapse the open-ended responses into categories. Earlier we did a consensus discrepancy scale and used these same figures as our example. If these figures were the findings for this scale, we would know:

Item #	Staff Rating	Staff Mean	Administrator Mean	Administrator Rating
1	3 5 1	3.0	2.6	5 4 1 1 5 1 1
2	1 1 1	1.0	4.9	5 5 5 4 5 5 5
3	5 5 5	5.0	2.4	1 2 5 1 2 5 1

For this measure, a deviation of .5 is considered agreement or disagreement from the other scores on that scale measure. For our example above, Item One = agreement; Item Two = disagreement; Item Three = disagreement.

Because we have chosen our level of rating before we administered the questionnaire, on item #1, the three workshop leaders gave ratings of 3, 5, and 1 for an average of 3. The staff gave it ratings of 5, 4, 1, 1, 5, 1, 1, for an average of 2.6. If ratings are less than .5 difference, they indicate agreement, and in this instance, the staff and users agreed on items #1. Administrators and staff agreed that reference interviews were conducted. However, the staff did not agree with administrators that information was provided in a timely fashion.

Questionnaires/Interviews: You might interview librarians in the immediate area or send them a questionnaire to determine their need for technology training. If so, responses to the questions in our suggested questionnaire could be simply counted to determine the numbers needing information in each category for the analyses involves only counting responses. If you sent 100 questionnaires and your responses were tabulated as shown below, you would plan your workshop for those needing very basic information on Internet and the World Wide Web. They should be given for as long as you can (to cover the content) but meeting the chosen "half-day" sessions.

> 1. My knowledge of the Internet is _90_ none at all _4_ basic _4_ can search easily _2_ have used for reference _2_ can teach the Internet to staff and patrons.
>
> 2. My knowledge of the WWW is _94_ none at all _0_ basic _2_ can search easily _2_ have used for reference _2_ can teach the WWW to staff and patrons.
>
> 3. I prefer workshops _40_ one hour only, _40_ a half-day, _15_ a full-day, _5_ shorter times over one or more days.

A questionnaire to patrons who are using the Internet can help to find the numbers of staff and their training needed to assist with a new technology. The question related to this (Item 7) one of several. If all patrons needed more training, staff would be trained and reassigned at least temporarily.

> INTERNET USE SURVEY
> This survey is being conducted to assess the value of providing Internet service to library users. Thank you for your help!
> 1. What is the purpose of your Internet session? Check as many as apply: (Responses omitted)
> 2. Please tell us about yourself. This anonymous information will help us analyze results.
> a. Are you a new library user? ___ yes ___ no
> b. Did Internet access bring you into this library? ___ yes ___ no
> c. How long have you used the Internet? ___ first time ___ less than a year
> ___ more than a year
> (Remaining responses omitted)
>
> 3. What information did you gain from your use of the Internet? (Responses omitted)
>
> 4. How useful was the information you found?
> ___ not useful ___ may be of some help ___ exactly what I need
> 5. How much relevant information did you find?
> ___ too little ___ just enough ___ too much
> 6. How satisfied were you with our Internet session? (Please circle your choice.)
> I___I___I___I___I___I___I___I___I___I
> 1   2   3   4   5   6   7   8   9   10
> low   so-so   high
> 7. Do you need more training on the Internet? ___ yes ___ no

Responses to this questionnaire would have some analysis beyond simple tabulation of numbers of responses and percentages. You might wonder who was most satisfied with responses, those with experience with the Internet or those who were new users. You might also wonder how many persons who were not registered users and who had come into the library for the first time were there because of the computers rather than regular users who also use computers. To do this, you will correlate variables.

When you design a survey and ask questions that relate to one another, this allows you to correlate the answers. If you were to survey your librarians after their training on the Internet, answers to the questions could be correlated in a number of useful ways. For example,

Correlate the number of librarians who completed the Internet training with their success in answering reference questions in general.

Correlate the training on the Internet and salary increases: In what way are they related? Does Internet application increase their value to the library?

Information on how to calculate and analyze correlations can be found in statistics books. This is not difficult, but statisticians, persons who do this type of work regularly, can be very helpful and you may wish to consult with someone who can help you both analyze and then report the findings.

Providing continuing education events has a cost attached to planning as well as presenting that is often neglected in assessing expenses. Calculating what staff make per hour and the number of hours spent BEFORE the continuing education event provides a more realistic picture of salary costs than assuming that because staff receive a salary, their time planning costs nothing. However, this is not true because when staff are planning, they are not doing another task that needs to be completed. Records on our tally sheet are analyzed below:

PLANNING TALLY SHEET
time expended in minutes

Activity:	# staff	# min	Total min.
Planning program	10	30	300
Phoning speakers	1	60	60
Arranging meals	1	15	15

Compute:

    A   ___ How many total hours per workshop were staff planning?

    B $___ Average hourly salary for staff

    A x B = C   costs per workshop for planning

<u>**Scales: Ranking and Rating**</u>: If you asked prospective participants what types of technology training they wanted and all 25 respondents wanted to learn all five choices, you might not know which would be considered the most important. To do that you would ask for a ranking. Answers to survey questions can easily be placed in rank order. Ranking responses begins with determining the modal response and listing other responses in order of decreasing frequency.

What is your preferences for technology training? Please rank from one to five with five your first preference and one your most preferred.

1. ___ e-mail
2. ___ learn to search the Internet.
3. ___ learn to FTP
4. ___ learn to search the WWW
5. ___ learn to create a home page
6. ___ learn word processing
7. ___ other, please specify: _________________

If you had 25 respondents to this questionnaire and these were your responses under each ranking, for 10 persons, e-mail was their first choice and for 6 e-mail was their second choice.

Service	1	2	3	4	5	6	7
E-mail					5	10	10
Internet					3	12	9
FTP	1	22				1	1
WWW			1	8	11	2	3
Home page	1	7	7	3			1
Word processing							1
Other	2	1	1	1			

After counting the number of hashmarks in each square, you multiply it by the rank. That is, e-mail had 10 first priority "votes," 10 second priority votes, and 5 third priority votes, that would total 10x7(70)+10x6(60)+5x5(25) = 155 points. FTP would have 1x7+1x6+22x2+1x1= 58, WWW= 123; Home page= 55, Word processing= 7 and other = 11. This would indicate that most potential participants preferred e-mail with the WWW a second preference. No longer do librarians seem to need word processing, nor do they seem to want to FTP (or they may not have understood this question.

Counting Items: If questions were raised and faster resources or more connections to the Internet would be helpful in responding to reference questions, a time measure that would indicate how long it was taking to answer questions would be an indication of need for additional training for technology. In the tally sheet below, poor search strategy extended the time to find an answer. This might also increase problems with "complexity" of the question in the next category.

<table>
<tr><td colspan="2" align="center">Time Measure
In-House Reference</td></tr>
<tr><td align="center">Date:</td><td align="center">Reasons for delay:</td></tr>
<tr><td>
Iiiiiiiiiii less than 5 minutes
iiiii   5-15 minutes
iiiii   15-30 minutes
iiiiiiii 30-60 minutes
ii   60 minutes
</td><td align="center">
No delay
Slow access to Internet
Used poor search strategy
Complexity of questions
Clarity of questions
</td></tr>
</table>

Observation: A participant observation aids in determining when and how well a task assigned is being completed. If you wished to analyze the degree of customer service given at the charge-out desk, a tally sheet similar to the one which follows could be adapted to meet your needs.

<table>
<tr><td colspan="6">Customer Service Analysis
At 10 minute intervals on ________________________ (date), the following was observed:</td></tr>
<tr><td>Task</td><td>Warm</td><td>Smiling Distracted</td><td>Stern</td><td></td><td>Ignored</td></tr>
<tr><td>Greeting patrons
Checking materials

Responding to questions</td><td>____
____

____</td><td>____
____

____</td><td>____
____

____</td><td>____
____

____</td><td>____
____

____</td></tr>
</table>

If few staff were give a "warm" or "smiling" ranking, staff development would be indicated. You might do a companion analysis by asking users how they rated service at the charge-out desk.

Relevance: Relevance measures to determine if training was important are essential to planning. When training offered is not perceived as relevant, participants will not wish to return to another program. Analyzing this measure requires counting responses to each question and assessing the answers. It may be that another survey of needs is required if training was judged to be not relevant. It may be that the content should be reconsidered to see what would make the presentation of more value.

Before/After Measures: Obviously what enticed participants to come to the session becomes the best choice of incentive for the next program. If students come because their employers pay their way and not because they need the information, it is less likely change will be implemented when staff return. If most participants indicate that continuing education credit is important to them, it is wise to continue to offer credit for programs.

Inflation/Deflation Index: A "Where we are" measure we have collected information on the average cost of our programs. The point here is that inflation in program signals a need for increase in budget or decrease in cost of programs or fewer programs. This is a very simple calculation:

$$\frac{1996\ cost - 1995\ cost}{1995\ cost} = annual\ \%\ increase$$

However, its simplicity does not signal an excuse to ignore the finding.

Focus Groups: Findings from focus groups are used to create or modify strategic plans. Results are recorded by paper and pencil, flip charts, computers, or any other available means. Reports from each working group are given to everyone and main points are selected for further consideration at that time or they are scheduled for consideration at a subsequent meeting. Care is taken that members who may have been absent at one meeting are given sufficient information that they do not "reinvent the wheel" at the following meeting when their very valid points were discussed although they were not present.

Focus groups were formed to help plan. The results of focus groups are analyzed by combining reports and using the findings to choose the best path to follow. Other action research plans may be put into practice to see if the chosen path does produce the success desired.

Quantitative/Qualitative Data Analysis: Confirming the quality of your continuing education programs usually involves the results from more than one action research study. An example of a quantitative collection that begins to give you qualitative data when you collect the data about specific activities six months after the event. You may ask questions such as:

1. I use the Internet to answer reference questions by:
   ___ sending e-mail to a colleague.
   ___ using information found directly on a Web Site.
   ___ sending a listserv request for information.

2. I answer reference questions on the Internet:
   ___ 15% of my time ___ 30% of my time ___ 50% of my time ___ 75% of my time ___ 90% of my

Finally, action research allows the reporting of data. A first question to answer is "Who needs the information?" Is it only administrators/funding authorities or should it be shared with other continuing education providers? Perhaps one of the purposes of this paper is to get members of this preconference workshop to make contacts so they can share both the outcome of their action research evaluations as well as the methods chosen to conduct the evaluation. All librarians benefit from learning about successes and they also need to be able to learn the final analysis of those events that are not as successful.

Action research allows us to cite programs that are of great value to participants, to share with administrators their value. Action research truly provides evidence of both the need and the value of continuing education programs.

REFERENCES

Carson, Terry (1990), "What Kind of Knowing is Critical Action Research?" *Theory into Practice*, Summer, 29, pp. 167-173.

Frost, David (1995), "Integrating Systematic Enquiry into Everyday Professional Practice: towards some principles of procedure," *British Educational Research Journal*, 21.

Herndon, Kathleen and Janice Fausko (1994), "Facilitating Teachers Professional Growth through Action Research," a paper presented at the annual meeting of the American Educational Research Association, New Orleans, Louisiana, April 4-8.

Isaac, Stephen and William B. Michael (1995), *Handbook in Research and Evaluation for Education and the Behavioral Sciences*, 3rd ed.   San Diego, California, p. 59.

McNiff, J. (1988), *Action Research Principles and Practice*, London, Macmillan, p. 57.

Robertson, Jan M. (1995), "Towards Leadership Praxis through Principals' Partnerships in New Zealand," a paper presented at the annual meeting of the American Educational Research Association in San Francisco, California, April 18-22.

"Secondary Perspectives: Classroom action research: The teacher as researcher," (1989), *Journal of Reading*, December, p. 216.

Tripp, David H. (1990), "Social Critical Action Research," *Theory into Practice,* 29, Summer, pp. 158-166.

von Manen, Max (1990), "Beyond Assumptions: Shifting the Limits of Action Research," Theory into Practice, 29, Summer, pp. 152-157.

PERSONAL PROFESSIONAL DEVELOPMENT: COMPETENCIES FOR THE SOLO LIBRARIAN

Sue Lacy Bryant
Information consultant

Abstract: The paper presents a comprehensive checklist of professional development needs for the 'solo' librarian in the twenty-first century.

INTRODUCTION

As the third millennium approaches, those information specialists competent and confident to manage information services alone (or with minimal support) should look to the future with optimism. A growing number can be expected to work on their own, managing small information units, acting as 'information brokers' within a team, or as consultants. To be successful, all these solo librarians must be high calibre professionals, able to keep pace with change.

Librarians who regard Continuing Professional Education as a 'fringe activity' (or worse still as 'unnecessary') are a danger to themselves, to clients and to the wider profession. For the solo librarian, perhaps more than any other, continuing professional development is "one of the most important resources ... to maintain competence" (Todd, 1987).

My aim is to demonstrate the significance of solo librarianship (now and in the years ahead), to discuss those areas in which solo information workers must be competent, and to describe a practical approach to personal development. Obstacles do need to be overcome, but should not be overestimated. All information workers (irrespective of the size of the service in which they work) benefit from taking a systematic approach to professional development.

THE PLACE OF SOLO WORKERS WITHIN THE PROFESSION

One-professional and one-person information services are common. The best estimates available for the United Kingdom suggest that perhaps as many as one in five qualified librarians and information specialists work solo - possibly an even higher proportion (Lacy Bryant, 1995). They work in every sector of the profession, from faculty libraries in higher education to information units in charities. Many special librarians are solo professionals - including roughly 50% of industrial, commercial and government library staff (East, 1983).   School libraries are almost exclusively one-person services.

Official statistics may underestimate areas in which solo professionals work, especially where they are at the forefront (or the fringes) of the profession and where they are employed part time. Similarly, independent librarians and consultants, who bring a portfolio of skills and experience to their clients, may not be fully represented. Significantly, estimates for special libraries (embracing services within health-care, charities and museums as well as government agencies, industry, and commerce) are acknowledged to be imprecise (LISU, 1996).

Although recent years have seen a modest expansion in the number of jobs in both education and medical libraries in the UK (LISU, 1996), declining employment in commerce and industry underlines the fact that solo librarians are vulnerable to the fortunes of the employing organisation.

THE FUTURE FOR INFORMATION WORK

Information is power. The twenty-first century will bring increased demand for skilled 'information operatives'. Stonier painted the broad picture: "knowledge has displaced the traditional land, labour and capital as the most important single input into modern productive systems." (Stonier, 1983). Less developed countries will strive to close the information gap. In the West, Stonier anticipates the expansion of both the 'knowledge' industries and the 'happiness industry' (encompassing education, leisure and social care) (Stonier, 1983). Handy predicted that in Europe "the new jobs" will derive from the "information-providing part of the service sector" (Handy, 1985).

Both authors define information work broadly, embracing every activity which processes, transfers or transforms information. Thus, conventional libraries will provide but a fraction of the new jobs. Nevertheless, there are many new areas in "which information brokers could make a significant contribution" (Lacey Bryant, 1986), actively "promoting information flow and exploiting the whole range of information forms and sources" (Valdez, 1974).

GROWING DEMAND FOR SOLO LIBRARIANS

A British study by EUCLID, a consultancy, confirmed that the world of information and libraries has a 'moving front', characteristic of expanding industrial sectors (Euclid, 1993). While the marketplace for 'new' jobs is small and highly competitive, more and more librarians are managing services single-handed, enticed by new roles and the responsibility, independence and job satisfaction that such work can offer.

Speaking at the Second International Conference, Prof. Wormell anticipated a role for information specialists as "individual experts .... making individual and team decisions based on their link-ups to various databases for various kinds of information" (Wormell,1993). St Clair has also predicted growing demand for expert information specialists committed to "providing the highest levels of service at the highest levels of quality" (St Clair, 1995).   Evidently the next century promises exciting opportunities for solo information professionals - but only for those prepared to grasp them.

PROFESSIONAL COMPETENCIES

As a consequence of their diverse responsibilities, the training and development needs of the solo information professional may be wide ranging. This breadth can be daunting. However, even though the analysis must be highly individual, solo workers can learn from research in 'mainstream' practice, as well as looking to what St. Clair has described as the developing theory and 'body of knowledge' of one-person librarianship (St Clair, 1995). They must also take cognisance of the views of employers.

The relevant strands of evidence from each of these three areas can be synthesised in a simple Checklist, as follows, to facilitate a methodical approach to professional development.

A CHECKLIST OF PROFESSIONAL DEVELOPMENT NEEDS

The Checklist of Professional Development Needs (Lacey Bryant, 1995) summarises those areas in which anyone managing a small information service might need to gain or enhance competence i.e. "the ability to carry out a task or practice a skill" (Harrod's, 1995). Indeed, as the framework derives from evidence in all sectors of librarianship, it provides a practical tool for self - assessment for any information professional planning for the future.

FIGURE 1.   *A Checklist of Professional Development Needs*

Core Areas	Competencies Needed	Action Plan
Organisational culture		
Management skills		
Interpersonal skills		
Communication		

Information technology

Library/information skills

Networking

Subject knowledge

Personal development

Some people may prefer to use the Checklist in conjunction with published guidelines, such as The Library Association's *Framework for Continuing Professional Development* (Library Association, 1992).

1. Organisational culture

It is crucial for managers of small information units to understand the purpose and culture of the organisation in which they are based, so that they can carve a valuable and valued role, which enhances the 'parent' body. The newly appointed solo information professional must discover where real authority lies, swiftly recognising stake-holders through whom developments can be influenced.

Slater's study of the special library sector revealed concern among managers that their information staff lack wider background knowledge (Slater, 1988) while Collins and Shuter reported that solo librarians found it difficult to find out 'what is going on' (Shuter, 1984). Clearly solo librarians must take personal responsibility in this area - and remain sensitive to changes within the organisation and in external influences upon it.

Induction training offers a 'window' on different aspects of the organisation. Where necessary individuals should instigate their own. Subsequently, networking plays a significant role in this area.

2. Management skills

Demand for management training (and also regarding information technology) dominates the market for continuing professional education in all areas of practice.

Five interrelated skills underpin every aspect of the management of a one-person or one-professional unit. Of these, the successful management of change, in response to what Roberts described as 'information circumstances' (Roberts,1979), is critical.

FIGURE 2.   *Management: core competencies for the solo information manager*

Core Competencies	Competencies Needed	Action Plan
Time-management		
Setting goals		

Planning and organising

Decision-making

Managing change

Individuals also require a portfolio of competencies relating to the management of tasks and of self. The following model, derived from work by Roobottom (Roobottom and Winkles,1985), is a useful basis for self-appraisal:

FIGURE 3.   *Task Management and Self-management*

Core Competencies	**Competencies Needed**	**Action Plan**
TASK MANAGEMENT		
Analysis of user needs		
Defining aims		
Prioritising		
Innovation		
Quality management		
Delegation		
SELF MANAGEMENT		
Self-analysis		
Self-motivation		
Stress management		
Awareness of learning styles		
Networking		

Various methods can be used to address weaknesses but the value of observation and experience should not be overlooked. Retrospection, taking the time to learn from incidents at work, allows us to avoid repeating mistakes and to programme success into future ventures.

Individuals will require specific additional competencies, for instance in handling statistics, financial management and increasingly, fund raising.

3. Interpersonal skills

Without excellent interpersonal skills the solo information officer or librarian remains an 'outsider', unable to anticipate or meet the information needs of clients effectively. Again, Roobottom's (Roobottom and Winkles,1985) model is applicable.

FIGURE 4. *People Management*

Competencies	Competencies Needed	Action Plan
Assertiveness		
Listening		
Giving/receiving feedback		
Challenging		
Negotiation		
Leadership		

Working with groups:
    meetings
    teamwork
    training		

Self awareness:
    personality
    personal style		

There are countless opportunities to develop competencies in these areas, in professional and in private life. These areas lend themselves to workshops and short courses which can illuminate personal experience.

4. Communication

Success as a 'gatekeeper' requires proficiency in many aspects of communication, including oral, written and interpersonal skills. Sadly Gash and Reardon found that employers are disappointed "with the level of personal transferable skills displayed by information graduates"(Gash and Reardon,1988).

The single-handed information manager may also need skills in desktop publishing, report-writing, user education, press work and displays, to name but a few areas. Marketing is crucial. Each of these competencies calls for appropriate approaches to professional development, from self-instructional packages to short courses, not to forget reading!

5. Information Technology

Williamson found that the staff of one-person units attached priority to training on information services, information retrieval and new technology (Williamson, 1988). Jago observes that proficiency in exploiting information technology is "the most marketable skill of all" (Foreman, 1992). As the microchip celebrates its' twenty-fifth birthday, the number of solo librarians operating without a PC and modem must be dwindling. Indeed, some find themselves in the vanguard, regularly exploiting technologies which have yet to become integrated into routine practice elsewhere.

A range of formal and informal methods can be used to develop sufficient competency. Meanwhile, it is sensible to 'hang on to the coat-tails' of colleagues in the organisation, or in other specialised libraries, while learning about new applications.

6. Library and information skills

Efficient practice of basic skills in librarianship, from acquisition through organisation to dissemination of information, is assumed. Much more important now is the way in which these skills are applied. The trend is against those who are not formally trained in librarianship or information science. The 1996 Institute of Information Scientists *Remuneration Survey* reported that "People without a degree or professional qualifications now earn less than other groups by a wide margin" (Cropley, 1996).

Modern information professionals require an entrepreneurial approach and the vision to perceive new opportunities. To quote St. Clair, employers require library managers who are willing to "respond to the authority of the customer", dispensing with "outmoded and tedious concerns" about traditional librarianship whenever appropriate (St Clair, 1995). Ojala foresees the new corporate 'Cybrarian', evaluating the quality of evidence, connecting "disparate pieces of information to originate new information" and delivering this in the form preferred by the client (Ojala,1993). Self-evidently, solo librarians must be confident in evaluating information services.

In Barcelona Prof. Wormell spoke of the "core strength of the information profession", which includes expertise and experience in the following competencies: concepts of the organisation of knowledge and theories of information transfer, information retrieval and the synthesis and dissemination of information plus an understanding of how to use information to competitive advantage, an appreciation of global sources and sensitivity to information policy issues (Wormell,1993). How extraordinary that so many librarians should seem so diffident about their skills!

7. Networking

Networking is a powerful antidote to the adverse effects of professional isolation. It is vital to invest time in making and nurturing links with other information specialists. Fortunately, personal networks develop naturally in the course of seeking and providing information. Formal networks may be organised geographically or by specialism; some operating independently, others under the aegis of a professional body. Membership of a professional association confers opportunities to participate in professional life and brings access to publications, meetings, training and advice.

Most people unconsciously call on the resources of an 'invisible college' of contacts made in the process of studying, working and recreation. Indeed, solo practitioners invariably become aware of other isolated information professionals who might welcome an informal initiative to benefit from mutual support, whether communicated by e-mail or in person. In Britain, membership of Aslib's 'One Man Bands Special Interest Group' remains small but steady. By contrast, the Solo Librarians Division of the Special Libraries Association of the United State of America has grown rapidly in recent years and now links single-staff librarians in many different parts of the world.

Networks open channels of communication in which all participants have a vested interest. Interpersonal networking forms a professional 'safety-net' for isolated librarians and information scientists, enabling them to keep up to date with developments within the wider profession and their own specialism.

8. Subject knowledge

Acquiring sufficient knowledge to meet the needs of the employer is always a priority for newly appointed 'solo's'. The broadening role of information professionals prompts many to develop expertise in other disciplines such as commercial subjects; a trend noted by research into employment patterns here in Denmark by Pors (Pors, 1990), and by Webb's later study of continuing professional development in UK professional firms (Webb,1991).

However, there is some concern that information professionals who acquire a highly specialised knowledge base meet barriers in transferring to other roles within the organisation or industry. Researchers at Robert Gordon University in Scotland, have been working on a Framework for Transferable Skills, to help librarians to develop their skills and strategies for career advancement.

9. Personal professional development

The overall success of a solo information service is governed by the public profile of its manager within the organisation. The importance of self-management and good communication, including interpersonal skills, have already been noted. Thus it is not surprising that solo librarians attach priority to opportunities for personal development. Regrettably, poor access to training was a common cause of concern among respondents to the survey by Collins and Shuter (Shuter, 1984). The need for self-motivation, and the advantages of formulating a plan for personal development are apparent.

IDENTIFYING PERSONAL DEVELOPMENT NEEDS

The Checklist is best applied to a three-part process of identifying personal development needs, involving self-audit, an evaluation of the information service, and forecasting the future needs of the employer.

Self-audit requires an honest look at oneself; recognising personal values, professional aspirations and motivation, along with personal style and personality traits. Compiling a personal profile can be a challenging process, highlighting contradictions which could hinder personal, professional and career development.

Certain aspects of library evaluation (both quantitative and qualitative) can be built into the service with minimal effort. It may be helpful to use further devices to gauge customer satisfaction. Where guidelines exist (for example 'The Value toolkit'(Urquhart and Hepworth, 1995) designed for healthcare libraries in Britain) so much the better, but there is no need to rely on 'magic formulae'. As Cronin said, evaluation is principally a process of "applied common-sense" (Cronin, 1982). Even the most brief and informal review of current performance, related to purpose and priorities, may highlight areas in which action is needed.

The library manager should already be familiar with the Political and legal, Economic, Socio-cultural and Technological (PEST) influences upon the organisation. A SWOT analysis, in the context of these external factors, reveals Strengths, Weaknesses, Opportunities and Threats from which it is possible to project future demands upon the service and its staff.

Working through the Checklist at each stage of this process will identify gaps and weaknesses, revealing areas in which new or enhanced competencies will contribute to professional development.

PLANNING PROFESSIONAL DEVELOPMENT

Securing the means to gain these competencies will pose challenges, best addressed with the same high standards of planning applied to the information service itself. It is essential to deduce the priorities for action (in the short-term and the longer-term) and to fix specific targets. These need to be real, realistic, valued by the individual, measurable and recorded (in writing, or to a confidante).

FIGURE 5   *Setting goals*

- List competencies needed
- Decide how to measure their achievement
- Make a note of the base-line
- Set a long-term goal, or goals
- Identify short-term objectives
- Identify the actions needed to achieve these targets
- Assess obstacles to be overcome

- Inform someone you respect of your aims

A personal development plan allows for progress to be monitored and discourages diversion of resources into those areas which are merely of greatest personal interest (or in which training is most readily available). Focusing on priorities encourages creativity and persistence in seeking out suitable means to strengthen competencies.

OPPORTUNITIES FOR PROFESSIONAL DEVELOPMENT

With sufficient aforethought most librarians in the West can avail themselves of appropriate opportunities for professional development, formal and informal, within the workplace and outside it. Colleagues in developing countries have a far harder task. Conferences, exhibitions and short courses may be few and far between. Furthermore, it may be difficult to access the professional literature, much of which lacks immediate application. Menou has challenged the information profession to respond to these practical difficulties, developing an "effective network by which strengths could be pooled in a free, flexible and decentralised fashion" (Menou, 1993).

Meanwhile, for isolated information professionals in all parts of the globe, the personal challenge is to explore every avenue available to develop the competencies required. Contrary to expectations, most means of gaining new competencies are relatively inexpensive - although, without exception, they call for "the commitment of time ; work time and personal time, time to prepare beforehand and time to reflect afterwards (Lacey Bryant, 1995). Recognition of preferred learning style is very helpful. Mumford argues that 'learning how to learn' is itself a managerial requirement (Mumford, 1988).

It is important to think widely. Work itself generates opportunities to seek the assistance of colleagues, request in-service training and maybe to benefit from mechanisms such as mentoring. Writing, research and committee work all demand competencies which can be acquired through practice, experience, or observation. To quote Segal, networking "presents an invaluable method for maintaining and updating one's professional competencies" (Segal, 1989).

Ritchie's survey of members of The Library Association, found that librarians favour practical, work-based activities, followed by liaison with colleagues, in-service training, and visiting other services (also useful as a form of benchmarking). Short courses and job rotation were ranked fifth, with professional reading in sixth place (Ritchie, 1988). It is particularly difficult for solo librarians to participate in courses as they require 'cover' as well as financial support.

FURTHER STUDY

Some will choose to remedy specific skill gaps with distance learning packages or computer assisted study programmes. Others will seek the intellectual rigour of pursuing a further qualification, in librarianship, within their chosen subject field or in management. The Institute of Information Scientists *Remuneration Survey* again reports that the greatest financial "benefits come with higher degrees or professional qualifications which are not information based" (Cropley, 1996).

The pursuit of professional qualifications may be a spur to further development, especially where there is a requirement to present evidence of satisfactory practice and awareness of current professional issues.

CONCLUSION

As the second millennium draws to a close, information remains of paramount importance to global society. There is an urgent need to close the 'information gap' between less developed countries and post-industrial economies. Meanwhile, new occupational territory is being opened up, offering greater scope to librarians and information scientists, especially those competent to manage information services alone. As the balance of the workforce shifts, there is a need to capture more reliable statistics depicting changes in the nature of information work and in patterns of employment - with enormous implications for both vocational education and continuing professional development. To quote Prof. Wormell, "the fundamental problem of education and training is not curriculum design, it is one of vision" (Wormell, 1993).

In the twenty-first century, as today, continuing professional development will provide the means by which successful information managers prepare for the future. To meet their complex needs and keep up to date in a fast changing world, solo information specialists (working freelance or in small organisations) must be skilled in managing their own development. Armed with a development plan designed to achieve concrete goals, the solo professional can 'move forward' - concentrating limited resources to best advantage, however difficult the 'information circumstances'.

Personal professional development "has to be tailor-made, patterned to meet individual needs"; flexibility in response to change and opportunity must be at its heart, and the improvement of professional practice its goal (Lacey Bryant, 1995).

REFERENCES

Cronin, B. (1982), "Performance measurement and information management", *Aslib Proceedings*, 34 (5), pp. 227-236.

Cropley, J. (1996), "Institute of Information Scientists remuneration survey 1996", *Inform*, 187, September, Supplement.

East, H. (1983), "Changes in the staffing of UK special libraries and information services in the decade 1972-1981; a review of the DES Census data", *Journal of Documentation*, 39 (4), pp. 247-265.

EUCLID (1993), *Feasibility Study for an Industry Training Organisation for Information and Library Services : a Report by EUCLID to the Information and Library Services Lead Body*, November 1993. Unpublished.

Foreman, L. (ed.) (1992), *Developing Professionals in Information Work :Personal and Organisational Growth in Libraries*, London: Circle of State Librarians.

Gash, S. and Reardon, D.F. (1988), "Personal transferable skills for the modern information professional: a discussion paper", *Journal of Information Science*, 14, pp. 285-292.

Handy, C. (1985), *The Future of Work : a Guide to a Changing Society*, Oxford: Basil Blackwell.

Harrod's Librarian's Glossary: 9220 Terms used in Information Management, Library Science, Publishing, the Book Trades and Archive Management, (1995), 8th rev. ed. Aldershot: Gower.

Lacey Bryant, S. (1986), "On the fringe : working as a Health Education/Information Officer", *Aslib Proceedings*, 38 (1), pp. 17-23.

Lacey Bryant, S. (1995), *Personal Professional Development and the Solo Librarian*, London: Library Association Publishing.

Library & Information Statistics Unit - LISU, Loughborough University (1996), *The L.I.S.T. : Library & Information Statistics Tables for the United Kingdom 1994/5*, Loughborough: LISU/British Library Research and Innovation Centre.

Library Association (1992), *The Framework for Continuing Professional Development : Your Personal Profile*, London: The Library Association.

Menou, M.J. (1993), "Requirements for international co-operation in continuing education for library and information work" in: B.Woolls (ed), *Continuing Professional Education and IFLA : Past, Present, and a Vision for the Future. Papers from the IFLA CPERT Second World Conference on Continuing Professional Education for the Library and Information Science Professions*, Munich: Saur.

Mumford, A. (1988), "Enhancing your learning skills - a note of guidance for managers", in S.Wood, (ed), *Continuous Development : the Path to Improved Performance*, London: Institute of Personnel Management, 1988.

Ojala, M., (1993), "Core competencies for special library managers of the future", *Special Libraries*, 84 (4), pp. 230-234.

Pors, N.O. (1990), "Employment patterns, the labour market and students preferences." *Libri*, 40 (2), pp. 112-125.

Ritchie, S. (1988), *Training and Management Development in Librarianship*, British Library, Library and Information Research Report 34.

Roberts, N. (1979), "Special librarians : job characteristics and work attitudes", *Journal of Librarianship*, 11 (1), pp. 4-14.

Roobottom, C and Winkles, T. (1988), "Self appraisal - a route to self-development" in: M.Pedler, J. Burgoyne, and T. Boydell, *Applying Self-Development in Organisations*, London: Prentice-Hall.

Segal, J.S. (1989), "Special libraries and multitype networks", *Special Libraries*, 80 (2), pp. 85-93.

Shuter, J. (1984), "The isolated professional", *Information & Library Manager*, 3 (4), pp. 106-113.

Slater, M. (1988), *Internal Training and External Short Courses : a Study of Informal Continuing Education in the Special Library/Information Field*, British Library Research Paper 52.

St Clair, G. (1995), "When less is more", *Library Manager*, October pp. 24-25.

Stonier, T. (1983), *The Wealth of Information : a Profile of the Post-Industrial Economy*, London: Thames Methuen.

Todd, F. (ed), (1987), *Planning Continuing Professional Development*, London: Croom Helm.

Urquhart, C. and Hepworth, J. (1995), *The Value of Information Services to Clinicians: a Toolkit for Measurement*, Aberystwyth: DILS, University of Wales, Aberystwyth.

Valdez, M. (1974), " An information broker as a member of a health service planning unit", *Aslib Proceedings*, 26 (12), pp. 473-476.

Webb, S.P. (1991), *Best Practice? Continuing Professional Development for Library/Information Staff in UK Professional Firms*, British Library: British Library Research & Development Report 6039.

Williamson, J. (1988), "One person libraries and information units : their education and training needs", *Library Management*, 9 (5).

Wormell, I. (1993), "Expanding professional horizons : the challenge of the FID in the 1990's" in: B.

Woolls (ed), *Continuing professional education and IFLA : Past, present and a vision for the future '*. Papers from the IFLA CPERT Second World Conference on Continuing Professional Education for the Library and Information Science Professions, Munich: Saur, 1993.

GROWING WITH THE CUSTOMER
CHALLENGES TO THE ESTONIAN LIBRARIAN IN THE 21ST CENTURY

Aili Norberg
Director of Library Services
National Library of Estonia

Abstract: The paper provides background information about the problems of library performance in Estonia. It focuses on the need for information, and that libraries can meet this demand and reports the findings of a survey concerning the role of libraries in establishing and developing an information base for training and scientific research work, as well as describing the problems of creating and maintaining an efficient system of communication.

INTRODUCTION

The population of Estonia is about 1,4 million. There are 745 libraries of different types and levels, which together have 560 000 registered users, including 100 000 users of the National Library of Estonia. Whether these figures should be regarded as large or small does not matter as much as the fact that all these people go to the libraries with very different needs and requests. It is important that they are not disappointed. Yet, this happens every day.

The role of information as the main resource of development in society is growing gradually. Knowledge and expertise form the foundation of every walk of life. Paradoxically enough, at the same time there is:

> too little information, when it comes to solving a particular problem,

and

> too much information, when one has to find their way amidst the whole mass of information.

The generation and movement of information in creative activities, be it the arts, science, or creation of consumable objects, has been compared to the circulation of blood in living organisms. Information will become an asset only at a certain level of organisation and concentration. If libraries which are undoubtedly there to support the circulation of information, want to function efficiently, then it is imperative for them to meet the demands of their consumers as precisely and fully as possible. Nowadays it has become virtually impossible to arrange, retrieve and analyse information without using modern information technology. The latter, in its turn, presumes certain material and intellectual resources.

An important facet of the problem is defining the level of general knowledge, professional skills, and analysing the potential of the librarians for them to assist in providing society with information. To be functional they need information themselves, mainly in the following two areas:

- a clear understanding of the needs and demands for information by their consumers,

- an awareness of the existing sources of information and modern information technology.

In what ways can a librarian keep in touch with the changing needs of the consumers of information? The easiest ways are to:

- collect feed-back information by means of inquiries, interviews, observations, conduct statistical analyses of the information collected, and rate the relevance of the information and quality of service as compared with the explicit needs of the consumers, using certain criteria;
- observe and analyse the actual service situation. Communicate with the consumer as a partner throughout the process of retrieval, be committed to the ensuing requests and obtain information on the needs (often the unconscious needs) of the users. This approach focuses on one particular person and provides much more precise information on the needs of each individual consumer.

Quite clearly the latter approach cannot be applied to very large groups of library users. Yet, it is necessary and feasible to use it in the case of smaller groups which have more specific interests, e.g. students, scientists, creative artists, or MPs, among the users of libraries. These groups, especially, considering their importance from the point of view of society.

Various inquiries involving large groups are taking place during the period of shaping or altering systems, as such extensive surveys enables the librarians to draw a general picture. Such methods have been used by Estonian libraries in periods of important restructuring, e.g. when starting the service systems in the new buildings of Tartu University Library and The National Library of Estonia.

At the present time various inquiries are being carried out in many libraries of the world into the changes in the paradigm of the global exchange of information in connection with the progress in the electronic dissemination of information.

One such study has just been completed in three of the largest Estonian scientific libraries - *"Academic Library Performance Measurement"*. Its internationally approved methods enabled the researchers to measure the quality of the performance of library services from the point of view of the needs and interests of different user groups.

THE FINDINGS OF THE SURVEY

During the past two years in which the study has been conducted, a large quantity of information has been collected which allows us to form conclusions about different user groups' satisfaction/dissatisfaction with the library services. It would be impossible to present here an exhaustive discussion of the whole body of the information collected. This paper will present some data as examples of the knowledge we can gain from this kind of research work. We focus on the information needs of certain specific user groups of the larger scientific libraries of Estonia, as well as their satisfaction with the organisation of user services.

70% of the active users of TUL are **students** who use the library primarily for the purpose of their studies. It is remarkable, that also 70% of the NL users point out that they visit the library in connection with their studies. In addition, 20% use the library's resources for their refresher or professional training courses. This is an indication of another facet of the National Library's functions - it has to be prepared to provide services to students on an equal basis with the university libraries.

Although not the largest user groups, the **scientists** are among the most intensive consumers of information. Scientists (including the teaching staff of the higher educational establishments) make up 5.4% of the total number of National Library (NL) users.   20% of the users identify themselves as having scientific interests, according to the recent inquiry. The corresponding figures for Tartu University Library (TUL) are 7.5 and 22.

Scientists constitute the most demanding, exacting, and pretentious (sic) group of users of scientific libraries, representing the highest level of information demand necessary for the nation's development. How do the Estonian scientists and people with scientific interests judge the content and processing of information in scientific libraries as well as the user services provided there?

The inquiries reveal the following as being the most significant problems for the users with scientific interests:

- **accessibility to library materials** (publications, electronic carriers of information, AV-material). It satisfies 75% of scientists at NL and 60% at TUL. Accessibility to materials and satisfaction with it may be somewhat influenced by the fact that the users at TUL can take books home. According to the inquiry this facility is also used by 12% of the scientific personnel of other higher educational establishments. On the days of the inquiry 69% of requests of study literature were satisfied, while only 58% of requests for scientific literature could be met favourably. The main reason for the negative responses to requests was that the required item was on loan. Thus, 26% of the interviewed users were not satisfied with the arrangements at the library. It was requested that at least one copy of every publication should be available to be used in the library itself.

At the National Library the main reason of dissatisfaction for the scientists (as well as other users) was the absence ,or insufficient provision, of needed literature or other material in the field. The open-access literature in NL is used intensively: 51% of the total user body, 54% of students and 41% of scientists and the teaching staff benefit from that facility, the corresponding satisfaction rates are 57, 51 and 73. A number of problems in the NL emerged from the process of ordering books from the stacks which is not acceptable for 16% of users; whereas it is found to be complicated by 30% of students and scientists who are the principal users of the library. 7 % of requested (and listed in catalogues) literature was not there - for reasons not specified.

It is obvious that the purposes for using the information from the library vary. For students the main purpose is their studies (77 %), then comes self-education (36%), scientific activities (22%) and interest in new acquisitions (16%).

In the case of the scientists the dominant purpose is research work (53%), then regular professional (teaching) tasks (44%), improvement of professional knowledge (28%), and acquainting oneself with the new acquisitions (30%);

- **reference and information services** which are more relevant for the scientists as compared to other user groups. 26% of reference information obtained at TUL is used for the purposes of scientific research work. Hence the more exacting demands concerning sources and the availability of information, as well as thoroughness of the replies. At TUL approx. 25 % of those who need information for their research work, were not satisfied with its availability, relevance, or exhaustiveness. Dissatisfaction related directly to an insufficiency of accessible source material and databases, while the helpful and competent assistance by the librarians deserved praise. Most requests for reference information at TUL were made in different reading-rooms by students (57 %), in the catalogue hall, and in reference and scientific information departments(by scientists - 14%).

In the NL reference information was most frequently required in the reading rooms for literature on law (20%), reference literature (16%), the humanities (12%) and periodicals (9%). Subject-wise most information is requested on legal matters (22%), economy(22%), history (17%), language and literature (13%), politics (11%) and arts (11%). Other fields are represented in smaller proportions.

CONCLUSIONS

Each event of looking for information to answer a request will make the librarian more aware of the profile of the needs of a specific user. The user will also discover new information sources and retrieval opportunities. Thus he is simultaneously prepared to cope on his own with solving his next task. Does this situation not endanger the position of the librarian?

Only if it stays unchanged without an attempt to make an improvement. Requirements for the range of skills of a librarian are great. Most of them are not library skills. They are in languages, computing, systems design, marketing etc. It is an obligation and a vital demand for a librarian (information officer) to be ahead of the consumers of information (library users), following the development of sciences and continuously obtaining knowledge about new sources of information, technologies and ways of service. Consequently, co-operation with an expert in a specific field brings about a better understanding of that field. As in any case of intellectual co-operation it results in creating synergy which is an essential lever for social development.

If libraries are to move towards this desirable situation, they have to learn that a prerequisite of success is a permanent process of learning and researching. If they are not to lose their lead ahead of the consumers of information, the libraries need to take several steps:

- arrange for the professional training of staff, especially in the field of the application of the developing electronic information technology;

- engage in converting the national information resource into an electronic database of Estonian National Bibliography (abstracts in English), which would allow fast information exchange at home and abroad;

- engage in statistical, bibliometrical, and scientometrical research, which would allow an estimation of the distribution of Estonian scientific and cultural thought and its impact in the world;

- turn the librarian into a key person in society together with satisfying the demands and responsibility;

- contribute to the training of young librarians. The library should be a good place for practice for students and to explain to them as many sides as possible, of the problems encountered in a modern library;

- develop an open-minded and democratic international outlook for the staff, and for everybody's sake, create an understanding of the role of information in the future - it belongs to everybody.

PLANNING PROFESSIONAL EXCELLENCE IN LIBRARY AND INFORMATION ORGANISATIONS - A SOUTH AFRICAN PERSPECTIVE

Fransie Terblanche
Senior Lecturer
University of South Africa
Pretoria, Republic of South Africa

Abstract: This paper provides the justification for the need to plan for the professional excellence of library and information services. It explains the importance of the competency of human resources in order to render an excellent library and information service.

INTRODUCTION

Achieving world class excellence and service depends on people - how well they are skilled, cared for, and managed. Human resources practitioners have a vital role to play in building up the country's economy by developing productive people who care about the services and, in our case, the information products which they supply.

To face the human resources challenges of today and beyond the year 2000, management will have to plan for excellence in the workplace. Professional excellence starts with the creation of an organisational climate in which people can operate as professionals, as well as making it meaningful for everybody to be part of the organisation. It is important for employees to feel equal and have equal opportunities for development in the working environment. Organisations should strive to be equal opportunity employers in offering an energetic work environment, a learning culture, and the opportunity for employees to fulfil their potential and work aspirations.

The role of human resources management is under the spotlight, as organisations increasingly recognise the importance of the human being as a valuable resource. The human resources management function has a key role to play in promoting and driving change and development, to meet the challenges of the future. The meaningful integration of human resources development into the whole managerial task demands a shift from the "marginalised personnel paradigm" to the "integrated human resources paradigm".

The marginalised personnel department paradigm is characterised by the following aspects:

- administrative personnel issues which do not add specific value to the achievement of strategic business goals
- it serves top management
- maintenance functions, e.g. recruitment, selection and personnel administration
- it has a short-term focus with limited vision or strategic focus - personnel practitioners tend to put people in "boxes" on organisational charts
- it can be regarded as a cost centre because it offers no development for employees or performance measurement of personnel's contribution to the overall vision and strategy of the organisation
- it is line management-driven with no human resources development objectives as rewardable measures
- has a more reactive operational focus on internal dynamics with a lack of clear, integrated human resources strategies.

The integrated human resources management paradigm is characterised by the following aspects:

- there is no differentiated human resources function, as such - its role is redefined in the context of world class requirements and continuous improvement of employees
- the human resources function serves all employees
- the contribution of the human resources function is seen in the context of change, providing

expertise and adding value to organisational performance - human resources development practitioners are interested in developing people for new "boxes" or getting away from the restrictiveness of boxes completely

- human resources management has a long-term, strategic focus which flows directly from the overall organisational vision and strategy
- human resources management can be seen as a profit centre, making a measurable contribution to improving organisational performance
- the organisation regularly engages in culture and climate surveys and measure the perceptions regarding human resource's ability to add value
- human resources specialists at managerial level participate at the highest level of decision-making which helps them in planning for human resources development needs and programmes
- because of the integrated approach, where open communication is essential, it is possible for any employee to participate in the strategic planning of development activities for staff members
- human resources development programmes and functions are proactive, strategic and focus on internal and external environments.

In making a comparison between the above paradigms, the second paradigm reflects the current requirements of human resources management and should provide the framework of human resources management in today's modern organisation. The overarching goal of human resources management should be to improve overall organisational performance by empowering every employee in such a way that the human resources of the organisation are optimally utilised. In order to do this, there are a number of key drivers which need to be in place. These key drivers are:

- A growth and development strategy.
- A performance management strategy
- Globalisation strategies.
- Strategies to integrate human resources management into the management of the information organisation, and within the context of the external environment of the organisation.
- A change management focus.
- Mechanisms through which human resources management and development can add value to the overall performance and service excellence of the library and information organisation.
- Strategically focused, technology-based human resources management and information systems.

With the above key aspects in place, the human resources in a library and information organisation and the organisation itself can grow and develop in order to become competitive in a global information world.

Planning towards excellence should focus on an emerging people management philosophy at macro and micro levels.

MACRO LEVEL

Effective human resources development in library and information organisations must in the first place be addressed strategically. **Strategic human resources development** means the process of changing an organisation, stakeholders outside it, groups inside it, and people employed by it, through planned learning and training so that they possess the knowledge and skills they need to be successful in their task and to deliver an excellent service to the library and information user and potential user.

To understand strategic human resources development, practitioners must first understand strategic business planning, because human resources management and development is only a tool for helping implement these plans. It is a holistic approach and the outcome is an organisational strategy for the human resources development effort which guides, unifies and provides direction to planned learning, training, development and growth.

The question of funding always looms over the plans for human resources development programmes, and it is easy to understand why training and development initiatives might be seriously hampered during times of budget reductions. However it is important to remember that if library and information management is willing to spend money on technology, they should simultaneously commit themselves to spend money and time on the training and development of staff in order to use the technology to offer and support an excellent service.

A philosophy which supports the holistic approach of strategic human resources development is that of the "learning organisation", advanced by Senge (1990). In simple terms a learning organisation places great importance upon intentional, continuous learning and transforming itself through both adapted and innovative learning (Callahan & Watson 1995, 377). Senge's philosophy, which has rapidly gained popularity in the corporate world, is equally valuable for library and information organisations.

The essence of strategic intent and thinking is the awareness of how factors in the external and internal environment as well as future conditions may effect decisions for the future. The time is ripe for human resources development practitioners to adopt a broader conception of their role - indeed, a strategic view - that they are agents who facilitate learning for organisations, groups/departments as well as individuals. Viewed from this broader strategic approach, attention will be given to important aspects on the micro level.

MICRO LEVEL

At the micro level, human resources management should engaged in a strategy to support individual and organisational development and growth. It often happens that money and other resources are wasted, because the training initiatives do not result in improved performance. To counteract this problem a situation analysis, or training audit, is a valuable starting point.

The purpose of the *training audit* is to systematically examine all major aspects of training and development activities. It assists the human resources development manager and his team to review what they are doing, and identifies what improvements can be made. The approach of the audit is to strengthen the theory and practice base of human resources development professionals so that they can enhance the performance of employees.

An in-depth needs-analysis aims to identify skill and competence requirements for the future. Competently executed training needs analysis often identifies needs that are best answered by non-training interventions. For example, interpersonal issues does not necessarily mean that there is a need for conflict-resolution programmes; it may simply indicate a need for a third-party consultation.

Many skills are learned at the workstation from people not necessarily qualified by ability or temperament to teach these skills. On-the-job training can be a neglected training aspect of a human resources development programme. The benefits of this method is that it can be focused to meet individual needs and the transfer of learning can be maximised by teaching skills where the work actually is done. During the training audit, key principles of effective on-the-job-training programmes are examined with a view towards integrating them into the human resources development programme.

The transfer of learning, as part of the audit, focuses on processes that ensure that applications move from the training room to the actual workplace.

Through a comprehensive *training and development strategy*, the provision of appropriate knowledge and skills in the identified core competence areas, will support and serve the organisation's vision, goals and objectives.

A training and development strategy should be designed which focuses on the *development* of knowledge and skills on all the key *performance areas* for the different employees.

A training and development strategy should also identify ways in which the organisation can better use the available human resources, e.g. through restructuring into high- performance or self-directed teams, multi-skilling, the implementation of appropriate succession planning and career development initiatives.

Non-competitive aspects in a library and information organisation can be outsourced. When outsourcing is appropriate, the library and information organisation should be creative in identifying and developing partnerships with local entrepreneurs. In the South African context much attention is paid to the development of entrepreneurial skills.

IMPLEMENTING A PROFESSIONAL EXCELLENCE STRATEGY

Implementing the professional excellence concept in a library and information organisation seems straightforward. However, changing the culture and attitude of people is not easy or quick. As a service expert has pointed out, "you cannot make happy customers with unhappy employees". For this reason it is a good idea to assess the climate of the organisation at the outset. By conducting employee surveys, interviewing specific work groups, one can determine the levels of morale, optimism and energy that will be encountered.

As the excellence process swings into action, it becomes appropriate to ensure that support systems in the organisation and in the external environment are aligned to the professional excellence concept. Amongst other aspects which are important for a climate in which professional excellence can flourish are:

Re-humanising the library and information organisation

In their struggle for survival and prosperity, organisations must be careful not to stampede over their people. Short-sighted bottom-line chases cause human resources to be confused with what can be called "human remains". It is important for management to realise that they have to deal with a complete human being. The spirits of the employees are the most important ingredient in the performance of the excellence process. It is the baking powder in the mix; it can make the organisation rise to any occasion, or it can make the organisation fall flat on its face. It is possible that the collective spirit of people will dictate the outcome of performance and excellence of the library and information organisation.

Three important organisational issues to be considered are:

- Organisational behaviour - the nature of the events that occur in the organisation will depend on the existing patterns of behaviour which emerge as the result of different attitudes that exist amongst the workforce. It is often the case that low performance is assumed, rather than properly explored. It is important to find the root causes for problems and address them, rather than treating the symptoms of problems. The problem could be a need for specific training or development programmes.

- Management role - the new management role shifts away from controlling to managing the total performance environment of the organisation and the employees. Through this shift, management becomes part of the team who can challenge systems, structures, procedures, and practices constructively to improve performance and excellence. The result could be a true learning organisation.
  The involvement of management in human resources development will result in a more transparent organisational climate, which establishes mutual trust and co-operation.

- Organisational transformation - the team approach is again applicable. Management and possible transformation committees should not work in isolation. Everyone must be involved and participate in the transformation process.

Empower or enable employees

The underlying theory for the empowerment of people, is leadership. Leadership is the ability to influence others to co-operate voluntary. The challenge of leadership faces every person in every role or position/level in any organisation. An organisation's ability to survive is directly dependent on growing leaders, and this in turn is dependent on meeting the needs of the human being - of putting humanity back into organisations. An organisation's ability, skills and commitment to enable, empower and liberate human resources will be a valuable source of competitive advantage in the future - especially in South Africa (Charlton 1992, ix).

The leadership role of management (management refers not only to the executive person, but it refers to those people in the organisation who have to guide and lead other people on various levels) is very important in the process of power sharing. Furthermore empowerment means, giving people the authority to carry out their responsibilities, as well as removing factors that hamper personal and organisational development.

This is a paradigm shift for management through which an *inclusive learning environment* can be created. An inclusive learning environment places everybody inside the learning environment, where every interaction is regarded as an opportunity to learn by the participants. The learning objective is no longer the "question that is asked to test if you know the answer" but rather the "question that stimulates discussion, dialogue and exploration around what the answer or solution, should be". Such a *workplace curiosity* is the foundation of a learning culture through which employees can empower themselves.

Key aspects in the empowerment of all employees include:

- ensuring that everybody understands the big picture
- encouraging employee involvement
- identifying potential to acquire competence - accelerated learning
- training, development, and empowerment should be seen as value adding
- empowerment which inspires and challenges employees intellectually

The involvement of management in human resources development will result in a more transparent organisational climate, which establishes mutual trust and co-operation.

Shared vision and values

It is the ideal that management should communicate its proposed vision to all employees and invite the whole staff to participate in the fleshing out of the vision and development of values which will give practical expression to the vision. Shared vision and values necessitate shared development of vision and values. Part of the development and implementation of shared vision and values is the participative evaluation of how well they are being fulfilled.

Mutual trust and respect

Mutual trust and respect is the result of treating others with trust and respect. It requires from everybody to take the first step, reaching out first and offering one's hand in trust and respect before demanding or expecting it from another. Viewed from within this context, mutual trust and respect in library and information organisations could be difficult, especially because of competitive initiatives. The only way of eradicating distrust is to initiate the type of actions and behaviours that demonstrate trust. This aspect links with the broader conception of the role of human resources development practitioners.

Unity in diversity

It is still all too often the case in multicultural societies, that specific levels or sections within the organisation are the de facto preserve of one or other group, or people from a relatively homogeneously background. Failure to recognise, practise and praise diversity is in itself an endorsement of discrimination. Lack of diversity is a guarantee that certain essential points of view, attitudes, and approaches will be ignored, or not allocated the importance that they deserve. The recognition of possible diversities in a library and information organisation will support the team approach and participative decision-making and management.

A SOUTH AFRICAN PERSPECTIVE

The transition to democracy in South Africa was without doubt, one of the greatest human achievements of the century. The people of South Africa got together, used their talents, and crafted a vision that is busy unfolding. In human resources development, a comprehensive framework being developed to redress imbalances of the past. The concept of an integrated approach to education, training and development forms the basis of the national training system. Such an integrated approach to education, training and development in one system requires a new pattern or paradigm of thinking in which they are not seen as separate entities, each with its own reason for existence, but as one life-long process of *learning*.

The *integrated approach* indicates an overall strategy with its vision to provide a human resource development system with an integrated approach to education and training, which will provide for the economic and social needs of the country as well as for the development needs of the individual. Education and training must, by means of a national qualification framework, empower individuals, improve their quality of life and contribute to the development targets in the national economic plan.

The national qualifications framework is based on a credit system for achieving learning outcomes. A learning outcome is in essence an ability developed by the learner that reflects an integration of knowledge and skills that can be transferred to different contexts. The learning outcome is a statement of learner *capability*. Thus, it does not only mean the mastering of skills. This capability is an integration of the ability to *perform* a task, and to *understand* it. That is, to become *competent*. The true meaning of *competency* is difficult to explain but one explanation is:

- a skill or a cluster of skills
- executed within an indicated range or context, and
- to specific standards of performance, integrated knowledge or understanding
- and the ability to transfer the skills to other related contexts (Bellis 1997, 32-33).

Competency is the integration of knowledge, skill, and value orientation, demonstrated to a defined standard in a specific context.

There are a number of important issues in this definition:

- It is integrative and consequently views human behaviour as holistic. While not disputing that competencies can be subjected to various types and levels of analysis; it is the integration of the components of a particular competency which is important.
- Knowledge can be defined as *what we know* which has been internalised, and also comprises *how we think and understand* ... it is information, theory, arguments, or concepts that have been conceptualised within our own particular mental and effective or emotional structures.
- Skills refer to *doing* or *the ability to do*. This may be abstract at a cognitive level, but the connotation around skills has been largely concerned with psychomotor activity. No one will argue that predominantly psychomotor skills include a cognitive element; but the physical expression of skills such as music, art, cabinet-making, typing or tasks done on the computer have been dominated by the concept of skill.
- Value orientation has received very little emphasis in the literature and debate on competencies; yet no activity or performance is value free. Value orientation can be seen as an essential component of competency and performance.
- A competency is only useful if it can be demonstrated or measured and this by definition requires standards of performance and statements of the parameters or context in which performance is required.

This is by no means a complete definition of competence as each context will require its own working definition. It does however, incorporate key concepts and can be applied in respect of the collective competence of organisations or teams, the individual competencies required by professions or specific jobs and those generic self-management competencies essential to individual functioning in a modern economy.

Such a view of competence can be seen as viable at all levels - both individually, organisationally and in terms of the national qualifications framework levels. Education and training based on this view can bridge the gaps in people development and organisational performance and professional excellence.

The National Qualifications Framework (NQF)

The legal basis of the NQF is the South African Qualifications Authority Act of 1995. The Act made provision for the establishment of the South African Qualifications Authority and tasked it with the implementation of the NQF. The basis of the NQF are *unit standards*. Each unit standard will be allocated a number of *credits at a specific level* and a qualification will be awarded when the learner has demonstrated an ability to meet the performance or assessment criteria specified in the required number and range of units. Unit standards can be seen as building blocks of a qualification. Unit standards include a statement of learning outcomes which the learner needs to achieve to obtain credits, towards a registered qualification.

Characteristics of unit standards

Well written Unit Standards internationally have the following characteristics:

- They include statements of the competency outcomes to be achieved.
- They will be endorsed by the relevant National Standards Bodies - which in South Africa acts under The South African Qualifications Authority - after acceptable consultation with stakeholders.
- They should reflect an integration of knowledge, skill and value orientation, that is, they should include:
- requirements to perform individual tasks as well as a number of different tasks within a function
- the requirement to respond to irregularities and breakdown in routines
- the requirement to deal with the responsibilities and expectations of the work environment, that are standards of professionalism, work ethics, and safety
- the ability to apply skills in new situations and changing work organisations rather than simply reflecting the tasks currently performed
- they should focus on the performance expected of the learner rather than the learning process and are independent of learning time constraints
- the performance criteria should be clearly understandable to the trainer and the learner
- subjectivity and ambiguous wording should be avoided
- The Unit Standards should be reviewed, and if necessary, updated regularly.

The library and information profession in South Africa, as well as the education and training institutions, are challenged to identify national, organisational, occupational and managerial competencies with the appropriate unit standards. This will enable the profession to create and develop new job profiles, since it is expected that the nature of jobs could change in future, as a result of technological and multi-cultural changes. This will make the library and information employee a more marketable and competitive person.

CONCLUSION

The success of future human resources activities in library and information organisations, will depend on integrating human resources development strategies with the overall organisational strategies on macro and micro level. In the new world of work, where there is great emphasis on the human being to offer an excellent service, competencies are becoming tradable commodities which have a market value. Competencies provide an integrating mechanism and focus for individual and organisational learning in the library and information profession.

REFERENCES

Bellis, I. (1997), "An interpretation of competence," *People Dynamics*, 15(1) pp.32-33.

Callahan, D. and Watson, M. (1995), "Care of the organisation: training and development strategies," *The Journal Of Academic Librarianship*, 21(5) pp. 376-381.

Charlton, G.D. (1992), *Leadership: the human race,*. Johannesburg: Juta.

Senge, P.M. (1990), *The fifth discipline: the art and practice of the learning organisation*, New York: Doubleday.

LIS PROFESSIONALS IN THE NETWORKED LEARNING ENVIRONMENT

Irene Wormell, FID/ET Chair
Royal School of Librarianship
Copenhagen
Denmark

Abstract: The paper aims to present the ways in which educators and trainers of information professionals have responded to the challenge of equipping professionals with the necessary learning strategies and flexible information skills adaptive to the reality of a networked/learning environment.

INTRODUCTION

The world of information has been under continuous change during the last decade and there is every reason to believe that the rapid changes will continue and that our involvement in the electronic information environment will increase.

This development requires an entirely new perspective, new strategies and new skills on the part of information professionals. In order to support the development throughout the world, information professionals need to learn new combinations of competencies and skills. Adaptation to the emerging electronic information environment demands considerable re-education of, and continuous learning by, all professionals, challenging their intellectual capabilities and requiring adjustment of their mental models and perceptions of work tasks.

In the last years in the FID/ET Committee work there has been strong emphasis on the competitive environment in which LIS professionals exist today and the vulnerabilities caused by the traditional definition of this profession. Since the place-bound character of the profession is weakening with the advent of electronic media, telecommunication and networking, many other information-related professionals are claiming that they hold the keys to the solutions of both content and form-related problems of the field. To support the ongoing professional developments the aim was to generate new diagnoses, treatments and inference methods to form a new foundation and a new definition for the profession.

1. FID/ET COMMITTEE ACTIVITIES

This strategic programme formed the basis for the FID/ET Pre-Congress Seminar in Tokyo, 1994, where *"Multifunctional Information Work. New demands for training?"* was the main discussion theme. The focus was on the synergetic effects of co-operative activities and the importance of having a multidisciplinary insight as regards working solutions for information problems. The *modern* LIS information professional was seen as a professional who constantly interacts with other professionals in the working environment

The seminar provided insight and knowledge about many ongoing activities where the integration of different skills and competencies of multifunctional information work has been successfully carried out by LIS institutions in co-operation with other academic institutions or private companies.

The topic of the 1996 FID/ET seminar in Graz, *"Working and Learning in a Networked Environment"*, was the new roles and functions that are emerging as a result of the new knowledge transfer practices which will be dominant in business and organizations within the next few years.

The aim was to stimulate the utilization of electronic information storage and network communication technologies to enhance professional competence and to provide the individual information professional with new operational and strategic capabilities. Because of the rapid changes in the working and learning environments of most organizations, the year 2000 will require an entirely new perspective, new strategies and new skills from information professionals. Most sectors within the information society are increasingly demanding flexible professionals who are capable of adapting themselves to fluctuating situations. It has been found that information skills in conjunction with independent learning behaviour strategies and co-operative attitudes are essential survival tools in modern organizations.

The seminar emphasized that the purport of education and training of modern information professionals is not only the adoption of new technologies but also a proper understanding of the flow of information and knowledge in modern society. The aim is to manage information as a critical resource which multiplies the value of other resources such as land, labour and capital.

The seminar had a very compact programme with 24 presentations, organized in three sessions.

1. Learning Environment
2. Working Environment
3. Managing Change in Careers and Workplaces

The presentations of the seminar are not published as a proceedings/monograph, but the papers have been submitted to relevant professional journals. Thus, a selection of full length papers related to the topic of "Learning in a Networked Environment" is published in the *FID News Bulletin* 1997 January as a special issue, providing the international readership of the journal with an interesting snapshot of ongoing developments in the field of education and training of modern information professionals.

Another selection of papers on the theme of "Working in a Networked Environment" is published as special issue of the *International Forum on Information and Documentation (IFID)* Vol.21, 1996 No. 4 December.

The future information professional

In designing the content of the Telework '96 course (tasks and sources), the designers chose information broking as a pilot application which combines skills from various competence areas where teleworking and information management work may synergise. In addition, account has been taken of a recent international survey on the state-of-the-art, the *Modern Information Professional* (FID, 1996), which identifies the following as critical skills and attributes for future information professionals:

- general ability to express knowledge, ideas and opinions with confidence and clarity to a variety of audiences for a variety of purposes (*communication skills*)
- ability to identify, use and critically access information sources based on the use of appropriate information technology (*information literacy*)
- ability to identify organizational and situational problems, analyse their main features and implement strategies and tactics for their solution (*problem-solving*)
- appreciation of the social and cultural context of a profession and understanding the ethical norms and standards which constitute professional integrity (*informed professionalism*) development of commitment to reflexive learning throughout one's professional life (*lifelong learning*). (Wormell, 1995b)

2. TELEWORKING - A NEW OPTION FOR MODERN INFORMATION PROFESSIONALS

One of the latest results of the FID/ET professional development programme is an international joint course between Queen Margaret College in Scotland and the Royal School of Librarianship in Denmark, which introduced undergraduate students to tools and issues that are relevant to teleworking. The approach was one of active learning, and the collaborative training programme lasted twelve weeks (September to December 1996). The course designers aimed to give the students experience in: 1) working and learning at a distance; 2) international broking across national frontiers; 3) working productively in teams with students from different educational traditions; 4) communication across national cultures and traditions; 5) acting as informed professionals.

Students were assessed according to the norms of the respective syllabi in each of the two participating institutions. Both Danish and Scottish groups, however, shared a common task: to produce a written evaluation report on the legislative, financial and social conditions of teleworking, both in Denmark and in Scotland. The purpose of this report was to review the conditions as well as the advantages and disadvantages of running this kind of business operation in the two different countries. The report was based on literature searches and analyses as well as the experience of the students themselves, combined with practical and theoretical knowledge in gathering and analysing information from various sources.

What did the course Telework '96 involve?

Two fourth year undergraduate seminar groups working together on an information broking business plan which would establish a framework for joint Scottish/Danish teams to gain experience of different aspects of electronic communication, networking and information entrepreneurship. The task was selected as an appropriate part of a training programme for a new generation of information professionals who can bid for transnational work within the EU and who are familiar with the practical conditions of broking and teleworking in different member states. The combination of broking and teleworking reflects the author's belief that information students must be aware of these emergent trends in professional information work. (Wormell, 1995a)

The students in both Scotland and Denmark had a background in information resources management, the role and function of information in business, the management and economics of information services, and teamworking. In addition to standard classroom and seminar support, a group of experienced and experienced international information brokers was recruited to act as mentors for individual students. The course designers offered this 'special resource', an electronic personal link for a given student to a senior professional with considerable experience and high level qualifications, with two aims in mind: firstly, these links would broaden students' communication skills, and secondly, they would lay the foundation for professional networking. The mentors have provided assistance in the form of seminars and short communications via e-mail in response to ad hoc problems, and they will review and comment on the final phase of the course work. Most importantly, they may be perceived as an inspiration and encouragement for students who may wish to enter the world of brokerage and fee-based information services.

The project is intended as a pilot for future active learning packages which may be made available to a wider clientele on the Internet. The active learning approach has encouraged the development of personal transferable skills in negotiation, in handling breakdowns in communication and planning and in coping with stress and cultural conflicts. These skills are often absent in LIS curricula, are difficult to foster in an academic syllabus but are highly sought after by employers. We feel they are particularly appropriate to the training of information brokers, i.e. independent intermediaries who must deal with unfamiliar clients and unfamiliar topics.

2.1 Background

The initiative was driven by both theoretical and pragmatic reasons. A series of academic studies of the social and managerial effects of teleworking, concomitant with such general predictions (Olson, 1988; Pratt, 1988, Huws, 1991; Solon, 1992), has defined and explored homeworking in terms of a range of scenarios. In the proposed course, we focus on homeworkers who work as members of groups, either ad hoc or as relocated employees of a larger institution. Students will experience tasks which are managed remotely and which lead to a marketable product or service. The course thus simulates the defining conditions of telework: geographical separation from management and from customers or clients.

Estimates in the previous decade of the extent of teleworking by 1995 have been grossly overgenerous. Fewer homes than anticipated have machines (Holmes, 1995; Ward, 1995), and the number has not increased according to the forecasts. But where households do have machines, many of these are used for work - most commonly extensions of the day job, a trend noted by Olson, 1988, and examined in detail by Wright (1990) in a study of behavioural scientists. The overestimates of previous years may have been premised on expected growth of an infrastructure that has only recently been established. The predictions of current forecasters may thus be better based than those of their predecessors. There is a growing body of 'testimony' from small-scale operators (Field, 1994; Bibby, 1995; Spinney, 1995).

Current forecasts of a major shift to home or teleworking in the US and the UK may be validated in an increased trend to contract out, or outsource service elements in both private and public sectors. Recent reports on the future workforce (The Institute for the Future, 1994), for example, indicate that by the end of the century, half of the working population will work from home, either attached to a corporation, or as self-employed agents. This is most likely to be the mode of working for workers over 45 years of age, many of whom may seek or may be forced into early retirement. Other potential client groups are women returning to work after child-rearing, and unemployed professional graduates (Crossan and Burton, 1993).

The author thus believes that there is a niche for training remote information professionals, and that, given a professional climate which seeks cost-effective service provision in LIS, they are likely to be able to compete in the market. (Lacity, 1994; Intner, 1994; Ogburn. 1994; Winters, 1994)

There are several types of task which we believe are suitable for teleworkers who will operate as information specialists. The *first* is work on 'standard' rule-based LIS tasks. indexing, abstracting, cataloguing and searching, where the role of a human mentor can be sustained remotely, as is demonstrated by the outstandingly successful Crossaig project. (Blaxter, 1995). The *second* area is management and planning tasks dealing with policy formulation, resource allocation and other areas characterized by discussion of loosely-defined alternatives, the use of a range of sources both local and remote, and decision-making (Caulkin, 1995; Blaxter, 1995). A *third* area is innovative problem-solving which will involve brainstorming and a discussion of realistic implementation patterns: sample tasks might be to design a research project or to write a specification for a new product or service.

2.2 The objectives

In the design of the course, it was aimed to develop skills identified in the recent FID/MIP survey (Wormell 1995b) by formulating *three* main objectives.

The first of these relates to the student experience; the second to the experience of the participating institutions as managers; the third to the experience of the lecturers as educators.

The course aimed to give the students experience in:

a) collaborative working and learning at a distance
b) acting, working and communicating with Internet and local network facilities
c) studying information broking across national frontiers
d) dealing with time management
e) dealing with cultural conflict
f) dealing with technology breakdowns

From the point of view of the participating institutions as managers (the second objective), the project would provide a working case study to establish technical and service level criteria for the delivery of collaborative courses. It would also allow both institutions to assess the management and costing implications of experimental collaborative learning packages. From the point of view of the participating institutions/lecturers as educators the third objective), the project would provide experience in integrating novel networked tools for collaboration into an approved syllabus in each of the participating institutions (e.g. IRC, CuSeeMe, Bookmarks and shared file management by means of FTP and home pages). In addition, it would also provide experience in integration (managing tasks and timetables for distance learning) across institutions and, thirdly, in negotiating with partners from a different culture with different first languages.

Phases of the course

The first phase of the project required students to establish work plans and to select from a range of tools to establish which was appropriate for what. This took two weeks of intensive laboratory work, though in future projects the time frame might vary as for example, students had greater or lesser experience of and access to Internet-based software tools. Students were assisted in this phase by technical experts.

In the second phase (about three weeks, with overlap with phase one). students acquired skills in home page development, and in building a Web-based resource platform which would allow them to   collaborate. Students drew again on the expertise of trained technical instructors and on Internet design literature.

In the third phase (about eight weeks, again with overlap with the previous phases), students addressed the main task: to compile two reports to be published on the Web using the collaborative platform established in the previous phases. The students were asked to take the role of international consultancy companies with Danish and Scottish team members, and the lecturers assumed the role of client organizations. The first part of the task was to prepare a tender document, requiring students to identify a topic for an evaluative report (which was the second part of the task) and to specify a workplan for the delivery of a report on that topic. In this phase (four weeks), students attended lectures and seminars led by experienced information brokers, and made on relevant study visits.

Sources and resources

The course designers with the aims outlined above, encouraged the students to use a range of sources. In addition to traditional printed material, both sites had access to web resources. The most important of these was a customised shared textual resource space, Telework 95, which was prepared in the previous year's teleworking class at QMC (http://www.qmced.uk/cis/telework/) and offers documentary support in the following areas:

business planning
project management techniques
costing and pricing
packaging and presentation
case studies

Telework 95 was supplemented by general Web resources including the homepages of sample information broking services and appropriate discussion lists and the resulting home page text,   Telework 96, can be accessed from the same QMC URL, and from the Danish page at http://www.ax.db.dk/telework/

In addition, students had access to human expertise in the form of the experienced international mentors mentioned above, who made themselves available on-line to offer advice as managers and consultants with established track records. Other brokers and technical experts were brought on board on an ad hoc basis and students were offered study visits to information centres and other relevant institutions.

As the pilot project had no external funds, the technology base for the management of shared resources and communication had to be cheap and easily accessible. We have used e-mail, Windows 95, Internet-based tools for file management and file transfer and conferencing - all of which were available in the public domain. We thus assembled a 'groupware platform' of our own with existing institutional resources. At both sites, a small development team designed tasks around locally assembled software, work stations and communication infrastructure.

2.5 Tasks

The course designers identified the following list of tasks as measures of competence to telework.

- to prepare home pages which present both personal and professional profiles
- to establish contact and negotiate responsibilities with a remote working partner (the course tutor in the first instance)
- to design a business plan over a period of weeks with this partner
- to identify on-line sources (electronic conferences, databases) for project work
- to identify sources of information about macro-level trends in society and the future of work
- to identify sources of advice to equip themselves as teleworkers

Competence in these tasks is, we think, indicative of experience in the following managerial areas:

- co-ordinating tasks
- managing time frames for group projects
- resolving questions of responsibility, accountability and ownership
- management of information to support project work
- tendering and costing issues for network work
- marketing

Successful completion of the tasks is also indicative of key technical competencies:

- presentation of oneself on the Internet
- searching skills: databases and Internet
- organizing and managing of jointly accessed local and remote file
- archiving and storing project work

2.6 Assessment

According to the criteria that obtain in each of the participating institutions, the students have been assessed on three dimensions:

1) task completion
2) managerial competence
3) technical competence

The tasks for the project were managed in a tight time frame. The task set included continuous work on a weekly basis on small tasks such as finding facts and data on the Internet, preparing a short essay on the essentials of broking such as personal characteristics, skills, working methods and working styles. In addition, students had to complete 'milestone' projects at six and at twelve weeks. These have been cumulative, leading to the final product, a business report, to be presented to the project managers (the lecturers and mentors) and assessed by them at the end of the course.

In mid-November, participants had an opportunity to work face to face for three days when the Danish participants visited Edinburgh. They worked on a mini-project in that week (a jointly prepared report on macro-level societal trends in the information society) which has been marked up as the first section of the final report. This joint project allowed students to compare face-to-face and electronic working and asses their experience of remote working to date.

3. CRITICAL ISSUES

The formal evaluation of the student questionnaires still has to be done, but based on weekly diaries kept by the Scottish students and verbal presentations by the Danish students at a feedback seminar in Edinburgh, there is an estimation of how successful we have been in carrying out our aims and objectives (discussed below as the three objectives described in Section 2.2.).

Technology failures

In spite of the efforts of the course designers, students at both sites have found the course stressful, largely because of technology failures: 'lost' e-mail and FTP failures; painfully slow Internet access at some moments; incompatible site licences. In the absence of back-up arrangements (lecturers providing access to fax and office telephones, for example) students felt frustrated. Neither side developed alternative channels of communication until relatively late in the course, when valuable time had been lost. In future courses, a workshop in the early stages on what can go wrong and how to cope may help to ease the stress of inevitable technology failures.

Working with strangers

With hindsight, both lecturers agree that assumptions were made about the ease with which students would be able to work productively with others outside the familiar course or college group. At both sites, however, students found working with strangers problematic; this is a common problem in computer-mediated groupwork, where more experience and skilled use of the facilities can help to overcome the initial barriers. In future courses the designers would include a session on professional etiquette and professional behavioural norms which may avoid manifest confusion in this year's cohort about the appropriate social register. Neither side had offered the other sufficient information about 'professional' competence - details of skills and aptitudes for example, and of how these had been acquired in the respective educational trajectories of each institution. At the face to face meeting in Edinburgh, it was suggested that arrangements for joint feedback sessions from the start should be included in the course design, to allow those participating in future versions of the course to identify early on failures in communication and information transfer.

Language and cultural boundaries

Working across language boundaries inevitably posed some problems, which in future versions of the course can be avoided by providing very specific instructions and ensuring in follow-up sessions that they have been clearly understood. Unfamiliar working habits were also a source of stress, for example, the 'flexible response' mode of working required each Danish/Scottish group to prepare a rapid report on macro-level societal trends in 48 hours. In future transnational versions of the course, profiles will be provided on the respective working habits and styles of the participating institutions.

Understanding the group task and one´s role in it

Understanding of one's role in the tasks which have been set for a team was enhanced by access to an archive of group transactions (the 'group text'). In the case of the Scottish/Danish project, shared bookmarks on the shared home page were intended to act as a 'group text' resource which would allow the class to reflect on the construction of joint texts and thereby gain a greater understanding of their own contribution *vis a vis* that of others in the group. The technological problems mentioned above have made this a less than convincing resource.

Management of time

A potential drawback in an electronic forum is the management of time, perhaps the most difficult aspect of team experience to accommodate in a computer-mediated system. While many participants in computermediated sessions appreciate that saving time in reaching consensus at different stages of task development is necessary, many also report feelings of 'premature closure', a phenomenon observed in some of the participants in Teleworking 96. Time management strategies vary according to circumstances: urgent commands, consensus building against the clock, diachronic and leisurely digestions and debate will all feature in the activity of a longitudinal group, and computer support will be more effective where participants understand that differing parameters are involved. A major issue for the students was time management when not in class - how much time they should devote to tracking down material in libraries, for example.

4. MANAGEMENT ISSUES

As a management exercise, the project allowed the course designers to identify several areas where problems may arise. The first of these relate to *technical and service level criteria for IT*. At local level, both sides had e-mail and internal communication problems and server problems which affected outside contact on occasions where neither the Danish nor the Scottish site alerted the other in time, lack of response to messages was misinterpreted as lack of interest or neglect. On several occasions, a link tried and tested by the technical assistants did not work when the group attempted to communicate in class time.

Issues relating to *levels of access* posed initial problems: permissions for who sees what must be established in a way that allows the lecturer/student relationship to work - if either is excluded from work which both must see (for assessment purpose for example), problems will arise. The first attempt to exchange tender documents via FTP for the lecturers at each site to evaluate, for example, failed completely. Our solution was to put everything - working drafts, finished assignments, work to be assessed, on the home page.

A third group of service level issues related to the *timing of access*. Technology in both institutions is heavily used, and access is thus to some extent restricted. Finding a timetable slot to allow synchronous communication for all participants proved impossible. Internet access was also subject to huge variations depending on the time of day.

A totally separate set of management issues relates to *costs*. The author chose to simplify this area by providing a rough calculation which does not include capital IT costs, as the project was based on platforms and toolkits already available at both sites. We have divided the costs of the human resource into three sections: academic, technical and support for the study visit. The estimates must be doubled to obtain the total costs as the hours listed apply for each of the participating institutions in Scotland and Denmark. Rough costs are as follows:

Academic support:
Pre-project meetings: 35 hours
Administration: 25 hours
Negotiation with mentors and local institution: 15 hours
Class contact time: 50 hours
Total: 125 hours

Technical support:
Setting up server and home page: 30 hours
Instruction and preparation: 20 hours
Total: 50 hours

Study visit:
Academic support: 10 hours
Class contact: 6 hours
Total: 16 hours

Our estimates indicate that design and administration are the resource intensive parts of the process, not the technology.

The third of our objectives (to provide experience in the design of innovative educational packages within and across institutions) proved less problematic in one of the two participating sites (Edinburgh), where the innovative web-based learning package for teleworking described above (a 'wired' inventory of resources and case studies) had been produced the previous year with help from an internal grant. This site thus benefited from the fact that students had clearer expectations of what might and might not be achieved and from expert technical help from an assistant who had worked on the previous project and was familiar with the working practices of the IT centre, and who had visited Copenhagen to inspect the technology base in the partner institution.

What has proved particularly challenging to both sides in TELEWORK 96 is international collaboration with a group of heterogeneous strangers, some at novice level, some more experienced in computer-based learning. One particular design issue is raised by such differentiated start-up skills: to what extent is a 'seamless' working environment desirable in the design of Internet-based learning materials? The course designers and their assistants did not attempt to provide this, as we felt it important that students should manage Internet tools and spaces, not have a 'management shell' supplied. With hindsight, this approach lost us valuable time on the completion of class tasks, and in the next version of the package, we may include a 'seamless workspace' interface borrowed from a parallel network-based course at QMC on Human Factors in Information Management. (Buckner and Davenport, 1996)

Feedback from the evaluation protocols will allow the course designers to adjust the resources and planning procedures and avoid some of this year's problems in future versions of the course.

ACKNOWLEDGEMENTS

The author wish to acknowledge the collaboration of Elisabeth Davenport, Senior Lecturer in Information Management at the Queen Margaret College, in the project as well as the assistance of the Danish and Scottish students who participated in the class, and the technical advice given by Dorthe D. Jensen and Alyn Jones in both the development and the implementation stages of the project.

REFERENCES

Alavi, M. (1994), "Computer-mediated collaborative learning: an empirical evaluation", *MIS Quarterly*, 18 (2), June, pp.159-180.

Blaxter, T. (1995), "Managing teleworkers: The Crossaig experience", *Managing Information,* 2 (5), May, pp. 30-32.

Buckner, K. and Davenport, E. (1996), "Support issues for case based learning in an undergraduate human factors class", in *Proceedings of the NetLinks Symposium on Networked Learner Support*, Sheffield, 18 - 20 May.

Caulkin, S. (1995), "Jobless bosses take to temping", *The Observer*, 5 February, Business Pages, p. 9.

Crossan, G. and Burton, P. (1993), "Teleworking stereotypes: 3 case studies", *Journal of Information Science*, 19, pp. 349-362.

Davenport, E. and McKim, G. (1995), "Groupware in LIS education", in M. Haycock Beaulieu and N. O. Pors (eds). *Proceedings of the 1st British-Nordic Conference on Library and Information Studies, Copenhagen 1995*. Copenhagen: Royal Danish School of Librarianship, pp. 167-180.

FID, (1996), " Modern information professional: worldwide survey", *FID News Bulletin*, 46, 10 October, p. 293.

Haddon, L. and Silverstone, R.(1994), "Telework: the changing relationship of home and work", in R. Mansell.(ed.), *The Management of Information and Communication Technologies: Emerging Patterns of Control*. London: Aslib, pp. 234-237.

Holmes, B. (1995), "This is the age of the microwave", *New Scientist*, 23 September, p. 5.

Huws, U. (1984), *The New Homeworkers: New Technology and the Changing Location of White Collar Work*. London: Low Pay Unit.

Huws, U. (1991), "Telework projections", *Futures,* January/February, pp. 19-31.

Institute for the Future (1994), *The Future Work Space. Summary Results, 1994*. Available from The Institute for the Future. 2744 Sand Hill Road. Menlo Park, CA94025 7020.

Intner, S. S. (1994) "Outsourcing: what does it mean for technical services?" *Technicalities*, 14 (3), pp. 3 - 5.

Lacity, M et. al. (1994), "Realising outsourcing expectations: incredible expectations, credible outcomes", *Information Systems Management*, 11 (4), Fall, 7 - 18.

Olson, M.H. (1988), "Work at home for Computer Professionals: current prospects and future prospects", *ACM Transactions on Office Information Systems*, 7 (4), October, pp. 317-338.

Pratt, J. H.(1988), "Socio-issues related to home-based work", in M. Helander, (ed.) *Handbook of Human-Computer Interaction*. Amsterdam: Elsevier Science Publishers, B.V.

Pratt, J. H.(1988), "Home teleworking: a study of its pioneers", *Technological Forecasting and Social Change*, 25, pp. 1 - 14.

Solon Consultants (1992), *Working at a Distance: Prospects for Telework,* London: Solon Consultants.

Winters, B.A. (1994), "Catalog outsourcing at Wright State University: implications for acquisitions managers", *Library Acquisitions: Practice and Theory*, 18 (4), pp.367-373.

Wormell, 1. (1995a), "Multifunctional information work - new demand for training?" in M. Haycock Beaulieu and N. O. Pors (eds). *Proceedings of the 1st British-Nordic Conference on Library and Information Studies. Copenhagen 1995,* Copenhagen: Royal Danish School of Librarianship, pp. 45-50.

Wormell, 1. (1995b), "Change, competence and organisation", *Education for Library and Information Services Australia (ELISA),* 12 (2), pp. 33-40.

Wright, P. (1990), "Homework: an international comparison of behavioural researchers' use of computers for work at home" in M. Feeney, (ed.), *Information Technology and the Research Process.* London: Taylor Graham, pp. 130-145.

RUSSIAN SYSTEM OF CONTINUING EDUCATION IN TRANSITION

Irina L. Klim
St Petersburg State Institute of Culture

Abstract: The paper recognises that the library profession is one that requires constant upgrading of knowledge and skills. It describes the changes that are taking place in Russia following research and legislative initiatives.

INTRODUCTION

The library profession is one, which by its nature requires permanent learning. Dealing with human knowledge and its endless development condemns librarians to lifelong study. Though the social prestige of the library profession has never been that high, the role of libraries has been highly esteemed. In managing large information resources, library personnel give life to them. We have to keep this in mind when thinking of the values which a library offers to society. Tremendous book collections, overwhelming electronic resources and the new channels of access to information have dramatically changed the traditional library world. They not only have enriched, but have also made the process of the way in which people communicate with knowledge more complicated. Is this not a challenge for the library profession?

All of the points mentioned above relate to libraries in Russia, though one factor needs to be added to the list - a historical move of the whole country from one socio-economic structure to another. The former components of the society are being revised according to new values and political interests. Library education is not an exception. After a century of growing expertise, which contained both positive and negative features, the educational system in Russia became an object for analysis and criticism by library experts and those outside our profession. In building a new structure it is always helpful to take note of the lessons of the past.

The professional development of librarians in the USSR was defined as being the *raising of the qualifications (RQ)*. To understand certain peculiarities of it we need to remember that libraries were considered as the active providers of the communist ideology, the official policy of the government. The pure mission of the libraries - to preserve, organize and to give access to information was also stated, but afterwards.

Consequently the mission of professional education resulted from the mission of libraries and contained the same premises. It was well-understood that to maintain effective performance, professionals needed to upgrade and renew their knowledge and skills. Appreciating the vital role of the libraries in the society, Soviet government spent a lot of money on establishing and supporting an effective system of professional development, which was called the raising of qualifications.

THE GOALS OF RAISING QUALIFICATIONS

There were three main goals underlying the former concept of RQ of the librarians:

1. Improvement of their communist ideology and competence in the soviet governments' policy.
2. Raising and updating their professional knowledge and skills.
3. Improvement in the general education of librarians with an emphasis on the social sciences and humanities.

STRUCTURE AND SUPERVISORS

The structure of the system was rather complicated and heavily centralized. It had a formal status in the field of librarianship, and was considered to be an important part of professional education and library policy. Its hierarchical structure was aimed to keep all institutions under an effective control by the ideological, government and professional authorities. Two main institutions headed this pyramid: the All-Union and the All-Russia Institutes for the Raising of Qualifications of Cultural Professionals which reported to the All-Union and Russian Ministries of Culture. Later on in 1971, there was established the Institute for the Raising of Qualifications of Information Specialists under the State Committee for Science and Technology. Its mission was to provide off-the - job training for the technical libraries' staff and information specialists. All three main institutes, in addition to their educational mission, had an extensive outreach to the system of RQ in the country.

The next level comprised a number of courses, centers and faculties in the different regions, and cities of the USSR which provided RQ programs for all practising librarians and library educators. They might be affiliated with libraries or educational institutions, or existed as separate entities. At the state libraries there were higher library courses within Educational Departments. Library courses provided basic knowledge and skills in librarianship to the subject specialists who came to work in the library. Along with the higher library courses Educational Departments organized on - and off the job training for all the librarians to update and develop their professional competence and skills. Most of the State libraries invited specialists from all over the country. Thus, the Lenin State Library was a center of this kind for the USSR, while the Saltykov-Schedrin State Public Library (now - Russian National Library) - for the libraries of the North-West region of Russia. Special libraries provided courses and organized seminars for the libraries within a related network.

The USSR consisted of 15 republics divided further into administrative regions. The system of RQ followed this geographic structure. Each region had a center of RQ, which operated as the co-ordinator for the libraries in the region. Two cities in the USSR had a regional status: Moscow and Leningrad (now St. Petersburg). Similar to the regional universal research libraries, the central city libraries in Moscow and Leningrad obtained the status of RQ centers within the library community in the city. In all these libraries the key role in professional education belonged to the departments of staff and library development. [1]

In the case of the other library networks: academic, scientific-technical libraries, various types of special libraries (theater, museum, school libraries, libraries for the blind, etc.) one was appointed (usually the largest or a state-level library) to act as a center for RQ.

Several faculties for RQ were opened at the Institutes of Culture [2]. The most famous were the faculties at the Moscow and Leningrad institutes. Some networks used these courses as their centers for RQ. As an example, we can note the academic libraries network in St. Petersburg, which made an agreement with Leningrad Institute of Culture to use its faculties for RQ to train university librarians from the city and the North-Western region of the USSR. In general, faculties for the RQ at the institutes of culture were, so to say, "inter-net" and inter-region courses.

Another type of course were the ones opened at the library collectors. Library collectors presented an interesting example of the Soviet type of library enterprises, which carried out a considerable part of the book purchasing and collection development business for the libraries, providing outsourcing services and products for them. The library collectors did not get a state budget, and carried out their business on a pay their own way basis. That is why the courses of the RQ offered only a fee-based training.

All RQ institutions in the first and second levels of the hierarchy provided off-the-job training and additional education for the librarians. But RQ, in general, was not understood only as being regular study at the courses. A lot of other on-the-job activities were considered to be raising qualifications. They were based in the libraries themselves, and constituted the third level of the RQ system. Each library, to a different extent, trained the staff, organized seminars, lectures, conferences, research works as important measures for the improvement of professional knowledge and skills.

STATUS AND BUDGET

All courses, whether they were independent or affiliated with the parent institution, had to get a license and to register their business at the local or federal authority. These departments approved their curriculum, and provided supervision.

Most of the courses, except those provided by the library collectors and faculties of RQ at the Institutes of culture, existed on federal and local budgets. The same related to the funds which libraries received from the parent authorities for sending their personnel to study at the courses of RQ.

Under the State legislation, each professional received off-the-job training on one of the listed courses once every 4-5 years. The length of the training was up to 2 months. Violation of this rule might result in administrative sanctions against both the supervisor or employee, whoever demonstrated ignorance.

FORMS OF RAISING QUALIFICATIONS

Summarizing all of the educational opportunities, provided at all three levels of the system, All-Union Institute of Raising Qualifications formulated five forms of RQ:

1. On-the-job short-term training.
2. Long-term training at the courses, faculties or institutes for the raising of qualifications (once every 4-5 years).
3. Study/training at the well-advanced libraries or information centers (in and out of the country).
4. Post-graduate study at the institutes of culture for a Ph.D. degree (aspirantura).
5. Study for another library position within LIS[3] (up to a one year course) (Vorobyov, 1991)

This list does not provide information about the many other forms of raising qualifications, which were well-developed by each library: seminars, conferences, participation in research projects. They should be added to the first point on the list.

CONTENT

The official approach to the RQ system put the main emphasis on the issues of upgrading, updating, and developing professional knowledge and skills. It was focused by the field of librarianship, or type of library. The RQ system in the Soviet Union did consider study for another position, but it was a rather small segment, because the change of major was not popular in professional career.

Looking at the goals of RQ we need to remember that a valuable part of each program related to the political issues. They were "a must" for creating any program whether they be for cataloguers, children librarians, bibliographers, not to mention library administration. At the same time, there were always the social sciences and humanities (literature, psychology) included in the curriculum as well.

The core courses in the curriculum were focused on the professional issues: new trends and expertise, international practice, and local librarianship.

The former system of RQ had both advantages and disadvantages, which have to be taken into account now, in a time of transition. The ADVANTAGES may be found in the wide involvement of the whole professional community in the system of RQ; it was well-subsidized by the government and also had alternative economic ways of management; state law ensured obligatory off-the-job training for each librarian on a regular basis; RQ was understood as being the development of both the professional and the general knowledge of the individual.

But in giving credit to the old system, we have to agree that it did not work as effectively as it could because of the following DISADVANTAGES: ideological premises and pressure; the small amount of initiative allowed to the RQ institutions; an overweighted system of courses with poor co-ordination causing duplication in different programs; regional and departmental barriers, preventing RQ patterns communicating; administrative pressures instead of motivation for study; separation of RQ activities from regular education and self-study.

The evaluation of the old forms by the new society is not a simple process in glorifying the good and punishing the bad. The existence and improvement of professional training appeared to be not only a matter of democratic changes and delegated freedom to the educational institutions. It is also a matter of money. The current economic crisis now causes certain losses of positive fundamentals in RQ, and has resulted in the closure of many institutions. The budgets for RQ and of the libraries have been drastically reduced. The gigantic system has been left all of a sudden without enough money, if any. The situation in professional education was aggravated by a wave of resignations - librarians were leaving the profession because of the lower than minimal salary. The replacement due to resignation reached 30-40 per cent per year so that the idea itself of a upgrading or lifelong study seemed odd.

The most difficult and vital years came at the beginning of the 1990's. It was a sort of an historical and economic test, or to say more - a test, about viability. During that period the hierarchy of RQ, set up by the soviet state, started to fall apart. Surprisingly (or probably not) the weakest part of it, which really disappeared, was the all-Union Institute of Raising of Qualifications of Cultural Professionals. Its funding had shrunk, and it died together with the All-Union Ministry of Culture, though All-Russia institute still exists. The same occurred to quite a few well-known courses and faculties, such as the Courses of RQ at the St. Petersburg Center for Information in Science and Technology, which used to be one of the most successful centers for raising qualifications for the information and library specialists. The last example reflects many trends in the new Russian economy, namely - a crisis in the industrial, military-oriented sector of it, severely affecting the network of scientific-technical libraries. In 1989 in St. Petersburg there were 740 scientific-technical libraries, operating within research institutes and industrials plants. As some scholars pointed out, it was a result of the "militarization" of the city economy (Akekseyeva et al, 1990). By 1996 the number of libraries had been reduced to 149 (Chalova, 1996). Experiencing a financial crisis, many industrial enterprises eliminated libraries as a ballast, less valuable when facing bankruptcy.

A current picture of the RQ system looks rather more like a mosaic than a former centralized hierarchy. It is made up of many courses, centers and institutes operating within libraries or independently, and mostly on a pay their way own basis. Even if being left in a state budget, the RQ institutions receive only about 50% of the money requested. Together with a dramatic shortage of students - librarians who came to study during the budget cuts made the institutions investigate the new ways of management and economic possibilities.

The most common solutions to the problems have been found in:

- *the tuition* being raised or brought in (if it was not before);
- *new programs and courses*, not necessarily for librarians, were announced to attract those who can pay;
- *regular education programs* were started, if the curriculum was approved by the licensing authority.

Some institutions made agreements with employment agencies, which paid the tuition for people registered as unemployed and who were willing to study for another profession to get a job.

It is quite remarkable, that even in the beginning of the new economic era, when a lot of "nouveau riche" (or the New Russians) came to the fore, demonstrating their success based not least on knowledge or education, the respect for education has not been lost. People still appreciate it not only as a social tool, but also as a means of personal development. So, using a business terminology, it might be formulated as - "demand brought action". Many institutes and courses of RQ started the programs, which gave the students, on completion, the official certificates or even diplomas in many popular fields: public management, accounting, computer and secretarial skill, interpreting, etc. The tuition at those courses might be rather high, and unfortunately not affordable for many. But the income it gave, helped the RQ institution to fill the gap in state funding and to continue teaching the librarians for a minimal fee.

Nonetheless the flow of librarians being trained at the RQ institutions has been reduced quite significantly, as well as the number of institutions of RQ that survived. In 1995 The Federal Government of Russian Federation issued a new Act on Additional Education for the Specialists, in which the former system of regular training has been consolidated (Postanovleniye..., 1995).

By contrast to the reducing number of state institutions, in the 1990s many commercial courses emerged. Operating on the for-profit basis, they managed to start programs in very popular fields such as: management, market economy and culture, computers and telecommunications, accounting, and foreign languages. Due to their high rate of tuition they could afford to invite well-known professors and specialists. Such centers were opened at Bibliomarket Co. (Moscow), Institute of International Banking (St. Petersburg), University of Economic and Finance (St. Petersburg), and the Moscow Library Association, to mention but a few. The courses for RQ at all the Institutes of Culture are still operating as for-profit educational units, bringing money for the budget of the whole institute.

When speaking of the transition of the Russian education for professionals, it is very important to mention these positive trends, which should greatly benefit the whole system when economic situation stabilises. The first of them relates to the new concept of professional development, which is actively discussed among Russian librarians and educators nowadays.

Rethinking the new <u>mission and goals</u> of the libraries and the status of the library profession Russian scholars and practising librarians provided several corporate research projects. They were guided by the major libraries: The Russian State Library, The State Public Library for Science and Technology (GPNTB), St. Petersburg, Moscow and Kemerovo State Institute of Culture, Central Research Library of Ukraine. The research results enriched our knowledge and understanding of the actual situation in the libraries and library profession at the end of the 20th century. It gave a good basis for rethinking the existing system of professional education as well. Though the system of RQ had not been that deeply analyzed we can get a picture of it from parts of the results of the research mentioned above, and from professional publications.

The most valuable impact on the concept of RQ has been made by the All-Union research "The Library Profession: State of the Art and Prospective" sponsored by the Ministry of Culture and headed by the St.Petersburg State Institute of Culture (Afansova and Sokolov, 1992). The Director of this project, Professor Arkady Sokolov (St. Petersburg), introduced to our profession the idea of a lifelong, never-stopped process of education, which he borrowed from pedagogic and foreign experience (Solokov, 1990). Instead of the former division: regular education at the library schools, and post-degree raising of qualifications, Professor Sokolov proposed to consider both of them together, plus a self-study component as the system of a lifelong education, which has to be considered as one entity. This idea became very popular as well as a new term, which in this paper will be translated as "continuing education".

The new system of continuing education, as it is proposed, is reminiscent of a circle rather than a strict one way process of professional growth. Continuing education consists of three major patterns:

REGULAR EDUCATION: school, secondary professional institutions, higher institutions,
    post-graduate study (aspirantura);
POST-DEGREE PROFESSIONAL DEVELOPMENT: on- and off-the-job study and training
    at the courses of RQ, and in the libraries;
SELF-STUDY: by each librarian on his own in the mainstream of professional and general
    education and personal development.

The concept of continuing education received legal support in the new Federal Law On Education approved by the government of Russia in 1992 (Zakon..., 1992). Continuing education considers all components to be interrelated, so that a regular education is never left somewhere behind. The rapid changes in library and information practice requires regular education even on a professional level. In the soviet times, only the RQ institutions could give new knowledge to the librarians: whether it be a simple updating, or study for another position within LIS. Now, as it used to be before, courses for RQ are trying to take over and to start re-qualification and regular academic programs. As the teaching potential and academic traditions of those institutions is rather low, and cannot be compared with the ones of the universities, why should new programs be created on accounting, management of the cultural enterprises, library automation etc., if there are well developed courses at the regular academic institutions? On the other hand, there was no tradition in Russian higher education to allow a student or professional to take just one, or several courses. One could apply only for the whole 5-year program. In the current situation with a rapidly changing library profession, re-qualification or additional education has to be considered by the academic institutions.

Thus, the concept of continuing education requires certain changes in a regular education as well. Jeffrey Huber pointed out: "... the continued growth and development of information technologies have made it more and more difficult to incorporate global view of practical application given the time constraints under which most MLIS programs operate" (Huber, 1995). While studying at the library school the students have to be oriented to, and be prepared for, lifelong, self-motivated learning. It is both a matter of willingness and skills and needs special training. The concepts of problem-based learning (Huber and Barrow, 1985) and critical thinking (Ennis, 1985) seem to be very important in educational methodology.

Looking at the structure of continuing education, we find that two patterns are found in the institutions: regular and post-degree education/raising of qualification. The third one, which is self-study, is for the individual, without any institutional support. In Russia it came from the former days, when the idea of professional development was reduced by RQ, and did not consider the active participation of individual. Some research revealed a decrease in professional reading among the librarians (especially in the small libraries) (Gorodilova and Mal'tseva, 1992). To improve the situation changes need to be made in the whole system of education: at the university - with orientation and obtaining skills for a future study; at the libraries - through the system of motivation for professional development. The Central Public Library in Kazant (Tatarstan) started permanent seminars to consider and discuss new professional publications as they did before with new books in the library collections (Abdalimova and Vodolazskaya, 1995). In the Statute of Professional Development of Personnel at the State Public Library for Science and Technology, it has been stated that library has to create conditions favorable for professional development (Arzukhanov, 1993). In the Central Scientific-Agricultural Library (St. Petersburg) the system of promotion was closely connected with the raising of qualifications (Abbakumova and Shlykova, 1995).

Another positive change in continuing education in Russia is the freedom given to the administration of libraries and educational institutions. It replaced the former administrative-command system of supervision, and gave way to initiative. Educators with whom I discussed this paper, told me that in soviet times they literally had no time in their curriculum for many professional issues, being pre-occupied by a lot of political campaigns (such as anti-alcohol), directives and acts, which the party and government issued tirelessly to guide society.

The initiatives delegated to the libraries made them really inventive. Instead of focusing on off-the-job training, libraries developed effective forms of professional training and learning. The most active are the state public and research universal libraries of the regions. Their past experience and the fact that these networks have survived without or minimal losses, helped them to maintain educational activities.

The programs of professional development for the state public libraries of St. Petersburg and Leningrad region are quite impressive. The system of public libraries in St. Petersburg contains 189 public libraries (the same as number as in 1989). The leading role in professional education for the librarians in all 189 libraries belongs to the City Central Library, and its department of staff and library development. The annual plans of the department contain such forms of professional development, as: a monthly roundtable for the directors of the central libraries, monthly seminars for the heads of the professional development departments, which take place not only in the Central library, but also in the other institutions according with the topic of the roundtable. If libraries get funds from the parent authorities (Committees on Culture within the municipal governments), they try to organize seminars - in the well-advanced libraries of the other cities, and even abroad.

For the other specialists: bibliographers, cataloguers, public services librarians such seminars and training are not so regular, but are scheduled within each year.

The Leningrad Regional Research Library is the center of professional education for 500 public libraries located in the towns and villages of the region. Because of the distance and lack of money which is greater than in St. Petersburg, regular seminars for the librarians are provided bi-monthly. In some regions in Russia, the initiative of the center for professional development has been taken over by the Institutes of Culture, as being the most advanced educational entities. As an example may be mentioned the Kemerovo Institute for the libraries of Altay region (Titaronka et al, 1996) and Khabarovsk Institute of Culture - for the Far East Region (Lopatina and Plenkova, 1994). Professors Lopatina and Plenkova from the Khabarovsk Institute stated that the problem for the librarians in the region relates to the distant location from the most courses and centers for RQ. Thus the institute sees its mission to help librarians. The recently held conference "Current theory and practice of Librarianship" and 10-day training for librarians within it, attracted a lot of specialists from all over the region.

The programs of professional study vary from region to region, but they contain a lot of common topics. Computer technologies, on-line searching of information, library management in a new economic situation, the psychology of personal communications and conflict management, public relations, international experience, the sociology and psychology of reading, reading in a new world - this is the list of the most common courses in the educational programs for librarians. Local studies are still very topical. In the annual program of raising qualification issued by the St. Petersburg Central City library we can find such themes as: the library system in St. Petersburg, publishers in St. Petersburg and its book market, the system of taxation in the city, books and reading in the city community, and many others. There is also a great interest in foreign practice and experience, so that in the program I found the names of the following countries: Germany, USA, Sweden, Norway, and Great Britain.

All five forms, that were mentioned regarding RQ, are still used in the new system. At the same time the priorities have moved from the regular training to a range in library activities: round tables, seminars, psychological training, situation games, open discussions, book markets and salons, excursions to counterparts.

I would place stress on the projects which many libraries (except small public and special) provide regularly. Annual conferences for the young specialists, and so called "big" research conferences at the all state and regional libraries attract those who carry out research and those who are interested in the results. Oriented to the library problems, they also benefit library performance.

Post-graduate study for a Ph.D. became less popular in an off-the-job basis. The stipend paid to post-graduates is much lower than a salary. That is why most of the professionals are doing a Ph.D. program while staying in their job. It takes more time to accomplish the research, but it still produces good results. Though the number of Ph.D. students has, however, fallen in last five years.

Summarizing my review of the system of continuing education, I have to state that the time of transition is still underway. To make the system logical and stable there needs to be a joint effort between the libraries and educational institutions, supported by considerable legislature. The system of advertising and providing information on existing educational opportunities has to be established to benefit both: librarians and educators. It will take time, but all the previous experience and good educational potential give us an optimistic view of the future.

FOOTNOTES

1. More precise but less understandable is a translation as Methodologic Department, which means the activities related to teaching librarians the new methods of work and providing a variety of professional supervision.

2. Institutes of Culture in Russia provide higher library education. In 1990s the Moscow and St. Petersburg Institutes were renamed consequently into the University and the Academy of Culture.

3. Library and Information Science.

REFERENCES

Abbakumova N.P. and Shlykova O.V. (1995), "Priglasheniye k diskussii", *Nauchnyje I Tekhnicheskiye Biblioteki,* (4), pp. 51-56.

Abdalimova T.V. and Vodolazskaya A.Y. (1995), "Mekhanizm upravleniya professional'nym samoobrazovaniyem bibliotekarey (na primere CBS)", in: *Kniga i Biblioteka v Kontekste Natsional'noy Kul'tury / Kazanskiy GIK.* Kazan: pp. 91-97.

Afanasova L.H. and Sokolov A.V.(1992), "Bibliotekar' - 90", *SovetskoyeBbibliotekovedeniye,* (3-4), pp.53-70.

Akekseyeva T.A., Zus'man O.M., Minkina V.A., and Starovoytova O.R. (1990), "Bibliotechnaya sistema krupnogo goroda", *Sovetskoye Bibliotekovedeniye,* (2), pp. 8-17.

Arzukhanov A.S. (1993), "Obespecheniye nepreryvnogo povysheniya kvalifikatsii kadrov GPNTB Rossii v usloviyakh avtomatizatsii informatsionno-bibliotechnykh protsessov", in: *Novyje i Usovershenstvovannyje Avtomatizirovannyje Bibliotechnyje I Informatsionnyje Tekhnologii*, Moskva: Sbornik nauchnykh trudov / GPNTB, pp. 45-50.

Chalova Z.V. (1996), *Godovoy Otchiot Prezidenta Sankt-Peterburgskogo Bibliotechnogo Obstchestva*. April 9.

Ennis, R.H. (1985), "A logical base for measuring critical thinking skills", *Educational Leadership*, 45, pp. 45-48.

Gorodilova E.N. and Mal'tseva T.N. (1992), "Professional'noye chteniye bibliotechnykh rabotnikov", *Sovetskoye Bibliotekovedeniye,* (1), pp. 34-39.

Huber, Jeffrey T. (1995), "Library and information studies education for the 21st century practitioner", *Journal of Library Administration,* (20), pp. 119-130.

Huber, Jeffrey and Barrow, H.S. (1985), *How to Design a Problem-based Curriculum for the Preclinical Years,* New York: Springer Publishing.

Lopatina O.A. and Plenkova G.N. (1994), "Povysheniye kvalifikatsii bibliotekarey Dal'nego Vostoka", *Bibliotekovedeniye,* (6), pp. 93-94.

Postanovleniye Pravitel'stva Rossiyskoy Federatsii, (1995), *Ob Utverzhdenii Tipovogo Polozheniya ob Obrazovanii Ucherezhdeniy Dopolnitel'nogo Pofessional'nogo Obrazovaniya (Povysheniya Kvalifikatsii) Spetsialistov,* 26.06.1005; # 610.

Sokolov A.V. (1990), "Nepreryvnoye bibliotechnoye obrazovaniye i nau chnotekhnicheskaya informatsiya", in: *Informatsionnoye Obespecheniye Nauchnykh Issledovaniy: Sbornik Nauchnykh Trudov,* Leningrad: Biblioteka Akademii Nauk SSSR,. pp.29-38.

Titarenko, Evgeny, Sbitnev, Stas, and Gendina, Natalia. (1996), "Training librarians at the Kemerovo Institute of Culture", *Journal of Education for Library and Information Science,* vol. 37 (1), pp. 67-71.

Vorobyov, A.K., ed. (1991), *Kontseptsiya Povysheniya Kvalifikatsii i Perepodgotovki Kadrov v Sfere Kul'tury*. Moskva, 145 pp.

Zakon Rossiyskoy Federatsii Ob Obrazovanii (1992), Vvedion 10.07.92; # 3267-1.

CONTINUING LIS PROFESSIONAL EDUCATION THROUGH DISTANCE MODE: PROSPECTS FOR INDIA

Uma Kanjilal
Faculty of Library and Information Science
Indira Gandhi National Open University
INDIA

Abstract: The paper describes the efforts bring made in India to provide CPD, and suggests a model and innovation techniques that might be employed.

INTRODUCTION

During the last two decades the proliferation of IT applications has brought tremendous changes to the total scenario of information storage, access and dissemination. The fast growth in the number of information institutions, increased investment and activities in the IT sector, and the rapid changes in information technology make it imperative for the information professional to acquire the basic skills of information handling and dissemination using computers and communication technologies. In the present day context of the 'Information Society' characterized by rapid social and technological developments, information professionals are facing the tremendous challenge of adapting themselves to the changing needs of the society. The information professionals having been employed for a few years need to update their knowledge and skills at regular intervals. The need for further training arises either from having to cope with the problem of occupational obsolescence, or to acquire specialized skills in some field or the other. Short term continuing professional education (CPE) programmes can play an important role in catering to this need. The offering of CPE programmes through the distance mode has become quite common all over the world and new modes of imparting them are being developed increasingly. The distance education system enables the learner to study at home, or any other place of their choice, at their own pace and time along with their normal job. Thus, the distance education system is characterized by greater flexibility and freedom of choice and can play a major role in providing wide range of continuing education programmes.

The IT revolution has already taken its root in India and this has profound implications for the LIS professionals, and the institutions providing education and training in the country. The distance education system is gradually evolving as an important component of LIS education in India. It is being considered as the most viable method of overcoming the problems faced in developing a competent LIS work force in the country. Advances in computer and telecommunication technologies have now helped in de-massifying delivery of education at a distance. Telecommunication based teaching is an effective means to reach out to geographically isolated clientele who could not otherwise afford educational opportunities. Moreover, distance education programmes with its quality of flexibility has a great potential to adapt to the changing needs of the society. This paper critically examines different efforts made in providing CPE programmes to the LIS professionals in India. It also attempts to suggest a suitable model and innovative techniques for imparting CPE programmes through the distance mode in India.

LIS EDUCATION IN INDIA

LIS courses are being offered at different levels in India. At present there are more than ninety universities offering BLIS, fifty seven universities offering MLIS and around thirty nine universities offering Ph.D. programmes in India (Table 1). The certificate and diploma level courses are being offered by the library associations, polytechnics, etc. Apart from these conventional courses there are associateship courses in Information Science by the Indian National Scientific Documentation Centre (INSDOC), New Delhi; and in Documentation and Information Science by the Documentation Research and Training Centre (DRTC), Bangalore.

Sl. No.	Level of Courses	No. of Inst./ Univ
1	Higher Secondary (10 + 2)	1
2	Certificate in LIS	87
3	Diploma in LIS	18
4	Bachelor's degree in LIS	91
5	Bachelor of Arts in LIS (3yr. duration)	02
6	Master's degree in LIS	57
7	M.Phil in LIS	05
8	Ph. D. in LIS	39
9	Associateship in LIS	02

Table 1: Number of LIS courses in India (Jagannathan and Kanjilal, 1995).

The fact that distance education can play a major role in providing LIS education in India is being gradually realized and efforts are being made to develop a quality education system through this mode. At present there are seventeen correspondence directorates and five open universities offering LIS courses through the distance mode at various levels (Table 2). Out of these twenty-two institutions, five are providing certificate courses, four diploma courses, fifteen bachelor's degree programmes and ten master's degree programmes.

The overall structure and curriculum of most of the library schools in India are almost similar, with more emphasis on classification, cataloguing, reference service and library management aspects. Though IT has become part and parcel of most of the libraries and information institutions, these aspects are not yet incorporated in the curriculum of most of the LIS training courses. The same sorts of courses are also being offered by the distance teaching institutions in the country. Courses offered by the correspondence directorates are generally based on print material. Some of these institutions are providing short term contact classes as well. The courses offered by the open universities on the other hand are quite innovative and involve multi-media packages for teaching and learning. Most of these institutions are using self-instructional course materials, audio and video cassettes, radio and television broadcasting, and counselling sessions. Apart from these facilities, the Indira Gandhi National Open University is using video conferencing on a regular basis.

Institutions Providing LIS Courses through Distance Mode	No. of Inst.
Total No. of Inst.	22
Open Universities	5
Correspondence Institutions	17
Certificate Courses	5
Diploma Courses	4
BLIS	15
MLIS	10

Table 2: No. of Institutions and Courses Offered through Distance Mode in India (Association of Indian Universities, 1996).

While discussing LIS education through distance mode in India, special mention needs to be made about the Indira Gandhi National Open University (IGNOU). It is a national university set up by an Act of Parliament in 1985. Apart from being a university, it also functions as an apex body for all the distance education systems in the country by co-ordinating and determining standards in distance education. IGNOU is presently offering BLIS and MLIS programmes. It is planning to launch the Ph.D. Programme within a years time. The LIS faculty at IGNOU is also planning to launch a 'Bachelor of Information Studies Programme'(BIS). This is being planned as a basic graduate degree programme of four years duration targeted for students completing school leaving examination (10+2). This programme is being developed, keeping in mind the present need for the information professionals in the emerging market.

IGNOU is the premier open university in the country which has developed a modern curriculum. While the BLIS course is a mix of both traditional and modern aspects of library and information science, the MLIS programme puts full emphasis on the information and information technology aspects. The curriculum for the MLIS also incorporates practical training in handling various modern information technologies. The LIS programmes of IGNOU have become quite popular within a short span of time and it has set a new trend of imparting LIS education through the distance mode in India.

CPE PROGRAMMES IN INDIA

The system of continuing professional education in India is still in the formative stages of development and is quite sporadic in nature. There is no set policy for the provision of CPE programmes for LIS professionals in the country. Though the Report of the Curriculum Development Centre in Library and Information Science (University Grants Commission, India, 1992) recommends that the teachers of LIS attend refresher courses of four weeks duration every 3 to 5 years, orientation programmes of short term duration in library automation /information technology ... etc. nothing much has been done in this direction.

With the changing technologies in the field of information gathering, storage, retrieval, and dissemination, many organizations in India are now grappling with the problem of maintaining and upgrading the competency of the LIS professionals. The curriculum for the LIS courses, still being traditional in nature, adds to the problem. As a result the need for well planned CPE programmes is being seriously felt by LIS professionals in India. Rapid automation of libraries, establishment of resource sharing networks and metropolitan library networks in the major cities of the country, increasing demand for information products and services e.g. online searching, CD-ROM databases, use of Internet, etc. has created a heavy demand for short term courses in computer applications.

The major effort in the provision of CPE programmes for LIS professionals have been taken up by institutions like the National Information System for Science and Technology (NISSAT), the Indian National Scientific Documentation Centre (INSDOC) and the Documentation Research and Training Centre (DRTC). The duration of the courses offered by these institutions range from one to eight weeks on subjects like Application of Computer and Information Technology in Library and Information Activities, Training in CDS/ ISIS, CCF etc. The DRTC and INSDOC have been advancing CPE programmes in the form of summer schools, workshops, seminars, etc. for the LIS teachers and librarians. The library associations like the Indian Library Association (ILA), the Indian Association of Special Libraries and Information Centres (IASLIC) and the Society for Information Science (SIS) have contributed to a great extent in the provision of CPE programmes in the form of annual conferences, seminars, workshops, study circles etc. Apart from these, some of the library schools also conduct summer schools and refresher courses of around one to twelve weeks duration for the LIS teachers and working librarians. In recent years a number of private organizations have also come up with CPE programmes in computer and information technology applications for LIS professionals.

Though there is a steady rise in the number of CPE programmes in the country, these are not yet able to cater satisfactorily to the needs of the LIS professionals. Most of these programmes are of short duration, informal and not very extensive in nature. Moreover, barring a few, most of these programmes lack proper infra-structural facilities and are developed with meager financial support. As a result, these are not really helpful in developing the skills and competencies required to meet the changing needs of the society. The system for CPE programmes for LIS professionals, therefore, urgently needs to be institutionalized in order to cater effectively to the rising demand for the modern information professionals in the country.

The distance education system which is found to be most suitable for imparting CPE programmes, has so far not been utilized for LIS continuing education programmes in India. The Open Universities in the country with their multi-media based teaching system, can play a vital role in this direction. The possibility of utilizing the distance mode of teaching for CPE programmes needs to be explored urgently to develop a well-planned LIS continuing education system in the country.

CPE PROGRAMMES THROUGH THE DISTANCE MODE: SUGGESTED STRATEGIES

The fact that a distance education system can play an important role in catering to the continuing education of the information professionals is being realized and efforts are taking place to provide such courses through the multi-media mode. Since nothing much has been done in this direction, the whole system needs to evolve in a phased manner. The following phases of development are suggested for the purpose:

Phase 1: Adapting the existing courses

The first step in this direction would be to identify already existing courses and adapting them for the purpose of continuing education. For instance IGNOU has developed its MLIS programmes on modern lines (Appendix). Each of these courses could be offered individually to acquaint the LIS teachers and working librarians to the latest developments in the profession. Courses like 'Application of Information Technology' and 'Information Processing and Retrieval' supplemented with practical hands on training could be specifically adopted for developing skills and competencies in these fields.

Phase 2: Developing generalist programmes

Latest developments in the field of information handling and IT application makes it imperative to develop such CPE programmes from time to time that could help the LIS workers keep abreast of the latest developments in the profession and acquire skills and competencies suited for the current job market. Therefore, certain generalist CPE programmes could be developed in areas, e.g., handling of various library automation software, handling of optical based information products, network related information services and activities (Internet, Intranet LANs, WANs), ..., etc. These programmes should be of three to six months duration and provide extensive practical training.

PHASE 3: PROVISION OF SPECIALIST PROGRAMMES

In the present day context, the market for the information professionals is not restricted to the librarians and archivists. It now requires wide range of specialists viz. computer and software specialists, database managers, DTP and graphic specialists, journalists, media personnel, etc. These specialization need to be incorporated in the form of CPE programmes as a part of further training for LIS professionals. Such specialized training may be of one year duration providing in-depth knowledge and skills.

The advantages of the distance education system for the CPE programmes are that:

- learners can undertake courses when they need to do so instead of waiting for the courses to be organized in their local area
- they can undertake the courses at their own pace, time and place
- study materials are always readily available, and
- the courses could be taken up along with their normal job (Clyde, 1991).

The basic disadvantage of such system is the separation of the teacher and the learner. However, this problem could be overcome with well-designed courses and judicious application of the educational technology. A variety of media is now being utilized for imparting distance education in India. The use of self-instructional print material, a/v materials, radio and television broadcasting have become quite commonplace. The tele-conferencing mode is increasingly being used nowadays. The Training and Development Communication Channel of IGNOU providing one way video and two way audio teleconferencing facility, could be taken up on a regular basis to impart CPE programmes (Kanjilal, 1996).

The latest trend in the distance learning is towards the use of networks. IGNOU being an apex body for distance education system in the country, needs to set up an Intranet connecting all its regional centres, study centres and other distance teaching institutions with the headquarters. This will enable the learners to directly interact with the teachers. This facility could be used for sending online lecture notes, newsgroups for discussions, e-mail for direct interaction with the student and the instructor, etc. A server could be set up at the headquarters for providing access to the Internet. The Internet seems to be another cost effective solution for reaching out the learners.

The availability of a wide range of innovative educational technology has now opened up the possibility of lifelong learning through the distance mode. These technological developments need to be tapped properly for providing continuing education to the LIS professionals.

CONCLUSION

The role of distance education in imparting CPE programmes has been recognized all over the world. India being a vast and developing country needs to implement such programmes on an urgent basis. CPE programmes developed for LIS professionals have to be tailored to the present needs of the society and the resources available for the purpose. The continuing education programme could become more significant when it is pursued meaningfully and progressively. Before launching any such programmes, it is essential to identify the areas in which the programmes are required. In the development stage, special attention needs to be given to the contents and skills that are to be imparted. It is also essential to select appropriate media based on the available technology for the purpose. A multi-media based distance education system, with its quality of flexibility, seems to be the future solution for providing continuing education for LIS professionals in India. All distance teaching institutions in the country, therefore, need to collaborate and make concerted effort in this direction.

REFERENCES

Association of Indian Universities (1996), *Handbook of Distance Education*, New Delhi: AIU.

Clyde, Laurel A. (1991), "Steps in the design and development of distance learning courses,": in Blanche Woolls, ed. *Continuing Professional Education and IFLA: Past, Present and Future...*, Munchen : Saur, pp.23-34

Jagannathan, Neela and Kanjilal, Uma (1995), "Library and information science courses for women", in *Speaking for Ourselves: Women in Distance Education*, New Delhi : Manohar Publications, pp.130-40.

Kanjilal, Uma (1996), "Human resource development in library and information science through distance mode : prospects for India" : paper presented in the 48th FID Congress and Conference. Graz, Austria. 22- 25th October, 1996.

University Grants Commission, India (1992), *Report of the Curriculum Development Centre in Library and Information Science*, New Delhi : UGC.

APPENDIX

List of MLIS Courses

    Core Courses :

Sl. No.	Course Code	Title of the Course
1	MLIS-01	Information , Communication and Society
2	MLIS-02	Information Sources, Systems and Programmes
3	MLIS-03	Information Processing and Retrieval
4	MLIS-04	Information Institutions, Products and Services
5	MLIS-05	Management of Library and Information Centres
6	MLIS-06	Application of Information Technology

Sl. No	Course Code	Title of the Course
1	MLIS-E1	Preservation and Conservation of Library Materials
2	MLIS-E2	Research Methodology
3	MLIS-E3	Academic Library System
4	MLIS-E4	Technical Writing

THE INTERNET AND CONTINUING PROFESSIONAL EDUCATION

Laurel A. Clyde
Faculty of Social Science
University of Iceland

Abstract: The paper describes the application of the Internet to continuing professional development, discussing models, tools and services, current practice, and issues, problems and challenges. There is a comprehensive list of sources appended.

1. INTRODUCTION

Within the formal tertiary education institutions, "the term distance education represents a variety of educational models that have in common the physical separation of the faculty member and some or all of the students"; (University of Maryland, 1996) or in other words, "distance education is instructional delivery that does not constrain the student to be physically present in the same location as the instructor". (Steiner, 1996) These definitions can also be applied to the continuing professional education context, where participants may undertake a course at a location remote from the institution or organisation that is offering the course.   The University of Wisconsin-Extension, Continuing Education Extension, Web page adds extra elements to the basic definitions, elements that are very appropriate in the context of a discussion of the use of the Internet in continuing professional education by distance education: "Distance education is defined as a planned teaching/learning experience that uses a wide spectrum of technologies to reach learners at a distance and is designed to encourage learner interaction and certification of learning". (1996)

Walsh and Reese (1995) have commented that "distance learning has become a core education strategy of the 1990s, with a reach that extends to a broad cross-section of institutions and curriculum providers around the world".   On the basis of an analysis of distance education networks in the United States of America, they claim that distance education can extend and improve the quality of an institution's educational offerings, provide substantial economic benefits, and "offer a strategic advantage in penetrating potential new market segments, including corporate education, continuing adult education, and job training". (Wellburn, 1996)

The Commonwealth of Learning in Vancouver, Canada, was established by the Commonwealth governments to give leadership and strategic support for distance education on the basis that "the deployment of modem communications and information technologies can be a major instrument for widening access to learning and for transforming the prospects for social and economic betterment around the world". (Commonwealth of Learning, 1995?) Hiltz (1994, p.25 1) has stated that "technology-enhanced distance education environments" facilitate collaborative learning and independent learning and are an improvement on the traditional classroom in terms of being able to "connect students and course materials on a round-the-clock basis".   Weiss (1994) and Walsh and Reese (1995 suggest that video is the key technology behind the success of modem distance education, but most of the arguments they give for the efficacy of video in distance education could also be applied to the Internet, while the Internet offers additional advantages, including possibilities for communication.   In relation to this, Leslie (1994) notes that "a broad range of studies seems to confirm the educational value of telecomputing networks", and Kinnaman (1995, p.86) comments that "the advance of technology makes constructing new and richer contexts for teaching and learning ever more tenable and more necessary".

Some of the advantages of the use of distance education techniques in continuing professional education are illustrated by an advertisement for seminars offered by Lucent Technologies Center for Excellence in Distance Learning (CEDL) in the United States: "How can your organization keep its workforce well trained without disrupting the daily routine?

How can 'grow Your own' experts from among your existing workforce? How can you be sure your entire international organization is getting the same message? The answer is distance learning." (Lucent Technologies, 1996) Although the learning materials provided through Lucent Technologies seem to be based largely on more traditional media, including print and videotape, they are using the Internet to advertise their services. With more and more organisations having access to the Internet, distance education opportunities offered partly or wholly via the Internet are becoming increasingly attractive to businesses and other employers.

2. MODELS OF INTERNET USE IN DISTANCE EDUCATION

It is possible to view the use of the Internet in distance education in many different ways. Among others, models of the educational process, models of the use of computers in education, models of information systems, and models of communication, all have something to offer as ways of looking at the present and potential use of the Internet in distance education. Two of these models will be introduced here, as examples and as a basis for further discussion of the use of the Internet in distance education.

There are, for example, different ways of looking at the use of computers in education, and, by extension, at the use of computers in distance education. Markwood (1994) has followed other writers in identifying four broad categories of the application of computers in distance education:

- **Computer Assisted Instruction (CAI),** in which the computer is used to present "lessons" or content and to provide practice or simulation of a real-world application, and/or testing;

- **Computer Managed Instruction (CMI),** in which the computer is used to keep track of a student's progress and achievement and sometimes to recommend additional remedial or extension work;

- **Computer Mediated Communication (CMC),** in which the computer is used as a tool for communication between student and instructor and/or among students, including use in individual and group communication strategies;

- **Computer-Based Multimedia,** a "still-developing generation of powerful, sophisticated, and flexible computing tools" in which "voice, video, and computer technologies" are integrated into "a single, easily accessible delivery system". (Markwood, 1994)

In recent years, the Internet, and particularly the World Wide Web, has come to be seen as having applicability in all four of these categories of computer applications in distance education, and particularly for the development of "computer-based multimedia" systems for distance education. "As more and more colleges, universities, schools, companies, and private citizens connect to the Internet ... more possibilities are opened for distance educators to overcome time and distance to reach students". (Gottschalk, 1995) In 1995, Engineering Outreach at the University of Idaho highlighted the following instructional applications of the Internet in distance education, based on this categorisation: using electronic mail for informal one-to-one correspondence; establishing a "classroom" electronic bulletin board; "engaging students in dialogue with other students, faculty, and researchers by encouraging them to join bulletin board(s) on topic(s) related to the class"; and developing a "classroom home page" with references, links, data, and other material that would be of use to students in the class. (Gottschalk, 1995) There are, of course, many other potential applications of the Internet in distance education, beyond those cited.

At the University of Maryland Institute for Distance Education (1996), three distance education models have been developed to "stimulate the thinking of educators who are faced with the problem of how best to serve learners who cannot or choose not to come to the campus". These models are based on an approach that is different from the one above; the

focus is not on the way computers are used but rather on the locus of control in the educational process. The intention is not to represent all possible forms of distance education but rather to represent points along a continuum from instructor control or institutional control of the educational process to student control. As with the categorisation of the use of computers in education that was considered above, these models have implications for the use of the Internet in distance education. The models are as follows:

- **The Distributed Classroom Model.** In this model, telecommunications technologies, including Internet-based services, are used to extend a classroom-based course from one location to students at another and distant location or locations. As is usually the case with classroom-based instruction, the instructor and the institution normally control the pace and nature of the instruction. The teaching/learning experience is usually designed to in-initiate the classroom in as much as that is possible. The communications technologies used are typically those for synchronous communication, that is, they require both the instructor and the students to be in a particular place at a particular time; they may include, for instance, two-way interactive video, audio and computer conferencing.

- **The Independent Learning Model.** The use of this model means that students do not have to be in a particular place at a particular time; they are provided with a variety of course guides and learning materials, and access to guidance and evaluation by a teacher/tutor. Students work independently, though there may be formal contact with the teacher or tutor through mail and communications technologies, and perhaps contact with other students through communications technologies. Students may work at their own pace, in a location of their own choice, and may have some control over the media they use for study and for communication. Learning materials may be provided through a range of media, including print, audiotape, videotape, computer disc, World Wide Web pages, CD-ROM. Communication technologies used may include fax, voicemail, electronic mail, among others.

- **The Open Learning Plus Class Model.** This model incorporates elements of the previous models, with course guides and learning materials to enable students to work independently, combined with the use of interactive telecommunications technologies for group meetings and discussions among students and with the instructor. The class sessions are usually "for students to discuss and clarify concepts and engage in problem-solving activities, group work, laboratory experiences, simulations, and other applied learning exercises." (University of Maryland, 1996) The technologies used will usually reflect those in the models above, with a range of information technologies from print to video and World Wide Web pages being used to deliver learning materials, and others, such as audioconferencing, computer conferencing, and chat used as the basis for interactive sessions.

Depending on how the distance education process is viewed, and the model or models on which it is based, the Internet can be used in a wide range of ways. It can be used, for instance, as a tool for the management of distance education - from advertising courses to providing the administrative infrastructure for communication with students throughout their course. It can be used in the course delivery process, as both a medium for delivery of learning materials and as a medium for interactive learning experiences. Used to the fullest extent, it can provide a multimedia, interactive learning environment through which students not only receive instructional or learning materials and work with interactive materials (such as online tutorials and simulations) but also work with fellow students and their instructor/s, submit assigned work, and receive feedback on their work and their contribution. This may involve the use of a number of different Internet tools and services, including electronic mail, the World Wide Web, listservs or newsgroups, and others. In practice, when the Internet is used in distance education at present, only part of the potential is realised; whether or not total use of the Internet is desirable will depend to a large extent on the nature of the course and its aims, and the potential participants.

3. INTERNET TOOLS AND SERVICES IN DISTANCE EDUCATION

Several different Internet tools and services can be used in distance education, for a range of instructional, communication, and management purposes. Some tools, like electronic mail, can be used for many different applications; others are more limited. Some tools that were once popular for the delivery of instructional materials are being replaced, as the Internet develops, by newer tools - for example, the text-based gopher system has largely been replaced by the World Wide Web as a means of providing multimedia interactive course materials for students. The following illustrate the present and potential applications of Internet tools and services in distance education, including continuing professional education offered by distance education.

- **Electronic mail** or email. Electronic mail can be used for one-to-one communication between an instructor and distant students, for the submission of assignments, and for the provision of feedback to students. It can also be used (through bulk mail servers) for the delivery of instructional materials to students. In addition, **listservs,** or electronic mail discussion groups, can be used for communication between the instructor and the class, and among class members. While most electronic mail systems are still text-based, it is possible to send image files and software as attachments to email messages, even through listservs. Recently, electronic mail systems have become available that allow users to send and receive images as part of the message itself, and to incorporate hypertext links into messages.

- **USENET Newsgroups.** While public USENET newsgroups can be used as a resource in distance education Oust as they can in a campus or institutional setting), it is also possible to create closed newsgroups for a particular purpose, such as delivery of course materials or group work on projects or other activities. As with electronic mail systems, recent developments have meant that some users are able to read newsgroups using software that allows them to see images and to follow hypertext links within the messages.

- **World Wide Web** (WWW) provides access to text documents, images, sound files, data, video, on the Internet, and also provides a medium of communication through links with electronic mail. Popular multimedia browsers such as **Netscape, Microsoft Internet Explorer,** and **Mosaic** have made the Web easier to use and much more attractive, and increased its functionality for purposes such as distance education. The World Wide Web can be used to deliver course materials, to answer student queries and encourage student response (for instance, through response forms as an integral part of the Web page), to lead students to other Internet resources (via hypertext links), and to provide management information. It can also be used to make student work available to others in the class, and to provide access to data (such as statistical data or pictures).

- **IRC, Chat,** and **Talk** are Internet systems that allow groups of people to communicate in "real time", that is, all at the same time, via computer. Any text typed by one person in the group will appear on the screens of all the others, and any person in the group can respond to the input of others. This means that these systems can be used to hold online meetings or seminars, formal or informal. The advantage over listservs and newsgroups is that feedback and response is immediate; the disadvantages are that all people must be online at the same time, and the participants have little time to reflect on points raised in the discussion while it is under way. In addition, there is usually no record of an IRC (or chat or talk) discussion, while this is readily available on listservs or newsgroups.

- **Computer conferencing** provides an extension of the text-based talk or chat systems, through the use of voice and video. Each participant in the conference has a video camera mounted on his or her computer, and sound capabilities on the computer. Using software such as **CUSeeMe,** the participants can see each of the other participants in a small "window" on their screen and hear each other. In addition, the video system can be used to display documents, pictures, slides, or images of three-dimensional objects such as specimens; it can also be used to present demonstrations, which can be saved to memory and replayed as necessary. Like IRC, this is a real-time system that requires participants to be online at the same time; however, it also allows images and video sequences to be saved for later use.

- MOO or **MUD** (multi-user environments). Through these systems, users can carry on a discussion or create simulations or play educational games. They allow users to play roles and to test theories about the way in which things happen in the real world. Increasingly, MUDs or M00s are being developed with multimedia features.

- **Telnet** allows Internet users to access and log on to remote computers, even though those computers may be very different from their own. A major application of telnet at the present time (December 1996) is to access and search the **catalogues of remote libraries,** and to request books and other materials from the library collection or through inter-library loans. While a few library catalogues can now be searched through the World Wide Web, it will be some time before this will be possible for library catalogues based on older mainframe software. Another application of telnet is to enable remote users to log on to **electronic bulletin boards** and to use them to communicate with others, to locate information, and to download files and software.

- **File Transfer Protocol (FTP)** is another older Internet tool that is gradually being replaced by the World Wide Web for casual applications. FTP allows a user to log on to a remote computer, locate relevant files or documents on that computer, and download them for use on his or her own machine. In distance education programmes, it has been used to deliver course materials, including text documents, images, and computer software to remote students. A major disadvantage, and one that has inhibited the widespread use of FTP in distance education, is that users need to have some knowledge of computer systems, and in particular some knowledge of UNIX systems, if it is to be used at anything other than the most basic level.

Other Internet tools and services that have some applicability in distance education include gopher, Internet radio, Internet telephone, and even very simple tools like finger.

4. CURRENT PRACTICE

Among the early applications of the Internet in distance education have been the use of the Internet to advertise and offer courses about the Internet. These have included courses for practising teachers and librarians. In 1993/4, a course about gopher, for librarians and others, called "Go-pher-it: Your Passport to the Internet" (by Thomas P. Copley) was offered by electronic mail. By 1996, universities and colleges were offering graduate for-credit and continuing education courses using a variety of Internet tools. In November 1996 the Jersey City State College posted an online advertisement to the KIDSPHERE listserv for a course called "Using the Internet in Education"; teaching tools included electronic mail, telnet, and the World Wide Web, so that the Internet was both the subject of instruction and the medium. In the same month, the School of Library Science at the University of Arizona advertised a course called "The Internet", to be "offered exclusively online" using "the software and resources being studied" as the instructional media. Internet tools to be used included electronic mail, the World Wide Web, USENET newsgroups, IRC, M00s, and FIP. Students were required to have "direct access to the Internet" as a prerequisite for registration. (Fitzner, 1996)

A search of the Internet (December 1996) revealed a wide range of applications of the Internet in distance education, whether in formal programmes of undergraduate and postgraduate study, or in continuing education. These applications include the use of Internet electronic mail in a distance education course, COMP 200 "Introduction to Information Systems and Technology" offered by the University of Alberta in Canada (Howard and van Duren, 1993); graduate and undergraduate degrees in business administration and management offered entirely online by the University of Phoenix; a course on "Navigating the World Wide Web" offered online (using the Web) by Penn State University's Program in Workforce Education and Development; and interactive simulations on the Web, such as the "Interactive Patient Examination" from Marshall University School of Medicine and the University of Toledo's "Equilibrium Dialysis Experiment". At AusWeb96 (the Second Australian World Wide Web Conference), Peter Evans of the University of Southern Queensland described the development and delivery of a Graduate Certificate in Open and Distance Learning programme via the World Wide Web, a programme that is "offered globally" for academics, professional trainers, and others involved in distance education and training. (1996) (See the reference list for the URLs of Internet sites mentioned.)

Meanwhile, within the professional associations concerned with distance education (such as the International Council for Distance Education and the Australian and South Pacific External Studies Association) and within the journals in this field (such as *Distance Education* and *Open Learning*) there has been considerable discussion of learning theory and pedagogical issues related to using the Internet in distance education, and there is a developing research base. The AusWeb96 Conference, with its "Education and Learning" stream, provided a forum for a discussion of the current "state of the art" in research and development. At this conference, Shirley Alexander (1996) presented an overview of current research related to Webbased teaching and learning strategies, while John Eklund, (1996) also from a basis of research, discussed cognitive models for developing learning materials and strategies for the Web. Ron Oliver and his colleagues (1996) provided guidelines (based on research and on design principles) for "creating effective instructional materials for the World Wide Web", but cautioned that "instructional effectiveness is not a proven characteristic for World Wide Web courseware", and while the potential of this medium is clear, "potential and reality are frequently not synonymous". Martyn Wild (1996) has noted that although the Web has "an ever-developing capacity to carry multimedia materials and information", neither the Web nor the Internet as a whole was necessarily an appropriate medium "for carrying experiential, empirical and theoretical forms of knowledge". Daniel Peraya (1994?), in an "overview of the state of the art in the distance learning domain", reviewed research based on communication theory and discussed its importance for understanding educational applications of the World Wide Web. He stresses that in a pedagogical context, delivering material is not sufficient; the learning environment has to include "a communication situation", that is, it has to include all the information, support and structures needed by the learner, such as content, explanations, activities, learning aids, and communication. Current research and development projects such as the European initiative EONT - An Experiment in Open and Distance Learning using New Information Technologies, which is partly funded by the European Union, are likely to tell us more about the potential and problems of using "computer networks and hypermedia systems" in distance education.

5. ISSUES, PROBLEMS AND CHALLENGES

While the Internet is being used by many universities and colleges for distance education applications, it is being less used at present for continuing professional education. This in itself is both an issue and a challenge. However, even in relation to university and college programmes, there are problems and challenges facing those who would like to make more use of the Internet, and a range of issues that need to be addressed. Not least among these issues is the question of access. This includes access both to the technology and also to the skills necessary to make effective use of the technology.

The Commonwealth of Learning "Communications and Information Technologies" brochure (1995?) notes that "given the nature of modem information technologies, which involve massive investments in systems and development costs, single institutions with limited resources and organisational reach cannot on their own exploit the economies inherent in large-scale communications networks, nor can they individually absorb the enormous costs of the necessary applications trials and training associated with the adoption of new technology". Thus the focus of the Commonwealth of Learning has been on "the strategic deployment of communications technology, training activities, and alliance-building ... designed to extract maximum value from the sharing of resources, joint planning and institutional co-operation". Through its technology programmes, such as its computer networking programmes, the Commonwealth of Learning helps "educational organisations identify and adapt innovative communications and information technologies and, by facilitating co-operation and resource sharing, enable them to take advantage of the benefits that can derive from large-scale communications systems" such as the Internet. Projects of the Commonwealth of Learning are often directed to finding innovative applications of current technology and to addressing "the challenges facing human resource development in developing countries". Thus 1994 saw the commencement of an Internet project in the Caribbean to provide inexpensive access to electronic mail for educational institutions, and other Internet projects are currently under way in Africa. While the Commonwealth of Learning is not the only organisation active in this field, it is a major player, and its activities and projects draw attention to a problem of access for people in developing countries (and, indeed, in some parts of more developed countries).

While access to technology and skills can be a problem for institutions that are developing distance education programmes, it is sometimes an even greater problem at the individual level, where people need Internet access in order to undertake the courses. Access to the Internet may be available in public libraries, in community centres, or in other public or semi-public places in a local community; nevertheless it can be very difficult for people to undertake distance education courses via the Internet (or partly through the Internet) if their access is not easy and convenient. If their access is at work, then support may be available, particularly base level technical support. However, if their access is at home, then technical support, including software support may be a problem. In addition, a certain level of information technology skills is normally required for participation in this kind of distance education, effectively limiting access to people with at least base level information technology skills (unless the course providers have developed strategies to address this problem).

While these access issues are of crucial importance in the context of today's distance education initiatives, there are also other issues and challenges associated with distance education, whether in the context of university and college programmes or of continuing professional education. One is the issue of "globalisation" of education; Richard Edwards has noted that Post-Fordism and globalisation, major trends in our contemporary world, encourage "cultural uniformity, while also giving greater importance to senses of the local and place, encouraging cultural difference". (Edwards, 1995) He argues that distance education is part of the trend towards uniformity under conditions of globalisation, while at the same time the rhetoric of open learning, often associated with distance education, is part of the trend that encourages difference and diversity. Inevitably, these different but converging trends will create ideological tensions when distance education is used for the provision of continuing professional education. The use of the Internet, a global communications medium that also provides individuals and groups with a powerful tool for presenting alternative or minority views, highlights this tension. This "raises issues for policymakers and practitioners in open and distance education alike". (Evans, 1995)

6. REFERENCES

Alexander, Shirley (1995), "Teaching and learning on the World Wide Web", Presentation given at AusWeb95, The Australian World Wide Web Conference,
http://www.scu.edu.au/ausweb95/papers/education2/alexander/

Commonwealth of Learning (1995?). "Communications and information technologies",
http:l/www.col.org/

Copley, Thomas P. (1994), "Go-pher-it: Your passport to the Internet", course offered by electronic mail, ror@netcom.com

Edwards, Richard (1995), "Different discourses, discourses of difference: globalisation, distance education and open learning", *Distance Education*, 16(2), pp.241-255.

Eklund, John (1995), "Cognitive models for structuring hypermedia and implications for learning from the world-wide web", Presentation given at AusWeb95, The Australian World

Wide Web Conference.
littp://www.scu.edu.au/ausweb95/papers/hypertext/eklund/

EONT (1996), EONT - An Experiment in Open and Distance Learning using New Information Technologies,
http://hyperg.softlab.ntua.gr/eont/

Evans, Peter (1996), "Development and delivery of a Graduate Certificate (Open and Distance Learning) via the WWW", Presentation given at AusWeb96, The Second Australian World Wide Web Conference,
http://www.scu.edu.au/ausweb96/educn/

Evans, Terry (1995), "Globalisation, post-Fordism and open and distance education", *Distance Education*, 16(2), abstract.

Fitzner, Sue (1996), "The University of Arizona - Internet course", Message posted to the Net-Happenings listserv on the Internet, 27 November.

Gottschalk, Tania H. (1995), "Distance education at a glance, Guide #7: Computers in distance education", Engineering Outreach, University of Idaho, http://www.uidaho.edu/evo/dist.html

Hiltz, Starr Roxanne (1994), Quoted by the Commonwealth of Learning (1995?) at
http://www.col.org/

Howard, Dale and Charles van Duren (1993), "Computer literacy at a distance", DEOSNEWS - The Distance Education Online Symposium, 3(9), October.

Kinnaman, D.E. (1995), "Cannibalism, convergence and the mother of all networks", *Technology and Learning*, November/December, p.86.

Leslie, J. (1994), "Kids connecting", *Wired Magazine,* online at
http://www.hkr.se/ihu/essays/wiredkid.html

Lucent Technologies, Center for Excellence in Distance Learning (1996), "Lucent Technologies:
Center for Excellence in Distance Learning (CEDL)", http://www.lucent.com/cedl/

Markwood, R.A. (1994), "Computer tools for distance education", in B. Willis (ed.), *Distance
Education: Strategies and Tools,* Englewood Cliffs, New Jersey: Educational Technology
Publications, pp. 199-211.

Marshall University School of Medicine, Interactive Patient Examination,
http://medicus.marshall.edu/medicus.htm

Oliver, Ron, Jan Herrington, and Arshad Omari (1996), "Creating effective instructional materials for
the World Wide Web", Presentation given at AusWeb96, The Second Australian World Wide Web
Conference,
http://www.scu.edu.au/ausweb96/educn/oliver/

Penn State University, Program in Workforce Education and Development,
hhttp://milkman.cac.psu.edu/~dlp/PS/psintro.html#contents

Peraya, Daniel (1994?), "Distance education and the WWW, TECFA, Faculte de Psychologie et des
Sciences de I'Education, Universite de Geneve,
 http://tecfa.unige.ch/edu-ws94/contrib/peraya.fm.html#HDRO

Steiner, Virginia (1996), "The Distance Learning Resource Network (DLRN)",

University of Maryland. Institute for Distance Education (1996), "Models of distance education: A
conceptual planning tool", Institute for Distance Education,
http://www.umuc.edu/ide/ide.html

University of Phoenix,
http://www.uophx.edu/online/

University of Toledo, Equilibrium Dialysis Experiment,
http://131.183.61.190/eqDial/Intro

University of Wisconsin-Extension, Continuing Education Extension (1996), Quoted in University of
Wisconsin-Extension, "Distance Education Clearinghouse",
http://www.uwex.edu/disted/definition.html

Walsh, J. and B. Reese (1995), "Distance learning's growth reach", *THE Journal, 22.*

Weiss, J. (1994), "Distance learning", Syllabus 1994, Campus Networking,
http://www.syllabus.com/archive/SyII94/07/

Wellburn, Elizabeth (1996), "The status of technology in the education system: a literature review",
Report for the Technology and Distance Education Branch, Ministry of Education,
Skills and Training, British Columbia, Canada, May,
http://www.etc.bc.ca/lists/nuggets/EdTech_report.html

Wild, Martyn (1996), "Developing educational content for the Web: issues and ideas", Presentation
given at AusWeb96, The Second Australian World Wide Web Conference,
http://www.scu.edu.au/ausweb96/educn/wild/

7. BIBLIOGRAPHY: INTERNET SOURCES

This list includes "meta-sites" that provide links to a wide range of distance education
resources and sites on the Internet, as well as electronic journals, online conference proceedings,
institutional and personal World Wide Web pages, and other Internet resources related to distance
education.

Africa Growth Network
http://www.agn.co.zal

Banks, Richard and Coombs, Norman (1995), "Your onramp to the Internet: The power of electronic mail", Presentation given at the 1995 Convention of the American Association for Higher Education,
http://www.sasquatch.com/flexlearn/onramp.html

College and University Home Pages - Alphabetical Listing
http://www.mit.edu:8001/people/cdmello/univ.html

The Commonwealth of Learning, Global Distance Education Sources
http://www.col.org/

Distance Education - An International Journal,
http://www.usq.edu.au/dec/decjourn/demain.htm

Distance Education at a Glance
http://www.uidaho.edu/evo/distglan.html

Distance Education Subject Guide, University of Alberta,
http://www.extension.ualberta.ca/atl/deg/deframe.htm

Distance Learning Resource Network
http://www.fwl.org/edtech/dlrn.html

Edith Cowan University, Department of Library and Information Science, Perth, Western Australia,
http://liswww.fste.ac.cowan.edu.au/

Eggleston, Steve (1996), "The Eggman's list of distance education and related links", The Nuance Group of Creative Associates, November,
http://www.access.digex.net/~nuance/distedl.html

European Association of Distance Teaching and the European Open University Network,
http://www.ouh.nl/eadtu/

European Distance Education Network (EDEN)
http://www.open.ac.uk/Partners/EDEN/

An Experiment in Open and Distance Learning Using New Information Technologies (EONT), SOCRATES Programme, European Union,
http://hyperg.softlab.ntua.gr/eont/

Finnish Association for Distance Education
http://oyt.oulu.fi/fade/

Indiana University, School of Continuing Studies
http://www.indiana.edu/~scs/dl.html

The Internet University - College Courses by Computer,
http://www.caso.com/

Learning Without Frontiers, UNESCO
http://www.cned.fr/

Monash University, Australia, Distance Education Centre,
http://www-mugc.cc.monash.edu.au/dec/

Open and Distance Learning Association of Australia (ODLAA)
http://www.usq.edu.au/dec/decjourn/odlaa.htm

Open Learning Australia,
http:l/www.ola.edu.au/

The Open University, International Centre for Distance Learning (iCDL),
http://acacia.open.ac.uk/ICDL-Facts.html

The Open University, International Centre for Distance Learning, Distance Education Database, http://acacia.open.ac.uk/Online.html

Stokes, Dawn (1996), Resources for Distance Education Using the Internet, The University of Texas at Austin,
http://www.tapr.org/~ird/Stokes/homepage.html

Technology and Distance Education Branch, British Columbia Ministry of Education, Skills and Training, Canada,
http://www.etc.bc.ca/

TeleEducation New Brunswick/TeleEducation Nouveau-Brunswick, Distance Education World Wide Web Sites,
http://ollc.mta.ca/teleedds.html

Tiedemann, D. (1995), A Select List of Organizations Using Internet to Deliver Education at a Distance, DEOS-L Resources Files (Send a message with the words SUBSCRIBE DEOS-L <yourfirstname> <yourlastname> to listserv@psuvm.psu.edu).

Tools for Publishing Courses on the WWW-WebCT
 http://homebrew.cs.ubc.ca/webct

United States Distance Learning Association (USDLA)
http://www.usdla.org/

University of Maryland, Institute for Distance Education, "Survey on Web-Enabled Instruction for Faculty and Designers",
http://www.umuc.edu/ide/websurvey.html

University of Southern Queensland, Australia, Distance Education Centre,
http://www.usq.edu.au/dec/

University of Wisconsin - Extension. Distance Education Clearinghouse,
http://www.uwex.edu/disted/home.html

Updegrove, Kimberly H. (1995), "Teaching on the Internet", Submitted in partial fulfilment of the requirements of N900 Nurse Midwifery Program, School of Nursing, University of Pennsylvania, August,
http://pobox.upenn.edu/~kimu/teaching.html

USENET Newsgroup: alt. education. distance

Westera, Gillian and John Frylinck (1996), "Interactive information literacy on the World Wide Web", Presentation given at AusWeb96, The Second Australian World Wide Web Conference, http://www.scu.edu.au/ausweb96/educn/

World Lecture Hall
http:l/www.utexas.edu:8O/world/lecture

THE IMPACT OF NATIONAL TRAINING REFORM AND THE RESTRUCTURING OF INDUSTRIAL AWARDS ON STAFF DEVELOPMENT IN AUSTRALIAN ACADEMIC AND STATE LIBRARIES.

Angela Bridgland
Director, Management Services
The University of Melbourne Library
Australia

Abstract: The paper reports on the National Training Reform Agenda, the restructuring of industrial awards, and impact on staff development in Australian academic and state libraries. It also addresses the impact of one aspect of the NTRA - national competency standards for the library and information industry, their impact on curriculum development, staff development and continuing education. The role of the Australian Library and Information Association is discussed in the light of the above.

INTRODUCTION

In 1988, the Australian Conciliation and Arbitration Commission (now the Australian Industrial Relations Commission) handed down an historic wage case, historic in that it established a structural efficiency principle (SEP) designed to help reform the Australian labour market. Education and training were seen to be critical to increasing the international competitiveness of Australian industry. Australian industrial awards were to be overhauled (restructured) to remove outmoded provisions and to make them more relevant and appropriate to the needs of modern industry and its workers. The three priorities of the restructuring process were to revise job classification structures, to multi-skill the workforce and, by bringing about major reforms to skill formation and training arrangements, to provide new career paths for employees.

The SEP which underpinned award restructuring required unions and employers to reach agreement on measures to increase the efficiency and effectiveness of their industries. These measures included establishing skill-related career paths which provided an incentive for employees to continue to participate in skill formation; eliminating impediments to multi-skilling and broadening the range of tasks required of an employee; and ensuring that working patterns and arrangements enhanced the flexibility and efficiency of the industry. These momentous changes in the Australian industrial arena were paralleled by changes in the profile of the Australian workforce and the nature of its work, and the development of a national training reform agenda, driven by the federal government and designed to complement award restructuring as a micro economic reform strategy.

There have been a number of recent reports on the potential, policy directions for Australian education. Reports such as the (then) Department of Education, Employment and Training's *Australia's Workforce in the Year 2001;* the Australian Education Council Review Committee's *Young People's Participation in Post-compulsory Education and Training* (the Finn Report); the Employment and Skills Formation Council's *Raising the Standard: Middle Level Skills In the Australian Workforce* and its *The Shape of Things to Come: Small Business Employment and Skills;* the Wiltshire report on the *Review of the National Board of Employment, Education and Training;* and the EPAC report, *Education and Training in the 1990s.*

Issues highlighted in these reports include the need for a convergence between general education and vocational training, the development of national core competencies, an emphasis on quality as well as quantity, a more accessible transition from the compulsory education system to the vocational skills training programs and the sharing of responsibilities. Many of these issues and recommendations have already been addressed and/or implemented through the national training reform agenda.

The changing nature of work and the need to make Australia more internationally competitive economically resulted in two microeconomic reforms, both based on skilling the nation. The National Training Reform Agenda (NTRA) was designed to deliver industry responsive curricula and to create nationally consistent approach to training delivery; award restructuring was designed to streamline and update existing awards so as to improve productivity and to provide improved career path opportunities for Australian workers. The need for improved staff development and training in libraries is compatible with both of these reforms.

In this context, I undertook research to examine the impact of large scale industrial change, with its underpinning economic and educational imperatives, on staff development in Australian academic and state libraries. At the time the survey component of this research was undertaken, the library industry competency standards had not been developed. There was, however, widespread knowledge that competency standards were imminent. This study also sought to examine the level of understanding of competency standards and how they might relate to staff development and training.

WORKPLACE REARRANGEMENT

Award Restructuring

Labour market reform was and is a key ingredient of the federal government's strategy to make Australian industry more productive, more competitive and more capable of generating longer term economic growth while at the same time expanding opportunities for individual workers and improving the quality of work life. The SEP, more commonly known as award restructuring, required unions and employers to reach agreement on measures to enhance the efficiency and effectiveness of their industry. Awards were seen as being restrictive, too narrowly defined in tasks assigned to different classification levels and with training needs aligned with the award rather than industry.

In theory, some of the problems arising from award classifications and other restrictions resulting from awards have been addressed by the process of award restructuring and subsequently by enterprise bargaining. SEP meant that everyone in the workforce who was subject to an award was required to undergo continual training throughout their career if they wish to progress to higher salary/wage levels.

Enterprise Bargaining

This moves the focus from industry-wide awards to actual enterprise or workplace level. It has been argued that only by improving the performance of each worksite will true microeconomic reform occur. An enterprise is usually taken to mean a single business with a single employer.

Enterprise bargaining is defined in the *Australian Enterprise Bargaining Manual* (1993, p.3202) as,

...a contract between an employer and the employees on wages and conditions of work in the employer's business or undertaking, entered into freely. In reality, the parties often seek assistance from government agencies, employer's organisations, trade unions and other sources in concluding agreements.

In *Enterprise Bargaining and Workplace Reform*, Teece (1993) explains that bargaining allows all employment conditions and work practices to be reviewed at a local level. Enterprise bargaining encourages management and their employees to take full responsibility for their own arrangements. They are expected to work out together what changes are necessary to improve the productivity of their organisation.

Enterprise bargaining does allow for wholesale change but it must take place within a legal framework. It is now included in the laws of all six States and the Commonwealth. These frameworks can be of two types :

- Enterprise Flexibility Agreements or
- Enterprise Bargaining Framework Agreements.

In the former, an employer negotiates directly with the employees. In the latter, the employer negotiates directly with the unions. Where enterprise bargaining has commenced within the university sector, the University administrations are bargaining directly with their unions who have formed single bargaining units. The key features of these Framework Agreements are that both employers and unions have agreed to bargain on issues of real substance; both have agreed that enterprise bargaining is about workplace reform and increased productivity; and there has also been agreement that there will be no disadvantage to the employee compared with his or her previous award.

Once enterprise bargaining is entered into, employees must understand that it is the only way to get a pay rise. A 2.9% pay rise is granted under the framework agreement. After this, future pay rises have to be funded from within the enterprise. In other words, productivity increases are seen as the means of generating greater profits which are shared by all. In non profit organisations, such as state libraries and universities, this must be seen in terms of benefits rather than profits. Although in the short term organisations may look to cost cutting, downsizing (or right sizing), trade-offs and one-off gains the longer term bargaining environment might address strategic goals, best practice, benchmarking, agreed performance indicators and changes in workplace culture.

NATIONAL TRAINING REFORM ISSUES

National Training Reform Agenda (NTRA)

In Australia, the combination of a changing workforce profile, the changing nature of work and industrial agreements, and the changing role of education and training, gave rise to the National Training Reform Agenda (NTRA). It can be described as a co-operative national response by government, unions and employers to economic and industry restructuring, including labour market imperatives and emerging requirements arising from workplace reform. The main aim is to increase the competitiveness and productivity of Australian industry through industry responsive reform of the vocational education and training system.

Flexibility to meet enterprise requirements within a stable and consistent national system was essential for reform to occur. The development of a National Framework for the Recognition of Training (NFROT) and nationally endorsed industry competency standards, along with The Training Guarantee Act (1990) and its companion, The Training Guarantee (Administration) Act (1990), were intended to ensure that the Government's major reform program for education and training for Australian industry took effect.

Key features of the NTRA are:

1. introduction of flexible training pathways to meet individual and industry needs;
2. transferability and portability of skills within/across industries, enhancing career path options;
3. establishment of nationally recognised qualifications and course accreditation procedures;
4. development of articulation and pathways between courses and institutions.

The principal elements of the NTRA designed to achieve these outcomes are :

- the establishment of the National Training Board in 1990 to promote, co-ordinate and endorse competency standards in industry;
- competency-based training (CBT), marking a shift away from time-serving as the basis for accreditation of training to testing for the attainment of specific competencies, including recognition of prior learning;
- the establishment of the Australian Standards Framework (ASF) in which competencies are allotted to eight levels across all industries;
- the establishment of the Australian Vocational Certificate Training System as a new pathway arrangement for entry-level training, incorporating apprenticeships and traineeships;
- the States and Federal Government agreeing to a national approach to vocational education and training matters, including the ceding of TAFE funding to the newly established Australian National Training Authority (ANTA) and an agreement for a national framework for the recognition of training (NFROT);
- an enterprise training stream, with the device of NFROT to articulate enterprise standards to national, recognised levels, and scope for enterprises to register as recognised training providers;
- various State Government initiatives in the training field, including the accreditation of courses and training providers; and
- initiatives in relation to the recognition of immigrants' qualifications.

There was also the introduction in 1990 of the Training Guarantee Levy which required all but very small firms to expend at least 1.5% of their payroll on approved training. This levy is currently in suspension.

A vocational training and education system which is more responsive to industry needs is seen as being essential to improving Australia's productivity and its international competitiveness. The training reform agenda focuses on the development of a nationally consistent, competency-based approach to vocational education and training, with a focus on workplace training. It is designed to complement and support other microeconomic reform initiatives, especially labour market reform which is occurring through workplace rearrangement (award restructuring and enterprise bargaining). The NTRA has been embraced by government, industry peak bodies, and public and private vocational education and training (VET) providers.

In summary, the objectives of this change are to achieve a multi-skilled workforce, improved career paths, develop closer links between education/training providers, a move to resource-based learning, a focus on life-long learning and the recognition of prior learning (RPL), competency standards and articulation between courses. (Arts Training Australia *Update 1* Winter/Spring 1993).

Competency Standards

The extent to which qualifications of professional and para-professionals in the information services industry are valued in the future could well be determined by the introduction of the *Library Industry Competency Standards*. The development of these standards has arisen as a result of the Federal and State Governments' push for national industrial and training reform.

This national training reform is intended to operate on competency-based training and assessment systems. The Mayer Committee adopted a broad definition of competence which recognises that performance is underpinned not only by skill but also by knowledge and understanding, and that competence involves both the ability to perform in a given context and the capacity to transfer knowledge and skills to new tasks and situations. (*Putting General Education to Work* October 1992-[Mayer Report]). The Mayer Committee identified a set of generic competencies which are intended to be achieved by the time a person leaves secondary school. They are as follows:

1. Collecting, analysing and organising ideas and information.
2. Expressing ideas and information.
3. Planning and organising activities.
4. Working with others and in teams.
5. Using mathematical ideas and techniques.
6. Solving problems.
7. Using technology.
8. Cultural understanding.

Three levels of competencies have emerged from these generic competencies. The three levels are developmental and each builds on the former. The three levels of competency to emerge are :

1. cross industry competencies;
2. nationally identified competencies for each industry; and
3. enterprise or workplace competencies.

The <u>industry level</u> competencies build on the generic competencies and address those areas of knowledge and skill which are industry specific. The <u>cross industry</u> competencies can be used by many industry sectors, e.g., training and assessment competencies. <u>Enterprise</u> competencies in turn, build on industry competencies and add any areas of knowledge or skill required specifically for that workplace.

Nicholls (1992, p.2) offers the following definitions of competence and competency-based standards:

> Competence: the attributes (knowledge, skill, attitudes) which enable an individual or group to perform a role or set of tasks to an appropriate level or grade of quality or achievement (i.e. an appropriate standard) and thus make the individual or

group competent in that role.

Competency-based standard: a level or grade of competence, understood in terms of a combination of attributes, which can be a basis for goals of personal and professional/vocational development and evaluation or appraisal or performance.

The definition of competency used by The National Office for Overseas Standards Recognition (NOOSR) emphasises those factors which are more relevant to the professions.

The competence of professionals derives from their possessing a set of relevant attributes such as knowledge, abilities, skills and attitudes. These attributes which jointly underlie competence are often referred to as competencies. So a competency is a combination of attributes underlying some aspect of successful professional performance ... Specifying the standard involves stating the kinds of tasks and context in which the required level of achievement is to be exhibited. (NOOSR, 1990, p.9)

As the body responsible for the recognition of professional and library technician courses in Australia, the Australian Library and Information Association (ALIA) has been deeply concerned to ensure that courses which it recognises are able to meet rigorous standards and criteria whilst at the same time ensuring that courses are responsive to marketplace needs. The ALIA was also aware that it needed to be involved in the development of the industry's competency standards if the standards were to be treated seriously or given any credibility by the industry as tools to design relevant training delivery. To date, the use of the competency standards for the basis of training delivery has not extended to first award, professional library and information courses. From the beginning of 1996, however, diploma courses preparing library technicians through the Technical and Further Education (TAFE) sector, are based on the industry's competency standards. There is also a glimmering of interest in the use of the standards as the basis of delivering on-the-job training as well, as reported at two recent national conferences on library and information competency standards (*Enterprise, Employment, Education: The Library Workforce in the 1990s* (1995) and *Future Challenge, Future Change: The National Library Competency Standards Conference* (1996).

Within the library and information industry, competency standards have the potential to be used in enterprise bargaining, recognition of prior learning, development of career paths, providing a basis for articulation within or across industries, as a means of identifying skill and training gaps, as a means of identifying training needs for industry/individuals, as a tool to assist with recruitment, to provide a clear statement of professional/technical work identity and to offer national benchmarks for training.

Use of Competency Standards in Continuing Professional Development (CPD)

Beyond entry level, competency standards offer considerable guidance for the longer-term development of the profession. CPD has been criticised frequently for lack of direction and/or rationale. The clear specification of what a competent professional needs to be able to do will provide a much sharper focus for CPD. Similar considerations apply to refresher courses for people returning to the profession after an absence or for people whose training is out of date. The value of competency standards for efficient and equitable recognition of overseas qualifications is also important.

Competency-based assessment will assist CPD by providing :

- a means of accrediting genuine self-initiated/self-managed learning that is relevant to the profession;
- a basis for national planning of CPD allocations from the resources of the profession; and
- evidence of the contribution of CPD to furthering of professional standards.

CBA will enable providers to set clear objectives for CPD programs that meet the real needs of the profession and delineate a career path from novice through to expert. By clarifying the role of CPD in relation to initial courses, CPD programs are able to adapt quickly to meet changing labour market requirements. The ALIA's Board of Education has prepared a set of principles for CPD which endorses the use of competency standards and CBA for the very reasons stated above.

STAFF DEVELOPMENT PRIORITIES

Prior to undertaking my research, an exhaustive literature review was conducted to ascertain what was deemed to be important to developing staff in libraries so they could cope with the ever increasing pace of change in their workplaces. What follows is a very brief synopsis of my findings.

There appear to be three key areas that should be addressed by libraries when developing training programs.

1) Technology training and education is seen as necessary to equip staff to manage technological change and to support and improve the effectiveness of the organisation.

2) The development of skills in interpersonal relations is seen as becoming increasingly important as the work environment becomes more interdependent resulting in the need to work with and influence others.

3) The changing nature of the concept of leadership is seen as a need to be addressed in terms of a shift in the idea of leadership as a management role to more "...personal responsibility for meaningful, creative change in the workplace" (Jurow, 1992, p.14).

A recurring theme in the literature is the need for change and flexibility. However, "...for change to occur as a result of professional development the individual has to be prepared to change" (Nicholson 1992, p.259). He/she must be motivated and see the need for change. As stated by Jurow (1992) much of the change occurring today, and in the future, "...is imposed" (1992, p.15). Therefore, the individual or organisation has little control in this situation. This has important implications for library managers and their management of human resources.

Jurow (1992) also stresses the importance of flexibility and the need to be able to respond quickly to changing conditions. The need for personnel to be able to function in a changing environment is seen as the greatest challenge facing academic libraries with a need to constantly update the knowledge and skills of personnel "...as the nature of the work and the library as an institution change" (1992, p.16). The need for the involvement of staff in the process of planning for change is stressed by Weaver-Meyers (1992) in order to produce well trained, supportive staff and in enabling libraries to cope with the new developments transforming the library profession.

FUTURE ISSUES FOR STAFF DEVELOPMENT

Changes in government policy resulting in award restructuring, the structural efficiency principle (SEP) and the resultant focus on multi-skilling and competency standards have resulted in a climate of uncertainty and confusion within the library profession. Added to this are the budgetary constraints resulting from the current recessionary climate and continual advances in information technology which require constant investment in new hardware, software and retraining.

This, as well as the trend towards funding allocation being increasingly determined by performance, suggests a need for a move away from the old models and paradigms of librarianship. In the academic library setting, the move away from the traditional view of "...the academic librarian... tied to the library's collections" is supported by Moore (1992, p.252). She discusses an innovative approach to academic librarianship trialled at the Royal Melbourne Institute of Technology (RMIT) libraries, which has librarians working in several different disciplines, in re-designed library positions. This model of cross functional, "customer-focused" teams of library staff is becoming increasingly attractive as more and more academic libraries in Australia adopt quality management principles.

Another issue of importance is the increased sophistication and expectations of library users. This is addressed by Nicholson (1992) who also sees a need for increased professional development in areas relating to delivery of service, such as communications and marketing. Line (1991) supports this view and stresses a need to consider the implications of increased user awareness of technologies and information access. He states that "...developments in the private information sector are perhaps leading people to have greater expectations of service" (1991, p.98).

Moore (1992) also has a strong opinion in this area and raises the issue of the quality of library service, with regard to quality management and strategic planning. The importance of this subject for academic libraries, in an era of increasing competition in the area of supply of information products, is stressed. Libraries must be able to compete with other information suppliers in providing access to information. It is imperative that this area be addressed in training and development programs. In addition, Nicholson (1992) sees the need to consider our position as an Asian nation. The resultant effects on initial courses and professional development programs is regarded as an increasingly important issue for the profession.

The importance of staff development and training as a means of career advancement and promotion is addressed by Ladd (1992). Bridgland (1993) discusses the need for realistic career path alternatives. At present, the career structure for library technicians is limited, so that qualification as a librarian is the only viable promotion option. Similarly, librarians who wish to advance must pursue a management direction, to which all librarians may not be suited or interested. There is a need for "...alternative career paths for professional and technical specialists which encourage them to remain within their areas of expertise" (1993, p.9). The necessary features of these alternative structures and the implications for staff development need to be carefully considered by both employers and the profession.

Effective staff development and training would appear to be viewed with increasing importance in the present climate. Shaughnessy (1992) suggests that increasingly time constraints and need influence the choice of options in staff development resulting in "... greater reliance on workshops, short courses and library sponsored events simply because of increasing job demands" (1992, p.288). Dyckman (1992) suggests that in order to provide increased opportunities for staff development "...libraries will use more in-house talent to train, requiring staff who attend outside workshops to bring back the information and help train others" (1992, p.88). The apparent preference for on-the-job and in-house training approaches to staff development and training is widely reflected in the literature, with time and cost seen as factors having most influence. My research endeavoured to establish whether award restructuring in libraries acted as a catalyst for these developments.

RESEARCH METHODOLOGY

For Australian libraries, the introduction of workplace rearrangement (particularly award restructuring) and the Training Guarantee Act (1990) (TGA) in the early 1990s brought with them a degree of confusion. There was confusion about what the broadbanding of classifications for librarians and library-technicians might mean for career paths and progression. At the time of embarking on this study, there was nothing written specifically for libraries on the implications of the NTRA, award restructuring and the TGA and many librarians responsible for staff development expressed the need for further guidance. Also at this time, members of the Board of Education of the Australian Library and Information Association were aware that the federal government's training reform initiatives had the potential to impact on:

- entry levels and qualifications in the library and information industry;
- on-the-job training in libraries;
- staff development in libraries; and on the
- continuing professional development of workers in the library and information field.

My research sought to ascertain the extent to which practitioners in libraries were aware of the underlying concepts of workplace rearrangement, the NTRA, the NFROT, competency standards and the TGA or of their potential impact in the workplace and on staff development in particular.

Four research questions guided my study:

1. Have the concepts of workplace rearrangement, the TGA and the NTRA affected the design, implementation and evaluation of staff development programs in Australian academic and state libraries?

2. What do those responsible for staff development in Australian academic and state libraries know/understand of workplace rearrangement, the TGA and the NTRA?

3. Have the education and training principles of workplace rearrangement and the NTRA (and, in particular, industry competency standards) been incorporated into staff development programs in Australian academic and state libraries?

4. What do those responsible for staff development in Australian academic and state libraries understand the term "staff development" to mean?

Data to address these questions were sought in three ways. Two national surveys of all Australian academic and state libraries were undertaken a year apart; (the number of respondents to the 1992 survey was 45; in 1993, due to the amalgamation of some academic libraries, there were 42 respondents); documents were examined, for example, staff development policy documents, and interviews were conducted, both to elaborate on survey data and to explore interviewee's meaning of the term, "staff development". At the time of the 92 survey, only 7 respondents' libraries had undergone award restructuring; by 1993 this number had risen to 22.

FINDINGS

Modes of Training Delivery

In 1993, as in 1992, almost all respondents used a combination of on-the-job, internal and external modes of training. On-the-job training was found to be, by far, the most common mode of delivery in 1992, whereas, in 1993, it was identified as most common mode for qualified library technicians by 13 out of 31 libraries (42%) and for librarians by only 11 out of 34 (32%). The most frequently reported "most common mode" for librarians was "external to the library" (14 out of 34, or 41%).

Perceived Present and Future Effects of Award Restructuring on Staff Development and Training

Respondents were asked how they felt award restructuring had affected, or would affect, their staff development and training. In 1992, only two of the seven libraries, which had implemented award restructuring, felt that it had already affected their staff development and training programs. In 1993, this increased only to 3 out of 22. Many of the recently restructured libraries commented that it was too early for effects to be felt but that they were expected in the future. Of the 4 libraries in the "Yes" group (i.e. award restructuring implemented by 1992) which responded in both years, responses were evenly divided and identical for both years.

On the future effects of award restructuring on staff development and training, 24 out of the 36 libraries who responded to this question in 1993 felt there would be changes, compared with 20 out of 35 in 1992. Of 6 libraries which in 1992 had already undergone restructuring, 4 (the same as in 1992) had either experienced or expected to experience change as a result of restructuring. From the 1993 responses, however, it is apparent that there is greater awareness among libraries of the potential effects of award restructuring on their staff development and training programs than a year ago.

Of the 24 libraries who expected future change, almost all predicted increases in several areas. The specific areas where future increases were most often expected were: the amount and quality of on-the-job and in-house training, the attendance of full- and part-time qualified library technicians and librarians at training, the budget allocations for training for full-time qualified library technicians and the amount of training in staff's own time.

Skill Development - Qualifications Vs Experience

The questionnaire attempted to discover whether formal qualifications or experience were emphasised in current library awards. The 1992 survey showed that restructured awards were less likely to emphasise formal qualifications than experience than unrestructured awards. As in 1992, unrestructured awards were more likely to emphasise formal qualifications. This is one clear example of the national training reform agenda having had an effect. Many restructured awards require libraries to employ staff who either have formal qualifications and/or relevant experience, thus recognising learning other than that implied by acquisition of a formal award.

SEP as a Catalyst for Change

As in 1992, the majority of libraries saw the SEP as facilitating change in the way staff development and training was conceived (26), planned (30) and implemented (25). Twenty-four respondents selected all three. Three-quarters of the restructured libraries saw SEP as facilitating change in these areas, compared with slightly more than half of the twenty libraries where award restructuring had not yet been implemented.

16 libraries added comments, including that SEP had led to an increase in the organisation's commitment to staff development and training, that it made training better co-ordinated, better documented and more directed toward the acquisition of specific skills, and that information from the SEP process had assisted in planning staff development programs. Two recently restructured libraries stated that the process had not yet addressed training. One expected that training would be "one of the negotiating points" in enterprise bargaining, a response which suggests the organisation sees training as being of benefit mainly to its employees, rather than a benefit to achievement of its goals. Of the unrestructured libraries, two felt that SEP would have little effect, as multiskilling and staff development were already practised in the library, while one doubted that SEP would be sufficient to improve a negative institutional attitude toward staff development.

Competency Standards

Most respondents saw the proposed development of Australia-wide library competency standards as having an effect on staff development (29 in 1992 rising to 32 in 1993). An increased number of respondents felt that the competencies, then being developed by Arts Training Australia (now CREATE), would provide clearer guidelines for future training strategies. Clarifying levels of achievement would result in more focused staff development and training programs which would give priority to the provision of training in the competencies.

However, the number of respondents with reservations about the national competencies increased (from four in 1992 to 12 in 1993). Many of these reservations concerned the process of identifying and defining competency standards, with some feeling the standards would be too vague, general or out of date, and others that they would be too restrictive. The interpretation, implementation and impact of these standards were also areas of concern.

Multi-Skilling and Productivity

As in 1992, most libraries saw multi-skilling as having numerous benefits. The number of respondents in 1993 recognising each benefit were :

Allow employers and employees greater capacity to adapt to the pressures of new technology (39)

Increase employee satisfaction through a greater variety of tasks (38)

Lessen demarcation between tasks (37)

Have a positive effect on career prospects (37)

Increase staff capacity for innovation (31)

Increase the scope of individual initiative through participation in goal setting (28)

Have a positive impact on job security (17)

Only job security was seen by several respondents (9) as being adversely affected by multi-skilling whilst, as in 1992, career prospects were seen, by most respondents, to benefit.

Effects of Award Restructuring and Enterprise Bargaining on Staff

Only two 1993 respondents believed that award restructuring was disadvantageous overall to librarians and qualified library technicians, compared with six in 1992. The number, who felt they were neither advantaged or disadvantaged, rose from five to ten, while 25 (26 in 1992) felt that staff were overall advantaged. These advantages included salary increases, improved career progression, and increased flexibility (e.g., in working hours). Among the libraries which had been restructured, opinion was evenly divided on whether career path opportunities for librarians and qualified library technicians had been improved under the new award. Libraries, which had not undergone restructuring, were more likely to see the process as improving career paths for library technicians by giving them access to higher levels, but they too were evenly divided on career paths for librarians. Although there were few changes from the 1992 results, respondents did seem more optimistic about career opportunities for librarians than a year ago.

Respondents were divided over whether enterprise bargaining would be generally beneficial to librarians and library technicians, with 15 replying "yes", 14 "no" and 13 either stating that they did not know or giving no response. However, many of those who answered "yes" or "no" added that they were unsure. The main benefit foreseen for staff in enterprise bargaining was that they could achieve more flexibility in terms of working hours and modes, although with the possible loss of penalty rates. Several respondents felt that the interests of staff would be subordinated to more powerful interests, and to the organisation's need to save money, while others felt that more articulate, or better performing staff, would gain, whilst others would be disadvantaged.

Other Important Issues for the Design and Delivery of Staff Development Programs

A range of influences were identified by respondents on other issues for the design and delivery of staff development programs. The responses, in ranked order, were financial resources (constraints), amalgamations, technology, release time for staff, access to appropriate training programs, and need for programs to be properly evaluated. The most important issues identified by the respondents for the design and delivery of staff development were the financial and human resource management policies of each institution.

It is helpful at this point to summarise the findings of the surveys against the key features of the National Training Reform Agenda (NTRA).

1.   *Flexible training pathways to meet individual and industry needs.*

Each survey asked respondents about their modes of delivery. In 1992, on-the-job-training was found to be the most common mode of delivery. In 1993, this remained true for qualified library technicians, while external training was more commonly used to train librarians. However, the move towards external training sessions was equally evident in libraries whether they had restructured or not. Thus, libraries seem to have embraced a range of training modes, the emphasis changing according to the level of formal qualifications of staff (and presumably the impact of qualifications on the type of work performed in each library). This could be argued as meeting both individual and industry needs.

As discussed in the findings above, in 1992 and in 1993, restructured awards were less likely to emphasise formal qualifications than those as yet unrestructured. This suggests a more flexible attitude to the incorporation of experience or recognition of prior learning as embodied in the national training reform agenda, through its National Framework for the Recognition of Training. This more flexible attitude of libraries which have undergone award restructuring would conceivably enable them to adopt competency standards as an alternative to formal qualifications for demonstrating ability.

Access to training can also be examined in light of the first key feature of the NTRA. In both surveys, part-time staff appear to have good access to training. Casual staff seem more likely to receive training if they are qualified librarians but the overall accessibility of casual staff to training declined slightly. Libraries will need to explore access of casual staff to training, particularly in light of the introduction of competency standards. Can a library afford to deny training to a valued casual if she or he cannot demonstrate competence in all areas of work?

2.   *Skills and career path options.*

Multiskilling as discussed in the findings above was viewed favourably by respondents in both 1992 and 1993. For many libraries, particularly the smaller ones, it was seen as essential and had already been the workplace norm for many years. Even in large libraries where the possibility of highly specialised staff exists, specialists are often required to perform other duties, for example, the curator of rare books is required to undertake administrative, training and promotional activities for the rare books collection. Thus this aspect of the NTRA was already embedded in library workplace practice.

As for career paths, in both surveys many respondents were not able to answer the question about career paths as the new awards were not yet in place. However, when asked if they thought career paths would improve in the future, the 1992 responses indicated that this would be so mainly for library technicians. In 1993, the margin of difference for those answering in the affirmative for library technicians and librarians had narrowed considerably. (See Table 13 above). This indicates a slow realisation that the restructured awards might be able to offer improved career track options for both professionals and para-professionals.

3.   *Nationally recognised qualifications and course accreditation procedures.*

In the Australian library industry, this already exists and has done for librarians for the past twenty five years via the accreditation or course recognition process undertaken by the Australian Library and Information Association. The ALIA has also ensured nationally consistent and portable qualifications for library technicians since 1978.   It is in the area of continuing professional development (CPD) that ALIA and the industry are looking to the NFROT principles and competency standards to provide a means of:

- accrediting genuine, self-initiated, self-managed learning that is relevant to the profession;
- a basis of national planning of CPD allocations from the resources of the profession; and
- evidence of the contribution of CPD to furthering of professional standards.

4.   *Articulation of pathways between courses and institutions.*

The surveys did not address this feature of the NTRA directly but this is possibly an issue which might be encompassed by enterprise bargaining, particularly if competency standards are introduced across the industry. Most respondents were unsure as to how enterprise bargaining would affect staff. Those who saw it as beneficial felt that it would create more flexibility in terms of hours and modes of working, allow rewards for good performance and would give staff a greater sense of involvement. On the negative side, the process was seen as threatening and purely driven by the desire to save money. It was felt that in the long term, it would affect overtime and penalty rate payments. One respondent commented :

Enterprise bargaining has been in effect [in this institution] since 1989. The overall effect for librarians is that those who could argue well have done better in the salary area than others. This has led to inequalities of salaries for staff with similar responsibilities. Library technicians have been inclined to accept what is on offer rather than negotiate anything more complex.

The 1993 open-ended responses on enterprise bargaining reflected that respondents were unsure as to how it would affect their staff.

CONCLUSION

Although about half of Australia's academic and state libraries have undergone award restructuring in the last few years, these two surveys have revealed very few changes in staff development and training policies and programs. For every library which reported a particular change there seemed to be one reporting the opposite. Those improvements which have occurred, seem just as likely to be related to modern management practices such as strategic planning, improved communication or more democratic organisational structures as to the implementation of award restructuring and the NTRA.

Many libraries found the award restructuring process long and arduous. But opinions varied as to its worth. Some saw few positive outcomes for staff or the library, reporting loss of morale and forecasting reduced salaries, conditions and career opportunities. Others saw far reaching long- and short-term benefits in improved career paths, more interesting work and more flexibility for staff, as well as improved efficiency and productivity through multi-skilling. It is likely that the experience of each institution depends largely on the actual local outcomes of the restructuring process, which in turn is affected by that institution's established philosophies and management practices as well as the local state of industrial relations. Regardless of whether award restructuring has been implemented, libraries appeared to be increasingly aware of the actual and potential implications of award restructuring and other industrial changes such as enterprise bargaining and competency standards on their staff development and training programs.

In conclusion it can be said that academic and state libraries in Australia were only just coming to terms with the large-scale changes introduced by workplace rearrangement and the NTRA. Whilst many respondents were unsure or unclear of the impact of aspects such as competency standards and enterprise bargaining, many of the other features of the reforms, such as multi-skilling, were well and truly embedded. It yet remains to be seen what the impact of competency standards will be. Uptake of their use across all library sectors in the country is slow, but this is not uncommon with major changes which are not enforced in some way.

As expected, financial resources and the organisation, with its policies, were seen as the most important issues which affect the design and delivery of staff development. The literature would indicate that staff development and training is largely the responsibility of the employer, so that the level of service is maintained and enhanced. Many libraries indicated that this was not the view of the organisation, but hoped that this would change over time. Once again these issues were the same both in libraries which had restructured and those which had not.

Other factors which were seen as important for the design and delivery of staff development and training were the availability of appropriate courses, and also the need for advance publicity to enable long term planning and budgeting. Respondents also were aware that there needed to be some form of evaluation to ensure that management and staff were not only working towards the same goals and objectives, but that their progress could be monitored. As is evident in the literature, there is a need to adapt to changes and industry requirements, as well as to clients' needs and evolving technologies.

The challenge for library managers is to devise programs which enable greater skilling and enhance the attainment of the library's strategic goals whilst avoiding a breach of the work requirements of the various classifications. Perhaps this will be easier when competency standards for the profession are embraced. In the meantime, those responsible for the design of staff development in libraries must adopt a position of creative diplomacy in order to multi-skill their staff without compromising work standards. The performance appraisal process and the application of Quality Management principles to work practices can provide a useful platform for this. Furthermore, staff development managers will have to design career paths which remove barriers to moving progressively through a classification structure. What is the point if the only career structure open to library technicians is to qualify as a librarian? They should not have to change their emphasis in order to gain promotion. Similarly, not all librarians want, or are suited to management positions. In any case, as flatter organisational structures replace more hierarchical ones, there will be fewer management positions for library technicians and librarians to take. There need to be alternative career paths for professional and technical specialists to take which encourage them to remain within their areas of expertise. To be attractive, these alternatives will either need to pay well, provide more job satisfaction, or both. This may also involve changing the way library staff view their careers, how successful they are and their value to the organisation. This, too, has implications for staff development.

Being aware of and responding effectively to the macro environment, including national initiatives such as training reform and workplace rearrangement are vital if libraries are to compete in information provision. Informed employers, employees, registered providers, tertiary institutions and professional associations can all play a role in determining staff development training needs. Partnerships among these providers can ensure the design and delivery of relevant, high calibre training and development products which are responsive to industry and client needs, thus helping libraries to continue to deliver and develop quality services and to survive and thrive in an increasingly competitive field.

REFERENCES

Arts Training Australia (1995), *Library Industry Competency Standards*, Sydney: ATA.

"Arts Training Australia" (1993), *Update* 1, Winter/Spring.

Australian Enterprise Bargaining Manual (1993), North Ryde, NSW: CCH Australia Ltd, p.3202.

Bridgland, A (1993), "Award restructuring, the Training Guarantee Act (1990) and staff development in Australian libraries", *Australian Library Journal*, 42, (3), pp. 205-213.

Carmichael, L. (Chairperson) (1992), *The Australian Vocational Certificate Training System: Report*. Canberra: NBEET

Department of Education, Employment and Training (1991), *Australia's Workforce in the Year 2001*, Canberra: DEET Economic and Policy Analysis Division.

Dyckman, A. (1992), "Library assistants in the year 2000", *Journal of Library Administration*, 17 (1), pp.77-90.

Economic Planning Advisory Council (EPAC) (1993), *Education and Training in the 1990s*, Background paper No. 31, Canberra: EPAC.

Employment and Skills Formation Council (1993), *Raising the Standard: Middle Level Skills in the Australian Workforce*. Canberra: NBEET

Employment and Skills Formation Council (1994), *The Shape of Things to Come: Small Business Employment and Skills*. Canberra: NBEET.

Enterprise, Employment, Education: The Library Workforce in the 1990s (1995), edited by Anne Hazell, Adelaide: University of South Australia.

EPAC report, (n.d.) *Education and Training in the 1990s*.

Finn, B. (Chairperson) (1991), *Young People's Participation in Post-Compulsory Education and Training*. Report of the Australian Education Council Review Committee. Canberra: AGPS.

"Future Challenge, Future Change. The National Library Competency Standards Conference. Melbourne, 4-5 December 1995 (1996), *Education for Library and Information Services: Australia*, 13, 1 May.

Jurow, S. (1992), "Preparing academic and research library staff for the 1990s and beyond". *Journal of Library Administration*, 17, (1), pp. 5-17.

Ladd, Y. (1992), "Continued and appropriate recognition for library technicians: grown-up perceptions", in *Libraries: The Heart of the Matter: Proceedings of the Australian Library and Information Association: 2nd Biennial Conference, Albury*, Deakin, A.C.T.: D.W. Thorpe, pp.177-180.

Line, M.B. (1991), "Library management styles and structures: a need to rethink?" *Journal of Librarianship and Information Science*, 23, (2), pp. 97-103.

Mayer, E. (Chairperson) (1992), *Putting General Education to Work*, Melbourne: AEC/MOVEET.

Moore, S. (1992), "The response of academic libraries to educational change" in *Libraries: The Heart of the Matter: Proceedings of the Australian Library and Information Association: 2nd Biennial Conference, Albury*. Deakin, A.C.T.: D.W. Thorpe, pp.251-254.

Nicholls, J. (1992), "Competencies, training and higher education, *Journal of Higher Education* 15, (2), pp. 2-4.

Nicholson, F. (1992), "Professional development programmes in Australia, United States and Great Britain" in *Libraries: The Heart of the Matter: Proceedings of the Australian Library and Information Association: 2nd Biennial Conference, Albury*. Deakin, A.C.T.: D.W. Thorpe. pp.259-262.

NOOSR (1990), *Establishing Competency-based Standards in the Professions. Research Paper No. 1*. Canberra: DEET, December.

Shaughnessy, T.W. (1992), "Approaches to developing competencies in research libraries." *Library Trends*, 41, (2), pp. 282-298.

Teece, P. (1993), *Enterprise Bargaining and Workplace Reform: Issues for Library and Information Workers*, Canberra: Australian Library and Information Association.

Teece, P (1993), *Enterprise Bargaining and Workplace Reform : Understanding Australia's new Industrial Relations System*, Canberra : ALIA, pp.2-3.

Weaver-Meyers, P.L. (1992), "The place of training in the process of change" in *Staff Development: A Practical Guide*. 2nd ed. Lipow, A.G. and Carver, D.A. (eds), Chicago: American Library Association, pp.12-15.

Wiltshire, K. (1994), *Review of the National Board of Employment, Education and Training*. Canberra: DEET

DISTANCE EDUCATION AS A NEW POSSIBILITY FOR LIBRARY AND INFORMATION SCIENCE EDUCATION IN ESTONIA

Sirje Virkus
Department of Information Studies
Tallinn Pedagogical University
Estonia

Abstract: The demand for continuing professional education for library and information professionals with the knowledge and skills of modern information technology will increase significantly according to the development plans for the libraries in Estonia. The paper reports the findings of a survey, and describes ways in which the needs will be met.

INTRODUCTION

The world of librarianship is in the midst of a "paradigm shift". Change is the most significant characteristic in this world. The virtual library, in which sources are accessible beyond the walls of the local library is bringing about fundamental changes in the way libraries and librarians serve readers and professionalism will necessarily entail a much higher level of technical knowledge as well. Adaptation to the electronic age demands a considerable re-education of, and continuous learning by, all professionals, especially information professionals. The education and training system has a key role in this new environment. Talk nowadays is frequently of the information society and it is essential to view the information society as a learning society which offers new opportunities for teaching and learning.

The systematic transition to the modern information technology in Estonian libraries started in 1992 when the plan for establishing information system for libraries was developed. On September 14, 1995 the major Estonian libraries signed an agreement for the establishment of ELNET, the consortium of the Estonian library network and the Charter of which was approved by the Government in 1996. The goal of the Estonian Library Consortium is to organise and co-ordinate the work on the library information system design and to solve organisational, legal, financial and other questions which will rise in the course of work. After a long evaluation and selection period the INNOPAC (Innovative Interface, USA) system has been selected for the unified integrated system for research libraries. The actual implementation of the system depends on funds and as the project has been insufficiently financed, the realisation has not succeeded according to the plan. The public libraries selected the system KIRJASTO 3000, for which substantial support was allocated by the Open Estonian Foundation.

According to the plan for the development of the libraries of Estonia, basic technology will be transferred to modern information technology during the period 1996-2005. As a result of that plan 1500 workplaces with modern information technology will be established in 591 libraries in Estonia. The demand for continuing professional education for library and information professionals with the knowledge and skills of modern information technology will increase significantly.

At present there are 1284 libraries in Estonia, among them 604 public libraries, 745 school libraries, and 141 special and research libraries. There are 3135 librarians working in Estonian libraries, and 48% of all librarians have been professionally educated.

To define continuing education needs at the present time a special questionnaire was distributed by the Estonian Librarian Association (ELA) among the members of ELA in February 1996. Almost 300 librarians answered the questionnaire. The analysis of the results showed that education and training is needed mostly in the fields based on modern information technology (computer handling, the generation and usage of computer-based databases, network training, integrated library systems, etc.).

In order to cope with the growing continuing education needs, a Centre for Information Work was established within the Department of Information Studies at the Tallinn Pedagogical University in June 1995. In addition to face-to-face courses, distance education as a new form and method of education has been implemented in the Centre.

Distance Education in Estonia

Distance learning, flexible learning, resource-based learning, open learning and computer-mediated learning are becoming commonplace in the progressive educator's vocabulary, but we should indicate that there is no widespread familiarity with the concept of modern distance education in Estonia. Distance education is still, by most people, associated with the kind of correspondence education that was offered under the old regime, and is often also associated with its most evident manifestation, i.e. technology. It is therefore important to convey an understanding of modern distance education to the Estonian educational systems (Distance..., 1993).

At their meeting on January 29 1993, The Nordic Council of Ministers made a decision to support the Action Programme for the Baltic Countries and neighbouring Areas. In this Action Programme provision was made for educational projects in distance education. For this reason the Council accepted an application from the President of EDEN (the European Distance Education Network) on behalf of the national associations of distance education in Finland, Norway, and Sweden to perform a Feasibility Study in the Baltic Countries (Distance..., 1993).

In March 1993 the Central and Eastern European Countries proposed within the framework of the Working Group on regional initiatives in human resources, to establish a Regional Distance Education Network in co-operation with PHARE. As a first step a feasibility study of the development of such a Regional Distance Education Network in Central and Eastern Europe was commissioned and the European Association of Distance Teaching Universities was contracted to carry out this study with the Ministry of Culture and Education of Hungary as co-ordinator.

Feasibility studies on the development of modern distance education were carried out in 1993 by groups of experts engaged by Nordic Council of Ministers and PHARE.

In October 1993, at a Seminar in Budapest for the official representatives of all eleven PHARE Countries, it was agreed unanimously that a Regional Distance Education Network should be set up with a long-term perspective. Following up the feasibility study, a financing proposal was agreed in 1994 for a 3 MECU pilot project called "PHARE Multi-Country Co-operation in Distance Education". The Pilot Project started in October 1994 and ended in February 1996.

The Estonian National Contact Point was established on 7th November, 1994 and Regional Centres were set up at Tallinn Pedagogical University, Tartu University and Tallinn Technical University within the framework of the PHARE Programme for Multi-Country Co-operation in Distance Education.

On 22nd of August 1996 an international seminar "Modern Training and University Education" was arranged at Tallinn Pedagogical University to draw some conclusions about what has happened in the field of distance education in Estonia.

The main obstacles to delivering distance education in Estonia were identified as being:

- a lack of appropriate literature and printed materials
- a lack of modern knowledge
- old-fashioned academic staff and subject oriented teaching
- a lack of ideology and/or policy at the strategy level about distance education
- few active learners (Jõgi 1996).

Still the rapid development of a national telecommunication network provides the possibility of making use of the most recent information technology in the field of distance education. Connecting the libraries, information centres, universities and schools to the Internet provides a good opportunity to disseminate distance education all over the Estonia.

DISTANCE LEARNING PILOT PROJECT FOR SCHOOL LIBRARIANS

For the transition from conventional learning to flexible learning specially targeted pilot projects will be used in the Centre for Information Work of the Department of Information Studies at the Tallinn Pedagogical University. The distance education pilot project for school librarians is the first project in the Centre adopting flexible learning methods.

Steps in the design and development of courses, identification of areas of need, selection of appropriate learning media, etc. had already begun in 1995. The distance education pilot project for school librarians started in May 1996.

THE AIM OF THE PROJECT

The aim of the project is to bring quality in-service and continuing education to school librarians in Estonia. This project also aims to enable the participants to become aware of the potential of network possibilities, to gain some basic skills about network information seeking and retrieval, publishing on the Internet via the World Wide Web, public relation and marketing, user education, etc. Today, from the computer at home or at the workplace, the educator or learner can access the vast number of library catalogues, journal indexes, reference books, full text of journal articles and books, art exhibits, employment notices, discussion groups, business data, etc. The learners in schools need help to convert information into knowledge, to avoid information overload, and to identify the best sources for the specific needs and abilities of each learner. We hope that school library will play an active part in the educational process of every school in Estonia and will support the work of teachers and students, showing them how to make use of the modern information sources available.

CHOICE OF TECHNOLOGY

Today there is a variety of technology available for the transfer of knowledge from competence centres to specific target group: print - electronic publishing; television and radio - broadcast: earth stations, cable & satellites; audio & video cassettes; computer based training; interactive video, CDI & CD-ROM; multimedia; telephony; audio conferencing; video conferencing; e-mail and computer conferencing; audio graphics (Bang, 1995). This technology offers the possibility to reach target groups, who - under normal circumstances - are disadvantaged regarding geography, economy, family, job and so on. We may say that recent innovations in technology have expanded distance education opportunities and even blurred the boundaries between distance and traditional education.

The Internet is a relatively new medium for enhancing and delivering distance learning courses. As a tool for distance learning, the Internet can both deliver content and serve as a multipurpose communications tool. The Internet also supports the open learning concept by providing students with the ability to connect to educational resources when it is convenient for them, to learn at their own pace, and allows students to explore the educational resources in an order that suits their needs.

The choice of media will depend on the nature of the subject matter and skills to be covered, the knowledge level and prior skills of the learners, and the learners access to replay equipment. The choice of instructional media depends greatly upon the budget of course developers as well.

Given the relatively high degree of access which schools have to computing facilities and electronic mail, electronic communication, especially the Internet, has an important role in the promotion of distance education to school librarians in Estonia. Many schools possess computers in Estonia and our schools are much more better equipped with information technology than our public libraries and the online aspect of distance education will continue to grow in Estonia as the number of schools equipped with telecommunications equipment and computers increases. There is a project called "Tiger-Leap" for school computerisation in Estonia. Teachers of informatics in schools have supported school librarians in their network learning activity as well.

There has been the experience of using the Internet at the Department since 1993, and delivering distance education through the Internet is also relatively inexpensive compared with other media in Estonia.

The Internet possibilities have been used for:

- presentation of the learning material
- delivering course materials
- interaction between the learner and the learning material, and
- communication between the learner and the teacher/tutor or among the learners themselves.

We have used synchronous communication possibilities for talk and asynchronous communication possibilities for electronic mail, listserv and WWW, telnet, ftp, gopher. Learning materials have been distributed as ordinary mail (as ASCII-files) - or as Attachments (for formatted documents) to learners. The learning materials also appear in the form of World-Wide-Web (WWW) pages accessible over the Internet, and students are encouraged to explore and draw upon the local and global networked information resources as well. We created a set of Web pages for the module with pointers to some useful information sources for school librarians.

In order to have communication during the courses when all the group members receive the same information, KR-LIST has been created for school librarians. It assists course discussions and the sending of questions or comments to teaching faculty or classmates as well. Students submit written assignments to the teaching faculty through e-mail, and assignments are returned with comments and suggestions in the same fashion.

CONTENT

The pilot project consists of four modules and topics covered include basic network concepts, Internet basic tools, services and search engines, network information seeking and retrieval, publishing on the Internet via the World Wide Web, public relations and marketing, user education, etc. Each module consists of 40 hours and includes self study, face-to-face session, and tutorial and group work. An introductory session of 16 hours was given during the first module using the traditional "face-to-face" method and 12 hours was offered in order to prepare students for the telematics-based components of the course. Key aspects of distance education were covered and terms such as distance education, flexible learning, resource-based learning and open learning were introduced to school librarians. An overview about the challenges and school possibilities was given as well.

Some of the advantages and difficulties experienced to date using the Internet for educational delivery have been described below.

Advantages:

- provides students with the ability to connect to educational resources when it is convenient for them
- the possibility to learn at their own pace
- allows students to explore the educational resources in an order that suits their needs
- a lower cost in the electronic publication of course materials compared to printing the same materials
- faster methods for electronically revising and re-distributing course material compared with print materials
- using the World Wide Web for delivering courses allows lecturers to develop content a single platform, yet the content is accessible by students using a wide range of computing platforms and WWW browsers
- an ability to re-use lecture materials by simply providing links to previous electronic course modules or externally stored resources materials on the Internet.

Difficulties:

- the school librarians experience of information and communication technology was relatively low, only one had practical network experience before
- it seemed to us that even when school librarians had access to computers and knowledge about them generally, they still needed a considerable time to master the techniques involved in using e-mail for discussions and communications
- not all students are suited for Internet-based education. Students may not be able to express themselves as well using the computer based communication methods as they would in direct conversation with their lecturers in classroom discussions. As a result, not all questions may be asked by the student when using computer mediated communications
- some students felt isolated, lacked confidence in their own abilities, and required careful support and encouragement. In general students have to be very highly motivated for personal competence development to study in isolation

- the cost of computer equipment and communications infrastructure limits the number of students that can afford an Internet-based course
- poor technical support or tutorial help can lead to incorrect usage of software tools needed to do assignments.

PROJECT ON DISTANCE EDUCATION FOR LIBRARY AND INFORMATION PROFESSIONALS "INFORMATION TECHNOLOGY IN LIBRARIES"

On 20th September 1996 the Department of Information Studies got support from the Open Estonian Foundation to start the long-term project on distance education for library and information professionals "Information technology in libraries".

The aim of the project: To deliver continuing professional education for library and information professionals using distance education methods in order to promote the realisation of the development program of Estonian Library Information System.

The Distance Education Project is planned for the period 1996-2000 and will include three stages:

- distance education for the scientific libraries
- distance education for central public libraries
- distance education for other public libraries and school libraries.

The project includes different modules: basic computer skills, integrated library systems, Internet basic tools, services and search engines, information seeking and retrieval in Internet and in commercial databases (Dialog, DataStar, etc.), generation of databases, electronic publishing, methods of analysing of information, reference work, Estonian information resources in network environment, user education and consulting, etc.

In addition to the technologies currently being used in the pilot project to deliver distance education to school librarians on the Internet, CU-Seeme videoconferencing software for the PC on the Internet will be used in this project.

CONCLUSIONS

This paper presents a brief overview of distance education as a new important field within the overall development of continuing education in Estonia. The Department of Information Studies of Tallinn Pedagogical University is currently exploring and developing new pedagogic models for learning, using electronic support and learner-centred approaches to provide education to remote students. Our department has taken a great interest in the use of network possibilities for distance learning purposes. The distance education pilot project for school librarians has indicated that the Internet has obvious distance education advantages, the difficulties in using this rapidly changing technology, and has given the experience to improve the quality of distance learning in the Department of Information Studies of the Tallinn Pedagogical University in the future and enable us to apply the ski.s and knowledge gained in the long-term project "Information technology in libraries" (1996-2000) and a the project of business information services (1997). Through the pilot project, the technology will be tested and evaluated in order to develop methods for use in the future.

REFERENCES

Bang, J. (1995), "Curriculum, pedagogy and educational technologies", *EADTU-News*, (18), pp.35-42.

Jõgi, L. (1996)," Introduction distance education possibilities in the Program for Continuing Training of Teachers Trainers in Estonia: distance education as a new possibility", paper presented at the international seminar *Modern Training and University Education*, 22 August, 1996, Tallinn/Estonia.

Distance Education in Estonia, Latvia and Lithuania, (1993), *Report on a Feasibility Study to the Nordic Council of Ministers* . Oslo.

Virkus, S. (1996), "Flexible learning on the information super-highway", paper presented at the international seminar *Modern Training and University Education,* August 22, 1996, Tallinn/Estonia. (In press).

Virkus, S. (1996), "Distance education in library and information science education in Estonia" in: *Papers of the 5th Congress of Baltic Librarians "Independence* and *Libraries,* October 21-22, 1996, Tallinn/Estonia.

Virkus, S. (1996), "Distance learning in a networked environment", paper presented at the FID/ET Seminar, 20-21 October, 1996, Graz/Austria.

EVALUATION AS HUMAN DEVELOPMENT FOR PROFESSIONALS IN THE TWENTY-FIRST CENTURY: A BRAZILIAN EXPERIENCE

Sueli Angelica do Amaral
University of Brasilia
Brazil

Abstract: The paper discusses the importance of evaluation as human development for professionals in the twenty-first Century. It shows an application form as an integral part of IBIS method. It relates the author's experience with this method, developed at the University of Brasilia, Brazil, and it is based on reflexive education.

INTRODUCTION

For a long time, as a developing country, Brazil has had a lot of problems concerning education in general. At this moment, the Brazilian government starts to evaluate the Brazilian educational system as a whole. If you look at the dictionary to search the meaning of evaluation, you can find that it means to assess the value of some activity or object. But this definition is not enough to understand about all approaches of evaluation. Some authors affirm that evaluation is a branch of research - the application of the scientific method to determine, for example, how well a program performs. Some writers look upon evaluation as an essential component of management; in particular, the results of an evaluation may help the manager to allocate resources more effectively. Others stress its role in decision-making: the evaluation gathers data needed to determine which of several alternative strategies appears most likely to achieve a desired result (Lancaster, 1993).

According to the Brazilian government's aims, the University of Brasilia established a program called the Program of Serial Evaluation (PAS). The philosophy of the program is to change the learning process in classrooms because we need students with a sense of criticism, prepared to answer intelligent questions. We hope that this kind of change will improve students' performance when they enrol at the University of Brasilia. PAS has about 25,000 students enrolled from 211 schools of 16 Brazilian states, besides 114 schools located in Federal District. There is a proposal to extend this project to other Brazilian federal universities.

The *Jornal do PAS*, volume 1, number 1, page 2, published on March of 1996, affirms that the program will provide a gradual and systematic selection from second level students. Because of this, the director of the Center of Educational Accomplishment and Development (CADE) of University of Brasilia (UnB) believes that in 1999, university students will be more integrated with the world's necessities required from professionals to work in the 21st Century.

CADE is a unit of UnB. Among its responsibilities, CADE evaluates learning and teaching at UnB. It promotes professors' evaluations, according to a special program, during the academic semesters. The process follows specific instructions, and professors need this typical periodic CADE evaluation to be attached to his/her administrative process at UnB. So evaluation is a permanent process at UnB.

According to this, it is impossible to think about learning and teaching and not think about evaluation. Since the beginning of my career as an assistant professor at University of Brasilia, Brazil, I have been concerned about learning and teaching, because I consider both as subjects very close to each other. Consequently, I realized the importance of evaluation in this whole process.

LEARNING AND TEACHING AND IBIS METHOD'S RESULTS

The twenty-first century is about to start, so teachers are preparing professionals to work in a new era, even when they have no idea about it. Demand for a new information professional education and training within the context of the new era must consider the relevance of information interdisciplinarity and the new profile of the information units by broadening the solely technical vision in favor of interaction that accompanies the development of knowledge and social changes. So, to exercise the role of information professional in the 21st century will be more than anything else a meeting of imagination with reality. Here, creativity and dialectic are dominant. Creativity leads to innovation. It is the practical application of ideas, the conversion of imagination into reality, from invention to product. Dialectic is the capacity to dialogue. Dialogue exercises argumentation and trains the professional to negotiate.

This new concept needs to be introduced into educational context in such a way that teaching and learning methods will assimilate these new principles. The new vision of reality hitherto is based on awareness about the interrelation and interdependence essential to teaching, learning and the self-knowledge process. Such a vision extends beyond present disciplinary and conceptual frontiers. New forms of thinking are now being developed which will be adopted in conformity to new principles and will be used by institutions, organizations, and communities in the process of creation or transformation.

Concern over these developments, together with observations on the need for awareness, sensitivity, quality and true simplicity in personal interaction served as the basis for stimulating the development of the IBIS method while, at the same time, it tries to set our present approach in the light of the evolution of society. It offers a challenge to professionals to adapt themselves with many behavior modifications so that they can react in an effective manner to this evolution. This discussion ranges over many aspects including an explanation of human perspectives, foundations for behavioral modification, and reflexive education.

The IBIS method was developed based on reflexive education. I have collaborated with Professor Tania Mara Botelho, developing research about it. The results of this research were showed in 1993 during the Second World Conference on Continuing Professional Education for the Library and Information Science Professions, sponsored by IFLA CPERT, in Barcelona, Spain (Botelho & Amaral, 1993). The other opportunity was in 1994, during the 47th International Federation for Information and Documentation Conference and Congress in Tokyo, Japan, at the FID Education and Training Pre-Conference Seminar about Multifunctional information new demands for training (Botelho & Amaral, 1994).

Nowadays, Professor Tania Mara Botelho is retired, but the IBIS method application continues. The method plays a fundamentally important role since it prepares an individual for an enhanced quality of life by meeting oneself in the work environment and in the profession.

THEORETICAL FOUNDATIONS

The theoretical emphases of evaluation placed on reflection in the educational process vary according to the characteristics of the setting in place and implementation of solutions, the use of particular cognitive bases, analytical skills, attitudes which facilitate the reflexive approach, levels of self-knowledge and self-determination, examination of values and ethical principles, and appreciation of ideologies and adversities. So, thinking as an IBIS method adopter, evaluation became an integral part of the way of learning and teaching with students.

Human beings want to be happy, so we need to develop all our own potential to enhance our senses to manage the success in our own lives. To get it, we need to develop self-awareness, trying significant changes of attitudes, values and habits. So, self-awareness is the result of a learning or re-education process. It is necessary to expand the macrovision of the world by means of interaction with personal and relational environment of organizations, as well as enriching one's microvision beginning with the interior world. Thus, a deepened knowledge of the environment will lead people to self-knowledge and will facilitate the interaction of each person with others.

We need to use our feelings, attention, observation, memory, intuition and reason to enhance our perception's capability. It is necessary to know how to see, to hear and to feel. We need to pay attention to develop our capability of observation. People are different, and it is important to understand it to succeed in interpersonal relationships.

The changes that occur and the new values that are assimilated bring better results for the students as they acquire a strategic vision of each situation. So, self-awareness in students regarding their role in society results in a broadening of their interactions with themselves and their varying environments: family, social, and professional. Achieving self-awareness embraces the perception of unity and totality. Self-awareness calls for the exercise of undivided attention, observation, and experience which leads to wisdom.

Self-motivation requires more than intention. It is necessarily a continuing and effective action to create a mental availability to construct. Students achieve self-motivation by exercising their creativity, their personal growth, reflexive education, and detachment. It is indispensable to be self-motivated in order to learn, to communicate, and to transmit ideas, in addition to understanding the complexity of a systematic approach to the universe. They need to abdicate any idea of dominating, or using force or manipulative power regarding other persons. It is necessary to communicate successfully and transmit ideas, above all, to know how to listen and see oneself in others, putting a spirit of empathy into play.

STUDENTS' EVALUATION FORMS

Since the beginning, I was interested about the ways to deal with evaluation, because the IBIS method involves reflexive teaching, and its approaches to professional training and development have been associated with notions of growth critical inquiry, analysis and self-directed evaluation. These notions must be associated with learning and teaching.

Evaluation of each student is made both at the cognitive and skills levels. The state of spirit of each student will be a manifestation of joy, happiness, and well-being. Self-expression will be reflected by a better knowledge and total use of the students' potential in their individual personal and professional activities.

That is the reason that leads me not only to evaluate students, but to make students participate in a whole process of the method approach at all. Because of that new point of view, they must understand how it is important to each one of them to realize their own development, to be prepared as an individual for enhanced quality of life by meeting with oneself in the work environment and in the profession.

The obtained results with the IBIS method were surprising in all aspects. It was very gratifying for me to see students' behavioral changes at the cognitive level of mastery with the measurement of necessary competence acquired from the course given the issues addressed during classes.

Although concerns about the initial proposed evaluation form remain, that was the reason that lead me to improve the evaluation forms. At first, I have had some personal difficulties in applying the first form proposed to students' individual evaluation sheets. Criteria mentioned in the form were aligned with instructional and learning variables of the IBIS method, and I have agreed with them but, in my opinion, the sheets did not have a simple layout, and I was misunderstood about the scale used. It was complex to fill them out at the same time that I was observing students' performance.

On the other hand, I have not agreed with the process as a whole, because only the professor has had the opportunity to evaluate. So, it was uncompleted, considering the premises of the IBIS method, including freedom to teach and freedom to learn. The students were not participating at all. They did not achieve self-awareness if they were missing circumstances which allow them to achieve the dynamic equilibrium in each one.

Since I have started my first class as a Librarianship professor at the undergraduate level, as Librarianship is taught in Brazil, I developed my own model appropriate for students' self-evaluation at the University of Brasilia where I work. I have always considered the principles and the premises of the IBIS method, primarily thinking about myself and my difficulties to distinguish personal from professional, and not permitting that subjectivity disturb the evaluation, when justice and impartiality are indispensable.

Generally, the students' evaluation is according to their performance considering attendance, work group, oral presentation, and written assignments. The percentage of each kind of performance depends on techniques used in order to achieve the goals of the course, number of students by classroom, availability of resources, and subject approach. In general, each kind of performance is evaluated following some criteria respecting the principles of the IBIS method, such as:

- Attendance (Students give themselves evaluations to be considered by the professor)

  1. Punctuality
  2. Regular attendance
  3. Interest and attention during classes
  4. Participation
  5. Reading texts

- Work group (Students give themselves and classmates evaluations to be considered by the professor)

  1. Group integration
  2. To know how to hear
  3. To know how to criticize
  4. Organizational capability
  5. Objectivity
  6. Leadership capability
  7. Respect for other classmates
  8. Criticism acceptance
  9. Planning capability
  10. Responsibility

- Oral presentation (Students give themselves and classmates evaluations to be considered by the professor)

  1. Content
  2. Creativity
  3. Used resources (handle with techniques, aesthetic form of presentation, and different resources)
  4. Use of time management
  5. Oral expression (language, clarity, capability to explain doubts)
  6. Body expression (posture and care with personal appearance)
  7. Presentation (explain how to develop the subject by group, interaction among components of the group during presentation, public communication)
  8. Flexibility (how to deal with the unexpected)

- Written assignments (Students are informed about these criteria used by the professor)

  1. Content
  2. Creativity and innovation of the approach
  3. Fulfilment deadline
  4. Presentation form (used resources and aesthetics form)
  5. Logical structure and chain of topics
  6. Writing and relationship between oral and written presentation
  7. Bibliography
  8. Bibliographic citation

Besides explaining all mentioned criteria, I talk about the meaning of evaluation and the importance of it to students' self-development, giving them opportunity to discuss their ideas about the subject in an open dialogue. Afterwards, I distribute the forms (Appendices 1-3), always during the first class of each course, when all students are invited to give me their opinions about them. These are the steps to inform all students about evaluation, and I give them every information about how many percentage points each kind of activity has in total.

Also, a collective evaluation class is the agenda at the end of each course. Everybody participates in this activity, and each student is invited to answer four questions about the course, which are distributed during the activity (Appendix 4).

Moreover, another type of evaluation is on the agenda, according to students' interest. Each student has an opportunity to make an individual evaluation appointment with me, if he or she wants it. It is up to them. This moment is planned to give them freedom to express their opinions without constraints. The students are treated as individuals and they have a chance to explain their critical opinions. This behavior is part of the process and it helps students to be conscious of their self-development, according to their own decisions. It is up to them, too.

Students are not accustomed to this professor behavior. It is a real "revolution," resulting from a new-found freedom and responsibility in teaching and learning. In general, they do not present any resistance and I was very grateful, appreciating students' behavior. They were completely amazed with this innovation, because they were not accustomed with that way to be treated. Most of the students enjoyed the new opportunities to express their feelings sincerely; they trust the process. After this takes place, all situations are put to good use in order to dismantle blocks and experience dialogue. Even the shyest were more confident.

The most interesting event is that not only students were touched. I was surprised when some professors were interested in this evaluation method, too. They asked me about the method and how to apply it. They started to use that approach and appreciated observing how students improve their behavior dealing with evaluation.

During the experience, testing the evaluation process of the IBIS method, one professor told me: "I have never seen the students so conscious of their own results. Even when their mentions are not the best, they agree with the results and they understand what is wrong in an easier way than before."

FINAL CONSIDERATIONS

The IBIS method allows the professor and primarily students to improve their relationship. It allows students to encounter their identity, sensitiveness of oneself and about the other, dialectic-participation, capability and evaluation of situations, and structuring of contents and systematic organization. Because of that, it is possible to consider its evaluation as human development for professionals. This evaluation of the growth process avoids judgements reached through rationalization that is harmful to the freedom of being in the 21st century in order to guarantee professional performance improvement as well as the social evolution and transformation demanded.

Obtained results with the IBIS method applications in 1993 (Botelho & Amaral, 1993) showed positive perspectives and it stimulates us to continue its application. From 1993 to 1995, I could apply the IBIS method to 221 undergraduate level students during 900 classroom hours observed at the University of Brasilia, Brazil. Most of the students demonstrated understanding of the aim of evaluation as a part of their self-development, and their participation was always increasing. The obtained results demonstrated a satisfactory involvement with the method and its evaluation.

In 1996-1997, I could not continue my observations about this process, because I was involved with my doctoral program and was not teaching during this period. It does not mean that the IBIS method evaluation project is concluded. At that time, I have evaluation forms to another professor interested in continuing the evaluation with that new approach. She shall test them with her students and report the results to me.

I will re-start teaching in 1998. I intend to continue applying the evaluation forms of the IBIS method. I have plans to enhance aspects related to case studies of the method, in order to intensify evaluation and the analysis of its results. The characteristics of the IBIS method demonstrate that the method can contribute to improvement of the profile of the information professional.

I realize that it will be necessary to adopt new paradigms about teaching and researching, valorizing flexibility, quality, harmony and consciousness to prepare new professionals under human development to act as professionals in the 21st Century. Professors must stimulate the self-awareness of each student in order to prepare the professional of the future to work, especially when they are teaching courses in which contents cover managerial techniques.

It will be necessary to develop teaching programs that valorize human beings in order to humanize the operational environment to develop technical abilities, stimulating innovation, creativity, and the new life values. This will suggest including these new life values in the content of the courses. Until that time, I would like to discuss my proposal and all suggestions about it will be welcome.

REFERENCES

Botelho, Tania Mara and S. A. Do Amaral (1993), "Continuing Education in the Information Profession: a Reflective Method, in Woolls, Blanche, ed. *Continuing Professional Education and IFLA: Past, Present, and a Vision for the Future; papers from the IFLA CPERT Second World Conference on Continuing Professional Education for the Library and Information Science Professions*, München: K. G. Saur, pp. 202-209.

Botelho, Tania Mara and Sueli Angelica do Amaral (1994), "Information Professional Education and Training for a New Management Paradigm in Developing Countries," in International Federation for Information and Documentation Conference and Congress, 47, Tokyo, FID Education and Training Pre-Conference Seminar: Working papers *Multifunctional Information New Demands for Training?* Tokyo: FID/UNESCO, pp. 20-28.

Lancaster, F. W. (1993), *If You Want to Evaluate Your Library*, Champaign, Illinois: University of Illinois, The Graduate School of Library and Information Science.

APPENDIX 1

University of Brasilia
FA - Department of Information Science and Documentation
Professor: **SUELI ANGELICA DO AMARAL**

Name of Student:..

SELF-EVALUATION FORM

ATTENDANCE

Evaluate your attendance and participation, considering each class if:
- Were you punctual?
- Did you pay attention during the classes? What about your interest for classes?
- Did you participate in class, asking or answering questions?
- Did you read all recommended texts?
- Did you get additional bibliography?
- How many absences do you have? Did you really need to be absent?

WRITTEN ASSIGNMENTS

The following criteria will be considered on written assignments evaluation by your professor:

1. Content
2. Creativity and innovation of approach
3. Fulfillment deadline
4. Presentation form (used resources and aesthetics form)
5. Logical structure and chain of topics
6. Writing, and relationship between oral and written presentation
7. Bibliography
8. Bibliographic citation

APPENDIX 2

University of Brasilia/ FA/CID
Professor: **SUELI ANGELICA DO AMARAL**
Date:...........................

' WORK GROUP EVALUATION

NAME OF EVALUATOR:...

NAME OF EVALUATED STUDENT:...

Observe your classmate following criteria below. Add up her or his points, considering one point to each criterion.

CRITERIA	POINTS
Group integration	
To know how to hear	
To know how to criticize	
Organization capability	
objectivity	
Leadership capability	
Respect for other classmates	
Criticism acceptance	
Planning capability	
responsibility	
TOTAL OF POINTS	

Fulfill your self-evaluation.

CRITERIA	POINTS
Group integration	
To know how to hear	
To know how to criticize	
Organization capability	
objectivity	
Leadership capability	
Respect for other classmates	
Criticism acceptance	
Planning capability	
responsibility	
TOTAL OF POINTS	

APPENDIX 3

University of Brasilia/ FA/CID
Professor: **SUELI ANGELICA DO AMARAL**
Date:....................................
NAME OF EVALUATOR:...
NAME OF EVALUATED STUDENT:..

ORAL PRESENTATION EVALUATION

- **Contents** (6 points)
- **Creativity** (2 points)
  (1 point)
- **Used Resources:** handle with

- **Body Expression:** posture and care with personal appearance

- **Presentation:** explains how to

techniques and aesthetics form of
presentation and different used
of
resources (2 points)

- **Use of Time Management** (1 point)

point)

- **Oral Expression:** used language,
- **Flexibility:** how to deal with
clarity, capability to explain doubts
(1 point)

develop the subject by group,
interaction among components

the group during presentation,
public communication (1

unexpected (1 point)

CRITERIA	POINTS
Contents	
Creativity	
Used resources	
Use of time	
Oral expression	
Body expression	
Presentation	
Flexibility	
TOTAL OF POINTS	

SELF-EVALUATION

CRITERIA	POINTS
Contents	
Creativity	
Used resources	
Use of time	
Oral expression	
Body expression	
Presentation	
Flexibility	
TOTAL OF POINTS	

APPENDIX 4

University of Brasilia / FA
Department of Information Science and Documentation
Professor: SUELI ANGELICA DO AMARAL
Course:..
Student:..
Date:.......................................

1. Did the course correspond to your expectations? Justify.

2. How much did the course contribute to your professional formation?

3. In your opinion, which mention do you deserve? Justify.

4. What do you suggest to improve the course?

AN APPROACH TO IDENTIFYING SKILLS WITHIN AN INFORMATION CULTURE: THE APPLICATION OF INFORMATION POLICY TO INFORMATION CULTURES

Michael Kristiansson & Leif Kajberg
The Royal School of Librarianship, Denmark

ABSTRACT: The paper identifies a future production unit that transforms ideas and objects into new ideas and objects. This production unit which will be treated in detail in the following is labelled information culture. The information culture which is suitable for meeting the range of challenges arising from the new global information-intensive economy increasingly gaining ground in these years is based on the theories on the learning organisation, leadership and teamwork. Also drawn upon in examining the nature of the information culture is the concept of the intelligent enterprise. In this context information culture is of interest since its provides an adequate framework for the study of professional skills as well as continuing education needs in the near future.

INTRODUCTION

In the present paper we have identified a future production unit that transforms ideas and objects into new ideas and objects. This production unit which will be treated in detail in the following is labelled information culture. The information culture which is suitable for meeting the range of challenges arising from the new global information-intensive economy increasingly gaining ground in these years is based on the theories on the learning organisation, leadership (Rasmussen 1995) and teamwork (Katzenbach & Smith 1993). Also drawn upon in examining the nature of the information culture is the concept of the intelligent enterprise (Quinn 1992). In this context information culture is of interest since its provides an adequate framework for the study of professional skills as well as continuing education needs in the near future. Within an information culture which functions as a team the group should be composed in such a way that the skills possessed by the participants are complementary. This observation is in no way a new one; it has in fact been relied on for years within industrial organisations. The recent development is that new work areas can be identified. For instance, Reich (1993) has singled out three job categories for symbolic analytic services: 1) problem-identifying, 2) problem-solving, and 3) strategic-broking. Together with these three job categories routine production services and interpersonal services could constitute a complementarity within the general workforce. For each of these job categories, a specific set of qualifications should be devised in addition to those qualifications that according to Reich should be possessed by all, especially the symbolic analysts, viz. abstraction, system thinking, experimenting and collaboration. These qualifications will not be given further treatment in present paper. What will be described in more detail is the concept of competence which must be ranked as a crucial skill in an information culture to be possessed collectively by the group. It is a lifelong learning process which should be facilitated by learning by doing.

For an information culture to be well-functioning, the principle of knowledge sharing must be adhered to and it is necessary that those people participating in addition to concrete skills are in possession of accountability and commitment (Katzenbach & Smith 1993). Hence, the intra and interpersonal skills - e.g. the individual's ability to be committed and to collaborate - are highly important to an information culture. In the context of library and information science, we think that there are two or three qualifications that could deserve closer examination but which will not be addressed here, namely data discipline and information responsibility which are related to the principles of knowledge sharing. Data discipline is very close to the universe of knowledge management and is justified by the wish for retaining the knowledge in the heads of the individuals in the enterprise even if employees leave the enterprise to seek employment elsewhere. Information responsibility to a large extent refers to the fact that individuals feel responsible that the information flow, and thereby the knowledge sharing processes, are functioning within the organisation. In this way knowledge sharing is closely related to elements of information policy (Knowledge as a competitive factor 1995).

In recent years information policy on a macro level increasingly appears on the agenda on a par with industrial and agricultural policy. Significant issues such as the development of IT-infrastructures, copyright and research have found there way into a range of national and international information policy programmes. Underlying the launching of the variety of recent information policy initiatives is not least the recognition that information and knowledge represent a resource of growing importance as well as competitive advantage. A similar development can be observed in private enterprises in which emphasis is increasingly being placed on information as a competitive parameter.

Information exerts a marked influence on the information exchange, information flows, power structures as well as the basic requirements for education and training in enterprises. This development is also reflected in the management literature which tends to ascribe more weight to leadership which involves a wide variety of information policy processes.

INFORMATION POLICY: A MICRO-MACRO PERSPECTIVE

In addressing the scope of information policy, Oppenheim and MacMorrow (1997) identify six major areas in which policies of relevance to informational activities can be developed. The areas singled out by the two authors encompass legislation, regulation, infrastructure, service provision, education and the cultural sphere. These main elements of information policy which are oriented towards the macro level, that is information activities at the national or international level, easily lend themselves to application at the micro level. They constitute a legitimate conceptual framework for developing an information policy for an information culture. It can be argued that the phenomena and activities at the macro level are recurring at the micro level.

Information culture is not that easy to delimit. It is an elusive concept since it could relate both to the culture within a formal organisation as well as to groups of employees operating outside the company but working on the same project and linked to the entire industrial complex with its subsidiary companies and its outsourced production or service activities. Information policy in this sense, and that means information policy developed specifically for an information culture as defined above, is designed for the purpose of strengthening and consolidating a culture in terms of information and information exchange. It is the same rationale that underlies the concept of national information policy, namely to contribute to the economic growth of the nation and to benefit the culture of that nation. In short, the information culture constitutes an area in which a policy can be developed. At the macro level, this means that an information policy will be a policy catering for the nation state. Thus, an information policy in this sense can be related to both a corporate environment, at group of employees or a specific project being undertaking within the formal organisation or outside.

As indicated above, the information policy thinking at the macro level can be transformed in order to fit the micro level. Hence, the legislative and regulation aspects constituting an important element of information policy addressing phenomena at the national or international arena are also essential in the context of information policy development for an information culture. Regulation within the company is necessary for e.g. handling security issues and for providing guidelines and rules indicating what employees are allowed to access specific files of information. Recent years have seen a shift away from the principle of providing individuals with information in a more controlled way, that is according to perceived and pre-defined needs - often decided about by the management. As opposed to this principle, a new one has been introduced which emphasises the idea of creating an information-rich culture providing individuals with a wealth of information resources. People is provided with as much information as possible and efforts are made to speed up information flows and target these information flows to the right persons. Implicit in this thinking is the idea that each employee should share and exchange information and adhere to the basic principle of information responsibility. Information should be available to everybody throughout the organisation in online accessible files and all pieces of information should be recorded within the company. To sum up, regulation is about hampering or stimulating information flows and this can be done by using a system of incentives.

The issue concerned with service provision is also of relevance to information policy formulation for an information culture. Viewed from the macro perspective, a range of information agencies such as different types of libraries, archives, museums, and other kinds of information centres produce various categories of information services whereas research institutes are producing knowledge. At the micro level, within an organisation, information-related services and products have traditionally been delivered by an in-house library or information unit and by the IT department. No doubt future organisational change within commercial firms will see a business process reengineering trend and a redefinition of the functions performed by the IT department and the library to allow for the development of more integrated service structures.

Another essential macro policy area is the infrastructure development which considers such issues as the development of national and international telecommunication infrastructures, the development of specific branches of the information industry as well as the establishment of relevant national information co-ordination organisations. Similarly, at the micro level, LANs constitute the backbone of the information infrastructure of a modern firm.

Not to be forgotten in a macro policy context is the cultural dimension including cultural information policies designed to help a nation preserve its heritage and develop, adjust and mediate the culture. Information policies with a cultural orientation consider institutions such as national libraries, public libraries, museums, national broadcasting services and other agencies concerned with cultural activities. At the micro policy level, priority is given to adjusting the organisational culture to the general economic competitive conditions. The concept of the information culture addressed here involves a synthesis between the communication infrastructure, the human capital, the organisational culture as well as the structure of the organisation. Information culture in this sense has been developed to form a competitive advantage within a company. From our perspective, an information culture needs to be currently developed and refined as a prerequisite of shaping a powerful organisation. As indicated below, developing the information culture involves the managerial aspects (leadership focus) and competence development.

In the classical macro policy context the role of education policies have been to ensure that people are properly qualified for the employment market and are prepared for being active citizens. In a modern information-intensive society, however, in addition to serving as a means for supplying the requisite manpower for the information sector, educational policies are also pursued for raising the awareness of information resources in the society at large and for promoting information literacy among the population as a whole. Entering a lifelong learning process is a must for the individual because of the constant flow of new knowledge (ideas and objects). Because of the abundance of information in the digital age, selecting the right information has become a greater problem and has increased the demands for information handling skills to be picked up by the individual or - and this is important - by a group. At the micro policy level, education policies are devised and implemented so as to develop employees' skills to make the information culture function. In addressing the educational policies developed for an organisation, particular attention will be given to the dichotomy between competence development and qualifications development. In the present paper the focus is on competence development because competence, as opposed to qualifications, constitutes the best means for handling complexity and for preparing oneself for tackling unexpected and unknown situations being the prevailing condition in the competitive climate typical of today's globalisation trends.

INFORMATION POLICY CHARACTERISTICS: HOLISTIC VIEW AND COHERENCE

Whether information policy is considered from a micro or macro perspective, it must be studied as an interactive and contradictory process involving as set of trade-offs. The reason for adopting a theoretical approach like this is that within the realm of information policy, different social goals are being pursued. At the macro level, it may be desirable to maximise information resources available in society in general. This aim which could be called the principle of dissemination of knowledge may however be contrasted with another principle, that of copyright. In short, on the one hand, the principle of copyright exists for the purpose of preventing misuse of intellectual works. On the other hand, copyright serves to encourage people to be more inventive, fore instance in terms of patent applications. In an economic context this is an illustration of two apparently contradictory economic considerations. Monopolies may be allowed for a specific period of time in order to stimulate the generation of knowledge but from another point of view point monopolies are an evil in that they interfere with free competition. Another example is the trade-offs between ensuring access to information and the protection of privacy. At the micro level, within commercial firms deserving the label "the intelligent enterprise" in the sense of Quinn (1992) as opposed to conventional industrial companies, there is a trade-off between the intention to allow employees to benefit from the free flow of information and the policy that the access to information should be restricted for security reasons. The company must not become too vulnerable externally because of a too high degree of empowerment of employees. There is a risk that too much empowerment among employees implying that inside information is circulated widely within the organisation and that employees are authorised to gather information, make use of it and to make decisions accordingly can be misused, e.g. Berings Bank in Singapore. In this case the solution is not to rely on a system of barriers and restrictions and to hamper the free access to information. It is important to secure a balance so that the principle of security is not being neglected but at the same time information must flow as freely as possible within the organisation; there should be very good reasons for introducing barriers to the unimpeded exchange of information. Limitations to the free flow of information will *ceteribus paribus* reduce employees' decision-making competence. It is important to devote attention to the concept of information culture. Information culture can be defined as a set of ideas. As corporate information channels change the information culture changes as well. A significant task to be solved by information policy is to develop the information culture so as to make it as competent as possible.

One basic condition to keep in mind is that the management in today's companies is faced with information overload and does not know how to cope with the current abundance of information. Hence, an appropriate strategy to be adopted in this respect is to recruit qualified people to handle this increasing complexity. This is what can be called decentralisation. The idea is that these particularly qualified employees are constituting a network within which they are actively exchanging information. They are the best persons for managing the in-house information flows. If the management attempts to handle these information flows they cannot be sure that they have selected the most appropriate way to do it. Adam Smith provides an excellent illustration of this problem. In the age of early industrialisation Smith argued that decentralisation of economic power should be effected and that market forces should be allowed the decisive influence on the economy relying on fact that citizens and consumers possess the best basis for decision-making regarding their own situation and for making the best decisions. The philosophy here is that everyone knows best where his own shoe pinches. In old days it was the economy which was beyond the control of conventional planning machinery's and consequently meticulous management and regulation efforts fell short because of increasing complexity and overload of information. Today a similar observation could be applied to the micro level, e.g. corporate contexts in which production processes involve an extent of information handling and cause a volume of complexity paralleling the industrial economy in the 19th century that make top planning measures insufficient. Consequently, consideration should be given to decentralisation and empowerment of employees. However, a far-reaching step like this certainly involves a risk that must be faced by the company. It is essential to make sure that employees are sufficiently committed to the survival of the firm. This is a real challenge to be faced. In order to prepare people for greater responsibility and to consolidate their relations with their workplace, various strategies could be selected including that of making people co-owners of the firm and making them share holders. When you formulate an information policy for an information culture it is essential to adopt holistic views and think in terms of coherence. When addressing the educational issues, it is necessary to consider several levels and aspects.

QUALIFICATIONS VS. COMPETENCE

When we speak of qualifications, we are dealing with the way in which we as human beings systematically unfold knowledge, insight and values. Human beings are capable of categorising their world ideally as well as materially and of combining these categories to form systematics. This can be achieved either through machines or by means of algorithms and administrative systems. The ability to systematise is one of the reasons for the great success of the human race. By systematising itself in its own network, human beings are able to maintain a high rate of repetition. We can reproduce ourselves with a very high degree of certainty. This manner of action has become the focus of greatest attention in western industrialised culture, in which repetition and standardisation has served as an important source of economic prosperity.

The production processes typical of the industrial age emphasised repetition and standardisation. Thus, companies relied heavily on machines, algorithms and administrative systems designed to repeat the same process over and over again. In an administrative aspect an apparatus was developed and refined so as to cope with repetitive situations occurring within the organisation.

To prepare individuals for their jobs in the companies of the industrial era great efforts were made to provide people with adequate qualifications. Qualifications can be regarded as a key concept of the industrial age.

Industrialisation leads to the development of a bureaucratic model which is well suited for the 20th century in that it assigns decision-making processes to a formalised system with emphasis on standardisation and repetition. The bureaucratic model implies that a qualified person is entrusted to make decisions at a specific level within the organisation. In this sense a qualified person means a staff member who is capable of making decisions in specific cases in harmony with repetitive and standardised procedures. The goals achieved in this manner emphasise uniform and qualified decisions within the organisations. The training provided for employees operating in this corporate environment typically aimed at enabling individuals to pick up such well-defined skills that allowed them to tackle analogous situations arising within the company.

In the digital age, however, we see a move from the organisational structures prevalent in the industrial age to a networked society. In contrast to the industrial society, organisations in the knowledge society are faced with the basic condition determined by the new, the unexpected, the uncertain and the hardly unpredictable.

Coping with contemporary and near future situations defined as they are by uncertainty and complexity requires that companies rethink the nature of qualifications needed by employees. Highly relevant in this context is the notion of competence which will be discussed below. The possession of competence allows people in a network to be better fit for tackling a complex and uncertain situation. In this way competence further enables people to generate new ideas from existing ideas in a competitive environment.

In the following, the definition of competence is examined from the perspective of the information culture. Competence develops within a network. Information culture represents the space or network in which a discourse is progressing and in which competence serves to transform complex flows of ideas and objects into new ideas and objects.

CULTURE

In order to underpin the concept of information culture and its relations with information policy theoretically, we shall take a closer look at the overall concept of culture. Two approaches to the concept of culture will be contrasted, namely the classic anthropological concept of culture versus a new view of culture as a complex process rooted in recent sociological research. The classic concept of culture implies a set of views, meanings and values expressed as a range of objects and ideas which are common, transmitted and occur as an integrated whole. This integrated whole is inherent in the cultural background of the individual members belonging to a specific culture and to which these members are being socialised.

In the present and past decades, the eroding effects of the global economy an other transitional processes on the national culture in the widest sense accelerated markedly. Very distinct are the impact of international financial markets and the expanding information and communication technologies on the national culture. It is evident that these developments are very significant and have exerted a strong influence on the individual's cultural background. It is obvious that the culture instilled in childhood has changed radically in recent years. More and more common cultural elements are finding their way into local cultures. Therefore, culture is changing and becoming less static and more dynamic because of the rapid exchange of ideas and objects across existing boundaries. Conceptions of values are constantly changing as well with implications for individuals as well as enterprises. This concept of culture applying to the digital age appear more relevant to us in examining the information culture and information policy in a time of increasing globalisation. According to this new view, culture is not a static phenomenon but should be considered as a complex process during which human beings are constantly creating, reinterpreting and negotiating cultural meaning.

In this context it is essential to focus on information cultures because their members are handling complex flows of information and are transforming existing ideas and objects into new ideas and objects. In this way the information culture is acting as a producer of cultural meaning.

From an information policy perspective, these processes are interesting and deserve close attention. They affect qualifications and ethical values. What people used to do, that is traditional habits, values, and views, etc. are no longer valid. They are being transformed and redefined, knowledge is becoming outdated quickly and value norms to which people tend to be socialised increasingly appear useless. Thus, an open attitude towards cultural influences is necessary. What is relevant today is an open culture in which views, ideas, values, etc. are currently changing and being regularly adjusted. Today people must be able to absorb these changes and new cultural patterns.

INFORMATION CULTURE

Industry and commerce as well as politicians increasingly ask for flexibility and innovation both in the production and in leadership since they are essential parameters in relation to competitiveness. The significance of these parameters to a great extent owe to the high degree of complexity in the information age. Modern and information-intensive companies can be viewed as organisations that suck in, in the one end, ideas and objects transforming these into meaning and ejects ideas and objects in the other end. An organisational structure performing like this is what we understand by an information culture. Thus, an information culture transforms a complex flow of ideas and objects into something meaningful. If the flow is less complex conventional organisational structures and administrative practice can be relied on. But the more complex the flow of ideas and objects is the less applicable traditional qualifications are for performing the tasks.

Hence, individuals, and consequently enterprises, must remain flexible, they must avoid regularity, abandon repetition and place their emphasis on innovation instead of the ability to change, in other words on conditions which are made possible by human competence. Humans can create sense in complex situations, and the potential which ensures that this is made possible is what we can call competence.

Definition of competence (leadership): A competent personal performance is an assembly of ideas that perspectives, arranges and organises a complex occurrence in such a way that a sense making state is brought about. (Rasmussen 1995, 61)

Definition of qualification (administration): A qualified personal performance is an unfolding of knowledge, insight and values, which systematises a complicated occurrence, in such a way that a specific state of objective is achieved (Rasmussen 1995, 61).

*Definition of information culture (*corporate context)

An information culture can be defined as a networked-based communications environment formed by a small number of people who are working together by means of information technology. Typical of these people is that they are working with digital information sources across organisational and geographical boundaries. As members of a small group they are communicating with each other and involved in a common activity, committed to a common purpose and working according to a common information policy for which they are ensuring mutual accountability. The leading principles of and information policy are 1) data discipline, 2) information responsibility and knowledge sharing.

The key activity is to transform a complex flow of ideas and objects into new ideas and objects and this production process is the very purpose of an information culture. Within this communications environment, a discourse is going on and this discourse is identical to the handling of a complex flow of ideas and objects. This information culture is not a static phenomenon but it is in a constant development process because the complex processes involved generate, transform and negotiate cultural meaning. To the individuals involved in an information culture this discourse means that they are part of a constant learning process. In composing the information culture, priority should be giving to recruiting group members possessing a set of complementary skills. At least three kinds of skills are expressed by Reich (1993) in his presentation of the three kinds of the symbolic analysts. In addition to possessing a range of qualifications, those working within the framework of an information culture must be equipped with a competence. Competence in this sense is the handling of certain complex and unpredictable situations involving the element of making sense through innovation in contrast to qualifications which enable the individual to handle less complex and known situations by relying on a formal logic action.

DISCUSSION

A model to cope with growing continuing educational needs should build on the concept of the information culture since this culture represents a modern production unit. Hence, studying how an information culture functions becomes important: mapping and analysing the variety of creative (ideas and objects) and political processes going on within the information culture. The nature of the information culture and the processes within it should constitute the framework for determining the qualifications and the competence which should be acquired by the participants. In this respect we distinguish sharply between qualifications and competence. Above we have tried to make clear that intra and interpersonal skills are important and that it is essential to think in wholes and in terms of coherence. It means that educational issues should be related to the following four core areas within information policy: formulation of rules, encouraging and hampering processes, developing information and communication infrastructures and developing organisational culture.

From an educational perspective, priority should be given to learning how to learn and to develop competence. Also, attention should be given to spotting the set of complementary skills necessary for an information culture for the purpose of determining the qualifications needed by the participants. These qualifications will differ markedly from those known so far. An essential challenge to be faced here is for instance: how do we educate librarians to act as problem-identificators of use to an information culture?

Besides, it is important to be aware of different trade-offs in connection with information policy. For instance, the efforts to ensure that employees are constantly developing and refining their qualifications and competence involve the risk that they will leave the enterprise to seek positions that are more attractive elsewhere thereby causing a brain-drain effect. Similarly, there is risk that the necessary empowerment of individuals within an information culture may lead to serious failures and losses and damage the enterprise. But these are just another type of problems that need to be remedied - what kind of education will serve to qualify individuals for tackling problems of this nature?

We know that enterprises articulate the wish for retaining the body of knowledge represented by the employees and for facilitating the sharing the knowledge among them. Thus, data discipline and information responsibility are vital areas that should be amplified and operationalised in order to give these areas an appropriate content for the purpose of identifying qualifications and intra and interpersonal skills.

REFERENCES

Katzenbach, J.R. & Smith, D.K. (1993). *The wisdoms of teams. Creating the high-performance organizations.* Boston, Massachusetts. Harvard Business School Press

Knowledge as a competitive factor (1995). Copenhagen. Arthur Andersen & Co.

Oppenheim, C. & MacMorrow, N. (1997). Information policy. In: *International Encyclopaedia of information and library science.* John Feather & Paul Sturges (eds.). London. Routled

Rasmussen, O. E. (1995). A strategy for the development of a theory of organisational leadership and administration. In: *Psychological Yearbook.* Vol. 2. Pp. 53-80

Quinn, J.B. (1992). *Intelligent enterprise. A knowledge and service based paradigm for industry.* New York. The Free Press

Reich, R. (1993). *The work of nations. Preparing ourselves for 21th-century capitalism.* London: Simon & Schuster. [Paperback].

CONTINUING EDUCATION FOR CROATIAN LIBRARIANS : NEEDS AND OPPORTUNITIES

Tatjana Aparac
Department of Information Sciences
Faculty of Philosophy
Zagreb

Dubravka Stancin-Rosic
National and University Library
Zagreb

Abstract   A brief description of the main aspects and objectives of professional continuing education (CPE) for the LIS professionals in Croatia is given. The need for improving the knowledge and skills of Croatian librarians and library assistants is highlighted as well as the opportunities for co-ordination and systematisation of all efforts which have been performed from 1970s up to day. An overview of the results of the 1996` survey conducted among Croatian librarians and library assistants - members of the Croatian Library Association - is given and the most interesting data are presented in a way that shed more light on the state-of-the-art in the field of education and CPE in Croatia.

INTRODUCTION

For the past twenty years the LIS profession in Croatia has been witnessing the gradual abandonment of tradition and the acceptance of new forms of organisational and educational systems. Tradition, and until recently, different socio-cultural reality, reflected in the case of Croatia in the relatively greater dependency on institutional context and on traditional methods and procedures, caused a higher degree of uncertainty when it came to the necessary changes and to the implementation of new information technologies in the field of the LIS education. But above all, the war and its consequences, resulted in a number of circumstances which are nowadays demanding a greater engagement of all intellectuals, and among them information professionals play a significant role. New possibilities, new market oriented economy, changes in the educational system, need for preservation of the national culture and public accessibility of the national cultural heritage, need to assure access to foreign databases and scientific literature, to name only a few elements of today's reality, demand from LIS professionals to be educated in such a way as to be prepared to perform difficult and varied tasks.

As is discernible, even from a casual glance at the situation in the field of the LIS education in Croatia, the dual system of entering into the profession is still present. The system of professional examination, which has been present in Croatia since early 1950s, apart from becoming a sort of parallel educational system to the university education, has become something between a basic professional and permanent education, not offering in neither of them satisfactory educational standards.

The only LIS Department in Croatia, established in 1976/77 at the Faculty of Philosophy, has been trying very hard since then to balance between tradition and new challenges so that professional examinations have been following since then the same approach. At the undergraduate level as a consequence of numerous limitations, which determine not only the programmes offered, but also Department's future development (for instance, insufficient number of faculty staff, restricted number of students accepted, inadequate and insufficient equipment, lack of basic literature both in Croatian and in foreign languages), the Department does not satisfy the present need for the library staff educated at the academic level, therefore the professional examinations still exist as an alternative way of getting a professional degree as a condition to keep a particular job for those already employed in the library.

Statistical data about library profession in Croatia

Statistical data show that there are about 1,500 libraries with 2,500 employed librarians, library assistants and technicians in Croatia. Croatian Librarians' Association, though, has about 1,280 registered members, not all of them engaged with the same interest and same amount of free time dedicated to the development of the profession.

For the purpose of this paper it is chosen to comment on the data and (non)existence of continuing education programs for the period from 1976 up to today[1] , taking into consideration the educational needs of today's working population and newcomers in Croatian libraries.

In the period from 1976-1996 9442 librarians and library assistants passed professional examination.

At the Chair for Librarianship[3], that is at the Department of Information Sciences, 249 students graduated till the end of 1996.

Teacher-training college in Rijeka, which had offered a programme for assistant librarians in the period 1964/65-1977/78, enrolled all together 335 graduate library students4 , most of them still working mainly in public, school and faculty libraries in the region.

MS degree in Librarianship in this period was obtained by 93 persons from special, public and university libraries and from the National and University Library.

Scientific degree in the field of information sciences, library science, was approved to approximately 20 persons with master's or doctorate degrees.

Although a number of candidates for professional examinations has been increasing lately and the interest for undergraduate study has been constantly higher than the allowed number of students, the statistical data show that there is still a considerable number of librarians and library assistants working in libraries and documentation and information centres without any professional knowledge or skills.

THE PAST EXPERIENCE WITH CONTINUING PROFESSIONAL EDUCATION (CPE)

However, the changes in today's networked society do not avoid Croatian librarians. New demands and new challenges could be answered only by following a development of the profession and by continuous widening and deepening of general and specialist knowledge and skills.

In such a situation the continuing professional education for LIS professionals in Croatia is not only of great importance regarding a broadly accepted approach everywhere in today's world, which declares it as an important element of the whole life learning process, but it should also serve as a sort of a corrective for oversights made in the previous period. Firstly, this relates to all those things meant to be very important for the profession, but not yet realised. Secondly, this relates to librarians themselves - to those already having a particular professional degree, but who need to gain more specialist knowledge in the field or learn more about new methods and techniques, especially information technology.

Croatian librarians have been aware of the changes in society in general and of professional challenges they have been facing for at least ten last years, and larger libraries and regional librarians` associations have been trying to find appropriate ways and modes for continuing professional education. In the mid 80` it was recognised that radical changes should be made in connection with approach, organisation and performance of continuing professional education. At the 26th Croatian Librarians` association (CLA) Conference (Pola, 1987) the main topic was CPE. Among conclusions and recommendations some were emphasised: awareness of the need for maximum co-ordination among the main creators of the CPE programs in Croatia (e.g. Department of Information Sciences - Chair for Librarianship, National and University Library in Zagreb and other major libraries, Croatian Librarians' Association and its regional chapters);importance of designing and verifying the national program for the CPE, based upon real needs of librarians of all professional degrees working in different types of libraries and other information instititions: recognition of the necessity of establishing a Centre for the CPE with a primary task to inform about all activities performed; importance of organising regional collections of domestic professional literature and assuring the availability of foreign professional literature for those librarians who might need it. Although the accepted recommendations clearly showed that the members of the CLA were determined to make a very much needed step forward to confront challenges of the profession, a number of subjective and objective reasons have influenced their execution, among them most important being: the destruction of a significant number of libraries during the war, the moving of the National and University Library to new premises and its organisational and managerial problems, lack of adequate number of professionals with experience and ability to adapt to the newly created circumstances. Ten years after the Conference the problems are still almost the same and the systematic CPE is badly needed.

As a result of all these moments and problems, the Section for Education and the CPE of the Croatian Librarians' Association agreed that specific steps have to be done in order to determine the needs for the CPE and possible teaching staff. The research which was undertaken during the Summer 1996 was thought to be a starting point for future actions.

NEEDS AND AIMS OF THE CPE IN CROATIA

The main objective of the above mentioned survey was meant to be collecting and analysing of as much as possible data about librarians and library assistants working in Croatian libraries, such as the level of their basic and professional education, career promotion and specialisation. No such data existed except the number of employed staff given regularly by the Croatian Institute for Statistics. Following this, it was intended to get information about different tasks professionals have been performing at their job. The issue of great importance for further planning of the CPE was necessary data about the number of employees being newcomers, or working already a certain period a time, or confronting a retirement soon.

It was also planned to get more data about previous CPE activities in Croatia, which were not regularly noted or collected, and to know more about individual needs and desires and their suggestions for further development of CPE.

To collect the data needed the questionnaire was designed and sent at the end of March 1996 to 1,280 persons whose names were drawn from the database of the members of Croatian Librarians' Association. The subjects were asked to answer the questionnaire in writing and to send it back in a self-addressed envelope until the end of April 1996. Telephone calls were made to those who did not answer until determined time, and then the calls were repeated only to the directors of libraries having more than five employers and to the presidents of regional librarians' associations asking them for help. A total number of returned questionnaires was 750 which made a 58 per cent of all subjects. The questionnaire was not anonymous because the respondents signed their names after answering questions. The data collected were organised and analysed using the SPSS.

The questionnaire was devised in three parts:

The first part was designed to enable collecting data about each subject questioned (e.g. his/hers educational level, basic graduate level, sort of professional qualifications, professional degree - rank, type of library or other information institution, type of professional duties, number of years in the LIS)

In the second part a number of questions was directed towards getting the data about training at the beginning of the professional career, about participation in the CPE program organised by various subjects, about participation, active or passive, at the professional meetings (e.g. conferences of the CLA, other conferences or workshops in the broader field of books and information). It was also interesting to get more information about a number and type of educational activities the respondents attended abroad. As number of courses are offered lately by different institutions and non-government bodies, apart from traditionally involved the CLA and Croatian libraries, it was important to reveal the reaction of libraries when it came to allowing their employees to participate and to pay for it.

The third part of the questionnaire was envisaged to be a source of information of respondents` opinions and suggestions in connection with the CPE. Especially, it was intended to gather more data about educational needs of Croatian librarians. In this sense it was felt to be of special importance to reveal what the respondents thought about the influence of non-appropriate professional education on the professional status of librarians in general, what they thought about the importance of the CPE and what they expected from the CPE. The data about the ways the respondents were keeping their professional knowledge and skills up-to-date (e.g. whether they read professional literature, domestic and foreign, which foreign languages they knew, who they turned to when it came to the question of consultancy and help). Finally, the subjects were asked to express their opinion about possible organisers of the CPE, about the ways of verification of the CPE program and about the sources of finance for the CPE program.

The most interesting results of the 1996 survey[5]

For the purpose of this paper the results are presented in a way that shed more light on the state-of-the-art in the field of education and professional continuing education in Croatia. Some of the results are presented in the form of tables which show the number of responses for particular question followed by percentage of the total answers. Other results are analysed from a point of view of the most significant findings.

Table 1. Level of Education Among academically educated professionals the majority of them came from the arts and humanities field or from social sciences (47, 9 per cent and 39,5 per cent); the others were from natural sciences (5.5 per cent), from technical sciences (3.1 per cent) and from medicine (0.7 per cent) working in special or university libraries (3.3 per cent of respondents did not answer this question).

Table 2. Professional Education. Among all professionals with a university degree 4.7 per cent of them succeeded in getting a promotion as senior librarians and 1.5 per cent as library consultants.

Table 3. Types of library in which the subjects were employed. The span of working experience of all surveyed subjects varied from 1 to 42 years, with the average working experience of 12.45 years. The highest number of answers related to 10 years of working experience (57 answers) which made it a dominant value.

The answers given in connection with the type of activities performed at the working place showed the highest percentage for reference services (71.4 per cent), followed by circulation process activities (58.7) and processing of library material activities (56.3). This has underlined our presupposition that the most known and most popular services in majority of Croatian libraries, regardless of their type, are reference services connected with circulation and processing of domestic material, the last one being performed in almost every library because of the lack of co-operative cataloguization projects. The collection-building process was done by 42.1 per cent of subjects, managerial job was performed by 38.2 per cent of the respondents and 36 per cent of the respondents were involved in preliminary preservation of the library material and technical activities. This especially draws attention to the fact that the respondents were coming from a high number of small and relatively small libraries, public or school, with mainly one employee. Activities like giving service in children's department, managing the local library collection, preparing special bibliographies, performing a professional consultancy service, were chosen by 23.1 per cent of correspondents under the possible answer "something else".

The second part of the questionnaire was directed to the ways and modes of the CPE regardless of the fact that this was offered within a purposely planned and designed program. The beginners in-house training organised on the basis of the program designed for and approved by a particular library institution was attended by 28.6 per cent of the respondents, while 44.3 per cent of them took part in specially designed in-house program for specific tasks they perform. All together 22.4 per cent of all respondents did not have opportunity to participate in any in-house training programs. These figures point out that a very high number of all employees did not get a proper start within in-house training.

In the period from 1987 until 1995 which we took for testing the recommendations given after the Pola Conference regarding the necessity to widen and deepen the CPE in Croatia, the data collected through the 1996 survey showed firstly that 27.8 per cent of all the respondents did not participate in any organised type of the CPE, and secondly that 57.9 per cent of them took part in the CPE only occasionally, twice or more times; 10.8 per cent of the respondents participated once in the CPE program. These programs were mostly offered by regional library associations (for 30.4 per cent of the respondents), by the CLA (for 37.0 per cent of the respondents) and by the National and University Library, mostly in connection with the CROLIST6 (for 37.8 per cent of the subjects). Among the institutions who were periodically offering the CPE programs were also the Department of Information Sciences - Chair of Librarianship (for 7.5 per cent of the respondents), the City Library in Zagreb or other city libraries (for 12.6 per cent of the respondents) and other organisations and institutions such as UNESCO/UNICEF, Open Society, Croatian Ministries of Education, of Science or of Culture.

In the above mentioned period (1987-1995) the four conferences of the CLA were attended regularly by 10.7 per cent of the respondents, 21.9 per cent of them were present there twice, three times participated 6.0 per cent of them and 57.1 per cent did not participate at all. When it came to the active participation, i.e. to the question of having a paper or presentation at the CLA conference in that period only 6 subjects answered that they regularly presented a paper, 4.8 per cent of them did so twice and 2.0 per cent three times. With 5.6 per cent not answering this question, there were altogether 13.2 per cent of the members of the CLA who took active part at the conferences. At the same time a number of respondents participated at the meetings or conferences organised by other institutions or organisations: only once participated 18.3 per cent, twice 9.6 per cent and several times 27.6 per cent of all the respondents.

Regarding the participation of Croatian librarians at the various programs of education abroad in the last 8 years they were attended once by 7.8 per cent of them and several times by 5.2 per cent of the subjects. With 4.8 per cent of those who did not reply to this question, 82.1 per cent did not visit foreign countries for the purpose of acquiring knowledge and experience. The most visited country in that sense was Hungary (2.8 per cent), followed by Great Britain and the USA (2.0 per cent), Slovenia (1.1 per cent), and Austria, Germany, Italy, Czech Republic and Spain, each of them less then 1 per cent.

Apart from the CPE programs in LIS, there were other types of courses attended by subjects surveyed, such as language courses (40 per cent of them), courses prepared for those working with children victims of war (7.2 per cent), basic courses about the CROLIST[6] (0.9 per cent). None of these or similar courses were attended by 51.7 per cent of subjects.

Of all those who were included in the CPE programs 0.6 per cent said that their own library institution did not authorise their participation at all; for 2.9 per cent the approval was given but they had to take their days off and 53 per cent were free to use their working days for such purpose every time they asked.

Regarding the tuition or registration fees 36.4 per cent of subject surveyed said that they did not get any financial support, 6.5 per cent of them succeeded to get it rarely, and 31 per cent got it every time they asked. Some of the respondents noted that they did not ask, but believed that the fees would be paid if they had asked, and 10 per cent did not answer this question.

In the third part of the questionnaire where the subject were asked to express their opinion about the CPE programs in general and to specify their own needs and expectations, we also hoped to get some suggestions for future plans.

Especially interesting was the opinion of surveyed colleagues about the influence of the professional education on the status of the profession as a whole and to their own status. Of all the respondents 5.1 per cent thought that the inadequate professional education did not lower the status of the profession, 53.1 per cent believed that it did only partially, and 39 per cent said that it lowered the status completely. Answering the second question in this section the majority of subjects believed that the professional education was very important for personal professional development; 49.1 per cent of them were of the opinion that this was important and for 39.8 per cent it was a very important issue, while for 10.5 per cent this was important but not a crucially important issue. None of the respondents thought personal education non-relevant for personal professional development.

Giving their opinion about personal expectations in connection with the CPE, 2.6 per cent of the respondents answered that they did not expect anything from it, 68.2 per cent thought that the CPE should widen the knowledge they already possessed and 18.0 per cent expected from the CPE to get a promotion. For 4.3 per cent of the respondents the CPE contributed to the better position in society and for 14.6 per cent of them this helped them to get a higher salary, while for 67.4 per cent the CPE was important for doing their job better. Some of the respondents underlined several other expectations such as getting security and confidence, or more information, or easier exchange of experience with colleagues.

In five other questions, related to the professional literature, the answers had shown in the first place that the professional literature was not as important as one should expect from professionals. Two journals issued by the CLA were not read at all by 7.6 per cent of the respondents, 46.5 per cent of them read these journals from time to time and only 44.7 per cent read them regularly. The answers were not given by 1.2 per cent of the respondents. Among these journals for those who were reading them Vjesnik bibliotekara Hrvatske (Journal of the Croatian Librarians, 1950 -) was important for 69.6 per cent and HBD Novosti (Bulletin of the CLA, 1989 -) for 23.1 per cent of them. Some other journals in the field of the LIS (such as Informatologia, Byte, Bug, for example) were not read by 27.5 per cent of respondents, 56.6 per cent of them read this kind of journals irregularly, while they were read regularly by only 12.6 per cent of the respondents.

By reading domestic professional journals 55.4 per cent of the subjects believed to be informed but not enough about new developments in the profession, while 8.5 per cent of them thought that they were not informed at all. For 26.7 per cent of the subjects surveyed professional journals were good source of information, and for 2.0 per cent they were a very good source of information.

Among foreign LIS journals, which were read by 13.6 per cent of the subjects, Library Trends was mentioned by 13, Information Technology and Libraries by 9, Special Libraries by 7, and Cataloguing and Classification Quarterly by 4 respondents. Other journals mentioned were Knowledge Organisation, IFLA Journal, Byte, Academic Librarianship, Alexandria, Libri, Program etc.

And finally, when Croatian librarians needed professional help 60.7 per cent preferred to ask a colleague at the work place, 57.5 per cent wrote or phoned colleagues in other libraries, 5.9 of them believed that help could be received from the Ministry of Culture, 21.6 per cent used the consultancy service at the National and University Library, 17.6 per cent used the consultancy service at the City Library of Zagreb, 21.4 per cent tended to turn to the consultants in relevant regional central libraries, 8.5 per cent got professional help at the Chair for Librarianship in the Department for Information Sciences in Zagreb, 6.3 per cent tended to ask someone in the CLA and 17.9 per cent asked any well-known expert in the LIS field. These choices were given in advance and when the subjects were asked to name other sources of professional help some of them underlined journals and handbooks or a well-known expert from abroad. Some of the respondents did not ask any professional help (1.1. per cent of them).

CONCLUSION

If one takes into account that being up-to-date in the LIS profession has become more and more difficult in the light of the socio-cultural changes and technological innovations, it is "...essential to consider who the beneficiaries of continuing education are, to what extent they benefit, and what the available options are, outside of formal degree programs, for self-improvement, updating, and lifelong learning."7 In case of Croatia a number of providers offer from time to time programs which could benefit the CPE in the LIS field. Among them the most important are, as the survey showed, Croatian Librarians` Association with its regional chapters, the National and University Library in Zagreb, the Department of Information Sciences - Chair for Librarianship at the Faculty of Philosophy in Zagreb and regional libraries which are obliged by law to give professional help to the libraries in their regions, to organise seminars, workshops and similar activities, and to co-ordinate library activities.

All these parties have been offering training within the frame of recognised needs and their abilities, but as it is discernible from the data collected, this is far from being enough. Furthermore, it has to be pointed out that the lack of the national CPE programme could cause more improvisations and unnecessary competition among these parties, instead of their working together to improve knowledge and skills of those who need them. One could also complain of many restrictive conditions for offering these courses, such as the lack of adequate infrastructure (organisational as well as financial) and lack of qualified instructors. In that sense a role of international organisations, such as the UNESCO and IFLA, EU and their relevant programs and private sponsored actions like those already being designed and organised by the Open Society, is very important especially in connection with the training for trainers programs.

It could be also noted that the status of the CPE for information professionals has not been yet examined carefully within the state legislation. One could only hope that the CPE of the LIS professionals in Croatia, after being examined from all its important sides which also understands further research and more detailed surveys, would see a brighter future.

FOOTNOTES

1   The period after the establishment of the undergraduate program in librarianship and renewal of professional examinations.

2.   Among them 581 librarians, 154 senior library assistants and 209 library assistants.

3.   The Chair for Librarianship was firstly introduced at the higher education level in Rijeka (in 1964/65), and only in the mid 70`s at the faculty level within the Department of Comparative Literature (Faculty of Philosophy, Zagreb), later becoming the Department of Information Sciences. The postgraduate study in Librarianship, Museology and Documentation, established in the early 60`s, offered within the program of librarianship basic courses similar at that time to the program of the professional examination except for the new courses introducing the computer science.

4.   In the period 1976-1978 there were 32 graduates.

5.   The results of the survey were presented at the CLA Conference, Primosten 26-28 September 1996 and are going to be published in the journal *Vjesnik bibliotekara Hrvatske* 39(1996), 3/4.

6.   CROLIST is a national computer based library programme designed and developed in the National and University Library in Zagreb.

REFERENCES:

Aparac-Gazivoda, Tatjana et al (1987), Bibliotekarski kadrovi, strucnost i obrazovanje kao pretpostavke za dalji razvoj bibliotecne djelatnosti u SR Hrvatskoj. *Vjesnik bibliotekara Hrvatske* 30, pp. 133-153.

Aparac, Tatjana ; Aleksandra Malnar ; Dubravka Stancin-Rosic (1996), Stalno strucno usavrsavanje knjiznicarskog osoblja u Republici Hrvatskoj. *Vjesnik bibliotekara Hrvatske* 39, 3/4 (in press).

Blazekovic, Tatjan (1979-80), Skolovanje visih knjiznicara na Pedagoskoj akademiji u Rijeci od skolske godine 1964/65. do 1977/78. *Vjesnik bibliotekara Hrvatske* 24, pp. 95-102.

Continuing professional education : an IFLA guidebook. München : K. G. Saur, 1991.

Markic-Cucukovic, Ljerka (1984), Library education in Croatia : state of the art and trends. *Informatologia Yugoslavica,* Sep. Spec. 6. Pp.11-15.

Stone, Elisabeth (1986), The growth of continuing education, *Library Trends,* Winter,pp. 489-513.

Weingand, Darlene, A. (1986), Continuing education programs and activities. In *Education for professional librarians* ed. by White, Herbert S., White Plains, NY : Knowledge Industry Publications, Inc., 1986, pp.223-235.

THE ACADEMIC LIBRARIAN AND SCHOLARSHIP: A VISION FOR THE TWENTY-FIRST CENTURY

Araxie Paula Churukian
University of California, Riverside
USA

Abstract: The focus of this paper is on professional practice, scholarship, and service. It discusses the challenges that academic librarians will face in the twenty-first century concerning how to achieve and maintain an educational level equivalent to and sufficient for that of their changing clientele. It describes required expertise, skills, and abilities that librarians will need in order to perform as professionals in the highly complex and dynamic environment of the Information Age.

INTRODUCTION

As we approach the twenty-first century, academic librarians must continue to assess their role in this exciting, challenging, technological, global information environment. This is an age in which both higher education and librarianship are in the midst of transformation. Michael D. Dolence's vision for higher education in the twenty-first century is applicable to librarianship too. To transform librarianship, we must realign it with respect to the changing nature of information, knowledge, and scholarship; the needs of individual learners; and the changing nature of work. These changes are critical to meeting the learning challenges of the twenty-first century (Dolence and Norris, 1995, p.22) In libraries the new developments in information technology are challenging and often overwhelming, but the real challenges that we will face are not technical in nature but personal. It is the change that will be required of individuals--administrators, professionals, support staff, and patrons--that will present us with the greatest challenges. Our institutions cannot afford to maintain the status quo and will ask as much of librarians as they do of other members of the campus community. If faculty, curriculum content, teaching methods, course organization, and scholarship have to change, the academic library and librarians will have to be among the first to change (Stoffle et al, 1996, pp.213-225). Librarians have to modify their vision as well as their activities and operations. The library's role should be characterized by visibility and vitality; librarians should be highly visible and well integrated into the academic governance of their institution and meet the needs of the community they serve.

In information technology, academic librarians in some institutions are already collaborating with the staff of the academic computer centers and exercising a leadership role in promoting and teaching electronic resources to students and faculty. A few years ago most librarians could only speculate about what it would be like to be a vice president for a major administrative unit other than a library. Today to face the technological challenges, many institutions of higher education are creating positions such as Vice-Chancellor for Information Technology, Chief Information Officer, Assistant Provost for Information Services, etc. (Mech, 1996). Consequently not only the nature of the services that librarians offer is changing, but the role of academic librarians is changing too. As technological innovations have encouraged the development of new, more intellectually demanding librarian roles, continuing and diversified education will give academic librarians the opportunity to advance their professional status in the academic environment.

LIBRARIANSHIP AS A PROFESSION

Is librarianship a profession? Are librarians doing professional or simply occupational works? Surprisingly, a clear definition of the profession has proved to be elusive over the years. According to the opinions of some scholars (cited below) there is still considerable disagreement on the subject. Harold L. Wilensky, writing in 1964 about "Professionalization of everyone?," argues that many occupations engage in a struggle for professional identification, but few of them "make the grade." Occupations that have been "established solidly" since the Middle Ages have been law, the clergy, and university teaching; some cases are still on borderlines--such as school teaching, librarianship, nursing, social work (Wilensky, 1964).   It seems that since then things have not changed much. In Lynn Curry and Jon F. Wergin's book *Educating Professionals* professions are divided into three clusters, the helping professions, such as nursing, social work, teaching, and the ministry, the entrepreneurial professions, such as journalism, business, and law, and the technical professions, such as architecture, engineering, and the military (Curry and Wergin, 1993). Apparently, some of those on borderlines have achieved professionalism, but not librarians. Furthermore, Margaret F. Stieg discusses the occupational categories that are designed by the U.S. census; librarians, it seems, do not fall under any professional occupation. She writes that of 77,205 full-time librarians employed year round, only 58 percent had five or more years of college, a figure that suggests that the term *librarian* does not, as ALA has tried to argue, carry with it a "connotation of professional" in the sense that professional tasks are those which require a special background and education (Stieg, 1992).

Stieg suggests one of the reasons that librarianship has not been recognized as a full profession is that often there is no clear differentiation of tasks among professional librarians and staff members. In the traditional library setting of the 1950s and 1960s, the tasks performed by the staff members were readily distinguished from the professional roles of librarians in cataloging, reference, and collection development. Today's technology, budget constraints, and administrative reorganization are creating new opportunities for library staff to assume more diverse and higher levels of responsibility . Therefore, the boundaries have become increasingly "blurred with growing of areas of functional overlap" (Sandler, 1996).

The opinions presented above hardly reflect the status of librarians. Academic librarians, with their knowledge of information organization, existing electronic resources, and subject expertise, are highly qualified to work as professionals and peers with the faculty on campus. However, they have to build profession-wide consensus on their own expectations for themselves as professionals. They have to change their basic philosophy of how they collect, process, synthesize, manage, and control information. They have to adhere to the core academic standards of their institutions. Even though commitment to service is the traditional hallmark of the profession, the time has come that they must be engaged more and more in teaching, research, and publishing. Most practicing librarians have the expertise to conduct scholarly research; they do not do so because their jobs do not require it to the extent that faculty jobs do. So few librarians actually engage in research. But to keep current in the fields of their own clientele, to change their image from being a passive keeper or retriever of library materials to a dynamic force in the creation and organization of knowledge, librarians must be researching and publishing. Research will increase the librarian's visibility in the profession and that increase in turn can increase the access to information for librarians, who will then pass the benefit along to their patrons. Such research will make a meaningful contribution not only to the library profession but also to scholarship in general. Besides, the benefits of research could, to quote Dale S. Montanelli and Patricia F. Stenstrom, include "job advancement, personal recognition when no advancement is possible, improved relationships with teaching faculty, increased responsiveness to change and openness to innovation, and better library service through shared knowledge and experience" (Montanelli and Stenstrom, 1996).

CONNECTING EDUCATION AND PRACTICE

No objective observer will deny that libraries have already responded in a variety of ways to the changing technology. As scholarly information continues its migration from printed to electronic formats, librarians confront the necessity of adapting their information mediation role to a completely different environment. This is a time of profound change in the information industry. Whereas a century ago libraries might have been considered to comprise the entire information industry, they represent only a portion today. Libraries' constituencies are changing the way that they seek and obtain information. Why would a patron search in the stacks for an article when he/she can retrieve it from a computer workstation or a personal computer in the library or off campus? Increasingly, information seekers will consult first the options that are easiest to use, fastest and most affordable. Librarians are sure to face competition for the information from an "array of Internet search robots, document delivery services, and increasingly decentralized data sources" (Wilder, 1996).

With the advance of technology, the attitude of the library's clientele is changing; they are becoming more and more sophisticated and demanding. They expect librarians not only to provide them with the information sources, but they also expect librarians to anticipate, interpret and analyze their needs. Librarians can no longer afford to play the role of just resource identifier, organizer, and acquirer. They have to play a variety of roles on the campus--such as researcher, synthesizer, teacher, mentor, and mediator. In order to play those roles, librarians need to look at patrons' needs and requests from the perspective of how they can make it happen rather than why they cannot. Carla J. Stoffle warns that increasingly librarians need to leave the "safe and familiar cocoons of their library buildings behind and work directly in classrooms, offices, and laboratories" (Stoffle et al, 1996, p.220).

Graduate library school programs cannot be expected to provide all of the knowledge, skill, and ability that librarians will need to work in an academic environment and to become an integral part of that institution. While the MLS has been considered to be the entry to professional librarianship, the concept of "terminal former education," is not only misleading, but also it sends a wrong message. Rather than "terminal" a more appropriate view would be that the master's degree in library science as the beginning of an educational process that will continue throughout a librarian's career (Weingand, 1994). Moreover, in the twenty-first century, current library educational systems and their associated accreditation may be neither sufficient nor even necessary to assure the survival of a particular school or program (Penniman, 1995). Therefore, the university library must accept the primary responsibility for continued development and training of its librarians.

Probably there has never before been a time when the effective role of the library depended on qualified personnel more than it does today. Library administration, in order to increase the library's efficiency and effectiveness, needs to allow librarians to pursue their scholarly objectives--to be engaged in teaching, research, study, and writing. To carry on those activities, librarians must have the campus and library administration's support--such as paid leaves, travel and per diem funding, and support for supplies, equipment, etc. To find out what kind of policy for academic professional leaves is in force in some U.S. university libraries, I sent informal inquiries to the campuses of the University of California and twelve university librarians in different states. From the responses I got, and from published research on the topic, it seems release time for research is lacking even in those libraries that encourage or require it for promotion and tenure (Koenig et al, 1996). One librarian, who does not believe that librarians should do research and publishing, complained that his university librarian once verbally promised him paid leave for a project, but his supervisor denied him the time off. One of the documents for leave that I received from research libraries, prepared in 1975, reads: "The Library must be in a position from both a staffing and a financial point of view to sustain the absence of a staff member who is to be on leave."

Since librarians form a large and diverse group, a wide range of opinions is sure to emerge. Some of them will clearly oppose any change in educational framework and work structure; they would prefer the status quo. Others will be for changes, particularly those who will invest their time and energy to bring changes, and probably there will be others in the middle, leaning in one direction or the other. Susan K. Martin, University Librarian at Georgetown University, defines the situation succinctly. She states that even though academic librarianship has only one qualifying degree--the MLS--practicing librarians have different approaches to the profession; there are those who are "no more than 9 to 5 librarians and those who come early, leave late, participate in professional activities and want a fulfilling professional career." Her solution is to create two distinct categories for librarianship--Professional and Occupational. Those librarians who want change are willing to invest their time, money, and energy; they see opportunities to be involved, to be innovative, and to make a difference both personally and professionally. These come under the category of Professional. Those who want to be Occupational would not be given the kinds of responsibilities, assignments, and promotions given to the Professional ones (Martin, 1993).

IMPLICATIONS OF THE NECESSARY CHANGES

Given their skills, experience, and abilities, librarians perform a unique and essential role in academe. They can have a bright future in the twenty-first century if they purposefully begin to change the nature of their work to adopt the emerging electronic access to information and restructure their workload. For example, they are still doing housekeeping activities or performing functions in the library that can be performed by the non-professional staff. They must relinquish or minimize some of their responsibilities and concentrate more on scholarly activities. They must openly address the matter of educational requirements. If they do not, in the twenty-first century the MLS may no longer be a useful credential given the nature of the technological and practical changes they face in everyday library work. Dolence points out that by the year 2000 a new level of learning will be needed for every member of the Information Age workforce who wishes to remain competitive and productive--"perhaps even to maintain basic employment" (Dolence and Norris, 1995, p.7).

Academic librarians must strive to achieve full faculty status. This, of course, is not entirely the responsibility of librarians as individuals but, according to the document prepared by the Academic Status Committee of the Association of College and Research Libraries (ACRL), the preservation and strengthening of faculty status is the responsibility of the profession as a whole, library administrations, university/college administrations, and other faculty members. The ACRL Document explains that faculty status is a means of achieving parity with other faculty in all academic institutions. "Parity in this context means access to tenure, sabbatical leaves, research leaves and funding, and any other institutional benefits that are accorded disciplinary faculty" (Faculty ..., 1993)

Charles B. Lowry's study of 1993 indicates that 67 percent of U.S. institutions of higher education have faculty status for their librarians (Lowry, 1993). The question is how many of them have equal status with the teaching faculty? One university librarian who responded to my informal inquiry explains that their librarians have faculty status; they are evaluated on the standards of teaching, research, and service. But he points out that they are not allowed to teach in a subject area, their research has to be related to library work, and they have no tenure. "Undoubtedly," he writes "if librarians have what faculty consider a symbol of highest achievement, the Ph.D., they [the faculty] are more likely to respect librarians. But as things are getting tighter in money, they ignore that similarity and emphasize the classroom teaching ... Librarians are support personnel and do not generate FTE. Sorry, but true."

I believe the only way librarians can achieve parity with the faculty is to work toward the objective of teaching not only courses of bibliographic instruction but in various disciplines. This is not an easy task. There will be resentment by the faculty, since university faculty traditionally have defended the uniqueness of their disciplines. In 1978, I submitted a proposal to the Department of History at the University of California, Riverside, to teach a course on "Contemporary Middle Eastern History." Perhaps some members of the history faculty were not happy to let me teach the course, but the real objection came from the Political Science Department. A faculty member with the advice of the chair wrote a memo to the dean of humanities. The memo did not mention my status as librarian, but it argued that Middle Eastern history after 1945 falls into the domain of the political science department. Fortunately, I had done my homework. I had already made sure that my expertise was needed by both the History Department and the campus--I had discussed the course with the chair of the Department of History, and as a Middle East specialist I was a member of the campus Speakers Bureau. I had also done the paperwork. I had written a justification, prepared a list of textbooks and readings, and a flyer for promotion, so I prevailed. Since then I regularly teach both lower-and-upper division courses. In his memo of November 25, 1996, the chair of the department, made the following statement: "She is not only a librarian but a trained historian."

The point that I want to make is that if librarians are going to achieve full parity with the faculty, they have to compete with them in the classroom, which means they have to build expertise by getting a master's degree or Ph.D. In their endeavor, librarians need the campus and library administration's support. Particularly, the approval and encouragement of the campus administration are crucial in demonstrating that they view librarians as peers of the faculty (Librarians ..., 1990). Institutions should provide an environment necessary for librarians to assess and promote their scholarly contributions to education. They should be given the opportunity to work with the faculty-- such as organizing seminars, workshops, team-teaching, joint projects, etc.

Another important issue, librarians' salaries, must be considered. Historically the work of librarians has been undervalued. This factor makes it difficult for university libraries to compete with special or corporate libraries or even with public libraries that benefit from civil service. Unfortunately, university libraries tend to try to improve local salaries by comparing them only with the higher salaries at peer libraries (Creth, 1986). Attaining full faculty status in every academic institution may be one method to improve librarians' earnings. If successful, academic librarians will join one of the oldest and best organized special interest groups, the faculty. "As early as the eighteenth century, Adam Smith recognized that faculty respond to the incentives accorded them " (Meyer, 1990).

CONCLUSION

There is no question that academic libraries' functions in 2000 and beyond will be dominated by technology. But terminals, hardware, software, personal computers, satellites, electronic communication, and so forth will not alter the fact that academic librarianship remains the life of the mind, not the life of the device (Veaner, 1985). This is not to suggest that technologies are not important; they are very important, particularly at research universities where they are essential. Even so, library effectiveness is far more dependent on the good work, dedication, and competence of all levels of library staff than it is on these "inanimate resources" (Shaughnessy, 1995). Therefore, the challenges that academic librarians will face in the Information Age should be viewed as a golden opportunity to advance and improve the status of librarians and to remain a vital force in the academic community

There should be concerted efforts at both institutional and national levels to create an academic environment where librarians will have the opportunity for and assistance with scholarly activities. At the local level, there should be a clear delineation of professional and support staff responsibilities. There should be well defined criteria for assessing scholarly contributions to the academic world. In general, an environment must be created that recognizes the interplay of activities in the three areas of performance--service, research, and teaching. Academic librarians should be visionary in conceiving of the present and in imagining the future, and they should be willing to take risks in translating their vision into action.

NOTE

Faculty status is a debatable issue. Today librarians are in a position to help scholars in their research. Because of the skills that this requires, many librarians themselves are researchers and scholars. In fact many of them also teach courses at their own and other institutions, and many publish as much as or more than some faculty. From an economist's points of view on the subject see Bruce R. Kingma and Gillian M. McCombs (1995), "The opportunity costs of faculty status for academic librarians," *College & Research Libraries,* 56 (May), pp. 258-264.

REFERENCES

Creth, Sheila D. (1986), "University research libraries," in: *Education for Professional Librarians,* White Plains, N.Y.: Knowledge Industry Publications, p. 23.

Curry, Lynn and Wergin, Jon F. (1993), *"Educating Professionals: Responding to New Expectations for Competence and Accountability"*, San Francisco, CA: Jossey-Bass Publishers, p. xiii.

Dolence, Michael G. and Norris, Donald M. (1995), *Transforming Higher Education: a Vision for Learning in the 21st Century,* Ann Arbor, MI: College and University Planning.

"Faculty status: 2001" (1993), *College & Research Libraries News,* 54 (June), pp. 338-339.

Koenig, Michael, Morrison, Ronald and Roberts, Linda (1996), "Faculty status for library professionals: its effect on job turnover and job satisfaction among university research library directors," *College & Research Libraries,* 57 (May), pp. 295-300.

"Librarians and campus administrators: working together to support the library," (1990), *Library Issues,* 10 (March), [1-3]

Lowry, Charles B. (1993), "The status of faculty for academic librarians: a twenty-year perspective," *College & Research Libraries,* 54 (March), pp. 163-178.

Martin, Susan K. (1993), "Raising our professional expectations with a two-track approach to librarianship," *Journal of Academic Librarianship,* 19 (March), p. 24

Mech, Terrence (1996), "Leadership and the evolution of academic librarianship," *Journal of Academic Librarianship,* 22 (September), pp. 345-353.

Meyer, Richard W. (1990), "Earnings gains through the institutionalized standard of faculty status," *Library Administration & Management,* (Fall), pp. 184-193.

Montanelli, Dale S. and Stenstrom, Patricia F, (1996), "The benefits of research for academic librarians and the institutions they serve," *College & Research Libraries*, 57 (September), pp. 482-485.

Penniman, W. David, (1995), "Preparing librarians for the Twenty-First Century - assuring that they will measure up," *Public & Access Services Quarterly*, 1, pp. 85-94.

Sandler, Mark (1996), "Transforming library staff roles," *Library Issues*, 17 (September), [1-2].

Shaughnessy, Thomas W. (1995), "Key issue: achieving peak performance in academic libraries," *Journal of Academic Librarianship*, 21 (May), pp155-57.

Stieg, Margaret F. (1992), *"Change and Challenge in Library and Information Science Education"*, Chicago and London: American Library Association, p. 55.

Stoffle, Carla J., Renaud, Robert and Veldof, Jerilyn R. (1996a), "Choosing our futures," *College & Research Libraries*, 57 (May).

Veaner, Allan B. (1985), "1985 to 1995: the next decade in academic librarianship, Part II," *College & Research Libraries*, 46 (July), pp 295-307

Weingand, Darlene E. (1994), "Continuing education: a voice from the field, Part II," *Journal of Education for Library and Information Science*, (Summer), pp 233-235.

Wilder, Stanley (1996), "Generational change and the niche for librarians," *Journal of Academic Librarianship*, 22 (September): 385-386.

Wilensky, Harold L. (1964), "The professionalization of everyone?" *American Journal of Sociology*, 70 (September), pp. 137-143.

MEASURING CONTINUING EDUCATION NEEDS: IDENTIFYING TRANSFERABLE SKILLS THROUGH MENTORING

Jane Farmer and Fiona Campbell
School of Information and Media
The Robert Gordon University
Scotland

Abstract: The paper reports the findings of a research project which identified the generic skills and competencies required by information professionals in the oil industry and health science sectors in order to focus their continuing professional development.

INTRODUCTION

Established theoretical models show that the skills which people acquire are complex and varied. Best, Abbott and Taylor (1990) describe three types of knowledge - *knowing how*, where there is an awareness that the individual possesses a skill; *knowing that*, which is concerned with whether the information is either intrinsic or contingent truth and *knowing why*, the principles which lie behind the skill. This theory is applicable to the ways in which people acquire relevant knowledge about their jobs and the skills which are vital to methods by which they carry out their tasks. The process model devised by Best, Abbott and Taylor (1990) describes a hierarchy of skills required for learning. These skills are,

(1) General, transferable, analytical skills
(2) Subject specific skills
(3) Instrumental skills (technological competence, research skills)
(4) General transferable personal, interpersonal and social skills (including communication and professional presentational skills)

(taken from Best, Abbott and Taylor, (1990), p29)

Sellen's (1980) *What Else Can You Do With a Library Degree*, recognised the problem of career development and advancement and readily acknowledged the core of transferable skills which information professionals possess. In her essay on using information skills, Autrey (1980) advises librarians to make a skills inventory, and to use self-assessment to identify whether they have acquired a great deal of specialisation or a broad range of peripheral skills and experiences. She emphasises that marketing of skills and competencies and by utilising techniques such as putting skills into a layperson's context and limiting the use of the term "librarian" is vital to changing management perceptions of the information professional's role and abilities. Recent work into self-marketing within the organisation has echoed this advice.

SOME DEFINITIONS

There are terms which have specific meanings within the context of the research which may need clarification.

  Skill - an aptitude or competency required for a particular job.[viii]
  Competency - professional ability and efficiency.[ix]
  Transferable skills - a core of generic skills that information professionals possess which can be transferred either to other roles or other sectors within the profession.[x]
  Mentoring has been defined in detail later in this paper.

The Need for a Transferable Skills Framework

Staff at The Robert Gordon University identified the need to help librarians and other information professionals to focus their continuing professional development in order to enhance their strengths and build up skills in areas of weakness. By aiming to identify the generic skills and competencies of professionals working within the oil industry and health science sectors the project allowed potential areas of career enhancement or progression to be revealed.

The project team surmised that in order to be able to move into a new position, whether that position is in a different aspect of the profession or a different role in the same area, it was necessary to identify which skills were transferable and which were not. These issues emerged,

Which skills needed to be refined in order to become transferable?

How much additional training or education would be needed to "top up" existing skills?

Which skills could be left behind with the old job (which skills were too subject specific or non-transferable)?

Which new skills would have to be acquired to make the transition to the new role?

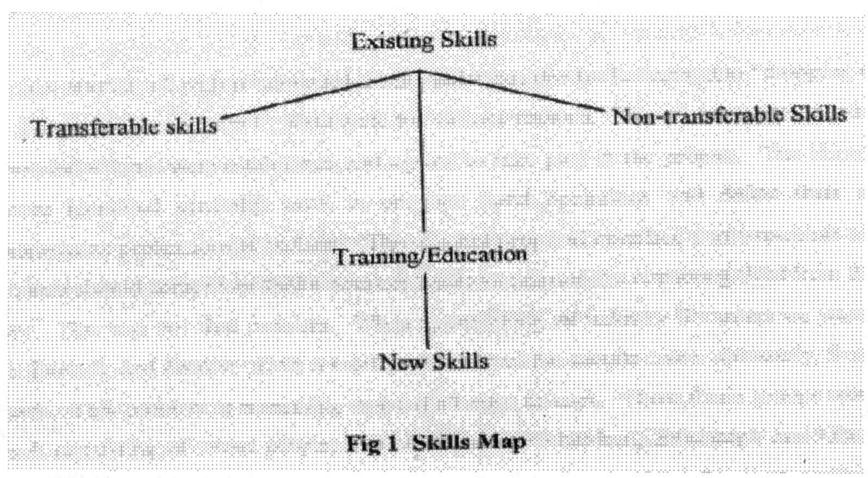

Fig 1 Skills Map

METHODOLOGY

The principal methodology for this research has been mentoring. We based it on Michael Tremblay and Andrew Wall's (1994) work with learning pairs. It was a technique they used at the University of Birmingham to investigate the ways in which managers in different types of health organisations perceive each other's roles. We adapted this method by tailoring it to meet the aims and objectives of the project. The project was designed to encourage the mutual understanding of two very different professional roles, through a series of mentoring meetings and plenary sessions. Further, it was initiated to facilitate librarians, in both the oil industry and health science sectors to build up a relationship with people working in other job areas. By enabling the learning pairs to explore each other's jobs and analyse each other's skills, a framework of skills which could be transferred from one job area to another was identified and validated.

HOW HAS THIS BEEN ACCOMPLISHED?

The term "mentoring" suggests a supportive relationship in which the mentoree is perhaps a company trainee seeking advice and organisational acumen from an older, more established employee. This traditional definition differs from the term as it existed within the context of the project. When we talked about mentoring we were describing a more equal relationship between two different professionals who were helping each other to identify skills which they may have had in common.

1. Identification of Participants

The project started off with twenty-six learning pairs but due to the inevitable "dropping out" period five people decided not to participate for various reasons. Twenty-one learning pairs i.e. forty-two individuals were established and agreed to take part in the project. The librarians who were identified generally work in one-man band operations and define their work environments as professionally isolated. The original proposal specified that two-thirds of the participants should come from health sciences backgrounds and the remaining third from the oil industry. This was our first problem. When approaching oil industry librarians we were met with disinterest and distrust. Only a small proportion of the sample came, ultimately, from the oil sector. This problem is something that I shall refer to later. Three focus groups were set up, each consisting of seven people, around centres in Aberdeen, Edinburgh and Glasgow. Introductory plenary sessions were run in each city to prepare and brief project participants about the course the research would take. These sessions involved initiating and facilitating discussion about careers, organisations and CPD. At this stage, people were informed that they were not obliged to commit to the project if they decided then that they no longer wished to participate. The purpose of these meetings, therefore, was to describe the project to the librarians and assist them in the first steps they would have to take.

2. Selection of mentors and establishment of learning pairs

The project team tried, as far as was possible, to encourage the participants themselves to suggest a mentor, so that they would feel that they had an input into the research and so that they would choose a mentor that they would feel comfortable with. We provided criteria for the selection of mentors such as - the mentor should not be a librarian, not work in the same environment as the learner, they should be one or two grades higher than the learner, and they should be in a position which the learner could reasonably aspire to. We suggested a number of different subject areas such as management, information analysis, information management, public relations, IT management, economic development. In many cases, the learners found it difficult to suggest any possible mentors and in these situations the project team, liaised with the librarian, identified the mentor and established the learning pair. The feedback which we received after the project indicated favourably that the librarians and mentors were generally satisfied with the matches made by the team. This was one of the main difficulties attached to the research. However, there were a few pairs which perhaps didn't work as successfully as we had hoped. These were people who had gone ahead and arranged their own mentors and generally the roles were perceived as being too similar. My role as research assistant was critical for the initiation and maintaining of contacts because it often took several attempts before a partnership was established. It was a bit like managing a dating agency.

3. The mentoring meetings

These meetings were arranged initially over a six month period but it soon became clear that not all the learning pairs would be able to finish the meetings within the allotted time.

Meeting I - was an introductory meeting with the researcher, as facilitator, present to help the pair get used to working together. The meeting took the form of a discussion, between the two people, about their respective jobs and what these entailed, the skills which they needed for their jobs, whether they perceived that they possessed transferable skills, what their definitions of "transferable skills" were and how these may or may not have differed from the definition put forward by the Library Association. The discussion also focused on career progression and allowed the respondents to "imagine" what they would like to do if they had the opportunity. Some time was also spent at this stage reviewing each person's career briefly with the help of their CVs, so that some mutual understanding could be gained of each other's career paths, the moves (sometimes radical changes) which had taken place. These meetings were straight forward and worked well because the learning pairs were generally well-matched and respondents felt at ease with each other.

Meetings II and III (work shadowing 1 and 2)

These took place when each shadowed the other at work for half a day.

The work shadowing involved completing three separate tasks or checklists of skills. **Task 1** evaluated the self and current skills. Respondents had to tick a five point scale which indicated whether they had a *low, limited, medium, confident* or *high* level of skills. This had to be completed before the work shadowing. Task 2 involved evaluating the skills needed to carry out the job effectively. Respondents were, again, required to complete the checklist and return this to the research assistant prior to the work shadowing. Task 3 was designed to be completed by the person who had done the shadowing - it acted as checklist of skills for the observation session. This was returned to the research assistant after the shadowing had been carried out.

The checklist, itself, was composed of eight skills categories and one set of attitudes needed for the job. These skills sections were, Information Technology, Self and Context Awareness i.e. organisational knowledge, Research Knowledge, Public Relations/Image, Interpersonal, Communication, Management, Office. We received favourable responses from the participants about this stage of the project. It was enjoyable and most people were interested in seeing what others do for a living. Further, the librarians mentioned that it was not only enlightening but also encouraging to shadow other information professionals. Some problems were encountered with the work shadowing but these will be addressed a little later.

Meeting IV The checklist tasks formed the basis of the analysis used at meeting IV. To identify the transferable skills it was necessary to carry out a number of different comparative analyses. A straight comparison where tasks 2 were analysed; perceptive comparison I where M3 was compared with L2 and perceptive comparison II where L3 was compared against M2.

A model was developed to describe the different comparisons between the skills tasks. L1 and M1 were used as background analysis.

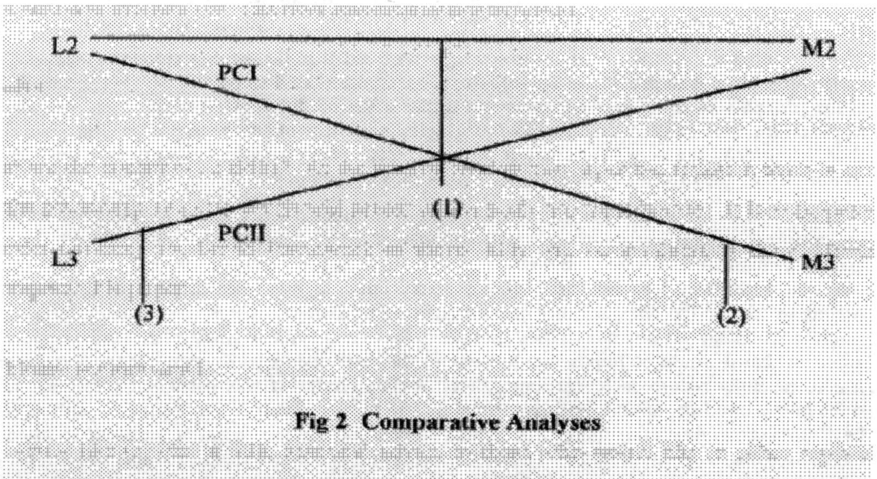

Fig 2 Comparative Analyses

(1) Straight Comparison. Identification of common/transferable skills i.e. the skills which could be used to transfer to other roles.

(2) This identifies how the mentor perceived the learner's role. Interesting to note how the mentors viewed "traditional" librarianship.

(3) Important. This describes how the learner perceived or misperceived the mentor's role. One of the barriers which prevents librarians from progressing to other jobs is the apparent misperceptions they have about the information jobs in other sectors.

(2) - (3) Perceptive Comparisons. These were designed to show
respondents how misperceptions sometimes occur about people's
jobs, skills.

From this fourth meeting, preliminary analysis of the skills tasks was carried out. Skills profiles for individual learning pairs were produced using this analysis.

Meeting V The fifth meeting was the final meeting of the skills programme. Like meeting I the session took the form of a discussion between the mentor and the learner. This discussion was open-ended and considered the skills profile, additional training needs and whether the librarians could or would make the transition to the mentors' roles. The project's objectives were re-examined and brought the empirical research to a conclusion.

RESULTS

What are the transferable skills? At the time of writing this paper the research team is carrying out the secondary analysis which will reveal which skills are transferable. It is anticipated that a leaflet outlining the broad framework of these skills will be available at the conference to accompany this paper.

PROBLEMS ENCOUNTERED

We would like to offer a little practical advice to those who would like to either replicate the study or use the methodology.

Firstly, it was interesting to note that many (but not all) of the librarians undertaking the CPD exercise tended to have quiet personalities and during the mentoring meetings would tend to put themselves down, betraying an air of inferiority when next to the mentor. This sometimes made facilitating the meetings difficult because the learner would be reluctant to put forward her/his opinion. The solution was to pair the learner with a friendly, outgoing, type of mentor.

Secondly, nearly all of the respondents agreed that the work shadowing sessions were not really long enough to provide them with anything more than a snap-shot of what the work was like. If the project was to be carried out again under a set of different circumstances, we would try to lengthen the time of the work shadowing. Having said this, of course, the shadowing had to be kept short in order to get people to commit to the project. Many people agreed to take part only on the condition that the meetings would not take up a substantial amount of work time.

Thirdly, we experienced difficulties both in identifying mentors to take part and in selling the project to potential mentors. A small minority of respondents felt mismatched with their mentors and on a couple of occasions the mentors pulled out at the last minute, indeed, when the programme was well under way, and we had to find replacements. It was often difficult to find other mentors willing to take on the responsibility of participating in a project which was nearing the conclusion of its empirical stage. It was due to these problems and the inevitable work related delays which made it apparent that it would be impossible to keep all the respondents progressing at the same rate and we had to carefully record each learning pair on a time chart. It was particularly difficult to arrange some of the meetings around holidays, time off and busy schedules. Furthermore, although it would have been gratifying and interesting, it was impossible for the research assistant to attend all the mentoring meetings (over 100). The respondents did seem to expect this and some felt aggrieved when they were told that this would be difficult.

Finally, we were disappointed by the fact that, despite their concerns about a lack of CPD, the Scottish oil librarians felt too busy, overworked, and disinclined to take part in the project. The research team tried hard to encourage them to take part (telephoning all major oil and support companies) but were met with a distinct lack of enthusiasm.

THE ADVANTAGES

The study was welcomed by all the respondents who took part. Their comments suggested that the study should be carried out again with wider parameters to include other librarianship sectors. It was felt that the work was worthwhile and that this type of on-going, developing research would benefit librarians to make and maintain contacts in other information roles. However, this kind of project requires a rigorous framework or system to control it and more project researchers would be needed to co-ordinate the large administrative tasks involved with the research. Having said this, the problems were relatively minor compared with the positive results of the project. One respondent admitted that without the research she would have been less likely to have evaluated her skills and competencies. It was through the mentoring meetings that she became more confident in her abilities and as a result she applied for a higher post and got the job.

Another respondent, the mentor, was considering different types of career development and having seen how content the librarian was in her job, via the work shadowing was tempted to take a lower salary for the benefits of a more rewarding career.

When asked about the worthiness of the research project the respondents gave generally very favourable comments. A selection of these follow,

"[The project]...has allowed me to speak about myself and my abilities in a more positive way. It has made me aware of certain, previously unrecognised, generic skills."

"It is important to promote the idea of transferable skills to the employer in the information field. I learned so much about myself, my skills, my role and have in fact decided on a change of career direction because of this project!"

"The opportunity for social interaction within the "mentoring" partnership discussions evolved outwith the respective job roles. [The project] ...allowed me to take stock of my own skills and moreover skills gaps that need to be addressed through my own staff development programme."

THE FUTURE AND CONCLUSIONS

The project has been designed to be practical. It was initiated in direct response to the dissatisfied cries of librarians working in the oil industry and health science sectors and to challenge complacency in the workforce. In my opinion it has succeeded in doing this. It is clear that the research has wider applicability and many librarians from other sectors have voiced their encouragement in the hope that the study will be replicated in public, school or academic librarianship.

The methodology could be extended to increase the length of work shadowing and cross-disciplinary pairings might be arranged to allow, for example, oil librarians to experience the work of health librarians. Academics are overly fond of telling practitioners to liaise with upper management in organisations and to promote themselves and their services more effectively - this is never as easy as it sounds. Robert Gordon's has tried to encourage and facilitate librarians to recognise their own professional worth by highlighting the many varied skills which they possess and through the British Library project we hope that others will be alerted to the importance and necessity of CPD in the workplace today.

REFERENCES

Autrey in Sellen, B-C (ed.) (1980), *What Else You Can Do With a Library Degree*, Syracuse, NY:Gaylord Professional Publications.

Best, R., Abbott, F. and Taylor, M. (1990), *Teaching Skills for Learning: Information Skills in Initial Teacher Education*, London: British Library Research and Development.

Sellen, B-C. (ed) (1980), *What Else You Can Do With a Library Degree*, Syracuse, NY: Gaylord Professional Publications.

Tremblay, M. and Wall, A. (1994), *Chief Executives Learning Together: a Report for the NHS Training Directorate*, Birmingham: University of Birmingham Health Services Management Centre School of Public Policy.

TRAINING THE TRAINER: A PERSPECTIVE FROM THE ALA/CLENE-RT[1]

Darlene E. Weingand
School of Library and Information Studies
University of Wisconsin-Madison
USA

Abstract: In an era of rapid change and technological development, the role of the librarian must also change. Such a transformation requires training, and much of this training occurs within the library itself. In addition, library staff also engage in training that is offered by library associations, universities, vendors, and so forth. But who trains the trainer? And what types of knowledge do trainers need in order to be effective? This paper offers insights into "training the trainer" that have been gathered by CLENE-RT over many Years. Areas covered include: how adults learn, collecting needs assessment information, designing learning objectives, determining quality in continuing education, and evaluating the learning activity.

INTRODUCTION

We are living in a time of unprecedented change. It is a time when information has become an increasingly valuable commodity and the means of accessing that information are tied to the rapid developments in technology. How can library staff cope with such a shifting environment? This is a question that has serious ramifications for the profession.

Libraries are staffed by individuals with many talents and skills. They occupy positions from administrators and professional librarians to clerks and shelvers. Each position carries its own element of importance, and it is the entire chain of interacting positions that makes the library operate effectively—or not. If there is a weak link, due to lack of training, then the entire operation will suffer and service will be compromised.

Therefore, training is an essential ingredient in addressing issues of accountability. It is no longer sufficient to consider fiscal stewardship as the primary definition of accountability. Libraries must be accountable to their funders and customers for how well the assets are managed--and library staff typically comprise 70-80% of any library's budget. These human resources are critical to good service and customer satisfaction, for they are the intermediaries between customers and information and/or materials. If staff are so important to library operations--and account for such a large percentage of the overall budget--than staff competence is more than a goal. It is a mandate.

However, academic degrees, in this time of rapid change, have a "shelf life" of approximately three years--and this figure keeps declining. This expectation can be assigned to any type of education or training. Therefore, not only initial preparation, but continuous re-training, is required throughout the worklife. Designing training that will deliver the knowledge, skills, and attitudinal approaches that are appropriate for specific audiences is a complex endeavor, but one that is vital if real learning is to take place.

How can training be delivered most successfully? How can trainers themselves be trained so that they are effective instructors? Are there strategies for teaching adults that help greater learning to take place? These are questions to be considered when any type of training is being planned. It is essential that training is designed with the learner in mind. Such design begins with knowledge of how adults learn.

HOW ADULTS LEARN

Malcolm Knowles, one of the foremost authorities on adult education, believed that adults learn differently than children. He dismissed the word, "pedagogy", as inappropriate, in that it means the teaching of children, and invented the term, "andragogy", which can be defined as the teaching of adults (Knowles, 1980). In J. R. Kidd's book on *How Adults Learn*, he quoted Knowles' analysis of the differences between children and adults:

"A child first sees himself as a completely dependent personality. He sees himself in his first consciousness as being completely dependent upon the adult world to make his decisions for him, to feed him, to change his diapers, and to see where the pin is sticking. During the course of his childhood and youth, that dependence is reinforced as decisions are made for him in the home, at school, in church, on the playground, and everywhere he turns. But at some point he starts experiencing the joy of deciding things for himself...To be adult means to be self-directing. Now at the point of which this change occurs, there develops in the human being a deep psychological need to be perceived by himself and by others as being indeed self-directing. This is the concept that lies at the heart of andragogy. Andragogy is based upon the insight that the deepest need an adult has is to be treated as an adult, to be treated as a self-directing person, to be treated with respect. Andragogy is student-centered and problem-oriented."(Kidd, 1973).

Therefore, adults learn best when the trainer understands the special attributes and needs of adults. Since adults bring many qualities to the learning activity, rooted in years of living, the trainer has a special challenge to incorporate these qualities into the entire educational design. The adult learner can be described as:

- <u>Ready to learn</u>. The movement is toward social and occupational competence. [Trainers] need to assist learners in filling perceived and real knowledge gaps; the attitude that no questions are "stupid" and that inquiry leads to opportunity is critical to effective [learning].

- <u>Caught climbing the mountain of time</u>. To the young, time is infinite; sometime in the middle adult years, the perspective changes and time is viewed as finite and increasingly precious...for many, time is more valuable than money and cash exchanged for information is considered fair and just.

- <u>Problem-centered in orientation to learning</u>. Motivation is directly related to the solving of today's problems and experiential activities are the most enduring. [Trainers] need to focus on the learner and the learning process. A shift in emphasis from facts to people brings strength and purpose to [the learning environment]. The stress on today's concerns and problems relates learning to reality and binds both into a motivational framework that works.

- <u>Self-directed</u>. Adults view themselves as capable and independent, and competent to direct and evaluate their own learning. The tendency of an instructor to project authority and enforce a variety of "shoulds" must give way to the scenario of the [trainer] as a learning resource and facilitator, seeking to meet learner needs through a collegial and collaborative relationship.

- <u>Experienced in life skills</u>. The adult's years of experience are incorporated into the learning process and mistakes are viewed as opportunities for learning. [Trainers] can capitalize on this treasure trove of experience by incorporating it into the learning activity. To reject this life experience is equivalent to rejecting the [student] as a person and must be avoided (Weingand, 1984).

Therefore, it is important for the trainer to keep in mind that the adult learner brings a wealth of resources to the learning activity. The wise trainer will build upon these resources when designing the educational event. The process of learning is further influenced by individual learner characteristics and needs, an awareness of the setting, the selection of learning objectives, the learning activities themselves, and evaluation. The successful trainer will understand the subject matter to be taught, how adults learn, and how various teaching strategies can be effectively applied to the learning process.

COLLECTING NEEDS ASSESSMENT INFORMATION

There are many options for collecting data about learner needs. *Surveys* of either individual learners or libraries are commonly used. In Appendix B, two surveys are summarized that have been distributed by the Australian Library and Information Association [ALIA] . The first survey of continuing professional development needs targets institutional members; the second survey is directed to personal members. This type of survey can be conducted by surface mail, telephone, personal interviews, or via the Internet.

Another method, the *focus group*, has become quite popular in recent years. The focus group technique is effective for gathering qualitative information, such as insights, reflections and reactions, in order to make complex decisions. It can be used to identify and define trends, issues, factors for resolution, reactions, differing points of view, and attitudes. Focus groups do not result in numbers or priorities, but participants have the opportunity to communicate what is on their minds. In addition, the process allows each participant to be a richer source of information--through interaction--than when responding alone (Wagner and Mahmoodi, 1994).

The focus group technique uses a discussion facilitator and a recorder. It is also helpful to use an observer. Some facilitators use a tape recorder, but this is not required. The structure of the focus group session typically includes a schedule of questions grouped into three modules similar to the following:

- Reflecting on the present -- what's happening
- Projecting a situation or problem into the future
- Evaluating strategies for addressing the issues of achieving the desired future.

The success of the focus group is dependent upon the selection of the participants, who should share some characteristic and/or knowledge of the area being studied, and the abilities of the discussion team members (Wagner and Mahmoodi, 1994). [See Appendix C for examples of questions designed to elicit information, insights and attitudes from continuing education providers].

A systematic and personal approach to learning is the self-assessment / learning contract developed by CLENE in the time before it became an ALA roundtable. [See Appendix D]. This combination of techniques focuses the responsibility for assessing needs and designing goals and objectives squarely on the shoulders of the individual learner. Self-assessment questions cover the areas of interests, needs, goals for professional growth, goals for personal growth (which may well affect professional goals), and a summary that selects areas for concentration in the next year.

Following this self-assessment, the learner analyzes overall goals, identifies skills needed to meet those goals, recognizes those skills that are already in place, and lists those skills that are still needed. Once this exercise is completed, a personal learning contract is developed that focuses on learning objectives.

DESIGNING LEARNING OBJECTIVES

Continuing the self-assessment discussion, the learner now creates objectives for the learning contract that address the following questions:

- Learning Objectives... "What am I going to learn?"
- Learning Resources and Strategies... "How will I learn it?"
- Evidence of Accomplishment of Objectives... "How will I know I learned it?"
- Criteria and Means for Validating Evidence... "How will I prove I learned it?"

Types of learning activities that can be 'plugged into' the contract include: formal workshops, courses, seminars, institutes; special activities, such as journal clubs, study groups, lecture series; non-supervised individual activities, such as personal use of audio-visual products, programmed materials, individual reading projects; teaching assignments; writing and publication; and professional association activities. Once the contract is completed, the learner strengthens the commitment by discussing its contents with a colleague.

Moving beyond the individual, designing learning objectives for activities that address the needs of clusters of individuals and groups requires a different approach. After information about the learners and their needs has been gathered, learning objectives should be developed for the activity. It is important to know why the educational event is being planned and what purposes are being addressed. In order to create appropriate objectives for an activity, three questions should be considered:

- By the end of training, what knowledge, skill, or attitude do you want participants to have?
- What observable behavior would indicate that they have learned this knowledge, skill, or attitude?
- What exercise might be used to allow participants to show this observable behavior?

The objectives themselves should be written in behavioral terms with observable outcomes, such as: *"Participants will assign Dewey Classification numbers to 25 books with a 92% accuracy rate."* If objectives are constructed in this manner, evaluation of the success of the activity is relatively straightforward [See Appendix E for a discussion of behavioral objectives].

DETERMINING QUALITY IN CONTINUING EDUCATION

Due to the rapid changes occurring throughout the information, library, and media fields--and the society they serve--library workers have sought means to keep abreast of the new developments. This demand has been acknowledged by various continuing education providers and the subsequent development of various continuing education activities. However, the quality of these activities has been uneven, as insufficient attention and inadequate experience were brought to the quality of the activities. Therefore, the CLENE-RT and the Continuing Education Subcommittee of the ALA Standing Committee on Library Education [SCOLE] created a set of "Guidelines for Quality in Continuing Education for Information, Library and Media Personnel," which were adopted by ALA Council on January 12, 1988.

The "Guidelines" note that delivery of quality continuing education programs appropriate to the needs of people involved in information, library, media services must be based on careful planning. A number of factors should be used in assessing the planning, design, delivery, and evaluation of these programs. These criteria can be applied by any person or group interested in providing quality continuing education opportunities (Continuing Education..., 1988)

The "Guidelines" offer criteria for various types of continuing education opportunities: group programs and activities; individualized programs and activities; instructional materials and technologies; continuing education providers; and learning consultants for individualized continuing education programs. Each type of opportunity is defined, followed by a selection of attributes necessary for an effective program. Each attribute has a specified criterion; for each criterion, a list of assessment factors is given. [See Appendix F for an outline of the "Guidelines."]

EVALUATING THE LEARNING ACTIVITY

The "Guidelines" specify that learning activities must be evaluated, both as a mechanism to assure quality and as a strategy for improvement of future activities. There are six steps to the successful evaluation of workshops and other learning activities (Shearer and Smith, 1992):

1. Know your purpose(s) in evaluation

- To meet a requirement of a funding body
- To determine participant satisfaction
- To improve future workshops
- To identify a market for future workshops
- To identify topics for future workshops
- To discover whether learning has been transformed into practice

Delineate what you need to discover

- What precisely needs to be learned about the identified purpose(s)

3. Identify who knows what you need to discover

- Learners
- Instructors
- Advisory committee
- Providers of food, housekeeping, etc.

4. Communicate what you need to discover to those who are best able to inform you

- Tell evaluation respondents about the purpose(s) of the evaluation
- Pre-test the questionnaire/form

5. Gather the information

- Seek a high response rate by using creative strategies
- Give reminders

6. Relate the findings to your purpose(s)

- Give special attention to negative comments
- Consider ways to improve the next workshops

The above points relate specifically to that type of evaluation that occurs when an educational activity has ended. However, there is another evaluation that takes place during the planning and implementing stages. Known as "formative" evaluation, this process monitors the development of the activity and helps to identify where changes should be made to enhance the quality of the event. Both forms of evaluation are essential and should be part of the educational design.

This paper has examined various attributes of continuing education design that must be considered when training the trainer to be effective in providing appropriate learning activities. The Continuing Library Education Network and Exchange Round Table has a history of focusing its efforts on aspects of training the trainer. The members of CLENE-RT have considerable expertise in networking, mentoring, training and continuing education. The ideas and strategies presented in this paper illustrate some of the contributions that CLENE-RT has offered to the profession. New members are always welcome [See Appendix A for further information].

APPENDIX A

ABOUT CLENE-RT

The Continuing Library Education Network and Exchange Round Table [CLENE-RT] of the American Library Association [ALA] provides a network, publications and workshops for continuing education providers. Open to all ALA members; dues: $15, individuals; $50, organizations. Contact CLENE-RT at ALA, 50 E. Huron St., Chicago, Illinois 60611, USA. Telephone: (312) 944-6780 or (800) 545-2433.

CLENE-RT has the following objectives:

1. To provide a forum for the exchange of ideas and concerns among library and information personnel responsible for continuing library education, training, and staff development;

2. To provide learning activities and materials to maintain the competencies of those who provide continuing library education;

3. To provide a force for initiating and supporting programs to increase the availability of quality continuing library education; and

4. To create an awareness of, and sense of need for, continuing library education on the part of employees and employers.

SURVEYS OF CONTINUING PROFESSIONAL DEVELOPMENT [CPD] NEEDS[2]

Survey 1:   Institutional Members
1.   Library staff and materials budget [check-off of choices]
2.   Type of library_______________________________   3.Postcode___________
4.   Number of staff:
Professional________Paraprofessional________Support/Administrative_____
5.   How does the institution support/provide staff in the library and information   service with CPD and   training?
6.   What do you consider have been the most successful recent programs provided to your library and information service staff?
        a. Content   [e.g., Internet/WWW, time management, competencies]
        b. Format   [e.g., short course, discussion group, workshop]
        c. Time [e.g., own time, business hours]
        d. Delivery mode   [e.g., in-house, retreat, customized program]
        e. Provider   [e.g., library staff development unit, consultant]
        Why do you consider these programs have been so successful?
7.   What do you perceive as the CPD and training priorities for library and   information service staff over the next three years?
        a. Content   [same examples as above...]
        b. Format
        c. Time
        d. Delivery mode
        e. Provider
8.   What employment related benefits do staff gain from undertaking CPD and training programs? [e.g., competency assessment, salary bonus, job advancement, staff review for development, job application techniques]
9.   Does your organisation market its training/CPD programs outside the organization?
10.   What areas of CPD/training needs do you perceive are not currently being provided?

Survey 2:   Personal Members
1.   What type of membership do you hold?
2.   In which year did you gain your first library and information studies qualification?_________
        Which type of library do you work in?________________
3.   What is your: Work Postcode_____________   Home Postcode_____________
4.   What two or three CPD activities that you have done recently have been most relevant to your professional development. Why?
        5.   What percentage of your continuing professional development is self-funded?
        6.   How does your employer assist you in your professional development?
7.   Please tell us what you believe are your CPD priorities for the next three years. Be as specific as you can.
        a. Content   [e.g., strategic planning, reference work, online skills, cataloguing, presentation skills]
        b. Level of content   [e.g., basic, intermediate, advanced]
        c. Format   [e.g., short course, discussion group, formal degree, conference]
        d. Time [e.g., own time, business hours]
        e. Delivery mode[e.g., in workplace, on campus, ALIA, distance education]
        f. Funding   [e.g., self-funded, employer-sponsored]
        8.   What are your incentives for undertaking continuing professional development?
9.   What barriers would you see to undertaking the CPD priorities you have identified?
10.   For which of your CPD needs (current and previous) do you believe there are   no appropriate courses/activities being offered?

APPENDIX C

CONTINUING EDUCATION PROVIDERS
FORECASTING LEARNING NEEDS & DELIVERY OPTIONS[3]

Focus Group Questions

A.   YOUR TOPIC NEEDS

1.   What were you doing recently when you felt you needed more knowledge, ability, or skill? What did you need to know or be able to do?

2.   What's happening in the future that you would like to be part of? What would you need to know or be able to do?

B.   FUTURE NEEDS OF OTHERS

1.   What critical events could happen between now and the year 2000 which would greatly affect the viability of libraries? What will library workers need to know or be able to do to affect that viability?

2.   What learning topics are emerging for those providing library, information, and school media services?

3.   What opportunities and challenges will meeting these learning needs present for continuing education providers and learners?

C.   DELIVERY OF CONTINUING LIBRARY EDUCATION

1.   How will the delivery of continuing education need to change? What will need to be retained? What additional changes are needed?

2.   To have effective library workers ten years from now, what will continuing education be like? How will it be delivered? What will the formats be? What structure will be needed? What will be necessary to make it all work?

D.   WRAP UP

1.   Thank you. Any other comments? What questions were you expecting us to ask? Do you have any questions now?

2.   If you have further insights, you may; contact us by _________________

CLENE: THE CONTINUING LIBRARY EDUCATION NETWORK AND EXCHANGE

SELF-ASSESSMENT AND THE LEARNING CONTRACT:
A SYSTEMATIC AND PERSONAL APPROACH TO LEARNING

This flyer has been prepared by CLENE members to give you a capsule version of two continuing education techniques which are becoming more popular with individuals in pursuit of their own learning. Since the primary focus of continuing education is the individual, self-assessment and the use of a personal learning contract are natural developments which we can expect to see more widely used. Self-assessment had a role in the 1978 CLENE state-wide continuing education institute and it was also the topic of our 1979 Assembly workshop at Dallas. We encourage you to use these techniques in planning your own continuing education program and to share the concepts with colleagues and friends at home.

Instructions:

The purposes of self-assessment and learning contracts are to better identify our learning needs in the context of personal life and work experience; to establish realistic learning objectives to meet these needs; to identify the ways in which we can best learn according to our own learning style and environment; and to establish the ways in which we will know how well we are meeting our learning objectives.

Your first step in this personalized approach to learning will be to find a good thinking place where you can spend some quality time with yourself. Consider your interests. specific educational needs (work or life related), and the personal and professional goals which you would like to prepare yourself for. Your interests and needs are considered separately because what you *want* to learn may not necessarily coincide with what you *need* to learn. A list of sample questions is provided here which will help you focus on these needs and wants in order to set priorities for your learning program. Throughout this flyer we have economized on space to give you the whole model, but in a shortened form. You will want to make your own question sheets and forms.

Self-Assessment Questions:

1. Interests

a.   Of my own personal interests, the following are most important to me:

b.   My professional interests tend to focus on the following areas:

2. Needs

a.   The skills or areas of knowledge which I most need to do a good job in my present work situation are (administration, research, storytelling techniques, computer technology. etc.):

b.   Among my list in 2a, 1 know the least about and should learn more about the following:

3.   Goals for Professional Growth

a.   Right now. my overall professional goals are:

b.   In order to help me work towards these goals. 1 need to learn:

4.   goals for Personal Growth (which may well affect professional goals too)

   a.   My personal strengths and assets are (physical, mental, interpersonal communication skills, etc.

5.   Summary of Assessment

Looking over the lists I have made, I would like to spend next year or so improving and growing in the following areas (one suggestion is to choose those of greatest priority and at least one from each of the four areas) :

While self-assessment is a very personal process. no one assumes that you won't need some help in identifying your own learning needs. Talk with someone who might have the experience or knowledge to help you identify what you should consider in this process. Let's assume you have decided it is time in your career to plan for becoming President of the American Library Association. You discuss this with past presidents, individuals who also ran, members of ALA council, Executive Board and staff of ALA. You may even want to talk with people who have been in this position in other associations. With this guidance. you can then rough out a way to isolate the needs you will base your learning program on.

My overall goals	Skills to meet goals	My skills	What I need
President of ALA	Political Leadership	Small group	Public speaking

Once you are satisfied that you have identified the learning needs which you should begin to address, it is time to develop a learning contract which will help you move towards the realization of your learning goals. The elements of this next step are listed with a framework to use in setting up your learning program.

<u>Personal Learning Contract</u>

Now that you have a starting place to build your learning program from, it is time to identify specific objectives and design a learning contract with yourself. You may well need help in doing this process as you did in identifying learning needs, and there are many places for this kind of help. If there isn't a librarian type to help you, you may get some assistance from a local Community-Based Educational Counseling for Adults (CBECA) program or its equivalent. Again, the brevity of this flyer allows us only to give you the general areas for consideration in the contract and a sample of what forms you may want to use.

LEARNING CONTRACT

Learning Objectives "What am I Going to Learn?"	Learning Resources & Strategies "How will I Learn It?"	Evidence of Accomplishment of Objectives "How Will I Know I Learned It?"	Criteria & Means for Validating Evidence "How Will I Prove I Learned It?"

I. What Am I Going to Learn--Specific Learning Objectives

Translate each of the learning needs you assessed in item 5 above into a learning objective and place this in column 1 of the Contract illustrated. Objectives should describe what is to be learned, not what is to he done. State your learning objectives in terms that are most meaningful to you-content acquisition, behaviors, or directions of growth. Remember to use action verbs and to be as clear as possible.

2. How Will I Learn it--Specify Learning Resources and Strategies

In column two of the contract, describe proposed ways in which you can best meet each objective. Identify the resources (material and human) and list the strategies (techniques and tools) to be employed in making use of them. Write down as many possibilities as you can. Several types of learning activities are suggested in this flyer to give you an idea of the many possibilities to choose from.

3. How I will I Know I Learned it--Specify Evidence of Accomplishment

In the third column, 'Evidence of Accomplishment of Objectives," describe the evidence you will collect to indicate the degree to which each objective has been achieved. Use measure which makes the most sense to you.

4. How Will I Prove I Learned it--Specify How the Evidence Will Be Validated

Specify criteria for each objective. Next, list the means proposed to use as evidence to judge according to these criteria.

5. Review Contract With Consultants

To strengthen the quality of the contract, review it with one or two friends, supervisors, or other expert resource persons and get reactions and suggestions.

6. Carry Out The Contract

As you work on carrying out the contract, notions about what is to be learned may be changed. If this is the case. revise the contract accordingly.

7.. Evaluation of Learning

One of the simplest ways to get some assurance that learning objectives have been achieved is to ask the consultants used in Step 5 to examine the evidence and validation data and give their judgment on your accomplishments.

You may want to set time limits for yourself to achieve each objective, depending on a realistic assessment of time available and your motivation.

As you proceed with your plans. keep a log of time spent and what you did. This log can be used in assigning continuing education credit. You may find it helpful to record your learning activity and your accomplishments even if you are not interested in credit. This kind of information provides additional guidance to your learning program.

RECORD OF LEARNING ACTIVITY

Inclusive Dates of Attendance	Provider (If Applicable)	Description of Learning Activity	No. of Hours

Types of Learning Activities To Consider In Meeting Your Learning Objectives*

1. Educational activities which are part of a planned program, sponsored by a 'responsible' provider (workshop, academic courses taken for credit or by audit, independent study, seminars, institutes, short courses, etc.)

2. Special activities not part of a planned program--(journal clubs, study groups, association meetings with specific educational objectives, lecture series, etc.)

3.   Non-supervised individual activities--(personal use of any A/V devices such as audio and video tapes, film-strips, films; programmed materials; individual reading projects).

4.   Papers, publications, books, presentations, and exhibits--(self-explanatory, but quality control criteria will specify how to assess this category activity).

5.   Teaching assignments.

6.   Other meritorious learning activity--(activities not covered in the previous categories but meet criteria for quality and show evidence of why it was chosen, how it was planned, how It was carried out, and how it was evaluated, as well as indication of any supervision).

7.   Association activities (projects. papers, educational programming).

    *CLENE's work on a national voluntary recognition system for your continuing education accomplishments will add to this list, clarify each activity, provide a general measurement concept for the activities and establish quality control criteria for evaluating activities as well as programs. To learn more about this Project, contact CLENE for the full report or Concept Paper #6, "Recognition For Your Continuing Education Accomplishment."

    If you want to learn more about the techniques of self-assessment and planning your own learning contract, the best place to look is a small book by Malcolm Knowles, <u>Self-Directed Learning: A Guide for Learners and Teachers</u>.

CLENE INC

CONTINUING LIBRARY   620 Michigan Avenue,
EDUCATION NETWORK   N.E.
AND EXCHANGE   Washington, D.C. 20064
                                                (202) 635-5825

BEHAVIORAL OBJECTIVES[4]

Behavioral objectives are educational objectives that are written in terms of observable behaviors. For example, the goal of a cataloging class may be that participants know how to use the Dewey Classification Schedules. To determine the objectives, we would ask ourselves what behaviors would indicate that the participant has obtained this skill. One of the best indicators would obviously be that they can actually use the schedules with a certain degree of accuracy. So a behavioral objective could be:

Participants will assign Dewey Classification numbers to 25 books with a 92% accuracy rate.

To write behavioral objectives for training:
1. Determine the knowledge, skill, or attitude that you wish to impart to the participants.
2. Determine what behavior would be indicative that the participants had learned that knowledge, skill or attitude.

Behavioral Objectives in Training. In traditional education, achieving a certain grade on a test is a typical behavioral objective. Trainers often cannot use such tests, so they need to be more flexible, and the objective often is built into the training as an exercise. For example, the above example of an objective could be re-framed as, "Participants will answer 50 reference questions at a 96% accuracy rate." One of the exercises then is for the participants to use the reference collection to answer 50 reference questions. After the exercise, the trainer gives the correct answers and quickly checks to see how many participants missed two questions or less. If most of the participants have achieved this level of proficiency, the objective can be considered achieved.

Behavioral Objectives in Experiential Workshop Design. Because behavioral objectives in training can be demonstrated through exercises, they are particularly useful in workshop design. Objectives typically will suggest exercises that could be used to measure the achievement of the objectives. Thus, behavioral objectives encourage a much more experiential form of workshop. Studies have shown that participants are more likely to retain knowledge, skills, or attitudes when educational methods that allow participants to actually experience or practice what they are being taught.

GUIDELINES FOR QUALITY IN CONTINUING EDUCATION FOR INFORMATION, LIBRARY AND MEDIA PERSONNEL [51]

The following outline provides the structure of the "Guidelines," including criteria; however, actual assessment factors are too lengthy to be included.

1.1   Group programs and activities

      1.1.1   Needs assessment

          Criterion: The specific needs of the client group should be assessed.

      1.1.2   Objectives

Criterion: Specific and measurable/observable learning objectives should be stated in one or more of the following areas: changes in attitude and approach to the solution of problems; acquisition (or mastery) of new knowledge or the revision of outdated knowledge in specific skills, techniques, and procedures.

      1.1.3   Design and presentation

          Criterion: The program should be systematically designed and delivered to meet the statement of objectives.

1.1.4   Timeliness

          Criterion: The program content should be current and timely.

      1.1.5   Promotion

          Criterion: The educational offering should be promoted responsibly.

      1.1.6   Evaluation

          Criterion: Evaluation should be an on-going and integral part of the educational offering.

1.2   Individualized programs and activities

      1.2.1   Needs assessment

          Criterion: The individual's specific learning needs or interests have been identified and assessed.

      1.2.2   Objectives

          Criterion: Based on the needs assessment, a set of clear, measurable, and/or observable learning objectives have been stated in one of more of the following areas: changes in attitudes; updating of outdated knowledge and/or attainment of new knowledge; and awareness or mastery of specific skills and techniques.

      1.2.3   Learning plan

          Criterion: An organized and coherent series of learning activities is systematically planned to achieve the individual's stated objectives.

      1.2.4   Evaluation

          Criterion: Evaluation is an on-going and integral part of the individualized continuing education activity.

1.3   Instructional materials and technologies

      1.3.1   Suitability

          Criterion: The instructional materials and technologies should be suited for the learning audience.

      1.3.2   Objectives

          Criterion: A set of clear measurable/observable learning objectives has been stated in one or more of the following areas: changes in attitude; attainment of knowledge; and awareness or mastery of specific skills and techniques.

      1.3.3   Learning strategies

          Criterion: The instructional materials utilized are suitable and appropriate for the objectives of the learning activity.

1.3.4   Timeliness

<u>Criterion</u>: The instructional materials are current and timely.

1.3.5   Learning environment

<u>Criterion</u>: The instructional materials are utilized in an appropriate facility and learning environment.

1.3.6   Package or module design

<u>Criterion</u>: An instructional package (or module), whether produced or purchased, is a complete and integrated unit and is well documented.

1.4   Continuing education providers

1.4.1   Administration

<u>Criterion</u>: A structure for systematic administration of the continuing education programs should be established.

1.4.2   Human resources

<u>Criterion</u>: Continuing education presenters, designers, and other human resources should demonstrate current expertise by training and experience in the pertinent subject matter and/or educational methodologies as appropriate to their function.

1.4.3   Facilities

<u>Criterion</u>: Adequate facilities conducive to good learning should be available for continuing education programs.

1.4.4   Financial resources

<u>Criterion</u>: The organization's financial resources should be adequate to support the educational program.

1.5   Learning consultants for individualized continuing education programs

1.5.1   Selection of a learning consultant

<u>Criterion</u>: Persons wishing to work with learning consultants for individualized continuing education activities should consider the following assessment factors in making their selection.

1.5.2   Assistance

[Persons wishing assistance in identifying a learning consultant may contact the ALA Office for Library Personnel Resources or the CLENE Round Table]

FOOTNOTES

{1}   American Library Association / Continuing Library Education Network and Exchange Round Table [see Appendix A].

{2}   Adapted from questionnaire distributed by ALIA, PO Box E441, Queen Victoria Terrace, ACT 2600, Australia, 1996.

{3}   Mary M. Wagner and Suzanne H. Mahmoodi (1994), *A Focus Group Interview Manual*, Chicago: American Library Association/Continuing Library Education Network and Exchange Round Table, p. 22.

{4}   From the handout materials of the CLENE-RT program, "Planning Continuing Education Events for Library Staff," presented by Gardner Hanks and Reneta Webb, American Library Association Annual Conference, New York, July 7, 1996.

{5}   Continuing Education Subcommittee of the Standing Committee on Library Education (SCOLE) (1988),*Guidelines for Quality in Continuing Education for Information, Library and Media Personnel*, Chicago: American Library Association.

REFERENCES

Continuing Education Subcommittee of the Standing Committee on Library Education (SCOLE) (1988), *Guidelines for Quality in Continuing Education for Information, Library and Media Personnel*, Chicago: American Library Association, p.5.

Kidd, J.R. (1973), *How Adults Learn*, New York: Association Press, p.36.

Knowles, Malcolm S. (1980), *The Modern Practice of Education*, New York: Association Press.

Shearer, Kenneth D and Smith, Duncan (1992), *Workshop Evaluation: Forms Follow Function*, Chicago: ALA /CLENE-RT..

Wagner, Mary M and Mahmoodi, Suzanne H. (1994), *A Focus Group Interview Manual*, Chicago: American Library Association/Continuing Library Education Network and Exchange Round Table.

Weingand, Darlene E. (1984), *The Organic Public Library*, Littleton, CO: Libraries Unlimited, Inc., pp. 33-34.

THE EFFECTIVENESS OF AN ACADEMIC LIBRARY AS A CONTINUING
EDUCATION PROVIDER

Abdus Sattar Chaudhry
Division of Information Studies
Nanyang Technological University
Singapore

Abstract: The paper reports a survey carried out amongst participants who have attended CPD programs organized by the Library of the King Fahd University of Petroleum and Minerals (KFUPM) which established a comprehensive continuing education program in 1987. A large number information professionals from Bahrain, Kuwait, Oman, Qatar, Saudi Arabia, and United Arab Emirates have participated in workshops, short courses, seminars, and other CE activities organized under this program.

INTRODUCTION

The Library of the King Fahd University of Petroleum and Minerals (KFUPM) is a medium size information support facility located in the eastern province of Saudi Arabia. It has a collection of approximately one million items of monographs, serials, a.v. materials, microforms, and electronic information sources for its user community of about 8,000 students, faculty, and researchers. It is fully automated and is using DOBIS/LIBIS, an integrated automated library system. The appointment and retention of highly qualified and competent staff has been the key strategy of the library in its efforts for the timely availability of information materials and provision of modern information services. The library administration has been concerned about the lack of adequate opportunities of continuing education for library and information professionals in the country. There was no active library association or other professional forum to take up the initiative for professional development activities in the information sector in Saudi Arabia as well as in the neighboring countries of the Arabian Gulf region. The schools of library and information science also did not show much interest in offering programs for the much needed continuing education of library and information professionals. To fulfill its needs for staff development and also to provide opportunities of continuing education to professionals in other information institutions in Saudi Arabia and other Arabian Gulf states, the KFUPM Library took an unprecedented initiative by starting a comprehensive staff development and continuing education program in 1987. Encouraged by its popularity, the CE Program was upgraded to a fully-fledged library training program in 1992. In 1993 Arabian Gulf Chapter of the Special Libraries Association was established. The Chapter has launched a professional development program. The KFUPM Library has also been collaborating with the Chapter in offering workshops for information professionals.

A detailed study of the needs of the library staff for training and continuation education was conducted before initiating the staff development and continuing education program at KFUPM. This needs assessment exercise solicited the views of the department heads on the extent and level of staff utilization, capabilities, and competencies. A working paper was prepared by a manager in the library and reviewed by a committee of senior staff. The committee recommended that immediate steps need to be taken for better staff development at KFUPM. A comprehensive staff development and continuing education program was initiated in pursuance of these recommendation. A conscious effort was made to keep library staff involved in the development and implementation of the program that ensured their full support for the program. A five-year action plan was developed and finalized after a review by the head of departments in the library. The program had two components: staff development and training and continuing education. The process of development and implementation of this program has been detailed (Chaudry et al, 1993).

The continuing education program was aimed at updating, refreshing, and upgrading knowledge, skills, and competencies of library staff through short courses, workshops, seminars and other professional development activities (conferences, symposia, training attachments, etc.). A senior manager with relevant experience was assigned as co-ordinator of this program with the responsibilities of conceiving and designing continuing education activities, initiation of communication with relevant agencies, identification of resource persons, publicity, and other logistic arrangements. Topics for various activities were selected in consultation with the library staff.

A major activity in the continuing education program was the conduct of short courses which were offered in collaboration with the Division of Educational Services of the university. One short courses was targeted to be organized each semester. Short courses have been offered on regular basis sine 1987 as planned. Topics and a time table were decided at the beginning of the year and communicated to the Educational Services Division for inclusion in the university-wide course catalog for wider publicity. In addition, a brochure was prepared for every short course which described objectives, outline of topics, participating faculty, registration requirements and other logistics. Senior library staff served as resource persons for topics related to library operations and services and collaboration was sought from the concerned academic departments of the university for coverage of theoretical aspects of various areas, e.g. management theories, computer fundamentals, etc. These courses were attended by information professionals from Saudi Arabia, Bahrain, Kuwait, Oman, Qatar and United Arab Emirates (UAE). The number of participants in the short courses ranged from 14 to 35. As was planned, approximately half of the participants in each course were from KFUPM while others came from other information institutions of Saudi Arabia and other Gulf states.

To assess the effectiveness of short courses, evaluations were conducted at the end of each course under the supervision of the Deanship of Educational Services. Some participants have suggested the extension of the course length from one to two weeks. They also emphasized the need for more practical sessions. As a result, necessary adjustments in the subsequent courses have been made. A time for informal meetings with the KFUPM library staff and a demonstration of the library automated system were also added as regular features of the short courses based on the suggestions made in the post-course evaluations. Though we encountered problems due to diversity of backgrounds, interest, and English language proficiency, the short courses turned out to be very valuable experience for the KFUPM library. Most of the time, these courses were highly praised by the participants.

Surveys were also conducted by the KFUPM Library staff to investigate employer perceptions and the perspectives of librarians about the needs of continuing education and suggestions for improvement (Ashoor, 1996; Chaudry, 1996). Suggestions were made that in addition to the post-activity evaluations, objective assessment of the overall utilization of short courses and other continuing education activities is very desirable. A study was therefore undertaken in the Fall of 1996 to investigate the overall effectiveness and utilization of continuing education activities by seeking input from the participants through a special survey. This paper reports the results of this assessment exercise. Based on participant perceptions, it reviews the fulfillment of objectives of the continuing education program and examines the relevance and application of skills and knowledge gained through CE activities to work in libraries and information centers. Possible improvements in various aspects of continuing education to enhance their utilization are also discussed.

METHODOLOGY

A number of papers in the professional literature have addressed the issues of evaluating continuing education activities in the field of library and information science. Conway has argued in favor of the intimate linkage between the effectiveness of continuing professional education programs and systematic evaluation (Conway, 1993). Chobot (1989) has suggested that an effective way to improve the quality of continuing education is to conduct sound evaluations of CE programs using standards and guidelines as tools. The American Libraries Association Guidelines for Quality in Continuing Education for Information, Library and Media Personnel have provide criteria for assessment of CE activities from perspectives of planning, design, delivery, and evaluation. Cavazza has recommended to replace the questionnaires by interviews to have clearer and more reliable feedback which can be used to design specific training in the biomedical library field (Cavazza, 1995). Pain-Lewins, Teng, and MacDougall (n.d.) have emphasized the need to focus on perceived benefits from continuing education in assessing CE programs using questionnaires and interviews. They have highlighted the important areas for evaluation including the reasons for encouraging/discouraging course attendance, identification and selection of courses, and perceived benefits obtained and defects of courses.

The above-mentioned papers have focused on questions relating to participant satisfaction about CE activities, adequacy of facilities, acceptance of quality of instruction and other aspects related to the conduct of programs. However, as Weingand rightly points out, little objective analysis of the quality and relevance of continuing education activities exits (Weingand, 1992).   It is difficult to judge how effective the continuing education event is as a means of professional development in the absence of objective analysis. The sponsors of continuing education would like to see the emphasis of evaluation on the impact of CE activities on the improvement of library and information services with eventual benefits to library users to justify the finances, time, and energy put in these activities. But little work seems to have been done to develop useful tools and appropriate methodology for assessment of the overall utilization of continuing education activities. We have attempted to investigate the extent of utilization of our CE program by seeking feedback from the participants. Using a specially designed form, input from the participants of short courses and other activities was sought through a mail questionnaire.   We hope further research will help refine data collection instruments for such studies. Procedural details of our survey have been described in the next section.

DATA COLLECTION AND ANALYSIS

A special questionnaire was designed to seek feedback from the participants of various activities conducted under the KFUPM Continuing Education Program. The questionnaire covers six areas: fulfillment of objectives, application of knowledge and skills in work, value of continuing education activities to participants and their institutions, reasons of non use of information/material, improvements needed for possible increase in utilization, and suggestions for overall improvement of the program. A copy of the questionnaire is given in Appendix A. Since effectiveness and utilization were central issues in the survey, questions in these areas contained a number of specific factors rather than an overall rating.

The KFUPM Library maintains a database of particulars of participants of its continuing education activities. A total of 203 professionals participated in various KFUPM CE activities during the period of 1987 through 1996. Many of these participants attended more than one activity. Taking into consideration the multiple participation, we mailed questionnaires to 117 potential respondents. Our later follow up revealed that a large number of participants had moved from their earlier jobs and could not be contacted to seek their input for this survey. This is related to the fact that the work force in the library and information sector in the Arabian Gulf Region is predominantly expatriate, and the turn over therefore is quite high. Consequently, receipt of questionnaires could be confirmed from only 86 respondents. As the continuing education activities under study cover a long period (10 years), we found out that several participants have gained higher positions after their participation in continuing education activities (most of them outside the library and information field). They were not enthusiastic to participate in the survey.   As a result the response rate for the survey remained quite limited (35 per cent) despite a number of follow up efforts.

The questions related to fulfillment of objectives, application and relevance, and value of CE activities (no. 1, 2, and 3) used a five-point scale to seek participant input (1 indicating lowest rating and 5 the highest).   Question no. 5 which relates to improvements needed to increase the utilization used this scale in a reverse order (1 indicating slight improvement and 5 substantial). Responses indicating raw scores were converted to weighted ratings and average scores were calculated for listed parameters.   It was assumed that in questions 1, 2, and 3 scores of 4 and 5 indicated positive agreement, 3 showed neutral response, and 2 and 1 indicated negative responses. In question 5, where scale was used in a reverse order, the ratings were limited to scores 1, 2, and 3 indicating that only slight improvements were needed in various aspects of continuing education offered by KFUPM. Most of the participants avoided to answer open-ended questions where suggestions were sought for improvement in general. These statistical data have been presented in four tables. The findings are discussed in the next section.

RESULTS AND DISCUSSION

Fulfillment of Objectives

Five areas were selected for examining the accomplishment of objectives. These included introduction of new concepts, encouragement to apply modern techniques, updating professional knowledge, development of skills for use of technology, and information exchange. As shown in Table 1, the fulfillment of objectives has been satisfactory in all the listed areas as the average score ranged from 3.6 to 4.0 (4 indicating that objectives were completely accomplished and 3.0 or above indicating that most of the listed objectives in individual activities were fulfilled). As stated elsewhere in this paper, updating professional knowledge was a major objective of the KFUPM Continuing Education Program. This objective has received the highest score reflecting the effectiveness of the program. However, the ratings were lowest for the objective related to development of skills for use of technology, which was the main reason for initiating the CE program. The possible reasons for this phenomenon have been discussed in a later section. Surprisingly, the area of information exchange (which was not a specifically stated objective in any of the CE events) also scored high (3.73). This might be an indication that the information professionals in the Arabian Gulf Region (where professional associations are not much active) are looking forward to any opportunity of gatherings of professionals to exchange ideas and information.

Considering participant perceptions about fulfillment of objectives as an indication of effectiveness, it can be safely concluded that this survey has confirmed that the KFUPM Library has been quite effective as a provider of continuing education.

Utilization of CE Programs

As shown in Table 2, the utilization of skills acquired and knowledge gained through CE activities were assessed in five areas including planning and management, staff training, professional development, initiating new products, and improvement of operations. Average score calculated on the basis of respondent ratings is higher (3.89) in the area of planning and management. This may be linked with the fact that most of the workshops and short courses offered were in the area of library automation, database development, use of microcomputers, and project planning and attracted professionals who were looking for such an opportunity to develop skills related to projects they were involved in. Surprisingly, the utilization remained comparatively low (3.43 average score) in the area of staff training. The potential of CE activities for developing staff training programs was always stressed. The participants were given complete course documentation to encourage them to repeat these activities in their organizations. One possible explanation of this situation could be that most of the participants in KFUPM CE program were from specialized information institutions where the smaller number of information professionals might have been an obstacle to make the repetition of CE activities a worth-while experience. The participants were asked to state reasons if they were not able to utilize information/material provided in the CE activities. However, most of the respondents chose not to answer this question. It would have been better if multiple-choice statement were provided instead of open-ended question. have been easier for respondents if multiple-choice statements such questions not be kept open-ended.

While the scores for utilization are lower in comparison with fulfillment of objectives, the fact that average scores in all listed areas are above 3 does indicate a reasonable utilization of CE activities. However, there is a need of further research in this area to probe the possible reasons and difficulties related to application of methods and techniques learned through CE programs in libraries and information centers.

Value of CE Activities

Even though the ratings for utilization of knowledge gained and skills acquired through CE activities were comparatively low, the perceived value of the KFUPM Continuing Education Program was rated highly by the respondents. As shown in Table 3, average score of value of CE activities from professional view point is 4.10 indicating that these activities are considered of great value by most of the respondents. A slight drop in the average score for value of CE activities from personal view point (3.86) might be linked with the relevance of topics to personal needs and preferences.

Higher average score for overall value of CE activities from the institutional perspectives indicate that the KFUPM Continuing Education Program has a great potential to contribute towards the staff development and training in the information sector of the Arabian Gulf Region.

Improvements for Increasing Utilization

The respondents were asked to indicate the extent of improvements needed in 9 major areas of CE program for further increase in its utilization on a scale of 1-5 (1 indicating slight improvement and 5 substantial). Their responses ranged from 1 to 3 indicating that they think only slight improvements are needed in different aspects of the CE program. Average scores for improvements are given in Table 4. Higher scores in this table have negative reflections. For example, in the 2 areas where the average score is above 2.0 it is an indication that more attention should be paid to improve the aspects of teaching methodology and publicity of CE events. Effectiveness of methodology is also related to lower average score for fulfillment of objectives for skill development to facilitate the use of technology (as pointed out in the earlier section). There always had been comments and suggestions that the short courses and workshops should be practical-based rather than lecture-based. We have compromised on this account with a 50:50 ratio for theory and practice but an overall shift from lectures to practicals was not considered advisable. An alternative was to increase the duration of these activities from one week to a longer period of time. This would have provided for sufficient practical training but the employers found it difficult to spare staff longer period of time. Steps are being taken to design programs in such a way that they build on each other and are offered in a sequence so that these can also be taken as long duration courses by those who can manage release from work. The other areas where higher average scores have been assigned include comprehensiveness of contents (1.97), physical facilities (1.97), logistics (1.97), and sponsorships (1.96).

Lower ratings indicate that only slight improvements are to increase the utility of continuing education. However, further investigations need to be carried out to be able to have specific suggestions to improve these important aspects of the continuing education program.

CONCLUDING SUMMARY

The feedback of participants sought through a special survey has indicated that most of the objectives of continuing education program at KFUPM have been fulfilled satisfactorily. An average score ranging from 3.6 to 4.0 has been assigned to the listed objectives on the basis ratings given by respondents on a scale of 1 to 5. The respondents perceive that the main objective of continuing education activities "updating professional knowledge' has been accomplished at a higher level in comparison with other objectives.

The participant have also indicated a higher level of utilization of knowledge gained and skills acquired through CE events. Their ratings yielded an average score of 3.43 to 3.89 to the various listed areas of use including planning and management, staff training, professional development, initiation of new products and services, and improvement of library operations.

The respondents of the survey think that professionally the continuing education activities are of great value for them as their ratings yielded an average score of 4.10 on this aspect. They also consider these activities of significant importance in the personal and institutional context as the average score on these aspects has been 3.86 and 3.93 on a scale of 1 to 5 (1 being low and 5 high). This indicates that the KFUPM Continuing Education Program has a great potential for staff development in the information sector in the Arabian Gulf Region.

The participant of various workshops and short courses organized under the KFUPM Continuing Education Program think that only slight improvement are needed in various aspects of CE aspects to further increase their utility. Their perceptions indicate that changes in teaching methodology, improvements in quality of instruction, increase in duration of training period, and better publicity and sponsorship arrangements can enrich the continuing education program. However, further research will have to be carried out to come up with specific suggestions for improvement in these areas.

It is desirable that additional evaluations are conducted of this program based on a larger sample as the response for the present study has been low despite several follow-up attempts. It will also be useful if feedback of employers can also be sought on the possible contribution of professionals in their work after their participation in continuing education activities.

REFERENCES

Ashoor, Mohammad Saleh (1996), "Employer perceptions about education for library and information science in the Arabian Gulf Region", paper presented at the *4th AGC/SLA Annual Conference on Human Resource Development in the Electronic Library Environment,* Kuwait, 15-17 March 1996.

Cavazza, L. (1995), "Training courses for medical librarians in Emilia-Romanga (Italy): a first evaluation, *Health Libraries Review,* 12 (1) pp. 63-65.

Chaudhry, Abdus Sattar (1996), "Continuing education of library and information professionals in the Arabian Gulf Region", paper presented at the *4th AGC/SLA Annual Conference on Human Resource Development in the Electronic Library Environment,* Kuwait, 15-17 March 1996.

Chaudhry, Abdus Sattar, Ashoor, Mohammad Saleh, and Rehman Sajjad Ur. (1993), "Development and implementation of an in-house continuing education program in an academic library", *Education for Information,* 11, pp. 47-56.

Chobot, Mary C. (1989), "Improving the quality of continuing education", *IFLA Journal,* 15 (3), pp. 210-217.

Conway, P. (1993), "Effective continuing education for training the archivist", *Journal of Education for Library and Information Science,* 34 (1), pp. 38-47.

Pain-Lewins, H. P., Teng, G. M., and MacDougall, J. J. (n.d.), *"Participation and Perceived Benefits from Continuing Education for UK Professional Librarians."* . British Library Report, Loughborough: University of Technology, Department of Library and Information Studies.

Weingand, Darlene E. (1992), "Surveying the effectiveness of short course provision in the professional development of library and information specialists", *Journal of Education for Library and Information Science,* 33 (3), pp. 249-253.

APPENDIX A

UTILIZATION OF CONTINUING EDUCATION ACTIVITIES

Follow-up Questionnaire

1. How well did the continuing education activities meet their stated objectives? Please indicate your assessment of accomplishment of objectives in the listed areas on a scale of 1-5 (1 indicating the lower level and 5 the highest):

Objective	Degree of Fulfillment				
	1	2	3	4	5

Introduction to new concepts and techniques

Encouragement to introduce modern information
 management techniques

Updating professional knowledge on selected topics

Development of skills for effective use of technology

Exchange of information among professionals

2.   How well did you apply the knowledge and skills gained through participation in CE activities in your work? Please indicate the extent of utilization of learning acquired in the following areas on a scale of 1-5 (I indicating minimum use and 5 extensive use):

Area of Use	Extent of Utilization				
	1	2	3	4	5
Planning and management of information services					
Developing training programs for staff					
Professional development					
Initiating new products/services					
Improving library operations and services					
Other ways of benefit (please specify)					

3.   If you were unable to make use of information/material presented in the CE activities, please explain why?

4.   How valuable were the CE activities to you on the whole? Please check the overall value of CE programs on the listed aspects on a scale of 1-5 (1 being insignificant and 5 extremely valuable):

Utilization Aspect	Assessment Scale				
	1	2	3	4	5
Personally					
Professionally					
Institutionally					

5.   Do you think improvements in various aspects of CE programs can further increase their utilization? Please indicate the extent of improvement needed in the following aspects of CE activities (1 indicating slight improvement and 5 substantial):

CE Aspects	Degree of Improvement				
	1	2	3	4	5
Appropriateness of topics					
Comprehensiveness of technical contents					
Effectiveness of teaching methodology					
Quality of instruction					

Duration of training

Physical facilities

Logistics

Publicity

Sponsorships

Other (please specify)

6.   Do you have any other suggestions about the continuing education activities offered by the KFUPM Library? Please give your suggestions briefly I the following space:

*We are grateful for your cooperation in completing this brief questionnaire. Please return it at your earliest convenience to **KFUPM # 2047, Dhahran 31261, Saudi Arabia.***

Table 1

Fulfillment of Objectives of CE Programs

n=30

Objective		Degree of Fulfillment			
			Weighted Rating		
	1	2	3	4	5
Average					
Introducing New Concepts 3.90	2	-	24	36	55
Inducing Participants to Apply Modern Techniques 3.97	1	6	15	32	65
Updating Professional Knowledge 4.00	2	-	18	40	60
Developing Skills for Effective Use of Technology 3.60	4	2	15	52	35
Facilitating Information Exchange 3.73	3	4	18	32	55

Table 2

Utilization of CE Programs

Area of Use	Extent of Utilization					
		Weighted Rating				
Average Score	1	2	3	4	5	
Planning and Management 3.89 n=28		2	4	9	44	50
Staff Training n=28	3	8	12	48	25	3.43
Professional Development n=30	1	6	12	52	45	3.87
Initiating New Products/Services n=29	1	8	21	32	45	3.69
Improvement of Operations n=30	3	4	18	56	25	3.53

Table 3

Value of CE Activities

Benefit Sector	Degree of Value					
Average Score	Weighted Rating					
	1	2	3	4	5	
Personally n=28	1	2	9	36	60	3.86
Professionally n=29	-	2	18	44	55	4.10
Institutionally n=29	2	2	12	48	50	3.93

Table 4

Improvements Needed for Enhancing Utilization of CE Programs

CE Aspect Average Score	Degree of Improvements Needed Weighted Rating					
	1	2	3	4	5	
Appropriateness of Topics n=30	11	26	18	-	-	1.83
Comprehensiveness of Contents n=30	11	18	30	-	-	1.97
Effectiveness of Methodology n=30	12	12	36	-	-	2.00
Quality of Instruction n=29	16	12	21	-	-	1.67
Duration of Training n=30	17	14	18	-	-	1.63
Physical Facilities n=30	7	34	18	-	-	1.97
Logistics n=30	7	34	18	-	-	1.97
Publicity n=30	8	26	27	-	-	2.03
Sponsorship n=29	10	16	27	-	-	1.96

APPLYING PRINCIPLES FOR EFFECTIVE STAFF DEVELOPMENT TO LARGE URBAN PUBLIC LIBRARY SYSTEMS IN CANADA: INTERSECTIONS OF RESEARCH WITH THE KNOWLEDGE, BELIEFS AND PRACTICES OF PUBLIC LIBRARY DIRECTORS

Ken Haycock
School of Library, Archival and Information Studies
The University of British Columbia
Vancouver
Canada

Abstract   Previous analyses of research in staff development in large not-for-profit organizations with multiple sites (Haycock, 1993) have led to the specification of guiding principles for effective practice. This work was extended to propose implications for large urban public library systems (Haycock, 1994).

Change in the information infrastructure and in the responsibilities of public libraries is resulting in demanding new roles and competencies for information professionals. These changes require investments in training and development. The purpose of this study was to determine the extent to which directors of large urban public libraries in Canada agreed with research-based principles for staff development as a result of their prior knowledge or personal beliefs, and the extent to which these principles were reflected in practice.

Previous analyses of research in staff development resulted in guiding principles for effective practice for large urban school systems and propositions for large urban public library systems (Haycock, 1993; this tertiary review included 35 research studies and over 120 citations, not reported here). This work was extended to incorporate recent research in staff development in library and information services and to expand on the implications for library systems (Haycock, 1994; ten additional studies in library and information studies were incorporated, also not reported here). The current study assesses the extent to which these guiding principles reflect the prior knowledge or personal beliefs of the 41 directors of large urban public library systems in Canada and the degree to which they are currently implemented in those systems; fifty-nine per cent (n=24) of the directors responded to a survey questionnaire, representing at least 50% of large urban public library systems in each area of the country.

Directors were asked to indicate the extent to which they agreed or disagreed with each of 50 statements, or guiding principles, on a four-point Likert-type scale [Strongly Disagree /Disagree /Agree /Strongly Agree] and the extent to which these statements were evidenced in their own systems, similarly on a four-point Likert-type scale [Not Implemented /Partially Implemented /Fully Implemented /Unlikely to be Implemented]. This paper clusters the guiding principles by theme and reports the extent to which directors agreed or strongly agreed with each principle, reported together, and the degree of perceived implementation, incorporating both partial and full implementation.

The extensive research literature in public education and more limited research in staff development in libraries and other information agencies provide considerable evidence and guidance as to what constitutes effectiveness in the implementation of change and in staff development (see, for example, Haycock, 1993 and Woolls, 1993), and provides a useful starting point for discussion of effective practice. For information professionals and their institutions, the evidence is worthy of assessment for relevance based on professional and institutional experience and for the questions it raises regarding value for investment in training.

The guiding principles for staff development were derived from the research literature. Staff development includes any activity or process intended to improve the skills, attitudes, understandings, or performance in present or future roles. A guiding principle is a comprehensive and fundamental truth or assumption which leads toward some desirable end or practice. Effective practice constitutes engaging habitually in the productive application of knowledge.

The review of the related literature was limited primarily to recent research and summaries which incorporate earlier findings. While the preponderance of studies examined were limited to the world of the professional teacher and reflect that context and culture they of necessity comment on the nature of learning by adults working in changing worlds with different expectations, and on the continual and continuing development of professionals and the institutions in which they work. Indeed, the findings from public education are in large measure replicated in studies in library management and staff development (see, for example, Smith, 1993 and Woolls, 1993).

CHARACTERISTICS OF STAFF DEVELOPMENT

Effective staff development has the commitment of the professionals involved, models positive human interaction skills and addresses personal concerns in a direct and sensitive manner. Effective staff development is also designed to suit its purpose. Participants are actively involved and are encouraged to observe each other to provide feedback on performance. Some believe that staff development is most effective when undertaken voluntarily but initial enthusiasm for training appears to have relatively little influence on learning.

Schools are both complex and powerfully resistant to change such that effective staff development involves working more organically within the individual school as an organization; this requires close collaboration between those inside and outside the local unit, such as in central administrative offices, meaning that the centralization of policy making and resources for staff development must be reconfigured; the role and relationship of agencies and services external to the local unit must be reassessed but it is unclear how autonomy and collaboration for the local branch or unit should be balanced; this raises the question whether large urban public library systems should also focus on individual branches or units or whether they or more unified and holistic than large school systems even though they serve the same diverse urban communities. Effective staff development requires that those involved also think and act more holistically about the personal and professional lives of employees as individuals and work continuously on the spirit and practice of life-long learning for all.

The guiding principles for effective staff development that follow are clustered around basic themes: philosophy and goals; focus; context; planning; support; content and processes; rewards and incentives; evaluation. Possible implications for library systems and library staffs are noted for each area as are the beliefs of directors of large urban public libraries in Canada and the extent of implementation of these practices in their systems. Reporting in this paper is limited to the extent to which directors agree or strongly agree, presented together, and the extent to which these principles are partially or fully implemented, again presented together.

PHILOSOPHY AND GOALS

Effective staff development is based on an organizational philosophy for staff development, is directed by organizational goals and is formally placed within the structure of the system. The focus is primarily on helping staff learn and use preferred approaches and strategies and on the expectations of the system. Objectives of effective staff development activities are clearly defined and the expectations for staff clearly stated. Expectations should be clear about what staff should be able to accomplish once the training is over, and how they will be evaluated. One would expect to find then, in library systems modeling effective practice from large public education systems, a clear statement of system goals, a specific staff development department and/or function in the organizational hierarchy and a focus on improved service. Expectations for the continued and continuing learning of staff need to be clearly set out. Recent studies in different types of libraries have also found that the presence of a co-ordinator results in improved staff development opportunities based on institutional needs but the factor with the greatest influence on the establishment of a training program and its effective implementation is the director's personal philosophy.

Beliefs and practices—
Directors of large Canadian urban public libraries endorsed these principles with agreement of 70% or more in each case with the sole exception of the influential nature of the director or branch head's personal philosophy. In spite of the high consensus of agreement, however, implementation, whether partial or fully, was much lower, particularly in the case of expectations for staff engaged in staff development activities being clearly stated, what staff should be able to accomplish once the training is over, and how they will be evaluated (67% partial or full implementation in each case). The influence of the director's or branch head's personal philosophy on the establishment of a

training program was recognized in 59% of cases. Further, while 87% of directors agreed that, like education and hospital systems, and corporations, large library system would do well to establish staff development and training divisions for professional and support staff and branches and to assist with the implementation of change, this was partially or fully implemented, according to directors, in only 45% of the systems.

FOCUS

Effective staff development focuses on the individual unit rather than the system, requires a local organizational effort, and occurs at the local site as much as possible, suggesting a shift of responsibility from central offices to individual branch libraries with central support. Staff development becomes a local organizational effort, tailored to the needs of the group; staffs learn together initially, support each other in implementation and continue to learn as programs are modified in practice; staff become more self-aware, self-analytic and self-renewing, in an ongoing effort. The local site is a low-threat, comfortable setting with a degree of psychological safety.

Effective staff development can empower staff to take control of their own professional development. The objective of staff development is to assist professionals to increase their repertoire of strategies and techniques, to raise their methods to a conscious level at which they can be examined and refined, and to encourage them to make a practice of discussing their ideas about their practice with colleagues. Learners participate in planning and carrying out plans for their own improvement with staff development only a provisional state that has as its object to make the learner or problem solver self-sufficient; learners need substantial freedom to direct their own growth in order to foster individual motivation and self-confidence. Professional development should be a cultural concept incorporating options, choice, authority and responsibility. The staff of a local school [or library] not only set goals for their education but are willing to go about training themselves and each other.

These principles would necessitate a major shift for many library systems, from *professional* development and continuing education for individuals to a balance with *staff* development for the branch or unit as a whole, from individual workshops sponsored by the central office to ongoing development by the department or branch to improve services and their delivery.

Beliefs and practices—
There was little disagreement that effective staff development empowers staff to take control of their own learning and development, incorporating options, choice, authority and responsibility and these principles are partially or fully implemented in more than 70% of library systems. There was, however, considerable disagreement about the appropriate locus of responsibility for staff development: 55% of directors believed that responsibility and resources for staff development should shift from the central office to individual branch libraries with central support, 50% agreed that the staff of the local branch library or division should set goals for their continuing education and go about training themselves and each other and one third agreed that effective staff development focuses on the individual branch or division rather than the system, requires a local organizational effort, and occurs at the local site as much as possible—this shift is implemented in one third to almost one-half of the systems (the discrepancy is accounted for in the random ordering of similar statements in the questionnaire).

CONTEXT

A climate which is characterized by the norms of collegiality such as expectations for shared work, of continuous improvement such as expectations for analysis, evaluation, and experimentation, and of collaboration, supports effective staff development. Collaboration, collegiality, and mutual adaptation are necessary ingredients but continuous staff development requires a healthy ethos— organizational health includes factors such as social climate, trust, open communication, and peer support for change in practice. Such a climate reduces the use and threat of external judgments from one's superior; adult learners are motivated to risk learning new behaviors when they believe they have control over the learning situation and are free from the threat of failure. Social cohesion and shared understandings facilitate a willingness to try out new ideas. The prerequisite of a receptive and positive climate allows professionals to flourish; the key associated aspect is the professional culture of the organization.

For the library system, effective leaders become accountable for developing an organizational culture which values collaboration and collegiality and focuses on learning together.

Beliefs and practices—

A climate characterized by the norms of collegiality, of continuous improvement, and of collaboration, supports effective staff development and effective library leaders are accountable for developing just such an organizational culture; all directors agreed and all believed that this is partially or fully implemented in their systems.

PLANNING

Effective staff development activities are part of an overall plan which is long-term, systematic, developmental, flexible and directed toward system goals. The staff development program needs to fit the long-term goals of both the individual library and its parent institution. This type of program takes place where dialogue, decision-making, action, and evaluation related to problems and issues occur.

Single session presentations can be invaluable for raising awareness and in helping individuals to make decisions about those areas where extended workshops would be beneficial but the long range program must provide for follow-up practice, peer assistance and coaching, and support in solving problems related to the implementation of new skills and behaviors as it takes time to implement new approaches. Staff development should be carried out in a sustained fashion over time.

The plan is based on both individual personal and professional needs and the needs of the organization. Needs assessments should be an ongoing part of an organization's operation, within a climate that encourages sharing and frank discussions of issues among colleagues and peers; these needs are assessed continuously to update knowledge and skills, and to improve the organization. Staff perception of needs is used as well as other criteria for individual and program needs; the focus is on job-related tasks that the participants consider real and important. It is crucial for staff developers to know the organization's structure and the particular individuals involved and where the participants are in terms of their feelings and present usage in order to match better the content with existing individual, group and contextual conditions.

There is a wide array of choices including peer centered options to accommodate individual differences and diversity of needs. Professional development includes professional dialogue, co-operative program development, peer supervision or consultation, peer assistance and coaching and action research, as well as local site-based analysis of problems, creative use of technology, opportunities to lead, and to be empowered to initiate new strategies or organizational structures based on their own diagnoses of problems.

Staff are involved in planning effective staff development activities. Participants take part in goal setting, implementation, evaluation and decision-making as objectives and activities planned by the participants are perceived to be more meaningful with a higher degree of clarity and acceptance. However, the effects of training do not depend on whether the professionals involved organize and direct the program.

Initial task-specific training is combined with ongoing follow-up activities. These follow-up activities allow for continued experimentation, staff collaboration and personal adaptation but require generous amounts of time, money and technical assistance for transfer to the workplace. The steps in effective staff development include the presentation of information and theory, modeling or demonstration of the desired change, an opportunity to practice, credible feedback, and peer observation, assistance and coaching.

Plans for effective staff development recognize that change is a gradual and difficult process and provide sufficient time to produce demonstrable results. Time is provided for sharing understandings, exploring applications of the content, and integration of new understandings into professional and personal perspectives. An atmosphere is created where risks can be taken by participants and presenters alike so that personal growth can occur for all. Time for learning is one of the most important investments a system can make.

Effective staff development provides staff time away from their regular responsibilities for planning, reflection, and assimilation.

Staff development is a long-term organizational effort requiring leadership, time and resources, commodities often in short supply for staff development in information agencies, even where it is a priority. Within the context of the library system's goals, staff development will be systematic but based at the branch or unit level, with time for collaboration and training for all staff together, and opportunities for practice, feedback and continuing on-site coaching.

Beliefs and practices—
Director were in agreement with these principles (more than 80% agreement in every case with 100% agreement on most). Implementation was similarly high, with more than 70% of the systems experiencing partial or full implementation. There was an even split on whether the effects of training depend on staff involvement in organization and direction of the program. A slight majority (57%) believe that staff development is systematic and based at the branch or unit level and a similar number saw this being implemented in their systems.

SUPPORT

The administration supports effective staff development by providing visible and continuing commitment to the program, by creating a supportive organizational climate, and by allocating time and resources. Administrators need to recognize the ability of staff to serve as leaders and to delegate more responsibility to them while providing appropriate support to counteract individual isolation and programmatic fragmentation.

The branch head facilitates effective staff development by building a healthy culture and encouraging staff. The head needs to become an organizational leader, skilled in assessing needs, facilitating group processes, identifying priorities, setting goals, and evaluating programs and needs to maintain a balance between attention to task and structure and attention to human needs. The head involves participants in the planning, operation and evaluation of professional growth activities, relies primarily on internal rather than external resources and participates in staff development activities in which staff are involved.

Effective staff development activities are facilitated by credible staff with time and expertise in both content and processes. The presenter comes to the subject from the participants' point of view, displays expertise, and conveys genuine enthusiasm for the subject; follow-up focuses on the context rather than the content of the change with assistance by someone trained in supporting staff development.

Beliefs and practices—
Again, 75% or more of the directors of large urban public library systems in Canada agreed or strongly agreed with these principles and believed that they were partially or fully implemented in their systems. Interestingly, however, only 59% of the directors agreed with the proposition that the library should rely primarily on internal rather than external expertise and resources yet 85% of the systems nevertheless do this. The reliance on internal staff development leaders rather than external expertise is based then less on the research base or the director's beliefs than on other considerations.

CONTENT AND PROCESSES

Effective staff development incorporates the principles of effective teaching, adult learning theory, and knowledge about the process of change. The content of effective staff development is research-based, proven effective, practical, and relevant to identified needs and problems faced in the workplace. "Research-based" clearly extends beyond experience and intuition: in improving reference services, for example, Dewdney (1986) reports that neutral questioning based on research in information-seeking behavior is more effective and more transferable than micro skills adapted for librarians from counseling; similarly, Smith (1993) reports on a Maryland (USA) Department of Education Division of Library Development and Services program which increased reference accuracy by focusing on librarian behaviors rather than library resources and on effective staff development practices, including coaching.

Effective staff development pays particular attention to the contexts in which participants work and is connected to the responsibilities and organizations of the participants. However, the training design is more important than where or when the training is held and who the trainer is.

Both academic library department heads and staff development officers, for example, believe that instructional design should be used in planning and preparing staff development programs but it is used less frequently than their opinions suggest.

Effective staff development relates theory and application by combining presentation with demonstration, practice and feedback. This training focuses on both the acquisition of knowledge and skills and the cognitions necessary for appropriate and integrated use of the practice. Staff development demonstrates the strategies that will bring about short and long term benefits to clients. Sessions may conclude with individual participant action plans to guide the application of learning.

Activities provide opportunities for participants to share experiences and expertise. Collaboration among participants and with the staff developer contains rich benefits for everyone who participates.

Effective staff development provides follow-up, on-site assistance to staff in the form of technical assistance, peer support and coaching. It also encourages reflection, collaboration, peer observation, risk-taking, experimentation, and adaptation. This is particularly effective through a collegial support system that values growth activities, provides moral support and facilitates small group interaction.

The content and processes of staff development are well-known to library systems but current research suggests a different configuration from common patterns. While focus on the unique concerns of different groups, such as reference librarians attending a workshop at the central library, might continue, there would also be a focus on professional and support staff together as a branch or unit, with due attention to assessing unique community and staff needs, team building, improving client service and ongoing evaluation. Coaching is more feasible when tied to on-site staff development and peer assistance than to an external consultant or colleague visiting on a fixed schedule. Peer assistance or coaching is an expensive ingredient in staff development programs but research suggests that substantive programs without coaching may very well be a waste of money.

Beliefs and practices—
More than 80% of the directors agreed with the principles for content and process of staff development but, again, there was only a slight majority (55%) that saw the focus of staff development on the branch or unit, with due attention to assessing unique community and staff needs, team building, improved client service and evaluation. Major discrepancies occurred in the delivery of staff development, however, with 87% of directors agreeing that instructional design and adult learning theory should be used in planning and preparing staff development programs but only 69% seeing this being implemented in their systems; similarly, 86% agreed that substantive staff development programs without on-site assistance and coaching may be a waste of money but this was practised in only 58% of systems to any extent whatsoever.

REWARDS AND INCENTIVES

Effective staff development identifies intrinsic rewards and incentives to encourage personal and professional growth. This might include pinpointing early progress indicators which participants can detect to counter premature discouragement and disillusionment. Informal rewards also become more powerful: satisfaction in interactions with clients; modification of the working environment; opportunities to engage in job-related experiences; opportunities to receive public praise; allocation of scarce resources; particular assignments; placement on decision-making bodies.

The most obvious rewards for library and information staff might include the satisfaction of personal growth and development, of improved service and of opportunities for leadership at the local level.

Beliefs and practices—
Effective library systems identify intrinsic rewards and incentives to encourage personal and professional growth (85% agreement) but only 65% of systems have made conscious moves in this direction.

EVALUATION

Evaluation is an integral component of effective staff development. Staff development programs are consistently monitored and evaluated for improvement and change of direction. Provision is made to document the planning, implementation and outcomes of all activities; outcome measures include documentation of changed staff behavior and change in the organization, as well as specific goal attainment such as client satisfaction or improved outcomes. Evaluation contributes to decision-making, modifications and improvement and is critical to resource allocation and accountability.

Beliefs and practices—
More than 80% of directors believed that evaluation was an integral component of effective staff development and that programs were consistently monitored and evaluated for improvement and change of direction and that evaluation contributed to decision-making and these were being implemented in more than 70% of the systems. However, while almost 80% agreed that provision should be made to document the planning, implementation and outcomes of staff development activities to determine the extent of changed staff behavior and apparent influence on the organization this occurred in fewer than half of the systems.

These principles capture the critical attributes and lessons learned from the research and the wisdom of "best practice" and as such can be helpful in summarizing, succinctly and thoroughly, the current state of the art in staff development. Of course, most of the statements are truisms with intuitive appeal; nevertheless, they do not find their way easily into practice. Indeed, other agencies—school systems, hospitals, large law firms—tend to have professional and staff development departments to assist units to become more effective.

The research literature supports a set of guiding principles for effective practice in staff development. These guiding principles have implications for relative roles and responsibilities of central administrative and branch staff, priorities for professional and staff development, branch-based management, and assessment and evaluation. Investment in human resource development is critical to the maintenance and enhancement of library and information services but must be based on demonstrably effective practice. For information professionals, nothing less should be acceptable. Directors of large urban public library systems in Canada agreed or strongly agreed with most of the principles, based either on their prior knowledge or personal values and beliefs. The degree of implementation varied markedly, however, with higher implementation of effective practices in establishing philosophy and goals, developing the institutional context, planning and support than in focus, content and process, incentives and evaluation. Several issues emerge for staff development and training, not the least of which is that some principles deemed impractical in qualitative statements by some directors are in fact being implemented in other systems; further, there was a high level of agreement about how staff development is translated into practice, for example through on-site assistance and coaching, yet there were lower levels of implementation here than elsewhere: the conclusion might be drawn that increased opportunities for staff development programs, whether seminars, conferences or in-house training, are more desirable than fewer, more focused programs delivered in more effective ways. Interestingly, more directors also agree with a shift of responsibility and resources from the system level to the branch level than is currently occurring, suggesting a likely direction for change.

There needs to be further research and elaboration on different types and degrees of decentralization of budgets and decision-making for staff development to local branches and the effect of these decisions on organizational roles and responsibilities, on central services and on performance outcomes, particularly in these large urban library systems.

REFERENCES

Dewdney, P. H. (1986). The effects of training reference librarians in interview skills: A field experiment. *Dissertation Abstracts International, 47*, 3598A. (Not available from University Microfilms)

Haycock, Ken. (1994). "Staff development in library and information services: Reconfiguring effective practice." *Education for Information Services: Australia*, 11(02), 3–16.

Haycock, K. (1993). Research in professional and staff development in education: A synthesis with implications for library and information science professionals. In B. Woolls (Ed.), *Continuing professional education and IFLA: Past, present, and a vision for the future; Papers from the IFLA CPERT Second World Conference on Continuing Professional Education for the Library an Information Science Professions* (pp. 90-100). A Publication of the Continuing Education Round Table (CPERT) of the International Federation of Library Associations and Institutions. Munchen: K. G. Saur, 1993. (IFLA Publications 66/67)

Smith, D. (1993). The greening of librarianship: Charting a new course for continuing library education. In B. Woolls (Ed.), *Continuing professional education and IFLA: Past, present, and a vision for the future; Papers from the IFLA CPERT Second World Conference on Continuing Professional Education for the Library an Information Science Professions* (pp. 11-23). A Publication of the Continuing Education Round Table (CPERT) of the International Federation of Library Associations and Institutions. Munchen: K. G. Saur, 1993. (IFLA Publications 66/67)

Woolls, B. (Ed.) (1993). *Continuing professional education and IFLA: Past, present, and a vision for the future; Papers from the IFLA CPERT Second World Conference on Continuing Professional Education for the Library an Information Science Professions*. A Publication of the Continuing Education Round Table (CPERT) of the International Federation of Library Associations and Institutions. Munchen: K. G. Saur, 1993. 365 pp. (IFLA Publications 66/67)

THE NEW ROLE OF LIBRARIANS AS INTERNET TRAINERS

Diann Rusch-Feja
Max Planck Institute for
Human Development and Education
Berlin
Germany

Abstract: The use of telecommunications and the influence of networked communication, such as the Internet, has expanded the role of librarians in the continuing education field. This paper investigates both the demonstrated expectations for user training for the networked communications based on a survey in a research institute and the continuing education possibilities for librarians to prepare them for this task. These include external seminars and workshops, formal CE courses at recognized librarian training institutions, and self-tutorials on the Internet itself, as well as more informal means of continuing education for librarians, such as in-service training and the utilization of networked discussion groups and forums. Plans for an international co-operation project to use existing CE Internet training materials from the University of New South Wales in Australia and offer them in English to German librarians via the Australian Centre in Potsdam co-ordinated with the Humboldt University in Berlin, Germany, will be reported upon. The educational value of this project lies not only in its content, but also in its aspects of participation in a self-paced tutorial employing a hands-on approach to networked information training combined with tutor mentoring by a German-language instructor. The paper concludes with suggestions for expanding such a program to non-librarian students to augment tertiary education programs and existing continuing education programs. Parallel to traditional subject bibliography courses required by undergraduate subject degree programs, such courses could be designed by subject specialist librarians in the appropriate fields and then offered as continuing education courses for students and practicing professionals with the additional mentorship of librarians.

INTRODUCTION

The use of telecommunications and the influence of networked communication, such as the Internet, has expanded the inherent role of librarians in the continuing education process. As in other special libraries - especially those in institutions serving high technology research institutions and institutions or companies with state-of-the-art computer technology and use of high technology in the research itself, our library was committed to keeping pace with major developments which would affect our abilities to provide relevant information in an adequate form and with the expected speed and efficiency demanded of us. During the first encounter with the Internet, the potential of the Internet as an extension of varied information resources beyond the physical information sources within the library or available through (often) expensive online hosts was very clear and we attempted to build on this. At first, the computer section of the Institute questioned why we wanted to be connected directly to the Internet and then, upon recognizing our involvement, felt somewhat challenged in their fields of competencies. Unnecessary conflict and competition was avoided by incorporating certain joint efforts which usually produced very positive results thanks to the co-operative efforts and commitment of all involved. Nevertheless, whether in relation to the computer department or to the users or within the library itself, new roles for us as librarians were and are still rapidly emerging. One of the most compelling of these is in "sharing the new wealth" as Internet trainers.

1. EXPECTATIONS OF USERS FOR TRAINING IN USE OF NETWORKED INFORMATION AND COMMUNICATIONS

In a survey our library conducted in January 1996 on the users' opinions on our library's services, we also asked questions regarding the user's familiarity and use of the Internet. The sampling represented fifty percent of the Institute researchers. Of that group, only one fourth had not already used the Internet at all (ca. 13 %) or had "just had a look" (10 %). Of those using the Internet (76 % of the sampling), over one third (38.7 % of the Internet users in the sampling) had had any training in using the Internet.(1) Of that group 6.4 % had taken an external course or seminar, 6.4 % were given training by persons in the computer department, 16 % had taken a two-hour introductory course offered by the computer department, 6.4 % had learned from colleagues, and 3.2 % had had a training course at a professional conference. Almost two thirds of the Internet users (64 %) said they had no training on the Internet at all or had taught themselves by trial and error (in two cases, adjustments have been made for multiple answers in the group indicating having had training).

Of the same group of Internet users, 54.8 % answered the question if they would like to have a training session with yes, only 19.9 % did not want any additional training for use of the Internet. Of those, who wanted training, only 11.7 % wanted a full day's training, 47 % said the training should be at most 2 hours long, 41.2 % said at most one half day. The results indicate the recognized need for such training - though they also reflect the schedule restraints of the researchers and their self-determined time allocation for increasing their own information retrieval skills. Unfortunately, due to the structure of the questionnaire, non-users of the Internet could skip over further questions on Internet use and were not thus confronted with the question if they wanted an introduction or training in using the Internet.

Although this shows a relatively small group of persons in our sample defining themselves as in need of training for using the Internet, similar self-estimated skills and capacities in using new technology such as CD-ROMs or fully utilizing the various aspects of a library OPAC sometimes reflect the level of sufficient user satisfaction. Not merely with the Internet, but also in other end-user retrieval services, we have notices that some users are satisfied when the search results produce a few good answers within in a relatively short period of time and without complex search mechanisms. This often depends on the level of subject familiarity (i.e., student, instructor, doctoral candidate, researcher), but necessarily. The end-user's willingness to learn and use more complex searching features also depends on the complexity and user-friendliness of the search modes, an interest in retrieval tactics, and frequency of use. On the other hand, one also encounters end-users who have responded to "advanced retrieval methods" seminars or in the case of the Internet trained themselves in using the resource discovery and retrieval tools so well that they feel they can organize, index, and search for the literature better than librarians. In terms of the Internet, these are usually academic professionals and researchers from the fields of mathematics, physics, computer science, etc., who also have a much stronger background in computer use than many librarians.

Despite exceptions, the shift to end-user searching, however, usually shows that the end-user, though generally satisfied with his search results, is not fully exploiting the contents of the data set being searched and does, in fact, need further training. This may apply with more validity to CD-ROM and closed database searching than to the Internet, but even here, the information professional has not become obsolete. Although this is a very delicate issue, the role and retrieval capacities of the information specialist must be transmitted to the end-user in such a way that the user recognizes and values the advantage of the information specialist's professional edge. One way to do this is to provide training courses for the end-user which emphasize the skills necessary to perfect search techniques. A further method is to set up separate sets of key Web sites of interest to the individual researchers with value-added aspects(2) and introduce this to the user. In our Clearinghouse for Project-Oriented Internet Resources (http://www.mpib-berlin.mpg.de/DOK/ech.htm), key Web sites which match the research interests of the Institute researchers are gathered, evaluated, structured, augmented by an annotation and made searchable on a project-oriented "resource page". In separate sections, links to library catalogs, search engines and official publications are listed. Our experience has been that some reseachers use this set of key sites customized to his or her research interests as a springboard to other meaningful sites, to keep up with developments in the field and to use as a ready reference for persons, institutions and if appropriate new publications.

Other observations have been made of those who have not yet become Internet users. The threat of the information flood, the lack of clear-cut, structurally defined quality criteria for assessing the information in the Internet has held many back from using it. Some feel that there is no appropriate information on their particular topics of interest in the Internet. In the beginning of more wide-spread Internet use, this may have been true, but the surge of Internet growth during the year 1996 and continuing now has shown that not only the amount of information and subject coverage is increasing, but also the informational quality. In talking to a non-Internet user, such resource pages as in our clearinghouse or other similar subject collection sites can be used to convince the user that there are appropriate information sources for him or her in the Net. This may then lead to an appointment for a more thorough introduction to searching in the Internet or to an invitation to a scheduled Internet course or seminar.

2. TYPES OF USER TRAINING TO DEVELOP INTERNET SKILLS

2.1. Internet Training Course from Computer Department

A general Internet course offered by the computer department of our Institute includes the history and theoretical basis of the Internet, its development, general characteristics and background understanding of the TCP/IP protocol, basic functions (ftp, telnet, gopher, WWW), use of the Netscape browser, HTML structure and features, etc. General examples are used, search engines are included. The course lasts 2-3 hours and has been scheduled approximately every 4 months. A separate course or individual training is available for help in setting up HTML-pages. Email training occurs at the same time as installation of the email program at the workstation of the user.

2.2. Internet Training Offered by the Library

Ad hoc introduction to user specific sites, use of the Internet, hints on information searching on the Internet, etc., and introduction to the Internet Resource pages in our Clearinghouse for Project-Oriented Internet Resources as well as in our Library Catalog's Resource Page (http://www.mpib-berlin.mpg.de/DOK/elib.htm and /ech.htm). We have also set pointers to several self-tutorials on the Internet (in general) and to at least one self-tutorial with specific subject-oriented searching, namely SOSIG (http://www.sosig.ac.uk).

Often the ad hoc introduction begins with a simple reference question which the library staff recognizes as a question best answered with the currency of a known Internet source. (Unfortunately, not all "known" Internet sources have been keep in the extended memory of the library staff in the bookmarks file of the public use computer or have been incorporated into the Internet services section of our Internet and Intranet services.) The library staff member usually sits down at one of the public computers with Internet access with the user and explains the steps while carrying out the search. In this way, the library staff member points to the links set up in the library resource pages for the Internet and also, if appropriate, explains certain structures, address formation, discovery and retrieval mechanisms, etc., to the user. After successfully gaining the answer to the reference question, the user is asked if there is time and interest in a short introduction to the Library and Research Documentation Unit's Clearinghouse of Project-Oriented Internet Resources. If so, this is done using examples of project resource pages belonging to the user's research area, as well as the general resource pages for that research area. Usually, the quality of the resources is discussed and the method of "allowing" the library staff carry out the initial searching to compile a set of basic starting points for this topic rather than have the researcher spend hours "surfing" or moving according to the principle of serendipity to find the very specific topics he or she is looking for. We try to emphasize that this is an inefficient and often unproductive method of searching in the Internet and offer to carry out even interdisciplinary and vague searches on the Internet for the researcher.

Introduction to the Clearinghouse services is also done with a specific project group or group leader when starting a new Clearinghouse resource page on the topic of that project.(3) Appointments for individualized training on the Internet can be made which usually then focus on an introduction to the principle of distributed information, search methods for the Internet (subject trees, browsing, virtual libraries, clearinghouses and other collective sites), the advantages and disadvantages of search engines, use of external library catalogs and of tables of contents services.

Our library staff has also provided training in setting up HTML-pages for other areas of the Institute. This has been on an individual basis and geared to the user's specific needs. It is obvious, that both in searching the Internet and in the function of assisting in setting up HTML pages, overlap occurs between the activities of the computer department and the library. This has not proven to be a problem, but rather often has complemented each other as different types of needs were often met by the library as by the computer department.

3. CONTINUING EDUCATION INTERNET TRAINING FOR LIBRARIANS

To prepare them for the task of training users in using the Internet, as well as using the Internet in their daily work, several types of CE possibilities for Internet training for librarians are available:

1.Formal (external) seminars, training courses and workshops (non-librarian specific)
2.Formal CE courses at recognized librarian training institutions or other librarian-specific Internet courses
3.Self-tutorials on the Internet itself
4.Informal CE for librarians, such as
5.- in-service training
6.- utilization of networked discussion groups and forums

3.1. Formal (external) seminars, training courses and workshops (non-librarian specific)

These seminars, training courses and workshops in using the Internet are for the most part not geared to the specific needs of librarians, although they usually do include information searching, search engines, etc. Nevertheless, they are often focussed more on other user groups and tend to thus be more general and include more technical information than may be necessary for a librarian (unless he or she is also responsible for the technical installation and maintenance of the Internet connection). In Germany, they are usually advertised by postal mail, some are conducted by information management consultants (often formerly special librarians) and some are endorsed by the German Association of Documentalists (DGD) or a business accreditation unit. The cost per day is usually double or more the cost of an equivalent seminar or workshop conceived for and often by librarians.

Another important source of Internet training at the CE level are the academic professional societies such as the APA, the German Physicists Society, and the Society for Information in Education in Germany (Gesellschaft Information Bildung) among many others are offering workshops and seminars within their annual conferences or as satellite programs in using the Internet. These events include not only the basics, but also highly subject-specific resources and resource discovery tools. In addition, there are various conference sessions at professional conferences and at general conferences on further vocational and professional education which focus on the influence and effects of the Internet in changing the respective professions. New professional designations such as "Internet librarian" and "Information Manager of Networked Information Resources" or in Germany, for instance, "Informationstechniker" (Information technologist), have become officially accepted and represent the beginnings of structural changes within the profession, as well as the challenge to the librarian and information management professions by the technical and related professions. New competencies are required to meet these new challenges and to fit this new role.(4)

3.2. Librarian-specific Internet CE courses, Workshops and Seminars

Librarian-oriented courses are offered not only by librarian training institutions, professional librarian and documentalist associations (in Germany, but also by regional information specialist groups called working groups for information - "Arbeitskreis für Information"), and professional library, information, and documentalist associations. In addition, Internet training seminars and workshops have been held in connection with professional conferences. It may also include commercial courses on the Internet developed for librarians. Examples of such courses include D. Scott Brandt's "Training and the Internet - Techniques and Approaches" (Online Information 96, London, December 2, 1996) and other professional development seminars at librarian conferences. Such courses range from various workshops and introductory courses on using the Internet, mastering HTML, designing individual Web pages, and navigating in the Internet.

3.3. Self-tutorials on the Internet

There are a number of self-tutorials on the Internet, the most notable of which was Patrick Crispen's ROADMAP, a ca. 30-session systematic introduction to the tools of the Internet with assignments, quizzes and tests given via the Internet over the course of ca. 5 weeks. The ROADMAP became so popular that multiple courses were running simultaneously and extended over a period of ca. 9 months from September 1994 to May 1995. The course was offered free of charge and in the initial courses, Crispen offered to pursue requests for obtaining college credits for successful completion of the course from the University of Alabama where he was a graduate student. Unless he neglected to notify the author to the contrary, no credits were granted. After the ROADMAP, similar courses have been offered on the Internet, often at a price ranging from US $25.00 to US $ 400.00 per course. These are usually advertised in appropriate discussion lists or via email.

The Internet Learning Resources Directory (NetLearn) assembled by Iain Middleton at the Robert Gordon University in Aberdeen is a list of links to resources useful in teaching Internet skills, annotated with abstracts and also includes materials in languages other than English (5). The Internet Resource Centre at the Heriot-Watt University in Edinburgh http://www.hw.ac.uk/libWWW/irc/index.html) provides links to various information sources on the Internet for learning and research, as well as to the Internet Resources Newsletter (http://www.hw.ac.uk/libWWW/irn/irn.html).

The ROADS program in the United Kingdom, as part of a national electronic library program and furthered by the Joint Information Systems Committee, has as one of its goals to supply not only key sites for Internet users, but also offer Internet trainers who make up training materials and even hold training sessions upon request across Great Britain. The SOSIG site for social scientists demonstrates this very well (http://sosig.ac.uk/). Another well-developed branch of the ROADS program is OMNI (http://omni.ac.uk/) which parallels SOSIG, but is directed at the medical profession.

The self-tutorial for social scientists at SOSIG (http://sosig.ac.uk/training/training.html) has already been mentioned. This is less formal and serves as a helping tool. Reference materials and documentation are also available. Two training officers and the director can be contacted and serve as mentors for Internet use by social sciences researchers.

In mid-1996, information specialists at Loughborough University evaluated interactive packages on the Web for Internet training with the following results: "At the CTILIS centre we have been looking at this area and have ... evaluated a number of "packages" on the web for Internet training. What we have come across has been very disappointing. Many "packages" are not interactive ... but two packages which are quite good ... are: http://www.globalvillage.com/gcweb/tour.html and http://K12.cnidr.org:90/htmlintro.html."(6) Loughborough also hosts a collective site for library introduction web pages with activatable links directly to the respective (American and British) library guides (http://www.lboro.ac.uk/departments/dils/cti/cti.html).

3.4. Informal CE for Librarians on-the-job

If Internet is to be part of the librarian's daily work, it is logical that in-service training and on-the-job application of Internet skills be emphasized.

3.4.1. In-service Training Sessions

In-service training sessions have certain advantages over external training seminars. Equipment that will be part of the job routine is used for the training and is usually available for practice outside the sessions. In-service training can be highly flexible and scheduled in intervals, small groups, at times most suitable to the trainees. If personal from the institution design and teach the sessions, there is direct continuance of contact with the trainer for follow-up and problem-solving.

The topics treated in our library in-service training for the Internet include
About the Internet - what it is, what it can be used for in libraries
Electronic acquisitions: publisher pages, book seller pages gray literature, official
    publications, statistical sources, data sets, archival material, digitized material
Document delivery services
        (commercial) (SWETS, UNCOVER, etc.)
        library consortia
        by email request (Univ. Saarbrücken SSGPsychologie, etc.
        ISI, database-connected services with references (DIMDI, SWETS, etc.)
        Searching in other library catalogs
Tables of contents service for journals

Contact with other libraries (Exchanges, Desiderata)
Reference work: any currency question especially re: people, institutions, projects, other
  library catalogs, services
Bibliographic verification, book finding
Dates, upcoming events, quick reference questions
Keeping up with further developments in librarianship.

This last point is usually treated individually (according to interest and language ability) with a visit to the Website of D-lib: The Magazine of Digital Library Research (at three mirrored sites http://www.dlib.org/ or http://www.ukoln.ac.uk/dlib or http://sunsite.nla.edu.au/mirrors/dlib/) or Ariadne (http://www.ukoln.ac.uk/ariadne/) Regular reading of these two solely electronic journals in particular not only fulfills one of the basic self-motivated continuing education criteria in the CE package for professional improvement developed by the (British) Library Association, but also challenges the reader to keep abreast the rapid developments in the realm of digital libraries and Internet information management.

3.4.2. Networked Discussion Groups and Forums

Depending on the individual discussion group, mailing list or forum, the following aspects of professional development and continuing education can be achieved:
> currency on library developments ;leading edge knowledge of developments on the net; gaining knowledge of the leaders in the field ;self-serving referral system (ask the experts, even if some would-be experts answer); time-saving ready reference source; knowledge of new terminology; practice in English obtaining an overview of where projects are being conducted, new developments have been implemented one's own input and testing of ideas is welcomed co-operation & joint ventures which can grow out of the discussion group, etc.

As a result of using the in-service training for the librarian staff, approximately 10 months after beginning the in-service librarian training courses, library staff is using email to order books, articles and journals, claim missing issues of journals, place interlibrary loan orders, search in library catalogs, establish contact to other libraries either in response to a specific question or a general question in a mailing list, or placing a question in a mailing list to help gain information or establish a consensus, maintain contact with other similar libraries via several MPG-mailing lists and also other subject specific or task-specific internet area listservs. In addition, almost the entire library staff searches in other library catalogs online to verify the existence of a book being ordered or to augment the bibliographic information. The lists or direct mailing between libraries may consist of gift listings or journal duplicates or serve to establish contact with individual libraries or maintain working contacts. Certain library-work oriented listservs or discussion groups are subscribed to by various persons in our library, though with few exceptions, extensive knowledge of English is a prerequisite for participation in such lists. Activatable links from the title entry in our online library catalog lead to "live" tables of content from publishers and suppliers in the Internet. So far we have been able to provide a link to the tables of contents for over 100 of our 730 current periodicals, but the links have had to be entered separately. The most frequent use of the Internet as a search assistant for information discovery and retrieval is still for reference questions, although there is growing use of the Internet for literature acquisitions.

4. CONTENT OF CE TRAINING FOR THE INTERNET

Our experience shows that the following points are essential to conducting an Internet training session for library staff who will be using services on the Internet in the future and assisting users with Internet skills and services:
> theory of distributed information systems & how to use them effectively
> functions of a browser; what can one do with the Internet (and what can't one do)
> types of Web sites:
> collective Web sites such as gopher, subject tree, virtual libraries, clearinghouses or
>>   subject gateways
> institutional Web sites

> key sites for library use (booksellers, publishers, union catalogs, library opacs, library
> suppliers, newspapers)
> key sites for general reference questions
> document delivery sites using search engines and other discovery and retrieval
> techniques and tools
> understanding HTML, links, bookmarks, downloading, printing, drawbacks of these
> structures
> use of images / graphics
> producing electronic publishing / publishing on the Web.
> services in the Internet
> how to find names, institutions (Finger, WhoIs+)

Other aspects could be included, especially for those who must install and maintain their Web-site themselves:

> Winsocks
> Win32x.dll
> eMail-Programme (Pegasus, Eudora ...)
> WinFTP
> WinNewsreader
> Netscape (installation)
> WinWord 6.0 (conversion to HTML)
> HTML.DOT
> Java, Hot Java

These topics were included in some of the Max-Planck-wide Internet seminars for librarians in the MPG as a service of the central administration of the MPG by the library co-ordinator. However, by this more computer-oriented nature, as opposed to direct library-oriented tasks, this course could also be delegated to the computer department.

Library staff also assisted in making model HTML-pages for Institute Internet site and training non-library Institute staff to set up effective and economical HTML-pages.

5. CO-OPERATIVE PROJECT FOR INTERNET DISTANCE EDUCATION ON THE INTERNET

Plans for an international co-operation project to use existing CE Internet training materials from the University of New South Wales in Australia and offer them in English to German librarians via the Australian Centre in Potsdam co-ordinated with the Humboldt University in Berlin, Germany, were made by representatives of the these institutions. Discussion began in the spring and summer of 1995 for a joint project in spring of 1997. In the late summer of 1996, teaching staff of the two universities involved (Humboldt and University of New South Wales met to discuss the curriculum content, requirements for student participation, course requirements, and procedural issues. Though it was envisioned to do the course in 1997, we may not be able to offer it until 1998. At the time of writing this paper, we have not yet been able to schedule this course for the current semester. Establishing reciprocal acceptance of the credits for course work is difficult because of the different educational structures and system. It is hoped that this project will be able to be realized by the end of 1997 or early 1998, though due to the rapid development of new search engines, the rapid growth of the Internet, and the increased basic knowledge of many librarians, it may be necessary to revise the content and course requirements.

The topic of the Internet was chosen because of the medium itself as well as the individual autonomy of the student in working at his or her own pace, while still having the opportunity to have relatively quick contact and feedback with not only the class instructor, but also the regional mentor/tutor and the other students participating in the course. It was planned that a discussion list be set up among the students (instructors and mentors could also participate) taking the course, with direct one-to-one email contact between the individual student and his instructor and regional language mentor. All assignments would be done in context of the medium itself. Students would chose one of a set of three subject areas - preferably one related to his or her previous field of study or academic interests - and pursue the class assignments and larger, more evaluative projects in this. The quality and selection of criteria, search method and critique of various resource discovery and retrieval mechanisms should be included in the final project report. Individual search results and reports on the search methodology would be posted for all participants.

The level of the course was geared for practicing librarians basically without any previous knowledge or direct use of the Internet, as well as for students in the library science program. The participant does not even have to have direct access to the Internet as this would be provided by the Australian Centre or the Humboldt University. However, it will be beneficial to have such direct connection to the Internet before completion of the course, otherwise the skills learned will dissipate without continued use, challenge, and expansion. The course was also conceived for unemployed librarians and documentalists in the former GDR states of Germany who are offered additional opportunities to enhance their professional qualifications and obtain reciprocal recognition of their degrees.(7) Since many librarians in Germany have just confronted the Internet or are just now being connected, such a course at the CE level would be very beneficial.

The educational value of this project lies not only in its content, but also in its aspects of participation in a self-paced tutorial employing a hands-on approach to networked information training combined with tutor-mentoring by a German-language instructor. A second advantage is the direct use of English for the German students within the "working context". In addition, at the instructional and institutional level, we are exploring the practical application and establishment of reciprocal recognition of a course conceived in one culture and offered within the setting of totally different structures and language.

Parallel to traditional subject bibliography courses required by undergraduate subject degree programs, such courses could be designed by subject specialist librarians in the appropriate fields and then offered as continuing education courses for students and practicing professionals with the additional mentorship of librarians.

The entire area of distance learning, self-paced learning and other issues of learning within the environment of computer networks has itself been treated as a grouped distance learning experiment sponsored and designed by the Institute for Educational Psychology and Empirical Pedagogics at the Ludwig-Maximilian University of Munich (KOoperatives Arbeiten und Lernen An der Hochschule http://infix.emp.paed.uni-muenchen.de/nic/seminar.html). Other initiatives are growing, for instance 'The Virtual Academy of Further Training,' which is being developed in Germany to focus on teachers professional development especially in Internet skills.(8)

CONCLUSION

The role of the librarian in Internet training will be defined by his or her own initiative among the users. Internet training can be incorporated into library tours and introduction to library services. It can be offered as a variety of small sessions focussing on various aspects of Internet work, or it could be offered as a subject-specific introduction to finding resources on the Internet. It may be necessary to establish a good basis for co-operation with the computer department in the institution in order to avoid competition. Librarian in-service training and CE professional development can focus not only on information discovery and retrieval, but also using the Internet in all aspects of library work.

With the advance of the Internet, the edges separating information retrieval tasks formerly ascribed to the librarian and information science professionals are blurring at incredible speed with the edges of the computer scientists, the informatics and the subject-oriented professionals themselves. The surging amount of information retrieval activities, database design, navigational expertise and involvement in developing net-based products among non-librarian, non-informationalist professionals is posing the question of the role of the librarian: could the librarian at an academic institution become obsolete as book-oriented tasks succumb to digital publication and in the end be reduced to archival maintenance? Does it mean that the subject professional will surpass the librarian - who is often lacking the indepth subject knowledge of the subject professional - in retrieval competencies and circumvent the library as the Internet accumulates increasing amounts of scholarly work with quality criteria that still remain to be defined for determining the digital impact factor? In an article relatively early on the Internet training scene, Bob Filipczak emphasized the major effect of the Internet as a permanent learning environment and stated, "It's a logical place for a trainer or training department to assert leadership."(9) This leadership will be the characteristic that defines the information professions in the future and CE training especially in the area of the Internet will help maintain that leadership role.

FOOTNOTES

(1)   This included external courses or seminars, group or one-to-one training sessions taught by the Institute's computer unit.

(2)   For this purpose, we have built up a Clearinghouse for Project-Oriented Internet Resources (http://www.mpib-berlin.mpg.de/DOK/ech.htm), see also the literature list of articles describing the concept and development of our clearinghouse at http://www.mpib-berlin.mpg.de/DOK/echlite.htm. A similar service was developed at the Applied Physics Laboratory with their own Information Navigation System (INS). See Amy M. DeBrower and Robert F. Skinder: Designing an Internet Class for a Scientific and Technical Audience. *Special Libraries* 87 (1996), p. 143.

(3)   Diann Rusch-Feja: Subject-Oriented Collection of Information Resources from the Internet: A Clearinghouse Concept to Support Researchers in a German Research Institute. *Libri* (1997) (in press).

(4)   Jamshid Beheshti, Ein systematisches Trainingsprogramm fuer den Umgang mit den neuen Technologien in den Informationsberufen. *Bibliothek: Forschung und Praxis* 20 (1996) 40-49 (also in English in *Educational Libraries* (1996)). See also Bibliothekar/Bibliothekarin an wissenschaftlichen Bibliotheken, Diplom-Bibliothekar/Diplom-Bibliothekarin an oeffentlichen Bibliotheken. Bibliotheken im Zeitalter der Datenautobahnen und internationalen Netze - Arbeitsplaetze der Bibliothekare im Wandel. ibv (Informationen fuer die Beratungs- und Vermittlungsdienste der Bundesanstalt fuer Arbeit (ibv), 3/97, 15. Januar 1997, 187-200, esp. 191-192.

(5)   See the compilations on this subject by Iain Middleton: http://www.rgu.ac.uk/~sim/research/netlearn/callist.htm; as well as Kathleen King: http://www.ed.ac.uk/~kk/ol-cat/ol-www-training-materials.html.

(6)   Contribution from Tracy Hopkins (t.hopkins@lboro.ac.uk) to the lis-link Mailing list on July 30, 1996 "RE:INTERNET TRANING MATERIALS".

(7)   A CE program to enhance the professional qualifications of former GDR librarians, who worked in a different structure as librarians in the former West Germany, already exists at the Humboldt University. This program runs over two years parallel to a full-time job. The content was designed to supplement certain deficiencies and includes the topic of Internet within course units on bibliography, information retrieval, document delivery.

(8)   Michael Drabe: The Virtual Academy of Further Training. Verein Schulen ans Netz e.V., Koordinierungs- und Beratungsstelle, Bonn (http;//www.SaN-eV.de).

(9)   Bob Filipczak: Trainers on the Net. Training (December 1994), p. 44.

REFERENCES

Bibliothekar/Bibliothekarin an wissenschaftlichen Bibliotheken, Diplom-Bibliothekar/Diplom-Bibliothekarin an öffentlichen Bibliotheken. Bibliotheken im Zeitalter der Datenautobahnen und internationalen Netze - Arbeitsplätze der Bibliothekare im Wandel. ibv (Informationen fuer die Beratungs- und Vermittlungsdienste der Bundesanstalt fuer Arbeit (ibv), 3/97, 15. Januar 1997, pp.187-200.

Brandt, D. S. (1995), What Does "Teaching the Internet" Mean? Computers in Libraries 15(8) pp.34-35.

DeBrower, Amy M., and Robert F. Skinder (1996), Designing an Internet Class for a Scientific and Technical Audience. *Special Libraries*, 87 pp. 139-146.

Filipczak, Bob (1994), Trainers on the Net. *Training,* (December) pp. 42-51.

Koch, Traugott (1995), Die Rolle der Bibliothek im Zeitalter des Internet: Provokation und Nachdenken. *Nachrichten für Dokumentation,* 46 pp.231-240.

Kovacs, Diane K., Barbara F. Schloman, and Julie A. McDaniel (1994), A Model for Planning and Providing Reference Services Using Internet Resources. *Library Trends,* (Spring) pp. 638-647.

Lipow, Anne G., and Sheila D. Creth (eds.) (1995*), Building Partnerships: Computing and Library Professionals*. The Proceedings of Library Solutions Institute No. 3, Chicago, Illinois. May 12-14, 1994. Berkeley & San Carlos, CA: Library Solutions Press.

Ohles, Janet A. (1994), Tips for the New Internet Trainer. *SpeciaList* 17,11 pp.1, 14-15.

INFORMATION EXCHANGE AND COMMUNICATION BETWEEN RESEARCHERS : THE SPECIALISED LIBRARIAN'S PART IN SCIENTIFIC RESEARCH

Viviane Couzinet and Arlette Bouzon
Laboratoire d'Etudes et de Recherches Appliquées en
Sciences de la Société
Université Paul Sabatier IUT
France

Abstract: This study of PhD students' use of scientific journals is being carried out within the framework of a seminar on communication and information exchange. It is part of a larger project dealing with researchers' use of scientific journals. The methodology involved the use of questionnaires, interviews and bibliometric studies.

INTRODUCTION

"Professional techniques which may be most in frequently observed in a student environment have most of the time something common with magic"

(Bourdieu, Pierre and Passeron, Jean -Claude, 1985)

The documentary practices of experienced researchers and of undergraduate and graduates students are, in France, a field for scientific investigation and study in librarianship. But there remains to be made an analysis of the documentary practices of researchers as beginners (preparing a PhD : first year of thesis) as users of information, or as more experienced (preparing a PhD : after the first year of thesis) who are users, as well as producers of information. The works written on the subject are more than scarce indeed. Thus, postgraduate students constitute the reservoir of researchers and teachers for tomorrow, who will pursue their practices through the processes of knowledge elaboration they used when preparing their dissertation. Elaboration of the thesis constitutes for the young researcher the important test for training in the field of research as well as a career in research itself. The thesis is a long and exacting task which demands the candidate's energy for about three or four years, and it must make a significant contribution to the scientific field concerned, in the theory as well as in the practical results which are published. It is only when the postgraduate student has gone through this process that he may become an experienced researcher.

The bibliography itself represents a major element in the thesis. The bibliography not only reflects the work that has been done, but it will also and mainly be, a starting point for other researchers to work on. A bibliography is not a simple collection of references. It is processed according to certain rules with a wish for coherence, legibility, and credibility. It is constructed as a working tool for the future reader and eventually for a future researcher interested in the subject. It assists in evaluating the work being done, and justifies its scientific worth. A bibliography must be complete, ready to use, and accurate. The choice of the listed references in particular is not made at random. It contributes to recognition of the references by jury members and, in case of a thematic bibliography, to the valorisation of its contents.

Articles from scientific journals especially are much appreciated references - even though the situation varies according to the different fields of sciences and to the scientific value of the journals quoted - as they occupy a central place in the appropriation practice of the researcher. References from journals play a significant part in the scientific validation of the work as well as in the future career of the researcher, and in the acknowledgement of the institution where he is employed.

We will then focus our study on postgraduate students and on the way they prepare the bibliography for their thesis as, in doing so, they accomplish a full process of research. We will limit our study to the use of journals articles, as they are a precious source of up-to-date knowledge as well as a privileged source for on going research on a specific topic. In that way we will try to examine the behaviour the young researchers adopt when it comes to document retrieval and what is their use of the scientific journals. But taking into account the present state of lack of investigation (theoretical and practical) on the postgraduate attitude towards reading, and documents chasing, the role of the information specialist in this process is less than clear and studying his role is a tricky job. We will nevertheless try to define the information officer's task as it is today, and to outline what it could be in the future when the construction of the thesis bibliography is carried out.

We start from the hypothesis that when the postgraduate student has received a training in information retrieval his practice in looking for what he needs changes for more autonomy, and his methodology for searching for bibliographic references and selecting adequate information improves. He becomes more secure and asks for some help from the information specialist. On the contrary if the postgraduate student works and stays alone with his investigations, his information retrieval practices stay approximate without any possible improvement. He will tend to ignore any proposal to be educated, and will not ask the information officer for help. Nevertheless in France, access to methods and methodologies of information retrieval essentially goes through the information specialist. In fact the teaching staff have generally little, if no time, to spare for methodology training. We will rely on the results of a study we led in Toulouse (the second university city in France) among the research group of the LERASS (*Laboratoire d'Etudes et de Recherches Appliquées en Sciences Sociales*) named "Information Communication between researchers" in the framework of a research program started in 1994 on the use of scientific journals by postgraduate students. As a first step we will focus on the role of the information specialist. Then we will analyse the documentary practices of the postgraduate students when they come to writing their thesis bibliography. Finally, we will study the role the information specialist could fulfil in the knowledge building process.

1. ROLE OF THE INFORMATION SPECIALIST INSIDE THE LIBRARY

Among the works that enlighten the contingent circumstances influencing scientific production, the sociology of sciences asserts that the social field interferes at the heart of the scientific content. The sociology of sciences insist on the social construction of scientific facts, focusing on the relevance of the networks the researcher will build to pursue and validate his investigation. We have centred on the place the information specialist occupies in the process of scientific production of postgraduate students. We will try to answer this question in studying the behaviour of researchers in information communication science. What are their dependency relationships with the information officer, what part they play in the process of scientific elaboration, this through quantitative tools especially bibliometrics?

1.1 General organisation of the library

In order to meet all the needs of the library users the information specialist must buy documents and has to keep alive the library collection. We see that today the documents available are numerous in term of quantity as well as in term of different types. The information officer has to ensure that documents are collected, classified, indexed and entered in the bibliographic catalogue. According to the changes in technologies of information and communication, organising and structuring the various fields of knowledge, as well as simplifying access to knowledge, is a vital issue. Except for a few uncommon cases, most of the documents have to be bought. The information specialist has to keep informed on what is published, what is commercially available, and to make choices according to the budget he handles and the requests he receives.

For the researcher, the information officer's role consists in giving him assistance with the retrieval. With this aim, he must listen to the query, he must have a dialogue with the researcher to guide him and assist him at every step of his investigation. But the information specialist might go beyond this assistance and provide the researcher with a method of information retrieval, as well as informing him of the main books and journals to be consulted step by step, helping him with the indexing vocabulary, with the use of the catalogue, or when dealing with an interlibrary loan.

The information specialist can also act by giving advice on the constitution and listing of the final bibliography of the thesis. But this pedagogical function is still not developed enough in France, and the kind of training that goes with it - a methodological training is too often missing.

1. 2. Educating in order to practice information retrieval.

It seems that there is a lack - complete or partial according to the different cases - in knowing the opportunity for assistance with information retrieval that the specialised library staff may provide.

The majority of postgraduate students indeed tend to ignore the capability of the specialised librarians, among them especially those of the university library staff. The staff from the university library appears to them to be less close than the staff of their own unit or laboratory. So it does appear that the help they may receive from the university library staff is less helpful than those of their research colleagues. As a consequence we do not observe a maximal use of the library resources by the researchers. One of the main reasons for this situation is that few researchers have benefited from training classes on how to chase books and journals, whoever the organiser might have been. If some privileged persons have had some training inside their laboratory, less than half of the postgraduate students (41%) of those surveyed (69 young researchers have been respondents) have attended a one day (at least) class of informative instructions on how to find the right information. Those who have attended did so more because the offer was there, than because they felt a need to look actively for this kind of training.

Half of the postgraduate students we questioned though, felt that their paper chase practices were good enough ; this tends to confirm the lack of interest in getting a proper training, not to speak of the lack of feeling towards the need to do so... Although the postgraduate student sees his career as the one of a researcher.

But taking into account the small number of researchers trained by specialised institutions, how does the researcher find the capacity to acquire for himself the existing resources ? Knowledge on available resources when it is there and whichever way it has been found should be related with systematic methods of information retrieval, more efficient in our opinion than empirical ones, and with the knowledge of what is a scientific journal. Thus the more trained a researcher is and informed on the available resources the more he is close to a network of searchers (friends, teachers) with whom he can regularly exchange information even though he may not be working within a research group (65 % of the researchers do not work in a research group). Postgraduate students who make most use of the library resources are the same as those who use scientific journals more than the others. These students go often (twice a month at least) to the library and stay there one hour (35 %) two hours or more (62%). They know which resources are available in the library. They use them, they use on-line databases, CD-ROM and they vary their sources of information in order to put a hand on the scientific literature (articles) needed. They make a systematic use of the university library catalogue, and often visit the library in their unit. The majority of them read more than three articles a month, photocopy them when possible, make interlibrary loan requests regularly, and take notes when reading.

These postgraduate students know that a journal is a periodical publication in which researchers publish the results of their investigations. So they use the journals for their study and to keep and update the knowledge they have. They know how to use the possibilities of existing services and do not need to take out personal subscriptions to scientific journals as they find what they need inside the library, making great use of the photocopying machine. On the other hand they might frequently buy a single issue of the scientific journal if it contains a specific author they are interested in (39%) covers a literature review, or gets deep into a theoretical model. Nevertheless these researchers scarcely request help from the information specialist. Even if half of the investigated group would welcome a training in document retrieval, the situation is such that 80 % of the persons questioned do not make a request; among them we find the postgraduate students that take no initiatives to be better informed or better educated and those who admit they ignore the available resources. The demand appears to be less than secured. What about the offer generating the demand ?

1. 3. The information specialist : a mediator?

The sociology of sciences has put social data into knowledge building, while differentiating the social from the cognitive. In the same move those studies which enlighten the contingent circumstances affecting scientific production (traditions, ideology, personal interest) a new stage has been passed, in asserting that social interferes at the heart of scientific contents. The identity of the scientific statement does not depend upon its existence in the absolute, but upon the sociocultural network in which it is inverted. Besides a scientific statement acquires the status of a scientific fact only if it is accepted *a posteriori* by the scientific community. The success of an investigation is thus linked to the network of relations that the scientist or the group of scientists will establish to support his works and obtain a large adhesion. The sociology of sciences theories insist in that way on the social construction of scientific facts and on the capacity the researcher has to defend his view points.

They centre on the networks relevance the researchers will have built and organise to valorise their investigation in an often broader environment than the scientific environment itself. It is in that frame that the information specialist acts with his capacity to help the postgraduate student in the constitution of this sociocultural network in which the postgraduate student tries to invert.

The knowledge of retrieval tools by postgraduate students does not seem well established. If more than half of them use systematic retrieval in catalogues, in the university library, or in their unit library, or laboratory library, they do so in a move which is erratic rather than orderly and which does not suppose a previously acquired methodology. They consult by themselves the catalogue and CD-ROM available. To question databases, they ask for the help of a person in the university library or in their laboratory. But this kind of query is not that much used as they give preference to the use of CD-ROM. We may suppose it is because CD-ROM does not require the intervention of a third party and provides free access, that they like it. But this media carries the question about the updating of the information it contains. If they are ready to rely on their peers and their thesis directors to find the adequate references, the young researchers still rely mostly on themselves. Truly enough a bibliography is a personal construction depending largely upon the studied subject.

The postgraduate students will equally ask their library staff or their professors. When an information retrieval training has been delivered inside the research laboratory where the postgraduate student works, this training has come with specific help on how to prepare a bibliography. This personalised work in order to accompany the new researcher, links closely the information specialist and the thesis director. This education goes for an enrichment of information retrieval practices : educated persons will make a larger use of databanks than of CD-ROM.

2 . CONSTRUCTION OF THE BIBLIOGRAPHY

The situation in which a student starting an investigation finds himself is the situation of a person completely overwhelmed by a large quantity of information with which he does not know where to start. His first work consists of building a basic bibliography on the studied subject. This bibliography will then be completed and refined until the final writing of the thesis. The student will then progressively build his research strategy. He will start with looking at general books acquiring knowledge of specific indexing vocabulary, then he will go and look at more specialised bibliographies, specific and current, sometimes scattered, in order to read the corresponding quoted documents. The formal listing of selected references will constitute the bibliography of the thesis and will be observed, discussed, eventually criticised when the thesis is presented. The specialised librarian may be an active person at all the stages of the investigation providing useful help. But the reality is often different. The documentary practice of postgraduate students reveals itself to be approximate enough. The part the information specialist plays, strongly linked to the limited way the postgraduate student sees him, is nearly non existent.

2. 1. The bibliography : helper to advanced research

The paper chase practices of postgraduate students are linked to a project (the thesis) which demands a coherent organisation for continued investigation. Thus the information retrieval know-how is first a material technique but it is not only a technique to search information, it is also a technique to make good use of contents, an intellectual technique which facilitates knowledge appropriation.

The word " bibliography " at first meant the physical knowledge of books "*biblion*" being the written document and " *graphein*" the description knowledge. In France to the word " bibliography " is opposed to the word "bibliology "which represents the theoretical knowledge about books (Meyriat, 1993). Bibliography is at the same time a technical knowledge for information professionals as well as the object resulting from it. In this study we will choose the terminology "references list" according to Jean Meyriat's recommendation. Jean Meyriat separates the lists of consulted documents which accompany most of the manuals and articles written for scientific purpose, from those written by information specialists. For the latest, AFNOR (*Association Française de normalisation)* definition is well adapted *"identification and documents description techniques, and classification of obtained documents"* (AFNOR, 1987) . Indeed, in the case that is of interest to us here, we care to adjust the descriptive instructions of the consulted documents to their function. These are not dedicated to inform various users with different objectives such as head librarians, archivists, booksellers or publishers, but to inform jury members, professors evaluating the postgraduate student work or peers i. e. other postgraduate students looking for references. For those, the physical description of the document will need to be simple enough, but other information will be given regarding the scientific contents of the documents (Meyriat, 1993). This role being played, for example, by an organisation of the subject of the bibliographic references. We will talk about the thesis bibliography as a helper for advanced research (Malclés, 1976). Indeed the thesis reference list aims at completing a work with relevant readings. It should prove the student's good knowledge of the investigation field, his ability to show that the study he makes brings innovative information through quoted references referring to an existing model. The student in that way possesses strong enough information to answer the jury's questions.

So, even if the bibliography is valuated with little consideration the effort it has cost is praised, as this bibliography is seen as useful and essential to intellectual research. The young researcher must prove he is able to acquire for himself the indispensable knowledge and in order to do so, he should be able to establish a list of the documents with which he nourished his investigation. This work done *a priori* and *a continuo* is a complete part of the investigation activity. The bibliography constitutes one of the material techniques for the intellectual work. These techniques are appreciated by Pierre Bourdieu and Jean-Claude Passeron, as they are professional techniques - used by the researcher - and without those intellectual work would only proceed from magic.

2. 2. A proof logic associated with a quantity logic

Scientific knowledge is no longer viewed as an accumulation of knowledge which would pile up and still we observe a great increase in the number of citations the past ten past years. We examined 28 thesis reference lists for 1984-1986 and 28 for 1994. For the majority of the thesis in the 1980's the references quoted were on average 175; this average reached 330 in 1994. The field examined, information and communication sciences, being still newly studied in France, the abundance of references is not a reflection of the scientific production but the recourse to other disciplines. This inflation is still emphasised by the fact that bibliographic references are listed by subjects inside subjects categories which lead to repeating documents references as long as they approach several aspects of the investigated field.

The introduction of investigation materials and tools facilitates this inflation. On the dissertations references list we observed that 52 % mix bibliography, research materials and research tools. If the specificity of the field studied might lead to confusion, studies relying basically on books or journals, show quite often in the references part, it was reported from interviews carried out during the survey. Bibliographical references are different from the research material - even though the latest list is also printed - which constitutes the starting point for observations. We are talking here of panels, a corpus, which are sometimes scrutinised with a magnifying glass, object of calculation and various analyses in order to prove the validity or inexactitude of an hypothesis. In the same way bibliographical references for the thesis differentiate themselves from research materials. Indeed references list are what we call " secondary documents" *documents that include signaletical or analytical data on source document,* or "tertiary documents" which are either *a synthesis of primary documents or a group of citations describing or analysing secondary documents (bibliography of bibliographies)"* (AFNOR, 1987).

Information retrieval tools which allow the access to the description of documents which will serve as the thesis bibliographical references and research materials form the same raw material the researcher extracts data from in order to analyse it. The postgraduate student who, paradoxically has taken himself on a path which leads to the career of a researcher does not make much use of the existing university papers or research production material : thesis, seminars papers, working papers. All these works seem to be ignored by young researchers, the same with proceedings of congresses or conferences.

When the postgraduate student is questioned, he says he reads a lot on his research subject, but also out of it, associating the reading of books as well as the reading of scientific journals. He seems to live through a bulimia of readings ; this bulimia goes along with trusting the professorial staff what ever the discipline taught, but it does not include the information specialist.

2. 3. A hardly noticeable advance in the scientific approach which does not care for the future reader.

Seen as a working instrument, the bibliography is not built once for all at the starting point of the investigation. Based on fundamental documents written in the field, the bibliography enriches itself on its way, refines itself though the working advance, and finally develops to thinner and thinner ramifications. This advance appears in a thematic presentation of references and serves as a working tool for the thesis evaluation. It is through the observation of this advance that evaluation takes place : evaluation that the important authors have been read, that network links have been seen, evaluation of the kind of approach. Little importance is given to the future reader as evaluator or novice research worker. This weakness is emphasised by the intricate way in which the references are shown. The general organisation does not care for the future reader. From 1994 on, the most common presentation for the references of a thesis is the thematic one. But it is often a doubtful thematic distribution including sometimes the media as a theme even though it is not the object of the query, or listing authors inside themes with an approximate alphabetical order. Bibliographical citations, sometimes not sufficient, may also prove incomplete. It is not always possible to identify the quoted document. Footnotes and bibliographical references are often confused. Bibliography shows itself with a number of "*opere citato* " which refer to several previous references, leaving the reader puzzled, as to the way to discover the quoted document is less than clear. But we also encountered virtuosi who easily combine alphabetical order, thematical distribution and media referencing.

3 THE ROLE OF THE INFORMATION SPECIALIST IN KNOWLEDGE BUILDING

3. 1. An offer which needs to be improved

Students which are at the same time research workers are not an homogeneous category. More than ever these are complex groups, numerous, intricate and changing as well. The information specialist will have to differentiate between them and adapt to researcher demand. Tomorrow even more than today, indeed the student, and of course the advanced researcher have already their subject basic knowledge that should be taken into account so as to complement it. The specialised librarian's role will be to listen and translate the request from the researcher, to have a dialogue with him in order to give a hierarchy to the elements requested and to guide and direct him at every stage of his work. As a first step the postgraduate student will need to be trained in paper chase techniques. A method will have to be shown to him as well as an indication of the main titles and tools he should work with, this all along with the working process. Then it will be needed that he receives a punctual help adapted to his specific demand. The information specialist approach will be a different one if he has to deal with an experienced researcher. Indeed a progression exists in the information retrieval process in a research strategy, in knowledge building. Learning how to differentiate between the demands is a necessity in order to give a correct answer.

Besides the investigation demands that the research worker uses different bibliographical instruments and moves from one another he will have to identify them in order to make use of them. The information officer may help to locate the main references or to foresee other trails to be investigated, but he should in our opinion, go beyond the answers to a query. He cannot just take care of the explicit requests and must propose a differentiate offer, causing demands of training. We have seen indeed how paradoxical can be the behaviour of some of the postgraduate students we questioned they were badly educated, satisfied though with their documentary practices as they knew no other and could not imagine they existed other ways. It is then a need to define a dynamic role for the information specialist which does not limit itself to providing information. This role should include the proposal of adequate training for references searching training being based on a cautious analysis of the demand expressed in interviews or group inquiries.

3. 2. Linking information and communication

What ever kind of information should be processed it cannot be dissociated from the communication means allowing to transcribe it. The communication includes the relationship aspect but also the technical knowledge being used. The coming of new medias and new information technologies will request from the information specialist an even more professional attitude to avoid the problem that the young searcher looses time, money, energy or be disillusioned. These technologies indeed constitute an excellent way to produce, disseminate, and dispatch information. They are also associated with a magic image which might lead to forget we speak only about tools... to be tamed. Information retrieval is also a time for communication between the postgraduate student and the information specialist who are interacting. If the information officer is ready to welcome the postgraduate student demands - an attitude allowing whatever questions to rise - the interaction will be rich enough and for the more efficient for the paper chase approach of the young researcher. Thus it will help the latest, and bring a lot of interest in the work of the information specialist.

3.3. Asserting the information specialist role in the information and communication network

The information specialist is not always seen as a full partner and he cannot alone undertake the different tasks we just mentioned. He must be inverted in a network including the teaching staff and among them the thesis director. Some research laboratories already include the information specialist in the work with postgraduate students, and have specific bibliographic instruction with individual accompaniment. These institutions are few in number, and this is to the regret of information specialist.

Besides today's postgraduate students are tomorrow researchers and they will go along with their current information retrieval practices, if the information officer doesn't take care. To remedy to this present state, one solution should be considered : to make a general use of education at a lower level of studies (masters degree for example) including the information specialist collaboration.

CONCLUSION

The information officer's position is nowadays changing and we can think of what this role will be tomorrow. The coming of new tools for information delivery will greatly change the situation. With the Internet for example, should we expect duplication or not of information delivery? The Internet might convert each researcher into a knowledge coproducer in a process of collective understanding.

Our research in its development brings out new questions to which we will have to answer. We intend to continue the reflection started during the 1994 LERASS seminar by a new one year seminar which will allow us - we hope - to look deeper into the results we obtained and to elaborate proposals for training in information retrieval. But the relevance of these proposals rely at first on a good knowledge of the erratic postgraduate students information retrieval practices. The librarian will then find himself in a position to offer the young researchers efficient daily helpers and training programs adapted to present or potential demands. Not only will he be seen as a specialist of information processing and dissemination who knows how to integrate new technologies, but also as a training person teaching reasoned practices of information retrieval. In changing his functions the information officer will have his role in the information communication network between searchers consolidated.

NOTE

[1] This university research group in France brings together teachers and researchers specialising in information communication science who train information officers.

REFERENCES

AFNOR (1987), *Vocabulaire de la Documentation*, Paris: AFNOR.

Bourdieu, Pierre and Passeron, Jean-Claude (1985), *Les Héritiers : les Etudiants et la Culture*, Paris: Les Editions de Minuit.

Boure, Robert (1992), "Le territoire incertain des revues scientifiques", in: La revue de sciences sociales et humaines, actes du séminaire : "la communication et l'information scientifique entre spécialistes"(1991-1992). Toulouse : *LERASS*, 1992. Vol.1, pp. 5-16.

Couzinet, Viviane, Bouzon, Arlette and Normand, Raoul (1995), "L'usage des revues scientifiques par les doctorants : entre démarche autonome et démarche erratique", in : *Lectures à l'Université, Langue Maternelle, Seconde et Etrangère, Toulouse* : Université des Sciences Sociales,15 et 16 September 1995 (in press).

Couzinet, Viviane, Bouzon, Arlette and Normand, Raoul (1996), "Les doctorants livrés à la recherche documentaire : la pratique de la revue scientifique", *Bulletin des Bibliothèques de France*, 41 (6), pp.54-59

Malcles, Louise-Noëlle (1976), *Manuel de Bibliographie*. 3 rev. ed., Paris : PUF.

Meyriat, Jean (1993), "La bibliographie" in: Robert, Estivals (ed.), *Les Sciences de l'Ecrit* : *Encyclopédie Internationale de Bibliologie*, Paris : Retz pp. 548-553.

INFORMATION SKILLS TEACHING IN THE AGE OF THE ELECTRONIC LIBRARY IN THE UNITED KINGDOM: IMPLICATIONS OF THE IMPEL2 ELIB AND OTHER RELATED ELIB PROJECTS

Graham Walton, Joan Day and Catherine Edwards
University of Northumbria at Newcastle

Abstract: This paper includes a review of the international literature on information skills teaching in the electronic library. It is followed by a description of the IMPELI project, an overview of the Electronic Libraries (eLib) programmes in the United Kingdom, and the IMPEL2 project specifically. Findings relating to information skills teaching in the electronic library will be examined and other relevant programmes will be described

INTRODUCTION

In the United Kingdom an electronic list was established in 1996 to engender discussion on the subject of information skills [lis-infoskills@mailbase.ac.uk]. Initially there was very little debate until a colleague of mine at the University of Northumbria, Ian Winship made the following statement:

> I have infoskilled for many years and believe that much of what we do,
> especially at the induction stage, is a waste of everybody's time....
>
> Please convince me that I am wrong! (Winship, 1996).

This succeeded in galvanising the list members into a wide ranging debate on the purpose, priorities and value of information skills. Much of the debate focused on the influence of electronic information sources on information skills teaching in higher education libraries. Looking through the archives of this list since Winship's original statement will provide a wide range of differing views on the areas.

This paper will include a review of the international literature on information skills teaching in the electronic library. This will be followed by background on the IMPEL1 project at the University of Northumbria at Newcastle (UNN). There will also be an overview of the Electronic Libraries (eLib) programmes in the United Kingdom and the IMPEL2 project specifically. Findings relating to information skills teaching, in the electronic libraries from IMPEL1 and IMPEL2 will be examined. Finally other relevant eLib programmes concerning information skills teaching will be described.

LITERATURE REVIEW

Information skills, end user instruction, bibliographical instruction, information literacy, user education: the concept of librarians teaching users the range of skills needed to retrieve, analyze and evaluate information is an area that provokes great debate. The following are an indication of the strength of views and opinions on the subject:

- Librarians need to develop 'more skills in promoting active learning and be prepared to give up control and encourage student led learning' (Atton, 1994).

- "....librarians will be involved in service to 'users' - that is, consumers of educational services - of a much more direct kind than hitherto"(Line, 1993).

- "Goals have changed from teaching tools to teaching concepts and from library instruction to information literacy and lifelong learning" (Tiefel, 1995).

- "Until academic libraries adopt an educational function as central focus of its service, user education will continue to be ineffective and academic libraries will continue to remain peripheral to the educational mission of the institution" (Wilson, 1994).

- "Information literacy will not be a unitary condition that one either possesses or does not; it will be a continuing process of learning, and instruction will be called upon to prepare students not only for the time they are in the education system but for a lifetime in the information age" (Dusenbury and Pease, 1995).

The importance of information skills teaching for students is loudly trumpeted by some authors. Atkinson and Scott (1995) argue that they are core skills because of the growing importance of resource based learning and the development of flexible and open learning styles. The concept of life-long learning is seen by Tiefel (1995) as the rationale for information skills programmes so users can become more efficient/effective and independent in their information seeking. The increase in the use of project work and tutorials justifies the development of information skills programmes.

Some writers have produced overviews of the area and also identified directions that should be taken. In 1986 Fleming wrote a review of United Kingdom literature on academic user education written between 1991 and 1985 (Fleming, 1986). In a far reaching article Tiefel (1995) describes the historical development of user education in the United States and makes various predications. This forecast approach is carried through by Dusenbury and Pease (1995). They look at how the information seeker, the technology and resources and the library/librarian will change. The focus is the interaction of these areas and how they will influence library instruction. A balanced review is supplied by Downard (1992). In her attempt to answer the questions on user education about why?, what form? and how? she concludes that despite all the research there is little consensus. A survey was undertaken in 1995 to establish an overview of user education for new library users and for existing library users in the UK HE sector (Hopkins, 1995). The initial analysis highlights the increase in demand.

In some cases librarians describe the user education programmes that they have established in their own institutions. Odini (1994) describes the constraints he works with when running the instructional programme at Moi University in Kenya. Another author outlines the development of a comprehensive orientation programme for education students at the University of Nevada (Master, 1995). A detailed information skills programme is examined by Atkinson and Scott (1995).

A common theme that emerges is the need for information skills programmes to be integrated into the curriculum if they are to be successful. Bober (1995) uses various studies which indicate that academic colleagues have a reluctance in accepting information skills as part of the curriculum. For the benefits of undergraduates McConnell (1993) argues that both "academic staff and librarians need to be involved in the arduous task of integrating library use and classroom instruction". Master (1995) identified the need for integration from the literature and used this to help plan the information skills programme she devised. The need for integration is again identified and stressed by Fleming in his review (1996).

Various librarians have used educational theories to underpin the structure and approach of the user education programmes they have devised. Critical thinking has been identified by several authors as an important concept. The major theorist in this area is Bodi (1988). Others have taken her ideas and employed them in structuring their own sessions (Atton, 1994; Walton and Nettleton, 1992). The principles of androgogy (adult learning) have been used by Wilson (1994) to structure an information skills programme. Kolb's experiential learning cycle was applied by Atkinson and Scott (1995) in their information skills teaching.

Evaluating user education programmes is regarded by many authors as essential but they acknowledge it is problematical. Werking (1980) completed a review of current thoughts in a 1980 evaluation. Bober et al (1995) proceeded to review the literature from 1980 to 1993. A pattern of limited systematic evaluation is described in both articles. The issue of few studies establishing the long term effects of user education is highlighted. Despite the difficulties in evaluation, librarians involved with teaching students are exhorted that 'outcomes assessment is one of the most important issues on the horizon' (Dusenbury and Pease, 1995).

A significant development in recent history is the development and adoption of information technology in information skills teaching. At Ohio State University the 'Gateway to Information' was developed by the Library (Tiefal, 1995). It is an expert system which allows students, via the OPAC, to 'identify, find, evaluate, and select the most useful information for their needs'. The CTILIS (Computers in Teaching Initiative Library and Information Science) survey (Hopkins, 1995) identified an increase in the use of computer based training packages. They provide a well argued justification for the continued development of these packages. Creanor and Dumdell (1994) describe the development and content of four computer assisted learning (CAL) packages designed to teach information skills in higher education. The potential of new communication technologies to integrate effective user education for remote students in Australia is explored by Wilson (1994).

Another area that has developed is the blurring between information skills and information technology (IT) skills. A somewhat idiosyncratic perspective on information technology skills teaching is given by Wall (1993). He does advise that the library should be involved: "anything the library is willing to take on that you can agree - go for it". Day (1991) provided a review of the provision of library use instruction for electronic information use. The increase in demand for end user services identified by East (1993) must have some implications for information skills teaching. Heijne (1992) identifies some of the problems in using networked information services and stresses the need for support from the library. The development of CD-ROM technology has posed specific problems for information skills teaching. Reese (1994) outlines very practical steps about how end users of CD-ROM can receive quality instruction. Challenges of different levels of IT, different cultural background and different learning styles will increase with the availability of CD-ROM (Jackson-Brown, 1993). Other librarians have become involved in teaching skills to students about Internet access (Rockman, 1993).   Sophisticated teaching laboratories in libraries have been developed specifically to teach these electronic information skills (Vasa and La Guardia, 1994). The initial stages of a project to develop CAL packages for using such sources as BIDS and CD-ROM have outlined recently (Wood et al, 1995).

It is likely that the issues surrounding information skills will continue to provoke the kind of debate described. Many authors agree that the demand for librarians to teach information skills will increase (Hopkins, 1995; Jackson-Brown, 1993; Tiefal, 1995). What will be interesting will be how librarians cope with this increase in a climate where a corresponding increase in resources is unlikely. Pacey (1995) has provoked considerable debate about 'user education' or 'information skills teaching.' He argues that user education is flawed, for instance in consisting 'far too much of training in how to jump over hurdles which ought not to have been there in the first place' and in the way it tends to be conducted in a vacuum, not answering the real needs arising from a student's course or project. He suggests that the creation of the 'self-explanatory library' would enable the encouragement of an environment where information skills are 'learned' rather than 'taught.' The debate will no doubt continue.

IMPELI

The IMPEL Project (IMpact on People of Electronic Libraries), now referred to as IMPELI was a 2 year project run from the UNN. Its subject was the human aspects of increased electronic provision in academic libraries. The study was managed jointly by the Department of Information and Library Management (DILM) and the Information Services Department (ISD), itself a fully converged library, computing and management information service. It focused on the impacts of electronic services on library and information service (LIS) staff working in an increasingly volatile Higher Education sector. IMPELI commenced in December 1993. The work was based on six higher education library case studies, sites being chosen by purposeful sampling rather random sampling. At total of 82 semistructured interviews took place with a range of library and related support staff. These were underpinned by questionnaires and scrutiny of documentation from each institution. IMPELI asked two basic questions:

- What are the impacts on you, your work and your environment of an increasingly electronic campus?
- What are the key issues surrounding the management of an increasingly electronic campus?

Information skills teaching did emerge as a key area for subject librarians. Other key issues that were indicated in IMPELI included:

>Contextual issues
>Institutional issues
>Strategic issues
>Organizational issues

Impacts on staff
Training and development
Impacts on users
Technological issues
Management of change
Cultural change

The approach was essentially exploratory and therefore very qualitative (Edwards, 1995 a-d). Interviews are in-depth, semi-structured, open and flexible, designed to get close to the real experience of people and the meanings behind their experience.

UK ELECTRONIC LIBRARIES PROGRAMME

In 1992 in the UK the Joint Funding Councils for Higher Education set up a Libraries Review Group under the Chair of Sir Brian Follett (Vice-Chancellor of the University of Warwick). It was established to review the future needs of academic libraries. The increasing availability of electronic information was a key factor in their deliberations. The findings of the Review emerged in what has become known as the 'Follett report' (Report, 1993). Many of its recommendations related to how libraries can cope with increasing demands on their services through information technology in electronic library. The Joint Information Systems Committee (JISC) established the eLib Programme. £15 million has been allocated for eLib over three years with a view to use IT to:

- improve delivery of information through increased use of electronic library services
- allow academic libraries to cope better with growth explore
- different models of intellectual property management encourage
- new methods of scholarly publishing

The eLib Programme Director, Chris Rusbridge, has given an overview of the work (1995). As at November 1996, 60 projects have been funded. They have been organized into seven broad areas: electronic document and article delivery, electronic journals, digitization, on demand publishing, training and awareness, access to network resources and supporting studies. The eLib URL is:

http://ukoln.bath.ac.uk/elib

IMPEL2: A JISC-FUNDED ELIB PROJECT

Following IMPELI funding was received from eLib for a two and half year continuation and expansion of the work under IMPELI, subtitled 'Monitoring Organizational and Cultural Change'. IMPEL2 is one of eLib's Supporting Studies. The scope has been broadened from IMPELI by approaching the subject from 5 directions:

- Project A: Impacts of the electronic library on library and related support staff (a longitudinal study)
- Project B: Impacts on academic staff and student users
- Project C: Impacts of Resource Based Learning policies on library and information services
- Project D: Monitoring the impact of the staff development needs of library staff
- Project E: Evaluating the impact and effectiveness of the Netskills and EduLib eLib projects

This has expanded the number of sites visited from the 6 in IMPELI to at least 28. IMPEL2 will be a much broader and deeper study than IMPELI but it adopts the same qualitative methodology as the earlier project. The projects are not completely different projects but contribute to one whole, as expressed diagramatically:

LIS staff

New roles   Technology   Teaching &
                          Cultural change   Learning

                              Users

At the centre of the circle linking lis, their new roles, the users of electronic information and trends in teaching and learning, are technology and cultural change. In this way it is clear how all the elements are inter-related and in-fact inseparable. They are all part of the changing culture in Higher education. This change involves the impacts of technology, trends in teaching and learning, the impacts of the mass higher education system coupled with financial stringency, quality issues relating to the academic curriculum and to research and increased accountability. Increased reliance on student centred learning, for whatever reason, means that students have to be proficient in information skills. Where the librarian fits into this process is central to IMPEL2. The IMPEL2 URL is:

http://www.unn.ac.uk/-liw5/impel2.html

INFORMATION SKILLS TEACHING AND THE OUTCOMES FROM IMPEL1 AND IMPEL2

An ever-increasing amount of electronic information requires students to have greater skills in information retrieval, analysis and evaluation. This, together with the growth in student-centred learning has meant that libraries are coming under increasing pressure to provide access, resources and support to end-users. The IMPELI project which looked at the IMpact on People of Electronic Libraries identified a number of key issues.

The amount of information skills teaching that is required by end-users varies quite considerably depending on a number of factors, such as the level of information skills they already have and the type of information they need to access. Some courses are more reliant on electronic services than others and require students to use their IT skills more frequently. IMPEL I highlighted the fact that there are varying levels of IT expertise and awareness among students and academic staff users. Many users were found to have a low level of IT skills: this was particularly so in the case of mature students.

Although all the institutions recognised the importance of user education, the amount and type of information skills teaching provided by institutions varied somewhat. All the institutions provided one to one instruction when required, but structured user education programmes generally consisted of various levels of end-user training to suit the needs of users at a particular time. Some user education programmes were found to be too ambitious in the amount of time and effort required and were later modified. The main difficulty in the provision of user education programmes was in the timing of the sessions: these should be given when the user needs the information.

The implications for library staff, particularly subject specialists, were that jobs were changing as they took on more of a teaching role and were expected to have more IT-related skills. Many staff felt that their current skills were not adequate. Liaison between library staff and computing staff varied, with some working jointly on information skills teaching programmes and others having no contact whatsoever. Liaison between library staff and academic staff was seen as important as the library role in teaching and learning increased. However, several academic staff seemed reluctant to work in conjunction with libraries to provide information skills teaching. Where both sets of staff did work together the results were usually highly satisfactory.

Data from IMPEL2 is being collected between September 1996 and March 1997 and will expand on that collected for IMPEL I.

TRAINING AND AWARENESS ELIB PROJECTS AND INFORMATION SKILLS TEACHING

When the projects in the eLib training and awareness programme areas are examined, information skills and the role of the librarian come through as being central. The training and awareness programme, as the title indicates, is not about delivering electronic information but is more concerned about skills needed to make effective use of electronic information.

One of the highest profile training and awareness projects is **EduLib** (URL http://www.hull.ac.uk/Hull/CTLS - Web/edulib/edulib.html), a collaboration between the University of Hull, the University of Abertay Dundee and the Staff and Educational Development Association (SEDA). The aim is to give EduLib participants the networked information skills and the teaching skills needed to work as training and support staff in the Electronic Library. The first stage has been to identify the skills needed for librarians' teaching and learning roles Training packages related to information skills teaching will be developed from this analysis. The cascade method will be used whereby participants will be expected to pass on their newly acquired skills to their colleagues.

Another high profile project is **Netskills** (UPL http:www.netskills.ac.uk) based at the University of Newcastle. Its remit is wider than EduLib in that it is concerned with the training needs of all users of electronic information. Its aim is to provide a comprehensive national network skills training programme aimed at shifting the culture within higher education towards awareness and widespread use of networked information resources. Library staff will be provided with materials and short courses to support then in training the users. This complements EduLib where the priority is about giving library staff the androgogic skills to develop fully their role as network trainers.

The other training and awareness eLib projects have some relationship with information skills but not at the same level as EduLib and Netskills. **TAPin** (Training and Awareness Programme in networks) (URL http:www.uce.ac.uk/tapin/tapin.htm) is a collaborative project based on a consortium of six universities in the Western Midlands part of the UK. The information skills focus will be when librarians in each of the six universities will be trained in the use and transfer of networked information resources. The trained librarians will then transfer these skills and resources to academic staff. **Netlinks** is being developed from the University of Sheffield (URL http://www.shefac.uk/-np/). The purpose of this project is to enable library professionals to acquire the knowledge and skills to successfully develop networked learner support. These will include teaching the networked learner the skills they need. A fascinating project on conveying information skills is being developed at Kings College. called CINE (Cartoon images for Network Education) (URL http://www.kcl.ac.uk/projects/cine/top.htm). This project will explore the potential of visual and animated media as a supplement or as an alternative to text. Animation modules covering the following information skills will be produced: text searching techniques, World Wide Web and Z39.50 operations.

SUMMARY

When discussing information skills teaching in higher education it is very difficult to not include the implications of electronic information. The whole issue of the relative importance of information skills invariably tends to polarise librarians. The above literature review highlighted some of the extreme views that librarians have about information skills teaching. When revisiting the archives of lisinfoskills@mailbase.ac.uk to see further reactions to Ian Winship's (1996) provoking comments the following can be seen:

> I too think a lot of 'user education' is utterly pointless, and for the librarians delivering it quite a depressing and futile business (Bradford, 1996).

> I think that part of the problem is that in the past many librarians want to turn end-users into pseudolibrarians (Wintrip, 1996).

> What I'm hoping my students will learn is an attitude rather than skill, a critical appreciation of information and hopefully a readiness to evaluate it - and not be frightened of it (Bainbridge, 1996).

It can be argued that this range of views and opinions is very healthy. Electronic information will ensure that this debate will continue, if not escalate. Information technology will effect information skills teaching in many ways. Users will need to learn about different electronic information sources that will become increasingly full text. They will need keyboard and other skills in order retrieve that information. Librarians will have more options in the ways skills can be conveyed. Users will need skills to evaluate and judge the information they have found, whether it be hard copy or electronic. The eLib Programme is very important in shaping how information skills teaching develops in the UK.

It has already been indicated that IMPEL2 is concerned with monitoring organizational and cultural change in the electronic library. T. S. Eliot, the writer, has given a very useful definition of culture:

Culture is not merely the sum of several activities *but a way of life*

Through gathering data in 28 plus sites IMPEL2 will develop a wide and rich picture of where information skills teaching fits into the *way of life* of academic librarians. These picture will help the sector establish how users of electronic information can best gain the skills and ability to be effective learners, teachers and researchers.

REFERENCES

Atkinson, J. and Scott, N. (1995), "Rethinking information skills teaching", *Learning Resources Journal,* 11 (2), pp. 45-48.

Atton, C. (1994), "Using critical thinking as basis for library user education", *Journal of Academic Librarianship,* 20 (56), pp. 310-313.

Bober, C., Poulin, S. and Vileno, L. (1995), "Evaluating library instruction in academic libraries: a critical review of the literature, 1980-1993", *Reference Librarian,* 51/52, pp.53- 69.

Bodi, S. (1988), "Critical thinking and bibliographic instruction: the relationship", *Journal of Academic Librarianship,* 14, pp. 150-153.

Bradford, C. (1 4 October 1996). *The value of user education - some jaundiced views.* [e-mail to lis-infoskills@mailbase.ac.uk], [Online] Available e-mail: c.bradford@ox-west.ac.uk (Christine Bradford)

Bainbridge, C. (25 October 1996). *Teaching info skills.* [e-mail to lisinfoskills@mailbase.ac.uk], [Online] Available e-mail: c-bainbridge@uwe.ac.uk

Creanor, L. and Durndell, H. (1994), "Teaching information handling skills with hypertext", *Program,* 28 (4), pp. 349-365.

Day, J. M. (1991), "User education for the media in UK academic libraries", *On-Line Kensaku,* 12 (4), pp. 187-196.

Downard, K. (1992), "User education in academic libraries", *Library Management,* 13 (3), pp. 29-38.

Dusenbury, C. and Pease, B. G. (1995), "The future of instruction", *Journal of Library Administration,* 20 (3/4) pp.97-117.

East, H. and Tilson, Y. (1993), *The Liberated Enduser: Developments in Practice and Policy for Database Provision to the Academic Community,* London: British Library Board. (CCIS Policy Paper no. 4. BLR&D Report 6 1 00).

Edwards, C. (1995a), *IMPEL Project. University of Wales College of Cardiff Library. Case Study Report,* Newcastle: University of Northumbria.

Edwards, C. (1995b), *IMPEL Project. University of Central Lancashire Library and Resources Service. Case Study Report,* Newcastle: University of Northumbria.

Edwards, C. (1995c), *IMPEL Project. Aston University Library and Information Services. Case Study Report,* Newcastle: University of Northumbria.

Edwards, C. (1995d), *IMPEL Project. University of Stirling Information Services (Library). Case Study Report,* Newcastle: University of Northumbria.

Fleming, H. (1996), "User education in academic libraries in the United Kingdom", *British Journal of Academic Librarianship*, 1 (1), pp. 18-40.

Heijne, M. (1992), "Networked services, user support and libraries: mutual benefits?", *Electronic Library*, 10 (1), pp. 47-51.

Hopkins, T. (1995), *User Education in Academic Libraries: Results of 1995 CTILIS Survey*, Loughborough:CTI.

Jackson-Brown, G. (1993), "The academic librarian's new role as information provider", *Reference Librarian*, (39), pp. 77-83.

Line, M. (1993), "Service and self service: the electronic library from the user's point of view", in: A. H. Hedal and J. Weiss, eds. *Opportunity 2000: Understanding and Serving Users in an Electronic Library: 15th International Essen Symposium*. Essen: Essen University Library, pp. 284-94.

McConnell, J.C. (1993), "Technology and teaching in academia", *Reference Librarian*, 39, pp. 31-40.

Master, N. (1995), "Taking the mystery out of the library: user education at UNLV's Dickinson Library", *Reference Librarian*, 148, pp. 115-129.

Odini, C. (1994), "Educating users at Moi University", *Library Information Development*, 10 (4), pp. 273-275.

Pacey, P. (1995), "Teaching user education, learning information skills; or, towards the self-explanatory library", *The New Review of Academic Librarianship*, 1, pp. 95-103.

Reese, J. (1994), " Practical tips for CD-ROM: end user instruction: making the most of your time", *CDROM Professional*, (January), pp. 59-60.

Report of the Joint Funding Councils' Libraries Review Group, (1993) (Chairman: Prof. Sir Brian Follett), Bristol: HEFCE.

Rockman, I. F. (1993), "Teaching about the internet: the formal course option", *Reference Services Librarian*, 39, pp. 65-75.

Rusbridge, C. (1995), "The electronic libraries programme", *Serials*, 8 (3), pp. 231-240.

Tiefel, V. (1992), "User education in academic libraries", *Library Management*, 13 (2), pp. 29-38.

Tiefel, V. M. (1995), "Library user education: examining its past, projecting its future", *Library Trends*, 44 (2), pp. 318-337.

Vasi, J. and La Guardia, C. (1994), "Creating a library electronic classroom", *Online*, 18 (Sept/Oct), pp. 75-84.

Wall, M. (1993), "The death of training: new strategies for user education", *ACM SIGUCCS User Services Conference*, 20, pp. 239-244.

Walton, G. and Nettleton, S. (1992), " Reflective and critical thinking in user education programmes", *British Journal of Academic Librarianship*, 7 (1), pp. 31-43.

Werking, R. H. (1980), "Evaluating bibliographic education: a review and critique", *Library Trends*, 29 (Summer), pp. 153-172.

Wilson, V. (1994), "Information literacy and remote external students: exploring the possibilities offered by the new communication technologies", *Australian Academic and Research Libraries*, 25 (4), pp. 247-252.

Winship, I. (11 October 1996). *The value of user education - some jaundiced views.* [e-mail to lis-infoskills@mailbase.ac.uk], [Online]. Available e-mail: ian.winship:unn.ac.uk

Wintrip, J. (14 October 1996). *The value of user education.* [e-mail to lisinfoskills@mailbase.ac.uk], [Online] Available e-mail: j-wintrip@wpg.uwe.ac.uk

Wood, F., Ford, N., Miller, D., Duffin, R. and Sobczyk, G. (1995), " Information skills for student centred learning: a computer assisted learning (CAL) approach: a second progress report", *ITS News*, (31), pp 33-40.

LIBRARIES AS LEARNING ORGANIZATIONS

Ganga B. Dakshinamurti
University of Manitoba Libraries
Canada

Abstract: The paper applies the theory of the learning organisations as presented by Senge and others, to libraries and argues that in an era of complexity and change in order to continue to develop and maintain the social, economic, educational and cultural fabric of our global community, libraries need to become learning organisations, where change is seen as a learning experience for all.

INTRODUCTION

You may be wondering whether there is a mistake in the title of my presentation - should it not be libraries as TEACHING organizations, rather than LEARNING organizations? After all, no matter what type of library - be it academic, school, special or public - the mandate for any library as an educational resource in practically any country is to be a reservoir for teaching tools.

At the same time, a library is essentially a service organization. It has a definite commitment for service to its users and its important assets are its human resources that provide such a service. It has become imperative for library workers to manage the changes that are buffeting libraries from all directions. To continue to be a viable presence in this changing world, and to fulfil its mandate, a library has to "adopt a new way of managing that is based on our organization's capacity to learn and change - consciously, continually and quickly" (Bennett and O'Brien, 1994 p.41). In essence, a library should be a learning organization, for "a continuous improvement requires a commitment to learning" (Garvin, 1996 p.19).

WHAT IS A LEARNING ORGANIZATION?

The concept of learning organization was proposed in the seventies by Argyris and Schon (1978). This was resurrected in the eighties by Peter Senge, who "redefined the organizational learning concept by broadening it into a more holistic theory which reflects the cutting edge of contemporary organizational management thought" (Worrall, 1995 p.351). Initially the concept was found to be nebulous, as stated by Calvert et al: "Trying to understand the concept of the learning organization is like trying to understand the concept of an elephant - while blindfolded. Your perception of the whole is determined by the part that is closest to you" (Calvert et al, 1994 p.38). A review of present literature shows that the discussion about learning organization has come to the forefront in business literature, and is now emerging in library literature as well, as shown by Worrell, who holds that the theory of learning organization as proposed by Senge "represents the natural evolution of decades of thought on participative management" (Worrell, 1995 p. 351). To this I would add the benefit of the considerable research on human resources development from the seventies and eighties that highlighted the need for continuous education to keep up with the changing world.

The definition of learning organization offered by Senge in 1990 in his Fifth Principle is often chosen as a comprehensive statement on learning organization, though some find it utopian in concept. Senge holds learning organizations as organizations "where people continually expand their capacity to create results they truly desire, where new and expansive patterns of thinking are nurtured, where collective aspiration is set free, and where people are continually learning how to learn together" (Senge, 1990 p.3).

I believe that the key concept in this definition is that in a learning organization, people are continually learning how to learn together. This helps in recognizing that all of us in an organization have to be continually learning, both individually and collectively, not because we are deficient in required knowledge and hence are in need to be trained, but because the environment keeps changing and we need to continually learn to adapt to these changes. For our organization to benefit from our learning, we need to learn to share such learning with our co-workers and to learn together so that all of us in an organization can help to move forward the mission and the strategic plan of our organization.

A bibliographic search on learning organization shows that several writers in the business world have elaborated Senge's concept further. Calvert et al conducted a series of focus group sessions to elicit ideas and perspectives on learning organization. The following tables (# 1 to 4) summarize succinctly their research findings (Calvert et al, 1994 pp.38-43):

Table 1. What Does a Learning Organization Learn?

Learning organizations learn

- to use learning to reach their goals
- to help people value the effects of their learning on their organizations
- to avoid making the same mistakes again (and again)
- to share information in ways that prompt appropriate action
- to link individual performance with organizational performance
- to tie rewards to key measures of performance
- to take in a lot of environmental information at all times
- to create structures and procedures that support the learning process
- to foster ongoing and orderly dialogue
- to make it safe for people to share openly and take risks

Table 2. What Does a Learning Organization Look Like?

A learning organization

- learns collaboratively, openly, and across boundaries
- values *how* it learns as well as *what* it learns
- invests in staying ahead of the learning curve in its industry
- gains a competitive edge by learning faster and smarter than competitors
- turns data into useful knowledge quickly and at the right time and place
- enables every employee to feel that every experience provides him or her a chance to learn something potentially useful, even if only for leveraging future learning
- exhibits little fear and defensiveness; rewards and learns from what goes wrong ("failure" learning) and right ("success" learning)
- takes risks but avoids jeopardizing basic security of the organization
- invests in experimental and seemingly tangential learning
- supports people and teams who want to pursue action-learning projects
- depoliticizes learning by not penalizing individuals or groups for sharing information and conclusions.

Table 3. How Does a Learning Organization Evolve?

A learning organization can begin by

- questioning current assumptions about learning
- getting an outside perspective
- tying the goal of becoming a learning organization to its organizational vision
- finding or creating a champion in top management
- looking for the "pain" in the organization - the place where more effective learning could help
- articulating learning-organization ideas plainly
- rewarding group as well as individual learning success and failure
- finding an external enemy to spur greater co-operative learning
- finding ways to collaborate internally in and unhampered by boundaries

Table 4. How Does a learning Organization Connect Learning to Profitability?

Organizations can use learning to better their bottom lines by

- using action learning to solve business problems or seize business opportunities
- reflecting on learning experiences, such as asking what prevented or permitted seeing better solutions
- improving processes by learning from more knowledgeable people
- developing awareness of the gains that can be squeezed from mistakes and successes
- shortening competitive cycles, as in developing new products more quickly
- helping management to recognize learning as a factor that affects the bottom line
- increasing individual and group accountability for learning
- leveraging key learning points, such as learning to acquire the most critical data.

The "bottom line" for a library is the effectiveness of its service to its users. If we substitute library in the tables above for a learning organization, every one of the characteristics listed fits to describe a proactive, user-oriented library. Library literature abounds with writings that call for continuous learning in order "to survive and prosper in the whitewater ride into the 21st century" (Bennett & O'Brien 1994) while we attempt to keep up with the changing technology. Proceedings of library conferences of all types and at all levels - provincial, national and international - declare with a sense of urgency the need for library workers to stay competitive through accelerated training. How can we ensure that libraries become and remain learning organizations as described above?

Senge's Five Principles:

Senge has prescribed five disciplines or "component technologies" as elements that unite to begin to form a learning organization. Starting from the individual level and leading to the organizational level, Senge outlines the basic principles of the theory of learning organization (source: Senge's The Fifth Principle):

1. Personal mastery:

A special level of proficiency in which individuals become committed to their own lifelong learning. The organization in turn is committed to the lifelong learning of its workers. Personal mastery involves people clarifying what is important and continually learning to see reality more clearly. By starting his set of principles at the personal level, Senge confirms that organizations learn only through its individuals; and learning, in order to be effective, has to start at the personal level.

Library literature has stressed the importance of lifelong learning at the individual level in these turbulent times. Learning organization will place a greater responsibility on the library workers to tie their learning to the library's goals and to share such learning with co-workers.

2. Mental Models:

Deeply ingrained assumptions that influence how we understand the world and how we take action based on our subtle patterns of reasoning, which tend to limit our thinking and acting. The concept here is to develop the kind of mental model that will accept the ongoing learning process. Learning organizations continually identify, test and improve their members' mental models.

Changing a mental model is not easy, but without such a change, no real learning can take place. On a day-to-day basis in libraries, essential changes are often resisted, because of a previously held mental model or assumptions about the change, or sometimes, about the person(s) proposing such a change. For a successful learning experience, it is critical we examine and evaluate the mental model we have about what is being learnt and prepare to have it changed through dialogues and discussions.

3. Shared Vision Building:

Sharing a picture of the desired future - in other words, the images people have concerning what the organization should be or what the members should be doing. There should be a shared sense of identity and mission.

Without building a shared vision of what is required based on what is learnt, the learning remains at the individual level and not lead to organizational development. Without sharing the mission of the organization, individuals can not form an effective functioning group, i.e. an organization. This sense of sharing is often missing in libraries within individual departments or among groups of individual workers, thereby leading to mistrust and biased opinions about each other, at departmental levels or at individual levels. Building a shared vision is highly required in all libraries. Open and purposeful communication is the key.

4. Team Learning:

The ability for individuals collectively to produce extraordinary results and allow individual members to grow more rapidly than they could otherwise. Using dialogue and the suspending of assumptions, the process calls for aligning and developing the capacity of a team to create the results its members want. In an organization, team building is often more important than individual learning because without teamwork, there is no organizational learning. Team learning functions as the microcosm for learning throughout the organization.

In libraries, it is all too common to find that while certain individuals will strive to learn further on their own, there may not be any deliberate sharing of such learning among co-workers, and thereby no team building either. What is needed is a formal and disciplined process as outlined by Senge. This calls for dialogue and discussions that establish and enrich team learning, so that the sum total of learning is more than the total of individual learning.

5. Systems Thinking:

A conceptual framework that sees all parts as interrelated and affecting each other, based on the understanding that organizational endeavours are of one system made up of interrelated actions. This is Senge's "Fifth Principle", crucial for the other four elements to develop together.

Many a library is known to lack systems thinking. Classic images abound in libraries about disputes between public services staff and technical services staff , who may be working in conflict without realizing that they form two halves of the whole organization. Attempts to raise awareness of this critical issue are much needed.

THE PROCESS OF IMPLEMENTATION

Throughout the process of becoming a learning organization as outlined by Senge with his five principles, concern about quality of work and openness to learning at all levels of the organization are critical for success. As pointed out by Dumaini, Senge's Fieldbook makes it clear that anyone who wants to be part of a learning organization must first go through a personal change, put aside their old ways of thinking (mental models), learn to be open with others by having open dialogue (personal mastery), understand how their organization really works (systems thinking), form a plan everyone can agree (shared vision) and then work together to achieve that vision (team learning). While none of these concepts are new, Senge has created something powerful by putting them together, so that individual workers can work together for the good of the organization (Dumani, 1994 pp.148-149). Worrell also paraphrases Senge's method thus: "The core disciplines describe an organizational culture in which individual development is a priority; outmoded and erroneous ways of thinking are actively identified and corrected; and the purpose and vision of the organization are clearly understood and supported by its members; within this framework, the application of systems thinking enables people to see how the organization really works; to form a plan; and to work openly together, in teams, to achieve that plan" (Worrall, 1995, p.352).

One approach that Senge strongly recommends is to have ongoing and structured dialogue among workers that would allow them to openly discuss conflicts in a constructive and creative way leading to solutions. "The goal is to move people away from their biases and deep seated beliefs that keep them away from focusing on the real problem" (Dumaini, 1994, p.156). This type of structured, and if needed, facilitated discussions and dialogues will help in any settings in libraries as not all libraries are generally known for having an open climate.

A review of Senge's five principles and an application of their process in libraries show that this process is much needed in libraries, as it brings together old tools such as training and organizational mission, in conjunction with concepts that may be known but are hardly implemented, such as shared vision and systems thinking. All these are combined in the concept of learning organization to form a powerful organizational tool. The following table (# 5) clearly shows how training has evolved as learning and education in a learning organization, where the emphasis is on thinking systematically and learning together as a team. The learning organization requires organizational learning in addition to traditional learning. Organizational learning is a set of processes and structures to help people create new knowledge, share their understanding, and continuously improve themselves and the results of the enterprise. In essence, organizational learning is not a program or a project; it is a management philosophy.

Table 5. The Evolution of Training in a Learning Organization

Traditional Training	Organizational Learning
Employees receive skills training; development Executives, development training	All receive learning support, lifelong
Training goals as per user requests needs	Learning goals as per corporate strategy, user
Addresses immediate needs/ short-term plans	Focuses on core competencies/ long-term strategic plans
Needs assessment by trainers/ managers	Needs assessment jointly by trainees, trainers and managers
Training locally or in classroom	Education at workplace or anywhere
Delivery as per periodic schedule	Delivery on real time, on request
Approach is a delivery of knowledge	Approach is learning experiences, workplace interventions
Instructor driven; specialists designed	Self directed; designed by participants
Trainers develop; trainees recipients developers	Educators facilitate, coach; trainees joint
Generalized content; often prescriptive trainees and	Content specific, applied; developed with trainers

(Source: *Personnel Journal* (1994), 73 (11) p.62)

Several people have listed the sequence of steps involved in establishing a learning organization. A review of these articles show that they are fully applicable to libraries. Two of the more frequently cited papers will be discussed here with a view for library applicability.

According to Garvin, "a learning organization is an organization skilled at creating, acquiring and transforming knowledge, and at modifying its behaviour to reflect new knowledge and insights" (Garvin, 1996, p.20). In other words, without the accompanying changes to the organization, the learning only creates a potential for improvement in the individual. A true learning organization becomes adept at translating new knowledge into new ways of behaving. This is accomplished by actively managing the learning process through distinctive policies and procedures to ensure that the learning occurs by design rather than by chance. What are these distinctive policies and procedures that serve as building blocks to form a learning organization? Let us review a couple of writers' statements about organizational development and consider whether they may be applied successfully to libraries.

Garvin's Building Blocks:

Garvin holds that the following five main activities that are integrated into the fabric of daily operations, and not left to happen/chance and isolated examples, will serve as building blocks for a learning organization (Garvin, 1996, p.20):

1. Systematic problem solving, that relies on facts, continually asks for accuracy and precision, and searches beyond symptoms for underlying causes.

2. Experimentation, that favours risk taking, that aims to move from superficial knowledge of "knowing how" to deep understanding of "knowing why".

3. Learning from past experience, that recognizes the value of failure that leads to better understanding, as contrasted with unproductive success, where nobody knows how or why success occurred.

4. Learning from others, by cultivating a receptive environment and benchmarking practices that lead to comparative study to gain new perspective.

5. Transferring knowledge, through reports, site visits, training, job rotation, etc.

While Garvin believed that these five building blocks will foster an environment that is conducive to learning and exchange of ideas, Bennett and O'Brien were concerned that "today's knowledge explosion and the galloping pace of change deserved an unprecedented learning response from organizations. Organizations and individuals alike must become continuous learners" (Bennett and O'Brien, 1994 p.40). The authors offer the following set of building blocks as preliminary benchmarks against which any organization can measure its capacity to support continuous learning:

Bennett's Building Blocks:

- Strategy/vision to support organizational learning
- Supportive behaviour of Executive Officer who holds oneself and others accountable for continuous learning improvement
- Management culture to ensure continuous learning and development, and to behave in accordance with the principle of continuous learning
- Organization's climate reflecting the sum of values and attitudes of members regarding learning; a climate of openness and trust
- Job descriptions that are fluid to respond to the changing demands of the external environment
- Information flow that is equitably and adequately distributed through use of advanced technology
- Individuals and team share their learning, mistakes are seen as learning opportunities, individuals take responsibility for their own learning, and progress is everybody's business
- Work processes that include creative idea generation in problem solving, constant questioning and disciplined thinking; and include benchmarking as a standard tool
- Performance goals and feedback, where feedback is valued and sought after and where performance evaluation is based on employees' contribution to the organization's goals
- Formal and informal training and action learning that allow people to learn new skills while solving day to day problems
- Individual/team development, where both the individual and the team are encouraged and empowered to learn and develop
- Rewards/recognition, that support and encourage individual and organizational learning; where risk taking is encouraged.

The authors recognize that no single organization can excel in all these twelve areas at all times, but they urge organizations to undertake continuous learning along these lines.

LIBRARIES AS LEARNING ORGANIZATIONS:

I believe Senge's theory on learning organization has considerable significance for libraries. As Worrell points out, "since the learning organization theory deals with universal organizational concerns such as problem-solving, communication, personnel and innovation, it should logically be applicable to libraries and other types of service organizations" (Worrell, 1995 p. 354). It is also true that many parts of the theory, such as systems theory, TQM, matrix management, etc. are already familiar to the library world, both in theoretical concepts and in practical application studies. What makes Senge's theory particularly noteworthy is that he has used all the familiar organizational developmental theories and has applied them to the concept of learning which up till now has been primarily left at the jurisdiction of the individual employee. While human resources development theories emphasized the importance of continuous training and development, it was still left to the individual to make use of the available opportunities. In these days of shrinking resources and ever changing technology, organizations no longer have the option to leave the choice and direction of staff development fully to individual aspirations. Management needs to take a much more proactive role in shaping the culture of the organization in such a way that continuous learning becomes a way of life for all members, not a project for a few for particular times.

The learning organization concept has combined many of the existing theories into, what Worrell calls "a holistic theory of organizational effectiveness" (Worrell, 1995 p.356), and has added the missing parts, such as organizational needs and systems thinking. Senge is particularly effective in calling for team learning. Individual learning is useful to an organization only to the extent the learning can be applied for organizational benefits. Up till now, such a persuasive argument has not been made for team learning and changing mental models. Senge's combination of learning theories on the one hand, with the sequence of personal mastery, mental model, shared vision, team learning and systems thinking, is at the individual level as they all call for the individual to be the initiator in mastering it. On the other hand, the process of implementing Senge's theory call for mutual trust among all within the organization, participatory management, open communication, motivation, rewards/incentives - all needing active participation and initiative by management. Both sets of learning theories call for change in organizational behaviour. At the individual level, learning would occur through on-the-job training, individual studying, etc. At the managerial level, support is needed to facilitate seminars, courses, conferences and workshops. It is particularly at the middle level where team work is needed to participate in meetings, committee work, structured dialogues and discussion, both the manager and the employees need to work together - managers with their expectations, and the employees with their willingness to participate. Regardless of the motivation of the employee, if the learning organization is to succeed, it is the manager who needs to first express her/his expectations. Team work and team learning will only take root and thrive where it is the expected and accepted mode of operation, as initiated in a collegial mode by the management to suit the whole system. For this, Senge's ten sets of system's archetypes or "nature's templates" (Senge, 1990 p.92) may be useful to implement system's thinking among library employees, and to diagnose organizational problems, as shown by Worrell (1995 p. 354).

At present, library literature contains little discussion about learning organizations and, except in a few instances, we need to draw from business literature concerning other organizations. Phipps has taken a leadership role in studying and applying to libraries the concept of learning organization (Phipps, n.d.) and is currently engaged in offering workshops in library conferences on applying this concept to libraries. Given the thrust in management literature to apply the concept of learning organization for systematic problem solving and benchmarking, and to accelerate organizational learning, it will not be long before this concept has a viable presence in library literature also, as individual libraries and library leaders start applying the learning process along the lines suggested by Worrell (1995 pp.355-356).

We no longer have a choice of not going this route. If we want to survive as a viable profession, libraries should become learning organizations, continuously learning and examining ourselves, both individually and collectively, as well as our policies and procedures, to fit the changing environment, even as we pursue our time honoured goals of providing the right information to the right person at the right time, *à la* Ranganathan. We can take comfort in the fact that ancient wisdom had long ago seen the correctness of doing great deeds together - we can not be too wrong following these footsteps:

"Asatoma sat gamaya
Tamasoma jyotir gamaya
Mrityorma amrutam gamaya
Sahana vavatu, Sahanow bhunaktu
Sahaveeryam karavavahai
Teejas vina vateetamstu mavidvisha vahai
Om Shanti, Shanti, Shantihi"

Let good deeds prevail over bad deeds
Let light (knowledge) prevail over darkness (ignorance)
Let immortality prevail over mortality
Let us be together, Let us eat together,
Let us do great deeds together
Without light, darkness will prevail; let us banish darkness
Peace, Peace, Peace.

(Ancient Hindu Prayer in Sanskrit)

REFERENCES

Argyris, C. and Schon, D. A. (1978), *Organizational Learning: A Theory of Action Perspective*, Reading, MA: Addison Wesley.

Bennett, J. K. and O'Brien, M. J. (1994), "The building blocks of the learning organization," *Training*, 31 (6), p.41.

Calvert, G., Mobley, S. and Marshall, L. (1994), "Grasping the learning organization", *Training and Development*, 48 (6).

Dumaini, B. (1994), "Mr. Learning Organization ", *Fortune*, 130 (8 October 17).

Garvin, D. A. (1996), "Building a learning organization," *Business Credit,* 96 (1).

Phipps, S. E.(n.d.), "Transforming libraries into learning organizations: the challenge for leadership" in: G.M. von Dran and J. Cargill eds. *Catalysts for Change: Managing Libraries in the 1990s*, New York: Haworth.

Senge, P. M. (1990), *The Fifth Discipline: the Art and Practice of the Learning Organization*, New York: Doubleday

Worrell, D. (1995), "The learning organization: management theory for the Information Age or New Age Fad?", *Journal of Academic Librarianship*, (September).

THE HIGHER SCHOOL OF INFORMATION SERVICE IN PRAGUE

Marcela Burilova
Vyssi Skola Informacnich Sluzeb
Czech Republic

Abstract: The paper describes the work of the Higher School of Information Service in Prague which is a new type of education in the Czech Republic.

INTRODUCTION

The Higher School of Information Services provides a new type of education in the Czech Republic. Its practical orientation differentiates this type of school from the traditional or Bachelor education. The latter are more or less theoretical and academic. The higher specialized education can be placed at a level between post secondary school and traditional university education.

The new system has been developed with the help of many foreign co-partner institutions, especially from the Netherlands and Great Britain. The Higher School for Information Services was one of the 12 higher vocational schools in Czech Republic. Its started its activities in 1992 based on the transformation of a secondary vocational school. After 3 years experimental time it was accredited in January 1996.

SCHOOL LEAVER PROFILE

Generally study at the level of higher vocational education prepares specialists and workers for a broad spectrum of functions in libraries, information centres, museums, and the newly emerging workplaces of information market. The students are prepared for top positions in management in medium-sized or small companies as well as for intermediate or senior positions in large organisations or firms. The students are also given specific knowledge that enables them to be self-employed. The school offers its students useful knowledge and skills. The course focuses its attention on computer techniques, foreign language teaching, communication techniques, and teaching management for information industry and information market. The decisive criterion of demand applying to the qualification of information workers, is the experience with the training and instruction of workers in modern information systems in advanced countries. The school-leaver is prepared for future work in all types of information workplaces.

At the present times there are three streams available:

services for information systems and agencies

services for libraries

services for museums and galleries.

The first school class is more or less same, the streams differ only in two optional subjects. The second and the third class have a much more diverse programme.

ORGANISATION AND FORM OF STUDY

The programme of study lasts for 3.5 years, and for part-time students 4 years. Each year is divided into 2 terms each of 18 weeks. The number of teaching hours is about 25 lessons a week. The period of examination at the end of each term lasts 3 weeks. There are approximately 5 exams for each period of examination. If they have not passed the exams, students must repeat the whole school year. To repeat a school year is possible only once during of study.

The study is provided partly in the classical forms of lectures and exercises, partly in seminars with small number of students, practical exercises in small groups especially with computer equipment, and individual consultation and individual work.

- the basic group has 15 students. It is a formula suited for language teaching, practical training with the computer, lessons in communication skills, information services etc. This is the maximum number that enables individual attention.
- the class of 25-30 students. It is used for subjects where formal teaching is used, but it enables occasional discussion with students. It is used for more or less theoretical subjects, for example statistics, logic, management, marketing etc.
- the class of 70-80 students. It is used for introductory theoretical lectures. The arrangement of the class enables contact with the students but provides very little opportunity for reaction from the students. It is necessary for students to overcome the problem partly by the study of the published literature.

The minimal number of students in a group is 15 in the first year, in the second and especially in the third year, it can be lower. The offering of optional subjects is subject to a minimal number.

The practical training lasts for 4 months and takes place in the 7th term. Students are trained at information institutions of their own choice. The School co-operates with nearly two hundred institutions. The best students have the opportunity to undertake their practical training at an institution in the Netherlands or Great Britain and we are trying to extend this offer to other countries.

MARKING

The students are evaluated using marks. The marks have the following scale:

1 - excellent

2 - very good

3 - satisfactory

4 - unsatisfactory

Student must achieve a mark of 3 to pass.

The evaluation method links with the university tradition of evaluation in the Czech Republic.

Individual subjects are evaluated in accordance with their nature, either orally or in the form of a test, some teachers include student' activity in their evaluation. The evaluation of individual subjects is a decision for the teachers, and they select the form of evaluation for themselves.

The final examination (after completion of the course) is complex. It is the only examination before a commission during the study.

SUBJECTS

The subjects studied differ according to the streams, but some of them are common for all three streams.

The most important part of study is work with computers, learning foreign languages and management for the information industry and market. Students learn the technologies of information services, the typology and structure of information documents and their resources, ways of identifying them, recording, preservation, selection and presentation. No less an important part of study are the communication skills. Students learn communication ethics and the specific rules of people behaviour in social groups.

In the second year there is a small number of optional subjects, the number increases in the third year. The choice of optional subjects is decided according to the practical demand.

EQUIPMENT OF SCHOOL

The School has very good equipment for its specialisation. It is one of the best technically equipped schools in the Czech Republic. There are 3 computer classrooms, each with 17 computers, parallel network UNIX and data line with connection to the academic network and Internet, the opportunity to work with CD ROM databases from any place in the school, a special classroom for desktop publishing and a very modern information centre. There are 50 study places, 6000 volumes of books and audio-visual documents, 40 periodical titles, 25 computers and two videos. This information centre serves students for the whole day over the week.

STAFF

The School has 30 internal teachers and about 15 external teachers. The workload of an internal teacher is 21 lessons a week, the external teachers are employed on optional subjects especially for the third class.

STUDENTS

The number of students is different in each stream and year.

Services for information systems and agencies:

> first class: 80 students

> second class: 40

> third class: 30

Services for libraries:

> first class: 60 students

> second class: 20

> third class: 15

Services for museums and galleries

> only 60 students in the first class, because this stream is new in this school year.

The interest in study at the Higher School of Information Service increases every year. The number of candidates last year was four times higher than The School could receive. Every candidate has to sit for an entrance examination. It consists of two parts:

- a foreign language test (English or German)
- an oral interview, where the candidate presents his interest in the profession and his ability to speak on a theme of their choice.

During the first class there is a relatively large decrease in the number of students, about a third of number. Some of these students do not pass the exams, some leave for colleges or universities. In the second class the group of students is relatively stabilised and the reduction in the number of students is minimal.

The experience with the new type of the higher vocational education is very good. There is a very great interest in the graduates of The School. But it is very early to draw conclusions. Time will show the success of this type of study.

1. class

- services of information systems and agencies
- services of libraries
- services of museums and galleries

		obligatory subjects	number of lessons a week
1.	1	First foreign language	4/4
2.	2	Second foreign language	3/3
3.	3	Bases of general and social psychology	2/3
4.	4	Bases of law science	2/-
5.	5	Bases of economy	3/-
6.	6	Select chapters of linguistic	2/-
7.	7	Bases of computer literacy	2/2
8.	8	Logic	2/-
9.	9	Mathematical statistics	2/2
0.	1	Information and society	-/2
1.	1	Teaching of resources	2/-
2.	1	Social communication I	-/2
3.	1	Management	-/2
4.	1	Sport	2/2

- services of information systems and agencies
- services of libraries

		obligatory subjects of stream	number of lessons a week
1.	1	Development of information systems I	-/2
.	2	Information technologies	-/2

- services of museums and galleries

		obligatory subjects of stream	number of lessons a week
	1	Museums and society	-/2
	2	Information technologies	-/2

Whole number of lessons is 26/26

2. class

- services of information systems and agencies
- services of libraries

		obligatory subjects	number of lessons a week
	1	First foreign language	4/4
	2	Second foreign language	3/3
	3	Social communication II	2/-
	4	Management	2/-
	5	Automated retrieval systems	-/3
	6	Databases	2/2
	7	Sport	2/2

- services of information systems and agencies

		obligatory subjects of stream	number of lessons a week
	1	Information technologies	2/2
	2	Information resources	-/3
	3	Programming I	2/3
	4	Internet	2/-
	5	Project of information systems	2/-
	6	Information services	2/2

- services of libraries

		obligatory subjects of stream	number of lessons a week
	1	Literature	-/2
	2	Automated library systems	-/2
	3	Development of information systems II	-/2
	4	Information resources	2/-
	5	Information technologies	2/-
	6	Information services	2/2
	7	Bibliographical description	2/-
	8	Subject description	-/2
	9	Project of information systems	2/-

Whole number of lessons is 25/24

3. class

- services of information systems and agencies
- services of libraries

		obligatory subjects	number of lessons a week
	1	First foreign language	6/6
	2	Second foreign language	4/4
	3	Marketing	3/2
	4	Seminar on graduate project	1/-

- services of information systems and agencies

		obligatory subjects of stream	number of lessons a week
	1	Desktop publishing	2/2
	2	Work with professional text	2/2

		optional subjects	number of lessons a

			week
.	1	Law information systems	2/-
.	2	Medical information systems	-/2
.	3	Ecological information systems	2/-
.	4	Geographical information systems	2/-
.	5	Municipal information systems	/2
.	6	Patent information systems	-/2
.	7	Market of information sources	-/2
.	8	Business information	2/-
.	9	Lotus Notes	-/2
0.	1	WWW and Gopher server relations	2/2

- services of libraries

		obligatory subjects of stream	number of lessons a week
	1	Literature	2/2
.	2	History of arts	2/2

		optional subjects	number of lessons a week
.	1	Law information systems	2/-
.	2	Medical information systems	-/2
.	3	Ecological information systems	2/-
.	4	Geographical information systems	2/-
.	5	Municipal information systems	/2
.	6	Patent information systems	-/2
.	7	Market of information sources	-/2
.	8	Retrospective conversion of records	-/2
.	9	Bibliographical description of special documents	2/-
0.	1	Public relations	2/-
1.	1	Internet	2/-

Total number of lessons is 26/26

CONTINUING EDUCATION OF INFORMATION PROFESSIONALS IN A CHANGING ENVIRONMENT: WITH SPECIAL REFERENCE TO BRAZIL

Tania Mara Botelho
Social Applied Studies
Brasilia University
Brazil

ABSTRACT: This paper discusses the issues of continuing education and some conceptual philosophical bases and approaches. It stresses the philosophical fundamental approach to continuing education in the graduate and post-graduate programs in library and information sciences. It poses the question of new scientific paradigms in education, stressing the need for a changing environment.

INTRODUCTION

Whenever it is mentioned that a cycle of changes is to be initiated, the first task is that of ascertaining the level of awareness of the individual in the society or group. In viewing this in a sociological context, this means in the context of the social, self-realizing, rational-economic, and self-motivated man. With regard to social man, there are assumptions that man is seen as being first motivated by economic incentives. As for the self-realizing man, when his other needs are relatively well met, he finds significance and realization in his work. The self-motivated man is capable of being mature without his work. Man is actually a more complex being than the rational-economic, the social and self-realizing types (Sampaio, 1984). The fact is that man is a viable being, capable of learning new motives, that he is motivated on the basis of many different kinds of needs, and that he may respond in many and different ways.

The evolution of society offers a challenge to professionals to adapt themselves with many behavior modifications so that they can react in an effective manner to this evolution. People enjoy living in an era of prosperity despite the fact that they are living in chaotic times caused by conflicts among nations, the fall of outdate regimes, racial clashes, problems between management and labor, and problems between individuals (Botelho, 1991). The changes that we are undergoing today call for a new logic and a new science which we should aim at an understanding of social and personal intelligence.

The new vision of reality hitherto discussed is based on the state of awareness about the interrelation and interdependence essential to teaching, learning, and the self-knowledge process. Such as a vision extends beyond present disciplinary and conceptual frontiers. New forms of thinking are now being developed which will be adopted with conformity to new principles and will be used by institutions, organizations, and communities in the process of creation or transformation.

CONCEPTUAL APPROACHES

The concept of continuing education in Brazil needs to be expanded to the scope of "apprendre a être" learn to be according to Edgar Fauré (1972) from Unesco and according to a report presented at the Club of Rome, entitled "We never end to learn" (Botkin, 1980). And that is because the very moment we are living Brazil, shows several challenges in social, economic and political life that needs a complete restructuring of the continuing education development and a new educational approach to continuing education programs. Those changes give opportunities to our profession in order to rethink the direction we want to go from now and on.

Library and information science schools are still offering courses at the levels of specialization, master and doctorate degrees. They do cooperate of privatization and budget situation at the Federal University in Brazil, that causes some anxiety for the development of continuing education problems. The private sector of our profession is small and there are few new enterprises devoted to continuing education activities.

This situation is paralleled by a change in the country and a concern with the future of educational institutions as a whole. The educational model adopted by the Brazilian universities does not fit the needs of the changing society environment. Theses changes have been caused by different sorts of variables such as government policies, social pressures technological innovations, obsolescence of human values. The question of freedom, democracy and cultural values has not yet been solved in Latin America and in Brazil. Scientific research needs leadership pointing the direction toward we must go. Nevertheless, this process of vertical hierarchical leadership does not contribute to all kinds of institutions. This cultural crack has to be studied and explored in order to give chances to the information professional to understand what continuing education can do for their lives.

The information profession is very much in the middle of a cultural barrier although it would be possible to implement the development of continuing education for community information programs to the information society works and users. Usually in Brazil the information professionals are an employee of a public enterprise. The private sector also has information professionals in their board but in a proportion of 20/80%. To understand the Brazilian situation we really need to understand the cultural environment we are living with.

In evaluating the role of continuing education in our professional in Brazil, we think that the practical approach of experience has been stronger than the theoretical. We believe this is due to the influence of the training class in librarianship. The information science profession needs a critical element to succeed in continuing education activities. Our opinion is that we need to approach continuing education with a new vision of reality. There are now being developed new forms of thinking which will be adopted in conformity with new principles and will be used by institutions, organizations and communities in the process of creation or transformation. Reflexive education plays a fundamentally important role since it prepares the individual for an enhanced quality of life. In meeting with oneself, in the work environment and in the profession. The theoretical emphasis placed on reflection in the educational process must be according to the characteristics of the setting in place and implementing solution for:

    (a) the use of particular cognitive bases;
    (b) analytical skills;
    (c) attitudes which facilitate the reflexive approach;
    (d) levels of self-knowledge and self-determination;
    (e) examination of values and ethical principles for the appreciation of ideologies and
        adversities (Botelho, 1993).

According to the studies of Carr & Kemmis (1986), research activity in education may be approached under four characteristics the process, the content, the prerequisites and the product. The process has to do with reflection on action and curricular deliberations. The content distinguishes the teachers own values, the social context and the educational theory. The prerequisites are the attitude toward reflexion within the tutorial context in which occurs. The product is considered to be effective learning, obtained by means of the emancipation and understanding of the relationship maintained among pre recognized values and practice as it was exercised.

The changes for the future of continuing education activities occur when the new values are assimilated for better results for the students, as they acquire a strategic vision of each situation. Emphases must be given to the importance of full attention being paid to all the developments and circumstances which allow the achievement of a dynamic equilibrium of each one. Self-awareness regarding the professional role in the information society results in a broadening of the student's interaction with himself or herself, with their varying environment: family, social, professional and human. Achieving self-awareness embraces the perception of unity and totality. It is indispensable to the self motivated, to learn, to communicate and transmit ideas in addition to understand the complexity of a systemic approach to the universe of the information society.

When these aspects are taken into consideration, the need for training information professionals in continuing education in such as a way as to bring about a new culture compatible with this approach involves the transformation of the existing paradigms in relation to educational and managerial leadership.

THE NEW PARADIGMS IN EDUCATION

Paradigms fundamentally involve the process of accepting ideas and concepts as given and guaranteed, without our noticing that this interferes with the free play of the mind, so essential to creativity. Throughout its centuries of existence, science has proceeded in this manner. So that even today it is considered normal for one revolution to replace another. Scientists believe that when several theories appear in order to explain the same phenomenon, only one of them can be the correct one, which implies the elimination of the others. The concept of creative plurality among ideas and theories leads to questioning the relationship of science to reality.

The new paradigm sees humanity in harmony with nature. It promotes individual autonomy in a decentralized society. Each person is seen as the administrator of his or her own potential. We are capable of imagination, invention and experimenting. We need only to exploit this potential. Human nature is neither good nor evil, but can continuously transform and transcend itself. The new vision of reality seeks to respect and live in harmony with all events: birth, death, learning, health, family, work, science, spirituality, art, community relationship, politics (Botelho, 1994a).

The paradigm proposed by Ferguson (1987) reflects the discoveries of modern science and the personal transformation in education. The author shows learning as process, a journey, with a relatively flexible structure and a belief that there are many ways to teach a given subject. Inner experience is seen as context for learning. The use of imagery, storytelling, dream journals, "centering" exercises, and exploration of feelings is encouraged. The education is concerned for the environment of learning: lighting, colors, air, physical comfort, needs for privacy and interaction, quiet and exuberant activities. Education is seen as lifelong process, one only tangentially related to schools, where the teacher is learner, too, learning from students.

In the field of Library and Information Science, Miksa (1992) has analyzed two sets of paradigms: (1) the library as a social institution, and (2) the information movement as a system of human communication. The first approach consists of a set of ideas relating the library as a social institution. The paradigm defines library as a social organization and expresses its functions in the social structure through material, organizational and intellectual properties. The second approach consists of set of ideas relating to the "process of information movement as a human system". This paradigm embodies the "idea of communication engineers and cybernetics theorists who had succeeded in expressing the properties of signal transmission system in mathematical" terms, that becomes the basis of the process of document citation retrieval". The author considered that the focus of this paradigm is the process of information movement that forms a system communication.

More recently the cognitive process are studied as a human process for human communication and transformed as information processing system to build specialist systems within the field of artificial intelligence. The modern organization is adopting the information resources management and the structure of distributed and neural systems networks inspired in those knowledge of cognitive sciences cited above. These new approaches make changes in concepts that affects our view of the information sector.

Whereas past theories emphasized production and human relations on a bidimensional plane, the new culture refers to the individual as a complete whole that is self-integrated and integrated with society in a multifunctional relationship   (Botelho et al, 1994) (Figure 1).

<table>
<tr><td>I</td><td></td><td>**THEORIES**</td></tr>
<tr><td>N</td><td></td><td></td></tr>
<tr><td>F</td><td></td><td></td></tr>
<tr><td>O</td><td></td><td>**RESEARCH**</td></tr>
<tr><td>R</td><td></td><td></td></tr>
<tr><td>M</td><td></td><td></td></tr>
<tr><td>A</td><td></td><td>**ENVIRONMENT**</td></tr>
<tr><td>T</td><td>S</td><td></td></tr>
<tr><td>I</td><td>C</td><td></td></tr>
<tr><td>O</td><td>I</td><td>**TECHNOLOGIES**</td></tr>
<tr><td>N</td><td>E</td><td></td></tr>
<tr><td></td><td>N</td><td></td></tr>
</table>

Figure 1: A Multifunctional Relationship in Information Science (Botelho and Amaral, 1994)

FINAL CONSIDERATIONS

In developing countries the cultural infra-structure demands a high level of creativity and flexibility due to the lack of resources and educational tradition. If on one hand we deal with resources difficulties, by the other hand we are very much open to the opportunities that are created to the innovative and creative processes. The so much known development gap derives for a cultural gap and finally to a consciousness gap. We believe that the route to overcome these kind of gap is education, innovation and arts.

These activities belong to an integrated project developed in the field of Educational Methods in Information Sciences that will be published in a book by the end of 1996.

REFERENCES

Botelho, Tania Mara (1991), "O espaço quartenário no setor de informação: significado e perspectivas", *Revista de Informação Legislativa*, 28.

Botelho, Tania Mara et al. (1993). "Continuing education in the information profession: a reflexive method" in: *IFLA CPERT - Second World Conference on Continuing Education*, München, K.G. Saur, pp.202-209.

Botelho, Tania Mara et al. (1994), "Informação e sociedade: uma sociedade inteligente em transformação?" in: *Congresso Latino Americano de Biblioteconomia e Documentação*, Belo Horizonte Brasil: pp. 438-467.

Botelho, Tania Mara et al. (1994), "Information professional education and training for a new management paradigm in developing countries": paper to Tokyo, FID/ET Conference, 1994.

Botkin, J.W. et al. (1980), *On Né Finit Pas D'apprendre: Le Fossé Humanin à Combler*, Paris: Pergamon.

Carr, W. and Kemmis, S. (1986), *Becoming Critical: Education, Knowledge and Action Research*, London; Palmer Press.

Faure, Edgar et al. (1972), *Apprendre à être*, Paris: Fayard, Unesco.

Ferguson, M. (1987), *Aquarian Conspiracy*, n.p., J.P. Tarcher.

Miksa, F.L. (1992) "Library and information science: two paradigms", in: *Conference on Conceptions of Library and Information Science*, London: Taylor Graham, pp.229-252.

Sampaio, Luis Sérgio (1984), *Informatica e Cultura*, Rio de Janeiro: Embratel.

THE LIBRARY AND BIBLIOMETRICS

Ona Voverienė
Vilnius University
Lithuania

Abstract: The paper discusses methodological issues and the importance of bibliometrics in library and information science.

A typical feature of the recent development of science is a rapid growth of attention to methodological problems. It is quite understandable. All over the world, and especially in post communist countries, many of the established paradigms, values and norms of science are being revalued, new trends in investigations are taking place, scientific communities are seeking to give a new quality, theoretical maturity and fundamentality to many branches of science. Library and Information science is not an exception.

The methodological aspect of investigations is especially constructive in this instance. One of its tasks is to stimulate a critical evaluation of existing theories, revealing weak points and problems, and improving, - even reconstructing - the existing theoretical paradigms and creating new ones.

The social function of the Library in society is the basic phenomena in Library science and the main object of its methodology.

The history of Library science shows, that the social functions of Libraries and librarians are different in different historical periods and different political, social and economic state systems. We can examine the ideas of the social functions of Libraries and librarians at the very beginning of Library science. It is already quite widely acknowledged, that the first ideas of Library science were born in Germany.

On the 30th of June 1644 the Professor of Theology and Director of the Library at Altdorfs University H.Koenig (1590-1654), spoke about the historical mission of Libraries, as scientific centres and librarians, as universal scientists, connoisseurs of the history of science in his inaugural speech on the occasion of opening this Library after its reconstruction (Library was founded in 1630) (Schmidaier, 1984).

The librarian, as a "universal scientist" was an ideal for many generations of librarians. The first encyclopaedia of science *"Polihistor"* was also written by a librarian D.H.Morhof (1639-1691). H.V.Leibnitz, one of the famous scientists of the world and the President of the First Prussian Academy of Science for many years was a director of the Royal Libraries in Hannover and Volfenbutell.

In the 19th century, to the function of Libraries and librarians "as universal scientists" were added the function of the management of the library. In 1820, for the first time a historian of science, F.A.Ebert, proposed the preparation of librarians as professionals. Only in 1893 did those ideas begin to be realised after the confirmation of Prussian Law, according to which scientific duties in Library had to be given only to persons having university education and scientific degree.

Libraries in Germany kept their scientific traditions and high prestige in society for a long time, almost till 1970. Some journals, among them *"Zeitschrift fur Bibliothekswesen and Bibliography"*, *"Beitrage zum Bibliothekswesen"*, *"Bibliothek und Wissenschaft"*, etc. have been issued for a long time until the present time. After 1970 many Libraries in Germany were turned into information centres and their scientific function began to fall into decay (Kerzum, 1989).

Quite a different situation was found in the Libraries of the former USSR. There the basic social function of Libraries was ideological. The main task of Libraries, beginning from 1917, was to propagate the Bolshevik's ideology and bring up younger generations in accordance to the main principles of this ideology. Historian V. Charlamov in his article "Phenomena of Ideology of Libraries" wrote, that the Soviet Libraries were the first helpers of the Government in bringing "soviet cultural revolution" to life. The ideology of Libraries was quite a realistic reflection of Bolshevik's ideology, which included such elements as:

1. There was limited strictly freedom of speech (In 1917 was accepted the Law of the press, the central censorship office, and special curators were founded).
2. The mystical values of the working class were adorated; moral values of peasantry were destroyed; the intellectuals were humiliated and reduced to status of servants to the ruling proletariat "Party and Government".
3. Culture was valued only from a utilitarian-utopian point of view and as means to solve political and economical problems.
4. Reality and history turned to be proletkult and sociorealism values; the outrageous lie become the official norm.
5. All spiritual life of society was deeply ideologised; all people were under ideological terror in accordance to the principle "Who is not with us - is against us".
6. The Russian nation was extolled groundlessly against other nations. Those were called as objects, which needs "cultural services".
7. Cultural activities and their material basis were considered from bureaucratic, centralistic and planning positions.
8. Soviet culture was developed as a closed system, isolated from the West and East and also from own culture of all historical pre-sovietical periods.
9. A placard and primitive perception of the world was propagated, "all cultural values" adapting to the needs of working people.
10. It was not acknowledged that there were different cultural level in different layers of society, and a difference between readers.
11. Apology of violence, authoritarianism and atheism flourished.
12. Terror, as a part of governmental policy and first of all genocide of scientific and cultural potential.

In all those processes, librarians willing or not, took part, and not only as object, but in most cases as a subject of this "cultural revolution", which means as destroyers of traditional national cultural norms and values. Librarians were not only victims of Bolshevik ideology, but most of them "builders of socialist society". That means that librarians are also guilty of destroying the consciousness of masses of people and mutilating the history of nations (Charlamov, 1991).

Such ideas were spread and requirements made in Library science and activities of all Republics of the USSR and all occupied countries.

Nevertheless after 1970, when the political climate become not so cruel, as was before, Library science in the USSR had the opportunity to be developed on a quite high scientific level. Works of I.Grigorjev, J.Stoliarov, A.Sokolov, T.Karatygina, E.Bespalova and others created a theoretical background of Library science, for further development of its theory, history and methodology, improving activities of Libraries and scientific researches. Ideas of Information science, methods and skills of scientific information activities, had a very important influence on Library science. As a result of this influence, ideas about the computerisation of Library and Information processes began to be developed, a programme of research in Library science was extended. The theory of Information science, its main results - system of concepts, laws and regularities, scientific methods, used in information researches, also new technologies were mastered into Library science. So Library science in the former USSR gained maturity and fundamentality. Russian scientists, and first of all J.Stoliarov, were much bolder than scientists in other Republics and after "perestroika" they refused and condemned the ideas associated with ideological violence (Stoliarov, 1989). I was happy to defend, in Russia, in Moscow State Institute of Culture my doctoral dissertation "Information science theory as methodological basis for professional preparing librarians" in which the main idea was how to harmonise new information technologies, rapidly coming into libraries, and bringing quite a different style of thinking and humanitarian values and norms of librarianship, which had been developed in Library science and librarianship for ages (Voverienė, 1992).

Lithuanian Library science and librarianship took quite different path of development, based on the West librarianship ideas, and first of all, on computerisation ideas. Of course, ideas of the computerisation of library activities are attractive, corresponding to the conception of a new modern library. They are important entering a new era of post-industrial information society. Only, new technologies entering libraries are bringing not only progress into them , but also new style of thinking in which there is no place for humanistic values and the spirit of the real library is "melting". It is quite evident in the practise of libraries in Lithuania and consciousness of librarians. Librarians, who had graduated from Vilnius University now are ashamed of being librarians. Even teachers in Vilnius University are calling themselves historians, informologists, managers of information resources, etc. but not librarians. The prestige of the profession and Library science is quite low, and we must do something in order to change this situation and raise the prestige of Libraries in society.

One of the most rationale way it seems to be changing of the social function of librarianship in society and returning to the beginnings of the development of Library science - to its scientific function.

There is no another social institution in the society such as Libraries, which posses so rich flows of literature and its bibliographic production. Bibliometrics, investigating the bibliographic characteristics of documents, using statistical and mathematical methods - is one of the most prominent scientific trends in all modern libraries which possess new technologies.

In Lithuania the concept of using bibliometric methods for different researches in libraries and bibliographical centres was suggested for the first time by V.Lyrov (Lyrov, 1970). He used to say that librarians those prospective methods in their research programmes will be able to understand many processes, which are taking part in science and will get unique opportunity to become scientists of equal worth to scientists of classical branches of science.

However those ideas have not find a place in the Libraries of Lithuania for more than twenty years. They were adopted in Information centres, and had success. Several trends of investigations emerged in Lithuania. Among them were:

- analysis of the information needs of users; their nature, structure and characteristics, dependence on branch of science, stage of investigation and type of scientific research;
- evaluation of the efficiency of information services in science; also evaluation of the efficiency of different methods of analysing the information needs of users;
- evaluation of the quality of scientific journals, among them abstract journals; analysis of the bibliographical culture of scientific journals issued in Lithuania;
- evaluation of the quality of scientific publications and the impact factor of scientists on the world literature;
- identification of schools in science, among them in Library and Information science;
- analysis of the relationships and interactions of Library science, Information science and Bibliography science; also relationships and interaction among bibliometrics, informetrics and scientometrics;
- improving theories of Information and Library sciences;
- analysis of the citations of Lithuanian scientists in the world literature;
- using "Science Citation Index" as rationale source for searching for new cited literature;
- identifying the priorities of the different branches of Lithuanian science, etc.

A group of scientists in Vilnius university and Library of Academy of Science are using bibliometric methods in their research. 5 of them defended their dissertations in which bibliometric methods were used. The peculiarity of bibliometric research in Lithuania is - all of them are made on volunteer basis: no laboratories, no helpers, no financial support. Some of volunteers to this trend of science devoted all their life.

It is pleasing to find out, that the Royal School of Librarianship has launched a Centre for Informetric Studies (Wormell, 1996). It gives a hope, that from Denmark the idea of bibliometrics will spread to all Libraries of the world and they will change the social function and prestige of Libraries in the world.

REFERENCES

Charlamov V.I (1991), " Fenomen bibliotecnoi ideologiji: S pozicij istorika", *Sovetskoje Bibliotekovedenije,* 1991 (2), pp. 41-46.

Kerzum I.V. (1989), "Bibliotecnaja professija v FRG", *Naucnyje i Techniceskije Biblioteki SSSR,* (7), pp. 38-42.

Lyrov, V. (1970), "Naukometrija i bibliografija", *Trudy Informatikov Litvy.* V, - (1), pp. 100-110.

Schmidmaier, D. (1984), "Bibliothekswissenschaftliche Bestrebungen an der Altdorfer Universitatsbibliothek zwischen 1630 und 1800", *Zentralblatt fur Bibliothekswesen,* 98 (1), pp. 17-22.

Stoliarov J.A. (1989), *Upravlenije Kulturoi: Organizacionno-Ekonomiceskij Mechanism,* M.: Ekonomika, 209 pp.

Voverienë O. (1992), " Teorija informatiki kak metodologiceskaja osnova professionalnoj podgotovki bibliotekarei-bibliografo", *Avtoref. dis. d-ra ped. Nauk,* V, 40 p.

Wormell I. (1996), Centre for Informetric Studies, *Managing Information,* (9), p.17.

POLISH EXPERIENCES IN CONTINUING EDUCATION FOR LIBRARIANS

Maria Kocojowa and Wanda Pindlowa
Institute of Librarianship and Information Science
The Jagiellonian University
Poland

ABSTRACT: The problems discussed include the concepts of the Polish model of continuing education for librarians at the present time, and the changes which should be made in the future.

Continuing education has been recognized for a good number of years as a very important part of the educational process.

SPECIAL COURSES

Initially Polish continuing education was introduced in the form of workshops for librarians. After World War II some courses were offered in Jarocin near Poznan, intended primarily for librarians in public and school libraries (several thousand personnel). Next important step was developed at the Center of Continuing Education in Warsaw which has branches in 18 provincial cities, as intermediate, post-matura education (matura being the diploma received upon graduation from an academic secondary school. The new model of courses started mainly in Polish academic libraries in the 1990's.

UNIVERSITY STUDIES

Continuing education *de facto* had its start in Poland with the introduction of university level education in full studies of library and information science: in Lodz in 1945, in Warsaw in 1951, and non-resident studies in Wroclow onwards from 1956. A quantum leap in education was made in connection with the negative findings of the state of qualifications of library personnel given in the *"Report of State of Libraries in Poland"* in 1973. As result of this sad state of affairs, to remedy the situation the Ministry of Education called for Librarianship and Information Science - LIS, to be offered in several localities, along with the Jagiellonian University in Krakow, which we represent. In the majority of localities regular and non-resident education were offered simultaneously. Post-diploma studies developed in Poland later in the 1980's as one of the ways of expanding the school which was threatened by the diminishing interest on the part of young people in regular studies during the years of economic crisis (1 - 2 years courses).

At the present time there are several educational centers including a full course of studies at the Universities of Katowice, Krakow, Kielce (The Pedagogical University), Wroclaw, and Warszawa. The cities of Lodz, Poznan, Lublin, Krakow and the Pedagogical University have specialities in the study of Polish philology or history. The Bachelorate, as called in Poland 'licentiate studies', were offered from 1994 in Torun and Olsztyn.

The introduction of computerization pointed to the need for change in university continuing education, and closer links with the changes taking place in the nation and the transformation of libraries. Day and non-resident studies had their curriculum approved by the Ministry of Education, which, in the cross-section, was similar to that of the Soviet bloc. At the present time the Polish universities are modifying their curricula, but the model has remained the same after deleting, naturally, the ideological subjects: the preponderance of historical knowledge over the professional knowledge relating to current library concerns. The exceptions to this structure are the University of Warsaw and The Jagiellonian University. These universities are basing their curricula mainly on that of the United States and United Kingdom, and in the last three years have radically modified their curricula in favour of information science and library automation. This modernization of Polish studies in the international context of Europe's Post- communist Countries is very important. The Institute of LIS at Jagiellonian University organized in 1995 the first meeting in Poland which reported the idea of High Technology in the education of library studies. In continuing education non-resident and post diploma studies play the most important roles for active librarians.

Non-resident Studies

Until recently, non-resident studies were considered in Poland to be second class. The didactic exercises were shortened to 1/3 of the time that day students were obliged to spend, and were conducted in a few meetings during the year, or, at best, monthly. The students were expected to gain the rest of the information on their own from their readings. With the lack of text books, this obligation soon became fiction, and the quality of the non-resident studies sank to a much lower level than that of the day studies. The introduction of tuition for non-resident studies in the 1990's began to change the situation, because, "he who pays has expectations", and the better paid faculty put more effort into the courses. These necessitate breaking through the mindset of the faculty as well as of the students, and there must be an honest desire on both sides, to gain not only the diploma, but real knowledge. Students, who are different from those admitted formerly, complicate these plans for reform. Instead of individuals chosen by libraries for advanced study, we have young people who did not gain entrance for day study deciding to pay for non-resident study in order not to lose a year. These are not always the best of candidates. At the same time, financial matters, such as continuing institutional problems with the budget, suggest this type of study, even when there is a lack of personnel, classrooms, modern equipment, etc.

In our opinion, it is important now to define the core and the level of these studies. It would be helpful to divide them into two steps (MA degree only for the most capable) as well as changing the number of hours of study - doing away with the 1/3 of the hours of the day student requirement. This measure, along with a very careful selection of curriculum courses favouring professional knowledge, should raise the standard of non-resident education from the professional point of view. The Institute of LIS at the Jagiellonian University introduced and conducted this curriculum from the academic year 1996/1997.

Under current consideration are the preparations which will lead to the conversion to a two-step system, as well as the redirecting of specialization more toward the demands of the labour market. Suggestions in this area from such organizations as UNESCO, IFLA, EUCLID (Conference in Bratislava at the end of 1994), suggested the undertaking of studies of the labour market of library specialists on a national level. The precursor in this regard was the Polish National Conference of the Institutes and Departments of LIS, organized by the Institute of LIS at the Jagiellonian University of Krakow in 1996. Considered there were the results of this type of survey in Southern Poland, and a discussion supportive of the transformation of curricula specialists in the day and non-resident studies. The proceedings of that conference were published in Krakow in 1996.

In the future modern technology and distance education should be helpful in supporting non-resident studies. Unfortunately, up to now there are no centres in Poland educating librarians which are provided with the appropriate equipment, and neither laboratories nor students in libraries and homes have a suitable technical environment, textbooks, etc. The Jagiellonian University endeavoured to obtain such equipment from the Ministry of National Education and National Committee of Research. The American, Australian and lately, the English experience points to the necessity of knocking down this barrier as quickly as possible.

POST-DIPLOMA STUDIES

A real support for continuing education librarians in Poland in these circumstances are the post-diploma studies, especially at Jagiellonian University and Warsaw University, one or two year studies for the conveying of up-to-date knowledge to library studies and information science graduates in the area of the "virtual library" (the automation of libraries, modern on-line technology in the development of information, World Wide Web, gophers, etc.) the special libraries (help for disabled, the preservation and conservation of collections, etc.).

The second trend in this education relates to active librarians who have an MA from a discipline other than LIS, for the purpose of professionalizing their knowledge and making them fully qualified librarians. In Poland at the Jagiellonian University we can boast about a successful experiment in this area in connection with the breaking down of barriers, namely, librarians' resistance to computerization and preparing the staff to introduce the VTLS system in the Krakow libraries. This task proved successful with foreign assistance from the Soros HESP program. The five-year plan of education is now yielding positive results, and the preparation of librarians to introduce the system ahead of the time allowed for the breaking up of psychological barriers and it has quickened the process of library automation in Krakow. Post-diploma studies have a diverse curriculum, depending on the possibilities of the educational institution. The tuition based system favours the needs of the public in relation to the changes in the work force (i.e. the retraining of teachers of Russian in connection with the disappearance of many positions in the schools, the meeting of the requirements for the second degree of specialization by teachers and librarians in schools in order to raise their salaries, etc.).

Taking part in post-diploma studies testifies to the professional ambitions of the environment and the desire to raise qualifications, as well as to the efforts of the administration to have professionally qualified personnel. It also makes it possible for individuals lacking a professional education to enter the profession, but who are useful in various sections of the workplace in libraries, (the so-called area librarians). Post-diploma studies at the moment are the most effective type of continuing education in Poland.

CONCLUSIONS

The rapid computerization of Polish library collections in the 90's increased dramatically a need for continuing education and training for librarians, especially in the use of modern technology, Internet connection, and in management and organization;

The need for professional development among librarians caused a change in university courses offered at the Departments of Librarianship and Information Science. In consequence the number of students in these programs went up dramatically, especially at Warsaw and Jagiellonian Universities;

The change of the economic system in Poland with a free market and private companies, created new jobs for graduate students from librarianship and information science programs. With computer skills and knowledge in modern technology and telecommunication they found employment in new sectors, such as business, computer firms and international organizations;

Research librarians and reference librarians need postgraduate courses in modern technology and information systems specific to the area of study, collection and system used by the institution or information centre (VTLS, MARQISE, TINLIB, GEAC etc.);

The postcommunist society left thousands of teachers of the Russian language jobless. Russian was obligatory in elementary and high schools. Many of those teachers choose now a "library-career". They now seek education at University's Library Department;

Programs have been changed at universities to accommodate students needs, but universities suffer from not having enough equipment necessary to teach students in the use of modern technology, especially in multimedia;

Another important organizational change is to combine courses in information with courses in management and organization under one university department's administration.

REFERENCES

Aletenberger, A. and Kocojowa, M. eds, (1995), *Modern Libraries and Librarianship in Poland.* Krakow, 112 pp.

Kocojowa, M. ed. (1995), *Edukacjaz Zakresu Bibliotekoznawstwa i Informacji Naukowej na Poziomie Wyzszym w Polsce. Status i przyszlosc [Teaching Librarianship and Information Science at Universities in Poland: The Present and the Future],* Krakow, 148 pp.

Kocojowa, M. and Wojciech, Zalewski, eds, (1996), *Libraries in Europe's Post-Communist Countries: Their International Context,* Krakow, 296pp.

Courier, J.(1995), " Information training. Workshop on Education and Training of Information Specialist in Eastern European and CIS Countries", General Information Programme *UNISIST Newsletter* 23 (1).

Kocojowa, M. ed, (1996), *Rynek pracy a studia bibliotekoznawstwa i informacji naukowej.* Krakow.

Pindlowa, W. ed, (1997), *Electronic Future of Academic Libraries,* Krakow.

Kocojowa, M. and Pindlowa, W. (1996), "The role of the Internet in the education of librarians and information specialists: paper to the Conference FID/ET in Graz, Austria 1996 "Working and Learning in the Networked Environment".

ASIAN INSTITUTE FOR EDUCATION IN LIBRARIANSHIP AND INFORMATION SCIENCE: A CONTINUING PROFESSIONAL DEVELOPMENT PROPOSAL

Russell Bowden

ABSTRACT: The paper presents a detailed proposal to overcome three library and information science educational problems: an ability to meet the needs for staff for new institutions, a need to modernise the content of courses; and to upgrade the standards of these programmes.

1. INTRODUCTION

From travels and work in Burma, China, Indonesia, Malaysia and Vietnam and discussions with eminent librarians and information specialists in India, Pakistan and Sri Lanka there has been identified a regional need that is currently not being met. In these countries and, I suspect others in the region were they to be surveyed, there are three major library and information science educational problems: an inability to supply the demand for new librarians and information scientists to staff new institutions as they are established: a need to modernise the contents of the courses currently being taught and an urgent requirement to up-grade the standards of these programmes. For instance in Indonesia there are only 10 departments of library and information science at the undergraduate level and only 3 at the postgraduate or Masters degree levels and only one offering qualifications above these for the whole of a nation that is the fifth most populous. The educational programmes are simply not keeping up with the demands for qualified and educated and trained professional librarians and information scientists that countries require. In some of the other countries listed above the demands in terms of numbers is being met but not in the quality of what is required. For instance in some of them erstwhile students leave a library and information science (LIS) course to immediately become lecturers without any opportunity to 'dirty' their hands in the real world of LIS work and therefore to teach from experience. Today the revolution in the operation of library and information services, resulting from the impact on them of the IT revolution (being as it is the "marriage" of telecommunication expansions with computer developments), requires major changes in the contents of the programmes in which workers for the libraries of the future are being educated. New educational philosophies, learning and teaching practices have been developing that have been ignored in the Departments of librarianship and information science. New skills in how to learn and the consequences of this on how to teach, therefore, need to be introduced.

These situations lead not only to governments becoming frustrated because of the lack of qualified professionals to fill posts in newly-created libraries, but also to posts being filled by unqualified 'clerks' or 'administrators' who simply add to the confusion already existing in the publics' mind as to what makes, and who are, librarians. These clerks and inadequately educated and trained librarians then move into library jobs to provide inadequate services to users and thus contribute further to the poor image, weak reputation and the resulting low status and poor salaries of the profession. Such situations have to be reversed.

That librarianship and information science is a profession there can, in my mind, be no doubt (although, unfortunately, it is not always recognised as such even within our own profession). It meets the characteristics of a profession drawn up by sociologists such as the six identified by Abraham Flexner in Shera's stimulating book on LIS education (Shera, 1972). It has its own intellectual foundation that encompasses a body of knowledge that includes principles, theories and increasingly laws drawn from science and learning that are unique to itself; in many countries it recognises the social responsibilities of the profession (witness IFLA's work in the Committee on Access to Information and Freedom of Expression); it communicates its knowledge and techniques through the educational programmes that are the subject of this paper; world-wide it has organised itself into professional associations (witness IFLA's membership); yet it still remains a very practical profession, building on its knowledge-base to educate and train workers in the skills, techniques and competencies necessary for the librarian to undertake responsibilities to provide services to readers and users. To provide such education teachers must not only have knowledge of these intellectual principles and theories that lie at the core of librarianship and information science but they must also have experiences from the workplace of their translation into the skills and techniques without which no library can successfully operate its services. In many cases, not only in Asia, this dichotomy remains unrecognised. It has to be addressed and remedied.

2. PROBLEMS

The problems, if they are to be resolved, lie in the educational institutions, usually in the departments of librarianship and information science (or some such title) in the universities and they rest with the teaching staffs. There are often not enough qualified teachers to allow the expansion of the intake on courses. In others the lecturers themselves have for such a long time been out of practice (or even out of touch with the latest thinkings) that their teaching programmes are out-of-date and urgently need updating and often also restructuring. Thirdly the philosophies and practices of the educational processes themselves used to teach librarianship are far out-of-date. There is little, if any, recognition of the major changes that have taken place and that have resulted in the learning processes being given priority over those of teaching and where education itself has now become 'student-driven'. Still in too many DLIS institutions 'chalk and talk' and the regurgitation of lecturers' duplicated notes for stifling examinations continue to serve as the educational process. In some places all these problems exist together.

For the sake of clarity a word or two briefly here on the differences between education and training. ('Briefly' because there is more than enough literature extant on the subject making it unnecessary to add more!). Education, simply stated, is about imparting the core of knowledge, the principles and theories of a subject without which the practice of that subject is deficient. Training follows education and is about obtaining the abilities to learn the skill, techniques and competencies to put those principles and theories into practice in a working situation. Medicine and engineering education are but two good examples. Librarianship and information science is analogous. Higher education institutions in Europe in the past concerned themselves almost wholly with the former ignoring the latter (that is perhaps one reason why it took so long for librarianship to find a respectable place in higher education institutions) but today with changes in educational philosophy the responsibilities of higher educational institutions for training related to the 'intellectual' contents of a discipline (outside the so-called elite institutions exemplified by the Oxfords and Cambridges and Yales of the university world) is clearer and less contentious. In most of Asia these issues still remain to be addressed.

3. WHY

Why are these problems needing more urgent attention at this moment in time than in the past? The answer is because the Information Technology revolution's impact on the operation of libraries and the provision of information services, and on the expectations of users (for instance from their access to the Internet), has speeded up the pace of change in the last decade. Also the urgency with which many governments are modernising their telecommunications systems is an example not only of this but also of the realisation that for many former Third World countries their successful economic take-offs have not been unrelated to their investments and improvements in their information services and libraries. Witness, for instance, the World Bank's current interests and financial support for academic library developments in China and Indonesia. Note also, by way of example, the Singapore Government's recent agreement to the expenditure of millions of dollars over the next four years to implement its Library 2000 and Information 2000 Plans. In addition, with the introduction of IT networks and computers into libraries - not only for "housekeeping" purposes (e.g. the registration of readers, the recording of loans, renewals, reservations etc.) - but more significantly for the collection, organisation and dissemination of information, people have begun to realise that the education of future professionals working in this automated and information intensive age requires new knowledge, expertise, skills and competencies some more related to information science than traditional librarianship. Given that it takes on average 9 years from the conception of a new course to the emergence from it of the newly educated cadres, capable of managing future services, to plan changes today is not to have the "product" working in libraries until the year 2005. The need, therefore, for changes and developments is now and is urgent.

4. SOLUTION

Each country facing these and related problems could find their own solutions to them. This would be wasteful. There is only a relatively small number of departments of library and information studies courses in existence in universities in Asia. In total not more than 85 institutions for all the twenty-two Asian countries listed in a recent IFLA publication (Fang et al, 1995), (of which 21 and 22 are in India and China respectively) leaving only 42 to turn out graduates or higher qualified librarians for the other 20 Asian countries.(Japan is not included because although part of Asia its problems are different). With not more, at a guess, than a maximum of 500 staff-members (of which at any one time only a proportion will require, or be available to take time out for, their knowledge and expertise to be upgraded) individual country solutions, to what may be seen to be only a national problem, are scarcely viable. Hence a regional solution as the answer. Compare, as an example, the situation in the UK, where there are eighteen recognised DLIS to meet the requirements of a single country and yet Asia's need for librarians is as great, if not greater, than the UK's.

In the early seventies a similar problem was identified (indeed it was the same problem, because it was not sufficiently solved before money ran out and other priorities intervened). It was resolved with Unesco, British Council, Leverhulme Foundation and UK Government assistance for the establishment in 1975 in the UK in Loughborough University of Technology of a Masters degree course in Archives, Library and Information Science and Education (MA/ALISE) jointly based in the Department of Library and Information Studies and the Faculty of Education. It operated for less than a decade before it lapsed but during that period it educated about 90 library school lecturers from about 12 countries. (Most of them today hold senior positions in their universities as Professors and Deans and Heads of Schools).

Thinking, in the intervening period, has changed and support for travel to industrialised countries for higher education is less popular and perhaps less well-regarded than in the '70's. Also the high costs of education there, the costs of intercontinental travel, accommodation and subsistence makes it increasingly difficult to find finances for this purpose. The solution, therefore, if not national or international would seem to be regional particularly if it encourages south-south, rather than north-south, relationships. In the libraries and information services fields in Asia these regional bonds already exist through CONSAL (Conference of South Asian Librarians) and the Asia and Oceania Regional Section and Office (in Bangkok) of IFLA. It is therefore a regional solution, to what has been discovered to be a common regional problem, that is here being proposed.

5. PROPOSAL

It is to establish an Asian Institute for Education in Librarianship and Information Science to serve the identified needs of the region. (In which country it might be based will have to be carefully considered). Its purpose would be to provide continuing professional education (CPD) opportunities for middle and upper-level and mid-career, or youngish, staffs from university-based library and information science departments in the region to re-educate and re-train them. To do this for four reasons; to expand national opportunities for LIS education; to modernise, upgrade and prepare educationalists to offer library education in their countries relevant to the new services that libraries and information services will need to develop if the Information Technology revolution is not to pass by and leave unaffected, not only the libraries and information services, but also the economies of some of these Asian countries. Thirdly, by undertaking these activities, to improve the standards of performance of LIS workers from their libraries and information services to their users. The Round Table for the Management of Library Associations and the Asia and Pacific Section's Delhi Pre-Conference IFLA Seminar in 1992 agreed that without improved standards of LIS services the status, reputation and image of the profession could never be improved (Bowden and Wijasuriya, 1994). A view, incidentally, supported by the results of a survey, based on original research, undertaken by social scientists (Prins et al, 1995). Fourthly to improve the learning and teaching provisions of the Departments by taking cognisance of the latest educational philosophies and practices.

Such an institution could serve to complement work done in the '80's for Unesco by Professor Neelameghan (from the Indian Statistical Institute, Documentation and Training Centre, Bangalore) in the University of the Philippines and also the courses offered today in the Asian Institute of Technology in Bangkok for which IFLA's ALP Core Programme provides scholarships and attachments. So this Asian Institute (AIFELIS) proposal could be viewed as an extension of regional co-operative programmes begun in the past and continuing to this day.

6. PROGRAMME

It is envisaged that the basis for the course would be the Loughborough MA/ALISE programme suitably updated and made relevant to the specific requirements of the Asian region. Without at this stage going into too much detail its foundation would be firmly based on that core of knowledge that is unique to librarianship and information science and that serves to distinguish our profession from any others. This will include the structure, organisation and classification of knowledge; the theory and practice of bibliography (including historical bibliography and software developments related to it etc.); the concept of professionalism especially concentrating on the social responsibilities of LIS such as protection of freedom of expression and protecting the rights of access to information as well as understanding the importance of achieving standards of performance in the delivery of services. The course contents will need to address many other problems for instance those associated with management such as quality control; job descriptions, assessments and performance measurements; with information services management and information delivery (e.g. accuracy, comprehensiveness, up-to-dateness, comparative access etc.); it will need to provide instruction on the structure of knowledge and information-flow in specific disciplines and how to inculcate information evaluation and analysis skills because if librarianship is to continue in the future to exist as a profession and not vanish and be superseded by workers with backgrounds from computing, soft-ware and network developments this is where its future has to lie. Also to be considered for inclusion will be some of the other impacts of developments in telecommunications and computers and their 'marriage' (the IT Revolution) on LIS practices through the development of networks and improved opportunities for ILL and resource-sharing. These proposals will, inevitably, in crude terms, move LIS education some distance away from librarianship and its concern for the management of buildings, stock, staff and money (although, of course not excluding them entirely) some distance nearer the laws, theories and skills that go to support information analysis, evaluation and therefore more towards information science.

It will have to place towards its centre the subject of international library and information services developments. Where in the past, in many institutions, this subject has existed only as an elective option it now has to become compulsory study. Because of the globalisation of information networks and sources international developments can no longer not be taught. Given that not all the Asian countries are rich, and certainly that their libraries are less than well-resourced, the management of resource-sharing needs to figure along with an understanding of the significance of co-operative practices and the importance of national LIS co-ordination and co-operation and the need for profession's nationally to develop library and information plans and policies. Preservation and conservation and disaster management are subjects perhaps even more important than in Europe because of the hostility of the Asian climate to documents and records.

These, and other subjects, will be taught with a view to the students teaching these subjects on their return, rather than managing actual libraries. In order to better so do students will need courses in the latest educational philosophies and they will need to learn how to motivate students in self-learning and how, themselves, to structure their own learning-teaching programmes on return to their own DLIS. The provision from their departments of continuing professional development opportunities will continue to be a significant need as the knowledge and practices of our profession continue to develop and change, perhaps faster than almost any other, reflecting advances in computers, telecommunications, information networks and publishing. If professional associations don't provide the opportunities then a responsibility will fall on the Departments to do so and teachers will have to know how to respond.

As always there will be far more to teach than time will permit so a secret to success will be not only the selection of priorities but a concentration on principles and theories eschewing the details that clog too many courses. Finding the correct balance between the 'old' (which will still be required) and the 'new' will be half the secret of success for the Asian Institute. Much more work on the contents of the curricula and individual courses will be necessary later and to some degree will depend on the human resources and skills available to the parent institution hosting the project and from elsewhere.

7. AIMS

In the short-term; through CPD to provide modern education and training and provide new knowledge and expertise for current teachers of librarianship and information science in the universities of the Asian region and for a few, specially selected, new entrants into teaching. In the long-term, through the provision of effective and modern LIS education, to provide librarians and information scientists for the future with the necessary knowledge, expertise, skills and competencies to successfully exploit the new technologies (made available by the developments in computer science and telecommunications) in the interests of better quality library services and information provision to users through networking and the sharing of resources, nationally and internationally, so that libraries and information services play more supportive roles in their nation's achievement of its economic and developmental objectives. (A concept, incidentally, that happily appears to be gaining wider credibility and acceptance with organisations like the World Bank and other NGOs than heretofore as the realisation takes hold that some of the 'economic tigers' of Asia owe a part of their economic success to the fact that libraries' and information services' developments have played not insignificant roles).

8. WHERE

Many of the countries so far identified as having these needs, and no doubt others, have in the main English as their second languages either through the accident of history or because they understand that English (perhaps more American than English) is the international language of communication today particularly on the new international information and commercial networks. Other criteria for selection of the host institution might include all, or some, of the following. Its academic standards must be high, well-known and well-respected. Its degrees must be recognised and the standards that they represent universally accepted. Ideally it ought to be near the geographical centre of the region, and well-connected through airlines with other countries not only in Asia but in Europe and America. Within the country there should be amicable contacts with international agencies that might be expected to provide some support to the Institute, such as those from France, Germany, Russia, the US and the UK as well as with Unesco and a number of other NGOs especially funding agencies.

9. BASE

It is not envisaged that a wholly new institution will need to be created. Instead it might be established within, or based upon, an existing institution. Additional criteria will be required here to assist with the selection of the institution on which to base it. These might include a survey of the practising professionals with internationally well-recognised reputations available locally to assist with teaching after suitable educational training. The programme will also need links with other departments, especially education, within the University enabling it to use this other expertise as well as with the practising professionals from libraries and information services outside the University. They must all be capable of teaching in English. Physical facilities, such as access to computers, learning resources, living and learning accommodation etc. will also need to be considered.

10. RESOURCES: HUMAN

It is envisaged that the majority of people to be involved will be made available from within the current resources of the selected parent-host institution. Where these are not available they will have to be brought in from the expertise available locally. Additional expertise will be required, particularly with up-to-date front-end developments in computers, telecommunications, systems and network development and other subjects. It is hoped that these could be made available from the countries at the forefront of these developments primarily in Europe, Japan, the US and the UK, through their agencies already operating in the country via aid programmes or, ideally, through formal "link" programmes with leading institutions from these countries.

11. RESOURCES: FINANCIAL

It is appreciated that there are likely to be problems in approaching Governments for new monies at this time - but that is nothing new! It would be naive not to think that some will not be needed but it is understood that a large call for new funding, however desirable and however much of a priority, is likely to go unanswered. However funds are likely to be required for buildings, equipment, stock and accommodation both for teaching and student accommodation. As a rough guide the host-institution might be responsible for in-country costs such as the provision of the Institute's physical infra-structure like buildings, equipment and local teachers (both university-based and from local libraries. External funding might be supplied for overseas teachers and advisors and for a 'link' programme and for learning resources and equipment and to provide financial support for students. However it might not be unreasonable to expect the universities and governments likely to benefit from the Institute to contribute all, or a portion, of their student's costs in the form of awards and scholarships. Exploration will have to be undertaken to see what joint-enterprises might be established with organisations in the private sectors not only in the host-country but also from others within the region and especially again from those that might expect benefits in the long-term themselves from the programme.

12. STUDENTS

They will all be recruited, with the exception of a few new and highly qualified younger practitioners having some work experience, from amongst reasonably senior and experienced university teachers of librarianship and information science. (So their accommodation will need to reach certain acceptable standards). Their entry qualifications to the course will need to be established to conform to current practices and norms of the parent university hosting the Institute. To encourage the widest participation and achieve the greatest attractiveness these might be at first degree level. However that in itself to some may appear to be unattractive and it may also be unacceptable to the host. So they might have to be, except in exceptional circumstances, no lower than a Masters. Exceptions may need to be made if the regulations are not to appear to hamper the main objectives of the Asian Institute namely, to help to raise a nation's library and information science teaching skills.

13. QUALIFICATIONS

If the lower qualification mentioned here is unacceptable and students enter the course with a Masters, or its equivalent, the qualification with which they emerge ought to be built upon that and certainly must be seen to enhance it. What this might be will have to be the subject of further deliberations with the institution selected to host the project. It might be another Masters (MA - ELIS i.e. an MA in Education for Librarianship and Information Studies) or, perhaps less attractively, a Postgraduate Diploma (e.g. PG Dip.ELIS). Ideally an MPhil or a PhD would be the most attractive and also most useful on the student's return home. But this may not be possible. All these suggestions will require much further consideration.

14. INTERNATIONAL SUPPORT

There is already some recognition amongst the international community of the problems in Asia that this proposal seeks to resolve. For instance within Unesco's Programme for Information (PGI) and within IFLA in both the Regional Section for Asia and Oceania and the Core Programme for the Advancement of Librarianship in the Third World funded in the main from the Nordic countries and the IDRC of Canada. (This proposal has already, informally, been discussed in some of these fora and interest, without commitments, expressed). FID and, to a lesser extent, the ICA both also have similar interests that might encourage increased co-operation. It is expected that the aims of a project like this will harmonise with the aims and objectives of some of the foreign agencies that have over the years been generous in their support for Asian LIS developments, such as the Asia Foundation, the Netherlands, German, US and British governments and the British Council. The World Bank has been supportive of academic libraries' developments in the region and is thought to look favourably on further similar investments as being worthwhile. Finally, as the concept of establishing "linkages" from one academic institution to another gains hold so such links might be investigated to support this project. Within the region already they are well-established in India,

Indonesia, Malaysia and Singapore and in China and they are not new concepts for countries like Vietnam and Burma. It is known, for instance, in the UK that a number of universities with well-established and well-regarded LIS educational programmes would be interested in further explorations. The same is probably true in Europe and the US.

15. SUMMARY

It is appreciated that this is a proposal still in the very earliest stages of development and that it leaves open many questions to which answers need to be found before any firm commitments can be entered into. It is an intention of this paper to tease some of them out into the open so that they may be more properly addressed. Nevertheless it is hoped that the paper provides enough information and ideas to justify a measure of support, in principle at least, and provides a basis for more work to take further forward the project.

It will be unnecessary to emphasise what a boost in Asia and internationally this Institute would be, were it to be established, not only for the country but also for the University that hosts it and for the reputation of the country's librarianship and information services.

REFERENCES

Bowden, Russell and Wijasuriya, Donald eds. (1994), *The Status, Reputation and Image of the Library and Information Profession: Proceedings of the IFLA Pre-Session Seminar, Delhi, 24-28 August 1992*, IFLA Publication 68, Munchen: K.G. Saur.

Fang, Josephine Riss, Stueart, Robert D. and Tuamsuk, Kulthida eds. (1995), *World Guide to Library, Archive and Information Science Education*, 2nd revised and enlarged edition, IFLA Publication 72/73, Munchen: K.G. Saur.

Prins, Hans, De Gier, Wilco, and Bowden, Russell (1995), *The Image of the Library and Information Profession. How We See Ourselves: an Investigation. A report of an empirical study undertaken on behalf of IFLA's Round Table for the Management of Library Associations*, IFLA Publication 71, Munchen: K.G. Saur, p. 32.

Shera, Jesse H. (1972), *The Foundations of Education for Librarianship*, New York: Becker and Hayes, p. 68.

LIBRARIANS CONTINUING EDUCATION IN THE LIBRARIES OF ESTONIA.

Krista Talvi
Estonian National Library
Estonia

ABSTRACT: The paper reports the findings of a survey of Estonian librarians which emphasised the need for life-long learning, and describes recent developments in librarianship in Estonia.

INTRODUCTION

Political and economical changes in Estonia have influenced all the spheres of life, and also the role of libraries in the society has changed.

In the 1920s and 1930s librarianship was still a developing science in Estonia. From 1944 till 1965 bibliography was taught at Tartu State University, beginning from the autumn of 1965 the teaching of bibliographical science was transferred to the Tallinn Pedagogical Institute. In 1992 it was renamed the Tallinn Pedagogical University. The graduates are awarded a Bachelor's degree. Specialists with appropriate higher education are trained at Viljandi Cultural College.

The role of a library as an intermediary of culture and information has increased due to the change in the social situation in the state. We must rearrange and develop the training of librarians in order to follow international standards and requirements.

Nowadays every person must practice lifelong learning in order to be successful in one's speciality and to have perspectives in the new fields of their occupation. In 1993 the Law on Adult Training was passed in Estonia and legal guarantees were established for the adult continuing education training and three directions were defined:

- general education
- employment – related education
- popular education.

The employment – related education of librarians is carried out on three levels: national, local and on the level of the professional association. These levels also offer popular education. General education is carried out in Tallinn Pedagogical University and in Viljandi Cultural College.

WHY DO LIBRARIANS WANT TO IMPROVE THEIR KNOWLEDGE?

- basic education, obtained ten years ago, is not sufficient for today's library work, and is not appropriate for modern society and its requirements and possibilities;
- the speed and profundity of change forces a specialist, capable of development, to understand that her/his education and training is a part of continuing education;
- the Law on Public Libraries prescribes that a head of a library can be only a person with library education;
- a decree of the Minister of Culture has enforced the educational demands for a librarian's post;
- another decree prescribes that librarians without professional education must pass a professional examination;
- professional requirements for librarians have been set down.

In 1995 3,851 staff worked in 1,294 academic, special, public and school libraries of Estonia. 3,171 of them (82 %), were professional librarians. The role of librarians with a specialised education in public librarianship, has grown as compared with 1990 (58 % in 1990, 65 % in 1995).

Of all library workers 45 % have a university degree, 25 % of them – in librarianship; 3 % have appropriate higher education. 2 % of them – in librarianship; 33 % have secondary education, 14

% of them – in librarianship. Librarians with secondary education (47 %) mostly work in public libraries.

Quite a number of people with a university degree in the different fields of the occupation, work in research and special libraries, the main reason for that is the specific feature of the work, and most of all, the implementation of new technology in these libraries.

THE FINDINGS OF THE SURVEY

It is never too late to learn and lifelong education is necessary for everybody. These viewpoints were expressed in the answers to the questionnaire survey in February 1996. The questionnaires were distributed among the participants of an ELA (Estonian Librarians Association) meeting and to the librarians who wanted to express their opinion about the duration of the courses and the subjects that would be discussed at the training courses.

The survey was initiated by the Education Committee of ELA. In delivering the questionnaires a representative sample was not intended. We wished to obtain the answers from the persons who were really interested in continuing education.

The total number of respondents was 302, divided by the type of library as follows:

- from county / city central libraries 141
- from branch libraries   119
- from research libraries   34
- from other libraries and institutions   8

18 fields of library activities were listed and the respondents had to mark the essential topics and add their own offerings.

The subjects were:

- acquisition and collections
- book market and price policy
- new information carriers in libraries
- new requirements for bibliographic description
- subject indexing
- classification
- library service
- library marketing
- public relations and advertising
- methods of research work
- library management
- elementary computer courses
- text processing
- creating databases
- information searching
- spreadsheet processing
- computer networks
- integral library systems

These subjects can be divided into two main groups:

I   **Use of information technology in libraries (computer courses, creating databases, etc.)**

II   **Innovative library activities (new requirements for bibliographic description, new information carriers in libraries, etc.).**

Besides these two main groups there is a third group – subjects in the general sphere of culture. This had the possibility of answering the need for learning foreign languages.

The respondents were aged between 20 and 63 years. The largest group was between 31-50 years of age. These made up 65 % of all respondents. By type of library the preferences for the topics for continuing education courses were different.

Generally the most requested subjects were:
(per cent of the respondents)

- elementary computer courses — 67 %
- new information carriers in libraries — 58 %
- new requirements for bibliographic description — 55 %
- classification — 50 %
- library service — 45 %
- creating databases — 39 %
- acquisition and collections — 36 %
- library management — 34 %
- information searching — 33 %
- text processing — 32 %
- public relations and advertising — 32 %
- subject indexing — 31 %
- computer networks — 30 %
- book market and pricing policy — 24 %
- library marketing — 23 %
- integral library systems — 20 %
- methods of research work — 20 %
- spreadsheet processing — 14 %

Librarians' preferences from county / city central libraries:
(per cent of the respondents)

- elementary computer courses — 74 %
- new information carriers in libraries — 60 %
- information retrieval in databases — 52 %
- new requirements for bibliographic description — 51 %
- classification — 47 %
- library service — 46 %
- public relations and advertising — 39 %
- creating of databases — 37 %
- subject indexing — 37 %
- text processing — 29 %
- computer networks — 28 %
- acquisition and collections — 28 %
- book market and price policy — 27 %
- library marketing — 26 %
- library management — 26 %
- integral library systems — 18 %
- spreadsheet processing — 13 %
- methods of research work — 5 %

Librarians' preferences from branch libraries:
(per cent of the respondents)

- elementary computer courses — 64 %
- new requirements for bibliographic description — 60 %
- classification — 59 %
- new information carriers in libraries — 57 %
- library service — 53 %
- acquisition and collections — 49 %
- library management — 47 %

- methods of research work   34 %
- book market and price policy   31 %
- subject indexing   30 %
- information searching   28 %
- creating of databases   24 %
- library marketing   24 %
- public relations and advertising   24 %
- text processing   20 %
- computer networks   18 %
- spreadsheet processing   12 %
- integral library systems   11 %

Librarians' preferences from research libraries:
(per cent of the respondents)

- information retrieval in databases   79 %
- creating of databases   56 %
- new information carriers in libraries   53 %
- new requirements for bibliographic description   53 %
- elementary computer courses   47 %
- text processing   47 %
- computer networks   44 %
- classification   35 %
- library service   35 %
- integral library systems   32 %
- acquisition and collections   32 %
- public relations and advertising   30 %
- library management   30 %
- subject indexing   26 %
- methods of research work   21 %
- library marketing   18 %
- spreadsheet processing   18 %
- book market and price policy   15 %

In the third group – continuing training in general spheres of culture,
the following themes were offered to respondents:

- ancient (classical) languages
- the history of culture
- the history of Estonian culture
- folk poetry
- the history of religion
- regional studies

The preferences given by different libraries varied to some extent.

The wishes of county/city central library workers were:
(per cent of the respondents)

- the history of Estonian culture   65 %
- the history of art 56 %
- the history of religion   30 %
- regional studies   23 %
- folk poetry   11 %
- ancient (classical) languages   9 %

The wishes of branch library workers were:
(per cent of the respondents)

- the history of Estonian culture   64 %

- regional studies   53 %
- the history of art   40 %
- the history of religion   19 %
- folk poetry   16 %
- ancient (classical) languages   13 %

The wishes of research library workers were:
(per cent of the respondents)

- the history of art   62 %
- the history of Estonian culture   62 %
- the history of religion   50 %
- ancient (classical) languages   32 %
- regional studies   27 %
- folk poetry   9 %

The inquiry also proved that there was a **great interest in learning foreign languages**. 30 % of respondents wished to study German, 26 % – English. The preferences were also for Finnish, Sweden, French, Spanish and other languages. It was also possible for respondents to name the topics that might be discussed at the continuing training activities. The subjects mentioned most often were psychology, literature, new research trends in medicine, semiotics, general history, etc.

The duration of seminars/courses was preferred to be 1-2 days (the wish of 70 % of all the respondents) and 3-5 days (24 % of the respondents).

As the most active respondents in all library types were people from 31-50 years of age and 42 % of them were librarians with university degrees or had secondary school certificate in librarianship, one can presume that the learning years of these people were in the 70s and 80s, the time when there was no computer science in the curriculum, and computers were an extraordinary phenomena in our lives. They also lacked a systematic review of the changes in librarianship. Language studies in the soviet time were obligatory, but the use of a foreign language remained passive.

The respondents to the questionnaire had to mention the courses, seminars, etc. they had attended in recent years. Very few had not taken part in any courses. Most of them had been organized by the National Library of Estonia, the Estonian Librarians Association, the Estonian Children's Library, the Ministry of Culture of Estonia.

As noted above, a system of library continuing education has been formed. It has been developed and improved.

Librarians' employment-related education is carried out on three levels:

- at a national level the training is organized for all Estonian librarians by Tallinn Pedagogical University, the National Library of Estonia, the Estonian Children's Library, the Ministry of Culture of Estonia, the Estonian Folk-Culture Development and Training Centre
- at a local level the training is organized by research libraries, county/city central libraries and special libraries for their own librarians
- Estonian Librarians Association organizes the training for its members.

The Centre for Information Work in Tallinn Pedagogical University, has arranged training courses from January 1996 in innovative subjects that are added to the curriculum of library profession. For decades the National Library of Estonia has been organizing continuing education activities. The National Library of Estonia and the Estonian Children's Library deals with general problems of librarianship and also with separate processes and methods of library activities. The Ministry of Culture of Estonia pays much attention to the organizing of joint international seminars.

The Estonian Librarians Association carries out excursions and advanced training courses, the Estonian Folk-Culture Development and Training Centre organizes courses for librarians to

introduce folklore and national culture. Many subjects must be offered on a local level such as work
with special literature of librarianship, the knowledge of fiction and language courses.

THE NATIONAL LIBRARY OF ESTONIA AS AN ORGANIZER OF CONTINUING EDUCATION

In the 1970s and 1980s the main organizer of continuing education was the National Library
of Estonia in co-operation with the Ministry of Culture of Estonia. The seminars and courses were
organized accordingly to the post of service, the training programmes for many years had been
worked out.

For instance, in 1984-1987 the continuing education seminars on management for the
directors of central public libraries were organized. Management psychology, role of a leader, laying
out the goals of the activities, interpersonal relationships, and communication psychology were the
matters of the greatest interest at that time. At the end of the 1980s, Estonian librarians widened the
contacts and co-operation with the library world abroad. This was reflected in the change of the
contents of the seminars. The libraries on the threshold of the 21st century, the education of the
librarians in Estonia and abroad, the construction of new library buildings and the automation of
library information service were the themes concentrated on. Also the seminars on the change and
innovation of Estonian agriculture, national problems, cultural themes and literature, aroused deep
interest.

Wide knowledge of local history has always been valued and has been considered to be of the
same importance as other fields of library work.

In 1984-1985 a seminar on regional studies was held both in Tallinn and in Tartu, resulting
in the review of the field's activities.

Every summer a seminar–camp has been held for the librarians of the public libraries. The
tradition goes back to 1963 when the first seminar–camp was held, the last in 1996. Summer seminars
for research libraries are held too, the conventional meeting place for this event since 1984 is
Lahemaa National Park.

In 1984 the School for Continuing Education for Culture Workers was opened in Tallinn,
now the Estonian Folk-Culture Development and Training Centre, and in addition to the seminars
organized by the National Library of Estonia, two-week courses were started for the librarians. Up to
1993 the National Library of Estonia regularly participated in the planning of the courses, drawing up
the programmes and in the realisation of the plan. From 1993 the organizing of the courses has been
divided between the Estonian Folk-Culture Development and Training Centre and the National
Library of Estonia. The Estonian Folk-Culture Development and Training Centre concentrates on the
matters of popular culture, folklore, and the development of popular education, the National Library
of Estonia deals mostly with professional themes.

The year of 1988 was a New Awakening Period for the Estonian nation. The desire for
national independence and reunion of the Estonian nation grew stronger.

Valuable book donations from Canada, Sweden, USA, Great Britain and Australia were sent
to Estonian libraries. At that time Estonian librarians' interest in Estonian exile literature and culture
deepened as well as their demand for continuing education in general. The seminars on exiled
Estonian writers who have helped to preserve Estonian national culture abroad were held. Numerous
librarians still took deep interest in the history of Estonia, Estonian literature, the Christian way of
life, the etiquette of behaviour and communication. A seminar group was usually made up of 40-50
people.

In February of 1993 the new building of the National Library of Estonia was opened to the
public – to all its readers as well to the colleagues from other libraries and official visitors. As the new
building is a modern one, equipped with the latest technology, the National Library of Estonia has
organized various seminars in the field of reference and information service, book repair, restoration
and binding, organizes guided tours on the premises, holds exhibitions and presents cultural events.

In co-operation with the Department of Information Studies of Tallinn Pedagogical
University and other relevant institutions, seminars on the most modern fields – advertising,

marketing, public relations, information society, information demand, library services for the handicapped persons – were organized.

In co-operation with the Ministry of Culture, the National Library has initiated four professional continuing education events of profound value in co-operation with Finnish colleagues. The development of innovation in Estonian librarianship is reflected in the automation of research and public libraries of Estonia, the changes in the library statistics of different types of libraries that has been adjusted to international standards. The Universal Decimal Classification (UDC) publication in Estonian has been compiled, of which a variant for public libraries is already completed and published. A universal subject index thesaurus has been compiled.

All the above mentioned innovations have demanded serious efforts of the relevant working groups, discussion meetings of various institutions and experts. Seminars on relevant fields and practical training courses have been held.

The Estonian library network has changed considerably: the libraries have been united and new libraries founded. The new libraries are in the centre of attention: new ways of service, new functions, visitor groups, co-operation, etc. of these libraries have been introduced to the public. Once a year an introductory tour to a new library has been organized. The Estonian Standard Library and the Estonian Patent Library have been introduced.

ARE THE CENTRES OF CONTINUING EDUCATION ABLE TO TAKE INTO CONSIDERATION AND PUT INTO PRACTICE ALL THESE WISHES AND NEEDS?

The Education Committee of ELA holds the opinion that the established system of Estonian continuing education enables them to be applied.

Transformations have taken place in our libraries, and implementation of information technology to speed the retrieval of information, no doubt, demand computer using skills from the librarians. But in library work we cannot consider only the development of technology, we have to take into consideration the changes that have taken or are taking place in political and social structures. We have to consider the development of engineering along with the need to change the attitude towards our work and libraries, the place where reader service is traditionally provided. Librarians have to know how to communicate, negotiate, and cope with management. In case of need the continuing education centres today have to be in a position to offer librarians all these services.

Organizing Committee

Niels Ole Pors, The Royal School of Librarianship, Copenhagen, Denmark.

Professor Patricia Layzell Ward, University of Wales Aberystwyth, UK

Professor Darlene Weingand, University of Wisconsin, Madison, USA.

Professor Patricia Oyler, Simmons College, Boston, USA.

Thelma H. Tate, Rutgers University, New Brunswick, USA.

Jens Thorhauge, The Danish Library Association, Copenhagen, Denmark.

Professor Blanche Woolls, University of Pittsburgh, Pittsburgh, USA.

APPENDIX B
AUTHORS OF THE PAPERS

Tatjana Aparac,
University of Zagreb,
1. Lucica 3
10000 Zagreb
Croatia
Phone: +385 1 6120 006, Fax: +385 1 513 834, E-mail: taparac@filozofffzg.hr

Tania Mara Botelho
University of Brasilia
SQN 316-E-202
ASA Norte
70775-050 Brasilia-DF
Brasil
Phone: +061-2724928, Fax: +55061-2747172

Arlette Bouzon
LERASS UPS-IUT
115, route de Narbonne
31077 Toulouse Cedex
France
Phone: 62 25 81 80, Fax: 62 25 81 97

Angela Bridgland
University of Melbourne Library
Parkville
3052 Victoria
Australia
Phone: +61 3 9344 5368, Fax: +61 3 9347 7243, E-mail:Bridgland@lib.uniinelb.edu.au

Sue Lacey Bryant
22 New Meadow
Aylesbury
HP21 7AN Bucks
United Kingdom
Phone: +01296 89256

Marcela Burilova
Vyssi Skola Infomiacnich Sluzeb
Pacovska 350
140 00 Praha
Czech Republic
Phone: +692 14 64, Fax: +692 1969, E-mail: burilova@sks.cz

Fiona Campbell
The Robert Gordon University
School of Information + Media
352 King Street
AB24 SBN Aberdeen
United Kingdom
Phone: +0044 1224 262957, Fax: +0044 1224 262969, E-mail: f.campbell@RGU.AC.UK

Abdus Sattar Chaudhry
King Fahid University of Petroleum & Minerals
31261 Dhahran
Saudi Arabia

Phone: +03 860-3000, Fax: +03 860-3018

Araxie Paula Churukian
University of California
Rivera Library
P.O. Box 5900
CA 92517-5900 Riverside.
USA
Phone: +909 787-3233, Fax: +909 787-3285, E-mail: araxie@ucracl.ucr.edu

Laurel A. Clyde
Faculty of Social Sciences
University of Iceland
101 Reykjavik
Iceland
E-mail: anne@rhi.hi.is

Clive Cochrane
The Queen's University of Belfast
Information Management Division
Lanyon Building (North)
Belfast B17 INN
Northern Ireland
Phone: (01232) 245133 ext. 3621, Fax: (01232) 248372, E-mail: c.cochrane@qub.ac.u

Viviane Couzinet
LERASS UPS IUT
115, route de Narbonne
31077 Toulouse Cedex
France
Phone: 62 25 81 80, Fax: 62 25 81 97

Ganga Dakshinamurti
University of Manitoba Libraries
127, Elizabeth Dafoe Library
Winnipeg, Manitoba
R3T 2N2
Canada
Phone: Fax: (204) 261 4580, E-mail: gdaksh@bldgdafoe.lanl.umanitoba.ca

Joan M. Day
University of Northumbria at Newcastle
Dept of Information + Library Management
Newcastle Upon Tyne
NE18ST Newcastle Upon Tyne
United Kingdom
Phone: +0191 227 4917, Fax: +0191 227 4572, E-mail: joan.day@unn.ac.uk

Gabriella Dotan
Beit-Berl College
Doar Beit-Berl
44905
Israel
Phone: 0972 3 540 3372, Fax: +972 3 540 6707

Catharine Edwards
University of Northumbria at Newcastle
Dept of Information + Library Management

Newcastle Upon Tyne
NE18ST Newcastle Upon Tyne
United Kingdom
Phone: +0191 227 4917, Fax: +0191 227 4572

Ken Eustace
School of Information Studies
Charles Sturt University
P.O. Box 588
Wagga Wagga NSW 2650
Australia
E-mail: keustace@wis.riv.csu.edu.au

Peng Feizhang
Wuhan University
School of Library and Information Science
430072 Wuhan
P. R. China
Phone: 86 27 7882712 (ext. 2529), Fax: 86 27 788 2661

Kay Flatten,
Faculty of Computing and Information Studies
University of Central England
Birmingham
UK

Paul Genoni
Department of Information Studies
Curtin University of Technology
School of Social Sciences and Asian Languages
GPO Box U 1987
Perth 6001
Western Australia
Phone: (09) 351 7256, Fax: (09) 351 3152, E-mail: paul@biblio.curtin.edu.au

Irith Getz
Beit-Berl College
Doar Beit-Berl
44905
Israel
Phone: +972 3 751 0177, Fax: +972 3 751 0177

Sally E. Gibbs
School of Information Management
Leeds Metropolitan University
Beckett Park Campus, Leeds
LS6 3QS Leeds
England
Phone: +0 1 13 283 2600 x 3552, Fax: +833182, E-mail: sgibbs@cmu.ac.uk

Anne Goulding
Department of Information and Library Studies
Loughborough University
Loughborough
LE 1 1 3TU Leics
United Kingdom
Phone: +01509 223056, Fax: +01509 223053, E@mail: a.goulding@lboro.ac.uk

Neil Greeve
Department of Information Studies
Curtin University of Technology
GPO Box U1987
6001 Perth
Western Australia
Phone: + 61 + 9 + 351 7694, Fax: + 61 + 9 351 3152, E-mail: Neil@biblio.curtin.edu.au

Ken Haycock
SLAIS
University of British Columbia
831-1956 Main Mall
Vancouver, BC V6T IZI
Canada
Phone: 604 822 4991, Fax: 604 822 6006, E-mail: haycock@unixg.ubc.ca

Oluremi Jegede
University of Lagos Campus
The Library - Nigerian Institute of Advanced Legal Studies,
P.M.B. 12820,
Marina,
Lagos
Nigeria
Phone: 234 1 862 833

Zhang Jin
Wuhan University
School of Library and Information Science
430072 Wuhan
P. R. China
Phone: 86 27 7882712 (ext. 2529), Fax: 86 27 788 2661

Leif Kajberg
Royal School of Librarianship
Birketinget 6
DK- 2300 Copenhagen S
Denmark

Uma Kanjilal
Faculty of Library and Information Science
Indira Gandhi National Open University
School of Social Sciences
Maidan Garhi, New Delhi - 110 068
India
E-mail: dk@nsc.ernet.in

Evelyn Kerslake
Department of Information and Library Studies
Loughborough University
Loughborough
LE11 3TU Leics
United Kingdom

Irina L. Klim
U.S. Cultural and Information Center
U. Millionaya, 5
St. Petersburg
Russia 191065
Phone: 7 (812) 325-8050, Fax: 7 (812) 325 8052, E-mail: ilkpete@usia.gov

Maria Kocojowa
Department of Librarianship and Information Science
The Jagiellonian University
Gotgcia 16
31-007 Krakow
Poland
Phone: 22 10 33 ext. 14 20 or 13 23, Fax: , E-mall: ikocoj@Filon.Filg.UJ.edu.pl

Michael Kristiansson
Royal School of Librarianship
Birketinget 6
2300 Copenhagen S
Denmark
Phone: +45 31 58 60 66, Fax: +45 32 84 02 01, E-mail: mk@db.dk

Aira Lepik
Tallinn Pedagogical University
25, Narva Road
EEOIOO Talinn
Estonia
Phone: +372 6 409 480, Fax: +372 6 409 118, E-mail: aira@lin.tpu.ee

Steve Morgan
University of the West of England
Bower Ashton Campus, Kennel Lodge Road
off Clanage Road,
Bristol B53 2JT
United Kingdom
Phone: 0 1 17 965 6261 ext. 473, Fax: 0 1 17 976 3 946, E-mail: s-morgan@uwe. ac. uk

Lesley M. Moyo
Department of Library and Information Studies
University of Botswana
Private bag 0022 Gaborone
Botswana
Phone: + 267 3552633, Fax: + 267 3552279, E-mail: moyoln@,noka.ub.bw

Aili Norberg
Estonian National Library
Department of Library Science
Tonismagi 2
EE 0100 Tallinn
Estonia
Phone: +372 6 307 122, Fax: +372 6 311 410

Augusta Maria Paci
Istituto di Studi sulla Ricerca e Documentazione Scientifica
Via Cesare de Lollis. 12
00185 Roma
Italy
Phone: + 39 6 44879 253, Fax: + 39 6 4463836, E-mail: paci@www.isrds.rm.cnr.it

Mihaly Palvolgyi
Konyvtar-Informatikaitanszek
Department of Library and Information Studies
Szombathely
4 Karolyi Gaspar ter
Hungary
Phone: +36 94 313 892, Fax: +36 94 312 248, E-mail: pami@kit.bdtf.hu

Wanda Pindlowa
The Jagiellonian University
Department of Librarianship and Information Science
Gotgcia 16
21-007 Krakow
Poland
Phone: 22 10 33 ext. 14 20 or 13 25, Fax: , E-mail: ipindel@filon.filg.UJ.edu.pl

Niels Ole Pors
Royal School of Librarianship
Birketinget 6
DK-2300 Copenhagen S
Denmark
Phone: +45 31 58 60 66, Fax: +45 32 84 02 01, E-mail: nop@db.dk

Ann Ritchie
Hollywood Private Hospital
Monash Avenue
Nedlands, 6009
Western Australia
Phone: (09) 346 6184, Fax: (09) 386 4735, E-mail: Hollylib@p085.aone.net.au

Maxine Rochester
School of Information Studies
Charles Sturt University
P.O.Box 588
Wagga Wagga NSW 2650
Australia

Eugenia Rossinskaya
Ministry of Culture of Russia,
Library for Foreign Literature
Nikolo Jamskaya Street, 1
Moscow, 109 189
Russia
Phone: 7 095 915 36 21, Fax: 7 095 915 36 37, E-mail: genieva@libfl.msk.su

Diann Rusch-Feja
Max Planck Institute for Human Development and Education
Lentzeallee 94
D-14195 Berlin
Germany
Phone: +49 30 824 06 230, Fax: +49 30 824 99 39, E-mail: ruschfeja@mpib-berlin.mpg.de

Trine Schreiber
Royal School of Librarianship
Birketinget 6
DK-2300 Copenhagen S
Denmark
Phone: +45 31 58 60 66, Fax: +45 32 84 02 01

Maria Silva
Federal State Library
Brasilia
DF Brazil
E-mail: marianeves@admass.senado.gov.br

Krista Talvi
National Library of Estonia
Tonismagi 2
EEO 100 Tallinn Eesti
Estonia
Phone: 6307 129, Fax: 6311 410

Agnes Teglasi
Konyvtar-Informatikai Tanszek
Department of Library and Information Studies
Szombathely
4 Karolyi Gaspar ter
Hungary
Phone: +36 94 313 892, Fax: +36 94 312 248

Fransie Terblanche
University of South Africa
Department of Information Science
Unisa P.O. 392
Pretoria 0003
South Africa
Phone: +27 12 429 6568, Fax: +27 12 429 3400, E-mail: terblf@alpha.unisa.ac.za

Jana Varlejs
Rutgers School of Communication
University of New Jersey
4 Huntington Street
NJ 08903 New Brunswick
USA
Phone: +908-932-1726, Fax: -908-932-6916, E-mail: varlejs@scils.rutgers.edu

Sirje Virkus
Tallinn Pedagogical University
Narva Road 25
EEOOOI Tallinn
Estonia
Phone: 372 6409 480, Fax: 372 6409 118, E-mail: sirvir@lin.tpu.ee

Ona Voverienë
Vilnius University
Naugarduko 45-4
2006 Vilnius
Lithuania
Phone: 370 2 63 40 18, Fax: 370 2 227 388

Clare Walker
University of the Witswatersrand
Private Bag XI
PO Wits 2052
South Africa

Graham Walton
University of Northumbria at Newcastle
Dept of Information + Library Management
Newcastle Upon Tyne
NE18ST Newcastle Upon Tyne
United Kingdom
Phone: +0191 227 4917, Fax: +0191 227 4572

Darlene E. Weingand
University of Wisconsin Madison
600 North Park Street
WI 53706 Madison
USA
Phone: +608 262-8952, Fax: +609 263-4849, E-mail: weingand@macc.wisc.edu

Blanche Woolls
School of Library and Information Science
University of Pittsburgh
Pittsburgh, PA 15260
USA
Phone: +1-412-6249435, Fax: +1-412-6487001, E-mail: WOOLLS@LIS.PITT.EDU

Irene Wormell
FIDIET Chair,
Royal School of Librarianship
Birketinget 6
DB-2300 Copenhagen S
Denmark
Phone: +45 31 58 60 66, Fax: +45 32 84 02 01, E-mail: IW@db.dk